Also in the Variorum Collected Studies Series:

HAIM GERBER
State and Society in the Ottoman Empire

A.R. DISNEY
The Portuguese in India and Other Studies, 1500–1700

JOAN-PAU RUBIÉS
Travellers and Cosmographers
Studies in the History of Early Modern Travel and Ethnology

RHOADS MURPHEY
Studies on Ottoman Society and Culture, 16th–18th Centuries

EKMELEDDIN İHSANOĞLU
Science, Technology and Learning in the Ottoman Empire
Western Influence, Local Institutions, and the Transfer of Knowledge

COLIN HEYWOOD
Writing Ottoman History
Documents and Interpretations

GEORGE D. WINIUS
Studies on Portuguese Asia, 1495–1689

W.G.L. RANDLES
Geography, Cartography and Nautical Science in the Renaissance
The Impact of the Great Discoveries

P.E.H. HAIR
Africa Encountered
European Contacts and Evidence, 1450–1700

URSULA LAMB
Cosmographers and Pilots of the Spanish Maritime Empire

DAVID A. KING
Astronomy in the Service of Islam

C.R. BOXER
Dutch Merchants and Mariners in Asia, 1602–1795

VARIORUM COLLECTED STUDIES SERIES

Travellers from Europe in the
Ottoman and Safavid Empires,
16th–17th centuries

Sonja Brentjes

Sonja Brentjes

Travellers from Europe in the Ottoman and Safavid Empires, 16th–17th centuries

Seeking, Transforming, Discarding Knowledge

This edition © 2010 by Sonja Brentjes

Sonja Brentjes has asserted her moral right under the Copyright, Designs and Patents Act, 1988, to be identified as the author of this work.

Published in the Variorum Collected Studies Series by

Ashgate Publishing Limited
Wey Court East
Union Road
Farnham, Surrey
GU9 7PT
England

Ashgate Publishing Company
110 Cherry Street
Suite 3-1
Burlington
VT 05401-3818
USA

www.ashgate.com

ISBN 978–1–4094–0533–7

British Library Cataloguing in Publication Data
Brentjes, Sonja.
  Travellers from Europe in the Ottoman and Safavid empires, 16th–17th centuries: seeking, transforming, discarding knowledge.
  – (Variorum collected studies series ; CS961)
  1. Learning and scholarship – Europe – History. 2. Islamic learning and scholarship – History. 3. Communication in learning and scholarship – History. 4. Travelers' writings, European – History and criticism. 5. Islam and science – Historiography. 6. Europeans – Middle East – History – 16th century. 7. Europeans – Middle East – History – 17th century. 8. Della Valle, Pietro, 1586–1652 – Knowledge – Middle east. 9. Middle East – In literature.
  I. Title II. Series
  303.4'824056–dc22

ISBN 978–1–4094–0533–7

Library of Congress Control Number: 2010923984

VARIORUM COLLECTED STUDIES SERIES CS961

Transferred to Digital Printing in 2014

Printed and bound in the United States of America
by Publishers' Graphics

CONTENTS

Preface   vii

Introduction   ix

Acknowledgements   xxx

I   The interests of the Republic of Letters in the Middle East, 1550–1700   435–468
Science in context 12. Cambridge, 1999

II   On the relation between the Ottoman Empire and the West European Republic of Letters (17th–18th centuries)   121–148
Proceedings of the International Congress on Learning and Education in the Ottoman World, Istanbul, 12–15 April 1999 (Studies and Sources on the Ottoman History Series 6), ed. A. Çaksu. Istanbul: Research Centre for Islamic History, Art and Culture, 2001

III   The presence of ancient secular and religious texts in the unpublished and printed writings of Pietro della Valle (1586–1652)   1–23
First publication

IV   Pietro della Valle's Latin Geography of Safavid Iran (1624–1628): Introduction (with Volkmar Schüller)   1–56
Journal for Early Modern History 10. Leiden, 2006, pp. 169–219

V   Early modern Western European travellers in the Middle East and their reports about the sciences   379–420
Sciences, techniques et instruments dans le monde iranien (Xe–XIXe siècle) (Actes du colloque tenu à l'Université de Téhéran, 7–9 June 1998), Tehran, 2004

VI	Pride and prejudice: the invention of a 'historiography of science' in the Ottoman and Safavid empires by European travellers and writers in the sixteenth and seventeenth centuries *Religious Values and the Rise of Science in Europe*, eds J. Brooke and E. İhsanoğlu. Istanbul: Research Centre for Islamic History, Art and Culture, 2005	229–254
VII	Peiresc's interests in the Middle East and Northern Africa in respect to geography and cartography *Preprint 269. Berlin: Max-Planck-Institut für Wissenschaftsgeschichte, 2004*	1–56
VIII	Astronomy a temptation? On early modern encounters across the Mediterranean Sea *Astronomy as a Model for the Sciences in Early Modern Times*, eds M. Folkerts and A. Kühne. Augsburg: Erwin Rauner Verlag, 2006	15–45
Index		1–22

This volume contains xxx + 320 pages

PUBLISHER'S NOTE

The articles in this volume, as in all others in the Variorum Collected Studies Series, have not been given a new, continuous pagination. In order to avoid confusion, and to facilitate their use where these same studies have been referred to elsewhere, the original pagination has been maintained wherever possible. The exception is article IV, which has been reset for the purposes of this volume.

Each article has been given a Roman number in order of appearance, as listed in the Contents. This number is repeated on each page and is quoted in the index entries.

PREFACE

This book and the articles it contains would not have been possible without the support and assistance of numerous friends, colleagues and family members.

My special thanks for long years of friendship, intellectual inspiration and collegial support of the greatest kind go to David A. King, Frankfurt. He assisted me in the last phase of my formal academic education many years ago. He was always there for me even beyond his retirement, whether I needed a microfilm, a letter of recommendation or a beer. Although our views of and approaches to the history of science in Islamic societies do not always agree and sometimes differ substantially, David was willing at all times to give my questions serious consideration, often spiced up by some teasing remark or challenging doubt.

My second 'thank you' goes to Lorraine Daston, Max Planck Institute for the History of Science, Berlin, who agreed to support my research projects during a period of severe difficulties, since after 1990 most of the posts in the humanities and social sciences in the territory of the former German Democratic Republic were destroyed and I lost my job at the University of Leipzig. I am not only profoundly grateful to her for her financial support, but also for the intellectual profit that I gained when listening to a broad variety of other research approaches offered in her Department 2. Without her my methodological experiences and my skills would not be those that they are today. Since I took a major shift in my understanding of history, science and the ethos of an academic during those two years in Berlin, I can say without exaggeration that Lorraine Daston proved to be another colleague of major importance to my academic development.

The third person to whom I wish to express my thanks and gratefulness publicly and with a wide smile on my face is my daughter Rana. Over the years, she became the most important woman in my life. She always wanted to distract me and re-orient my academic interests from philology and mathematics, two domains she found of little interest to herself, to adventure in the form of travel, images, maps and people outside the formal canons and institutions of academia. She agreed to support me in my pains of analyzing and interpreting historical sources, listening time and again to my various ideas about how to understand a particular piece of evidence, only to be exposed the next day to yet another trial. Since her English is much better than mine, she has also acted as my translator, proof-listener and critic. She challenged and teased me, offering postmodernist and modernist attacks from cultural studies and art history alike on my ways of doing things anchored in philology, modernist history of science and Quellenkritik. She took my indignation, rejection and acquiescence with good will pierced by bouts of impatience. Countless evenings, she was rocked to sleep by listening to ever evolving versions of my papers. Any mistakes that remain in my texts and their English are without doubt mine.

There are many more friends and colleagues who deserve to be mentioned for various kinds of support, help and inspiration to my work. In particular I wish to thank Erhard Scholz, Wuppertal; Liba Taub, Cambridge; Rivka Feldhay, Tel Aviv; Friedrich Steinle, Berlin; Willem Floor, Bethesda; Živa Vesel, Paris; Karin Rührdanz, Toronto; and Feza Günergun, Istanbul.

SONJA BRENTJES

Seville
April 2010

INTRODUCTION

During most of the twentieth century, our historiographical perspective on contacts between Christian, Muslim and Jewish scholars working in domains such as arithmetic, algebra, geometry, astronomy, astrology, geography, medicine or philosophy emphasized two periods, two types of knowledge as well as objects of knowledge exchanged during those contacts, two unilateral directions of their flow and two types of relationships between those who participated. The first set of elements comprised the twelfth and thirteenth centuries, scholarly texts and the occasional instrument, Arabic to Latin, 'Orient' and 'Islam' to 'Occident' and 'Latin Christendom', the transfer of 'preserved ancient Greek' knowledge from the 'Arabs' to its (only rightful) 'European (Christian) heirs' and Catholic clerics arriving from abroad and desiring Greek knowledge, heading the translation efforts to which Jewish scholars fleeing religious persecution, converts to Catholicism and 'natives' speaking vernacular forms of Arabic and Latin contributed as mediators and adjuncts. A second, largely independent and slightly later series of encounters between 'Arabic, Islamic' knowledge and 'foreign recipients' in this time of contact was seen in activities among Jewish communities when scholars who grew up in Islamic societies translated the scholarly literature they had been taught for their brethren in communities of the Provence and neighbouring Mediterranean regions from Arabic into Hebrew. Although the kind of knowledge and type of objects (texts and instruments) transformed into Jewish knowledge were very similar to those acquired by Catholic clerics, sponsored at Castilian, Norman or Hohenstaufen courts and later taught at universities in Bologna, Paris, Cambridge, Oxford and elsewhere, the emphasis on the ancient Greek knowledge 'preserved unchanged' in the Arabic intermediary culture was less pronounced and did not obliterate other elements in the acquired knowledge and other interests of the acquiring scholars and their communities. Jewish scholars were not seen as members of European, i.e. Catholic, intellectual history and their later Protestant and secular successors and hence did not need to be constructed as 'genuine heirs' of Greek knowledge. The same applies to Arabic speaking and writing Muslims, Christians and Jews in European Islamic societies. Even today they are not recognized as full objects and subjects of European history. Their acquisition of Greek knowledge was transitory at best. This knowledge was not theirs to keep and transform. Their role could only have been to pass it on.

The second set of elements consists of the late eighteenth and nineteenth centuries, a continuous flow from the 'West' to the 'East' of French, English, Austrian and German armies, colonial administrators, scholars trained in the centres of Europe 'bringing' with them 'modern Western' science for reforming and subsequently replacing 'ossified' and inferior armies, schools, medical institutions and knowledge plus members of the local educational, administrative and political elites. The transferred knowledge and its accompanying institutions and technological applications proved the colonizers' intellectual, social and racial superiority over 'Semites', 'Turks', 'Mongols' 'barbarians' and 'hordes' as argued by academics of the nineteenth and the first half of the twentieth centuries and propagated by politicians and ideologues, a line of thinking taken up again in the academic justification of the 'war on terror' in the last decade. Ernest Renan's Islamic 'tribes' of Asia threatening progress and civilization in Europe share at least one feature with Bassam Tibi's 'fundamentalists' threatening the allegedly same civilization in the 'West'.[1] All of them are incapable of rationality and appreciation of 'modern' science and its concomitant political and moral values and modes of living, although the precise elements used to define this civilization differ between the two academics of the late nineteenth and late twentieth centuries. The incapability of their subjects of study rests in their race, their language, their religion and hence their culture. They are not, never were and never will be 'genuine' heirs to ancient Greek or modern 'Western' science.

The centuries between these two periods of contact did not draw serious attention among historians of science of whatever period and region since it was believed at best that nothing happened that merited such attention and at worst that the worlds and cultures were tightly sealed off from each other, the blame usually being laid at the door of the (Ottoman) 'Turks'.[2] Furthermore, with the circumnavigation of Africa and the colonial division of the world between Spain and Portugal, the Mediterranean and the overland routes linking southern Europe to Asia were thought to have lost out as areas of European-Asian commerce and cultural exchange in comparison to transatlantic conquest, African slave trade and south and south-eastern Asian spice trade. Authors and exhibition curators emphasizing the important role of Asia for early modern

---

[1] Ernest Renan, *L'Islamisme et la science*, Université de la Sorbonne, 29 March 1883, published in Discours et conférence, Paris: C. Lévy, 1887, pp. 375–409< Reprint BiblioLife, LLC ; (digitalized http://www.archive.org/stream/a605828800renauoft#page/n387/mode/2up); Bassam Tibi, *The Challenges of Fundamentalism. Political Islam and the New World Disorder*, Berkeley: University of California Press, 2002.

[2] See for instance the panel 2 of *Discoveries* on the web presentation of the exhibition encounters, V&A, London, 23 September – 5 December, 2004: (http://www.vam.ac.uk/vastatic/ microsites/1196_encounters/exhibition/text_panel/text_panel_2.html).

and hence could be evaluated and possibly appreciated according to the norms and values of the host culture. Their authors often configured the narrative between two rather rigidly distanced points of measurement – inferiority and superiority. A culture that appropriated foreign knowledge through translating texts, copying images and transferring craftspeople for reproducing technical goods was normally seen as inferior to the culture where the appropriated forms and products of knowledge had originated. Depending though on the kind of appropriated forms and products of knowledge as well as the geographical location of the originating culture, the appropriating culture could be seen to achieve a superior status when it mastered theoretical disciplines, in particular philosophy, mathematics or astronomy, and their arsenal of methods, and when the level of comparative knowledge achieved in the same period in some Catholic and later also Protestant countries in Europe was judged as lower than that of the other culture. If either of the two or both were not in place, the appropriating culture was judged as remaining inferior. Characteristic of this kind of academic as well as political evaluation was the fact that the levelling board for the comparison was always and exclusively a Catholic, Protestant or secular society of Europe. It is only recently that Hindu scholars have begun to apply the same kind of value laden comparison between what they perceive as their 'own' scholarly past and that of other, above all Islamic, societies.

The new approaches to telling stories about the appropriation and adaptation of foreign knowledge, in contrast, are less interested in such a comparative evaluation. They rather look at the fascinating and difficult cross-cultural processes from a perspective of mutual learning, interpreting and transforming knowledge products, the practices of generating them and the values that make them desirable and permit them to be used. In short they study the complex context that comes into play when people leave their own environment and cross a multitude of boundaries either in search of knowledge abroad or offering their own learning, skills and values to a new patron or new colleagues. Exchange began also to be studied within one society, in particular when it comprised different religious groups such as the Ottoman Empire.[7] The 'discovery' of the 'local' as a central epistemological and historiographical category demonstrated that processes of transfer, translation, distribution or dissemination not only take place on macro levels, i.e. between cultures separated by different world views or social organizations, but are an important ingredient in any effort to introduce new ideas, a different form

---

[7] Ekmeleddin Ihsanoglu, Kostas Chatzis, Efthymios Nicolaidis (eds), *Multicultural science in the Ottoman Empire*, (*De Diversis Artibus: Collection de travaux de l'Académie internationale d'histoire des science/Collection of Studies from the International Academy of the History of Science* 69) (N.S. 32), Turnhout: Brepols, 2003.

of practice or a new manner of representation.[8] The flow of knowledge in early modern Catholic and Protestant Europe was not at all free of conflicts, misunderstandings or rejections simply because all participants subscribed in general terms to the same religion or wrote most of their academic treatises in the same scholarly language. The same applies to the flow of knowledge in and between early modern Islamic societies. That being the case, the main question to be answered for processes of boundary crossing is not any longer one of comparative cultural, let alone civilizational standing. It has rather become one about the activities that were undertaken and the values that were applied during the act of boundary crossing as well as one about the processes that made some parts of the identified and acquired foreign knowledge sustainable as explicitly recognized parts of the knowledge of their own cultures, while others were camouflaged, 'denaturalized' or excluded.[9] These two questions give rise to a third one that addresses the changes that the previous owners of the foreign or the 'own' knowledge and their cultures underwent as a result of such processes, i.e. how the foreign and the 'own' knowledge cultures began to move in different directions, subscribing to modified values, being practiced in modified institutional environments and being remembered in altered modes of verbal or visual narration.[10]

My own work was formed by these changes of academic practice in multiple ways. I came to recognize that our previous meta-narrative of the intellectual relationships between the 'West' and the 'East', in particular between 'Europe' and 'Islam', was flawed on several levels. In my own intellectual journey, the four most important of these levels concerned our presuppositions, the criteria and methods for analysing historical evidence, the questions we do and do not ask and the answers and judgments we do and do not construct. Categories like inferiority and superiority or the mostly implicit beliefs that progress is the only 'natural' trajectory for science and that societies to which this 'axiom' does not apply are intrinsically flawed were part of the criteria upon which we built answers and evaluations. The search for the 'primeval locus or form' of a method, a subject matter, an institution or an observation or the reduction of the matter of inquiry to scientific content and usually only one of the cultures and

---

[8] Steven J. Harris, 'Introduction: Thinking globally, acting locally', in Mario Biagoli, Steven J. Harris (eds), *The Scientific Revolution as Narrative*, (*Configurations* 6.2) (1998), 131–39.

[9] See, for instance, Marc Fumaroli, 'The Fertility and the Shortcomings of Renaissance Rhetoric: The Jesuit Case', in John W. O'Malley, S.J., Gauvin Alexander Bailey, Steven J. Harris, and T. Frank Kennedy, S.J. (eds), *The Jesuits, Cultures, Sciences, and the Arts 1540-1773*, Toronto, Buffalo, London: University of Toronto Press, 1999, pp. 90–106; Nicolas Standaert, S.J., 'Jesuit Corporate Culture as Shaped by the Chinese', in ibid., pp. 352–61; Harold Cook, .

[10] Peter Burke, Ronnie Po-Chia Hsia (eds), *Cultural Translation in Early Modern Europe*, Cambridge: Cambridge University Press, 2007.

its representatives involved in producing such kinds of knowledge dominated our repertoire of questions. The assumption that certain concepts such as fact or objectivity possess no history, but are universal and unchangeable, belonged to the arsenal of widely shared beliefs as does the conviction that humans live in blocs of culturally defined, but fundamentally and permanently different identity such as 'Occident' and 'Orient', 'West' and 'East' or 'Christendom' and 'the Islamic world', to name only those of immediate relevance for my research.

Once I began to realize that our historical narrative of the intellectual encounters between Catholic, Protestant and later secular societies in Europe and Islamic societies in Europe, western Asia and northern Africa was highly selective in its choice of topics, periods and actors and often negatively inclined towards Islamic societies, I began to pay more attention to the stories told in the historical sources that I studied and the methods that were applied to compose them. I began to understand that our concept of humanism was too narrow in its exclusive focus on the role of Greek and Roman authors. While many scholars of the sixteenth and first half of the seventeenth centuries, the period I investigated, studied rhetoric and preferred Greek and Roman texts over Latin translations of Arabic treatises, not all were of the opinion that the philological faults and rhetorical shortcomings of these translations meant that the Arabic sources had to be abandoned. Patrons and scholars of the newly founded societies and academies paid substantial attention and funding to the acquisition of Arabic, Persian and Ottoman Turkish scientific, literary, historical, religious and philological manuscripts, as much or even more as they directed their sight and purse towards collecting Greek or Latin manuscripts in the same domains. The planned and officially funded missions sent to western Asia looked for manuscripts in all those languages (and others) on the entire range of subject matters together. Travellers acquiring manuscripts by their own financial as well as social means merely differed in quantity, not in outlook and purpose. The Graeco-Latin humanism of Catholic and Protestant universities and other circles of learning, the interest for 'Asian' and 'African' languages and the search for their texts were not situated in separate areas, but were exercised, financed and organized by the same people who were also engaged with contributing to the new scientific practices. They represented an 'Oriental' humanism that combined philology with religious studies as well as medical, mathematical, astronomical, geographical, historical and philosophical interests. This 'Oriental' humanism and the collecting of Oriental manuscripts were themselves new practices, linking science with commerce and reputation building in the *Republic of Letters* as well as among the secular and religious nobility. Francis Richard, Justus Witkam and other colleagues working on Arabic, Persian, Ottoman Turkish, Hebrew or Samaritan manuscripts extant today in major European libraries whose collections go back to this new early modern form of mixed socio-cultural practice, have investigated painstakingly the details of the history of these collections in Paris, Leiden, Cambridge, Oxford and Rome.[11] They identified buyers, traders, owners, users and intermediaries who (re-)moved individual manuscripts from their previous private, educational, courtly or religious libraries in the Ottoman Empire, Safavid Iran, Mughal and other Islamic domains in India as well as northern Africa to Italy, France, England, The Netherlands and German speaking countries into private and courtly libraries, for study, display or private pleasure alone. A new geography of knowledge is thus on the verge of emerging that will not replace the ones we are already familiar with for Catholic and Protestant Europe. Nor will it overshadow the newly established ones for East Asia. It will enrich, modify and qualify these better known geographies. Papers I, II and VII discuss aspects of this new geography of knowledge.

Early modern Catholics and Protestants did not only travel to western Asia and northern Africa for buying manuscripts for trade and for rich patrons. Unpublished letters, travel accounts and diplomatic reports show that numerous well-known scholars, many unknown men and a few women from London, Cambridge, Oxford, Paris, Dieppe, Leiden, Berlin, Tübingen, Rome, Venice, Naples, Lisbon and other cities in Catholic and Protestant European countries planned to travel to or did indeed visit the Ottoman Empire, Safavid Iran and occasionally even Mughal India. The belief in the superiority of ancient authors, if not necessarily as scholars, but at least as writers, expressed in their

---

[11] Francis Richard, *Catalogue de manuscrits persans, I, Ancien fonds*, Paris: BnF, 1989; Francis Richard, 'Les manuscris persans apportés par les frères Vecchietti et conservés aujourd'hui à la Bibliothèque nationale', *Studia iranica* IX.2 (1980), 291–300; Francis Richard, 'Achille de Harlay de Sancy et ses collections de manuscrits hébreux', *Revue des etudes juives* CXLIX.4 (1990), 417–47; Francis Richard, 'Les frères Vecchietti, diplomats, érudits et aventueriers', in Alastair Hamilton, Maurits van den Boogert and Bart Westerweel (eds), *The Republic of Letters and the Levant*, Leiden: Brill, 2005; Jan Justus Witkam, *Jacobus Golius (1596–1667) en zijn handschriften*, Leiden: Leiden University Library, 1980; Jan Justus Witkam, 'The Middle Eastern holdings of the library of the University of Leiden', *British Journal of Middle Eastern Studies*, 8.1, (1981), 60–64; Jan Justus Witkam, 'Precious books and moments of friendship in 17th-century Istanbul', in Mustafa Kaçar and Zeynep Durukal (eds), *Essays in honour of Ekmeleddin Ihsanoglu*, Volume I, Societies, cultures, sciences: a collection of articles, Istanbul: IRCICA, 2006, pp. 467-474; Jan Justus Witkam, *Van Leiden naar Damascus en weer terug. Over vormen van islamitische lees- en leercultuur*, Leiden: Leiden University Library, 2003; Jan Justus Witkam, 'The Golius Collection', in Jan Justus Witkam, *Inventory of the Oriental Manuscripts of the Library of the University of Leiden*, Volume 1, Manuscripts Or. 1–Or. 1000, Leiden: Ter Lugt Press, 2007, pp. 11-12; Arnoud Vrolijk and Kasper van Ommen (eds), *All my Books in Foreign Tongues*, Scaliger's Oriental Legacy in Leiden 1609–2009. Catalogue of an exhibition on the quatercentenary of Scaliger's death, 21 January 2009. With an introductory essay by Alastair Hamilton. Leiden: Leiden University Library, 2009.

published writings about the physical or intellectual travels was by no means a cultural imperative that shaped implicitly the writing, observing and arguing habits of these early modern writers about Islamic societies in western and southern Asia. Comparisons of unpublished letters, diaries and travel accounts with published writings of the same kind show deep differences between the sources that were given centre-stage in each of the two categories and the arguments, frameworks and languages that were considered authoritative and hence permissible to be relied upon by the author. In his studies of other kinds of sources, not touching upon the exchange of knowledge with Islamic societies in western Asia and northern Africa, Peter Burke has labelled 'classicizing' one of the three processes that he recognized as having been at play in early modern translations from foreign languages. Following translation theorists, he defined the two other processes as 'domestication' and 'foreignizing'.[12] Although Burke's usage of the terms relates primarily to issues of language, all three processes characterize other acts of 'cultural translation' as well, as I argue for the first of them in papers III, IV and V, taking up the complexities of early modern writing about western Asia and the scientific tradition(s) of Islamic societies.

Criticizing ancient authors for their alleged or true lack of knowledge in geography or history was also not a cultural imperative when writing about Islamic societies in western Asia and northern Africa. The geographical and historical written depiction of both regions rather reinstated ancient authors as the primary authorities. Thus early modern Catholic and Protestant writers designated, by their choice of sources and authors, the two regions' ancient identities as those that claimed precedence over the new, contemporary identities shaped by people of different languages, origins, histories and beliefs. Unpublished documents leave no doubt that this written depiction was indeed a conscious process of reinstating the authority of ancient authors against collected, observed or learned local knowledge of the visited Islamic societies that was presented visibly and with pride in the authors' diary entries or letters. In paper III, I present an analysis of the unpublished documents of one of the wealthy, educated and curious travellers of the early seventeenth century, Pietro della Valle. Unpublished documents also show that not all visitors of foreign lands were indeed interested in their nature or culture. Nor did they bother with ancient authors. Mapmakers working in Catholic and Protestant cities, in contrast, preferred the new, local knowledge over the old, written one found in ancient authors. Hence, a mixed and not fully stable geographical

---

[12] Peter Burke, 'Cultures of Translation in Early Modern Europe', in Burke, Po.Chia Hsia, *Cultural Translation*, pp. 7–38, in particular pp. 26–9, 34–5, 37–8; Peter Burke, 'Translations into Latin in early modern Europe', in ibid., pp. 65–80, in particular pp. 79, 80.

discourse emerged that delighted in often uncertain and unfounded efforts to compare and equalize ancient names and localities with contemporary ones. While this need to compare and equalize ancient and contemporary concepts was accepted by some early modern educated men as a component of knowledge, others questioned the validity of its results or even ridiculed both need and results. This geographical discourse mixed with history and politics, with religion and war, with intellect and emotion. It was not a debate of 'pure' knowledge about mountains, rivers and woods or cities, villages and peoples, nor could it have been so or become so. The conscious return of its speakers to ancient secular and sacred books and the authority of their authors brought with it the devaluation of their own recently acquired foreign knowledge and of the cultures that had produced it. The allegory of the luxurious and wise, but static and inert Asia was born in this scripting praxis that re-integrated ancient authors through visits to libraries at home into an author's (oral or written) travel account and obliterated (partially or fully) the newly acquired foreign knowledge as I have suggested in paper III. In paper IV, on the other hand, I present, together with my colleague Volkmar Schüller (Berlin), a different approach chosen by the same traveller whom I discuss in paper III (Pietro della Valle) to the vexing question of how to mediate between different systems of geographical knowledge. While still privileging ancient norms, della Valle gives wide range to his own learning activities and the object(s) of his learning in the Ottoman and Safavid Empires in a text originally composed for a Jesuit missionary from Bohemia serving in India and subsequently in China, an example for my argument later in this introduction about the relationships between visitors to western Asia and missionaries in India and the Far East. The manuscripts prepared for print and the lack of success in publishing this geographical text point to the difficulties that a more balanced form of representation could encounter in the face of censorship, ideology and the politics of overseas missions.

 This complex early modern discourse took its inspiration and information from many diverse sources, the veracity of which its speakers had no means yet to evaluate. The limitation of judgment resulted from a lack of familiarity with other intellectual traditions, languages, customs and natures. It was sustained by the as of yet only limited capability of self-reflexive questioning of the own intellectual traditions, languages and customs. The continued dominance of knowledge drawn from books for elaborating and defending one's views added a further constraint, even when only relatively 'simple' issues were at stake like that of names of places such as Baghdad versus Babylon, Tabriz versus Ekbatana, Tunis versus Carthago or Istanbul versus Constantinople. The first two of these hotly debated identifications are false. Three of the four concern the identification of the past known through ancient secular and sacred books with the foreign present. One continues the battle for the long fallen capital of the Byzantine Empire with discursive means denying the city its contemporary cultural identity. The antiquarian status of the three other examples does not signify, however, that no political and religious currents were at play in the refusal of numerous authors to acknowledge that Carthago had disappeared many centuries ago and that Tunis, while not exactly at the same locus, had now taken its place as a coveted, feared and despised centre of sea power in the Mediterranean. The mixed composition of its lords and sailors made up of local Muslims, voluntary and involuntary converts from Italy, France, the Iberian Peninsula, German speaking countries or The Netherlands plus some Ottoman reinforcement added to the emotive as well as intellectual problems authors had when talking about the city and its port. The temporary loss of former friends or colleagues to the 'other side' due to captivity and subsequent slavery was emotionally difficult to bear and costly to end. The voluntary decision not to return to the native society and one's former friends brought pain to those left behind who rarely understood the rationale of such a step. Those men, usually disparagingly called renegades and often severely punished if they returned, nonetheless served not only as go-betweens between their own families and their new companions, but were put to good use by scholars in Catholic or Protestant countries who wished to buy manuscripts, acquire animals or drugs, participate in lucrative trade or receive a description of an eclipse. In paper VII I discuss one of the well-known scholarly brokers of exchange between the Islamic and the Catholic and Protestant dominions of the *Republic of Letters*, Nicolas Fabri de Pereisc, and his network of interests and contacts in northern Africa and western Asia, among them voluntary converts to Islam.

Collecting manuscripts, medals, coins, drugs, plants, animals or observing comets and measuring latitudes were activities that connected many of the travellers to the Ottoman and Safavid Empires, whether they were merchants, missionaries, scholars, diplomats, adventurers or people in search of paid positions, with the then standard practices of scholars in Catholic and Protestant countries. Travellers, in particular long-term travellers like missionaries or diplomats and in the case of Venetian consulates also their officially attached physicians, did not only collect matters of scientific interest in their foreign environments, but brought such objects with them from their places of origin, among them scientific manuscripts, instruments, books and plans for observations and other scholarly activities. They were connected to colleagues, friends or patrons at home and in several other cities in Catholic and Protestant countries with whom they corresponded, to whom they sent parts of their collections and from whom they received instruction, information, letters by other scholars or the occasional book or instrument.

Networks have become a privileged concept in history of science for describing the comparable settings in as well as between Catholic and Protestant countries or the overseas missions of the Jesuits in China or Japan within the Jesuit Society.[13] As a rule, historians of science overlook that the same relationships characterized the travels, missions and consulates in the Ottoman Empire and Safavid Iran. Western Asia has been systematically neglected in Anglophone studies of scholarly activities of Catholic and Protestant travellers abroad. Even works such as *The Jesuits, Cultures, Sciences, and the Arts 1540–1773* (1999) whose editors and contributors undertook their writings as a reflection of and contribution to the changes in historiography at large and in regard to the Jesuit order in particular did not realize that many of the people they studied did not arrive in China or Japan by ship via southern Africa and Goa alone, but crossed the Mediterranean and then travelled overland through western Asia, starting mostly in Aleppo or Istanbul, moving on to Basra, Bandar 'Abbas or Isfahan and once they had arrived in Surat, Goa or Agra could have crossed the Indian subcontinent by foot were they chosen for further travel to Siam (Thailand), Cochinchin (Vietnam), China or Japan. In many cases theirs were no continuous travels. They often spent a year or more in one of these main stations of combined marine and overland journeying, serving in the houses of their orders or learning languages. Learning Arabic was seen, at least in the seventeenth century, as a necessity for many missionaries sent to Asia. Thus a good number of them were trained for a shorter or longer time in Rome, Aleppo or Cairo by their own brothers, missionaries from other orders or Arab native speakers, mostly Maronite Christians. Hence western Asia was not exempted from the overseas missions, neither of the Jesuits nor of that of other orders such as the Carmelites, the Capuchins, the Augustinians or the Franciscans. It rather played an important role as a place for education, transfer, political 'lobbying' and missionary activities among the various Oriental Christian as well as Jewish communities. Francophone studies of Catholic missions have paid more attention to western Asia as well as Islamic societies of India, a fact perhaps explained by the role played by men like Cardinal Richelieu, Cardinal Mazarin and Jean-Baptiste Colbert in these missions as well as commercial ventures abroad.[14]

---

[13] Steven J. Harris, 'Long-Distance Corporations, Big Sciences, and the Geography of Knowledge', *Configurations* 6.2 (1998), 269–304; see as another example the short description of the research project *Mapping the Republic of Letters* at Stanford University: http://shc.stanford.edu/collaborations/supported-projects/mapping-republic-letters.

[14] Francis Richard, 'L'Apport des missionnaires européens à la connaissance de l'Iran en Europe et de l'Europe en Iran', *Etudes safavides*, Tehran: IFRI, 1993, pp. 251–66 (Bibliothèque iranienne, 39); Francis Richard, 'Les missionnaires français en Arménie au XVIIe siècle', *Arménie entre Orient et Occident*, Paris, BnF-Le Seuil, 1996, p. 196–202; Philippe Le Tréguilly

Catholic missionaries in the Ottoman Empire may have participated only as comparatively marginal figures in the exchange of knowledge that took place during the early modern period. Their activities in this respect covered, however, a wide variety of topics. Jesuits had arrived in the late sixteenth century in the Ottoman Empire, followed by Carmelites and Capuchins in the first decades of the seventeenth. The presence of Catholic orders in Iran began in the first years of the seventeenth century, when the Augustinians and Carmelites, then the Capuchins, and with nearly half a century delay, the Jesuits, applied for permission to the Safavid shahs to settle and open their houses first in the capital and later in other cities of the realm. The Jesuits and Capuchins opened schools for boys of the Christian minorities, for instance, in the province of al-Shām (Syria), teaching there Arabic, Greek, Italian and catechism. A primary field of exchange of knowledge, to which the *Propaganda fide* in Rome and the *Missions Étrangères* in Paris contributed successfully, was the compilation, printing and dissemination of grammars and dictionaries. They were mostly derived from Arabic, Greek or Persian antecedents. Oriental Christians who had migrated to Rome or Paris contributed to their compilation, proofreading and preparation for print. Missionaries investigated languages little known at the time in their home countries, measured geographical latitudes and participated in the transfer of books and instruments from Rome or Paris to Aleppo, Sayda, Istanbul and Isfahan for purposes of conversion and inter-faith competitions, as I show in paper VIII.[15] In addition to those institutionally backed activities, individual missionaries cooperated in Nicolas Fabri de Peiresc's projects of astronomical observation (see paper VII), acted as doctors and pharmacists and supported members of the *Republic of Letters* in their search for Arabic, Persian, Ottoman Turkish, Armenian, Coptic, Syriac, Greek or Ethiopian manuscripts. The superiors of the houses as well as those in Rome or Paris often looked with displeasure upon such activities, regarding them as detrimental to the ministry and as overstepping the boundaries of the missions' officially condoned practices. Special dispenses were required for administering drugs and other medical treatments and for leaving the mission for observations of the sky and nature, dispenses that were not always given in time or at all.[16] In Basra, Isfahan and elsewhere, missionaries studied medical, astrological or

---

and Monique Morazé (eds), *L'Inde et la France: deux siècles d'histoire commune, XVIIe–XVIIIe siècles: histoire, sources, bibliographie*, Paris: CNRS éditions, 1995; *Science et présence jésuites entre Orient et Occident, autour de Fronton du Duc*, Paris: Médiasèvres, 2004.

[15] Sonja Brentjes, '"Renegades" and Missionaries as Minorities in the Transfer of Knowledge', in Ihsanoglu, Chatzis, and Nicolaidis (eds), *Multicultural Science*, pp. 63–70, in particular pp. 64–6.

[16] Brentjes, '"Renegades" and Missionaries ...', pp. 66–8.

geographical manuscripts as a means of learning the local languages, copied or bought them, translated them into Latin or one of the European vernaculars, compiled dictionaries with their help or wrote treatises in which they merged their own education with that available in their new environments.[17]

Questions that are too seldom asked, but proved to be of relevance to my own research project, concern the how, where and with whom visitors of the Ottoman and Safavid Empires acquired the necessary communication skills and learned where to look for the kind of knowledge and objects they wished or had been told to buy, copy or appropriate otherwise, what problems they encountered in these undertakings and how they solved or sidestepped them. Who were their intermediaries and brokers of introductions, contacts, permissions and safe guards? What were the concepts and methods of teaching and learning the various languages spoken and written in western Asia? How can we corroborate the veracity of the travellers' accounts about the adventures, friendships and dangers, that is, what was 'fact' and what 'fiction', and what choices could and did the writer make when drafting his letters, diary entries or accounts? With whom did he cooperate in which activities abroad and at home? In short, which were the many little and bigger steps a traveller had to take physically and metaphorically in order to arrive at the chosen stations of his journey(s) and reap the gains of his courage, curiosity, patience and boldness?

I address some of these questions in papers I–V. Others need further reflection and research. In the geography of knowledge of Catholic and Protestant visitors of early modern western Asia Istanbul, Aleppo and Cairo were nodal points of learning and contacts in the Ottoman Empire, while Isfahan played the same role for Safavid Iran. The broader range of possibilities available in the former results on the one hand from the larger and culturally more complex territories that it covered and on the other from a less centralizing approach to foreigners on its soil sharing their surveillance with the provincial governors. The Safavid shahs, in contrast, followed mostly the precedence set by 'Abbas I at the beginning of the seventeenth century who prescribed locations for the missionaries either in Isfahan or its Armenian suburb New-Julfa and granted only sparingly the permission to open trading posts in his ports for merchants from Europe, while Indian traders seem to have fared better. Only under 'Abbas II did a larger network of missionary

---

[17] Michel Bastiaensen (translated and annotated by), *Ange de Saint-Joseph dans le siècle Joseph Labrosse: Souvenirs de la Perse safavide et autres lieux de l'Orient (1664–1678). En version persan et européenne*, Faculté de Philosophie et Lettres XCIII, Brussels: Éditions de l'Université de Bruxelles, 1985; Francis Richard, 'L'Apport des missionnaires européens ...', 1993.

houses and trading posts begin to arise across the country, providing other Catholic and Protestant visitors with more addresses for accommodation.

Several Ottoman and Safavid cities housed small Christian communities from Europe, trading in the southern and eastern Mediterranean by then for almost half a millennium, and larger Christian populations formed by native inhabitants or resettled groups from other parts of the two empires. These communities, as a rule, provided the individual traveller with places of contact or lodging, although the Safavid shahs preferred to prescribe accommodation for visitors from among the properties of their courtiers. The language training of missionaries, if they were sent from Rome, began at the city's Maronite College and was continued by the Carmelites in Aleppo. Individual travellers and the occasional diplomat learned Hebrew, Turkish and occasionally Arabic in Istanbul, apparently above all with leading Jewish scholars as well as merchants. Some also took Arabic classes in Cairo. Most of the later prominent professors of Oriental languages though, who spent a longer time in the Ottoman Empire, studied with members of the scholarly elite in Aleppo. At times, contacts with Maronite Christians served the same purpose. Another group of men who came to the Ottoman Empire to learn Oriental languages were court translators and interpreters or their sons whose patrons wished them to improve their skills. Venice as well as Paris pondered repeatedly the need and possibilities for opening language schools for young boys, prospective interpreters for their embassies. Although in particular Venice indeed undertook such a formal training for some time in Istanbul, the schools were not very successful during the period that I studied. In Iran, the centre of language studies for European travellers was Isfahan. They approached scholars for introductory as well as advanced classes. A few of them who stayed on for longer periods of time themselves gave classes to newly arrived missionaries or passers by, once they felt sufficiently at ease with their new skills.

Sometimes, travellers like Pietro della Valle complained about the difficulties of learning a different language, in particular when the distance between their experience with Indo-European languages and the new language was as great as in the case of Ottoman Turkish where they had to master an agglutinating language with many loan words from a Semitic as well as an Iranian language that also were unknown to them. They expected language classes that fitted their own upbringing and grammatical training, i.e. a conceptual framework and terminology that agreed with Latin grammar. Jewish (and probably other) teachers of Turkish at best taught the language in the conceptual framework and terminology of Arabic grammar, if they were inclined at all toward a formalized teaching material of the various tenses and ways to express clauses, cases and similar categories of Indo-European languages. Della Valle describes comical scenes in his encounters with his first

Jewish teacher of Turkish, whom he dismissed after the third session since the teacher simply could not comply with the traveller's demands and the traveller was incapable of fitting into the unfamiliar form of doing things. His saviour was a highly educated Jew, the teacher of the French ambassador Achille de Harlay de Sancy, to whom della Valle had turned for help. He read and spoke fluently the three literary languages of Ottoman elite society. He also had a certain grasp of Latin grammar since the ambassador had taught these rules to him for easing his own learning of Turkish, Hebrew and perhaps also Arabic. Hence, even the acquisition of something so basic, for communicating in a foreign environment and picking up foreign knowledge, as learning how to speak the foreigners' language was fraught with difficulties in the early modern period. It could only succeed if both sides taught, learned and were willing to cross the boundaries that limited the partner. People with extraordinary skills or of special origin had to be found in the foreign society in order to help the visitors to reach their goal.

Della Valle's second Jewish teacher of Turkish was a leading scholarly member of his own community and a merchant. He could not always be in Istanbul and spend all his time with Christian foreigners. Hence, della Valle was once again without a teacher. The replacement came once more through the ambassador's mediation. Having had no previous experience in teaching Turkish to Catholic visitors, della Valle was suspicious about his new teacher's capability to perform well. 'Bizarre' (as della Valle called them) situations arose between the two men. The teacher translated what he knew into Spanish or perhaps rather Ladino, Judaeo-Spanish. Born in al-Quds (Jerusalem), he might have been a descendant of Jewish emigrants from the Iberian Peninsula after their expulsion by their Catholic Majesties of Spain and Portugal. Turkish words that this new teacher did not know in Spanish he modified by adding a Spanish ending. Della Valle had to transfer these into Tuscan, which he did not always achieve and hence was left second guessing. It took, however, only a few weeks before della Valle wrote to his friends in Naples that he could already chat with the ladies.[18] Other travellers imply that they learned some of their basic or advanced Turkish from members of other minorities and in a much less formal environment than della Valle, although apparently with at least partially the same purpose, i.e. to engage with the ladies.

In contrast to earlier times, a good number of extant fragmentary or completed dictionaries, interlineal or newly composed grammars and collections

---

[18] Sonja Brentjes, 'Western European Travelers in the Ottoman Empire and Their Scholarly Endeavors (Sixteenth–Eighteenth Centuries)', in Hasan Celâl Güzel and C. Cem Oğuz Osman Karatay (eds), *The Turks*, Volume 3, Ottomans, Ankara: Yeni Türkiye Publications, 2002, pp. 795–803; p. 796.

of basic conversation exercises by Italian, French, English or German visitors of or temporary residents in the two Islamic societies have survived in various European libraries. Most of the dictionaries and conversation books focus on very elementary bits and pieces meant to help with mastering everyday life needs in a foreign environment. Many also contain basic Christian vocabulary. Some fragmentary dictionaries go beyond the norm and provide insights into the special interests of their compilers. A short anonymous French-Arabic dictionary, for instance, teaches mainly words needed when engaging in relationships with the other sex, a purpose that brought a good number of young and not so young Catholic and Protestant visitors to the Ottoman Empire. Istanbul and Cairo reigned supreme in this respect as private letters, Capuchin records and legal broadsheets in the Chamber of Commerce in Marseille attest.

The complete dictionaries, in particular those concentrating on Persian vocabulary, were often the work of missionaries. They show that language material compiled by Jesuits in India was highly appreciated outside the order too. This leads to the question to what degree the orders engaged in overseas missions indeed differed in their policies, at least in respect to their own education in the local languages and the study of works of local scholars. It should also be asked how much Carmelite and Capuchin policy of cultural adaptation was encouraged by what is called in Jesuit studies the 'cultural imperative', i.e. the framework for missionary work provided by the host culture, and what made them choose Jesuit material if the relationship was as tense as often implied.[19] The dictionaries compiled by missionaries in Isfahan confirm that their intellectual framework in the mid-seventeenth century continued to be that of Aristotelian philosophy and only very elementary arithmetic, geometry and astrology, not enough to engage a Shi'i scholar of the period into a serious debate about nature, the cosmos, the influence of the planets or mathematics. The Persian and the less extensively present Arabic and Turkish vocabulary leaves little doubt that the people with whom the missionaries collaborated when compiling those scholarly tools did not come from elite educated circles and had in all likelihood not passed through a madrasa education.[20]

Della Valle who also compiled collections of Persian words used, like the missionaries, Jerónimo Xavier's dictionary of religious terminology composed in Agra in the early seventeenth century, but went beyond them by learning some

---

[19] Standaert, 'Jesuit Corporate Culture ...', pp. 356–7; Erik Zürcher, 'Jesuit Accommodation and the Chinese Cultural Imperative', in D.E. Mungello (ed), *The Chinese Rites Controversy: Its History and Meaning*, Monumenta Serica Monograph Series XXXIII. Nettetal: Steyler Verlag, 1994, pp. 31–64.

[20] MS Città del Vaticano, Biblioteca Apostolica, Borg. 14.

basic vocabulary of the mathematical sciences as used in scholarly manuscripts and discussions. He continued his search for adequate vocabulary at different stations of his many years of travel and even after his return to Rome. Still, when writing in Persian in Goa after an interview with the Jesuit astronomer and visitor of Siam, Cristoforo Borro, on recent new ideas about the universe discussed in Italy and elsewhere for his friend from Lar, the astronomer Mullā Zayn al-Dīn, his vocabulary often enough was not taken from the scientific terminology familiar to his friend, but from daily life. Hence, acquiring access and a fine understanding of the mathematical, astronomical and astrological knowledge of his friend and other Safavid scholars proved beyond della Valle's possibilities and perhaps lastly also his interests. An unfinished translation extant today in the Archivio Segreto, Vatican City, of the elementary astrology of another friend of his from Lar, Quṭb al-Dīn 'Abd al-Ḥayy b. al-'Izz Ḥusaynī, widely distributed in libraries of Iran, India and Europe, and the probably never implemented plan of translating an elementary Ottoman Turkish introduction to astronomy and astrology also testify to the limits that della Valle faced in his efforts to master two languages, specific technical terminologies and corresponding domains of scholarly knowledge.[21]

When sent at the age of sixteen to the Ottoman and Safavid Empires to learn Arabic, Ottoman Turkish and Persian, it took François Pétis de la Croix nine years of intensive studies in Iskanderun, Istanbul and Isfahan, mostly with madrasa scholars, to achieve the good understanding of the disciplinary canon of Islamic higher education that an anonymous dictionary extant at the *Missions Étrangères* in Paris reflects, despite the fact that his father François de la Pétis Croix, royal interpreter of Arabic and Turkish, trained him from his early childhood to become his successor. His later career as secretary and translator of French ambassadors and armies in northern Africa, professor of Arabic at the Collège Royal de France and finally heir to his father's position at court confirmed his philological achievements. This was not the only knowledge, though, that his study with madrasa scholars allowed him to acquire. He also became well-versed in various matters of protocol, courtesy and etiquette. These skills made him a very able and successful negotiator between the courts and their armies.[22] There is no reason to assume that penetrating the scientific parts of this canon of higher Islamic education demanded less dedication and intimacy than that of the literary and religious disciplines. Hence, most travellers who stayed for much shorter periods of time had little chance to grasp more than the objects that embodied such knowledge, not the

---

[21] MS Archivio Segreto, Città del Vaticano, Della Valle-del Bufalo 51.

[22] http://www.institutkurde.org/en/conferences/kurdish_studies_irbil_2006/Chris+KUTSC-HERA.html

knowledge itself. Their comments on the local scholarly life and the quality of the scientific knowledge need to be taken with extreme caution. They have to be balanced by an independent study of available Arabic, Persian or Ottoman Turkish manuscripts of the period.

In addition to the barrier that the lack of language proficiency meant for those travellers who were seriously searching for scientific knowledge, texts, instruments and related objects, the usually old fashioned information about authors and titles that they possessed due to their studies of medieval Arabo-Latin translations of philosophical, medical, mathematical, astronomical, astrological and other treatises proved yet another hurdle to their quest. Some travellers tried to lower it while still at home or while on their way to the Mediterranean shores. They contacted well-known Maronite Christians who had studied in Rome and were familiar with the scholarly literature on both sides of the Mediterranean or at least in part, such as Gabriel Sionita. However, since these educated informants were Christians they could not provide the travellers with letters of recommendation to Ottoman madrasa teachers. They apparently did not even know the scholarly world and the book markets of the capital and other big cities very well, since they provided no counsel as to where to go and whom to ask for guidance. Hence, if a traveller wished to buy objects of knowledge he turned first and foremost to compatriots among the merchant and diplomatic communities of Istanbul, Aleppo, Damascus, Cairo or Alexandria. The conditions varied from city to city. In Aleppo, merchants were able to solicit help from professional scribes and private library owners to acquire copies of important mathematical manuscripts. Rumours or written complaints about ingratitude or worse of the scholarly recipients of such largesse emphasize that refined social skills were needed on this level of exchange too. In Istanbul, Muslim bibliophiles even loaned their manuscripts to Catholic scholarly visitors, some of whom conveniently forgot to return them intending to use them to further their own carrier and income. The German traveller Christian Rau is the best known example for this ungentlemanly behaviour. Conflicts on book markets between Muslim onlookers and Muslims sellers as well as Jewish and Christian buyers point in the same direction. However, reports about them are difficult to corroborate given their narrative functions in the travel accounts. Language teachers proved to be major mediators between public as well as private book sellers and Catholic or Protestant buyers. They also copied texts themselves for their foreign students. In some cases, as letters to Jacob Golius in Leiden and John Greaves and Edward Pococke in Oxford document, such connections lasted over many years, continuing even after the departure of the foreign scholars.[23] Witkam has argued that the condition of the

---

[23] Witkam, *Inventory of the Oriental Manuscripts* …, Vol. 1, pp. 19–21.

book market in Aleppo changed significantly during the seventeenth century. Valuable and finely illustrated mathematical and other manuscripts, not for sale in the 1630s, were available for another Dutch buyer a few decades later.[24] He also showed that Golius and his teacher, the dervish Aḥmad b. al-Ḥājj Ḥusām al-'Akalshānī, worked together when copying important texts. Aḥmad wrote the texts. In a number of cases he also copied the diagrams and marginal notes. In another exemplar, a copy of a collection of mathematical texts made in Aleppo in 1036/1626 from a manuscript copied in Maragha only thirty (?) years after Naṣīr al-Dīn al-Ṭūsī's death, from an autograph of this important Shi'i scholar, Golius drew most of the diagrams himself and added further glosses. Witkam suggested considering this manuscript as a working copy, for Golius meant to protect the precious Ilkhanid collection from damage.[25] A careful and systematic study of all scientific manuscripts brought to Catholic and Protestant countries of Europe in the sixteenth and seventeenth centuries in addition to, and beyond the information already available will provide us with numerous new insights into the contacts that travellers were able to build and maintain, the circulation of scientific manuscripts in the early modern Ottoman and Safavid Empires and even into economic aspects of the book trade in the period. Such an investigation will strengthen the geography of knowledge that linked Europe, western Asia and northern Africa in these two centuries.

A closer look at the intellectual relationships between Catholic, Protestant and Islamic societies in Europe, northern Africa and western Asia in the early modern period thus modifies our historiographical perspectives in four directions. Islamic societies lose their odour of being eternally hostile to the outer world and more or less rigidly sealed off towards any visitor from abroad, merely dealing with their Christian (and other) neighbours through wars and conquests, while being internally on a path of intellectual decline and social decay. This applies first and foremost to the Ottoman Empire that has received so much 'bad press' since the sixteenth century and continues even today to be seen not only by the European and Arab public, but also by academics working on other cultures and societies as the enemy *par excellence* of Christian Europe, the Arab world and science, progress or civilization at large. A less parochial view of the intellectual changes in the early modern period opens our eyes to the important material, intellectual and ideological roles that the Ottoman Empire, its various cultures, territories and peoples have played in them. As I argue in papers I and II, the Ottoman Empire, or to be more precise, several of its cities, were part of the *Republic of Letters*, the network that underpinned and sustained much of early modern Catholic and Protestant

---

[24] Witkam, *Jacobus Golius* ..., p. 63.
[25] Witkam, *Inventory of the Oriental Manuscripts* ..., Vol. 1, p. 20.

scholarship. At the same time, the Ottoman Empire was consciously portrayed by its foreign educated visitors as a land from which they could learn little, a society that not only did not have the same educational institutions as the home countries of those who wrote about it, but one whose 'uneducated warrior elite' destroyed even the tradition of learning of the 'Arabs', despite the fact that they shared the same religious creed. Much of our own historical perspective on the sciences in late medieval and early modern Islamic societies has been formed by the narratives invented by early modern Catholic and Protestant travellers and their colleagues at home and their subsequent modifications as I argue in paper VI. Serious and careful deconstruction of these narratives, as well as a better understanding of the practices that led to their construction, is needed to recover the past on its own terms.

ACKNOWLEDGEMENTS

Grateful acknowledgement is made to the following persons, institutions and publishers for their kind permission to reproduce the papers included in this volume: Cambridge University Press (for Paper I); Dr Halit Eren, Research Centre for Islamic History, Art and Culture, Istanbul (II, VI); I.B. Tauris, London (III); Volkmar Schüller and Koninklijke Brill N.V., Leiden (IV); the Institut Français de Recherche en Iran, Tehran (V); the Max Planck Institute for the History of Science, Berlin (VII); Erwin Rauner Verlag, Augsburg (VIII); and the History of Science Collections, University of Oklahoma Libraries, Norman, OK, for the images reproduced in Chapter VIII.

I

The Interests of the Republic of Letters in the Middle East, 1550–1700

The Argument

The "raison d'être" of this paper is my dissatisfaction with current portrayals of the place and the fate of the so-called rational sciences in Muslim societies. I approach this issue from the perspectives of West European visitors to the Ottoman and Safavid Empires during the sixteenth and seventeenth centuries. I show that these travelers encountered educated people capable of understanding and answering their visitors' scholarly questions in non-trivial ways. The travels and the ensuing encounters suggest that early modern Muslim societies and their institutions, their ways of producing knowledge, the types of their knowledge, and their material resources contributed important elements to various early modern West European approaches to gaining knowledge about nature, history, and politics.

Crossing boundaries — and the impact it had upon the formation of scientific concepts, disciplines, their practices, modes of expression, and the roles scholars played in various social and cultural settings — was a major theme of medieval Muslim historical, religious, and political writings. Modern students of the history of science in Muslim societies are accustomed to accepting and applying boundaries drawn by medieval sources. One problem with these boundaries is their static character, which was caused, for instance, by relegating all contrary evidence about them into the footnotes of modern research papers. This treatment consequently marginalized that information which did not support the privileged perspective of the boundaries. To redraw the lines in a more dynamic configuration requires more than merely reintegrating the marginalized evidence into the main body of a research paper. It necessitates a deeper historical study of the ways in which medieval authors erected those boundaries and talked about them, including their motives for proceeding as they did, and the rewards gained. However, this presupposes breaking down the boundaries that characterize the modern history of science in Muslim societies.

The boundaries erected and accepted by most modern historians of science in Muslim societies are defined by an almost complete lack of contextual and local analysis, by the methodological prison into which the sciences in Muslim societies are confined, and by the practice of categorizing medieval writers according to different modern disciplines. The most widespread methodological approach to the history of science in Muslim societies consists in investigating and evaluating it in (explicit or implicit) comparison with ancient Greek and Hellenistic traditions and early modern West European developments. Thus, the sciences in Muslim societies are constrained to fit into alien patterns and to live up to standards of other cultural and social origins. The disciplinary-bound training of modern historians of science in Muslim societies often separates Muslim scholars and their works into modern disciplinary categories neglecting any compartments that are not directly linked to the modern researcher's qualifications and interests.

One possible way to question these boundaries is to study the early modern perceptions of the sciences in Muslim societies. This would provide a perspective different from that of medieval and contemporary Muslim sources which at the same time is different from our own views. Sixteenth- and seventeenth-century West European and Ottoman sources give testimony of intensive commercial, political, religious, military, and cultural encounters and engagements with changing alliances between West European states and the Ottoman Empire. Analogous information is contained in sources dealing with the Eastern neighbor of the Ottomans — the Safavids. It is with such information, its context, and its results that my paper will be concerned. Despite the many preconceptions and prejudices about early modern Muslim societies that permeate European sources, these sources are nonetheless valuable for a study of early modern Muslim societies and their relations with Christian states in Europe. They inform us about the aspirations the travelers pursued in these empires and what activities they carried out. They describe which social, cultural, religious, political, administrative, and material sources they tapped to gather information and to acquire different sorts of material items. They illuminate how they behaved to get access to such sources. They also show what differences characterized the portrayal of Muslim societies by European travelers. With respect to the Muslim societies, they tell us in what ways the officials interfered in the travelers' activities and what support they lent, or with what kind of reactions the local scholars, merchants, or peasants responded when they were approached and interrogated by the travelers.

A variety of sources such as travel accounts, letters, dictionaries, bibliographies, textbooks, instruments, or paintings support the thesis that scholarly studies and practices in early modern Western Europe to a remarkable extent looked for and depended upon the contemporary Muslim societies across disciplinary, geographical, and professional boundaries. My focus with regard to contemporary Muslim societies will be the Ottoman and the Safavid Empires. The West European perception and usage of these two early modern Muslim societies was fairly broad and multifaceted. Its scholarly forms took place either through traveling, diplomacy, commerce, and war, or through reading books and collecting all sorts of items brought or sent home by sailors, merchants, envoys, missionaries, adventurers, or mercenaries. Early modern Muslim societies and their institutions, their ways of producing knowledge, the types of their knowledge, and their material resources constituted essential elements in various early modern West European approaches to gaining knowledge about nature, history, and politics.

Most information and material resources acquired by West European scholars from Muslim societies came from and was obtained from the Ottomans. Certain Ottoman customs filled West European visitors and residents with awe, admiration, and respect, and were imitated in the travelers' own cultures and transformed into local habits such as drinking coffee, creating public gardens and animal houses, and applying certain medical practices. The many wars between the Ottoman Empire and several Christian states of Europe contributed to sharpening the long existing Christian polemics against Islam. With regard to the sciences in the Ottoman Empire, it gave rise to a rhetoric which denied that Muslim subjects of the Empire had any true interest in the sciences or any skill in the arts. If there was anything worthwhile to notice in this respect, it had been either introduced by so-called Christian renegades, i.e., converts to Islam, or by immigrant Jewish refugees from European Christian states.

The ambiguous relationship between the Christian states of Western and Central Europe and the Ottoman Empire is reflected in such cultural practices as the use of models of human heads in Turkoise forms for training the cavalry. They were introduced to demonstrate publicly the wish and the will to overcome the enemy. At the same time, military ceremonies and courtly practices of the Ottomans were duplicated at Christian courts for entertainment and to exhibit the courts' ability to reproduce Eastern splendor. After the Ottomans' defeat at Vienna and other towns, the skulls and other bodily parts of dead Ottoman soldiers were displayed and sold at West European market places alongside living animals and humans from other parts of the world. The flesh and certain organs of Ottoman soldiers were transformed into drugs and other "useful" objects and sold to apothecaries, libraries, cabinets of curiosities, and museums.[1]

The West European interest in the Middle East is a historical phenomenon which the current perception of the history of the sciences in Muslim societies is unable to cope with. If the rational sciences in Muslim societies were marginalized,

---

[1] "Zedler's Universal-Lexicon of 1745 knows to report that traders brought entire barrels full of 'Turkish heads' to the New Year's fair at Leipzig in 1684, which stemmed from the battle field at Vienna last September. They sold them for four, six, eight Reichstaler. As trophies of victory, they ended in the 'most noble cabinets of curiosity and libraries of Europe'. ... Even more drastically master Dietz, barber in the Brandeburgian regiment, described the evening after the conquest of Ofen in 1686: In most cases, the massacred 'were skinned, the fat was burned out, the membra virilia was cut off, dried and kept in large sacks. From this, the most valuable mumia is produced. They were also often cut up and their entrails were searched to see whether swallowed ducates could be found'" (Heller 1996, 46). About the skull of the Ottoman grand vizier Kara Mustafa executed in 1683 and buried in the courtyard of a mosque in Belgrad, Heller reports: "The skull was excavated by Jesuit monks after the assault of Belgrad in 1688 and presented as a gift to the bishop of Vienna, Kollonitsch. It is preserved as an object of exhibition until today in the Historical Museum of the City of Vienna" (ibid., 46-47). The translation here and in all later cases is mine. It is often too flat to render adequately the early modern style in all its peculiarities. S.B.

had withered away, or were extinguished by so-called Orthodox oppression before the sixteenth century, how could the European scholars and collectors acquire what they were looking for in the contemporary Muslim societies and why did they find people trained in the mathematical, geographical, occult, medical, and philosophical sciences capable of talking to their West European visitors in meaningful ways despite all linguistic, religious, cultural, and political differences and enmities?

Out of the abundant material evidence for the broad range of interests of the Republic of Letters in the Middle East, I have chosen three domains to discuss here. The first domain focuses on the travels of physicians and botanists into the Ottoman Empire who pursued goals more narrowly confined to scholarly subjects. The motives that drew the scholars to travel to the Middle East, their approaches to knowledge available in the region, and the use they made of their experience will be treated in section 1. The second domain includes the travels carried out by gentlemen travelers and merchants both to the Ottoman and the Safavid Empires. These were not primarily for scholarly purposes. In section 2, I ask what interests did such travelers pursue in the two Muslim societies which proved to be of value for the Republic of Letters, what were their sources of information, and how did they evaluate the collected data and their provenance. The third domain is West European political theory exemplified by the earliest scholarly expedition for the sake of the humanities (or, anachronistically speaking, the social sciences). This expedition was described in the account of an English gentleman who traveled to the Ottoman Empire to do research on the fundamentals of political theory. A comparison of this novelty with the more widespread Western European evaluation of the political system in early modern Muslim empires is the subject of section 3. I will ask what these different ideas about political theory meant for the West European construction of a narrative about the sciences in these societies.

The three sections are held together by one main point which I intend to emphasize: Contrary and complementary to most modern histories of early modern sciences in Western Europe, the Muslim territories, their cultures, their economies, their written, oral, instrumental, and gestural knowledge, their forms of patronage, and their scholarly networks were important for the search for ancient, medieval, and contemporary Greek, Latin, Arabic, Persian, Turkish, Armenian, Coptic, and Hebrew religious, historical, literary, and scientific sources, for the acquisition of curiosities, plants, animals, and archeological items, for the determination of chronologies, the observation and measurement of astronomical events, geographical coordinates, meteorological phenomena, or architectural monuments, as well as for the trade in drugs, mummies, manuscripts, instruments, coins, and other things of relevance for the Republic of Letters. The implementation of these interests of the Republic of Letters in the Middle East depended upon the acceptance, cooperation, and support by the authorities of the visited states as well as by local inhabitants and foreign residents. The depiction of these reactions of the administration of the Ottoman and Safavid Empires and of their individual subjects provides us with glimpses, if not deeper insights, into the state of the sciences, their limitations, boundaries, and vivacity in the two Muslim societies.

1. Middle Eastern Interests of Physicians and Botanists

During the sixteenth and seventeenth centuries, several Italian, French, and German physicians and botanists such as Andrea Alpago (d. 1522), Pierre Belon (1517-1564), Leonard Rauwolf (1535-1596), Prospero Alpini (1553-1617), or Joseph Pitton de Tournefort (1656-1708) traveled to the Ottoman Empire to collect plants, animals, vocabulary, drugs, or remedies for their literary studies, their cabinets of curiosity, their gardens, or for commercial purposes. The Italian scholars worked as physicians for the Venetian consuls in Damascus and Cairo and studied the language and the medical knowledge available there. Alpago was a student of the Damascene physician Ibn al-Makki, and Alpini profited from talking to other Italian physicians who were already living in the region for a longer period as well as to some unnamed Cairene doctors. The French scholars were supported or sent by powerful clerical or royal patrons such as the Cardinal François de Tournon or the French king Louis XIV in order to gain knowledge of Mediterranean plants and animals as well as of the names and uses ascribed to them by the contemporary inhabitants of the Mediterranean world. Rauwolf's travel was part of a commercial mission financed by his uncle, a well-off merchant of Augsburg.

These scholarly travelers published a series of books based on their Middle Eastern experiences. Some of them, such as Belon, Rauwolf, or Tournefort, described their travels in the Middle East. Others such as Alpago or Alpini discussed and applied the newly gained knowledge in new editions or translations of Arabic medical texts of Ibn Sina and his commentators such as Ibn al-Nafis (d. 1288), in descriptions of Egyptian diseases, the country's natural history, or the highly valued drug *balsam*. The specificity of the travelers' interests shaped the contents and structure of their publications as well as the use they made of the plants, animals, and drugs they had collected abroad.

The entire text of Belon's travel account (published in 1553) is permeated by his preoccupation with contemporary names of plants and animals, their pictures, their medical usage, and their relation to the names and medical applications given by ancient Greek authorities. Three motives appear to have been central for his travel and the structuring of its account. The first was his wish to write in French about medical, botanical, and zoological issues based on the ancient Greek nomenclatures, an endeavor not undertaken before as he claimed in the introduction.[2]

---

[2] "I take it for granted that nobody can justly criticize me for not having translated things from others than the good ancient authors; and from those I have often taken help in expressing the names of animals and plants and other similar things which are called by proper names. Since such things

The second was the inspiration Belon drew from what he declared to be the application of false names to plants or animals in the vernacular. Such misuse needed correction because it brought forth, for instance, the medical application of the wrong herb and because it contradicted the ancient Greek authorities. This theme obviously was dear to Belon since it figures prominently in his travel account. Belon devoted the entire second chapter to it (Belon 1553, 1b), and treated it repeatedly not only in his travel account, but also in his other writings.

Underlying these two incentives is Belon's humanistic zeal to emulate ancient Greek authorities whom he refers to time and again as "the good authors." In the preface and introduction to his account, Belon legitimized traveling for the sake of knowledge as one of the standards of ancient Greek authors. It is, however, not only the travel at home in the nearby mountains and valleys which lends credibility and reputation to a scholar, but above and foremost travel in distant, strange territories such as Egypt, India, or "Chaldea" (Belon 1553, c). The exemplary Greek scholars are portrayed as traveling students, eager to acquire practical and theoretical knowledge in major disciplines of their own canon. A similar attitude is reflected in Belon's description of his activities in the Ottoman Empire. It differs from the model insofar as Belon claims that his presence and his knowledge also proved to be useful for the inhabitants of the visited country (Belon 1553, 22b–23a). A second humanistic motive invoked by Belon is the *return to the sources*, which he applies to the world of nature:

> Because in most cases the singularities taken from the plants, animals, and minerals are sent to us through the benefit of the peregrinations, without which it is difficult and at all impossible for us to partake in the gifts and riches of the foreign lands, I decided to go to see them at their birth-places. In order to make it easier for me to recognize them, I wanted first to draw the perspective of their images from the books of our ancestors for imprinting it into my mind. Then I dared to undertake the search for them far away in foreign countries not hoping for any other recompensation for my pains than to see them in vigor. (Belon 1553, c ij)

Belon added a further dimension by placing his travel within the commercial explorations of the Indies, both the West and the East Indies, and the commendable acquisition of Eastern wealth. In particular, he was interested in spices and drugs (Belon 1553, 23a). Thus, the acquisition of knowledge, material specimens for investigation, and objects of trade represents different aspects of the same project, the humanist's travel to the East.

Belon's aim to restore the proper names to plants, drugs, or remedies caused him not only to quote ancient Greek authors extensively and to compare their information to each other and to his experiences collected while traveling. It also induced

---

have been never before examined nor put into our vulgar French in accordance with the writings of the ancient authors, the difficulty for me was much more cumbersome" (Belon 1553, 1a).

him to visit the shops in Constantinople to see what the *Turks*[3] sold there and to inquire what they were interested in buying. To find the answers, Belon sought out *un scauant Turc, docte en Arabe* whom he asked to go with him to the market "to write for him a table of all the kinds of merchandise, drugs, and other matters which were sold in the shops of Turkey. It contained the table of Avicenne, written in the Arabic language, encompassing in sum all the things which are brought to them from foreign countries" (Belon 1553, 22b).

Not knowing Arabic or Turkish, Belon proceeded in a rather ingenious way:

> When the said table was established, the Turk read for me all the words, the one after the other. As he read them to me, I wrote in my letters the same word which he had written in his vulgar (tongue), in such a manner as he had loudly read them for me in Arabic. Thereafter I let me show the thing which he had named for me for after having seen it I might write in my language below his writing the thing which I had recognized. By this means I wanted to be able to ask (further questions) if I needed it. (Belon 1553, 22b)

Belon also described the habits and customs of the numerous religious and ethnic groups living in the Ottoman Empire. These parts include information about the bazaars and their drug shops, about the literary sources of Jewish and Muslim medical education, the relative merits of both groups of physicians, and a general, but brief evaluation of the Muslim system of education. Belon reports with surprise that girls are taught to read and write, repeatedly stresses his preference of *Turkish* over *Jewish* physicians and druggists, and states in general terms that the teaching of philosophy and other sciences did exist in the Ottoman Empire of the mid-sixteenth century. What gives these descriptions of customs and habits an individual touch is their linkage with Belon's specific interests in natural history and medicine. Manners, customs, and beliefs, Belon thought, shaped local interests in plants, animals, and stones and their medical, emblematic, or commercial use, and as a consequence, the character and thoroughness of human knowledge. Because the peoples of the Mediterranean world preferred fish rather than meat on their tables, they recommended fewer diets based on meat in cases of disease, and were much more informed about the biology of fishes than that of forest animals.

Belon's approach in all his botanical and zoological writings is characterized by the way he combined philological, botanical, zoological, medical, anthropological, and historical inquiries in order to gain reliable knowledge about the species. This can be seen, for instance, in his *L'histoire naturelle des Estranges Poissons Marins, Avec La Vraie Peinctvre & description du Daulphin, & de plusieurs autres de son espece* (published in 1551). This natural history of the sea fishes shows as well that Belon's travel to the Ottoman Empire had allowed him direct observations of certain animals, such as the hippopotamus, which had attracted much attention in West European writings and paintings, but were not well known to the authors (Belon 1551, 48b–49a).

---

[3] I use italics in this and analogous cases to indicate the language of the travelers.

Rauwolf's travel account is less saturated with philological and zoological discussions. Its textual authorities with respect to botany and medicine are several ancient Greek and Roman authors such as Dioscurides, Theophrast, or Pliny; medieval Arabic writers such as Ibn Sarabiyun (ninth century), Abu Bakr al-Razi (865–925), Ibn Sina (d. 1036), or Ibn Rushd (1126–1198); and contemporary scholars such as Carolus Clusius (1526–1609). Its dedicatory epistle in some respects resembles Belon's arguments for justifying travel. Ancient authorities such as Plutarch and Diogenes Laertios are cited to demonstrate that traveling in far away countries, above all Asia and Egypt, was an indispensable part of Greek scholarly practice. These ancient testimonies for the usefulness of travel do not suffice, however, to justify Rauwolf's medical and botanical travel to the Middle East. The Bible's frequent references to plants useful for healing found in the Middle East are needed to strengthen the case.[4] The Christian character of Rauwolf's commercial and scholarly travel is stressed repeatedly. Early modern collectors of herbarii are summarily mentioned as *pilgrims* for the sake of knowledge who suffered for gaining new insights and collecting new drugs. Rauwolf saw himself in the same mental space as a *pilgrim* to improve his material stock for medical practice ready to suffer for the sake of it and, even more so, to prove himself a worthy member of the community by stressing the multitude of dangers and pains he experienced while traveling in the Middle East. Apparently that is why he does not portray himself as an eager student of the knowledge available in the Ottoman Empire. He even failed to mention the help he received from an Arab botanist from Tripoli in determining the local names of the plants he had collected during his travel. The only learning in the Ottoman Empire Rauwolf admitted to have done was his own observation of nature.[5]

The motif of the *pilgrim suffering as Christ* shaped the mentality of many early modern West European travel accounts about the Middle East. It linked educational and professional travel with the religious pilgrimage to the Holy places. Traveling to gain knowledge, expertise, and stock obviously could not be sufficiently legitimized by referring to ancient scholarly customs, but needed to stress the traveler's readiness to relive to some extent Christ's sufferings in the same region and in a similarly hostile environment.[6] The direct, personal experience of

---

[4] "After I had seen such things in the authors who had written about it and in whose books also more strange and medically useful herbs for instance from Greece, Syria, Arabia, etc. can be found, and after I had read more and thought about it, I took a liking of them the more I saw of them if they were shown together with their places in the beautiful and fertile Orient which are remembered by many writers, but in particular in the Holy Book. The more (I read and saw) the more I desired to visit them also at the places where they grew with the idea also to observe and perceive the inhabitants of those countries, their life, mores, customs, (civil) orders, religion, etc." (Rauwolf 1582, unpaginated).

[5] "After I had decided to undertake this far away travel above all in order to see and to learn to recognize myself the beautiful and foreign plants which are remembered once in a while by the authors at these ends and places, I accepted gladly the good opportunity which I got to this end through my lengthy stay at Aleppo" (Rauwolf 1582, 111).

[6] "Then, after my defunct brother in law, Melchior Manlich senior, proposed to travel to the Orient with his ships in order the investigate the countries' drugs, matters, and other things useful for his trade and promised to cover the expenses and also to pay a suitable salary, I took the often desired

the Holy Land and its adjacent countries, the traveler's sufferings there, and witnessing the "devastation" of Jerusalem, Babylon, and other places once praised as wonderful, lively, and rich enabled him to understand God's wrath and admonished him to bear the hardships of life at home without moaning. Rauwolf defends the publication of his travel account with this potential to better his compatriots' attitudes towards life and to further truly Christian morals. At the same time, he praises it as a handbook of sorts for the appropriate behavior in Ottoman prisons and as proof that there are people living in the Ottoman Empire who are of good heart and easily convertible to the true Christian faith. Thus, traveling to the Middle East does not only improve commerce, science, and individual Christian experience, but contributes to improve and enlarge the Christian commonwealth as such. This combination of individual, local, and — so to speak — geopolitical aspects of commerce, science, and faith characterized many scholars of the sixteenth and seventeenth centuries who directed their attentions towards the Middle East. To separate their scientific from their commercial, political, and religious motives and interests is to create boundaries that either did not exist or were publicly disclaimed.

Rauwolf's account contains a series of fairly detailed enumerations of trees, fruits, vegetables, flowers, and herbs grown in the gardens and the fields in Syria. These enumerations are explicitly linked to Rauwolf's commercial and scholarly interests in drugs and spices. Rauwolf often gave transliterations of what he understood to be the local names of the plants, food, or clothing: "Except of these they have other sweet drinks which they prepare from red jujube fruits [Brustbeerlein] (Cibeben, which drink the inhabitants ... call Hassaph)" (Rauwolf 1582, 105–106).

Ignorant of Turkish and Arabic, Rauwolf obviously had access to people who knew the local languages. Some of them might have been merchants who worked as factors in major Syrian towns. Rauwolf undertook together with other West European travelers and residents at least one of his excursions through the natural environment of Tripoli (Rauwolf 1582, 111). Other informants may have been the interpreters who worked for the French and Venetian consuls and their entourage (Rauwolf 1582, 33). Merchants at the bazaar shared with Rauwolf their knowledge of the simples and of true and false stones or drugs (Rauwolf 1582, 63, 95–96). In some cases, Rauwolf claimed to inform his reader about local medical uses of the plants or herbs he had seen during his excursions or about the local procedures to make soap (Rauwolf 1582, 95).

Rauwolf's most important source for these various forms of local knowledge, however, was the already mentioned Arab botanist. Rauwolf met him after his return to Tripoli in 1575. The two men were brought together by Rauwolf's friend

---

occasion ... and directed my path in the name of God straight towards the Orient. What I suffered, saw, and experienced within three years (which I spent there) under great danger, pain, and labor at water and land, all this I have carefully noted into a small travel book day for day as it happened and as I saw it to keep it as a memorial for my life" (Rauwolf 1582, unpaginated).

Johann Ulrich Krafft, factor of the Manlich emporium in Tripoli from 1573 until its bankruptcy a year later, who was the only one to describe this encounter in his own travel account (Dannenfeldt 1968, 125, 148, 305). Rauwolf showed the Arab the dried plants he had collected during his travels and talked to him through a Jewish interpreter. Rauwolf's silence about his encounter with the Arab botanist fits into the general picture the traveler drew of the state of the sciences in the Ottoman Empire.

Despite the commercial interest in new herbs and drugs from foreign countries, which made Rauwolf's travel possible, his account mainly concerns the species and commodities that were well known at home either as part of the literary heritage on the *materia medica* or as drugs approved of in medical practice. More than once he refers to having seen unknown plants or drugs, but often he abstains from describing them. His focus as he wrote was on those plants and drugs which are found in *Autoribus* (Rauwolf 1582, 63).

Rauwolf's preference for authorized knowledge reflects problems that West European botanists faced when encountering unknown plants. The usual practice of identifying singular plants by name compelled Rauwolf time and again to return to books on botany, medicine, natural history, and *materia medica*. It also fueled his desire to learn and to write down the names of the plants he had collected as they were used by merchants and scholars in the Ottoman Empire.

Plants unknown in the textual traditions of West European knowledge of nature could only be transferred into new knowledge when put into a class already known. Local names, while important to Rauwolf, apparently were not considered sufficient for this purpose. In some cases, Rauwolf preferred to identify the unknown plant on the basis of Pliny or Theophrast in contradiction to what the local names implied: "I have asked for this herb, but they do not know to give it any other name than *Lubie Endigi*, that is, Indian beans. As I recognize it, however, I take it more for Trionum, which is remembered in particular by Theophrast in several instances. Who cares can continue to search for it" (Rauwolf 1582, 193).

Because the descriptions of plants, drugs, their locations, and uses, were motivated by the specific interests of the travelers, these descriptions are more detailed than Rauwolf's general surveys of the state of the arts and sciences, which are as brief as Belon's, but offer evaluations opposite to those of the French traveler. Rauwolf also claims that girls were taught to read and write, but there were no *liberal arts* in the Ottoman Empire, because the *Arabs* and the *Turks* considered them a waste of time and preferred frivolous entertainments such as listening to historical narratives which praised their own ancestors and deeds and denigrated their enemies (Rauwolf 1582, 91). The *Turkish* physicians were few in number and badly educated, because they knew only their own language. The *Jewish* physicians dominated the field, were proficient in a series of languages necessary for the study of medicine, above all Greek and Latin, but were unreliable in times of epidemics and were *covetous*. The character flaws of the latter served to explain and to legitimize Rauwolf's successful practice of medicine in Aleppo not only among the

West European merchants, but also among noble Ottomans, that is, among infidels. Crossing religious boundaries in healing was an activity repeatedly and severely criticized and controlled in German medical writings, papal bulls, or Spanish court documents. Infidel physicians were not supposed to heal Christians and vice versa.[7]

Traveling in the Middle East, collecting plants, animals, and stones there, and comparing their features and names with those found in ancient Greek and Latin and in medieval Arabo-Latin authorities contributed to the restoration of the ancient *materia medica*, the import of new simples into botanical gardens, museums, and pharmacies, the regulation of drug production, and the acquisition of authority. Prospero Alpini was the scholar whose reputation and power to determine, for instance, the "authenticity" of certain drugs was most closely linked to his stay in the Middle East. His books about Egyptian plants, Egyptian diseases, Egyptian natural history, and Egyptian balm enjoyed a wide readership and repeated reprints for more than a hundred years. After his return from Cairo in 1584, he had a successful career as a professor of medicine and a botanist. He taught medicine at the University of Padua (1594–1616) and was the director of its botanical garden where he read public lectures and showed foreign visitors around, among them the young Nicolas Fabri de Peiresc.

Balm, the oriental drug most often talked about by even non-expert travelers to Egypt, established Alpini's special reputation. In 1594, he was asked by two Mantuese apothecaries, Giovan Paolo and Antonio Bertioli, to certify that the *balsamo orientale* produced by them was the much sought after ingredient necessary for the theriac. Alpini was able to comply with their demand since he was convinced that he had brought an "authentic" sample of the balm plant from Cairo and planted it in the botanical garden at Padua.[8] Most travelers in the second half of the sixteenth century, however, reported that the "true" balm trees near Cairo had ceased to grow. As a result, different agents such as Jewish merchants, Ottoman pashas, or pilgrims were said to have replaced it with imports from Mecca.

Prospero Alpini's *Natural History of Egypt*, published posthumously, contains the most detailed information about the scientific life in the Ottoman Empire provided by a European traveler in the sixteenth century. Alpini gave Chapter II.1 of his work the title *De scientiis quibus Ægyptii delectantur*. He emphasized that he indeed had chosen this title purposefully since he had already reported in his earlier book about the diseases of the Egyptians that this people very much liked to study. Then he explained that they studied three languages, namely Arabic, Persian, and Turkish, followed by a variety of disciplines which, according to Alpini almost matched the university curricula in Western Europe, but in fact

---

[7] An example of this attitude can be found in the book by Christian Trewmundt who also cited papal bulls against the consulting of Jewish or infidel physicians by Christians (Trewmundt 1598, 95).
[8] This episode has been described and interpreted by Findlen, 270–271.

partly surpassed it in scope, for it included topics such as logic, metaphysics, theology, philosophy, rhetoric, medicine, mathematics, and magic. He named several sources the general public and the educated elite had available in their philological training and called the al-Azhar mosque the most important school in Cairo (Alpin 1735, 85). His description of the disciplines taught there and which of the arts and sciences were most favored corresponds rather well with what we know, for instance, about the teaching of Ibn al-Akfani (d. 1348) in fourteenth-century Cairo.[9]

Alpini also asked whether the Egyptians knew necromancy. While all the former disciplines mentioned by him are confirmed by classifications of the sciences in Arabic, such as the already mentioned fourteenth-century *Irshad al-qasid ila asna al-maqasid* of Ibn al-Akfani or the mid-seventeenth-century *Kashf al-zunun 'an isama al-kutub wa'l-funun* by Hajji Khalifa (d. 1657), Alpini's quest for necromancy reflects the interests of his native society rather than that of Egypt. However, Alpini claimed that many Egyptians adhered to this discipline in a particular form by linking it with *astronomy* (Alpin 1735, 88). This understanding of necromancy stems from a medieval Latin tradition which identified necromancy with the science of astrological talismans.

In the same chapter, Alpini reports that other Italian physicians traveled to and in the Middle East to collect material for Arabic-Latin dictionaries with the purpose of improving the indices to editions of Ibn Sarabiyun and Ibn Sina based upon a distorted reading of Alpago's work:

> Jacobus Manus Salodiensis who seven years before me passed his Medical exams with magna cum laude in a Venitian nation and who is also a man well trained in Arabic whom I met in Cairo told me once that he possessed an Arabic dictionary with all the words used in medicine and brought it into Latin adding some of his own observations to rouse up the souls of the students to higher (things) and also to correct the words of (Andrea Alpago) Bellonensis' indices to Serapion and Avicenna which have been misread seeing that the Arabs do not understand a (single) word pronounced by us in these. (Alpin 1735, 86)

---

[9] "I said elsewhere when I started to talk about the famous Cairene temple that they call Gemelazar that in it the universal academy of almost all the disciplines is (maintained) at huge expense in which the professors and students are nourished at no cost with food, clothes, and even books. I say in this famous gymnasium almost all disciplines are taught such as logic, natural and supernatural philosophy, rhetoric, mathematics, medicine and natural as well as supernatural magic. But most of all they teach the work of judicial astrology and all the divining arts. Of this kind is physiognomy (proceeding) in the same way as the philosophers are accustomed to practise it in particular from the lines of a face, but also by other (accidental) properties, and chiromancy (doing it) from the lines of the hands which offers the possibility of divining. But among all geomancy is what they prefer. This art takes its judgment from the variants of points which are formed by them into the aspects of figures [Omnibus vero præferunt Geomantiam, quæ ars supra punctorum varios, quæ ab ipsis formantur figurarum aspectus, suum habet judicium,...]. They believe that it becomes more certain with regard to these configurations of points, if it will be shaped for the celestial scheme (the common man calls it genesis), calculated by the astrological art, of that (person) with respect to whom or in whose favor the geomantic figure has been made" (Alpin 1735, 86–87).

In the early seventeenth century, interests similar to those of Alpini motivated Mario Schippano from Naples to learn Arabic and to urge his younger friend Pietro della Valle (1586-1652) to search for Arabic dictionaries, manuscripts of Ibn Sina's *Canon*, and other Middle Eastern medical and pharmaceutical texts in various regions of the Ottoman Empire.[10]

Alpini's career also reminds us that the Ottoman Empire not only provided space, nature, history, and scholarly traditions as areas of study and means to collect ingredients useful to further one's own reputation at home. The Empire's commercial and political interdependence with several West and Central European states also created paid scholarly positions at the residences of commercial and political representatives of those states, which proved more valuable for gaining an intimate knowledge about professional practices and the methods and means followed in the Middle East than the knowledge that was picked up by short-term travelers. The courts of local rulers, in particular in Morocco, presented a further outlet, for instance for French physicians, as the case of Etienne Hubert at the beginning of the seventeenth century demonstrates.

These examples of the various interests of physicians and botanists in the Middle East indicate with sufficient clarity that Middle Eastern knowledge and the practices of gardening, pharmacy, medicine, botany, and zoology were indeed essential in major scholarly endeavors during early modern times. They also show that flower gardening was an important feature of early modern Ottoman culture,[11] contrary to Cunningham's claim (Cunningham 1996, 41). West European travelers, collectors, and merchants brought home from the Middle East bulbs and seeds of flowers unknown in their countries and planted them in their gardens or displayed them in their museums.

The inducements to transplant plants from the Eastern and Southern shores of the Mediterranean into West European gardens arose not only from their medical and scholarly significance. Courtly culture in the Muslim lands played a role too. Ottoman flower culture gave rise to a specific form of early modern West European

---

[10] See, for instance, Della Valle 1674, part I, 168, 172 etc. Alpini's and Della Valle's testimonies suggest that the willingness to learn Arabic and to travel to the Middle East for this purpose was not that rare a feature of sixteenth- and seventeenth-centuries Italian physicians as Siraisi claims with respect to Ramusio and Alpago. See Siraisi 1987, 138.

[11] See, for instance, the following description given by Rauwolf: "In the gardens, the Turks diligently grow beautiful flowers which they use to enjoy themselves and to put them on their hats. I was able to see the beautiful plants which come to light there daily in December as our March violets with black-brownish and white flowers which they presented to me at this time in several posies. Furthermore the tulips, hyacinths, narcisses, which they still know under the old name Nergies. But in particular I saw a beautiful gender with yellow filled flowers called Modaph. Furthermore a strange winch mit leaves like ivy und huge purple coloured bells which grow into round bolls as one can see at the rue Hamala with three different compartments wherein the black coloured seed is to which they ascribe the property to purge the phlegm. This is found at times in our gardens and is called by the inhabitants Hasmsea, the Persians Acafra, and Serapion in chapter 273 Habalnil, but by the Latins Granum Indicum or Carthamus Indicus. Who wants to know more therefrom may look at the authors themselves at the above mentioned places. Avicenna, chapter 306 and Rhases, 208. Moreover, I found a beautiful gender Amaranti which several believe to be Pliny's Symphoniam because of its colours und therefore call it "feathers of the parrot." (Rauwolf 1582, 124-125).

floral art — the so-called *coronary* flowers. According to Harvey *coronary* flowers are those which are suitable for a wreath or a garland. The name of the art came into fashion in England soon after 1600 (Harvey 1994, 297). While Harvey deems it necessary to consider medieval predecessors in Muslim societies (al-Andalus and Persia) in horticulture and flower gardening, all his evidence for the English art of *coronary* flowers comes from sixteenth- and seventeenth-century Ottoman Empire and English commercial and diplomatic activities there. The originators and patrons of Ottoman flower art were Sultan Suleiman's Grand Mufti and religious adviser Ebussuud Efendi (Abu l-Su'ud, d. 1574) and Suleiman's son and successor Selim II who made Istanbul, as Harvey writes, the greatest plant center west of China (Harvey 1994, 299). Flowers described by Alpini in his book about Egyptian plants and a variety of flowers from other parts of the Ottoman Empire or brought to Western Europe via the Ottoman Empire are registered in lists of *coronary* flowers composed by English scholars in the middle of the seventeenth century.

The floral knowledge of the Ottoman court and its practice of creating purposefully varied blossoms and colors were regarded as an art that produced nobility through selection. This property made Ottoman flowers a worthy component of early modern practices of collecting, display, and courtly art. Most English travelers to the Ottoman Empire brought or sent bulbs, seeds, or saplings home and planted them in the Oxford Botanic Garden or on private soil or displayed them in dried form in museums and cabinets of curiosity. Together with the plants, written sources on Ottoman and earlier Muslim floral knowledge were acquired and sent to England.[12]

Similarly, but almost incidentally, Findlen's book on museums, collecting, and scientific culture in early modern Italy illuminates the fact that the Middle East constituted an indispensable reservoir for the collectors, natural historians, physicians, and their patrons. The examples presented above illustrate that the attention devoted by Italian scholarly communities to the Middle East had already spread in the middle of the sixteenth century to France and a few decades later to the German-speaking territories. One can easily add more examples of botanists and physicians from France or England traveling during the sixteenth and seventeenth centuries to the Middle East to collect specimens and to buy manuscripts. Others such as Conrad Gessner, Carolus Clusius, or Nicolas-Claude Fabri de Peiresc stayed at home and collected the relevant knowledge through the exchange of letters, drawings, or plants collected or bought through middlemen in Middle Eastern lands.

---

[12] Harvey lists roughly 12 kinds of "true" coronary flowers which came to England before 1590 and six kinds which arrived there between 1600 and 1640. He also documents that almost all English visitors of the Ottoman Empire since the late sixteenth century whether merchants, physicians, botanists, or chaplain-arabists sent bulbs or seeds home (Harvey 1994, 300–302).

2. Gentlemen Travelers and Merchants in the Middle East

In most modern history of science in early modern times, accounts of the Muslim territories are conspicuously absent despite the general acceptance that traveling was an essential feature of scholarship of the period. Two centuries earlier, however, Boucher de la Richarderie had claimed in his *Bibliothèque Universelle des Voyages* that most of the travels carried out by West Europeans within Europe were undertaken in the European parts of the Ottoman Empire.[13] He listed 182 titles plus their various editions and translations concerning the European regions of the Ottoman Empire alone for the period from 1550 until 1808. He gave roughly as many with respect to its Asian regions. Recently, Yerasimos has compiled a list of almost 450 travel accounts, military reports, surveys of ambassadors, and letters describing travel in the Ottoman Empire and Northern Africa from the fourteenth to the end of the sixteenth centuries both by Ottoman (30) and non-Ottoman subjects (419). It shows that while most of the travels of non-Ottoman subjects in the fourteenth and fifteenth centuries were undertaken as pilgrimages, the travels of the sixteenth century were inspired by diplomatic and apostolic missions as well as commercial aims. The sixteenth century also saw the first scholarly journeys to the Ottoman Empire (11).[14] In a time where a journey just for the sake of seeing the places out there or for transferring letters from a West European court to its ambassador in Constantinople[15] took at least several weeks, while many travels took several years, this figure is impressive and demonstrates that the Middle East was an area not totally irrelevant for Western Europe and its scholarly culture(s), commercial prospects, and political ambitions as implied by most modern accounts on early modern history of science.

Not all the accounts published about the Ottoman Empire, however, were based on travels. Some were built exclusively upon earlier texts. Even in the accounts published by authors who had indeed traveled, a literary tradition of composing travel accounts was at work. Since at least the late sixteenth century, this tradition was fed by the evolution of the so-called *apodemic* literature. This theory of the way to travel and to write about it recommended the traveler to keep at least one, better two diaries to write down all immediate impressions which had to be ordered under headers in more leisurely times during the voyage. This second diary was meant to prepare the later account. The theory prescribed not only how to organize the travel report, but also what was to be visited and asked for.

The outcome of the theory and of decades, if not centuries, of published travel

---

[13] "No country in Europe, even not Italy and Switzerland, has been visited so often by travelers of all classes as the European Turkey" (Boucher de la Richarderie 1808, tome IV, 50).
[14] Yerasimos broke this total number down in several tables showing the "national" (geographical, ethnic, or religious) origin of the travelers, the motives for traveling, and (less complete) their social status (Yerasimos 1991, 9–12).
[15] The first regular West European ambassadors to the Ottoman Empire came from the German Empire (sent in 1527, officially recognized in 1530) and France (in the 1530s). The first English ambassador arrived in 1583 (Yerasimos 1991, 11).

450

reports was a degree of standardization that some travelers to the Middle East such as Henry Blount felt bored with already in the first half of the seventeenth century. The standardization of travel literature stabilized and extended West European prejudices towards Muslim societies, both negative and positive. The Ottomans often are depicted in more or less negative terms as the destroyers of kingdoms and the world — cruel, lazy, stupid, or greedy. If there was something good in the Ottoman culture, Jewish emigrants or Christian renegades were often considered its source. This feature applies above all to scholarly and technical knowledge and practices. With regard to social, religious, or legal elements of Ottoman culture, the differences to the traveler's own society more often were positively evaluated and attributed to the Sultan's tolerance with regard to the diverse communities of the Empire and their religious creeds or to the efficiency of the Muslim juridical system. The Safavids, on the other hand, are presented often with more sympathy as endowed with messianic features, polite, and educated. On the other hand, both dynasties were regarded as being truly splendid. Their courts, their gardens, their hippodromes, and their harems never ceased to attract attention, both physically and mentally. Most travelers sought eagerly to gain access to either of these places by joining the ambassador of their country when he went to an audience or by paying fees, bribing Ottoman officials, and other efforts.

With respect to the description of the sciences, these travel accounts differ remarkably. While most reports about the Safavids agree in presenting the sciences there as flourishing, albeit less developed or at best in parts and attitudes different from those in Europe, the majority of the accounts on the Ottomans remains silent about this subject or denies that the Ottomans had any science or art. Even the few authors who found something worthwhile to say about this topic, such as Pierre Belon, Nicholas de Nicholay, Prospero Alpini, Henry Blount, or Ismael Boulliau (1605–1694), are very brief and much more sterile than the accounts on Persia. The denial of sciences in the Ottoman Empire developed into a topos which was recognized as such early on. In the seventeenth and early eighteenth centuries, the English astronomer and orientalist John Greaves or the Italian military expert, war prisoner, and political adviser Luigi de Marsigli publicly contradicted such evaluations. In the late eighteenth century the topos and its recent repetition by the French traveler of Hungarian origin De Tott urged the Italian Father Toderini to travel to Istanbul for an *in situ* investigation. He found out what Greaves and Marsigli already had claimed and what is confirmed by modern research: the Ottoman Empire had a rich literary and scientific history and its intellectual life in the seventeenth and eighteenth centuries was quite vibrant. The absence of the sciences in West European travel accounts on the Ottoman Empire and its presence in those on the Safavid dynasty which steadily increased during the seventeenth century are particular signs of the expressed difference in West European political and religious rhetoric towards the two Muslim societies.[16]

---

[16] I do not think, however, that the Christian polemics against Islam and the wars between

A major activity of gentlemen travelers and merchants which contributed to satisfy the curiosity and to provide material for the research interests of various members of the Republic of Letters in Western Europe was to collect Greek, Arabic, Persian, Turkish, Coptic, Syriac, Armenian, Hebrew, Judaeo-Arabic, and Judaeo-Persian manuscripts on biblical themes, liturgy, stories about prophets, early church history, profane history, legal subjects, literature, medicine, the (pure and mixed) mathematical sciences, the occult disciplines, and philosophy. Major components of Italian collections of Oriental manuscripts came from what such travelers as Pietro della Valle or the two brothers Gioambattista (1552-1618) and Gerolamo Vecchietti (1557-c. 1640) bought at the end of the sixteenth and in the early seventeenth century in Egypt, Istanbul, Persia, and India. Besides various valuable religious texts of Jewish and Coptic communities and several volumes of mystic and profane Arabic and Persian poetry, the three travelers bought extracts of two of the major astronomical handbooks produced by Muslim scholars, the so-called *Ilkhanid Tables* compiled by Nasir al-Din al-Tusi (d. 1274) and his colleagues in Maragha and the so-called *New Tables* compiled by the Timurid prince Ulugh Beg (1394-1449) and his collaborators. They also brought some mathematical and medical texts to Italy, among them the rare treatise on arithmetic by al-Tusi's colleague Sharaf al-Din al-Samarqandi (thirteenth century) and parts of Ibn Sina's medical encyclopaedia. Moreover, Della Valle, who had lived almost ten years in the Ottoman and Safavid Empires, brought home several Persian and a few Turkish texts written by himself which testify to his scholarly and religious interests and contacts in Persia — some treatises defending Catholic doctrines against critic by Safavid theologians, an Italian-Persian dictionary, a Turkish grammar, love poems in Persian styles, and a Persian summary of a Latin work on Tychonic cosmology written in 1613 by the Italian Jesuit Christofero Borro (1583-1632).

A feature which applies to travel accounts written in the seventeenth century irrespective of the Middle Eastern region visited are reports about geographical data, debates about the etymology or provenance of names of towns, and efforts to identify famous historical cities or regions of the Bible or of ancient Greek profane histories and geographies with those of seventeenth-century Arabia, Asia Minor, or Persia. It is in such reports that Muslim textual, oral, instrumental, and cartographic sources are more or less regularly used. They are either referred to as a generic type of source such as *the new Persian geographical tables*,[17] or as *the*

Christian states and the Ottoman Empire were the only reasons which contributed to this rhetoric. I have argued elsewhere that differences in patterns of travel, distribution of European settlements, degree and types of access to the courts, length of stay in the region, knowledge of the local languages, and other factors were involved too (Brentjes 1999).

[17] Chardin who included the geographical data in the description of the travel route remarked for instance with respect to Abhar: "Abhar's distance from the equator is 36 deg. 45 min. and from the Fortunate Islands 48 (sic., instead of 84) deg. 30. min. This longitude and all the others which I mention are taken from the newest Persian tables" (Chardin 1686, 312).

astrolabes of the Persians,[18] or attributed to specific authors or informants, or not given any name.

Thomas Herbert (1606–1682) — an English gentleman who as a private member accompanied the mission sent by England's king Charles I to Safavid Persia for obtaining trade concessions — in the account of his travel to Persia in 1627 praised some of the qualities of Persian towns with reference to unnamed Arabic geographers and relied among other sources upon Ulugh Beg to argue that Shiraz was a big town already in long-gone times. For the matter of evidence, Herbert did not discriminate between Western Christian and Muslim sources. He treated Ulugh Beg as well as a so-far-unidentified Ibn Ali as authorities of equal standing with the two late fifteenth-century Venetian ambassadors Contarini and Barbaro to the Aq Qoyunlu ruler Uzun Hassan, the late sixteenth-century Portuguese traveler Pedro Teixeira, the sixteenth- and seventeenth-century West European scholars Philipus Cluverius and Wilhelm Schickard, and the early seventeenth-century Catholic convert Juan of Persia, a former Shi'ite and secretary of shah Abbas' I embassy to the pope and several West European rulers (Herbert 1928, 69). Jean Baptiste Tavernier (1603–1689), a French Calvinist merchant in Persia and India in the middle of the seventeenth century, included in his travel account an entire table of geographical data on Persia (Tavernier 1681, 151). D. King identified it as transmitting predominantly an extract of a lost medieval geographical table on Persia called *Kitab al-atwal wa'l-'urud li-l-furs*. It is likely that Tavernier got this data, as he claims, during his stay in Persia.

Geographical tables and maps seem to have been an item that Persians preferred to give as a gift to European travelers. Other visitors such as the French Calvinist merchant Jean Chardin (1643–1712) or the German physician Engelbert Kaempfer (1651–1716) also reported that they had received either tables or maps. In most cases, we still do not know which Muslim sources the travelers had access to nor what those maps that they claimed to have seen in Persia looked like. Herbert, for instance, reported that a map from Abu l-Fida's *Geography* was offered for sale at Gambrun while we only know of tables of geographical latitudes and longitudes and circular diagrams with inscribed place names as components of this work.[19] Chardin, although he asserted that the *Persians* were ignorant of the art of map-making, nevertheless described in his itinerary a meeting with Rustam Beg, the Safavid military commander in chief, during which Rustam Beg showed Chardin maps that he himself had drawn and claimed that they were much more accurate with respect to Azerbayjan than the West European maps that had only recently been published in Europe and were in the commander's possession.[20]

---

[18] "The elevation of the pole above its horizon is marked on the astrolabes of the Persians as 38 degrees and 40 minutes, and the longitude as 81 degrees 54 minutes" (Chardin 1811, vol. II, 300).

[19] An additional problem is that this remark is found only in later editions of Herbert's account.

[20] "They possess neither globes nor celestial maps as well as no terrestrial maps" (Chardin 1811, vol. IV, 327). "*On Geography and History*. ... They have diverse authors who have written on it: nonetheless, they know very little, above all with regard to the part of this art which is called *the map*" (Chardin 1811, vol V, 116f). Langlès who produced the scholarly informed edition of Chardin's

These travel accounts enrich our until now rather scarce knowledge of Safavid scholarly life during the seventeenth century. Some intriguing problems are embodied in the ways the travelers described and used the Persian or Arabic geographical data. One concerns the apparent ease with which the travelers claimed to have been able to communicate about these and other intellectual matters with Safavid scholars. Even if the travelers or, for that matter, the Safavid scholars had almost no inkling of the languages of their counterparts, the travelers' accounts still maintained that the two sides communicated sensibly about Euclid, about constructing an astrolabe, or about terrestrial maps.

Della Valle reported that his Muslim friend of Lar, the astronomer Zayn al-Din, plied him to send Latin books on cosmology, astronomy, and mathematics. Despite a very limited Latin vocabulary which Della Valle had taught him, Zayn al-Din thought that diagrams and numbers were essentially the same in Western Europe and in Persia. This feature would have enabled him to understand the main contents of the books he asked for. Similar claims were made by Olearius, Tavernier, or Chardin with respect to maps, astrolabs, and tables.

Such claims are not entirely ridiculous, since the two cultures indeed shared related traditions, practices, concepts, and objects. On the other hand, such claims were gross exaggerations and contributed to rash judgments on both sides about the value and usefulness of the products of the other scholarly culture and led to the neglect of such components that appeared to be incommensurable.[21]

Another interesting aspect of the ways that travelers talked about and used Persian and Arabic geographical data is the claim that the two cultures produced maps that were similar and easily readable for each other, easy to compare with maps of their own making, and easy to evaluate. Given the very premature kind of knowledge of Safavid cartography presently available, this claim is somewhat surprising. The only Persian regional map with respect to Iran I know of is found

---

account in 1811 annotated the last quotation with a footnote claiming that Askery-Khan, the Qajar ambassador, who had recently visited Paris had brought a map as a gift which Langlès considered as showing the Persians' recent improvements in this art (Chardin 1811, vol. V, 117).

[21] This concerns, for instance, West European complaints about the lack of precision of geographical data in Arabic texts. The perceived, as well as the factual, lack of precision is not only the result of the manuscripts that the informants accepted, the instruments used, and the practices applied to determining the coordinates, but also the expression of changed standards and expectations as well as the consequence of a lack of experience and qualification in dealing with Arabic and Persian manuscript sources on the part of West European scholars. Another example is that astrology was regularly ridiculed in West European travel accounts on the Safavid and to a lesser extent the Ottoman Empires. This led to a neglect of the mathematical methods and concepts developed and applied by Muslim astrologers and timekeepers. Thus, the sophisticated astronomical models of Nasir al-Din al-Tusi available in early modern Italy, England, and France were for the first time investigated by a West European scholar during the nineteenth century. The treatises on similar models by Ibn al-Shatir or Qutb al-Din al-Shirazi equally available in early modern Europe attracted the attention of Western scholars only since the early 1950s. In early modern Muslim societies, certain Western European scholarly and technological devices were rejected because they either did not reflect the cultural function attributed to their Muslim counterparts or stood in conflict with courtly norms. In Safavid Iran, the Western design of a compass was ridiculed since it did not concentrate on providing the direction to Mecca. At the Moghul court in India, European glasses were used as a tool of punishment for involuntary digressions from protocol.

in manuscripts of Hamdallah al-Mustawfi al-Qazwini's *Nuzhat al-qulub* (c. 1340). As catalogs of Persian manuscript collections indicate, this text was read and copied more than once in Safavid times. However, whether it triggered a mapmaking tradition lasting into the seventeenth century is unknown.

On the other hand, already a cursory glance at major sixteenth- and seventeenth-century West European maps of Western Asia such as those by Gastaldi, Ortelius, G. Mercator Jr., De Jode, W. Blaeuw, or N. Sanson, to name only a few, shows that Persia was represented by most of them, albeit differently, in terms of Islamic geographical works — those by al-Idrisi and Abu l-Fida as well as yet unknown sources.[22] West European cartography of Persia obviously had no difficulty turning its back on the Ptolemaic tradition since the 1550s. This is not the case for West European cartography of the former Byzantine parts of the Ottoman Empire and the Holy Land, nor for the travel accounts and missionary reports on the Safavid Empire and bilingual or trilingual dictionaries composed in the first half of the seventeenth century in Isfahan and Basra by missionaries and Muslim partners. There, either ancient Greek geographical and historical authorities, divisions, and names, or biblical and related traditions dominate the cartographic and verbal scenery. Some travelers such as Chardin pretend to use such knowledge characterized as old-fashioned in place of the contemporary local knowledge to serve their West European audiences and ease their way into strange and unfamiliar territories. However, all those texts, including that by Chardin, describe at length and in detail the ongoing debates and controversies among West European members of the Republic of Letters on the subject of which of the famous cities and provinces of ancient Persia can be recognized in contemporary Safavid cities and provinces or found nearby. In late sixteenth and early seventeenth centuries, the mental landscape of the Republic of Letters and of the Catholic Church with regard to Persia was essentially that of Ptolemy, Strabo, Herodotus, and other ancient Greek authors. What then seduced the cartographers to abandon this landscape in favor of Islamic perspectives and what made this change so persistent and commercially successful?

3. Asian Rulers, Aristotle, and Political Theory

As studies of *despotism* have long shown, Aristotle's *Politics* and its early modern usages profoundly shaped West European political and historical theories and in particular West European perceptions and interpretations of Asia.[23] Not only did

---

[22] This is also true for the Arabian Peninsula and to a lesser extent for Northern and parts of Sub-Saharan Africa. The differences between ancient Greek geography and the type of Islamic geography used by the West European cartographers consist above all in the chosen values of geographical coordinates including the prime meridian, the number and names of indicated towns, rivers, mountains, or deserts, and the political subdivision of the states or regions depicted.

[23] See, in particular, Grosrichard 1979 and the bibliography he assembled.

it form the core of the political views of West European literates and theoreticians of government, but it also provided the most widely used frame of reference for travelers, diplomats, merchants, and missionaries when evaluating the culture, social structure, morals, or the sciences in the contemporary Ottoman or Safavid Empires. It still works its silent influence in the current history of science in some of the most basic assumptions about the sciences of early modern Asia, but also of early modern Western Europe.

The early modern West European interpretation of the Ottoman style of government was set by Aristotle's verdict in Book III, 14, § 6 that the "Barbars are more servile in their nature than the Greeks as the peoples of Asia, in turn, are more servile than those of Europe; and they therefore will tolerate despotic rule without any complaint" (translation by Koebner 1951, 277).

As Koebner has shown, humanists differed in their renditions of the term *despotic* on philological and political grounds. But they agreed that two contemporary peoples fitted best the Aristotelian claim — the *Turks* and the *Muscovites*.[24] Thus, within these theoretical boundaries, the Ottomans could not provide a feasible object for studying the fundamentals of human affairs, because they represented a form of government which was no part of the typology of governments, but characterized each of the three types (tyranny, demos, oligarchy) in their degenerated stages (Koebner 1951, 277).

Reports by missionaries, letters and accounts by travelers, or speeches given by diplomats confirm that West European political evaluations of the Ottoman and Safavid Empires were deeply permeated by ancient Greek theories of government and history. These theories shaped their attitudes and perceptions at least as profoundly as religious rigidity. In his report, *L'Estat de la Perse en 1660*, which remained unpublished until 1890, but not secret, the French Capuchin missionary Raphael du Mans (1613–1696) combined Aristotelian concepts with West European notions about the dependence of the welfare of a state from the existence of nobility, historico-geographical assumptions about the civilizatory capacities of people living at opposite ends of the world and in between, medieval theories about the stages of the rational soul, and firm belief in Catholic Christianity as the only true religion. Introducing the form of government in Persia, he claimed:

> The government of the kingdom is despotic, monarchic, the King having the absolute command over his entire kingdom and over all his subjects (*Raiet*), the right of life and death without fear of revolt or rebellion. The reason being that all the grandees are people who are the first and usually the last nobles of their race, the king elevating and denigrating them, the one as easily as the other. (Du Mans 1890, 42)

---

[24] Other examples were taken from history such as ancient Persia or from myth such as the empire of Prester John (Koebner 1951, 284–249).

In his assessment of the civilizatory value of Safavid society, Du Mans added:

> In order to understand well the state of this country, one has to compare the two extremes together, that is, this of the anthropophages, *margaiats*, where the strongest is the master and where the disorder is the order which governs; the other is that of the West where the reason and the natural goodness and the true religion has drawn us from being animals in order to bring us to that of the angels. Then take the medium between these two to form the idea of this one here. Furthermore, this medium has to be geometrical, not arithmetical, so that the difference will not be as distant from the brutal as from the angelical. (Ibid.)

Travel accounts such as those by Tavernier or Chardin make clear that the travelers as well as the missionaries knew that high ranking positions in Safavid Iran often were occupied by subsequent members of the same family. They were aware of the different legal status of the military forces recruited among the Qizilbash and the special royal forces introduced by shah Abbas I, the former being free members of tribal groups and similar social compounds, the latter being slaves mostly from Georgia and adjacent regions. They experienced the interference of different military and civil factions into the selection of a new ruler after the last had passed away and criticized such activities severely. They also were informed of at least the basic features of the legal system and its being part of the religious organization of the society. Thus, they knew that although several shahs had struggled to subordinate the forces competing with them for power, none had ever become the absolute despote which Du Mans chose to be the political category characterizing Safavid government. In political writings of the eighteenth century, these insights of travelers based on experience were recast into the claim that *despotism* in its pure essence never existed (Grosrichard 1979, 65ff.).

Nonetheless, most travelers of the seventeenth century shared Du Mans' evaluation of the type of government existing in Safavid Iran. They also agreed that the only way to describe the foreign society, its social structure, and its culture was to compare it with the structures of their own society and its culture, which provided the norms of evaluation. This was not necessarily intended to denigrate the other society. According to Th. Hentsch, however, during the seventeenth century there occurred a major rift that set Western Europe apart from the Middle East. While the former became defined more and more as the only geographical and historical region where modernity took place, the latter was cast increasingly in terms of a glorious, but long gone past. As a consequence, the contemporary Muslim societies were discarded as immobile and despotic, with nothing to offer the West European observer except the ruins of ancient times (Hentsch 1992, 83–94).

A major vehicle that carried the changing West European perceptions of itself and the Middle East was the description of the state of the sciences. Hentsch emphasizes in this respect above all Chardin's claim that Safavid science not only knew nothing of the novel West European discoveries, but would improve its undeniably extant intellectual prowess if it applied West European methods and disciplinary compartmentalization (Hentsch, 90-91). While the travel accounts of the seventeenth century indeed indicate shifts in West European perspectives, this concerns not so much Safavid society itself, but Western Europe and its scientific enterprises. The travelers seem to reflect more of the competing attitudes towards the sciences within Western Europe than within Safavid society. Surprisingly, however, none of them refers explicitly to the major changes in the Republic of Letters during the seventeenth century and in particular during its second half. The only West European scholar of importance to the so-called scientific revolution mentioned in the travel accounts and missionaries' reports on Persia is R. Descartes.

At the same time, the travelers were able, at least to some extent, to recognize difference and to appreciate it. The travelers' feelings of undoubted superiority with regard to science were still tainted by the heritage of the Oriental past and by West European contemporary insecurities. At the beginning of the seventeenth century, Herbert tried to describe the otherness of Safavid teaching, interpreting it in terms of what was thought to be ancient Greek and Latin traditions. This identification enabled him to appreciate what he observed:

> Berry is a village which promises much at a distance, but, when there, deludes the expectation: howbeit, not a little famous through the Persian territories, both from the immunities that an ancient learned Syet endued it with, confirmed by succeeding princes, and from an Arabic school which is there kept and distinguished into several classes of civil law, astrology, physic, and what leads to Mecca: commendable in their Pythagorean silence, practising to discourse by winks, nods, and dumb signs; for babbling and noise in all Arabic schools is detested. ... Some schools I visited, and observed (as I formerly mentioned, near Lar) that, according to the old adage *necessarium est silentium ad studia*, they effect silence, and sitting cross-legged wag their bodies, imagining that such motion advantages study and serves for exercise. (Herbert 1928, 63, 245)

In the second half of the century, Du Mans was equally keen to point to the otherness of Safavid teaching. Different from Herbert, he no longer thought to compare what he experienced with ancient traditions. His sole foil was France. In this comparison, he painted a trajectory rising from open criticism at French conditions and appreciation of Safavid attitudes to unabashed glorification of France and denigration of Persia. Du Mans' entry into the subject was directed towards what he thought were unwarranted developments in attitude and style in French education:

> Their manner to teach and to take lecturing consists in choosing who appears to be good as his schoolmaster. Because here, teaching is of the highest degree of honor. The most elevated (persons) do not wish to deprive

themselves from it and to this end they distribute, ordinarily more of the purse than of language, the science and the wisdom to acquire for themselves the name of a scholar [docte]. There, in France, this word of teaching is unable to free itself from the latest insult of the world, which is "pedant", and it is not much envied either for the glory or the profit. (Du Mans 1890, 128–129)

In the following paragraphs, Du Mans took back most of his praise of Safavid education. He started by ridiculing the otherness of Safavid teaching with regard to social behavior, attitudes towards authorities, and contents. But he felt able to do so only by alluding to mockeries meaningful only in his own culture:

There, the professor [Monsieur le docteur] is on his backside sitting like a taylor, the student is also sitting, but on his knees out of respect. He reads two or three lines of the book he has brought. The professor explains (them) to him in Persian. (The student) takes up (the reading), and in this manner (it continues) alternatively for two thirds of an hour. Thus, if the student not comprehending Orléans' gloss bothers his professor too much, he starts to embroil him into a long discourse beginning — as one says — to deduce the two wars of Troye from an egg. The well advised student has to asquiesce and to lie saying "at the moment, I understand very well, this is very clear, I do not believe that anybody in the world could explain this in a better manner; and if *Aristu* (Aristotle) would be alive he could not render the issue as clearly." (Du Mans 1890, 169)

Then, Du Mans chastised the lack of disciplinary compartmentalization in a downright mean tone that effectively turned the tables on the Safavids. While the French attitudes towards teaching might be condemnable compared with those in Persia, if the French teach science they do it in the only right way. By doing so, they created success that elevated the status of France to be the leader of all the nations of the contemporary world. The Safavids, however, despite their eagerness to study and to teach were superficial, flimsy, and thus achieved no lasting results.[25] At the end, drawing conclusions from his observations and comparisons, Du Mans told his readers whoever they were[26] that if the Safavids would teach the sciences as in France, that is, if the Safavids were French, they would surpass the

---

[25] "A student does not limit himself to a lecture on one kind of science. On one day, he will make a pot pourry of logic, physics, theology, grammar, etc. In the same way the masters proceed who believe themselves dishonored if they refuse to teach any science which they are asked for even if they have never heard of it before: it is sufficient that the student reads. Since he understands the language and has a bit more of science and babil than his student he always knows how to help himself. This is not like in the West where it is necessary that a professor after having picked up the meanings and the opinions of all the good authors extracts the honey therefrom by limiting himself to only one science at a time. This makes us successful up to the point where France is at the moment, the chair and the bar having given us the advantage over all nations" (Du Mans 1890, 169–170).

[26] The two editors, Ch. Schefer in 1890 and F. Richard in 1995, differ in their opinions of who might have been the addressee of Du Mans' report — Colbert or the superiors of the French branch of the Capuchin order.

The Republic of Letters in the Middle East 459

latter in scientific success, that is they would be better French. Although his evaluation stresses the superiority of French scientific, religious, and technological standards, beliefs, and practices, France is not yet a paragon of virtue and strength with no need to take advice from other cultures:

> One has to admit — to take an expression from here — *ez haq ne miton kouzachte*, "that one cannot avoid the truth." If these people here had the veritable belief which is the principle of the heaven's benedictions, the printing, as we do, for the easy communication of what each one wishes to give to the public, the order in lecturing and taking lectures and studies, the goods which our graduates usually pursue, they possibly could equal us, if I do not even say surpass us, because they study since their childhood until senility, while we others in France after we have been powdered a bit in the classes until the age of eighteen or twenty years — and this by force, because one expects an affront or surprise from behind — we do not continue to deepen the sciences as we could do it, as if there were too little delightful writings which are our luminaries. And what concerns most of our modern authors, they are only plunderers of the ancients, disguised and put in other postures and other gravies in order to give the taste of novelty to the reader. (Richard 1995, vol. 2, 128–130)

In Du Mans' last lines we relocate Chardin's theme of the lack of modernity in Safavid science and its doubtful valor in Western Europe stressed by Hentsch who abstained from questioning the given qualification as the major expression of the rift in West European perceptions of the contemporary Middle East. Twenty-four years later, in a third report, Du Mans not only added some specifics with regard to the West European novelties the Safavids did not know, but raised more severe criticisms of the Safavid scholarly system while omitting all critical comments on French attitudes towards teaching and the vanity of novelties.[27] Among other things, Du Mans characterized now the algebra taught in Persia as ancient and added that the Persians knew nothing of Cartesian (geometry?) and (mathematical)

---

[27] "The colleges at Isfahan are more than one hundred, but they do not resemble ours with their subordinated and fixed classes. ... Each college is presided by one principal, moudarres, who, having the habit of a scholar and being elected, has to teach publicly. The students can choose according to their wishes whomsoever they want for a teacher, Akron, or leave him at will again and turn to another one. ... Here, anybody is allowed to teach what he knows and what he does not know. During the course of one single day, a person teaches seven or ten different lectures in order to have as many disciples as possible to spread publicly like trumpets the master's science, status, and gains. There is no method in their studies. Here, someone can offer a work on theology or physics who has never seen or learned before any rule of logic. The European method to acquire other sciences imitates the honey producing bees which after having plundered the fields and flowers carry the honey collected from wherever to their beehives. From all the good authors, our professors compose a summary of all the honey known and believed in. Then, step by step, they open the eyes of their students who write with such diligence, sincerity of the soul, and charity that, after the course is completed, the majority of the students is also capable (to occupy) the teacher's chair. Here, among the Mores, things are done otherwise. One of the students reads with clear voice one, two, etc. lines of one of the authors to his co-students, the professor explains (them) and adds whatever comes to his mind in a rather longwinded sermon. May understand who is capable!" (Richard 1995, vol. 2, 302).

analysis.[28] These remarks indicate Du Mans' keeping in touch with what went on in the (mathematical) sciences at least in France. Thus, his silence with regard to the deficits in French teaching and the immodesty of modern authors might be read as signaling shifts in attitude in France both towards teaching and towards innovation after 1660.

The changing descriptions of the state of the sciences in Safavid society by West Europeans in the course of the seventeenth century should also be regarded in juxtaposition with what they wrote about the political systems of the Ottomans and the Safavids. Such a perspective shows that the conceptual limitations of early modern West European political and historical theories and the wish to understand oneself and the other by making comparisons were factors that reinforced their tendency to misrepresent Safavid society as fundamentally different from West European societies in political terms and as rather similar, but in tendency inferior to them, in cultural terms.

A different approach was chosen by the English gentleman Henry Blount (b. 1602). On May 7, 1634, he embarked at Venice to travel to the Levant. After his return about two years later, he became one of the gentlemen-pensioners of England's King Charles I, who knighted him March 21, 1639. In a collection of various travel accounts published in 1752 it is said that "He was esteemed, by those that knew him, a gentleman of a very clear judgment, great experience, much contemplation (tho' not of much reading), and of great foresight into government" (Churchill 1752, 511).

He had acquired his *foresight into government* by studying law, but most of all as he himself had claimed, by his travel to the Levant. In his account of this journey, Blount declared boldly that to capture the fundamentals of human social relations traveling to other Christian countries was useless. Only the study of a world perceived as substantially different would reveal the secrets of *society*:

> Intellectual complections have no desire so strong, as that of knowledge; nor is any knowledge unto man so certain and pertinent, as that of human affairs: this experience advances best, in observing of people whose institutions much differ from ours; for customs conformable to our own, or to such wherewith we are already acquainted, do but repeat our old observations, with little acquist of new: so my former time spent in viewing Italy, France, and some little of Spain, being countries of Christian institution, did but represent, in a several dress, the effect of what I knew before." (Churchill 1752, 511)

---

[28] "Besides books on grammar (*tesrif*) they have their logic (*mentek*), physics (*tebiai*), theology (*elahi*), moral (teaching) (*fekke* [sic]), mathematics (*riasi*), arithmetic (*elme hisab*), geometry (*hendese*), astronomy (*nejom*), ephemerides (*tekvim*), mean motions (*zige* [sic]) according to Ptolemy's (*Betlemious*) system, ancient algebra. Nothing of the Cartesian (doctrines) and analysis [Nihil de Cartesiana et analisi] is here in usage. (They use) Euclid's works, Menelaus' and Theodosius' spherics, Ptolemy's Almagest from antiquity; from their moderns most books have been composed by Khwaja Nasir (*Coja Nessir* — Nasir al-Din al-Tusi). He flourished 400 years ago in the province of Persia Khorassan (*Corasson*) and has treated all the sciences." (Richard 1995, vol. 2, 304).

Reciting the ancient Greek theory that men are formed by natural dispositions shaped by the climate they inhabit, Blount claimed that it was nature that guided him in his pursuit of knowledge:

> Then seeing the customs of men are much swayed by their natural dispositions, which are originally inspired and composed by the climate whose aire and influence they receive, it seems natural, that to our north-west parts of the world, no people should be more averse, and strange of behaviour, than those of the south-east. (Churchill 1752, 511)

Nature's recommendation to study the Ottoman Empire in order to understand Christian society was supplemented by the unique form in which modernity was shaped by the Ottomans. Their Empire was the only appropriate place in the entire world to discover and memorize human society at its most splendid elevation:

> Moreover, those parts being now possess'd by the Turks, who are the only modern people great in action, and whose Empire hath so suddenly invaded the world, and fix'd itself on such firm foundations as no other ever did; I was of opinion, that he who would behold these times in their greatest glory, could not find a better scene than Turky. (Churchill 1752, 513)

Identifying the Ottoman Empire as the only feasible object for his research, Blount appears to have been to some extent innovative in his treatment of Muslim society.[29] His point of departure laid outside the boundaries of the learned political discourse of the time which was most concerned with the readings of Aristotle's *Politics* by its early modern translators and commentators. As his geographical legitimization of traveling for the sake of political inquiry shows, Blount's mental configuration was also influenced by Aristotle's *Politics*. Despite his bold depiction of the Ottoman Empire as the only object worthwhile to be studied by the political theoretician, Blount also considered the sultan to be a *despotic ruler*. However, he did not find the cause for this political system to be the Asian climate and the henceforth ensuing eternal natural characteristics of its inhabitants, but the Empire's composition of many diverse nations and religions not bound to each other by any feeling of sympathy, affection, or shared customs. This composition resulted from Ottoman military strength and its drive to conquer. To govern such a heterogenous conglomerate, it was better to apply strict enforcement of the will of the ruler rather than lenience and civility. For Blount, this point was made perfectly clear when one compared the Roman Empire with its many civil wars to the Ottoman Empire with its stability due to having effectively subdued its many conquered subjects. *Despotic* rule appears to have been in Blount's eyes more a matter of expediency and political insight than a state prescribed by nature.

---

[29] Perhaps Blount was influenced in his approach by sixteenth-century Italian authors such as Giovanni Botero about whom Cochrane wrote that he: "treated the Ottoman state as a modern equivalent of the model states of antiquity — that is, as one capable of furnishing lessons in political wisdom" (Cochrane 1981, 333–334).

With regard to the state of the arts and the sciences, Blount was one of the few early modern West European travelers in the Ottoman Empire who not only saw buildings used for teaching purposes such as the *madrasa* (so-called "college") but also referred to them in his travel account.[30] Most travelers ignored the madaris and described only the mosques and other buildings of Ottoman towns.[31] Numerous woodcuts of Istanbul whether illustrating travel accounts or published separately only show the major mosques but not the madaris which surrounded them. Despite this attention to educational architecture, Blount was barely interested in the contemporary sciences of the Ottoman Empire. He only mentioned sciences as part of his investigative and narrative program in connection with Cairo's ancient reputation as "the fountain of all science and civil arts."[32] Thus, he has nothing of consequence to report on them. He even believes there are none to speak of except for some poetry and mathematics. This conviction is, however, not based on any concrete investigation. It is the result of a set of assumptions on Mohammad's goals in shaping the basic tenets of Islamic doctrines, the nature of the "Turkish nation," the historical course of the sciences through different regions of the earth, and the function of the sciences within society.

Blount reflects on the sciences in the Ottoman Empire in his portrayal of Islamic religion which he perceived of as the second most important Ottoman institution, the first being the Empire's army. He believed that only very few men are gifted with intellectual faculties that can rise above mere passions. Rational reflections about the world are the only means to prevent them from otherwise dangerous activities:

> Now the greatest number of men being governed by passions, in all people

---

[30] Blount wrote, for instance, about Edirne: "Beside this meskeeto, there is another brave one with four spies, built by Sultan *Selim*, and many other of two a-piece, with fair colleges, cloisters, and baths, equal to the monasteries of any one city in Christendom for quality, though not in number; it hath also many fair hanes, all covered in like manner; so likewise are their Besesteins, or Exchanges, whereof it hath four or fives, some not much inferior to ours in *London*, especially one, which I guessed half a mile in length, and richly furnished with wares: ... After ten days stay in *Adrianople*, we rode up and down as business required, to *Burgaz*, *Churlo*, and divers other pretty towns, all of them adorned with dainty meskeetoes, colleges, hospitals, hanes, and bridges: for it is in Turky as in other kingdoms; the nearer the imperial city, the more stately is the country inhabited" (Churchill 1752, 519-520).

[31] See, for example, the rather detailed and appreciative description of the mosques of Istanbul given by the French traveler Carlier de Pinon in 1579 (Pinon 1920, 79-81).

[32] "The last and choice piece of my intent, was to view Grand Cairo, and that for two causes; first, it being clearly the greatest concourse of mankind in these times, and perhaps that ever was; there must needs be some proportionale spirit in the government; for such vast multitudes, and those of wits so deeply malicious, would soon breed confusion, famine, and utter desolation, if in the Turkish domination there were nothing but sottish sensuality, as most Christians conceive. Lastly, because Egypt is held to have been the fountain of all science and civil arts, therefore I did hope to find some spark of those cinders not yet put out; or else in the extreme contrary, I should receive an impression as important, from the ocular view of so great a revolution; for above all other senses, the eye having the most immediate and quick commerce with the soul, gives it a more smart touch than the rest, leaving in the fancy somewhat unutterable; so that an eye-witness of things conceives them with an imagination more compleat, strong, and intuitive, than he can either apprehend, or deliver by way of relation" (Churchill 1752, 513).

The Republic of Letters in the Middle East

they have been entertained, for the present life, with justice; for the future, with religion: yet there were found some few intellectual complexions, in whom the understanding prevailed above passions. Those discerning wits could not receive the gross supposals upon which the heathenish superstitions relied; wherefore, to train them in such ways as civil societies require, they were instructed in a seeming rational way, wherein they were amused about an intelligible world, stored with rewards of honour, virtue, and knowledge; with punishments of infamy, vice, and ignorance. These were to them instead of *Elysian* fields, or infernal rivers, and, as some scoffers think, but of little better assurance, only righter framed to such capacities. By these speculations, contemplative heads, who else might dangerously have busied themselves about state affairs, were finally moped and diverted. (Churchill 1752, 539)

The *Turks*, who were still in the beginning phase of state building, preferred the sword over the letters which Blount considered effeminating. In a later stage, he conjectured, due to greatness, indolence, the impact of the climate in certain of the Ottoman possessions, intermarriage, and the order of natural things set by the path of the sun, learning will be appreciated by the *Turks*.[33] This process of effemination and infiltration was already underfoot in Blount's time: "I have often seen copies of love-verses, and some few pieces of mathematicks, pass amongst them with much applause. I saw one for singing, and composing of two or three sonnets, hath at a feast in *Belgrade* at *Hungary*, a horse given him worth near twenty pounds *English*" (Churchill 1752, 539).

While he has nothing to say about the *Turks'* attraction to mathematics, their love of poetry together with fiction and music follows universal patterns formerly observable in ancient Greece and England. Superstition, that is religious prescriptions, will forever prevent the Ottomans from sculpting and painting,

> but as for other learning, it is like to insinuate but by degrees, and with many repulses, as a corruption most pernicious to their religion, especially the searching parts of philosophy, which stomach that sensual paradise, as hath

---

[33] "To which purpose I have often considered, whether learning is ever like to come in request among the *Turks*, and as far as conjecture may venture, I doubt not thereof, for learning is not admired in the beginning of empires — *emollit mores, nec finit esse feros*, and so weakneth the sword: but when once that hath bred greatnes and sloth, then with other effeminacies come in letters. Thus, in *Rome*, at the first, philosophers were banish'd as unactive, but upon the conquests of *Carthage* and *Greece* they crept in; and the *Turkish* empire consists much of those countries, whose air makes speculative wits, and which of old bred the greatest divines, philosophers, and poets of the world: wherefore, though for some ages the *Turkish* race may retain its own proper fierceness, yet in time those subtile climates and mixture of blood with the people thereof, will gentilize and infect it with the antient softness natural to these places. ... Now the natural course of things much follows the sun, who gives life to all; wherefore this *Cyclopaedia* hath been observed to run from east to west. Thus have most civilities and sciences came, as some think, from the Indian gymnosophists into *Egypt*, from thence into *Greece*, so into *Italy*, and then over the *Alps*, into these faint north-west parts of the world, whence if the inquisition hinder not, perhaps they may pass into those new plantations westward, and then return in their old circle among the *Levantines*" (Churchill 1752, 539).

been noted in *Averroes*, *Avicenna*, and others, who could not endure it: thereupon the academy, which began to rise up at *Bagadat*, was suppress'd; yet let no man conclude that this can hinder philosophy, for there can never want wits able to bend it to religion with them, as well as Plato with the *Grecians*, and *Aquinas* with the *Romanists*. (Churchill 1752, 539)

The supposed loss of medieval Muslim philosophical traditions, which was accepted as a historical fact among Christian writers of Europe since Riccoldi da Monte Croce, Blount ascribed to a much wider set of factors than any of his contemporaries among the travelers to the Ottoman or Safavid Empires: language, tyranny, war, ecclesiastical interests, and in particular the profound differences in Turkish and English mentalities.[34]

Thus, while in terms of concrete information about the contemporary state of the sciences and the arts in the Ottoman Empire, Blount's account does not differ much from other writings of the period, his particular programmatic approach to the Ottoman Empire combined with several medieval concepts of religion, philosophy, history, and science in general and Islam in particular contributed to his portrayal of the Ottomans as principally capable of mastering and contributing to science and art, the latter's characterization as a retrograde step in civilization rather than as progress, and the lack of one-sided evaluations of the perceived differences in mentalities.

4. Conclusions

The Republic of Letters — its territory with its centers and peripheries, its population and their hierarchies, its values, norms, and codes of behavior, and its cognitive projects — has been described in recent studies by Bots, Waquet, and Goldgar as universal, but West European; as non-denominational, but Western Christian; as liberal, socially mobile, and apolitical, but authority-worshipping, group-conscious, and involved in politico-religious intrigues and battles; and as favoring "right" behavior over "right" knowledge. In other words, it appears to have been a fairly close-knit community which by weaving various conflicting hopes, dreams, and beliefs into patterns of "correct" behavior and speech tried to gain independence and protect itself from the harsh West European social, religious, economic, and political realities.

While there is no reason to doubt that the members of the Republic of Letters indeed tried to cope with life by drawing clear and at times even solid boundaries,

---

[34] "(Their) wits seem more abstruse, and better fix'd for contemplation, but ours more nimble and ready, so as their discourses are more profound, ours more superficial and plausible; and were I to account for the loss of their antient authors, I should not only accuse language, tyranny, war and ecclesiastical interest, but especially this different relish, and strain of our fancy from theirs, for I have found it in conceits, as in airs of musick. In great part that takes not with them which much affects us; our very reason differs" (Churchill 1752, 539–540).

the description of those boundaries as given by the two mentioned studies and a number of other studies on early modern history of science is, as the material presented and discussed in this paper indicates, much too rigid. It tends to simplify the complexity of the relations between the values, norms, and codes of behaviors and the quests for knowledge that governed and motivated the Republic of Letters.

The territorial, cognitive, and religious boundaries were much more flexible and permeable than their confinement to Western Europe implies. Knowledge in specific forms and appearances was a good so eagerly sought and so highly cherished that it allowed not only Oriental Christians entrance into the Republic, but also Jews, Muslims, and heathens, as individuals and as texts or other material evidence. The Republic was much more universal and non-denominational than thought. The judgments about what knowledge was worthy to serve as the entrance ticket, however, were made by West European members of the Republic and the tools they used were their very own scholarly traditions and orientations. Hence, the Republic of Letters was local inasmuch as it postulated the existence of only one feasible, albeit complex set of knowledge that was valid for all mankind. This postulate permitted exchange and transfer of knowledge. But it also contributed to putting those parts of non-Western knowledge that shared similar historical traditions on a lower level in the value-scale and to pushing beyond the limits the ones which either served unfamiliar or disapproved of ends or were altogether different.

Regarding the sciences in Muslim societies and the boundaries supposedly separating them from religious, legal, and philological studies, the material discussed in this paper not only shows that in the sixteenth and seventeenth centuries, people in the Ottoman and the Safavid Empires studied philosophy, astronomy, mathematics, or medicine. It also indicates that their knowledge was of a quality that enabled them to enter into a meaningful communication with West European scholars, a communication that was a dialogue, not a monologue. Obviously, the sciences in these two Muslim societies had not died out nor were they deadly sterile, but they were lively parts of the cores of society — the court, the army, the *madrasa*, and the local urban culture.

References

Alpin, P. 1735. *Prosperi Alpini Historiæ Ægypti naturalis*. Lugduni Batavorum: Apud Gerardum Potvliet.
The 'Arabick' Interest of the Natural Philosophers in Seventeenth-Century England. 1994. edited by G. A. Russell. Leiden, New York, Köln: E. J. Brill.
Belon, P. 1551. *L'histoire naturelle des Estranges Poissons Marins, Avec La Vraie Peinctvre & description du Daulphin, & de plusieurs autres de son espece, obseruee par Pierre Belon du Mans*. Paris: Regnaud Chaudiere.

Belon, P. 1553. *Les Observations Singularitez et choses memorables, trouuées en Grece, Asie, Judée, Egypte, Arabie, et autres pays estranges, Redigées en trois Liures, par Pierre Belon du Mans.* Paris: Gilles Corozet.

Blount, H. 1752. "A Voyage into the Levant." In *Collection of Voyages and Travels. Some now First Printed from the Original Manuscripts, Others Now First Published in English. In Eight Volumes. With A General Preface, Giving an Account of the Progress of Trade and Navigation, from its First Beginning. Illustrated with Several Hundred Useful Maps and Cuts, Containing Views of the Different Countries, Cities, Towns, Forts, Ports and Shipping: Also the Birds, Beasts, Fish, Serpents, Trees, Fruits and Flowers; with the Habits of the different Nations, all Elegantly Engraved on Copper-Plates.* London: Printed by Assignment from Messierus Churchill, For Thomas Osborne in Gray's Inn. MDCCLII, vol. VI.

Bost, H. 1994. *Un "intellectuel" avant la lettre: le journaliste Pierre Bayle (1647–1706).* Amsterdam, Maarssen: APA-Holland University Press.

Bots, H., F. Waquet 1997. *La République des Lettres.* Paris: Belin, De Boeck.

Boucher de la Richarderie, G. [1808] 1970. *Bibliothèque universelle des voyages ou notice complète de tous les voyages anciens et modernes dans les différentes parties du monde: publiés tant en langue française qu'en langues étrangères, classés par ordre de pays dans leur série chronologique; avec des extraits plus ou moins rapides des voyages les plus estimés du chaque pays et des jugemens motivés sur les relations anciennes qui ont le plus de célébrité.* 6 volumes; volumes 3, 4. [Paris: Treuffel et Würtz.] Genève: Slatkine.

Brentjes, S. 1999. "Early Modern West European Travellers in the Middle East and Their Reports about the Sciences." In *Travellers in Egypt and the Near East,* edited by P. and J. Starkey. Ithaca, in press.

Chardin, J. 1686. *Journal du Voyage du Chev.^{R} Chardin en Perse & aux Indes Orientales. Par la Mer Noire & par la Colchide.* London: Moyse Pitt.

——. 1811. *Voyages du Chevalier Chardin, en Perse, et autres Lieux de l'Orient.* Edited by L. Langlès. Paris: Le Normant.

Cochrane, E. 1985. *Historians and Historiography in the Italian Renaissance.* Chicago, London: University of Chicago Press.

Cultures of Natural History. 1996. Edited by N. Jardine, J. A. Secord, E. C. Spary. Cambridge, New York, Melbourne: Cambridge University Press.

Cunningham, A. 1996. "The Culture of Gardens." In *Cultures of Natural History,* edited by N. Jardine, J. A. Secord, E. C. Spary, 38–56. Cambridge, New York, Melbourne: Cambridge University Press.

Dannenfeldt, K. H. 1968. *Leonhard Rauwolf. Sixteenth-Century Physician, Botanist, and Traveler.* Cambridge, Mass.: Harvard University Press.

Du Mans, R. 1890. *Estat de la Perse en 1660.* Edited by Ch. Schefer. Paris: Ernest Leroux.

Findlen, P. 1994. *Possessing Nature. Museums, Collecting, and Scientific Culture in Early Modern Italy.* Berkeley, Los Angeles, London: University of California Press.

Goldgar, A. 1995. *Impolite Learning. Conduct and Community in the Republic of Letters, 1680–1750*. New Haven, London: Yale University Press.
Grosrichard, A. 1979. *Structure du sérail. La fiction du despotisme asiatique dans l'Occident classique*. Paris: Editions du Seuil.
Harvey, J. 1994. "Coronary Flowers and Their 'Arabick' Background." In *The 'Arabick' Interest of the Natural Philosophers in Seventeenth-Century England*. Edited by G. A. Russell, 297–303. Leiden, New York, Köln: E. J. Brill.
Heller, H. 1996. "Muslime in deutscher Erde: Frühe Grabstätten des 14. bis 18. Jahrhunderts." In *In fremder Erde. Zur Geschichte und Gegenwart der islamischen Bestattung in Deutschland*. Edited by G. Höpp, G. Jonker, 45–55. Zentrum Moderner Orient, Berlin, Arbeitshefte 11.
Hentsch. Th. 1992. *Imagining the Middle East*. Montréal, New York: Black Rose Books.
Herbert, Th. [1634] 1971. *A Relation of Some Yeares Travaile, Begvnne Anno 1626. Into Afrique and the greater Asia, especially the Territories of the Persian Monarchie: and some parts of the Orientall Indies, and Iles adiacent. Of their Religion, Language, Habit, Discent, Ceremonies, and other matters concerning them. Together with the proceedings and death of the three late Ambassadors: Sir D. C. Sir R. S. and the Persian Nogdi-Beg: As also the two great Monarchs, the King of Persia, and the great Mogol.* [London: Printed by William Stansby, and Jacob Bloome.] Amsterdam, New York: Da Capo Press, Theatrvm Orbis Terrarvm.
Herbert, Th. 1677. *Some Yeares Travels into Africa, Asia, ... especially ... Persia and Industan*. 3rd. ed., London.
———. 1928. *Travels in Persia 1627–1629*. Edited by W. Foster. London: George Routledge & Sons.
Jardine, N., J. A. Secord and E. C. Spary, eds. 1996. *Cultures of Natural History*. Cambridge, New York, Melbourne: Cambridge University Press.
Koebner, R. 1951. "Despot and Despotism: Vicissitudes of a Political Term." *Journal of the Warburg and Courtauld-Institute* 14: 275–302.
Nellen, H. J. M. 1994. *Ismaël Boulliau (1605–1694). Astronome, Épistolier, Nouvelliste et Intermédiaire Scientifique. Ses Rapports aves les Milieux du "Libertinage Érudit"*. Amsterdam, Maarssen: APA-Holland University Press.
Piemontese, A. M. 1989. *Catalogo dei Manoscritti Persiani Conservati nelle Bibliotheche d'Italia*. Roma: Istituto Poligrafico e Zecca dello Stato, Libreria dello Stato.
Philologica Arabica. Arabische studiën en drukken in de Nederlanden in de 16de en 17de eeuw. 1986. Catalogus. Tentoonstelling Museum Plantin-Moretus: Antwerpen.
Pinon, C. de 1920. *Voyage en Orient*. Publié avec des notes historiques et géographiques par E. Blochet, Paris.
Rauwolf, L. 1582. *Leonarti Rauwolfen/der Artzney Doctorn/vnd bestelten Medici zu Augsburg. Aigentliche beschreibung der Rai?/so er vor diser zeit gegen*

Auffgang inn die Morgenländer/fürnemlich Syriam, Iudaeam, Arabiam, Mesopotamiam, Babyloniam, Assyriam, Armeniam, &c. nicht ohne geringe mühe vnnd grosse gefahr selbs volbracht: neben vermeldung vil anderer seltzamer vnd denkwürdiger sachen/die alle er auff solcher erkundiget/gesehen vnd obseruiert hat. s. l.

Richard, F. 1995. *Raphaël du Mans missionaire en Perse au XVIIe s. Moyen Orient & Océan Indien XVIe-XIXe s.* 9, Société d'Histoire de l'Orient. 2 Bände, Paris: L'Harmattan.

Russell, G. A., ed. 1994. *The "Arabick" Interest of the Natural Philosophers in Seventeenth-Century England.* Leiden, New York, Köln: E. J. Brill.

Starkey, Paul and Janet. In Press. *Travellers in Egypt and the Near East.* Ithaca.

Tavernier, J. B. 1676. *Les Six Voyages de Jean Baptiste Tavernier ... en Turquie, en Perse et aux Indes.* Paris.

——. 1681. *Beschreibung der Sechs Reisen Welche Johan Baptista Tavernier, Ritter und Freyherr von Aubonne. In Türckey/Persien und Indien/innerhalb vierzig Jahren/durch alle Wege/die man nach diesen Ländern nehmen kann/verrichtet.* Genf: Johann Hermann Widerhold.

Toomer, G. 1996. *Eastern Wisdome and Learning. The Study of Arabic in Seventeenth-Century England.* Oxford: Clarendon Press.

Trewmundt, Ch. 1598. *Dess Christiani Trewmundts Gewissen=loser Juden=Doctor/In welchem Erstlich Das wahre Conterfeit Eines Christlichen Medici, und dessen nothwendige Wissenschafften/wie auch gewissenhaffte Praxis, Zweytens Die hingegen Abscheuliche Gestalt Dess Juden=Doctors/Wie auch dessen Unfehigkeit zur Lehre und Doctors-Würde/und die schad=volle Bedienung der Krancken Aus geist= und weltlichen Rechten/mit unumstösslichen Gründen vorgestellet wird.* Gedruckt zu Freyburg/Im Jahr M DC LXXXXVIII.

Valle, P. della 1674. *Petri della Valle, Eines vornehmen Roemischen Patritii Reiss-Beschreibung in unterschiedliche Theile der Welt.* Genf: Johann Hermann Widerhold.

Yerasimos, St. 1991. *Les Voyageurs dans l'Empire Ottoman (XIVe-XVIe siècles).* Publication de la Société Turc d'Histoire, Série VII, No 117, Ankara.

II

ON THE RELATION BETWEEN THE OTTOMAN EMPIRE AND THE WEST EUROPEAN REPUBLIC OF LETTERS (17th - 18th centuries)[1]

Traveling to meet members of the Republic of Letters and to converse with men of influence in the world of courts was one of the main features of early modern West European scholarly cultures, as has long been recognized in history of science studies. Travelers venturing to remote parts of Asia and the New World and guided by commercial and apostolic interests are also acknowledged as an important aspect of the contemporary quest for knowledge.

Traveling to the Middle East, however, has as a rule been ignored in current histories of scientific cultures in early modern Western Europe. Yet there is a surprisingly large number of sources describing such travels and the various motifs which attracted the travelers to the Middle East. These sources suggest modifying the portrayal of the scientific cultures in early modern West European and Middle Eastern societies.

The aim of the paper is to contribute to such a modification. In particular, it addresses the position formulated by Nellen in his paper on West European scholarly travelers to the Levant who wrote about the travelers and the Ottoman Empire:

> Operating from the tiny, isolated western colonies, they hesitantly entered a foreign world that frightened as well as fascinated them. From the 16th century onwards, however, Turkish society gradually turned against the West. Its receptive and cosmopolitan attitudes increasingly gave way to a strong inclination to isolationism, a slow but irreversible process that was mainly determined by religious rigorism. If western intruders did manage to make contacts, their ignorance of the language proved a hindrance to the informal and fruitful exchange of ideas. In addition to this, in the Ottoman Empire there was no autonomous scholarly life such as was developing in the West more or less independently of Church and State. ... Although mention must be made of intermediaries like the Greek dragomans and the many renegades that had worked their way up in the administration of the Empire and therefore symbolized the possibility of mutual penetration of the two cultures, the distance between Islam and Christianity remained great: there was no room for more than an incidental - let alone an institutionalized - exchange of information and ideas. (Nellen 1996, p. 210)

---

[1] I thank David King, Frankfurt am Main, and Ekmeleddin İhsanoğlu, Istanbul, for their help.

II

I believe that Nellen's statements are fundamentally wrong. Despite the profound religious differences, despite the numerous wars and political frictions between West European states and the Ottoman Empire, there was room in more than only marginal cases for an exchange of information and ideas. I even believe that this exchange was rather substantial, although its impact upon the two scholarly communities differed. To substantiate these claims, West European sources of the 17th and 18th centuries which speak of personal encounters between scholars from France and the Ottoman Empire as well as literary encounters of French scholars with Ottoman scientific traditions have been studied.

The number of travels to the Middle East devoted primarily to scholarly goals started to increase in the second half of the 16th century. The two major areas of interest which brought West European scholars into the Ottoman Empire and adjacent countries were studies of materia medica related matters and the acquisition of manuscripts in all the major languages of the past and contemporary Middle East on a broad variety of topics, ranging from religion to history and literature to the mathematical sciences, geography, and philosophy. Scholarly ends were also pursued in travels devoted to commercial, religious, or political aims. During the 17th and 18th centuries, a substantial number of merchants, diplomats or gentlemen traveling for education or entertainment contributed to the acquisition of manuscripts, seeds, coins, medals, inscriptions or recipes. They also were eager to meet local scholars and to exchange with them information and ideas on different scholarly topics. An important contribution to this exchange of knowledge and its material means came from diverse Christian communities in the Ottoman Empire. Among them, several Maronites played an active role in the translation of religious, historical, philological and geographical texts.

The material documenting diverse activities of these scholars, travelers, merchants, missionaries, and diplomats implies to modify the current portrayal of the scholarly cultures in the Ottoman Empire and their interaction with the Republic of Letters in Western Europe in three ways:

1. West European scholars in the 17th and 18th centuries pursued a variety of intellectual goals in the Ottoman Empire using the means provided by missionaries, merchants and diplomats as well as by the local scholarly communities, merchants and Ottoman provincial rulers treating some of the latter as if they were members of the Republic of Letters;

2. There were scholarly communities in the Ottoman Empire engaged in a variety of scientific endeavors;
3. Muslim scholars and members of the state, civil and military as well as of the religious elites in the Ottoman Empire allowed and sought encounters, debates, and exchange of knowledge with West European travelers.

This paper will discuss these three claims based upon travel accounts, letters and geographical activities by Balthasar de Monconys, Ismaël Boulliau and Jean-Baptiste Bourguignon d'Anville. To indicate that these three examples are not exceptional I refer to the efforts made since the middle of the 16th century to publish, translate and exploit Arabic and Persian geographical manuscripts. In this time, a copy of the *Taqwim al-buldan* by Abu l-Fida' was brought to Western Europe by Guillaume Postel. There it came first to be kept by the Palatine Library, Heidelberg. Other copies were brought during the 16th and 17th centuries to Italy, Austria, France, and Britain. In the late 16th century, an incomplete copy of al-Idrisi's *Geography* arrived in Italy where it became part of the Medicis' library. Both texts were repeatedly accessed by West European and Maronite scholars from the 16th until the late 18th centuries for utilization of their information for cartography, geographical dictionaries, historiography and the revision of latitude and longitude values.

Among the scholars who either printed the one or the other text in Arabic or in Latin translation, completely or in extracts, or produced manuscript translations we find during the 16th and 17th centuries Bernardino Baldi, Wilhelm Schickard, John Greaves, Thomas Hyde, Laurent d'Arvieux in cooperation with M. de la Roque and Melchisédech Thévenot, the Maronites Johannes Hesronita, Gabriel Sionita, and Abraham Ecchellensis who were followed in the 18th century by Jean Gagnier, Abraham Schulte, Johann Bernhard Koehler, Johann Jacob Reiske, Johann David Michaelis, Friedrich Theodor Rinck, and others. Not all of these works have been published and almost none of them has been investigated by a historian of science.

Among the geographers and cartographers who exploited (or claimed to have done it) the one or the other text for dressing new maps of Northern Africa, Western Asia, the Caspian Sea, etc., Jacopo Gastaldi, Abraham Ortelius, Nicholas de Sanson, Guillaume De l'Isle, and Jean-Baptiste d'Anville have to be mentioned. Pierre Bertius, Pierre Duval and d'Anville used the one or the other text for producing historical maps.

II

Additional geographical sources in Arabic and Persian, for instance, Hamdallah al-Mustawfi al-Qazwini's *Nuzhat al-qulub*, Ibn al-Wardi's *Kharidat al-'aja'ib*, the geographical coordinates given by Nasir al-Din al-Tusi, Ulugh Beg or Ali Qushji, as well as anonymous texts, have been tapped by Jacob Golius, Adrien Reland, Gilbert Gaulmyn, Antoine Galland, John Greaves and Thomas Hyde. Several Arabic, Persian, and Syriac historical works were translated - at least in extracts - during the 17th and 18th centuries and scrutinized by cartographers for their geographical information. Gottfried Wendelin even learned of a new determination of the latitude and longitude of Constantinople made during the reign of Murad III which brought for the latitude and the longitude the values 41° 30'; 56° 47', and informed Pierre Gassendi in a letter preserved in the Bibliothèque nationale de France about it.[2] These values, however, deviate from those known from Taqi al-Din's observations carried out under Murad III.[3] Thus, Wendelin's values pose an intriguing question not only concerning the sources of Wendelin's knowledge who claims to have got the information from Constantinople, but also whether there was another measurement of the two values made during Murad's reign. West European travelers such as Pedro Teixeira, Thomas Herbert, Adam Olearius, Jean-Baptiste Tavernier, or Jean Chardin contributed to spread geographical knowledge from Persian tables, astrolabes and perhaps even maps and to introduce the names of Nasir al-Din al-Tusi, Abu l-Fida' and Ulugh Beg to a larger West European public.

These literary and cartographic activities undertaken in Western Europe were accompanied by geographical and astronomical measurements and the dressing of maps and city-plans which West European missionaries, merchants, travelers, members of embassies - in particular physicians and engineers -, and researchers from the academies and scientific societies carried out in the Ottoman Empire and many of which have not been investigated yet.

1. Balthasar de Monconys (1608?-1665)

De Monconys was a royal legal counselor in Lyon who traveled from the late 1620s to the late 1640s widely all over Western Europe and the Ottoman Empire. He was in personal and written contacts with several European courts and numerous major members of the Republic of Letters such as Nicolas Fabri de

---

[2] Ms Paris, BNF, Dupuy 663, ff 27a-28b; see, in particular, f 27b.
[3] 41° 15'; 60°.

Peiresc, Pierre Gassendi, Jacques and Pierre Dupuy, Ismaël Boulliau or Marin Mersenne.

The framework for French scholarly interest in the Middle East since the middle of the 16th century was set by François I's efforts to win Süleyman as an ally against Charles V. Several French ambassadors were sent within a brief period of time to the Sublime Porte. Most of the scholarly travelers were members of their entourage, partly because of the passports, letters of recommendation and financial means needed for such a journey. From this time on, French scholarly traveling into the Middle East transgressed the simple structures of a sponsoring patron and a sponsored scholar. Individual noble patronage, personal scholarly interests and needs, state and church concerns, and the courtly and commercial accumulation of wealth and prestige met in the organisation and implementation of scholarly travels to Muslim empires.

In the first half of the 17th century, scholarly interest in the Middle East or the lack thereof often reflected religious and political positions and ambitions within French interior politics. This was the case, for instance, in the quarrels surrounding the edition of a polyglot Bible or the public denunciations of Boulliau's interests in Islam by Théophraste Renaudot, Jean B. Morin and others. On the other hand, the reciprocal support of political and scholarly traveling to the Ottoman Empire which had gained a more steady footing with the establishment of regular and permanent French ambassadors in Istanbul in the second half of the 16th century was a social asset appreciated by the ambassadors as well as the scholars. Gassendi, for instance, was invited and accepted to be a member of such an ambassadorial entourage, although the entire project failed because of unknown reasons. Gassendi can be taken as a token of the immense attraction the Ottoman Empire exercised on the French scholarly world during the 17th century. In 1629/1630, he himself together with his friend François Luillier started to study Arabic hoping to access texts Gassendi's mentor and friend Nicolas Fabri de Peiresc had acquired from Cairo, Aleppo, Sayda and other Ottoman towns.[4] Other friends, students, or contemporaries of Gassendi such as Joseph Gaultier, Jacques Gaffarel, François-Auguste de Thou, Gilbert Gaulmin, Claude Hardy, Melchisédech Thévenot, Marin Mersenne, Ismaël Boulliau, or François Bernier either learned (some) Arabic, Persian or Turkish to study texts of various genres, traveled to Muslim countries, or sought to acquire from there manuscripts and

---

[4] Ms Paris, BNF, fr 9536, f 213a.

II

other material deemed necessary for their own research. Boulliau even had hoped to travel together with de Monconys to the Ottoman Empire.

In 1665, after de Monconys' death, his son edited and published at Lyon his father's journal of travels through Western Europe and the Ottoman Empire in the late 1640s and early 1650s. Since the late 1620s, de Monconys had wanted to travel as far as India and China. According to his son, in this time de Monconys

> auoit vne forte passion pour la Chymie, qu'il estimoit la clef de la Nature qu'elle nous ouure par la dissolution des corps. (De Monconys 1665, p. 2)[5]

After some time he discovered his error, but vowed that not all had been in vain since:

> ... de l'epreuue de tant de secrets, dont les Charlatans abusent le Monde, il auoit acquis d'autres lumieres qui payoient assez sa peyne & son argent: semblable aux Geometres à qui la vaine poursuite de la quadrature du Cercle a fait quelque-fois inuenter en chemin des propositions plus vtiles que leur grand oeuure. (Ibid.)

In this spirit, he did everything to get to know the most occult and the most strange arts, being curious to the excess. In Egypt and in the Levant,

> il ... s'informa diligemment des Iuifs, des Arabes, & des Indiens, s'il rencontreroit parmy eux quelque reste de l'ancienne Cabale des Egyptiens, ou de la Philosophie de Trismegiste, & de Zoroastre, que Pythagore & Platon piquez d'vne pareille ardeur y auoient autrefois recherchée en leur ieunesse. (Ibid., p. 3)

According to his son, the results were less than satisfying. He claimed that this caused his father to turn his back to the occult disciplines in favor of the mathematical and physical sciences:

> Mais enfin n'ayant peut (sic) rassassier son esprit d'vne nourriture si creuse, & si legere, il tourna ses pensées à la belle Physique, & aux Mathematiques, qui de toutes les Sciences humaines, sont celles où il y a plus de proffit, & de solidité. (Ibid.)

The published travel log, however, paints a somewhat different picture. During his travels, de Monconys was already interested in both the occult and the mathematical and physical sciences. He met, for instance, with Ottoman astronomers and mathematicians. Moreover, according to what de Monconys

---

[5] I quote all the extracts in the original spelling of the sources.

wrote right at the beginning of his travels about a visit to a woman diviner in Tours, his aim while traveling was rather to prove the futility of the occult arts:

> Au retour du Plessis ie fut voir vne femme, qu'on m'auoit fort vantée pour scauoir des choses extraordinaires & surnaturelles; & comme i'auois resolu pendant mon voyage de ne point laisser passer d'occasion de m'esclaircir de la fausseté de tous ces contes & dela vanité de toutes ces sciences, ie commencay par elle le catalogue des ignorans, que i'ay trouuez en ces matieres; ... (Ibid., p. 6)

The same attitude is displayed in a letter de Monconys wrote on July 13, 1647 from Cairo to de Champigny in Lyon:

> ... leur ignorance est extréme, & c'est ce qui leur fait croire aussi bien qu'ailleurs qu'il y a des charmes & des sortileges; i'ay eu vne curiosité toute particuliere pour cela, i'ay veu tous ceux qu'on estimoit Magiciens, que i'ay recognûs de tres-grosses bestes, & il faudroit des iours entiers pour vous entretenir sur ce chapitre; ... (Ibid., p. 188)

He met with numerous experts of various occult arts, Muslims, Jews, Copts, Greeks, and Armenians, men and women, in Alexandria, Cairo, Aleppo, and other towns of the Ottoman Empire:

> Le 4. (Mars 1647) ie fus le matin auec Grillet chercher Soliman Magreplil afendi, qui vint chez moy l'apresdiné; il disoit qu'il feroit voir des Esprits: puis ie fus au Bazar à Cancali, & toute l'apresdiné auec le Pere Elsear.
> ...
> Le 6. (Mars 1647) ie fus prendre des cendres & oüir Messe aux Capucins: puis auec Rabi-Isac voir Soliman Magrepli à son Diuan; l'apresdiné j'oüuis le Sermon du Pere Elsear, & vis vn Iuif qui disposoit quelque nombre que ce fut dans neuf rangs, en sorte que de tout costé on trouuoit toûjours le mesme sens;
> Le 5. (Iuin 1647) ... & fus chercher vn aveugle lequel est estimé grand devin, ie ne le trouuay pas.
> Le 6. ie fus le matin chercher hors du Zebekier la femme qui devine, mais elle n'y estoit pas: ie vis au retour vn Cofti en grande reputation pour cela, qui me dit des choses entre deux, mais il ne reüssit pas au miroir: il me donna vn papier, & me promit de m'apprendre beaucoup de choses: ...
> Le 7. ie fus le matin chez le Devin aveugle, auquel ie ne pùs parler, à cause de la quantité de femmes qu'il y a voir: ...
> Le 8. ie fus voir vne femme qui disoit la bonne fortune dans les masures d'vne maison rompue à la porte d'vne mosquée: elle estoit entourée d'vne infinité de pauvres femmes; ie luy donnay mon mouchoir (comme c'est la façon), & elle me dit des sottises: ...
> Le 9. (Iuin 1647) apres la Messe ie fus chez vn vieux Kofti qui fait profession des sciences curieuses, lequel m'offrit de m'enseigner beaucoup de choses. (Ibid., p. 197, 260, 262)

II

Most of the time, he is silent about what he exactly asked these experts to do for him. But almost always he informs his readers that they failed to meet either what he wanted them to perform or, interestingly enough, what they, approaching him on their own, had volunteered to carry out:

> Le 8. (Mars 1647) ie demeuray tousiours au logis, iusques à ce que Soliman Magrepli m'enuoya son valet, ie le fus trouuer auec Rabi Isac, mais ie vis qu'il ne sçauoit rien, quoy qu'il soyt estimé Magicien, & qu'il eust mesme dit qu'il feroit voir des esprits en quelque forme qu'on voudroit, & qu'il parleroit quel langage qu'on voudroit; il me vouloit voir, & souhaitoit mesme d'apprendre le moyen de trouuer des thresors, ce qu'il croyoit que ie sçeusse. (Ibid., p. 198)

Apparently this repetitive declaration that practical examination of the best known experts of the occult arts of all religious groups, male and female, in the Middle East had yielded one negative result after the other was not yet sufficient to satisfy de Monconys. Almost at the end of his travels he conveniently met with one Ottoman scholar who had even changed his faith more than once and therefore possessed a wide array of connections or insights. This scholar ensured de Monconys that he too had had only negative experience with the experts of the occult arts. August 18, 1648 de Monconys wrote in his travel log:

> ... ie fus voir Monsieur Mazerat où ie trouvay vn Medecin Turc, iadis Chrestien, & puis Iuif; qui est sçauant en Medecine, Philosophie, & Mathematiques, & qui a cherché autant que moy sans rien trouver; ... (Ibid., p. 424)

Reading de Monconys' travel log a bit more carefully illuminates that there is more to the story than these open efforts to discredit the occult arts. Almost everywhere, de Monconys bought precious stones, eyes of fishes and cows, and other material of alchemyical interest. He met some of the experts of the occult arts numerous times, spending entire afternoons and evenings discussing and carrying out experiments. He talked with them about religious questions which often were beyond his understanding, about philological issues, astrology, drugs and alchemical recipes, and topics he only managed to describe in terms of Western European constructs, such as the *perpetuum mobile*:

> Le 10. (Iuillet 1648) ... l'apresdiné ie fus visité de deux Turcs curieux, l'vn aux Mechaniques & l'autre en Astrologie; le premier Mahamet Cherebi me donna vn bitume de Perse, quil nommoit Momie bonne à remettre les os cassez à ce qu'il me dit; il auoit vne des plus belles, viues, & eclatantes cornalines que ie vis iamais; il me parla du mouvement perpetuel qu'il me promit de me faire voir.
> Le 14. ... l'apresdiné ie fus aux Deruis voir Mahamet Cherebi, qui ne me montra ny l'aymant, ny le mouuement perpetuel dont il m'auoit parlé; ... (Ibid., p. 403)

II

He claimed that by promising and keeping his silence he protected Jewish, Coptic or Muslim magicians from being found out as cheats by their communities. He acknowledged that some people were better skilled to perform occult acts than others, and that there were different sorts of techniques according to which the occultists were classified. He differentiated between diviners operating on the streets and experts sharing their knowledge in privacy, in a Sufi convent, or on the basis of written or oral recommendation by other experts. According to his reports, he freely used the networks of scholarly and other social connections generously offered by Muslim, Jewish and Eastern Christian subjects of the Ottoman Empire and by Western European residents. Thus, his activities display a much more complex structure than that being simply directed towards disproving the scholarly solidity of the occult arts. Moreover, they suggest that the French traveler behaved as if he was within the confines of the West European Republic of Letters investigating, acquiring and sharing whatever was of interest for the traveler and for those who stayed at home.

The impression that de Monconys conceived of the Ottoman Empire as some sort of an extended Republic of Letters is strengthened by what he wrote about his activities in the fields of mathematics or physics. He paid visits to mathematicians, natural philosophers interested in dynamics and hydro-mechanics or in collecting plants and other curiosities, astronomers and physicians. He carried with him to the Middle East treatises on Galilean dynamics the contents of which he lectured about to Capuchin missionaries at Cairo:

> Ie mis au net pour le Pere Elzear cette Demonstration que l'on m'auoit donnée à Florence.
> DIMOSTRAZIONE TROVATA DAL
> gran Galileo, l'anno 6139. (sic). (Ibid., p. 169)

There and elsewhere in the Ottoman Empire, he received and wrote letters from and to West European scholars about further questions of physics, the behavior of the Nile, the pyramids, the customs and manners of the visited peoples, and his evaluations of their civilizational merits or flaws:

> Ie receus lettres de Monsieur de la Senegerie qui contenoient ces curiositez fort rares alors, & qui ont esté apres plus communes.
> FIGVRE DE L'INSTRVMENT D'HYDROTECHNIE, ...
> Il adjoute, qu'on luy a promis de luy faire voir vn Polifile notté de la main du dit deffunt M. Tole, portant l'explication de tout le secret de l'art, & qu'il me le communiquera lorsqu'il l'aura
> On me rendit ensemble cette lettre de Monsieur de Busenas.

129

II

PERILLVSTRI, AC OMNI SCIENTIARVM
genere Claro, GALILAEO GALLO, Philosopho incognito & patrono meo Colendissimo.
...
LETTRE DE Mr DE MONCONYS à vn de ses Amis, sur les Pyramides & les Mumies d'Egypte.
... , au retour ie receus lettres de Monsieur Magis & Piscatoris du 18. Ianvier & 16. Feurier. (Ibid. pp. 171, 175, 183, 200)

He prepared instruments such as a telescope for the specific purpose to carry out astronomical observations in the Middle East. When they got lost at sea he ordered new ones made in France which he received by ship from Marseille only a few weeks later in Cairo. There, he also bought instruments which may have been telescopes. While using the telescopes indeed for various astronomical observations, de Monconys also applied them to satisfy his social and sexual curiosities by spying from afar into the backyards of Ottoman houses. In his visits to native experts, he often was accompanied either by other French travelers or by one of the missionaries, consuls, their physicians, and interpreters. Those experts of the occult arts with whom he met more often also came to visit him in his lodgings within the West European communities or to share his dinners together with Capuchins, travelers, and other West Europeans:

> Le 8. Ie fus le matin à la Chambre de M. Gombaud, au Caué, à la Messe aux Capucins & saluer le Pere Elzear Capucin: puis voir vn Pere Cordelier reformé Chapelain du Consul me vint voir ensuite, Isaac Leon dina auec nous l'apresdiné le Pere Elzear me vint voir, & apres ie fus voir M. de Bermond iadis Consul. (Ibid., p. 164)

Despite this claimed transparency and permeability of the boundaries between various groups of experts, scholars, diplomats or religious men, de Monconys apparently preferred to communicate with scholarly minded Western European residents of the Middle East. He took two Italians to teach him some basic Arabic, a behavior very different from that of Western European travelers who came to the region to learn the languages. They usually addressed local people with a scholarly training in standard Arabic and learned the colloquial with servants. De Monconys' choice of the teachers apparently was dictated by his wish to learn alchemical secrets and to search markets, libraries and private houses together with the teachers for all sorts of useful items. He rarely, if ever, criticized Western Europeans in the Middle East who also pursued the occult arts, but reported in more appreciative tones of the experiments carried out with them, quoted the recipes they had given to him, or mentioned stones and other items shown to him:

> Le 23. (Feurier 1647) ie fus me promener le matin auec mon Me: l'apresdiné i'alla voir Mr le Consul qui me montra ses Patentes du grand Seigneur, ses escuelles de bezoar mineral, & d'agate, puis chez Mr Portel qui me donna vne pierre de la iaunisse & de la colique. ...
> Le 19. (Mars 1647) Ie fus le matin auec Sieur Pietro mon Maistre voir vne maison dans la contrée de Venise, & chez vn Turc qui aime les mathematiques: puis l'apresdiné ie fus pour passer le loüage que le Maistre remit au lendemain: apres le Sieur Pietro m'ayant apporté de l'argent congelé au suc d'herbe, ie le fixay en lune. ...
> Le 20. I'arrestay la maison, & le reste ie couppelay le Mercure fixé dont il resta peu, & de couleur d'amatiste à la touche: ie donnay au Sieur Pietro pour auoir de l'herbe deux piastre. ...
> Le 26. Ie fus a la caue auec Isaac & mon Maistre, acheptay vne cassette 85. medains. me fis raser, experimantay mon tire-poil que i'appris le soir à mon Maistre: ...
> Le 28. Ie fus au Basar auec vn Iuif: Ie vis vne pierre grise qu'on disoit estre vne espece de bezoar ...
> Le lendemain Pietro fie sa congelation deuant moy. Il fit chauffer dans un creuset plein de craye blanche le mercure, puis ... (Ibid., p. 193, 201f)

He also carried out such experiments himself. De Monconys was most enthuastic about father Elzéar de Samsaye, the superior of the Capuchins at Cairo, whom he frequently met. It was with him that de Monconys discussed the latest developments in Italian physics. For him he copied a Galilean text on the fall of a body on the inclined plane and to him he talked about Torricelli and other Italian natural philosophers. But he also talked about astrology, alchemy or divination with father Elzéar who seemed to have approved of such talks and activities:

> Le 18. (Feurier 1647) le Pere Elzear me lût vne Comedie qu'il avoit composée: ie luy promis les autres demonstrations que i'avois escrites à Florence & à Pise, & nous resolumes d'aller voir ensemble vn Grec n'aguere arrivé, qu'on disoit estre fort curieux: l'apresdiné nous y fûmes, & apres vne conversation en Italien de divers sujets, il me dit que dans les Isles de Grece les femmes vsoient d'vn secret pour faire meurir les figues qui a quelque chose de particulier. ... (Ibid., p. 177)

The missionaries as well as the orders caring for the churches in Jerusalem and other places in Palestine at least partially pursued alchemy in close contact with healing practices and the search for cosmetical recipes.

In the eyes of de Monconys, the veracity of the occult arts or their futility depended not only upon a sufficient technical training, the correct application of technical procedures, or sufficiently succinct claims, but also upon the origin and to a certain extent the gender of the experts. Western European religious or university trainees were better qualified or at least more reliable than Middle Eastern experts. Representatives of high culture knowledge who according to de

II

Moncony were exclusively male were preferable over those of low culture knowledge who came from both sexes.

Ms Paris, BnF, fr 25280 entitled "Alcoran, Théologie Musulmane, etc." contains several extracts of Turkish geographies in Arabic or Latin letters as well as two brief summaries from de Monconys' travel log and Jean-Baptiste de Tavernier's account of his travels to the Ottoman Empire, Persia and India, besides a variety of other fragmentary texts and notes, among them the fragment of a French translation of the Quran, texts on the creeds of Oriental Christian communities, a refutation of Islam by a Spanish convert of the mid-15th century, Arabic and Turkish fragments of grammar, and French fragments on astronomy, mathematics, philosophy and related topics. According to the catalogue of the French manuscripts of the BnF, the writer of these various pieces was Antoine Galland (d. 1715) who worked twice as a secretary of the French ambassador in Istanbul in 1672-73 and 1679-80.

The brief summary from de Monconys' text concerns his travel from Aleppo to the Black Sea. Galland stripped de Monconys' report down to its bare geographical information. He evidently tried to identify the names de Monconys mentioned by using French and Turkish sources. The former is made clear by the interlinear gloss "*selon Belon yrchilirmak*" referring to a small river by Adena called by de Monconys "*Ioutteum*".[6] The latter is implied by the transformation of several of de Monconys' names into a form closer to their Turkish pronounciation: *bouladin* for Blaudon, *husrev pacha khani* for le camp de Cosrou Bacha, *eski cheher* and *yeni cheher* for Aschichaer and Enguichar respectively, and *isnik* for *la Ville de Zenie*.[7] Galland was clearly not only interested in learning Turkish, but also in improving his geographical knowledge of the Ottoman Empire by comparing Western and Eastern sources. This attitude was characteristic of a number of French geographers, historians and scholars of other disciplines during the second half of the 17th and the 18th centuries. Gilbert Gaulmyn, Melchisédech Thévenot, Guilleaume De l'Isle and Jean-Bapiste d'Anville are only a few names to be mentioned in this respect.

2. Ismaël Boulliau (1605-1694)

Boulliau was a student of Pierre Gassendi, a member of the Parisian erudite circle of the brothers Jacques and Pierre Dupuy, an active astronomer and

---

[6] Ms Paris, BNF, fr 25280, f 299a; de Monconys, p. 371.

[7] de Monconys, pp. 379-382; Ms Paris, BNF, fr 25280, f 299a.

astrologer, a classicist, and as many of his scholarly colleagues and friends, a (Catholic) priest. He traveled to Smyrna in December 1646, to Constantinople in January 1647, and returned from there to Smyrna in May 1647. From both towns, he wrote letters to France and Italy, for example, to Jacques Dupuy, and there he talked about his expectations and experiences. In 1649, he took up an exchange of letters with Prince Leopold of Tuscany whom he had met in Florence in fall 1646. In his second letter, dated June 17, 1649, Leopold invited Boulliau to compose for him a "relation of his travels to Asia", because such an account would stimulate "the reflexion on a variety of curious matters".[8] In an undated letter, Boulliau responded to this invitation and attached to it a report of almost 46 pages which does not describe merely Boulliau's experience while traveling to the Ottoman Empire, but discusses also geographical and physical subjects such as Galilei's works on the rotation of the earth and its connection with the tides. In his letter dated February 4, 1651, Leopold affirmed its arrival.

The depiction of Boulliau's impressions of Smyrna and Constantinople in his letters to Jacques Dupuy differs occasionally substantially from the statements in his report to Leopold. This concerns above all the evaluation of Smyrna and the level of education of its Greek and Muslim inhabitants. Furthermore, some information given in the letters is not found in the report and vice versa. In the report, Boulliau claimed to have pursued the idea to travel to the Ottoman Empire already ten years before he actually went there. The occasion arose when, on January 1, 1635, François-Auguste de Thou was ordered – much to his surprise as well as disappointment - to go as royal ambassador to Constantinople.[9] François was a son of the historian Jacques-Auguste de Thou, his father's heir as the head of the Royal Library in Paris, and had bought a commission as a royal officer. In 1628-1629, as a young men, he had visited several towns in the Ottoman Empire, among them Constantinople, Jerusalem, Sayda, Cairo and Alexandria. This travel - a mixture of tourism, pilgrimage and pursuit of political and scholarly purposes in the interest of Nicolas Fabri de Peiresc and Jacques Dupuy - gave him much pleasure, but also strengthened his rejection of the Ottoman state.[10] The mission as an ambassador never materialized. While preparing himself for it, de Thou not only requested the newest information about the state of affairs in the Ottoman Empire from Peiresc who acquired a report from his collaborators in Egypt, but

---

[8] Ms Paris, BNF, fr 13039, ff 7a-7b.

[9] Ms Paris, BNF, fr 9537, ff 351a-351b.

[10] ibid., ff 289a-306a.

II

also received offers from scholars such as Boulliau or the Silesian physician Elichmann to accompany him as members of his entourage.[11]

This context of Boulliau's desire to pay a visit to Constantinople permits one to expect a description of the Ottoman Empire which differs to some extent from those of the average West European traveler to the Middle East. Indeed, several of the letters and also certain parts of the report for Leopold contain less prejudices and more specific stories about encounters with Ottoman educated men than several other contemporary accounts. Nonetheless, Nellen perceived of Boulliau's descriptions of the Ottoman Empire as mainly negative:

> In quest of ancient remains he was constantly confronted on his journey by a total cultural decay, and as his research for valuable Greek manuscripts had little success, his evaluation was primarily negative. This negative view was reinforced by the realisation that the Turks deserved no respect as exponents of natural sciences and astronomy; they were in his eyes pitiful dilettantes. Although the climate in cities like Smyrna and Constantinople was very agreeable and these regions provided the local population with an abundance of life's essentials, it was difficult to enjoy such advantages. Boulliau soon missed the company of his Parisian friends. Man, he wrote in a contemplative passage of a letter, was after all created for contact with other reasonable people. The Greeks and Turks were certainly not lacking in common sense, but compared with westerners who were at all civilized they were unreasonable. (Nellen 1996, p. 215)

Nellen added that as a priest Boulliau was disturbed and fascinated by the "erotic atmosphere" of the Levant and "revelled in stories about the perverted love life of the foolish sultan Ibrahim".[12] He emphasized that Boulliau had a very positive opinion of the administration of the Ottoman Empire, that the Ottomans understood best the art of government, and that "the secret of their approach lay in a policy of religious tolerance".[13] Nellen interpreted - certainly not unfounded - Boulliau's appreciation of Ottoman administration as a "barely concealed criticism of abuses Boulliau saw around him in France".[14] But he ignored that these and other topics had acquired already a topical character. Almost every West European traveler commented on them in one way or the other. Nellen also saw no need to discuss Boulliau's ambivalent sentiments towards the Ottoman Empire expressed in his letters and his later survey. Boulliau's letters from Italy, written in 1645 and 1646 during the first two years of war between Venice and the Ottoman Empire over Crete, are full of comments on this war, Ibrahim's "obsession" with

---

[11] ibid., ff 351b, 356a; Ms Paris, BNF, fr 13039, f 11b.
[12] Nellen 1996, p. 215.
[13] ibid., p. 216.
[14] ibid., pp. 216-217.

this war and the lack of unity and interest in liberating the Holy Land among the Christian states of Europe. Despite his fierce opposition against the Ottoman attack of a Venetian "property", Boulliau was very eager to travel to Constantinople and repeatedly wrote to Jacques Dupuy that there was no danger involved in such a voyage since he did not intend to meddle in affairs of the state or religion. On the other hand, having barely arrived in Istanbul and describing to Jacques Dupuy what places he planned to visit in town and outside, Boulliau spoke of returning home at the nearest possible occasion. In the following weeks of his sojourn in the Ottoman capital, Boulliau's emotional configuration changed again. The pleasant climate, the beautiful location, the impressive features of the Aya Sofya and of the major Ottoman mosques, as well as the warm reception he received in the French embassy and in some Ottoman circles made him relax visibly. As his letters testify, Boulliau surprisingly rarely described his experience in the Ottoman Empire in terms of the standard Western-European views of this state and its political and religious culture.

He made use of them, above all, in his letters written during his first stay in Smyrna. Twice, Boulliau complained about the lack of education among the inhabitants of Smyrna whether Greek or Muslim.[15] In the first instance, he supported what he perceived as a loss of knowledge in relation to ancient Greece by a similar statement by Lukian.[16] In the report to Leopold, he replaced these remarks by a lengthy story about a Portuguese Marrano who had studied medicine and the mathematical sciences in Portugal, Spain and Italy and who had come in search of an adequate wife to Smyrna where fate caught him in a trap and made him convert to Islam.[17] This difference not only indicates that Boulliau finally found educated people in Smyrna, but also suggests to take his first sweeping statements not completely at face value.

In his later letters from Constantinople and from his second stay in Smyrna, Boulliau had somewhat different stories to tell. He appreciated the warm-hearted welcome he received by several Muslim religious, military or literary men. He paid their generous friendliness back by a behavior according to the best norms of the Republic of Letters. He reported some impressions which he thought contradicted the standard expectations of his compatriots. As a consequence, he worried that certain of them would belittle his experience or even try to negate it.[18]

---

[15] Ms Paris, BNF, Dupuy 18, ff 168a and 170a-170b.
[16] ibid., f 168a.
[17] Ms Paris, BNF, fr 13039, ff 25a-26b.
[18] Ms Paris, BNF, Dupuy 18, f 185b.

II

He enjoyed not only the Aya Sofya, but also the major mosques of Constantinople whose architectural relationship to the Byzantine building he emphasized.[19] In only one of these later letters, Boulliau adhered to a standard West European prejudice - the idea that the contemporary Greek population in the Ottoman Empire, in particular, its priests, was almost illiterate.

Having left Smyrna on January 23, 1647 and arrived at Istanbul on February 3, he wrote in his second letter from there, dated Febraury 21, to Dupuy that he had been received very friendly by the ambassador Mr. de Vantelet, his secretary Mr. L Empereur, and other members of the ambassador's household. L'Empereur who had started his career in the Ottoman Empire as French consul in Jerusalem was well known to the brothers Dupuy and their friends since the late 1620s when Francois-Auguste de Thou had made his grand tour through the empire. In the following decade, de Thou, Dupuy, Peiresc, and Mersenne exchanged repeatedly letters with L'Empereur asking him for political news and for help in their quest for manuscripts and other curious and useful items. While in Istanbul, Boulliau visited with him various historical sites and relied upon his support in arranging introductions to the Greek Orthodox patriarch of the city and to the head of a dervish order in Pera, Adem Efendi. Boulliau obtained the permission to study the manuscripts and books available in the patriarchal library among which he mentioned in particular an almanach of the year 995 written in majuscules. He also spent several afternoons with Adem Efendi and some of his followers in Pera, drinking coffee together, discussing - occasionally with much precaution on Boulliau's side - religious topics, and inquiring about what Adem Efendi knew about astronomy, the calculation of a calendar, and meteors or comets. He accepted the dervish as a "scholar according to their fashion" and learned from him the allegedly Qur'anic notion that meteors were fiery stones thrown by the angles at jinn who eavesdropped at the gates of heaven. Adem Efendi showed his French visitor a calendar prepared, as Boulliau wrote, by the Ottoman Müneccimbaşı, i.e., the head of the palace astronomers, on the base of the Jalali era. Boulliau also informed Dupuy that he suffered to some extent under cultural differences, since he could spit nowhere during his encounters with the dervishes nor when visiting mosques.[20] Three weeks later he reported that he had

---

[19] ibid., f 178a.

[20] ... Je vous ay donné aduis par ma precedente qu'apres 52 jours de seiour a Smyrne jen partis le 23 Januier & j'arriuay icy le 3 du courrant, ou je saluay Monseigr l'Amb<assadeur> incontinent apres que je fus debarqué auec le Cap<itaine>. S. E. m'a receu en sa maison & m'a voulu tant fauorizer que de m'y loger; je luy en suis tres-estroictement obligé et a Mons. de Gremonuille qui m'auoit recommandé par ses lettre & par vne dont jestois chargé. Monsieur l'Empereur m'ai faict & continue encores a me faire mille courtoisies & ciuilités. Il m'a mené promener en plusieurs lieux tant dedans que dehors Constantinople. Je vous ay escrit que jauois esté au

seen all the major mosques of Istanbul, including the Aya Sofya - many; travelers before and after regularly accused the "Mores" or the "Turks" to hinder all Christians from visiting their mosques -, had visited the Akmeidan, the Hippodrome, and the arsenal. With the help of an interpreter of the Ottoman court, Mr. Panagioti - who, as Boulliau wrote somewhat condescendingly, "as a Greek who never had left Constantinople was quite well educated" -, he had searched for Greek manuscripts, in particular the works of Menander. His search, however, remained unsuccessful since the contemporary Greeks supposedly limited their reading to the homilies and similar kinds of texts.[21]

After Boulliau had left Istanbul to sail via Smyrna back home, he described his experience in a letter from Smyrna dated May 22, 1647 as quite

---

Patriarchat ou j'auois veu leurs liures quils ont de reste MSS. et entre autres vn evangelion de lan 995 de Nre seigr J. C. escrit en lettres majuscules. J'ay veu l'Hoc-meidan cest dire (sic) le camp de la fleche, ou les Turcs s'exercent a tirer de l'arc, & ou ils font leurs prières publiques & de sermon en quelque nécessité publique. J'ay veu tournoier les Dreuiches (sic), qui est la chose la plus inguliere de ce pais, & mercredi 20 du courrant, j'allay auec Mr de Vantelet voir le superieur ou Abbé de ces Moines Musulmans qui s'appelle Adam Efendi qui est fort estimé de ceux du pais. Il est scauant a leur mode. J'appris de luy par vn Drogman que les estoilles tombant que les Grecs appellent asteres diattontes, sont des feux du ciel que les anges jettent sur les diables lors que ces malins esprits veulent s'eleuer vers le ciel & auec ces lances a feu ils les repoussent dans l'enfer. Mr Guyet voudroit voir les plumes des vns & les cornes des autres pour croire ce que nous a dict cet Adam Efendi. Je luy parlay par le Tergiman ou Drogman de leur Kalendrier, il envoya querir son almanach qui a esté faict par vn Mungi (sic) Bachi (cest a dire le prince des Astrologues du G<rand> S<eigneur>) qui a estudié en Europe. Ils obseruent soigneusement l'Equinoxe du Printemps, & si le temps se monstre beau ils font entr'eux allegresses & resjouiances aussy bien qu'anciennement a Rome. a ce jour la celebrabantur Hilaria, quód Sol Aequinoctium superans diem nocte longiorem effecerit. Les Turcs qui augmentent tant qu'ils peuuent leur langue de l'Arabe et de la Persiene ont pris de celle cy le mot de Nevruz ainsi appellent-ils l'Equinoxe, & se seruent de l'annee Persiene de Sultan Gelal eddin. Il nous accusa d'auoir falsifié l'Euangile & d'auoir trunqué le passage qui parle du Prophete. nous romprimes le discours per ragione di buon gouerno e per non sentire cose chi hauessero potuto ramaricarci l'animo. Il est homme au reste moralement bon & honneste homme & qui nous fit grande ciuilité. il nous donna le caué a boire & vn serbettres (sic) delicieux & nous parfuma d'Aloes. Nous les rencontrasmes dans vn petit cabinet tout couuert de tapis luy assis dans le coing enuironné de dix de ses Dreuichs qui discourroient en prenant le tabac tous assis comme des cousturiers. je patissois en deux poincts, pour ne pouuoir m'asseoir comme eux, & pour n'ozer cracher, chose quils abominent lors quils sont sur le Soffa ou dans la mosquée, ou il faut bien se donner de garde de cracher, s<ous> peine de remporter quelques bastonnades. Ce bon Abbé en discourrant ne laissoit pas de dire son chappellet et de prononcer par interualle ellemdullillahi louange de dieu. L'vn doibt me mener aux Santons qui celebrent leurs orgies de nuict, qui s'agitent d'vne facon tout autre & plus violente que les Dreuichs. Voyla ce que je peux vous escrire attendant que j'ays le bien de vous reuoir qui sera dieu aydant dans la fin du printemps comme jespere. ... (ibid., ff 176a-177a)

[21] ... J'ay peu de choses a voir apres auoir consideré Ste Sophie autant qu'il a pleu a M[rs] les Imans de me la laisser voir. j'ay veu a mon aise yegny chanisi c'est la mosquee neufue du Sultan Achmet, Sultan Soliman & Cha zadé, l'Jup ou le G.S. prend son espee. apres Sainte Sophie c'est la Suleimanie qui a le plus d'architecture, & qui luy ressemble le plus, la neufue a la place de l'Atmeidan ou Hippodrome qui la rend fort belle. J'ay esté aux eaux douces ou l'on fabrique la poudre a canon. et le premier beau jour est destiné pour aller jusques a l'emboucheure de la mer noire. ...J'ay faict quelque enqueste touchant les liures mais il n y en a plus. Vn Drogman du Residens de l'Emp<ereur>, qui a nom Panagioti et qui, po<ur> vn Grec qui n'est jamais sorti de C.P., y a asses bien estudié, ma dict qu'il auoit faict perquisition par toutes les Bibliotheques anciennes qui restent, po<ur> apprendre des nouuelles du Menandre, mais il n'a jamais pû en rien trouuer. Ce qui reste aux gens de deca, qui ont encores quelque petite teinture de literature, ce sont homilies des PP. ... (ibid., ff 178a-179a)

II

pleasant because, against all misgivings and suspicions by Jacques Dupuy, he had encountered not a single unpleasant incident. Boulliau emphasized that, on the contrary, he had met "very modest" men who were "much more moderate than our French (compatriotes)". He remembered with pleasure his repeated visits with Adem Efendi and his meetings with Ismail Efendi Emin from the arsenal who favored Boulliau since they both shared the same first name and with Salah (?) al-Din Efendi, a poet and man of letters, very similar in nature to Boulliau's, Gassendi's, and Dupuy's friend Francois Lhuillier. All these Muslim acquaintances sent Boulliau their best greetings and farewells to Smyrna, a social nicety which Boulliau appreciated highly. He hoped that his report would set Dupuy's spirit at rest, but feared that minor spirits of "the nature of toads and spiders" would turn all his words into venom.[22]

Some of Boulliau's claims in these letters such as the Müneccimbaşı's training in Europe are surprising and difficult to corroborate. In 1647, the Müneccimbaşı of the Ottoman court was Hüseyin Efendi who was in office from 1630 to 1650.[23] A copy of the calendar made by him in 1054 A.H./1644-45 is extant in Paris.[24] In 1668, it had been transferred from cardinal Mazarin's collection to the Royal Library. Another surprising information can be found in Boulliau's survey of his travels which, however, is corroborated indirectly by an earlier similar experience of the Oxford mathematician, astronomer and orientalist John Greaves. In his report, Boulliau repeated the story about the origin of the "shooting stars", albeit in a somewhat altered version.[25] He reported that Adem Efendi was born in Antalya and characterized him as follows:

> Is linguarum Persicae & Arabicae apprime peritus, Philosophiae et Astronomiae non ignarus erat. (Ms Paris, BNF, fr 13039, f 23a)

---

[22] ... Vostres souhaits desquels vous vous serez sans doubte retracté, n'ont pas esté accomplis, car par la grace de Dieu je n'ay faict aucune mauuaise rencontre dans CP. au contraire j'ay trouué des hommes tres modestes & plus moderés que nos francois, outre que j'auois des-ia faict des cognoissances auec des personnes, qui en cas de mauuaise rencontre m'eussent serui, j'en ay l'obligation a Mr l'Amb. & a Mr de Ventelay auec lequel j'ay esté plusieurs fois chéz Adam Ephendi Directeur des Dreuichs qui est vn ... des gens de condition & des beaux esprits de C.P. Vn entr'autres Hismahil Ephendi Emin du Tersenal me faisoit grandes caresses a cause que nous auons mesme nom, & souuent que nous nous sommes rencontrés, il me donnoit du Sabalihhair Ismail Celebi & me faisoit tousjours ciuilité. J'ay aussy cogneu vn autre homme qui est aphis c'est a dire homme de lettres & poete qui a nom Teleatin Ephendi qui a beaucoup du genie de Mr Luillier. J'ay receu des baisemains de leur part depuis que je suis de retour en cette ville & principalement d'Adam ephendi. J'ay bien voulu vous dire toutes ces particularités pour vous mettre l'esprit a repos, car je scay bien que vous m'aymés trop pour me souhaitter du mal. Je prevoy neantmoins que certains esprits de la nature des crapaux & des araignees conuertiront en venin tout ce que je viens de vous dire la dessus, ... (ibid., ff 185b-186a)

[23] For a brief description of his scholarly life see Aydüz 1993, pp. 171-174.

[24] Ms Paris, BNF, Turque 181.

[25] Ms Paris, BNF, fr 13039, f 23b.

II

Then, Boulliau described a later meeting with Adem Efendi during which he asked the dervish whether he knew anything about Copernicus and his planetary system:

> Ab Adamo illo quaesiui, num de nostris Philosophis & Astronomis aliquid intellexisset, de Pythagoricorum systemate per Copernicum restituta Terraeque motu annuo ab Europae Astronomis peritioribus asserto. (ibid., f 24a)

Although Boulliau adhered to the astronomical theories of Copernicus and to Galilei, he nowhere - neither in his letters nor in his later account - explicitly derided Adem Efendi's religiously motivated rejection of the heliocentric system. His position towards Adem Efendi's explanation of the origin of meteors, however, changed over time and space. While he had not commented on it directly in his letters from the Ottoman Empire, he had reported that one of his companions had made fun of the Quranic notion by asking for remainders of the wings of the shooting angles and the like displaying the lack of familiarity of the French visitors with the various descriptions of the possible appearances of jinn and the differences between the category of spirits and Satan. In his account to Prince Leopold, however, Boulliau ridiculed and sniffed at Adem Efendi. He accused him and his colleagues of having considered their visitors as so feeble-minded that they would agree to what the dervishes had declared being a well established doctrine while rejecting as vulgar and erroneous the opinion introduced as Muslim belief by the ambassador's son, namely that "shooting stars" fall to earth when the soul of a Muslim wishes to leave its body:

> Tam vacui capitis nos credidere, vt gravem eiusmodi verissimilemque opinionem rudis ac impeiti vulgi eironeae traditioni oppositam admitteremus. (Ibid., f 23b)

Boulliau's voyage to Smyrna and Constantinople were not his only encounters with Muslim scientific traditions. In his astronomical writings, he also exploited Latin and Greek translations of Arabic and Persian astronomical tables, among them the so-called Persian Syntaxis by Georgios Chrysococces which is based to a substantial extent upon Nasir al-Din al-Tusi's "Ilkhanid Tables".[26] During his visit to Florence, before his travel to Smyrna via Livorno, Boulliau had worked repeatedly in the library of the Medicis. There he found a commentary on the "Persian Syntaxis" which - according to Boulliau - contained information not present in the text in the Royal Library in Paris with which he had worked before:

> Je continue de voir la librarie du Grand Duc, laquelle n'est pas assortie de tant de liures Grecs que celle du Roy. ... Ily en a vn qui explique sintaksin persikon astronomikon

---

[26] See Mercier 1984.

II

dans lequel jay trouué beaucoup de choses qui ne sont poinct dans le Georgius Chrysocca entr'autres j'y ay trouué le Kalendrier des Arabes, & des Perses auec les festes qu'ils obseruent dans leur Musulmanisme. Il y a aussy quelque eu de chose touchant le calcul des années des Mogors quils appellent Mogoulios & de ceux du Chatay quils appellent Khathedes. j'ay transcript ces endroits la, & les noms des mois de 17 differents villes ou peuples de Grece & d'Asie. (Ms Paris, Dupuy 18, ff 160a-160b)

A comparison with Mercier's survey of Chrysococces' work implies that the version studied by Boulliau in Florence indeed differed from what is today regarded as Chrysococces' proper work.[27]

Finally, in his correspondence with Leopold, Boulliau asked the prince to look for manuscripts of Apollonios' *Conics* and for works by Archimedes. Leopold informed Boulliau about the Books V-VII of Apollonios' work which were extant in an Arabic paraphrase and told him that the Maronite scholar Abraham Ecchellensis and the Italian mathematician Alfonso Borelli cooperated in translating this Arabic paraphrase as well as that of the *Liber Assumptorum* ascribed to Archimedes. In six letters (1658-1660), Boulliau and Leopold talked briefly about this project and its progress.[28] A seventh letter touching this issue was sent by Boulliau to Vincenzo Viviani, one of the mathematicians at the ducal court.[29] Finally, in a letter dated August 18, 1660, Leopold was happy to inform Boulliau that the first folios of the translated *Conics* had been printed.[30] The completed book appeared, as is well known, in 1661 in Florence.

3. Jean Baptiste Bourguignon d'Anville (1697-1782)

D'Anville was royal geographer, member of the Royal Academy of Inscriptions and Letters and of the Royal Academy of the Sciences in Paris, and secretary to the duke of Orléans. Over a period of more than 40 years, he studied Arabic and occasionally Turkish and Syriac geographical and historical texts because of three interrelated research interests: the dressing of new and of historical maps and the determination of historical geographical measures. The regions in respect to which he consulted these texts encompassed mainly the Ottoman Empire and some of its more prominent parts such as Egypt or Syria. But he also used them for his research about the size and location of the Caspian

---

[27] ibid., pp. 46-49. Whether this commentary indeed refers to the Moghuls, as Boulliau claimed, needs to be checked.
[28] ibid., ff 73a-76a, 79a, 80a-81a, 166a-168b.
[29] ibid., f 164a.
[30] ibid., f 168a.

Sea, the name and place of the historical capital of the Uighur kingdom, or to draw a map for a history of the Ayyubid Salah al-Din.

The texts d'Anville drew upon most often were al-Idrisi's and Abu l-Fida's geographies. Furthermore, he exploited al-Farghani's introduction into astronomy, the geographical tables by Nasir al-Din al-Tusi and Ulugh Beg, Ibn al-Wardi's cosmography, al-Maqrizi's and Murtada b. al-Khalil's histories of Egypt, the Turkish *Jihan numa* by Hajji Khalifa, or Barhebraeus' Syriac history. As far as his notes extant in Mss Paris, BNF, fr n. a. 6502-6503 testify, d'Anville accessed all these sources through Latin or French translations:

> On trouve dans l'Edrisi une route qui de Tobbat dont jai remarqué que la position convenat à Kashgar, conduit à la ville capitale d'un pays dont le nom se lit Bagharghar dans la version des Maronites, Tagargar dans celles des Elemens d'Astronomie d'Alferganie per le docte Golius. Le nom de la ville se lit aussi diversement: Tantabéc dans l'Edrisi; Tencabash dans les Tables Astronomiques de Naseruddin et d'Ulug-beg. entre les villes d'al Torc, ou du Turquestan." (Ms Paris, BNF, fr n. a. 6503, f 341a)

> Abulfeda dans sa description du pays de Masr, ou de l'Egypte: Il y a plusieurs lieux dans le Royaume Masr, qui s'appellent du nom de Bousir. Il y en a un dans la province de Fioum, que l'on appelle Bousir Kouridas, où l'on dit que Maruan el Hamar, dernier des Khalifes de la race d'Ommiah, fut tué. Vn autre dans le pays de Bouseh. (Item) Bousir, suivant Jacout est un des pays du Royaume de Masr, comme il est marqué dans les Cartes. ... (ibid., f 546a)

> Ben al-Wardi, la Perle des Merveilles. Ptolémée donne 18000 Stades de circonférence à la Terre qui font 24000 milles, ou 8000 Farasanges, la Farasange étant de 3 milles. Le Mille est de 3000 Drah ou Coudées royales. La Coudée est de 3 Aschbar, ou Palme, chaque Aschbar est 12 doigts, le doigt est de 5 grains d'orge rangés l'un contre l'autre, ventre contre ventre. La largeur du Schaira ou grain d'orge est de 6 poils de mulet.

> Schantariah est habitée par des berbers et un mélange d'Arabes. Il y a des mines de fer, et de la pierre Zaram. Elle est separée d'Alexandrie par un grand Desert. ... (ibid., f 465a)

Idrisi's and Barhebraeus' works had been translated partially by the Maronites Johanna Hesronita, Gabriel Sionita, and Joseph S. Assemani in 1619 and 1762-66. For his study of the life of Salah al-Din, d'Anville used the partial Latin translations of Abu l-Fida's geography made by Albert Schulten and those made by Jean Gagnier as well as at least one or more French versions. The determination of the latter needs further study since the two French versions by Laurent d'Arvieux and Melchisédech Thévenot which appeared in different editions in 1663, 1696, 1717 and 1718 concerned only Arabia and India.Murtada's history of Egypt was available to d'Anville by the French translation made by

II

Pierre Vattier (1666). Ibn al-Wardi's cosmography d'Anville excerpted in a French version called *La Perle des Merveilles* whose translator I could not identify yet. It was, perhaps, a part of Galland's translations of extracts from Arabic, Persian, and Turkish historical and cosmographical writings. This might also apply to al-Maqrizi's history of Egypt. Hajji Khalifa's geography d'Anville apparently accessed through its French translation made by Pierre Armain, student of the language school founded by France in Constantinople in 1668, then royal interpreter in Alexandria, and attached to the Royal Library since circa the 1730s.[31] He apparently knew Thomas Hyde's edition and Latin translation of the tables of Tusi and Ulugh Beg and al-Farghani's *Introduction into Astronomy* in the translation by Jacob Golius from which he used repeatedly also Golius' notes. Additional information about Middle Eastern geographical knowledge, d'Anville gained from Barthélemy d'Herbelot's *Bibliothèque Orientale* and from references by Golius and Edward Bernard to unpublished Arabic manuscripts:

> Bibliothèque Orientale, p. 347. Il y avoit, autrefoi, selon le Geographe Persien, un lieu proche de la ville de Colzum, qui portoit le nom de Kiosck-Feraoun, c'est-à-dire le Balcon ou le Portique de Pharaon." (ibid., f 474a)

> Golius dit avoir lû dans Al-Teifashi, auteur Arabe, que le prémier ou plus ancien nom d'Alexandrie; suivant les monumens des Coptes ou Egyptiens est <u>Racod</u>, et que ce nom se trouve encore dans les Glossaires ou Vocabulaires Coptes. (ibid., f 505b)

> Mais, on a tout lieu de croire, qu'Eratosthene a trop épargné le nombre des Stades dans cette distance d'Alexandrie à Syene; ce que j'attribue à une défalcation trop forte sur les Distances itinéraires pour en conclure une mesure directe et aerienne. Il étoit peutêtre prévenu du même principe que Abu Rihan, qui du nom de sa patrie a été surnommé al-Biruni; selon ce principe, le cinquiéme d'une distance itinéraire est à deduire pour l'employer en droite ligne. Mais, quoiqu'Al-Biruni ait été approuvé en ce point par le docte Edward Bernard, dans son Traité de <u>Ponderibus et Mensuris Veterum</u>, je suis persuadé que cette déduction est trop forte, spécialement à l'égard de l'Egypte, où je la croirois plus convenable sur le pied d'environ un huitième (d'Anville cancelled here his former belief: d'un dixième ou environ neuf ou dixieme). (ibid., f 651b; extract from his draft of a paper on the ancient Egyptian measure called "schoene": Continuation de ce qui concerne le schoene Egyptien, et discussion de la Mesure de la Terre par Eratosthene. ibid., ff 650a-651b)

Although d'Anville did not know any of the Middle Eastern languages, he joined French translations or explanations to numerous Arabic geographical names:

---

[31] Ms Paris, BNF, fr n. a. 888-889.

142

Ben al-Wardi, la Perle des Merveilles. ... Alaki, montagne, près d'une rivière sans eau. Encreusant dans le fes de celle riviere on trouve l'eau. Bahr-bela-ma: mare-sine aqua ...

Nahr-Eddahab, ou fleuve d'or, dans la contrée de Damas et de Halep. Les habitans de Halep croient que c'est le Wadi Bathman. Il se perd dans un marai." (ibid., ff 465a-465b)

Batn, qui est la denomination de plusieurs lieux en Syrie et en Arabie, signifie proprement en Arabe venter, le ventre. Et apparement il se prend en figuré pour un lieu profond et renfermé. (Ms Paris, BNF, fr n. a. 6502, f 271a)

He either consulted French orientalists or cooperated with one of Arabic scholars or one of the so-called Jeunes des Langues affiliated to the Royal Library, or acquired this knowledge from the royal geographer Philippe Buache, a relative of Guillaume De L'Isle, who could read and write some Arabic - not always correct - as his notes preserved in the Library of the Institute de France testify.[32]

D'Anville used the described sources to determine distances, locations, names and geographical coordinates of towns, villages, islands, rivers, mountains and mineral mines in Egypt, Syria, Yemen, Iraq, Turkey, the Mediterranean Sea, Persia and China. To this end, he compared his various sources with one another and translated the information drawn from texts into local maps of distances, provincial maps of towns, rivers, and mountains, or linear or curvilinear representations of itineraries.[33] In a series of papers read at the Royal Academy of the Sciences and at the Royal Academy of Inscriptions and Letters d'Anville formulated his conclusions and, in some cases, evaluated his sources. Some of the information d'Anville applied in his printed maps of the region, such as al-Idrisi's data about distances between towns in the delta of the Nile.[34]

Contrary to the current assumptions about the value of Arabic, Persian, or Turkish sources for 17th or 18th-centuries West European sciences, d'Anville's indiscriminate treatment of the mentioned texts illustrates their immediate relevance for his research projects. He considered them as reliable sources and regarded the variations found in them with regard to geographical coordinates or names of geographical objects with the same attitude as he approached the variations found in ancient Greek or Latin texts and in 17th and 18th-centuries travel accounts, maps, or research papers and books - as a possibility to guide his

---

[32] Ms Paris, Institute de France, 2302, piece 1, ff 1b, 2a, 5b; piece 14, f 2b.

[33] Ms Paris, BNF, fr n. a. 6502, f 107a; Ms Paris, BNF, fr n. a. 6503, ff 498a, 507a, 582a; Ms Paris, BNF, Département des cartes et plans, Ge DD 2987 (6739, 7810).

[34] Ms Paris, BNF, Département des cartes et plans, Ge DD 2987 (7801).

II

research and as variations he had to sort out by comparing as many sources as possible including measurements and observations carried out by his contemporaries. D'Anville never formulated this attitude explicitely, but it is what he did by making extracts of the described variety of texts and by collecting letters from French physicians and scholars of other disciplines traveling to the Ottoman Empire for geographical and historical purposes. D'Anville's approach to geographical research also included appreciating his various sources without an explicit a priori preconception, for instance, a blind preference of one type of source over all the others. His criticisms or praises as expressed, albeit rarely, in his notes and extracts were author- or subject-oriented. This made him prefer occasionally information drawn from Arabic sources over conjectures proposed by contemporary scholars as it was the case with regard to the name and location of the historical capital of the Uighur kingdom:

> La capitale de l'Eygur anterieur étoit nommée par les Chinois Kia-ho-tchin, ce qui signifie la ville du confluent, parceque deux rivieres après avoir embrassé cette ville, se joignoient ensemble sous ses murs. On veut que ce soit la même ville qui est aujourd'hui désignée par le nom de Turfan, et on allegue sur cela le témoinage des auteurs Chinois. Mais, ce temoignage ne signifie peutetre autre chose, que Turfan tient aujourd'hui le meme rang dans l'Eygur, que Kiao-ho-tchin tenoit autrefois. J'ai déja formé quelque difficulté sur ce sujet dans un mémoire donné à l'Académie sur le Li mesure itinéraire des Chinois. Ce qu'il y a de positif c'est que la situation actuelle de Turfan ne répond point à la circonstance que demande le nom de Kiao-ho-tchin, puisque les cartes que nous devons aux missionnaires Jesuites de la Chine, assez circonstanciées dans les environs de Turfan pour y marquer de foibles ruisseaux, qui perissent, a peu de distance à leur source, n'en mettent point à Turfan, et je crois cette raison peremtoire. Je soupçonne fort que la grande ville de Lop dans Marc-Pol, est l'ancienne capitale de l'Eygur. ... Ce que dit l'Edrisi de la situation de Tantabec ou de Tenkabach, sur un grand fleuve, courant vers l'orient, convient parfaitement à la ville de Lop. L'Edrisi ayant ecrit sa geographie vers le milieu du douzieme siecle et du vivant de Roger I. roi de Sicile comme un passage de son ouvrage le fait connoitre, la ville dont il parle comme de la principale d'une contrée particuliere, et ayant selon sa relation douze portes de fer, ne peut être que la residans des Idikou qui regnoient alors dans l'Eigur, et souverainement, puisque la domination de Zinghiz Khan. (Ms Paris, BNF, fr n. a. 6503, f 341a)

Besides his study of texts, d'Anville cooperated with contemporary travelers such as the Jesuit Claude Sicard in dressing maps based upon the results of their investigations in the Ottoman Empire, collected and excerpted letters by French consuls and missionaries in the Ottoman Empire such as Jean-Jacques Le Noir du Roule, consul of Damietta, or the Jesuit Brevedent who traveled to Southern Egypt and Ethiopia together with Jacques Charles Poncet, a surgeon in the service of the French consul of Cairo, and wrote instructions for research travelers such as the physician Bellet about geographical observations to be conducted there.[35] Bellet, for instance, wrote to Louis-Philippe, Duke of Orléans who patronized his voyage:

> ... Dans les instructions qui m'ont éte données par Mr Damvile par ordre de Monseigneur, on me demande quel est aux environs d'Andrinople le cours des riviers qui sy reunissent. jay lhonneur d'envoyer a Monseigneur un plan de cette ville, Monseigneur y trouvera ce qu'il a desiré. Ce plan a este levé sur les lieux par un ingenieur, qui est a la suite de M. Le Comte d'ulefeld ambassadeur d'alemagne et qui par ordre de sa cour a levé celuy de toute la route de l'ambassadeur sur les terres otomanes.
>
> Jay trouvè icy un Drogman qui a fait le voyage de georgie. je luy ay montré la carte que me donna Mr Damvile. ce Drogman ne trouve pas que le phare y soit bien placè non plus quelques lieux situez sur ses bords. jay pris ses memoires, mais ils ne peuvent-me servir encore que pour me conduire dans les questions que je dois proposer. (Ms Paris, BNF, fr. n. a. 6502, ff 165a-165b)

Bellet traveled together with the Jesuit Duchateland, member of the entourage of the French ambassador, professor of hydrology in Toulon, and honorary member of the Academy of the Arts at Lyon. About Duchateland's astronomical activities, the journal *Mercure de France* reported in April 1742 (p. 768):

> Observations astronomiques faites dans les mois d'Avril et Mai 1741 à Constantinople sur la latitude et la longitude de cette mesme ville, par le R. P. Duchateland (Academicien honoraire de l'Academie des Beaux-Arts de Lyon) pendant le sejour qu'il y a fait a la Suite de l'Ambassadeur de France.
>
> Il y a trouvé la latitude de 41 Degrés 8 Minutes 30 Secondes, et la Longitude de 27 Degrés 30 minutes, ou de une heure cinquante minutes de tems orientale, à compter pour premier meridien celui de l'Observatoire de Paris. (ibid., f 14a)

D'Anville also seems to have interviewed a Muslim convert about his knowledge of the topography of the Ottoman Empire:

> Le 28. mars, 1726. apris de Pierre Achmad, Turc converti.
> Villes de Roumeli, scavoir, <u>Scople</u> ou <u>Scopia</u>.
> <u>Manastir</u> ou <u>Monasterio</u>
> <u>Stib</u> ou <u>Stephanos</u> c'est la même signification
> <u>iol-Kioster</u> ou <u>Castorîa</u>
> vers laquelle il y a une ville de Belgrade, que les Turcs noment <u>Arnaout-Beligrad</u>, ou Belgrade des Albanois.

---

[35] Ms Paris, BNF, fr n. a. 6502, ff161a-166, 187a; fr n. a. 6503, ff 583a-586b, 608a-608b.

II

> ...
> De Belgrade sur le Danube à la mer noire, on passe à <u>Izalgik</u>, <u>Vidini</u>, <u>Nicople</u>, <u>Silistra</u>.
> De Silistra, si on veut suivre le Danube jusqu'à la mer, on passe <u>Demir-Capi</u> ou la Porte de fer. C'est un endroit du Danube ou le fleuve est resserré entre deux montagnes, et où le lit du fleuve est ambarassé de rochers. C'est la raison du nom qu'on donne à cet endroit-là.
> De Silistra à Andrianople on compte près de sept journées. ... (ibid., ff 1a and 2a)

In the same volume, almost 100 folios later, a sketch of all the places mentioned by Pierre Achmad can be found.[36] However, d'Anville himself never seems to have payed a visit to the Middle East, but drafted all his maps based on the knowledge he acquired from the textual studies and personal contacts described above. Among the many maps extant from d'Anville in the Bibliothèque Nationale de France in Paris and showing his efforts to translate what he had read, collected, excerpted, or inquired about, finally two maps shall be mentioned in particular. The first is based upon Abu l-Fida's *Taqwim al-buldan*:

> Carte Manuscrite d'Arabie dressée uniquement de la Description qu'en a faite Abuffeda Ismaël Sultan de Hamah en son livre de Geographie intitulée Takouim al Buldan qu'il acheva d'écrire vers l'an de l'ère Chrétienne 1321 dressée en 1720. (Ms. Paris, BNF, Département des cartes et plans, Ge DD 2987 (6661))

This map was not available to me since it was sent to be microfilmed. The second has no title, but states:

> Dressé le 7 Novembre 1725. D'Anville, Geogr. Ord^{re} du Roy. (Ms Paris, BNF, Département des cartes et plans, Ge DD 2987 (6739))

It depicts Khuzistan and Luristan (Chosistân and Laurestan) showing 42 places, several rivers, and three major mountains. Its size is 15.5 cm times 16 cm. A rectangular grid drawn by pencil is still visible in which three latitudes (30°; 31°; 32°), but no longitudes are marked. The complete grid runs from 29° 30' to 33° 30'. D'Anville used different sources to draw this map, among them the Latin translation of al-Idrisi's geography. Numerous, but not all, of the 42 places and 3 mountains are given in the same transliteration and with distances coming close to those given in this translation.

---

[36] ibid., f 107a.

II

Conclusions

The three examples of members of the West European Republic of Letters exchanging knowledge directly or via intermediaries with inhabitants of the Ottoman Empire and sharing with them texts, authorities, concepts, or practices produced within the scientific traditions of the two cultural regions indicate a substantial distortion of our own perceptions of the past. Since other fields of historical inquiry do not share with the history of science this lack of awareness of the close contacts between Western Europe and the Ottoman Empire before the French scientific expedition to Egypt in 1799, the question as to what caused this loss of historical knowledge has to be raised. Presumably, several different components contributed to produce this result. According to my experience, a major aspect is the deep impact West European travel accounts and their standardised negligence of the sciences in the Ottoman Empire had for a long time upon West European historical research about the Ottoman Empire, in particular, and the West European public opinion about the Ottomans, in general. As my introductory quotation from Nellen's paper illustrates, the latter continues to subscribe to this view even nowadays. A second important factor is the way in which history of science became institutionalized in Western Europe during the 19th and 20th centuries - as a sort of annex to the sciences constructing their historical confirmation and legitimation and serving to enhance their communication with the non-specialized public. A third component consists in the involvement of West European scientific communities in spreading the patterns of social, political, economic, or religious *modi vivendi* of their own societies into non-Western cultures, including the Ottoman Empire, and in stabilizing and maintaining them there. This involvement included the construction of at least two sorts of narrative - one which insisted that the export of Western sciences meant social, cultural and scientific progress for the recipient cultures and the other which emphasized exchange with the scholarly traditions alive in the non-Western cultures and the raising of the native scholars up to the standards of their Western peers. While in the case of India, both discourses were at work, with regard to the Ottoman Empire, in particular its Arabic provinces, the first narrative seems to have dominated. But other, less direct trends also contributed to forgetting the close scholarly contacts between Western Europe and the Ottoman Empire of the 17th and 18th centuries. Examples are the growing specialization and differentiation within the sciences, their loss of exchange with the humanities, the almost complete exclusion of the actors from the final narrative about research and its results under the impact of scientific positivism, or the separation between the historiography of Western and non-Western cultures within European

II

universities and other academic institutions such as the professional societies or the curricula. As a result, history of science - despite and partly because of all the changes in style, focus, and approach during the last decades - is mainly a historiography of the sciences in Western societies, above all Great Britain, France, Germany, Italy, the Netherlands, and the USA, today more so than twenty years ago.

Bibliography:

Aydüz, S. 1993: *Osmanlı Devleti'nde Müneccimbaşılık ve Müneccimbaşılar*. Istanbul Üniversitesi, Istanbul
Bots, H., F. Waquet 1997: *La République des Lettres*. Paris: Belin, De Boeck
Bougerel, J. 1737: *Vie De Pierre Gassendi*. Paris; reprint Genève 1970
Cultures of Natural History. 1996. (Eds.) N. Jardine, J. A. Secord, E. C. Spary. Cambridge University Press: Cambridge, New York, Melbourne
Findlen, P. 1994: *Possessing Nature. Museums, Collecting, And Scientific Culture in Early Modern Italy*. University of California Press: Berkeley, Los Angeles, London
Goldgar, A. 1995: *Impolite Learning. Conduct and Community in the Republic of Letters, 1680-1750*. New Haven, London: Yale University Press
Goodrich, Th. C. 1990: *The Ottoman Turks and the New World, A Study of Tarih-i Hind-i Garbi and Sixteenth Century Ottoman Americana*. Wiesbaden
Inalcık, H. 1973: *The Ottoman Empire. The Classical Age 1300-1600*. Weidenfeld and Nicholson: London
Mercier, Raymond 1984: The Greek 'Persian Syntaxis' and the Zij-i Ilkhani. In: *Archives Internationales de l'Histoire des Sciences* 34, 35-60
De Monconys, B. 1665: *Iovrnal Des Voyages de Monsievr De Monconys, Conseiller du Roy en ses Conseils d'Estats & Priué, & Lieutenant Criminel au Siege Presidial de Lyon. Où les Scauants trouueront vn nombre infini de nouueautez en Machines de Mathematique, Experiences Physiques, Raisonnements de la belle Philosophie, curiositez de Chymie, & conuersations des Illustres de ce Siecle; Outre la description de diuers Animaux & Plantes rares, plusieurs Secrets inconnus pour le Plaisir & la Santé, les Ouurage des Peintres fameux, les Coûtumes & Moeurs des Nations, & ce qu'il y a de plus digne de la connoissance d'vn honeste Homme dans les trois Parties du Monde. Enrichi de quantité de Figures en Taille-douce des lieux & des choses principales, Auec des Indices tres-exactes & tres commodes pour l'vsage. Pvblié par le Sieur de Liergves son Fils. Premiere Partie. Voyage de Portugal, Prouence, Italie, Syrie, Constantinople, & Natolie*. A Lyon, Chez Horace Boissat, & George Remevs.
Nellen, H. J. M. 1994: *Ismaël Boulliau (1605-1694). Astronome, Épistolier, Nouvelliste et Intermédiaire Scientifique. Ses Rapports aves les Milieux du "Libertinage Érudit"*. APA-Holland University Press: Amsterdam & Maarsen
Nellen, H. J. M. 1996: "Such is my rambling destiny": travellers to the levant in the seventeenth and eighteenth centuries, in *Commercium Literarum. Form of Communication in the Republic of Letters 1600-1750*. Edited by Hans Bots & Françoise Waquet. APA-Holland University Press: Amsterdam & Maarsen, pp. 207-258
Ormond, H. 1902: *Missions Archéologiques Francaises en Orient aux XVIIe et XVIII Sciècles*. 2 vols., Paris
Rossi, E. 1948: *Elenco Dei Manoscritti Persiani Dela Biblioteca Vaticana. Vaticani - Barberiani - Borginai - Rossiani*. Città del Vaticano
Tolmacheva, M. 1995: The medieval Arab geographers. *International Journal of Middle East Studies*, 27, 141-156
Tolmacheva, M. 1996: Bertius and al-Idrisi: an experiment in Orientalist Geography. *Terrae incognitae* 28, 36-45
Manuscripts and Manuscript maps:
Ms Paris, BNF, Dupuy 18
Ms Paris, BNF, Dupuy 663
Ms Paris, BNF, fr 13039
Ms Paris, BNF, fr 25280
Ms Paris, BNF, fr n. a. 6502
Ms Paris, BNF, fr n. a. 6503
Ms Paris, BNF, Ge DD 2897 (6661, 6739, 7801, 7810)
Ms Paris, Institute de France, 2302

III

The Presence of Ancient Secular and Religious Texts in the Unpublished and Printed Writings of Pietro della Valle (1586–1652)

In 1561, on his second journey to the Safavid Empire, Anthony Jenkinson carried a letter from Queen Elizabeth that greeted Shah Tahmasp in the following manner:

> Elizabeth, by the grace of God, queene of England, &c. To the right mightie, and right uictorius prince, the great Sophie, emperor of the Persians, Medes, Parthians, Hyrcanes, Carmaranians (sic), Margians, of the people on this side, and beyond the river of Tygris, and of all men and nations between the Caspian sea and the gulph of Persia, greeting, and most happie increase in all prosperitie.[1]

From the maps of the World, Asia and the Safavid Empire drawn by Giacomo Gastaldi between 1546 and 1562 in Venice, the early modern observer could learn that the realm of the Safavids comprised very different provinces than Elizabeth had imagined. The map called *Persia Nova Tabula* drawn by Gastaldi for the Italian edition of Ptolemy's *Geography* in 1548, for instance, is covered not only by ancient Greek names such as Partia, Persia or Ircania, but the reader could find in it also new names such as Azimia, Corazani, Lar or Mar di Bachau.[2] The map of the first part of Asia, that is the region from the Black Sea and the eastern part of the Mediterranean Sea to Kabul, produced by Gastaldi eleven years later, is in the Safavid realm completely purified of ancient Greek names and covered with local names such as Servan, Gilan, Taperistan, Mesandaran, Cusistan, Lurestan, Arach, Chirman, Corasan, Sigistan or Mare de Bachu. Some of the names are incorrectly spelled such

---

[1] Hanway, Jonas, *An historical account of the British trade over the Caspian sea: with a journal of travels from London through Russia into Persia; and back through Russia, Germany and Holland. To which are added, the revolutions of Persia during the present century, with the particular history of the great usurper Nadir Koala* … (London, 1753), vol. 1, p. 6.

[2] *La geografia di Clavdio Ptolemeo Alessandrino*, Con alcuni comenti & aggiunte fatteui da Sebastiano Munstero Alamanno, Con le tauole non solamente antiche & moderne solite di sta<m>parsi. (Venice, 1548).

as Tares, Tarsi, Mare Coruzum or Adilbegian, while others are misplaced, outdated, explanatory or misunderstood such as Rabia, Djargument, Ieselbas or Circan. But all of them go back to local names used in the medieval or the early modern period in Iran.[3]

Gastaldi's maps were very successful. They influenced the Western European cartographical portrayal of Safavid Iran until the Empire's demise in the 18th century. Cartographers adopted both ways of naming Iran and its parts found in Gastaldi's maps – mixing ancient Greek with medieval plus early modern Persian names in transliterations of all kinds and applying exclusively transliterated medieval and early modern Persian names. Western European cartographers of the early modern period loved to indulge themselves and their clients with local names from as many foreign languages as possible. An example for this attitude of going native in the case of Iran is the legend inscribed in the Caspian sea in the maps of Abraham Ortelius (1570 and following editions) and Gerhard Mercator as edited by Jodocus Hondius (1607 and following editions).

> For the Hyrcanian or Caspian sea, one has need of various names today. The Ruthenians call it Chualenska (sic) More; the Mores Bohar Corsun (sic) (a word shared with the Arabian Gulf), which means closed sea. I see that it is called by others in other ways, as the sea of Bachu, Cunzar, Giorgian, Terbestan, Corusum, namely after the denomination of the neighbouring regions and places. The lake is the largest of the entire world and salty. It is rich in fish.[4]

Elizabeth's letter and the maps of Gastaldi, Ortelius and Mercator set the stage for my paper. When we compare early modern printed travel accounts with early modern maps produced in Catholic or Protestant Europe, we discover that cartographers and map-printers preferred more often the use of local names, while authors of printed travel accounts favoured clearly ancient names. This does not mean that cartographers and map-printers after Gastaldi never used ancient names. But when they used them they identified them mostly as names of the past by writing, for instance, 'Fars (or Farsistan) olim Persis'. Authors of printed travel accounts, in contrast, employed ancient names as guiding principles, as the names that truly mattered. The local names, which never were absent, were mostly presented as of secondary,

---

[3] Iacopo Gastaldi 1559, *Prima Parte della Asia*; Re-edition Antonio Lafreri, (Rome, 1570).

[4] Abraham Ortelius, *Theatrum Orbis Terrarum*, (Amsterdam 1570). *Persici sive Sophorum Regni Typus*, Staatsbibliothek Berlin, Preussischer Kulturbesitz, Berlin, B 219.

derivative relevance and needful of being placed in the context of the ancient names in order to become meaningful. The structural dominance of ancient names over medieval and contemporary local names was accompanied by explanatory and interpretative stories taken from ancient secular and religious sources. These stories strengthened the ascription of meaning to localities in Safavid Iran (as well as in the Ottoman Empire). They also identified the Safavid presence as an unchanged duplicate of the Achaemenid past seen through the eyes of ancient Greek and Latin writers.

Modern historians tend to take the dominance of ancient geography and history in early modern printed travel accounts about Safavid Iran at face value. They often declare that the geographical knowledge of early modern travellers about Iran was solidly anchored in ancient geography. They accept so-called eyewitness accounts of nature, culture and peoples as descriptions of observations made and told by the early modern traveller himself. They tend to repeat evaluations of Safavid society given by early modern travellers without questioning their validity, context and history. This readiness to trust the narrator is particularly strong when scientific subjects are described and judged.

The surviving papers of one of the most eminent early modern Western European travellers to Safavid Iran, Pietro della Valle (1586–1652), prove beyond doubt that the picture drawn in printed travel accounts is a construction caused by censorship and academic aspirations. This construction did not permeate the system of beliefs of the Italian traveller as is shown by his unpublished private and semi-public writings. While travelling, Pietro della Valle was much more interested in learning local names, histories, customs and modes of life than remembering what ancient authors had written. A comparison of della Valle's unpublished letters to his friends and family, his original letters to Mario Schipano before they were printed and his travel diary with the printed letters and with his Latin geography of Iran prepared for print reveals that the printed letters turn upside down della Valle's views and actions in three major points: the image of the Orient, the image of della Valle himself and the image of ancient secular and religious knowledge and values. Introducing quotes from and references to ancient authors and texts achieved this profound reconfiguration of della Valle's letters to Mario Schipano. In the following sections of my paper, in order to prove the claims just made, I will present the results of my comparative analysis of the four types of texts della Valle produced in Iran and in Italy.

III

4 Ancient Secular and Religious Texts in the Writings of Pietro della Valle

1 Della Valle's published letters to Mario Schipano

Della Valle quoted from or referred to 83 ancient, medieval and early modern texts or authors in his letters published in 1650, 1658 and 1663. Ignoring della Valle's references to his own letters, the remaining 82 texts comprise the Bible, the Qur'an, four other books on religious subjects, texts by 38 classical Greek and Latin authors, 31 books by medieval and early modern Catholic writers – more than the half of them editions and collections of or comments on classical authors, seven works by medieval and early modern Muslim scholars and one book by a medieval Armenian Orthodox, then Catholic writer. Thus, the majority of the works quoted by della Valle in his printed letters treats secular and religious topics of Greek and Roman antiquity, of Judaism and Christianity. The prevalence of this kind of literature and issues is also shown when we ask which texts or authors are most often quoted by della Valle.

Table 1

Title/author	Letters from the Ottoman Empire	Letters from the Safavid Empire	Letters from India
the Bible	112	33	–
Strabo	26	16	10
Vergil	26	21	–
Pierre Bélon	44	–	–
D. Siculus	15	19	4
Herodotos	17	9	3
Xenophon	6	18	–
Filippo Ferrari	10	12	–
Pierre Gilles	16	–	–

All of the quotes from Ferrari serve to identify a certain town, region, river, mountain or king with an ancient name and most quotes from Bélon and Gilles either concern Egyptian antiquities, ancient identities of early modern Arabic towns, villages and rivers or refer to Byzantine monuments in Istanbul and environment. Hence, it is not exaggerated to claim that most of della Valle's references to books and manuscripts serve to structure, interpret and identify the places, objects and peoples he had encountered on his voyage as well as their histories, beliefs and customs in terms of ancient classical and biblical perspectives.

Della Valle used Ferrari, Strabo and Siculus to offer his own identifications of contemporary Arabic, Turkish or Persian geographical names with ancient Greek or Latin names, to criticize what he considered wrong identifications by Ferrari and to remind his readers of shared geographical perspectives on the Safavid Empire as well as the two other regions he visited. He wrote, for instance, about Mazandaran:

> But before we go ahead I describe the location of Mazanderàn in general that it may be possible for you to recognize it in geographical maps and to see whether it is truly ancient Hyrcania or a part of Hyrcania or another province close to that as I think it more likely.[5]

Della Valle applied Herodotos, Xenophon, the Bible, Strabo and Diodorus Siculus as a means to identify contemporary customs and habits in the Ottoman Empire, the Safavid Empire and Western India with customs and habits already described by the ancient authors. The second identification more so than the first one creates the impression that nothing has changed in those countries since classical times, an insight not left to the reader's astuteness, but formulated explicitly more than once.[6] The value of this

---

[5] 'Ma, prima che passiamo innanzi, descriuerò il sito del Mazanderàn, in generale; accioche V. S. possa riconoscerlo nelle carte Geografiche, e veder, se veramente è l'antica Hircania, ouero parte dell'Hircania, ò pur altra prouincia a quella vicina, come io più tosto penso.' De'*Viaggi di Pietro della Valle il Pellegrino Descritti da lui medesimo in Lettere familiari All'Erudito suo Amico Mario Schipano. Persia, Parte Prima.* (Roma, 1658), p. 177.

[6] When, for instance, telling Schipano that the Safavids take their dinner on earth sitting on fine carpets, della Valle commented: 'Ma, che maraviglia? Anche in tempi anchissimi, non ci narra Senofonte (1) che quella bella ed onestissima Pantea, moglie del re de'Susiana, quando fu presa dall'esercito di Ciro, fu trovata ne suo padiglione, insieme con le sue ancelle, in terra a sedere? E che I tappeti servissero in Tiro a'suoi tempi appunto per sedervi sopra, non l'abbiamo da Ezechiel profeta (2)? ... (1) Cyropaed., lib. V. (2) Ezech. XXVII, 20.' Della Valle: *Viaggi*, vol. 1, p. 632. An analogous statement can be found only a few pages later when talking about

III

6   *Ancient Secular and Religious Texts in the Writings of Pietro della Valle*

judgement is not explicitly negative. The absence of historical change in any of the visited territories and cultures does not mean for della Valle immobility and backwardness. His rhetoric points more to continuity, reliability and accessibility for the outsider endowed with classical sources. When discussing the ethnic origin of the Mughals, della Valle wrote for instance about the heirs of Chingiz Khan:

> This Chingiz, ..., having made himself finally the master of a huge state and quasi of all Tatary which encompassed the one and the other Scythia; divided it when dying among his sons. To Giagatà, who was his second-born son, he (gave) the country of Samarcand with the entire Sogdiana and diverse other areas (close by); & these were called after his proper name Giagataio and Giagataini all the people which remained under his rule. It is a most ancient custom of the Scythians to give to the countries subjected by them the name of their princes as one can see well in Diodorus Siculus.[7]

The qualitative picture sketched in the published letters about della Valle's scholarly attitude towards the areas he had visited and lived in for several years is one of personal experience safely secured within the boundaries of ancient secular and religious knowledge and wisdom. The personal experience is portrayed as one of cultural superiority of the traveller himself and of his native country. The latter is most often identified with the hometown of the recipient of his letters, that is Naples. Most towns and cities, della Valle visited were less beautiful than Naples. Only Isfahan could compare with the Italian city. Most inhabitants of the Ottoman and the Safavid Empires della Valle met were less civilized than himself. Even Shah 'Abbas, to whom della Valle later devoted a eulogy, is described as less witty and less well mannered

---

ambassadorial gift giving in Safavid Iran: 'Ed è costume fra di loro antico, poichè Filostrato ci accenna che I re medi, anche al tempo di Apollonio (1) non si andavano a vedere senza doni. ... (1) De Vita Apoll., lib. I, cap. 19' Della Valle: *Viaggi*, vol. 1, p. 650. There are several more remarks of this type in other letters of della Valle, all of them connected with quotations from or references to ancient authorities.

[7]   'Questo Cinghiz, ..., fatto si al fin padrone di vn'immenso stato, e di quasi tutta la Tartaria, che comprende l'vna e l'altra Scithia; lo diuise poi morendo à suoi figliuoli. A Giagatà, che era suo figliuol secondogenito, toccò in sorte il paese di Samarcand, con tutta la Sogdiana, e diuerse altre terre di là intorno; & egli dal suo nome proprio lo chiamò `Giagataio, e Giagataini tutti i popoli che restarono sótto al suo gouerno. Costume antichissimo de'Scithi, di dare à i paesi à loro soggetti il nome de'lor Principi, come ben si vede in Diodoro Siculo. Lib. 2,' *De'Viaggi di Pietro della Valle il Pellegrino Descritti da lui medesimo in Lettere familiari All'Erudito suo Amico Mario Schipano. Parte Terza cioè L'India co'l Ritorno alla Patria.* (Roma, 1663), p. 38.

than the Roman patrician. Della Valle portrayed himself as superior since he adhered to the only true faith, spoke alone a cultured, courteous language and adored women in a more appropriate style than the natives. Ancient knowledge lent authority to his information about contemporary Ottoman and Safavid geography, culture and history. Arabic and Persian texts and authors are portrayed as reliable when della Valle wished to point out false beliefs of contemporary Italian writers on geography and history, but were of no great use when ancient history of Iran was discussed. They remain a minority voice in della Valle's printed letters. The modern geography of the Ottoman and Safavid Empires, della Valle wrote about to Mario Schipano, was in no need of justification and legitimization by Arabic, Turkish and Persian scholarly works. It was della Valle's personal experience with these territories that provided the new knowledge and it was his own intellectual capacity which allowed equating the new with the familiar knowledge found in ancient works and in recently printed books taken along from Italy.

This insistence on his personal vouchsafing for the reliability of the new knowledge is the cause that – despite the great number of quotations from or references to ancient secular and religious works – della Valle's published letters drown ancient geography and history in a flood of early modern Oriental names and activities when looked at the relationship from a quantitative angle. Numerous letters do not contain a single reference to any work, but Oriental names appear in growing frequency and are often fully independent from any kind of foreign imprisonment. Della Valle's printed letters undoubtedly show no steady effort to anchor Ottoman or Safavid geography, history and customs in an ancient harbour. Despite the immense work della Valle carried out in Rome to enhance the status of his letters by quoting many ancient authors and texts, he could not and perhaps did not wish to silence his genuine efforts of learning the local contemporary geography on its own terms undertaken while actually travelling.

2 Ancient authority in della Valle's Latin geography of Safavid Iran

The anchorage of contemporary Iranian geography in ancient knowledge and wisdom is much stronger in della Valle's Latin geography of Iran called 'About the regions subjected by the recent empire of the Persians'. He wrote a first, apparently lost version of this treatise for the Bohemian Jesuit Vincislaus Pantaleone Kirwitzer (d. 1626), a missionary in China and then in the

8

Philippines, whom he met in Goa. Barely back in Rome, della Valle decided to publish the text.[8] This intention never was implemented despite della Valle's continuous efforts to improve the text. The text of the fine copy prepared in 1628 shows many parallels with the printed letters and was apparently revised accordingly. The frame of della Valle's description of each of the 17 territories he dealt with consists of identifying the contemporary local name of the region with an ancient designation and providing an etymology for the local name that more often than not is wrong. This frame is filled with different ingredients among them the physical and natural endowments of the area, major cities, major monuments, borderlines and political events.

> The region of Babylon, together with some of the adjacent territories, still called by its ancient name in the Holy Scriptures, is called by the contemporary Persians Araq. The meaning of this name is sweat, first, because the heat in these areas is most excessive during summer time. Perhaps too because these areas are made fertile not only by cutting irrigation ditches from the rivers, but also by much sweat, after they have been completely soaked by a few rainfalls. But Araq has two meanings, i.e. Araq of Arabia and Araq of Agiamia. Those regions subject to the power of the Persians are called Agiam, or Agem. Araq of Arabia refers to Babylonia and the adjacent areas, presently subject to the empire of the Turks. If you turn towards the east, you travel from Araq through the high rising mountains of the region of Kurdistan. These run from north to south, with the Taurus Mountains as a kind of branch, and divide the Persian Empire from the Turkish Empire. Araq of Agiamia is thus the first region under Persian control, and includes the province of Hamadan, whose capital is the city of the same name. This province is, I assume, part of ancient Persia or Susiana in the borders set by the Medes.[9]

---

[8] 'Li II. Aprile per essere il giorno del mio Natale, feci di questo dì la data della lettera dedicatoria nel mio Trattato. *De Regionibus subiectis recentiori Persarum Imperio*, che haueuo animo di mandare in luce.' Penultimate letter to Schipano, Rome, 11 July, 1626. Della Valle: *Viaggi* III, p. 498.

[9] 'Babylonia regio, cum aliquot ex adiacentibus terris, a recentioribus Persis ad hanc usque diem antiquo nomine in sacris litteris memorato, Araq nuncupatur; cuius nominis interpretatio est sudor tum quia vehemens in illis terris calor est aestivis temporibus, tum etiam fortasse quia paucis admodum humefactae pluviis, non nisi deductis a fluviis magno quidem sudore rivis, terrae illae fertiles redduntur. Verum quia Araq nomen duplex est: Araq nimirum Arabia et Araq Agiamia (Agiam enim, sive Agem, universas Persarum dominio subiacentes dicunt regiones); pro Araq Arabia Babyloniam et adiacentes terras Turcarum hodie imperio parentes intelligunt. Unde recto tramite si orientem versus proficiscaris superatis montibus regionis Kurdistan qui, Tauri quodammodo rami, a septemtrione in meridiem excurrentes Persicum imperium a Turcico disterminant, statim Persicae dictionis prima occurrit regio Araq Agiamia et eius pars provincia Hamadan, cuius metropolis est Hamadan civitas eaque pars, ut opinor, antiquae vel Persidis

The framing of Iranian geography by ancient concepts and spatial arrangements reminds the reader – through its continuous repetition – that the guiding principle of geographical writing had to be ancient knowledge.[10]

---

vel Susianae in finibus Medorum.' Della Valle, P., 'De recentiori imperio Persarum subiectis regionibus'. (ed.) Gamalero, E. *Studi Iranici* 17 (1977), pp. 287–303; 288. The English translation is from Sonja Brentjes and Volkmar Schüller, 'Pietro della Valle's Latin Geography of Safavid Iran (1624–1628): Introduction', *JEMH* 10, 3–4 (2006), pp. 169–219, p. 189.

[10] See, for another example, della Valle's description of Azerbaijan: 'Adherbaigian, cuius interpretatio est ignis cultores, procul dubio Media est antiquorum seu potius, ut melius dicam, pars eius praecipua et magna; regio est montana, per quam institutum superius iter norduestem versus prosequendo, transgresso primum haud <sperendae magnitudinis> fluvio qui in Caspium exurrens persice nunc Sepid-rud, hoc est albus fluvius, turcico vero nomine vulgo Qizil-uzen, quasi rubeus natans vel aureus natans appellatur, sed quis nam esset apud antiquos non facile reperio, praeter alia permulta loca minus memoratu digna, insigniores reperiuntur civitates duae: Ardebil nempe magis ad orientem sita, peregrinationis meae ex ea parte terminus, Persarum hodie sanctuarium regumque hisce temporibus in Perside regnantium<. M>ausoleum ob insignem quemdam ex eorem maioribus virum celebremque populis sanctimoniae fama quem, licet ipse rex non extiterit, nescio tamen an religionis an progeniei dignitatis gratia seu quia proprio sic nomine vocaretur, passim Sciah Sofi, hoc est regem selectum et sincere amicum sive religiosum, quod idem est apud illos, appellant et regum qui nunc regnant progenitorem et Sciaitarum rectae in Agiamia nisi primum auctorem, praecipuum certe resuscitatorem ibi sepultum.

Magis vero ad occidentem in eodem quasi paralelo sita est Tebriz civitas, sedes et ipsa olim regum, frequentibus bellis inter Persas ac Turcas saepe vastata, saepius hinc inde capta, saepissime oppugnata, adhuc demum permanens iisdem de causis fama super aethera nota. Reliquas Adherbaigian civitates, cum eas ipse non viderim, sub silentio praetereo; tantum subiungam Adherbaigian regionem habere ab oriente maiore ex parte Araq Agiamia<e>, ab occidente septemtrionem versus Armeniam, cuius portio Persici imperii pars est hodie et Turcis confini, a septemtrione autem Ghilan et alias antiquae Mediae spura mare Caspium magis septemtrionales partes, ubi olim Caddusii, Mardi et his similes memorabantur, a meridie vero Araq similiter partes, ni fallor.' Gamalero: 'Della Valle', pp. 288–9; the acute parentheses indicate a correction of the edited text according to the manuscript.

(Translation from Brentjes, Schüller: 'Pietro della Valle's Latin Geography'; pp. 190–91: 'Adherbaigian, a name that means worshippers of the fire, is doubtless the Media of the ancients or, as I prefer to say, its greatest and most excellent part. The region is mountainous. If one follows the upper road leading northwest, one crosses first a river of remarkable size which flows into the Caspian Sea. This river is called now in Persian Sepid-rud, i.e. the white river. But in Turkish it is commonly called Qizil-uzen, i.e. water that runs blackberry-red or golden-colored. What river this may be according to the ancients, I cannot easily discover. Besides many other places barely worth mentioning, this region has two important cities. To the east lies Ardebil, the termination of my peregrination in this area. There one finds the sanctuary of the Persians and the mausoleum of the kings who reign today in Persia, owing to a man who stood out among their greatest, and was famous among the population through the legend of (his) pious life, even though he was not himself a king. He was everywhere called Sciah Sofi, which

III

10   *Ancient Secular and Religious Texts in the Writings of Pietro della Valle*

Authors were not of prime importance. They are even almost invisible in della Valle's text. He merely quotes three times from Vergil, once from Strabo and once, perhaps, from Pliny without saying so and refers to Diodorus Siculus. Throughout the text, he keeps, however, the reader engaged in a debate about what ancient identity could and should be ascribed to each and any contemporary Iranian town, river or mountain. In this debate, again, della Valle insists upon his personal experience and, occasionally, on the authority of Persian and Arabic texts for deciding cases of dispute, for instance the troublesome question of whether the ancient Porta caucasia, Porta ferrea and Porta caspia were built at one and the same place and whether this place was modern Derbend on the Western shores of the Caspian Sea.[11]

---

can mean either "chosen and upright king" or "pious king." Whether he was so called due to his faith and the dignity of his descent, or because this was his proper name, I do not know. They also call him "the ancestor of the kings reigning today." He who is buried in Ardebil was at least the outstanding restorer of the Shi'ite sect in Agiamia, if not its first founder.

Situated more toward the west (in Adherbaigian), and almost on the same parallel, is Tebriz, once a royal seat; it is known to the heavens above, for during the repeated wars between the Persians and the Turks it was often devastated, captured, or besieged by one side or the other. The remaining cities of Adherbaigiàn I pass over with silence since I have not seen them myself. There is so much the region of Adherbaigian borders on: in the east the larger part of Araq of Agiamia, in the west, towards the north, Armenia, part of which is now included in the Persian Empire, bounded by the Turks. In the north it is bounded by Ghilàn and other more northern parts of ancient Media at the Caspian Sea, there where once dwelled Caddusians, Mardians, and the like; in the south, if I am not mistaken, it is bounded by parts of Araq.'

[11] 'Alia est Derbend, quod nomen persice sonat quasi <P>ortae <L>igamen, ut ut Latinius <seu Caspiae> seu Caucasia<e> seu Ferrea<e> Porta<e> nuncupe<n>tur. Sed cum confusione scriptorum et quoad situm et quoad nomen huius urbis aliqua inducta sit obscuritas, non incongruum mihi videtur quod repperi apud orientales auctores hic aperire. Tria haec profecto valde confundunt Latini civitatum nomina ita ut non facile sit dignosci quae fuerint antiquorum Porta Ferrea, quae Porta Caspia et quae Porta Caucasia. Turcae hanc de qua loquebamur Derbend, portae nominis, ut puto, similitudine inducti, eorum lingua Demircapi, Ferream nimirum Portam communiter appellant, unde forsitan recentioribus nostris orta est confusio. Arabes vero et Persae geographi, Turcis procul dubio eruditiores, alteram ab altera clarius distinguunt, nam quae a Persis Derbend nuncupatur ab Arabibus dicitur Bab el abvàb, id est porta portarum et diversa nimis recensetur a Porta Ferrea; quam, huiusmet significationis vocabulo, Arabes Bab el hadìd, Persae autem Der Ahanin appellant et longe amodum a Derbènd, Caspioque mari magis orientalem, in tractu quarti climatis reponunt, plusquam viginti sex graduum longitudinis; et septem fere latitudinis differentia. Derbend enim quam commemorabamus in quinto climate ab iisdem constituitur, ad litus, ut dixi, Caspii maris occidentale; et cum illa sub imperio Chacqàn (magni scilicet cuiusdam orientalium Tartarorum regis) describatur, haec Persis paret, et ultima est hodie Persarum ditionis prope Caucasios <M>ontes; ....' Gamalero: 'Della Valle', p. 291.

III

Ancient Secular and Religious Texts in the Writings of Pietro della Valle 11

3 Della Valle's travel diary

Della Valle's notes from and about his travels, contained in Ms Città del Vaticano, Biblioteca Apostolica Vaticana, Ottoboniano latino 3382, are almost void of any authority except his own and that of other travellers from Catholic and Protestant Europe whom he met in the Ottoman and the Safavid Empires. A few late medieval and early modern authors and once or twice the Bible can be found mentioned in the text of the diary, while the few references to ancient authors were almost all added at second thought and hence can be found in the margins or between the lines. The authors della Valle mentions in the entries are Torquato Tasso, Pierre Bélon and Filippo Ferrari. Once, he also reports about the Persian treatise *Ketab-e vajebat-e zaruriye*.[12]

In the margins della Valle refers to two classical authors, Strabo and Justinus, to four early modern writers – one French and three Portuguese – , Pierre Bélon, Pedro Teixeira, Father Negrone and a Father whose name I cannot decipher correctly, and to four Persian books – the *Ketab-e masalek al-mamalek* of Abu l-Hasan Sa'id b. 'Ali al-Jurjani (d. ca. 881h/1476), the *Si fasl* by Nasir al-Din al-Tusi (d. 672h/1272), the *Taqvim* by 'Inayat, the brother of

---

[12] (Translation from Brentjes, Schüller: 'Pietro della Valle's Latin Geography'; pp. 195–6:' The other city is Derbend. This name means in Persian something like the hasp of a door, although the Latins call it the Caspian, Caucasian or Iron Doors. But the confusion among writers with regard to the position as well as the name of this city has created a certain lack of clarity; hence it seems not inappropriate to present here what I have discovered in the books of oriental authors. The Latins have thoroughly confused three names of the city, so that it is not easy to differentiate which cities the ancients named Porta Ferrea, Porta Caspia, and Porta Caucasia. What we speak of as Derbend the Turks call in their language Demir-capi, influenced, I think, by the similarity of the word "door." This means undoubtedly Porta Ferrea, a fact that perhaps caused the confusion among our contemporaries. But the Arabs and the Persian geographers, without doubt more learned than the Turks, differentiate the one clearly from the other. The city the Persians call Derbend the Arabs call Bab elabvàb, that is, door of the doors. This is completely different from Porta Ferrea, which the Arabs call Bab elhadid, and the Persians Der Ahanin. They situate it far from Derbènd, and indeed east of the Caspian Sea, namely, more than 26 degrees longitude and almost seven degrees latitude away, in the fourth climate. Derbend lies in the fifth climate, on the western shore of the Caspian Sea, as I have said. While Der Ahanin or Bab elhadid is said to be under the rule of the Chacqàn (i.e. the great king of the eastern Tartars), Derbend is subject to the Persians. Today, it is the outermost border of the Persians' dominion, near to the Caucasian mountains.'

[12] Ms Città del Vaticano, Biblioteca Apostolica Vaticana, Ottoboniano latino 3382, ff 3b, 7b, 12a–13a, 15a, 22a, 36a, 36b, 38a, 38b, 124b.

the astronomer Mulla Zayn al-Din from Lar and Yahya b. ʿAbd al-Latif al-Qazvini's (d. 962h/1552) *Lubb al-tavarikh*.[13]

There is only one exception to this rule. The entry 13 October, 1621 reports about della Valle's journey to Chehel Minar after the crossing of the river Kur via the so-called new bridge, that is, Pul-e no. In the text of this entry, della Valle claimed that the people of the country did not have any good history of the ancient times, but Don Garçia da Silva y Figueroa, ambassador of Spain and a man well-versed in history, had told him that Quintus Curtius did not mention the place as one already very ancient.[14] Della Valle added that he had no access to Curtius' book nor could he consult any other book.[15] Later, when the traveller discovered that the author meant by the ambassador was not Quintus Curtius, but Diodorus Siculus, he wrote the latter's name in-between the lines. A second reference to Diodorus Siculus in-between the lines is found earlier in this very same entry where della Valle talked about the location of Chehel Minar with regard to some mountains. This interlinear addition is marked by a siglum to be integrated into the original text of the diary.[16] All of these references are verbal and do not contain any specific indication of the number of the book or chapter where the remark could be found.

The style of della Valle's references to authors and texts differs in the various textual environments where they appear – the text of the diary, the margins of the diary, the space between the lines, the text, margins, interlineal space of and notes to the original letters, and the printed letters. In the text of his diary, della Valle simply wrote remarks such as 'che descrivo il Tasso', 'come dice Belonio', 'della quale Belonio fa mentione' or 'come benissimo dice L'Epitome Geografica'.[17] In the margins, all references are marked as notes which say 'see the book of this or that author'. In the case of the two

---

[13] Ms Città del Vaticano, Biblioteca Apostolica Vaticana, Ottoboniano latino 3382, ff 24a, 39a, 52a, 59b, 83a, 84a, 138a, 150b, 154b.

[14] Ms Città del Vaticano, Biblioteca Apostolica Vaticana, Ottoboniano latino 3382, f 150b: 'Don Garzia da Silua y Figheroa, che fu in Persia Ambas.ʳ di Spagna, et era huomo dotto d'historia, diceua che Quinto Curtió ne fa mentione come di cosa antichissima anco altro tempo; ...'

[15] Ms Città del Vaticano, Biblioteca Apostolica Vaticana, Ottoboniano latino 3382, f 150b '... ; Io non ho qui Quinto Curtio per uederlo, ne altro libro da potei consultare, ...'

[16] Ms Città del Vaticano, Biblioteca Apostolica Vaticana, Ottoboniano latino 3382, f 150b: '... Cehil minar a pie (sic) del Monte che gli sta congiunto per leuante, : e della cui pietra é facta la fabrica, ... : come a conto dice Diodoro Siculo ... .'

[17] Ms Città del Vaticano, Biblioteca Apostolica Vaticana, Ottoboniano latino 3382, ff 22a, 36a, 38a, 38b.

Ancient Secular and Religious Texts in the Writings of Pietro della Valle 13

ancient authors, the references are more specific saying 'Vedi Strabone lib. 16. in principio' and 'Vedi Giustino hist. lib. 32 ...'.[18] The two interlinear references to Diodorus Siculus correspond to the references in the text of the diary.

Most of these notes in the diary can be recognized as later additions. Some have been added clearly a long time after the respective entry had been written. One such case is della Valle's note to the entry for 19 October, 1616 in which he referred to his Latin translation of the Shi'i creed carried out three years later in Isfahan.[19] A second example is his reference to al-Jurjani's *Ketab-e masalek al-mamalek* for al-Mada'in at a moment when he had not yet left the Ottoman Empire, not yet learned Persian and not yet bought the manuscript.[20] A third example is the reference to Negrone's book on India, which, according to Della Valle's note, was still in the process of printing in Rome. It is attached to the entry for 8 December, 1618 at the end of the folio, separated from the text by a siglum and dated by della Valle's remarks that Negrone passed through Persia in 1619 and that he saw him later in his place, that is in Goa. The form in which della Valle wrote about this later meeting suggests that he made the addition to his diary some time after this meeting. I am inclined to think that he did it in Rome. In this added reference, della Valle used the first form of his quoting style for the margins: 'Vedi de gli Indiani le relazioni del Pre' Fra Francesco Negrone francescano, scritte in portoghese ...'.[21] A fourth note in della Valle's diary confirms that this comment has been added only after the traveller had returned to Rome since variants are also found in Ms Città del Vaticano, Biblioteca Apostolica Vaticana, Ottoboniano latino 3384, a collection of reworked letters and excerpts from studied books and manuscripts, and in Ms Città del Vaticano, Biblioteca Apostolica, Ottoboniano latino 3385, a two-volume manuscript with long excerpts from books and manuscripts studied by della Valle.[22]

---

[18] Ms Città del Vaticano, Biblioteca Apostolica Vaticana, Ottoboniano latino 3382, ff 52a, 165a.

[19] Ms Città del Vaticano, Biblioteca Apostolica Vaticana, Ottoboniano latino 3382, ff 47a, 124b.

[20] Ms Città del Vaticano, Biblioteca Apostolica Vaticana, Ottoboniano latino 3382, f 55b.

[21] Ms Città del Vaticano, Biblioteca Apostolica Vaticana, Ottoboniano latino 3382, f 83a.

[22] 'Ho qualche ... che possono esser la ruina di C...fonte Citta famosa ... Vedi la Geographia Persiana intitolata (in Persian: Mesalik Memalik) alla Città (in Arabic: Mada'in).' Ms Città del Vaticano, Biblioteca Apostolica Vaticana, Ottoboniano latino 3382, f 55b; 'Mesalik Memalik Geografia Persia: Medain, che in Arabico uel dir due città, uuol che sin. Tesofontes in Persiano, dunque bene, secondo Strabone, Seleucia e Tesifonte. erano ... in un luogo : e però due città p<er> (?) Clima 3. Madain.' Ms Città del Vaticano, Biblioteca Apostolica Vaticana,

III

14 Ancient Secular and Religious Texts in the Writings of Pietro della Valle

In his printed letters, a few general references of the type as in the text of the diary can be found too, but all references discussed in section 1 add in the margin a note like 'Lib. 8', 'Lib. 1, cap. 2' or 'Gen. Lib. 2'. Hence, the diary's references to the ancient authors may have been added only when della Valle had made up his mind about the form of quotation to be used in the published version of his letters, that is, in Rome.

The almost complete absence of ancient secular and religious authors and texts in the text of the diary – if we ignore the Bible and the reference to Quintus Curtius – and their very occasional presence in the diary's margins is truly surprising. Given the small number of della Valle's references to any author in the text of his diary, a few remarks in this text pointing to a Greek or Latin poet, historian or geographer and some references to the Bible could be regarded as a mere difference of genres. Della Valle's almost complete silence about his classical and religious education and beliefs, however, implies that more is at stake, in particular since it is not only the authors and books which are absent. The geographical and historical frame guiding della Valle's geographical treatise and suffocating the landscape of oriental toponyms in his printed letters is also rarely visible. In his diary, the traveller wrote about the territories he passed through with caravans in a style where local names, often misspelled and later corrected, dominate over classical learning. In territories better known to early modern travellers such as Istanbul or the Arabic provinces, he rarely bothered at all to give an ancient name. Only in cases such as Homs or Hama did he write 'A tre hore di giorno arriuammo ad Hhams, ouero H̶h̶a̶m̶u̶s̶ "hams" (Arabic), che anticammente si chiamaua Emissa' and 'a tre hore di giorno o poco più arriuammo ad Hhamà anticamente detta Apamea.'[23] In territories della Valle was less familiar with, his major effort was directed towards learning the local names of towns, villages and camps and trying to memorize them by writing them down in Latin and Arabic letters according to what he had understood by listening.[24] Smaller rivers, villages and small towns he only remembered by the local names. When he discovered that allegedly correct identifications between ancient and local names proved to be wrong such as identifying Baghdad with Babylonia, he made a note

---

Ottoboniano latino 3384, f 79b; 'Medain <repeated in Arabic>/ Tesdid …/ Medain é (sic) Ctesiphon secondo la Geografia Persiana.' Ms Città del Vaticano, Biblioteca Apostolica Vaticana, Ottoboniano latino 3385, vol. 1, f 64a.

[23] Ms Città del Vaticano, Biblioteca Apostolica Vaticana, Ottoboniano latino 3382, ff 38a–b.

[24] Ms Città del Vaticano, Biblioteca Apostolica Vaticana, Ottoboniano latino 3382, see, for instance, ff 64a, 67a, 68b.

saying so.²⁵ Provinces, major rivers and mountains of the Ottoman Empire he often described by their ancient names.²⁶ During the first months of his stay in the Safavid Empire, he combined ancient and native names as in his identification of Arac with Parthia and Mazandaran with Hyrcania. In this fashion, the diary continues until 1619/20. Then, ancient names occur only very rarely, for instance, when discussing the problem of the two rivers called Kur. Only very seldom did della Valle seem to have felt the desire to check with Ferrari's lexicon what the ancient name of a town, province, river or mountain may have been. Even his excursions into ancient Persian history, in particular his visit to Persepolis and Naqsh-e Rostam, did not induce him to mention a single author in the long notes describing his observations. Authors and books, in particular ancient authors and printed books from his own culture, were not at the forefront of della Valle's mind while living in the Ottoman and Safavid Empires.

4 Della Valle's original letters to Mario Schipano

A comparison of the diary with the single letter attached to it and with the material found in Mss Città del Vaticano, Biblioteca Apostolica Vaticana, Ottoboniano latino 3383–3385 and Archivio Segreto. Archivio Della Valle – del Bufalo 51 shows that the situation of the text of the diary corresponds more closely to that of the original letters of della Valle than to that of the printed version of the letters. These manuscripts reveal that the character of the printed letters was the result of della Valle's intensive study of ancient secular and religious texts as well as of medieval and early modern texts in several languages. This study was carried out almost entirely after his return to Rome. The only exceptions were his studies of Persian, Arabic and Turkish manuscripts in Iran and India that he continued in Rome and integrated partially in his printed letters.

These manuscripts also show that ancient secular and religious authors are more visible in the original text of the letters than in the diary. In his letter from Farahabad, which he dated in the printed version 'July 25, 1618 Qazvin', della Valle quoted implicitly from Vergil (2), Plato (1), the Bible (1), Ovid

---

[25] Ms Città del Vaticano, Biblioteca Apostolica Vaticana, Ottoboniano latino 3382, f 48a.
[26] Ms Città del Vaticano, Biblioteca Apostolica Vaticana, Ottoboniano latino 3382, ff 40a, 45b, 77b,

(1) and explicitly from Ferrari (5).[27] He did not add references to individual books or chapters, in full accordance with the fact that he was writing letters, not the manuscript for a book proper. When he decided to give his letters into print rather than rewrite them as a coherent monograph, the situation changed. Now, explicit references to books were not only appropriate but also necessary if the contemporary standards of scholarly book writing should be met. These standards were apparently less formalized and less standardized than one often assumes. Della Valle, at least when starting to prepare his letters for print, had no clear rules in mind which he wished to follow. As the changes in and the notes to della Valle's letter from Farahabad illustrate, the revision of the letters was not done in one single process of work, but evolved over time. Explicit and numerous quotes from ancient books were not among the changes della Valle started with. A number of newly produced versions of his original letters contained in Ms Città del Vaticano, Archivio Segreto, Archivio Della Valle – del Bufalo 51 do not yet show a single one of such explicit quotes. References to ancient and early modern authors can be found in the revising notes attached to the letter from Farahabad/Qazvin, but they are only a fraction of what can be found in the printed letter purporting to have been sent from Qazvin. The references also do not appear yet in the form used in the printed letters. The 42 numbered and several other additions penned down on six folios, including one long addition at the beginning of the letter covering the description of 'Ashura, contain seven references: ancient authors (5), the Bible (1), Ferrari (1). Six of them are in the verbal style of the text of the diary. The seventh is in the later style of the printed letter. In the additions found in the margins of the letter, there is a second new verbal reference to Ferrari.[28] In the printed letter, only one verbal reference to an ancient author (Vergil) can be found, while there are 29 references to ancient authors, five references to the Bible and eight references to modern authors, seven of which concern Ferrari. Hence, della Valle decided possibly within a first round of serious work on his letters that ancient secular and religious authors needed to be seen more often. He may have shown his first revision to some friends who may have suggested increasing the visibility of ancient secular and religious texts even further. Thus, della Valle rewrote his annotated and reworked letters fully by his own hand and then started

---

[27] Ms Città del Vaticano, Biblioteca Apostolica Vaticana, Ottoboniano latino 3382, ff 263b, 265b, 266a, 285b, 286a, 290b.

[28] Ms Città del Vaticano, Biblioteca Apostolica Vaticana, Ottoboniano latino 3382, f 277b.

Ancient Secular and Religious Texts in the Writings of Pietro della Valle 17

a new round of annotations and corrections introducing more and more quotations from and references to ancient authors and texts. Another possible explanation of the multiple corrections introduced into his letters by della Valle may be the person who signed the imprimatur for the first volume of the letters, that is, the letters from the Ottoman Empire – Leo Allaci. Allaci was a well-known scholar with a high reputation in the classics. Della Valle, with his close relationship to the papal court and the Propaganda fide, may well have learned while working on the letters that Allaci was going to decide upon the fate of his letters and hence decided to make the letters respond more closely to the taste and interests of this one special reader.

Additions were not the only changes della Valle imposed on his original letters. He formatted their outward appearance by numbering them, giving them a title, omitting the form of the header typical for a letter and dividing them into numbered sections. He corrected Italian, Latin, Arabic, Turkish and Persian spelling, kept only the transliterated forms of the Oriental words, omitted several drawings found in the original letters as well as in his diary, worked on the elegance of his style and cut out numerous passages longer than one line. The cancelled passages often talked about geographical, historical and political subjects without being too intimate, provocative or revealing as della Valle had pretended in the preface to his letters.[29] Some of these passages were replaced by newly formulated statements, which repeated some of the previous information. In the case of the letter from Farahabad/Qazvin, della Valle deleted 23 passages rephrasing only three or four of them. One major result of the process of cutting out original passages is the decrease of visibility of the Orient and della Valle's continuous and intense efforts to get to know the foreign lands in their own languages and concepts. One important example of this belated oppression of Oriental reality and della Valle's newly acquired knowledge is his cancelling of two folios of Persian toponyms describing his itinerary from Isfahan to Farahabad and his efforts to assemble a list of Safavid provinces and districts and equate them to classical names.[30] Finally, the printed letters contain occasionally additional material, which has not been indicated in the notes and comments to the original letters. The printed letter from Farahabad/Qazvin shows one such

---

[29] Ms Città del Vaticano, Biblioteca Apostolica Vaticana, Ottoboniano latino 3382, see, for instance, ff 265b, 278b, 281b.
[30] Ms Città del Vaticano, Biblioteca Apostolica Vaticana, Ottoboniano latino 3384, ff 130a–131a.

unannounced addition with two summarizing quotations from Justinus.[31] These unannounced additions indicate a third round of proofreading and correction of the letters before they were given to the printer.

Mss Città del Vaticano, Biblioteca Apostolica Vaticana, Ottoboniano latino 3384 and 3385 contain what is left from the products of della Valle's reading. They show that the traveller spent much time copying quotations from the Bible, Strabo, Herodotos, Xenophon, Diodorus Siculus and many other authors, including some, such as Schickard or Gassendi, whom he did not integrate into the printed version of the letters. Almost all of the authors and books he quoted in the printed letters are present in these two manuscripts. Ms Ottoboniano latino 3384 also contains several newly written forms of della Valle's letters called 'Rimesse'.[32] It is here that the references to the used books adopted the form we later find in the printed version. This form is also present in two folios of quotations from 30 ancient and modern books, including one Persian history.[33] Immediately after this list, a new one follows entitled 'Modo, come cito in margine gli Autori'.[34] The list starts with Vergil and offers two options: 'Eneid. 3./ouero Virg. Eneid. 3/ Egl. 2'.[35] A look in della Valle's printed letters shows that he worked with both variants.[36] Folios 76a–80b in Ms Città del Vaticano, Biblioteca Apostolica Vaticana, Ottoboniano 3384 finally contain a list entitled 'Noue de mettersi nell' India'.[37]

After della Valle had finished the extensive revisions of his letters to Schipano, he gave them to his sons for producing fine copies. Then the letters went to the Inquisition for receiving the imprimatur. As a result, numerous

---

[31] Ms Città del Vaticano, Biblioteca Apostolica Vaticana, Ottoboniano latino 3382, f 291a.

[32] See, for instance, Ms Città del Vaticano, Biblioteca Apostolica Vaticana, Ottoboniano latino 3384, ff 33a–37b (Rimesse nella 3 Lettera da Sphahan), 53a–56b (Rimesse nelle Lettere della Persia. Lra. i. Sphahan), and 57a–b.

[33] Ms Città del Vaticano, Biblioteca Apostolica Vaticana, Ottoboniano latino 3384, ff 70a–71b.

[34] Ms Città del Vaticano, Biblioteca Apostolica Vaticana, Ottoboniano latino 3384, ff 72a–72b.

[35] Ms Città del Vaticano, Biblioteca Apostolica Vaticana, Ottoboniano latino 3384, f 72a.

[36] See, for instance, *Viaggi di Pietro della Valle Il Pellegrino Descritti da lui medesimo in lettere familiari all'erudito suo amico Mario Schipano divisi in tre parti cioè La Turchia, La Persia e l'India colla Vita e Ritratto dell'Autore.* (Brighton, 1843), vol. 1, pp. 12–13.

[37] Ms Città del Vaticano, Biblioteca Apostolica Vaticana, Ottoboniano latino 3384, ff 76a–80b.

changes had to be introduced.[38] Hence, we may conclude that the enormous amount of time and labour invested by della Valle into revising his original letters was partly caused by expectations about possible demands from the Propaganda fide before granting the imprimatur. Della Valle wished to make sure that this time the Inquisition would allow his work to be printed and not, as many times before, withheld the permission or even set the printed book on the index as happened to della Valle's book about Shah 'Abbas printed in 1629. A second factor may have been his assumption that a 'good history' needed to be based on ancient authors, at least for the members of the Republic of Letters. As della Valle has written time and again in his letters, he wished to become famous and immortal by publishing them. A wish as deeply felt as this one could cause an author to spend much money, time and ink for revising substantially many of his 54 letters written between 1614 and 1626.

5 Reflections on the conflicting usage of ancient authority in della Valle's writings

In the published letters, della Valle complained occasionally about the lack of books which prevented him from identifying the ancient name of a certain river or mountain.[39] One of these complaints appears in the letter from Farahabad/Qazvin. There it is encapsulated within a passage referring to ancient authors and their books in the form he chose in Rome.[40] This location suggests to consider the complaint as a later added statement too and to regard such a complaint as almost topical. However, such regret is explicitly expressed in his original letters too, for instance in one written from Baghdad on 23 December, 1616. In this letter, he reports about his arrival in a town called by the Arabs 'el Her'. His Arab informants also told him that Jews founded the town in the time of Solomon. Della Valle doubts

---

[38] 'Il testo ... non è passato integralmente nelle varie edizioni per gli interventi della censura ecclesiastica che modificò alcune espressioni che sembrarono troppo vivaci o sconvenienti e cancellò alcuni passi che attaccavano un certo tipo di politica missionaria ovvero apparivano equivoci o compromettenti; solo dopo queste modifiche – poco numerose per la *Turchia* e per l'*India*, molto più frequenti e importanti per le *Lettere dalla Persia* – l'opera fu data alle stampe.' *I Viaggi di Pietro della Valle. Lettere dalla Persia*. Tomo I. A cura di F. Gaeta e L. Lockhart, (Roma, 1972), pp. xix–xxi.

[39] See, for instance, della Valle: *Viaggi*, vol. 1, pp. 448, 625, 646, 780.

[40] Della Valle: *Viaggi*, vol. 1, p. 780.

that one can trust the tradition and history as told by the 'ignorant Arabs'. God alone knows. But he himself, della Valle sighs, cannot recover the truth from the mist of change because 'beside the "Epitome geografica" I have no other book nor any help in these countries'.[41] Other than Filippo Ferrari's *Epitome geografica*, della Valle mentioned Pierre Bélon's travel report, Giovanni Baptista Raimondi's Arabic alphabet, the French translation of Pietro Andrea Mattioli's commentary on Dioscorides' *De Materia medica*, Franciscus Raphalengius' Latin-Arabic dictionary, Thomas Erpenius' Arabic grammar and a book of Marc Anton in French translation, which he either carried along since Naples or encountered in Iran.[42] His cursory way of talking about such encounters between him and European books in Iran indicates that he did not search for them. It also indicates that most of the sources he quoted in his printed letters were not directly accessible to him while travelling even if we allow for his using some books available in the libraries of the French and Venetian ambassadors in Istanbul and of the missionaries in Isfahan or Goa. The lack of any quotation from ancient secular and religious sources in his printed letters from India except the first one from Surat suggests rejecting the hypothesis that della Valle used such libraries when writing his original letters to Schipano. Although he browsed occasionally in his copy of Ferrari's geographical dictionary in order to identify modern Iranian rivers, towns or mountains while writing his letters in Iran, his only explicit statement that he spent time in the Carmelite convent of Isfahan explains that the purpose of his visit to the convent was to work on his translations of Persian treatises into Latin while sitting at a table because there was no European-style table in his house.[43] Some of his rare references to Ferrari in his original letters imply that in the first years of his travels he identified himself with this book as the authority guiding him on his difficult travels through the less familiar parts of the Ottoman Empire and Safavid Iran.[44] Later letters from Iran indicate that della Valle's attitude changed over time. The traveller encountered too many

---

[41] Ms Città del Vaticano, Archivio Segreto, Archivio Della Valle – del Bufalo 51, letter from Baghdad, 18 December, 1616, unpaginated. Della Valle kept this passage unaltered in his printed letters, see della Valle: *Viaggi*, vol. 1, p. 357.

[42] See, della Valle: *Viaggi*, vol. 1, pp. 509, 605, 737, vol. 2, pp. 50–51.

[43] Della Valle: *Viaggi*, vol. 2, p. 226.

[44] See Ms Città del Vaticano, Archivio Segreto, Archivio Della Valle – del Bufalo 51, letter from Istanbul dated 27 June, 1615 where della Valle calls Ferrari's book 'our Epitome geografica' although it did not provide him with what he was looking for – the name used in Western Europe for Bitlis.

contradictions between the early modern geographical and historical reality of the two Islamic countries and the knowledge found in Ferrari's book as well as in Western European maps. He became increasingly sceptical about such information and began claiming that the knowledge he collected while visiting the region himself and while reading and translating Persian and Arabic sources could contribute substantially to correct such faulty Western views.[45] Parallel to his rising distrust in early modern Western European knowledge of Iran, della Valle's original letters not only express an increasing familiarity with the landscape of Iran and its nomenclature, but a decreasing need for comparing this nomenclature with names found in ancient sources.

Della Valle also integrated ideas and judgements other than his references to ancient, medieval and early modern authors and texts into his letters when preparing them for print. A striking example is his report about a meeting between himself and Father Negrone, a Portuguese Franciscan, in Goa. This report is part of his letter from Surat written before della Valle ever set foot on Goan soil. Hence, this report cannot have been a part of his original letter. If he had carried this first letter to Goa and then added the report, it would have appeared as a postscript since this is how he proceeded in similar cases. The presence of this report in his letter from Surat can thus only mean that della Valle added it in Rome when preparing his letters for print. The function of this added report is to open a venue for a comment. In this comment della Valle declared that good historical texts, in particular if they concerned Indian matters, had to be based upon two elements: ancient history, geography and other humanistic studies plus local sources accessed by the writer himself after having learned the local language(s). In both respects, della Valle exclaimed, Negrone was lacking and thus were his books.

> But I had a somewhat longer talk with him in Goa, which I did not do in Persia. I found him of very little foundation in the matters of ancient history and geography in accordance with all the religious (men) from Spain, and mostly the Portuguese, who give themselves little to other studies except for those that serve for preaching. I do not know, (however), how it can be possible to write good histories, and in particular about things of the Indians, about which he could gather information

---

[45] See della Valle: *Viaggi*, vol. 2, pp. 219, 264 et al. In his letter from Shiraz written on 27 July, 1622, for instance, della Valle distanced himself from the very same book, now calling it 'Ferrari's Epitome': 'Fra Filippo Ferrari nella sua Epitome geografica attribuisce il nome di Bendemir al fiume, il quale crede (1) che dai Latini fosse detto *Bagradas* o Brisoana, ma s'inganna, chè Bendemir è nome del ponte, e non del fiume, ed io nel suo libro che ho appresso di me ve l'ho notato in margine.' Della Valle: *Viaggi*, vol. 2, p. 264.

only through an interpreter, a method – as I have proved by experience – through which one accumulates often many errors.[46]

Della Valle's methodological claim by virtue of having been added to the letters only when they were prepared for print suggests that it was meant to apply only to printed histories, not, however, to every kind of report about India and by extension Iran or the Ottoman Empire. Hence, the fact that della Valle's private and semi-public writings show a fundamentally different outlook indicates that the high visibility of ancient secular and religious references in his printed letters and his Latin geography of Iran does not signify an intellectual mentality, but a convention of printed learned literature propagated by the Republic of Letters and kept in place through various forms of censorship.

Because the printed letters differ in many aspects from the originals sent by della Valle to Schipano, the question arises whether they differ also in spirit, something denied by della Valle's assurance that he only omitted private, slippery and politically sensitive statements. Given the enormous difference with regard to the presence of authors and books in the two versions of the letters, this question can be only answered with yes. The letters as originally composed by della Valle had a much more private and much more Oriental outlook than the letters given to the printers. Many facets of the original letters' Oriental character have been annihilated, including della Valle's researches into the administrative geography of Safavid Iran. As a consequence, the prominence of ancient geographical and historical names, quotations and judgements is much stronger than in the original letters. The description of Safavid Iran as the unchanged duplicate of the ancient Iranian Empire of Cyrus or Darius is exclusively the result of della Valle's reading in Rome. Concepts of ancient geography, however, were present in the original letters for a long time and did never disappear completely. Della Valle was often preoccupied in his letters to determine whether a certain ancient name, territory, mountain, river or city corresponded to one he encountered in his own time. The original letters also indicate that the longer he lived in Iran

---

[46] 'Ma hauendo io in Goa discorso con lui più à lungo, che non feci in Persia, l'hò trouato molto poco fondato nelle materia d'histories antiche, e della Geografia, conforme à tutti i Religiosi di Spagna, e massime di Portogallo, che poco si danno ad altri studij, fuorche à quel che serue à predicare: onde senza buon fondamento d'historia antica, e di Geogrfia, e d'altre lettere humane, non sò come possa scriuer bène historie, e particolamente delle cose degli Indiane; de'quali anco solo per Interprete hà potuto informarsi; nel qual modo io per isperienza hò prouato, che si pigliano spesso molti errori.' Della Valle: *Viaggi* III, p. 85.

the more grew his reluctance to trust in Filippo Ferrari's knowledge about Oriental geography. He repeatedly criticized him explicitly or implicitly for not being correct with regard to the spelling of Oriental names, their locations and even their existence.

Della Valle's printed letters were used by French geographers in the second half of the 17th century as sources for new knowledge about the Ottoman and Safavid Empires which was capable of modernizing their maps. If they had worked with the original letters rather than with the French translation of the printed letters, the impact of della Valle's knowledge acquired while travelling could have been much greater. The French mapmakers restored, however, in some sense the spirit of della Valle's original letters since they ignored all references to ancient names and concepts and focused upon local contemporary knowledge.

This difference between the qualitative and the quantitative relationship between ancient sources, contemporary Oriental geography and della Valle's own role as an agent of knowledge results from the fact that in the original letters as written from the Middle East, ancient authority was almost completely absent. Della Valle had no use or need of ancient books while travelling through the Middle East. The books were not only too heavy to carry around; they also made no sense when travelling with a caravan through the Arabian Desert or riding with his new wife to inspect the ruins of ancient Babylonia in order to prove that Baghdad was a different city. Even remembering what he had learned by heart from ancient religious and secular books was rarely worth the effort.

IV

Pietro della Valle's Latin Geography of Safavid Iran (1624–1628): Introduction

by
Sonja Brentjes and Volkmar Schüller

In the seventeenth century, numerous visitors from Catholic and Protestant countries in Europe came to Safavid Iran. Most were ambassadors, merchants, and missionaries. Almost all contributed bits and pieces to an increasing cultural exchange between Catholic and Protestant Europe and Safavid Iran. The European-style paintings in Isfahan in the palace of Cehel Sutun and in the Armenian church of New Julfa – as well as the lovely Safavid miniatures extant in Rome, Leiden, Paris, London, or Vienna – are wonderful witnesses to this process. The exchange was by no means limited to the arts. The *Propaganda fide* in Rome and *Missions Etrangères* in Paris sponsored the printing of religious pamphlets and brochures to support the missions as well as dictionaries and grammars to improve the missionaries' skills. Merchant families sent young boys with one of their relatives to Iran in order to learn the Oriental languages where they were spoken, together with the secrets of the trade. Safavid shahs and their courtiers encouraged mixed Muslim-Christian sessions at the court or in public and enjoyed good disputes.

The resulting manuscripts and books were widely distributed with institutional support, both in Safavid Iran and in Catholic Europe. Missionaries in Iran translated medical writings from Persian into their own languages and compiled encyclopaedic dictionaries and accounts of the country's flora and fauna, history, language, contemporary politics, religion, and culture. Several missionaries repeatedly claimed that the mathematical and astronomical-astrological education widespread among the Safavid elites induced them to exploit their own knowledge in these disciplines as a vehicle for their apostolic mission. When we look at the books produced by the missionaries and at the Safavid manuscripts on the sciences acquired by Catholic and Protestant visitors from Europe in seventeenth-century Iran, we discover, however, that mathematics and astronomy together with astrology constituted only one of the many scholarly subjects that attracted the visitors' attention and money.

Geography and medicine appear to have been a much greater attraction to the Europeans than the mathematical sciences. The collecting of plants and seeds served scholarly as well as commercial purposes and was thus pursued by scholars, merchants, and adventurers alike. In comparison to these activities, discussing mathematics, astronomy, and astrology was of rather little relevance and attraction. The diverse dictionaries produced in the seventeenth century support the claim that the exact sciences, contrary to the missionaries' claims, were by no means central to their exchange with Safavid nobles and scholars.

Most of the activities described above apparently took place primarily as oral communication. Written results of an exchange of scholarly knowledge are rather scant in number and quality on both ends of the cultural spectrum. This article presents an English translation of one such extant witness to the impact oriental written and oral sources had upon the collection and appropriation of knowledge of Safavid political, physical, and cultural geography. This witness is the Latin geography of Iran by the Italian nobleman and adventurer Pietro della Valle (1586–1652). It was first composed in 1624 in Goa, the capital of Portuguese India, and addressed to a Jesuit missionary, Vincislaus Pantaleone Kirwitzer (d. 1626), whose center of activities was first in China and then in the Philippines. Della Valle had met him while waiting in Goa for a ship bound to Europe. According to a letter written to his friend Mario Schipano after his return to Rome in summer 1626, Della Valle meant the treatise to be printed, although its publication never materialized.[1] In Rome, Della Valle continued to work on this text, adding some of the latest information he had received from Iran and Georgia, polishing his Latin style and grammar, and introducing, albeit very briefly, the notion of a wider audience he wished to reach. He also substantially revised the letters he had sent from Naples to the Italian physician Mario Schipano, one of his friends and a co-member in the Accademia degli Umoristi. Because there is a close relationship between several passages in the revised letters, as published by Della Valle, and in his geography, it seems likely that the two later versions of this treatise, which Della Valle produced in 1626 and 1628 in Rome, also differ substantially from the original Goan version, which is lost.

---

[1] "L'undici aprile, per essere il giorno del mio natale, feci di questo dì la data della lettera dedicatoria nel mio trattato *De regionibus subiectis recentiori Persarum imperiò*, che haueuo animo di mandare in luce." Penultimate letter to Schipano, Rome, July 11, 1626. *Viaggi di Pietro della Valle Il Pellegrino Descritti da lui medesimo in Lettere Familiari all'Erudito suo Amico Mario Schipano Divisi in Tre Parti cioè: La Turchia, la Persia e l'India colla Vita e Ritratto dell'Autore*, ed. G. Gancia, (Brighton, 1843), 2:934.

The Innovative Character of Della Valle's Text

Della Valle's geography of Iran has been described by a reviewer of this essay as offering to present-day historians no new knowledge about Safavid Iran, its neighbors, or Europe. This may be true from a purely "factual" point of view. We are not at all convinced that it is correct with regard to anthropological details mentioned by the Italian traveler. We are sure, however, it is wrong with regard to intellectual history in Europe. The issue at stake here is Della Valle's decision to describe Iran under Shah Abbas in a scholarly treatise about the country's geography. The most important aspect of his approach is the relative importance of geographical concepts and names from classical antiquity versus geographical concepts and names of local provenance. A second aspect is the relative importance of written versus oral information. A third aspect concerns the relationship between different sorts of practices used by the traveler to gain, evaluate, and order information.

Della Valle's geography of Iran thus differs markedly from earlier attempts by authors from Catholic and Protestant Europe to describe their geographical knowledge of this region. It also stands apart from others of Della Valle's own writings.

Iran in geographical and cartographic sources of Catholic and Protestant Europe

Iran as Iran does not appear in geographical texts and maps made in Catholic or Protestant Europe before the early nineteenth century. In the 1820s and 1830s, a few French and some German maps name the territory of present-day Iran by this name, while English and most other maps continue to call the region Persia. Persia had been the standard name for Iran in western maps and geographical texts since the mid-sixteenth century. Before this time, the region carried no single name, but was divided according to classical authors into seven or more provinces, one of them being Persia. This classical division was reinforced when Ptolemy's *Geography* was translated into Latin at the beginning of the fifteenth century. A second name, given to Iran in western sources since the beginning of the sixteenth century, was "the kingdom of the Sophi," with Sophi being a transliteration of the Persian epithet of the new ruling dynasty (the Safavids). The first known map carrying this new name is a portolan chart made for the king of Portugal in 1519.[2]

---

[2] Miller Atlas, Ms Paris, BNF, Cartes et Plans, Rés. GE DD 683, f 2r.

Medieval maps produced in Catholic Europe that showed Iran often had nothing to say about the geographical details of the country. Portolan charts from the early fourteenth century made in Genoa and at Majorca are an exception to this rule. These charts not only show coastal towns, ports, bays, capes, and islands as most portolan charts do, but also display towns, mountains, rivers, peoples, and rulers in the interior space of the regions depicted. While most portolan charts focus on the Mediterranean Sea, parts of the Atlantic Ocean, and the Black Sea, the portolan charts from Genoa and Majorca also depict parts of the modern Middle East up to the shores of the Caspian Sea. One member of this group, the well-known Catalan Atlas, includes all Asia and hence all of Iran. This is true too for those of the world maps of the fourteenth and fifteenth centuries that are closely related to this group of portolan charts. Despite all differences in detail, these two groups of maps give place names for Iran too. Marco Polo's book, the reports of papal and royal envoys to the Mongol or Timurid courts, and oral information collected by Genoese and Venetian merchants who sailed on the Caspian Sea from the later thirteenth century, are most often considered the sources of the portolan charts' rather limited knowledge of Iran.[3] A new, recently proposed view is that maps produced by Arabic and Persian scholars, in particular those working at the Ilkhanid court in the second half of the thirteenth century, were more likely the fountains from which this knowledge was appropriated.[4]

A closer look at the two groups of maps indicates that maps by Iranian authors may indeed have been involved in the process of collecting local geographical knowledge about Iran, not so much for features that actually existed as for misunderstood geographical symbols. The Catalan Atlas and later portolan charts and world maps related to it show, for instance, a connection of lakes Van and Urmia to the Persian Gulf through a straight river, fed by arms springing from the two lakes. The lakes are represented by two circles of medium size, a feature common to numerous Arabic and Persian maps, in particular regional maps by Abu Zayd Ahmad b. Sahl al-

---

[3] R.V. Tooley, Charles Bricker, and Gerald Roe Crone, eds., *Landmarks of Mapmaking: An Illustrated Survey of Maps and Mapmakers* (Amsterdam, Brussels, Lausanne, & Paris, 1968), 106–9; R.W. Karrow, Jr., *Mapmakers of the Sixteenth Century and Their Maps: Bio-Bibliographies of the Cartographers of Abraham Ortelius, 1570/ Based on Leo Bagrow's A. Ortelii catalogus cartographorum* (Chicago, 1993), 239.

[4] Fuat Sezgin, *Mathematische Geographie und Kartographie im Islam und ihr Fortleben im Abendland*, in *Geschichte des Arabischen Schrifttums*, 12 vols., (Frankfurt am Main, 2000), 10:300–20.

Balkhi (d. 934), Abu Ishaq Ibrahim ibn Muhammad al-Farisi al-Istakhri (d. 364), or Abu l-Qasim Ibn Hawqal (fl. 943–988). The river system with its main river and two branches does not reflect a set of natural objects. It was taken either from an earlier map or from a geographical text. Two main possibilities exist as to which kind of source could have been used. Regional maps of Khuzistan and Arabic Iraq are one possibility. In these maps, the two regions are separated by a borderline, which bifurcates at its northern end.[5] The river system may represent a slightly reshaped misunderstanding of this borderline between Iraq and Khuzistan. The second possibility is Ptolemy's *Geography*, which talks of a river Eulaios to the Persian Gulf. This river has a source in Susiana and another one in Media.[6] The familiarity of Genoese and Majorcan mapmakers and monks with either of the two sets of possible sources cannot be proven with certainty. Until now, historians of cartography have believed that Ptolemy's *Geography* came to be known to the Latin world only at the end of the fourteenth century when the Byzantine scholar Manuel Chrysolaras brought a copy of the work to Florence. Possible familiarity with the maps of al-Balkhi, al-Istakhri, or Ibn Hawqal, from the ninth and tenth centuries, or their later copies, has not even been discussed.

The local place names used in the portolan charts and world maps, on the other hand, point rather to intermediary sources from the mapmakers' own cultural environment. "Marga," for instance, cannot possibly be considered a transliteration of a written form, since a transfer of all written Arabic letters of this name (Maragha) would include an a between the *r* and the *g*. Chesi, on the other hand, comes almost undoubtedly from Marco Polo, who spells it Chisi. In the portolan charts, Chesi is situated on the Iranian coast of Khuzistan, near Abadan. No Arabic or Persian map known to me shows a locality with a similar name in this area. The only place name that shows some similarity is Shiniz. While a misreading of the Arabic letters *n-i* into *s* is possible, it is nonetheless unlikely that Shiniz is the ancestor of Chesi, for the sound value of *ch* in Italian dialects is *k*. Chesi was placed on the coast of Khuzistan close

---

[5] H. Mžik, *Al-Iṣṭakhrī und seine Landkarten im Buch "Ṣuwar al-Aḳālīm" nach der persischen Handschrift Cod. Mixt. 344 der Österreichischen Nationalbibliothek*, ed. R. Kinauer and S. Balic, (Wien, 1965).

[6] *Claudii Ptolemaei Geographia*, ed. Carolus Fridericus Augustus Nobbe (Leipzig, 1843, reprinted Hildesheim, 1990), 90. Sonja Brentjes, "Revisiting Catalan Portolan Charts: Do They Contain Elements of Asian Provenance?," in Philippe Forêt and Andreas Kaplony (eds.), *The Journey of Maps and Images on the Silk Road*, Brill's Inner Asian Library, vol. 21 (Leiden, 2008), pp. 181–201.

to Abadan because Marco Polo had reported that travelers wishing to go from Baghdad to India went to Chisi and from there they sailed to India.[7] He added that the people from Persia brought horses to Chisi, Ormus, and many other cities on the coast of the Indian Ocean in order to ship them to India for sale.[8] These two statements, when combined, suggest that Chisi or Chesi was situated at the coast of Khuzistan close to Abadan. The place Marco Polo talked about was, however, most likely the island of Kish in the Persian Gulf. Furthermore, the localities named in the portolan charts and world maps for Arabic Iraq are often wrongly placed, although the names are most often easily recognizable and occasionally correctly spelled. None of the slightly varying orders of placing the localities in the western maps can be found in any of the Arabic and Persian maps of this region that we are familiar with. As studies of the Dominican and Franciscan missions in the thirteenth and fourteenth centuries reveal, some Italian towns, in particular Pisa and Genoa, had close ties with Mongol Iran through bishops and their *fratres* who resided, starting in the late 1310s, alternatively in Maragha, Sultaniye, Tabriz, and Kirnë in the province of Nakhcivan.[9] The missionaries had, not surprisingly, a much better understanding of the spelling of Iranian place names like Maragha than the mapmakers, as the example "*episcopus Maragensis*" in documents of the orders indicates.[10]

While the sources of these portolan charts and world maps are obviously complex, the maps themselves share one feature that is important for understanding the background of Della Valle's Latin geography of Iran. In contrast to earlier medieval world maps, these maps made room for oriental local knowledge, even if it was misunderstood, misplaced, and mediated through western travelers. An opposite process took place in the fifteenth century after a Byzantine manuscript of Ptolemy's *Geography* had been brought to Florence and translated into Latin. Starting in the 1430s, portolan chart makers like Andreas Bianco in Venice added a Ptolemaic-type world map to their atlases of portolan charts.

Portolan charts of the first half of the sixteenth century overflow with classical nomenclature while retaining orientalizing images of rulers

---

[7] Gian Battista Ramusio, *Navigationi et Viaggi* (Venice, 1563–1606), ed. R.A. Skelton and George B. Parks, 3 vols. (Amsterdam, 1967), 2:6.

[8] Ibid., 6f.

[9] Angelo M. Piemontese, "La via domenicana verso la 'Cronaca d'Europa' di Rašīd al-Dīn," in *Turcica Et Islamica*, ed. Ugo Marazzi (Naples, 2003), 707–29, 719.

[10] Ibid., 719.

and applying this kind of iconography to kings in Russia and Poland too. On the other hand, the extant copy of Fra Mauro's world map, produced in 1459 for the king of Portugal and considered the finest specimen of medieval cartography, criticizes Ptolemy and expresses its maker's belief that the geographical knowledge of the ancient astronomer was insufficient for mapping the world as known in 1459. Fra Mauro compensated for Ptolemy's deficiencies by searching for the oral knowledge of seamen and travelers like Niccolo Conti, and by drawing on knowledge from Arabic and possibly other Asian sources.[11] This means that Fra Mauro, who composed his complex world map shortly before Portuguese sailors circumnavigated Africa and were led by Arab pilots across the Indian Ocean, recognized, from studying books and talking to experienced travelers, the out-of-date status of ancient geographical knowledge.[12]

Moreover, the Latin manuscript tradition of Ptolemy's *Geography* indicates that interested readers and copyists of the text replaced the 27 known maps of the standard series with non-Ptolemaic maps that drew for knowledge of Asia or northern Europe on portolan charts and possibly oral information.[13] These anonymous consumers of Ptolemy's *Geography* seem to have shared Fra Mauro's opinion. As a result, a contradictory, multi-layered picture emerges in respect to what was considered appropriate to write, draw, or say about the geographical knowledge of classical authors with respect to Asia, a major part of the Old World. While it became standard after 1500 to criticize ancient geographical knowledge when discussing the New World and South or East Asia, western Asia was recast as a domain where ancient geographical knowledge was applicable and continued to carry valid meaning.

A further trend reinforced this tendency. Producers of Ptolemy's *Geography*, mapmakers, and university scholars of the sixteenth century joined in their efforts to improve the Latin translation of the Greek text made by Manuel Chrysolaras and his student Jacopo d'Angelo between 1397 and 1409, and also to modernize the classical text and its Byzantine maps. One way to approach this complex goal was the introduction of new knowledge into the world maps joined to Ptolemy's book. Another way consisted in the addition of maps of regions that did not belong to the standard series of 27 maps, such as

---

[11] *Il Mappamondo di Fra Mauro*, ed. Tullia Gasparrini Leporace (Rome, 1956).
[12] Tooley, et al., *Landmarks of Mapmaking*, 53–4.
[13] Marica Milanesi, *Tolomeo sostituito: Studi di storia delle conoscenze geografiche nel XVI secolo* (Milan, 1984).

Palestine, Scandinavia, or Lorraine. A third way was to add maps that claimed to modernize one or more of the 27 standard maps. Examples are maps of Italy, Spain, or Sclavonia. A fourth procedure was to insert annotations to Ptolemaic place names that comprised of alternative classical or Biblical names, names from travel accounts, historical treatises, portolan charts, and knowledge grounded in contemporary war and politics.[14] This procedure restored knowledge of the local geographical features (real or imaginary) of contemporary Islamic societies to the textual body of western geography. In a sense, the correctors and modernizers of Ptolemy's *Geography* in Germany and Italy returned to the standard of fourteenth-century Genoese and Catalan portolan charts and fifteenth-century portolan style world maps.

Efforts to modernize Ptolemaic geography climaxed with the Italian translation of Sebastian Münster's corrected edition of Ptolemy's *Geography* (translated by Pietro Andrea Mattioli) and the maps by Giacomo Gastaldi that were produced for this translation. Gastaldi transferred a series of names collected and added by Münster into the new maps he produced for regions of Africa and Asia hitherto not included into the process of modernization. He also looked for sources for collecting additional local names used in Africa and Asia in the middle of the sixteenth century. He collaborated with the secretary of the Venetian government, Giovanni Ramusio, and one of the governmental translators of Turkish, Michele Membré, in a series of shared projects, such as mural maps for the Palace of the Doge, small-sized maps for Ramusio's collection of travel accounts, world maps for the Ottoman court, the so-called Hajji Ahmet map, and a not yet identified or found map of Asia. Gastaldi created completely new maps of Asia and Africa that used Arabic, Persian, and Turkish geographical knowledge insofar as it was available in Venice. As a result, his map of Anatolia and the representation of Iran in his maps of Asia (parts one and two) come, in fact, much closer to the geographical reality of these two territories than any earlier map produced in Catholic Europe. Gastaldi's maps of Africa and Asia are accompanied, either on the maps themselves or in form of separate sheets, by long lists of names that aim at equating ancient names of places, provinces, mountains, and rivers with contemporary names. Gastaldi exploited Münster's previous work and added his newly acquired knowledge as expressed in the maps. The diversity

---

[14] Tooley, et al., *Landmarks of Mapmaking*, 55–6. Marica Milanesi, "La 'Geografia' di Claudio Tolomeo nel Rinascimento," in L. Lago, *Imago mundi et Italiae: La visione del mondo e la scoperta dell'Italia nella cartografia antica (secoli X–XVI)*, (Trieste, 1992), 1:93–104.

of sources used by Münster and Gastaldi created a potpourri of names and equations, the quality and validity of which differed greatly.[15]

Efforts to identify and match ancient and contemporary cities with each other are recorded in much earlier western sources. Venetian diplomats visiting fifteenth-century Iran already argued for Tauris being ancient Ecbatana. Clerical travelers to the late Abbasid caliphate, like Riccoldo da Monte di Croce, argued for the identity of Baghdad and ancient Babylon. The sixteenth century, however, saw the transformation of such efforts into a kind of game, which occupied western European writers on geography and history until the later years of the eighteenth century. Gastaldi was not the only producer of maps with name-lists.[16] Editions of Ptolemy's *Geography* and the new kinds of atlas, like Abraham Ortelius's *Theatrum Orbis Terrarum*, were adorned with appendices listing ancient and modern names.[17] Separate dictionaries connecting modern to ancient names were compiled from the middle of the sixteenth century.[18] Serious disputes over who got the game right shaped the geographical discourse about the Ottoman and Safavid Empires in the later decades of the sixteenth century and were carried over into the seventeenth century. The disputes showed that there were no agreed-upon rules by which

---

[15] For a survey of Münster's sources, see, for instance, Tooley, et al., *Landmarks of Mapmaking*, 62.

[16] *La Geografia di Claudio Ptolemeo Alessandrino: con alcuni comenti & aggiunte fatteui da Sebastiano munstero a la manno, con le tauole non solamente antiche & moderne solite di staparsi, ma altre nuoue aggiunteui di Meser Iacopo Gastaldo Piamotese cosmographo, ridotta in volgare Italia no da M. Pietro Andrea Mattiolo Senese medico eccelletissimo* (Venice, 1548). Giacomo Gastaldi, *I Nomi Antichi E Moderni Della Seconda Parte Dell'Asia* (Venice, 1561); Giacomo Gastaldi, *I Nomi Antichi E Moderni Della Prima Parte Dell'Asia* (Venice, 1564).

[17] *Descrittione di tutta Italia di F. Leandro Alberti Bolognese, nella quale si contiene il sito di essa : l'origine, & le Signorie della Città, & de i Castelli, co i nomi antichi, & moderni, i costumi de popoli, le conditioni de i paesi. Et piv gli huomini famosi, che l'hanno illustrata, i Monti, i Loghi, i Fiumi, le Fontane, i Bagni, le Minere; con tutte l'opere marauigliose in lei dalla Natura prodotte. Con somma diligenza corretta, & ristampata* (Vinegia, 1553). Orazio Toscanella, *I nomi antichi e moderni delle provincie, regioni, città, castella [sic], monti, laghi, fiumi ... & isole dell'Europa, dell'Africa, & dell'Asia : con le graduationi loro in lunghezza e larghezza & una breve descrittione delle suddette parti del mondo* (Venice, 1567). Abraham Ortelius, *Theatrum orbis terrarum [De Mona druidum insula antiquitati suae restituta ... epistola ... Humberti Lhuyd ... Synonymia locorum geographicorum, sive antiqua regionum ... urbium... nomina, recentibus eorundem nominibus explicata ... (a Arnoldo Mylio)]*, (Antwerp, 1571). *Clavdii Ptolomaei Alexandrini ... opus Geographiae castigatum & emaculatum additiōibus. raris et inuisis. necnon cum tabularum in dorso iucunda explicatione ...*, ed. Laurentius Phrisius (Strasbourg, 1522).

[18] Fr. Philippo Ferrario, *Lexicon geographicum ...*, ed. G. Dillingham. *Adnectitur tabula longitudinis ac latitudinis urbium ... per totum terrarum orbem, ex ejusdem Philippi Ferrarii "Epitome geographica" desumpta* (London, 1657).

equivalency could be determined. Any argument was admissible – quotations from the Bible, ancient history books, Arabic geographies, Persian astronomical tables, accounts written by western and eastern travelers, oral information, popular etymologies, and geographical coordinates were all treated equally in principle.[19] The choice of how to rate their reliability and importance was in the hands of the individual author. The disputes did not lead to a shared consensus, either on the rules or on the names and their equivalents.

In the second half of the seventeenth century, while continuing the game, travelers, missionaries, and scholars pretended that the game was old-fashioned, and that they subscribed to it merely because of habit and custom among their readers.[20] A deeper look suggests, however, that the rules had not changed substantially and that no new approaches had emerged for introducing more reliable criteria for deciding which modern locale was situated on top of which ancient village or town. A decisive break from the early modern rules of the game was achieved only in the first half of the eighteenth century, at least for the Greek and Anatolian parts of the Ottoman Empire, when scholars started to investigate more closely archaeological remains and tried to interpret ancient texts in light of these material remnants.[21] A second turnabout accompanying this change in the rules was the resetting of the goal. Now the purpose of the game was to identify ancient names with the help of modern localities and their names.[22]

Della Valle's diary, his original letters, and his geographical treatise mark an important intermediary stage in the process of creating in Catholic and Protestant Europe a body of geographical knowledge that depicted contemporary realities. The original form of his letters, before being revised for printing, shows a profoundly different procedure followed by the traveler while in the Ottoman and Safavid Empires, as has been shown elsewhere.[23]

---

[19] For the discussion of examples in an early seventeenth-century English travel account, see Sonja Brentjes, "Early Modern Western European Travellers in the Middle East and their Reports about the Sciences," in *Sciences, techniques et instruments dans le monde iranien (X–XI siècle)*, ed. N. Pourjady and Ž.Vesel (Tehran, 2004), 379–420.

[20] *Voyages du Chevalier Chardin en Perse, et autres lieux de l'orient*, 10 vols., ed. L. Langlès, (Paris, 1811), 2:154–5, 330–39, et al.

[21] Patrick Jager, "Voyageurs au Levant à la recherche de l'antiquité," *Dix-Huitième Siècle* 27 (1995): 89–98. *Homère en France après la Querelle (1715–1900): Actes du colloque de Grenoble (23–25 Octobre 1995)*, ed. Daniel Sangsue (Paris, 1999).

[22] See Jean Baptiste Bourgignon d'Anville, *Géographie ancienne abrégée* (Paris, 1768).

[23] Sonja Brentjes, "The Presence of Ancient Secular and Religious Texts in the Unpublished and Printed Writings of Pietro della Valle (1586–1652) ," paper III in this volume..

Rather than following closely one of the few books he carried around with him, which was Filippo Ferrari's *Epitome geographia*, a dictionary identifying modern places by ancient names, he preferred to collect information and to create knowledge by his own observations, questioning local people, scholars, peasants, and nomads alike, and learning the Arabic, Turkish, Kurdish, or Persian names of the day. Most of his energies went into the acquisition of first-hand local knowledge, whether oral or written, and the philological skills necessary to access it. If he used books at all, it was a travel account from the sixteenth century by the French druggist Pierre Bélon. Della Valle employed Bélon both as a source of information and a chance for displaying his own, new knowledge contradicting the statements of the French traveler. The same kind of skeptical and occasionally outright critical attitude Della Valle applied to the geographical dictionary by his compatriot Ferrari in the few instances he referred to it. He wrote long discourses about the inappropriateness of the identification of Baghdad with Babylon and in favor of the identification of Ktesiphon with al-Mada'in on the basis of his visits there, as well as knowledge learned later from a Persian geography.

Della Valle's attempts to acquire and present geographical knowledge of Iran

Della Valle produced five different sorts of sources that speak of his efforts to acquire geographical knowledge of Iran and to describe this newly gained information. His diary is the document nearest to his immediate acts of collecting information while traveling through the Ottoman and Safavid Empires. Closely connected to the diary are his original letters written during this travel to Mario Schipano in Naples, and to some extent also his letters written to Cardinal Crescentio Crescentis in Rome and other friends, family members, and acquaintances in Istanbul, Naples, Rome, and Aleppo. The letters sent to Schipano were published 26 years after Della Valle returned home in 1626. During these 26 years, Della Valle studied and excerpted a substantial number of manuscripts and printed books from antiquity, the Middle Ages, and the early modern period written in Latin, Italian, French, Portuguese, Persian, Arabic, and Spanish. Works by ancient Greek authors and the occasional Hebrew sources Della Valle studied in Latin translations.

As we have shown elsewhere, Della Valle acquired geographical knowledge while traveling from three kinds of sources: oral information from native inhabitants of the territories he traveled through, a travel account by the sixteenth-century French druggist and natural historian Pierre Bélon, and manuscripts in local languages that he bought during his journey.[24] Della Valle's focus while acquiring this knowledge was on learning local names of towns, villages, rivers, lakes, plains, and mountains, memorizing their local spelling, and transliterating them correctly into the Latin alphabet. A second effort aimed at rectifying errors in Bélon's report. A third task Della Valle shouldered with some delight was to criticize identifications made at home of ancient towns with contemporary place names in the Ottoman and Safavid Empires. A major problem for the two processes of correction and critique was the necessity to confirm the veracity of the new information and to place the verified information into the canon of knowledge familiar to Della Valle and his countrymen. Della Valle believed that written sources were necessary for verifying orally acquired knowledge. His diary and the letters to Schipano testify to the unhappiness he felt over the very few books from his own culture that he could access while traveling.[25] He thought to balance this shortage by buying Arabic, Persian, and Turkish manuscripts about geography and other scholarly fields.[26] Indeed, he bought Persian manuscripts about geography, history, and astronomy, Arabic and Turkish manuscripts on astronomy, astrology, and medicine, as well as dictionaries, poetry, and literature in all three languages.[27] Lacking books as means of proof, Della Valle had to find another device for handling acquired local information. Depending on whether he possessed knowledge about a region, a river, a place, or a monument learned at home, he compared the old and familiar knowledge with the new information. The printed letters do not indicate that he invented a single rule for how to handle the comparison. When it suited him, he chose the old and familiar knowledge over the new information, while on other

---

[24] Sonja Brentjes and Volkmar Schüller, "The Safavid Court in the Seventeenth Century: A Place of Learning and Exchange of Knowledge?," unpublished manuscript 2002.

[25] Ms Città del Vaticano, Biblioteca Apostolica Vaticana, Ottoboniano latino 3382, f 150b: "... Io non ho qui Quinto Curtio per uederlo, ne altro libro da potei consultare ..."; Ms Città del Vaticano, Archivio Segreto, Archivio Della Valle – del Bufalo 51, letter from Baghdad, December 18, 1616, unpaginated. Della Valle kept this passage unaltered in his printed letters, see Della Valle: *De'Viaggi di Pietro della Valle il Pellegrino Descritti da lui medesimo in Lettere familiari All'Erudito suo Amico Mario Schipano. Persia, Parte Prima* (Rome, 1658), 357.

[26] Ms Città del Vaticano, Biblioteca Apostolica Vaticana, Ottoboniano latino 3382, ff 24a, 39a, 52a, 59b, 83a, 84a, 138a, 150b, 154b.

[27] See Ettore Rossi, *Elenco dei manoscritti persiani della Biblioteca Vaticana* (The Vatican, 1948).

occasions he opted for devaluating the old knowledge in favor of the new.[28] If he applied a yardstick at all, it was social hierarchy. Courtiers of Shah Abbas are portrayed as more reliable in their knowledge about Iran, its geography and history, than peasants or local elites.[29] A comparison between the diary and the original letters to Schipano and the unpublished letters to Crescenti reveals that the need for verification depended on the type of text Della Valle composed. The need for verification is rarely visible in his diary and his letters to the cardinal. It is much more prominent in his original letters to Schipano. It is overwhelmingly present in the printed version of Della Valle's letters to Schipano. Its presence is the result of the long years of study of books and manuscripts that Della Valle undertook in Rome after his return. The excerpts from his reading enabled Della Valle to revise his original account on what he did and cared for while traveling. The traveler's expressed motif was his wish to improve his account's quality to ensure his fame while alive and after his death.[30]

In the middle between these two sets of documents stands Della Valle's geographical treatise. It evidently drew on his original letters when first written in Goa. Later in Rome, it underwent a similar process of revision as the letters without getting infused with the same heavy dose of classical and biblical sources. In the geographical treatise, Della Valle portrays himself as the decisive source for reliable knowledge. Local written and oral information is presented as plausible and at times even superior to what Della Valle had learned at home or what his countrymen believed in.[31] Ancient authors and the Bible are rarely explicitly mentioned, but occasionally quoted without quotation marks. Della Valle knew what his readers could recognize as metaphors, similes, lines of verses, or other bits of shared education and belief. The combination of common, familiar knowledge with the explicit self-presentation as the owner of reliable, but foreign knowledge is Della Valle's central strategy in the geography of Iran for ensuring the credibility of the new knowledge he offered.

---

[28] Pietro della Valle, *Voyages de Pietro della Vallé* [sic]: *Gentilhomme Romain, Dans la Turquie, l'Egypte, la Palestine, la Perse, les Indes Orientales, & autres lieux*, 7 vols. (Paris, 1745), 2:109, 133, 188–9; 4:115–16.

[29] See ibid., 6:148.

[30] See the analysis in Sonja Brentjes, "The Presence of Ancient Secular and Religious Texts," paper III in this volume.

[31] See the translation below.

The different status of the three types of documents within Della Valle's career as a traveler and writer lies at the heart of Della Valle's different approaches to the portrayal of Iran's geography and history. Della Valle's original letters to Schipano and, to a lesser extent, his letters to Crescenti are filled with information about local geography. In the case of his letters to Schipano, this information is visually highlighted as oriental knowledge acquired by the traveler through witnesses and written sources. The traveler assured his addressee of his continuous efforts at improving the quality of such knowledge by studying local languages, buying local manuscripts, talking to local scholars and nobles, and undertaking excursions to verify that the local information that contradicted beliefs at home was indeed correct. Knowledge from classical sources played almost no role in the diary or in the original letters. Given that such knowledge permeated Della Valle's education as a member of Roman nobility, the repeated reference to a shortage of books can only be seen as a stratagem. The traveler could have used Filippo Ferrari's *Epitome geographia* given to him by Schipano in order to place new information into the framework of classical and early modern knowledge available at home. That he referred to Ferrari's geographical dictionary less than ten times in his original letters, while doing so more than twenty times in the printed version, affirms his lack of interest in such a bookish practice of gathering knowledge while traveling.

The printed letters show a remarkable unevenness in their treatment of geography and history in the Ottoman and Safavid Empires. Filled with hundreds of quotes from ancient secular and sacred books, they transform the seventeenth-century Middle East into a pre-Islamic cultural domain described from a Hellenistic and Christianized perspective. Below this level, the contemporary physical and cultural geography of the Arab territories of the Ottoman Empire and the western and central regions of Safavid Iran are visible in the languages of the courtly elites and merchants. In the process of revising his original letters to Schipano, Della Valle tried to do what he had mostly avoided while traveling. He sought to identify modern places, mountains, rivers, and ancient ruins with names long lost, but preserved in ancient writings.

Della Valle's Latin geography of Safavid Iran represents a synthesis between the procedure followed while traveling and expressed so proudly in his original letters and the re-alignment of modern oriental geographical reality to ancient knowledge and perception through the study of books expressed so loudly in the printed letters. In marked contrast to the printed letters and most of the printed travel accounts of the seventeenth century, Della Valle's Latin geography of Iran does not coat an Oriental foundation with a classical perspective, but presents both forms of geographical reality and depiction as of equal importance, the meaning and relationship of both has to be explored by means of philology, sources from all three cultural realms (the ancient one, the Oriental one, and the early modern western one), and oral local information. Mathematical and astronomical criteria, while praised in Della Valle's printed letters and applied in his own observational practice, both while traveling and later at home, are of minor relevance in his Latin geography of Iran. This treatise, written for a fellow-traveler in the East, may well have taken this form because the fellow-traveler had to cope with the non-familiar landscapes and cultures of Asia like Della Valle himself, rather than sitting at home, expecting to read about foreign lands in familiar terms. The repeated revision of the text in order to prepare it for publication in Italy, the insistence on Persian, Arabic, and Turkish vocabulary, and the lack of explicit references to ancient books and authors indicate, however, that Della Valle had intentionally kept a structure that invited the Italian reader at home too to recognize Oriental (written and oral) depictions of Iran's cultural and physical geography as of equal standing with ancient texts. With this decision, he broke away from the humanist preference for ancient knowledge over oriental knowledge and re-introduced, through the medium of the traveler's individually gained knowledge, the scholarly relevance of oriental sources for western writings about Iran.

Della Valle's return to humanist literary practice in the printed versions of his letters to Schipano invites us to read other printed travel accounts of the period as equally grounded in a literary tradition rather than as the expression of the travelers' practices of gathering new knowledge while traveling. Della Valle's Latin geography of Iran affirms that less stifling approaches to describing new knowledge about Islamic countries were possible in the seventeenth century. This contradiction raises the question as to what motivated the travelers to adopt the literary fiction created by applying ancient Greek and Latin geographical concepts and names to early modern Islamic countries when they turned into authors who planned to print their accounts. Travelers turned into authors had to face the knowledge available to their compatriots. Those who employed ghost-writers or worked with editors – like André Thevet in the sixteenth century or Jean-Baptist Tavernier and Jean Chardin in the seventeenth century – had to cope with what these ghost-writers or editors knew, understood, and accepted.[32] Those travelers who acted as ghost-writers, like Adam Olearius, could impose their own views about what a good travel account should look like upon their fellow-travelers. Censorship was a third element that needed to be accommodated. Many travelers who wished to publish their accounts wrote for a well-defined audience. Pilgrims to Jerusalem and other places in the Ottoman Empire described their travel most often in the framework of earlier books on pilgrimage. The contemporary realities of the Ottoman Empire did not matter in such a framework and appeared merely to mark the beginning and the end of the journey, as well as the real and imagined hardships suffered during it. Young men traveling in the entourage of an ambassador – or extending their so-called grand tour through Catholic and Protestant countries of Europe to the territories of the Ottoman Empire – wished to show off the fruits of their learning while traveling and their piety while following the stations of the pilgrimage route. For them, classical authors and the Bible proved indispensable tools for presenting themselves as refined and well educated travelers. Scholars visited the Ottoman Empire because they wished to gather information about new commercial commodities, in particular drugs, plants, and animals, to collect sources and objects of knowledge (manuscripts, coins, seeds, animals, etc.), to free ancient knowledge from its vernacular impurities by comparing their books with oriental nature, and to restore ancient knowledge to its fullest by acquiring translations of classical texts into Arabic from Oriental libraries and booksellers. When they published accounts of their travels, they did not always use the humanist style of writing about knowledge, but occasionally made more room for Oriental knowledge. Those who adopted the humanist style often did so because their predecessors had chosen this style. Borrowing heavily from successful travel accounts was a commercially viable strategy. It was also considered good scholarly behavior. Others, finally, were narrow-minded bigots who could not and would not find a single good hair on the foreign bear. As a result, a multi-layered image of the early modern Islamic world in Northern Africa and western Asia was created, one that colonized these regions intellectually, deprived them of their own linkage with classical antiquity, and denied their peoples and rulers the right to belong to the same geographical spaces as the writers of the accounts and their readers.

---

[32] See, for instance, Frank Lestringant, *André Thevet, cosmographe des derniers Valois* (Geneva, 1991), as well as Langlès's preface and notes to his edition of Chardin's account, *Voyages du Chevalier Chardin*, 1:xvj–xvij, xxxvj, et al.

Della Valle's Latin Style and Grammar

In his introductory phrases, Pietro della Valle described his treatise for Father Vincislaus as a small work which he had already written some years ago, but which he intended to send to him now in a revised and enlarged form. Hence, his geography of Safavid Iran was not a text written spontaneously, but a well-considered, carefully formulated treatise which evolved through several revisions, perhaps from earlier notes written spontaneously. This process of repeated revision could not but have a clear impact on the chosen wording and style. Whereas in spontaneously written notes, the style of the language is very much like the style of spoken language, the language in a carefully worked out treatise will usually be much more complicated. In the spoken language, the sentences are not very long, the syntactic constructions are not too complicated, and the vocabulary mainly consists of frequently used words whose sense is easily recognizable. The author of a carefully planned treatise will choose his wording much more consciously. Which style of language an author favors depends on many circumstances. As a rule, s/he will decide in favor of a style s/he can assume is well understood by the reader. One basic aim of writing is to make the content and the message of a text accessible to the reader. Many authors often choose, however, a style that indicates that they are learned and educated men or women. Such a choice is often accompanied by a lack of attention to whether the formulations in their text are clear and unambiguous. Pietro della Valle was one such author.

A treatise is a well formulated text when its statements can be understood completely and unequivocally by the reader. Unfortunately, Pietro della Valle violated this principle repeatedly. In translating the Latin text, we frequently wondered whether the original reader of this treatise could truly understand the content of a phrase as meant by Pietro della Valle, even if one grants the reader a thorough knowledge of (classical or early modern) Latin and its stylistics. By formulating long and difficult Latin sentences, Della Valle obviously endeavored to give his treatise the appearance of a classical Latin text. Even if early modern scholars actively spoke Latin, it was no longer spoken as a living language. Educated native speakers form their sentences as a rule instinctively and choose the right grammatical construction automatically. If the language is, however, only spoken as a scholarly language, the grammatical constructions and connections in longer and more complicated sentences tend to be increasingly incorrect. This is particularly true if an author did not truly master Latin grammar. Such a deviation from classical Latin grammar makes the understanding of a text more difficult. Because Della Valle often ignored the rules of classical Latin, understanding his text was not easy. In several cases, we could understand passages only by checking the translation with the help of other sources, for example historical encyclopaedias and dictionaries. Therefore we admit frankly that there are some passages in the translation where we are not quite sure whether we have understood them correctly.

Della Valle loved to embellish his text with short phrases and expressions that he borrowed almost literally from Virgil, and to which we refer at the corresponding places in the translation. In the early modern period, any person educated in the Latin language knew Virgil's poetry. This does not mean necessarily that many authors chose to insert the poet's words without attribution in order to improve the quality of their own texts. Quoting from Virgil in this way served to impress the reader with the author's reading, if not his good style. In those days too, such poetic formulations in scientific texts or reports may have appeared to the readers as stilted and ornate. In addition to Della Valle's implicit quotations from Virgil, there are certainly further expressions and short phrases in Della Valle's treatise taken over from other famous Latin authors that we were unable to identify.

In 1628, when Della Valle wrote his last revision of the text, Vincislaus Kirwitzer had been dead for two years. Hence, he never saw the final version of Della Valle's geography of Iran and could not judge for himself the traveler's efforts to improve his very first draft composed while in Goa.

Translation[33]

On the regions which are subjected to the present empire of the Persians
Pietro della Valle, the pilgrim, warmly salutes the Honorable Father Vincislaus Pantaleone of the Society of Jesus

---

[33] The last version, obviously prepared for publication, is contained in Ms Bibliotheca Estense di Modena, Modena, γ.S.1.10 (Fondo Campori 698) (hereafter Ms Modena γ.S.1.10). An earlier version can be found in Ms Bibliotheca Estense di Modena, Modena γ.U.1.22 (Fondo Campori 699) (hereafter Ms Modena γ.U.1.22), but it is barely legible.

Remark: The edited Latin text of Della Valle was based exclusively on the latest manuscript compiled by him in 1628. The editor, Enzo Gamalero, did not prepare an apparatus, nor did he say that there was an earlier manuscript available in the same library. His edition contains several errors, ignores all the Persian glosses compiled by Della Valle with much care, and neglects a few of Della Valle's additions, changes, and notes. These omissions have been corrected wherever necessary. We indicate in our translation only such changes of the edition that are wrong or

IV

This is a small work about the regions subjected in our time to the Persian Empire. I wrote it four years ago in Goa following your wish, and I now send it from Rome for you to read in the farthest corner of China, where you are living now: I would have loved to present this small gift a long time ago, but I hope that it will not be unwelcome now, because of the material that has been added.

One addition you will meet as the preface. Two others are added as appendices. The preface explains how certain proper names (places, ranks, and men) that appear here should be pronounced in Latin. I mean not the ancient pronunciation, which has been completely abandoned, but in our own Latin, i.e. in that proper to the people who now dwell in Latium. Though the peoples of Europe all use Latin letters in writing, they do not pronounce certain of the letters in the same way; rather, each nation pronounces them in its own manner. That is why I felt it necessary to explain this to you, a man of Austrian origin, and to other readers. Pronunciation will be marked by accents in the style of the Greeks, as is the rule in lists of words in (foreign) languages (made) by travelers. This way, one will know on which syllable the accent rises or falls. This (method) shows best how an expression should be pronounced in a correct und unadulterated way. Furthermore, as one can see, I have placed these words in the margin (where) they are not only written in Latin, but with the correct Persian signs too, so that there will be no doubt about the proper pronunciation of Persian speech.

The first appendix I have added deals with Baghdad.

The city of Baghdad, with the entire adjacent region of Babylon which was occupied by Abbàs, king of the Persians, and added to his kingdom about the time I was writing this text in India, or a few months earlier. The Turks have thus far not been able to recover it, despite having created huge armies

---

alter the meaning of the edited text. As to what concerns the translation, we have tried to follow in a first translation the edited text as closely as possible, but chose to deviate wherever necessary due to Della Valle's cumbersome style. Such deviations include the introduction of full stops and other punctuation, which we do not mark specifically. They also include adding, replacing, or omitting words. These are not marked, unless substantial. The result was a text that was difficult to read and hence more or less inaccessible to the modern reader. That is why we gratefully accepted James Tracy's generous offer to edit our English text. As a result, the text below is strictly speaking not a translation, but a modernized rendition of the content of Della Valle's geographical treatise. Substantial changes we carried over from the manuscript used by Gamalero for the edition are pointed out in footnotes. We preserved Della Valle's historical orthography of Persian, Arabic, and Turkish words as well as the royal title of his own culture, i.e. king, for the Safavid title shah and the Ottoman title *sultan*.

in recent years, and exerting all their force toward this objective. We were informed of this matter, i.e. the subjugation of Babylon by the Persians, in May 1624 shortly after you had left town. <It is thus no wonder that our text describes this region as subjugated to the Turks, for such had been the case previously.>[34]

The other point I wish to add is that the noble heroine Ketevan Dedupali, the mother of Teimuraz, one of the Georgian princes, who will be mentioned twice honorably in this small work, and about whom we have often spoken, has finally (crowned) the exalted deeds of (her) previous life with the most glorious martyrdom, after she patiently suffered great tortures with admirable perseverance until the very last gasp. (This happened) in the same city of Sciraz where she has been detained already for a long time, in hopes of inducing her to renounce her belief in Jesus Christ.[35] I do not know why, but the king of the Persians finally ordered the prefect of this province to subject her to compulsion.[36]

More I do not have to add. Good-bye: please inform me about the affairs of the Chinese and about the spread of the Christian faith in that very far region of the east and remember us in your prayers to God.

Rome, the place of my birth, the third day after the Ides of April 1628.[37]

The region of Babylon, together with some of the adjacent territories, still called by its ancient name in the Holy Scriptures, is called by the contemporary

---

[34] Ms Modena γ.S.1.10, f 3a, 11–14.

[35] Ketevan was killed September 12, 1624. Nodar Assatiani and Alexandre Bendianachvili, *Histoire de la Géorgie* (Paris & Montréal, 1997), 188.

[36] Della Valle tends to ignore the larger political and military contexts of the imprisonments of the various Georgian hostages. Before he came to Iran, during his stay there, and after he had left, the war between the Safavids, Ottomans, and various Georgian factions concerning who would rule the Caucasus went on almost incessantly. According to Assatiani and Bendianachvili, Abbas ordered Ketevan's conversion for humiliating his Kakhetian enemies and to weaken their resistance. Assatiani and Bendianachvili, *Histoire de la Géorgie*, 188. Kalistrat Salia believes that her death in 1624 was caused by Abbas's uncontrollable temper after Teimuraz and his ally Saakadze had again escaped annihilation. Kalistrat Salia, *History of the Georgian Nation*, ed. Nino Salia (Paris, 1983), 298. All three writers take an explicitly nationalistic stance. Their common source was probably the eighteenth-century Georgian historical chronicle of Wakhucht, published in 1856 by M. Brosset, *Histoire de la Géorgie depuis l'Antiquité jusqu'au XIX siècle: Traduite du Géorgien* (St. Petersburg, 1856), 2:166. Torturing and killing captured enemies and sending their heads to allies as proofs of success were standard practices among the Georgians, as well as the Ottomans. The same applies to killing prisoners who had lost their value, or who proved to be an obstacle to a new political endeavor.

[37] April 16, 1628.

Persians Araq. The meaning of this name is sweat, first, because the heat in these areas is most excessive during summer time. Perhaps too because these areas are made fertile not only by cutting irrigation ditches from the rivers, but also by much sweat, after they have been completely soaked by a few rainfalls. But Araq has two meanings, i.e. Araq of Arabia and Araq of Agiamia. Those regions subject to the power of the Persians are called Agiam, or Agem. Araq of Arabia refers to Babylonia and the adjacent areas, presently subject to the empire of the Turks. If you turn towards the east, you travel from Araq through the high rising mountains of the region of Kurdistan. These run from north to south, with the Taurus Mountains as a kind of branch, and divide the Persian Empire from the Turkish Empire. Araq of Agiamia is thus the first region under Persian control, and includes the province of Hamadan, whose capital is the city of the same name. This province is, I assume, part of ancient Persia or Susiana in the borders set by the Medes.

Hamadan is a city half way between Baghdad, the royal seat of Babylonia in earlier times, and Sphahanum or Isphahan, which has recently become the magnificent seat of the entire Persian monarchy. There, namely in Hamadan, the tombs of Esther and Mardochei are preserved until this day. Many Jews from neighboring places and from all over come there to pay their respects at the tombs. Sphahanum, a city also in the region of Araq, has a latitude of approximately 32 degrees. When one travels from there toward the middle between Arcturus and west, as I believe, i.e. toward the northwest, one comes to the cities of Kasciàn, Qom, Qazvin, Abher, Sultania, and Zengian, still in the region of Araq. Zengian is the borderpoint of the regions of Araq and Adherbaigian.[38] At the end of this treatise I give the height of the pole for these and some other cities, according to the results of various observers of my time, who determined them in different ways and whose opinions often differ. It will suffice to state that, at least in my view, the region Araq of Agiamia borders in the east on Choràsan; in the west on Araq of Arabia; in the north partly on Mazanderan and the other provinces located on the (south shore of the) Hircanian (Caspian) Sea, and, farther west, as the Sea curves, on

---

[38] "... et Zengian ultra quam terminus erat Araq regionis et Adherbaigian." Pietro della Valle, "De recentiori imperio Persarum subiectis regionibus," ed. Enzo Gamalero, *Studi Iranici* 17 (1977): 287–303, here 288. In the manuscript, the explanation added to Zengian is put between commas. In his letters to Schipano, Della Valle identified Sultaniyya as the place where the province of Iraq terminates and Azarbayjan begins. Pietro della Valle, *Voyages de Pietro della Vallé* [sic]: *Gentilhomme Romain, Dans la Turquie, l'Egypte, la Palestine, la Perse, les Indes Orientales, & autres lieux*, 7 vols. (Paris, 1745), 4:115.

Adherbaigian; finally, in the south it borders on Persia proper, the greatest and most excellent part of which is today called Fars or Farsistan.

Adherbaigian, a name that means worshippers of the fire, is doubtless the Media of the ancients or, as I prefer to say, its greatest and most excellent part. The region is mountainous. If one follows the upper road leading northwest, one crosses first a river of remarkable size which flows into the Caspian Sea. This river is called now in Persian Sepid-rud, i.e. the white river. But in Turkish it is commonly called Qizil-uzen, i.e. water that runs blackberry-red or golden-colored. What river this may be according to the ancients, I cannot easily discover.[39] Besides many other places barely worth mentioning, this region has two important cities. To the east lies Ardebil, the termination of my peregrination in this area. There one finds the sanctuary of the Persians and the mausoleum of the kings who reign today in Persia, owing to a man who stood out among their greatest, and was famous among the population through the legend of (his) pious life, even though he was not himself a king. He was everywhere called Sciah Sofi, which can mean either "chosen and upright king" or "pious king." Whether he was so called due to his faith and the dignity of his descent, or because this was his proper name, I do not know. They also call him "the ancestor of the kings reigning today." He who is buried in Ardebil was at least the outstanding restorer of the Shi'ite sect in Agiamia, if not its first founder.

Situated more toward the west (in Adherbaigian), and almost on the same parallel, is Tebriz, once a royal seat; it is known to the heavens above, for during the repeated wars between the Persians and the Turks it was often devastated, captured, or besieged by one side or the other.[40] The remaining cities of Adherbaigiàn I pass over with silence since I have not seen them myself.[41] There is so much the region of Adherbaigian borders on: in the east the larger part of Araq of Agiamia, in the west, towards the north, Armenia, part of which is now included in the Persian Empire, bounded by the Turks.

---

[39] According to H.L. Rabino di Borgomale, the ancient name of the river was Mardus. It originiates in Curdistan where it is called Qizil-uzen. Its name in Gilan is Sefid-rûd. H.L. Rabino di Borgomale, *Les Provinces Caspiennes de la Perse* (Paris, 1917), 46–7.

[40] In Virgil's *Aeneid*, I:379: "... fama super aethera notus"; Della Valle, "De recentiori imperio Persarum subiectis regionibus," 289: "... iisdem de causis fama super aethera nota." We follow the English translation of Virgil's *Aeneid* by H. Rushton Fairclough: *Eclogues, Georgics, Aeneid I-IV* (Cambridge, MA and London, 1953), 267.

[41] Although this phrase seems to suggest that Della Valle had seen Tabriz, this is not the case, as he states clearly in his letters to Schipano. Della Valle, *Voyages de Pietro della Vallé*, 4:73.

In the north it is bounded by Ghilàn and other more northern parts of ancient Media at the Caspian Sea, there where once dwelled Caddusians, Mardians, and the like; in the south, if I am not mistaken, it is bounded by parts of Araq.

I wish to speak less about Armenia than possible, because I have visited this region too little. It suffices to mention the better known cities: Nachcivàn and Irovàn, which have been attacked in recent years by the Turks, albeit without success. The small but densely populated province of Alingià is a neighbor to the city of Nachcivàn. Its inhabitants, though speaking Armenian, adhere to the Roman-Catholic faith. Several of them perform the service. They have a number of small churches that are cared for by the brethren of the Dominican order who live under (the guidance of) an archbishop of the same nation and constitution. (The archbishop) is usually ordained in Rome.[42] But (their number) decreases day by day. They do not receive assistance from Europe. Little by little, crude and countless errors creep into the faith among them, because of ignorance since they are illiterate and have no scholars. Nonetheless I hope that in future the spiritual needs of these Armenians and all the other Christians, wherever they may be in the world, will be taken care much better, by the work of the exalted congregation (De Propaganda Fide) established in recent years by the cardinals and other pious folk, under papal supervision, and which works seriously for the spread of the faith.

While the great difference in language also causes difficulty, it is particularly disruptive that those who were sent here from Rome a few times to teach them do not stay long, because they hate entirely the rude way of life of the Armenians (as I myself have seen occasionally). On the other hand, those pious Armenians do not easily bear the far more delicate mores and the more exact teaching of our fathers.

Under the jurisdiction of Irovan is Three-Churches, the highest patriarchate and sanctuary of all Armenians.[43] It was built in olden times not far away from a mountain on which – as one believes – Noah's ark was stranded. The altar stone of the larger of these churches was cut from the place where Noah after the deluge was ordered to offer the first sacrifice to Deus Optimus Maximus. They say that these things were told in a dream to Saint George, the apostle of the Armenians (they call him Lusavereius, that is, the illuminator, because he enlightened the people here with the light of the Gospel long ago).

---

[42] Compare to Della Valle, *Voyages de Pietro della Vallé*, 3:127.
[43] Della Valle talks here of Etchmiadzin.

After many of the Armenians had been joined by war to the empire of the Persians, King Abbàs, who rules today, ordered this stone to be brought into the interior of the kingdom for greater security. Together with relics of the saints which were in the possession of the Armenians, he had the stone brought to Sphahan, promising that he will erect there, for pious keeping of the stone, three other churches similar to the old ones. His hope was to prevent the Armenians from returning to their homeland, out of love and veneration for the stone. While no church has yet been built under the name of Three-Churches, many others have been built. The aforementioned stone, together with the other relics, is preserved in the city of the Armenians called New-Ciolfa. This is one of four cities that form the beautiful Sphahanum, the tetrapolis. They are separated from each other by a very narrow space; the river Zende-rud forms a natural boundary running from sunset to sunrise, while the lovely Cehar Bagh street runs from north to south. The river and the street cross at the bridge, very artfully constructed across the river. In addition to the cities of Armenia already mentioned, Old-Ciolfa was memorable for being at all times rich in commodities. Its inhabitants traveled throughout the world for profitable trade, just as the Genoese did in the dominions of the Catholic King. They were the founders of the new Ciolfa which, as I have said, has been joined to Sphahan.

Among the cities of Armenia beyond the Araxes, Van is famous in the nation of Agiamia. Others, under the power of the Turks, are also famous; but with these I have no business, because my aim is to describe the regions of the Persian empire, bounded by the Araxes. Of these regions, the one situated in the direction towards Armenia is very fertile, rich in all that is good, easily the best under Persian rule, were it not for its close proximity to the foe. For to Persia's west lie Assyria and other regions subjugated by the Turks, who are always hostile towards the Persians. To the north are the Georgians, a Christian people, who have also been hostile to the Persians in recent times. Thus while Armenia was easy to invade, it has been difficult to protect. King Abbas, prudent and calculating, thought it best to rule safely over a people without land than to abandon country and people to the danger of invasion by the foe.[44] Thus the cities of Armenia joined to his empire were

---

[44] Savory explained the forced dislocation of the Armenian inhabitants of Julfa in 1604 due to the commercial and economic interests of the shah and his entourage. In exchange, the Armenians received major privileges, among them the distribution of funds from the court for building St Joseph's cathedral in New Julfa, religious freedom, a form of self-government, and interest-free loans. Roger Savory, *Iran under the Safavids* (Cambridge, 1980), 174–5.

depopulated almost completely, by the dislocation mentioned above. That is why Old-Ciolfa and Nachcivàn are completely destroyed and have become hiding places for robbers and wild beasts.

Irovan, though it is the residence of a *chan* (that is, governor and military commander of the region), is less populous than before. Nonetheless, the fertile soil here supports towns and villages and other settlements, as well as isolated peasant houses. We can add to them the city of Ghiengé, which is not unknown, and owes its wealth to the silk trade. Teflis, a city said to lie either in Armenia or in Iberia on the borders of Armenia, was once the residence of one of the Christian princes of the Georgians called Luarsàb. His grandfather was that famous Simon who is mentioned often in our history-books.[45] But in later years, when this prince's good fortune began to wane, while still at the height of his power he surrendered on his own initiative to the King of Persia, though without his wife and children; the necessity of war made him do this.[46] After being kept prisoner for several years, he died in my time, murdered in prison.[47] His territory the Persians made into a province ruled

---

[45] Compare to Della Valle, *Voyages de Pietro della Vallé*, 5:142. Simon and Luarsab (1592–1622) ruled the kingdom of Kartli. After being defeated by an Ottoman army, Simon was brought to Istanbul where he died in prison. Luarsab, fighting against Shah Abbas, was taken prisoner and died in a fortress in Shiraz. See Assatiani and Bendianachvili, *Histoire de la Géorgie*, 183–4 and Salia, *History of the Georgian Nation*, 283.

[46] In his letters to Schipano, Della Valle gave an almost identical description of Luarsab's place of origin, voluntary surrender to Shah Abbas, imprisonment, and later strangulation. In this report, he said more clearly than in his geographical treatise that Luarsab had neither wife nor children. See Della Valle, *Voyages de Pietro della Vallé*, 6:19. However, according to Assatiani and Bendianachvili (183–4) and Salia (283), Della Valle erred with regard to Luarsab's family, as well as with regard to his voluntary surrender. The common source of the two modern histories of Georgia again may have been Wakhucht's historical chronicle from the eighteenth century, which claims that Luarsab had been lured by Shah Abbas into leaving his exile in Imereti, accompanying him to Iran, and then putting him into prison since he did not agree to convert to Islam. Brosset, *Histoire de la Géorgie*, 50–51.

[47] Luarsab was strangled by a bowstring in 1622, the result of a series of political and military events in Kartli and Isfahan. He had fallen into the shah's hands in 1615 and was held as a royal hostage for a long time in Astarabad. Muslim Georgians from Kartli, as well as the tsar, interceded on Luarsab's behalf. This pressure made Shah Abbas insist upon Luarsab's religious conversion for securing his submission; this, however, the prince declined. Therefore, he was brought to Shiraz in Southern Iran. Nonetheless, ongoing anti-Persian activities in the subjugated region of Kartli were ascribed to Luarsab's intrigues against Abbas. Parallel to the events in Kartli, a conspiracy against Abbas was discovered in Isfahan involving a number of Georgians. In this situation, Abbas considered it appropriate to kill Luarsab. See Salia, *History of the Georgian Nation*, 286, 288, 292. Compare also to Della Valle, *Voyages de Pietro della Vallé*, 4:74.

by another prince, undoubtedly of the same family, but a Muhammedan; he governs no longer as a supreme ruler, but as one subordinate to the king of the Persians.[48]

This province is bordered in the east by another territory of the Georgians called Kacheti, oriented towards Iberia or Albania, and governed by Teimuràz. This prince has now fled to the Turks and is still alive, but neither he nor the Persians govern. After this great rebellion in which many Georgian nobles were killed, the prince had opened to the Persians this prosperous and naturally fortified region. Since he could not hope to maintain permanent control of the region, King Abbàs led away almost all of the inhabitants as prisoners, to the interior of his empire. At the same time, two small children, sons of prince Teimuraz, as well as his mother called Ketevàn, whom they give the title Dedupali, that is, queen, were sent to the king himself, though this did not win him over.[49] The mother of Teimuraz, exceedingly constant in

---

In a later letter, Della Valle named Luarsab's successor Simon Chan, son of Bagred Mirza. Ibid., 4:20. For the administrative and political structure of the Georgian kingdoms conquered by Abbas, see Klaus Michael Röhrborn, *Provinzen und Zentralgewalt Persiens im 16. und 17. Jahrhundert* (Berlin, 1966), 4–5, 75–8.

[48] Della Valle's earlier (1626) statement adds: depending on him (i.e., on the Persian shah): "... nec amplius absoluto, sed tanquam Persarum Regi subdito, ab eo dependente gubernatur." Ms Modena γ.S.1.10, f 8b, 14. In 1615, Abbas appointed Bagrat as governor of Kartli. When he died in 1619, his son Simon followed him as governor. The situation was, however, very troubled, and both governors were rather unsuccessful in subduing Kartli. Simon turned to Abbas for help and was sent in 1620 with a counselor, Giorgi Saakadze, and a huge army back to his province. Saakadze had changed sides in an earlier war between Abbas and Kartli and was appreciated as an ally by Abbas. Now he again changed sides and led, together with Teimuraz, the Georgian troops fighting against the Persians in the battle of Martqopi, which the Persians lost. Teimuraz was proclaimed king of Kakheti and Kartli. Abbas sent a fresh, larger army, which defeated the Georgians in the battle of Marabda and reestablished Simon as the khan of Kartli. In 1625, Teimuraz and Saakadze returned for organizing a new insurrection. Saakadze became the de-facto ruler of Kartli, which displeased Teimuraz. As a result, a deep conflict evolved, and Teimuraz and Saakadze started fighting against each other rather than against the Safavids. Saakadze lost the battle despite his turning for help to the Ottomans, who beheaded him in 1629. Teimuraz ruled for the next six years over Kakheti and a part of Kartli, the remaining part being under Simon's rule until 1629 when Abbas died. Salia, *History of the Georgian Nation*, 291–3, 297–8, 300–301. See too, Della Valle, *Voyages de Pietro della Vallé*, 5:142–3.

[49] Della Valle summarized in this paragraph events that took place between 1613 and 1624; he did not always respect the order of the events. In late 1613, Teimuraz sent first his mother and elder son as hostages to Abbas upon the shah's demand and under the pressure of the Kakhetian nobles, and upon a second demand his younger son plus children of the nobles too. Thereafter, Abbas demanded that Teimuraz come to him in person, but Teimuraz refused to obey and tried to fight the Persian army. He lost the war and fled first to Kartli and then

Pietro della Valle's Latin Geography of Safavid Iran (1624–1628)

Christian piety, is now guarded as a hostage, but treated honorably in the city of Sciràz. But the youths have been inducted into Muhammedan rites, not, according to rumor, according to their own wishes. They have been turned – oh, hideous crime – into eunuchs, far from their grandmother's face, lest the hope of progeny nourish in them any thought of restoring their family's former state.[50] After Teimuraz was attacked unexpectedly, he and a few other Georgians fled into neighboring Christian territories also ruled by Georgian princes. The once fortunate region of Kacheti, destroyed and devastated, was subjected to the incursions of the Lexghi, the Georgians, and the Persians; a fertile land thus lies uncultivated.[51]

---

to Imereti. Salia, *History of the Georgian Nation*, 284. Moreover, Abbas's demand for sending Teimuraz's mother as a hostage not only reflected the then standard procedure of securing compliance of an enemy, but responded too to her role as leader of the anti-Safavid rebellion against the Safavid protégé Constantin from 1605. Assatiani and Bendianachvili, *Histoire de la Géorgie*, 185.

[50] The two children were castrated in 1620. In his letters to Schipano, Della Valle commented repeatedly on the shah's purpose for castrating the two boys; once, for instance, in 1618, although at that time, the two boys were not yet mutilated: "… ed i figliuoli, che erano piccoli, gli hanno fatti maomettani, e, se è vero quel che si dice, anche eunuchì, acciocchè non pensino più a successione di stati." Pietro della Valle, *Viaggi di Pietro della Valle Il Pellegrino Descritti da lui medesimo in Lettere Familiari all'Erudito suo Amico Mario Schipano Divisi in Tre Parti cioè: La Turchia, la Persia e l'India colla Vita e Ritratto dell'Autore*, ed. G. Gancia (Brighton, 1843), 1:663. The origin of Della Valle's premature report about the castration is his dependence upon hearsay, as he implied in this letter and confirmed in a letter written in 1622. See Della Valle, *Voyages de Pietro della Vallé*, 5:143. In this later letter, Della Valle reshaped the explanation about the castration into an act of *raison d'état*, of a kind of political generosity – in essence, in lieu of taking their lives and for protection against future suspicions. In contrast to Della Valle, Salia considers this deed to have been an act of vengeance committed in "an access of impotent rage" against Teimuraz for his continuous fight against Abbas and, in particular, for his role in the abortive Ottoman-Safavid war from 1618. Salia, *History of the Georgian Nation*, 291–2. This interpretation seems to be, however, not very likely since two years had passed between the two acts and no state of rage, however intense it may have been, could have lasted for two years. Della Valle's interpretation does not seem very likely either since Abbas did not so much act in order to prevent future events, but in order to suppress present insurrections, punish his adversaries, and further his immediate political aims.

[51] This phrase apparently refers at the same time to the war of 1613–14 and to the war of 1615–16. It was after the first war that Teimuraz and a few of his adherents fled to Kartli and then to Imereti. At best, this attack of Abbas can be dubbed "unsuspected" because the war in the Caucasus Mountains was part of the Ottoman-Safavid fight for supremacy, and in 1612 a peace treaty had been signed between the two sides after almost ten years of battles, skirmishes, invasions, and expulsions. The destruction and depopulation of Kakheti, however, took place only in the second war. The shah divided the province of Kakheti into two parts. The eastern part was now ruled by Peikar, the khan of Ganja, and the western part by Bagrat, khan of Kartli

Bordering this region and to Armenia, more to the east and somewhat north of Armenia, I believe, lies the region of Scervàn, near by the Caspian Sea, thought by some to be the ancient Atropatene. Its capital is the city of Sciumachi. Not far away from it there are two cities on the west coast of the Caspian Sea; I believe they belong to Albania. One of them is Bah Kuia, famous for its white, public oil-well. It is also called, as some prefer, by the Persian name Vahcuh, that is, the open mountain. Since the sea seems to enter here the interior of a very high mountain, despite the wall that surrounds the port, the image was formed of a mountain somehow lying open. The other city is Derbend. This name means in Persian something like the hasp of a door, although the Latins call it the Caspian, Caucasian or Iron Doors.[52] But the confusion among writers with regard to the position as well as the name of this city has created a certain lack of clarity; hence it seems not inappropriate to present here what I have discovered in the books of oriental authors. The Latins have thoroughly confused three names of the city, so that it is not easy to differentiate which cities the ancients named Porta<e> Ferrea<e>, Porta<e> Caspia<e>, and Porta<e> Caucasia<e>.[53] What we speak of as Derbend the Turks call in their language Demir-capi, influenced, I think, by the similarity of the word "door." This means undoubtedly Porta Ferrea, a fact that perhaps caused the confusion among our contemporaries. But the Arabs and the Persian geographers, without doubt more learned than the Turks, differentiate the one clearly from the other. The city the Persians call Derbend the Arabs call Bab elabvàb, that is, door of the doors. This is completely different from Porta Ferrea, which the Arabs call Bab elhadìd, and the Persians Der Ahanin. They situate it far from Derbènd, and indeed east of the Caspian Sea, namely, more than 26 degrees longitude and almost seven degrees latitude away, in the fourth climate. Derbend lies in the fifth climate, on the western shore of the Caspian Sea, as I have said. While Der Ahanin or Bab elhadid is said to be under the rule of the Chacqàn (i.e. the great king of the eastern Tartars), Derbend is subject to the Persians. Today, it is the outermost border of the Persians' dominion, near to the Caucasian mountains. Presently barbarian people, namely of Tartar origin, it is said,

---

(appointed to this position in 1615). Peikar brought Turcoman and Tatar nomads into his new dominion as a means to secure the area for the Safavids. Lezghians from Daghestan also moved into Kakheti and settled in a number of abandoned villages. See Salia, *History of the Georgian Nation*, 283–4, 290–91.

[52] Ms Modena γ.S.1.10, f 10a, 5.
[53] Ms Modena γ.S.1.10, f 10a, 13.

inhabit the areas which stretch from the Black Sea to the Caspian Sea. The designation as Tartars is given to them as infidels not inappropriately by the neighboring Christians, in particular the Georgians. Presumably because the Tartars were the first Muhammedans encountered by people in these parts, they call all who devote themselves to the perfidy of Muhammed Tatar, that is, Tartars.[54]

Be this as it may, the barbarians who inhabit this part of the Caucasus are more properly called Lexghi or Legzi; like boundary stones, they divide the Persian empire and the Georgians from the Circassians. I could not learn clearly enough whether most of them are Muhammedans or pagans, or whether some of their people may be Christians, if they are worthy of this name, for among the Georgians and the Circassians there are also Christians. I think, however, that it is better to assume that they are nearly atheists, and that few among them can be found who confess any sect without guile. What we know for sure is that they are robbers, infesting all boundaries in a hostile way. They continuously plague with attacks either the Georgians or the Circassians, and they enjoy stealing human beings more than anything else. Prisoners of all ages and both sexes they either return, for the ransom they seek, or sell for ransom to the Muhammedans in the city of Derbend and perhaps elsewhere. Some nobles of this people, adherents of the Muhammedan perfidy, have lived in the name of hospitality with King Abbas, and are held in great respect at the Persian court. When I was a guest of the king I have often seen them during pleasant banquets, and have spoken with them in polite company.

---

[54] Della Valle's speculation has no substance. The Tatars were not the first Muslims in the Caucasus Mountains. They only came there during the fifteenth century. The European name Tartar for the Tatars is a corruption and a misled derivation from Tartaros, the ancient netherworld, leading to the identification of the Tatars in the Middle Ages with Satan and his offspring. We chose to translate Della Valle's "perfidia" as "perfidy" because there is no single word rendering the complex meaning ascribed to Muhammad and Islam in the early modern period. Muhammad was then considered in Catholic and Protestant Europe as an impostor, liar, and seducer. Islam was seen as a falsehood, a treachery, and a superstition. Muslims were denounced as dishonest, scheming, thieving infidels.

Beyond the city of Vacuh, at the western end of the southern shore of the Caspian Sea, lies the region of Ghilàn.[55] This names means mud.[56] The earth here is namely very muddy and humid and hence, as I believe, abundant in snakes, although they are not dangerous. The soil is also very fertile in the production of silk thread and the fruits of the earth, and is the only region in all of Agiama to grow olives. But the air is rather unhealthy. The sea here is also rich in fish; the best salmon is exported to Sphahanum and other areas. As I have said, Ghilàn is bounded on the north by the Caspian Sea, and has Scervàn as its neighbor to the west, and Adherbaigiàn to the south. Between Ghilàn and Adherbaigiàn runs a long range of mountains, the Taurus, a very strong bulwark against hostile invasion from this side. Finally, to the east of Ghilàn lies Mazanderàn, a region worthy of being known, but thus far little known to us.[57] Since I have traversed it myself, I have decided to describe Mazanderàn very carefully, hoping that my prolixity will not vex the honored reader.

I know not the meaning of Mazanderàn, for nothing about it can be found in the dictionaries of the Persians, other than that the word is plural in form (as are most Persian names for cities and regions), and that the name is proper to this region.[58] It lies exactly in the middle of the southern coast of the Caspian Sea, though in my opinion it stretches a bit more to the east. To the east it borders on Esteràbad, to the west on Ghilàn, to the north on the Caspian Sea, and to the south on Araq. Mazanderàn is securely divided from Araq by the same range of mountains [the Taurus] that runs between Ghilàn and

---

[55] "Supra civitatem Vah-cuh …"; "Supra" is taken here to mean "southern," following Pliny 2, 73, 75, 183: "Simili modo tradunt in Syene oppido, quod est supra Alexandriam…."

[56] This invented etymology is based upon taking the word as a plural form of *gil*, which indeed means "mud." According to Rabino di Borgomale (see note 7), the name of the region is derived from the Avestan word "Varena," which designates a region north of mount Elburz; *Les Provinces Caspiennes*, 17.

[57] i.e. della Valle's compatriots in Catholic Europe.

[58] According to Rabino di Borgomale, Mazandaran also comes from an Avestan name of a region bordering Varena. The form of Mazandaran and Gilan does not represent a plural, as Della Valle believed on the basis of modern Persian, but comes – according to Rabino di Borgomale – from the adjectives "Varenya" and "Mazainya." The two expressions indicated that these regions were inhabited by bad spirits. *Les Provinces Caspiennes*, 17.

Adherbaigiàn. These very high mountains, everywhere almost inaccessible,[59] provide for the traveler coming from Aràq only one entrance, through a narrow valley that extends for a distance of about two days' journey over a fairly smooth and easily defensible track between steep slopes. About half way, where the track rises toward more humid peaks, is the city of Firuz-cuh, that is, Victorious Mountain. This city is thought to mark the border between Mazanderàn and Aràq. It is worth mentioning here that the mountains, whose slopes stretch north into Mazanderàn, are entirely wooded, being planted with slender trees; because of the blossoming herbs they also have a green hue, strongly resembling Italy's Appenines at their most beautiful. But to the south, towards Aràq, the slopes are arid, like the whole region; without water, trees, or herbs, they have an inhospitable aspect. After Firuz-cuh the track for travelers to Araq divides in two; one road runs northwest, or rather west, under plane-trees without number, notably tall, giving shade, through the city of Taheràn, and on to Qazvinum. The other runs directly south to Kascianum, across the mountain called Siah-cuh, that is, Black Mountain. Before reaching the track into the mountains one comes to a large, marshy plain, fed by streams from all sides, with a particularly large stream in the middle, whose water is bitter, and flows under a bridge. Since it was in former times very difficult to traverse this area – men and animals dared not pass, due to the depth and viscosity of the mud – King Abbàs, with his customary care for the public good, has caused the track to be paved with broad stones, making a road of some five miles that looks very straight to the eye.

On the track leading into the Siah-cuh mountains one encounters another plain, having a whitish, salty surface that is very dry in summer. Because the salt reflects the sun's rays, this plain is nowadays almost impenetrable due to the extreme heat. Hence travelers usually take another route. This track is covered in winter by salty water, sometimes as high as the bellies of the animals, but it is easily passable nonetheless: not only is there no complaint due to the simmering heat, but the earth below the water, forming the track, is firm enough for horses and pedestrians to proceed without difficulty. To make the track recognizable, lest wayfarers stray into areas having deep and viscous mud, the way is marked by black stones that are set erect, like pillars, and in a straight line, so that the traveler can see from one to the next.[60] This

---

[59] We follow the manuscript, which has "inaccessus," rather than "inascensus," as the edition. See Della Valle, *De recentiori imperio Persarum subiectis regionibus*, 292.

[60] Della Valle wrote literally: "(the stones) … look at each other from afar." See also Della Valle, *Voyages de Pietro della Vallé*, 3:177. This road that connected Abbasabad Siahkuh with

place is called in Persian Nemek-zàr, that is, "the place of the salt," or "the salt-works." Here people coming from Araq find two tracks: one goes north through Siah-cuh and through the narrow valley I mentioned, to Mazanderàn; the other goes east to Chorasàn. This track crosses the Taurus Mountains, which not only separate Araq from Mazanderàn, but also continue to the east, separating Araq from Chorasàn.

Now let us turn to Mazanderàn, from which we have briefly turned away, although not without reason or sense. The soil here is very much like that of Ghilàn, humid and muddy, so much so that there are places where in winter time camels sink in up to their bellies. I once followed this track from sunrise to sunset, but during the whole day, because of the obstacles the camels had to endure, I could not pass more than two *ferseng* (that is, Persian *parasangs*, which correspond to Spanish miles). Still, the soil is fertile, rich in all kinds of plants and trees; I have seen there chicory, borage, and other excellent herbs known in our climes, which I have not found anywhere else in all of Agiamia. The supply of fruit is huge; quinces and lemons, especially beautiful, are brought for sale even to Sphahanum. Wild vines, mostly in the woods, also offer grapes to the traveler. The growing of wheat is less successful here, I believe because of the humidity. This is why the cities and villages that are very numerous here are especially populous along the track that leads to Araq; many natives have been induced by the king to come down from the mountains and settle along the track, for the greater convenience of travelers[61].[62]

I should add that in the villages almost no bread is made from wheat, rather it is made from rice; rice aplenty is available, due to the humidity. In the larger cities (these are few) there is some bread made from wheat, but it is consumed more by strangers than by natives. The frugality of these people[63] I cannot pass over in silence. They mainly eat fish, of which there are many sorts, and plain rice, boiled in water and flavored with vinegar or other sour juices. They eat no meat, almost no bread, and no food to which fat has been added; this last they consider unhealthy, although, having spent some time there myself, my experience was different. In summer the air is

---

Garmsar was built between 1600 and 1610. See Wolfram Kleiss, "Die Karawanenwege in Iran aus frühislamischer Zeit," *Studia Irania* 5 (1987): 142.

[61] We follow here the manuscript that has "peregrinantium," not the edition that has "commoditatem." See Della Valle, *De recentiori imperio Persarum subiectis regionibus*, 293.

[62] See Della Valle, *Voyages de Pietro della Vallé*, 3:209.

[63] The manuscript has "gentium" ("de earum gentium sobrietate"), the edition "gente." See Della Valle, *De recentiori imperio Persarum subiectis regionibus*, 293.

rather unhealthy. This comes from the strong evaporations of the Caspian Sea, I believe, which rise upward and are blown across the regions by winds, until they are stopped by that continuous chain of mountains I have so often mentioned; since these vapors cannot be scattered elsewhere, through the air, they undoubtedly bring about considerable corruption. Whether it be for this reason, or because of their modest diet, I know not, but the faces of the natives are rarely of a ruddy complexion, mostly ashen or at least colorless. Even so the women are very beautiful, because of their white skin, and the charm of their black eyes and black hair. Although they mainly live in villages, they are very sociable and civilized. Because all people of both sexes are very obliging, and welcome strangers, I never had to pay for anything in the entire region. As soon as night fell, we were hospitably received in some noble place in the next village or town to which we came. Thanks to my wife, all the men and most of the wives of the notable men at once took an interest in how we fared. They brought us not a few gifts which we subsequently reciprocated, giving from among the things we carried with us presents that were pleasant to them, my wife to the women, and I to the men. We passed with them many a gay night, with splendid dinners, long speeches after dinner and many merry songs, sung by girls or (as the evening progressed) sung in chorus. Only at sunrise did we leave behind our many friends, content with the comparable gifts we had given them more for honor's sake than for the sake of value. We made it a point to follow this rule, so as to part as people who, if ever returning along the same route, would be welcome in the houses of our very same hosts. They would consider the rules of hospitality violated if it were done otherwise. This received and laudable custom is preserved as holy and inviolable throughout the empire of the Persians.[64]

Mazanderàn's capital is presently Ferhabàd, a name meaning *laetitia colonia*. King Abbas began[65] to build it a few years ago, but it is not yet finished. It is less than two miles away from the Caspian Sea, situated on both banks of a medium-sized river spanned by a well-built bridge. This river is called by the inhabitants Tegginé-rud (with a three-syllable pronunciation only, the sound of which cannot be expressed easily by our letters), a name that means something like rapid river.[66] It originates from various sources in the mountains

---

[64] Compare to Della Valle, *Voyages de Pietro della Vallé*, 3:213.

[65] We follow here the manuscript, which has "coepta," while the edition has "capta." See Della Valle, *De recentiori imperio Persarum subiectis regionibus*, 293.

[66] According to his remark in the original letter from Farahabad and Qazvin, written at the beginning of May 1618 and finished July 25, 1618, Della Valle meant to say that he could not

separating Araq from Mazandaràn; then it runs through deep rounded valleys, also through ponds and even fields of rice. That is why its water is now rather unhealthy. Finally, it descends a short slope to the sea. From the Caspian the river is navigable to a small city called Sarù or Sarì, that is, saffron-colored, with small boats, mostly carved out from a single tree trunk, and no doubt also with flat river-barges capable of transporting large cargo.[67] This city is four *ferseng* from Ferhabad, not far from the mountains, on the road that goes to Araq. Between it and Ferhabad lies a wide plain, cultivated mainly by Georgians; it was once forested, but those moving in cut down the trees. Settlements in this region are almost all villages. Even the capital, Ferhabàd, is not walled, as is true for almost all the other cities of the Persians.[68] But it is large enough to have several broad, straight avenues running miles from one side of town to the other; the avenues cross over canals that carry away the water and dry out the mud. Because of the excessive humidity, the mud is very deep, and causes great inconveniences. This was why, even when I was there, they had begun to pave many of the streets with stone.

In my time there Mazenderàn was so populous that the inhabitants of the cities were numbered not in persons but in families: among people brought here from elsewhere are counted first those of the Muhammedans having been brought there from the region of Scervàn, 25,000 families; then 12,000 Georgian families. They were Christians originally, but not having righteous shepherds to care for their souls, very many converted daily to the perfidy of Muhammed, partly due to poverty, partly due to ambition. Next 40,000 Armenian families, of the same kind of fidelity towards Christ; and 7,000 Jewish families, brought from Georgia where they originated. These numbers do not include natives of Mazanderàn and Ghilàn, or the courtiers and

---

transliterate "Tejne" easily into Italian. The present-day spelling of the river's name is "Tajan," but it has no connection whatsoever with "fast, quick" or similar words.

[67] Compare to Della Valle, *De recentiori imperio Persarum subiectis regionibus*, 234–5.

[68] Della Valle claimed in his letters to Schipano that all towns in Persia were without walls. See ibid., 4:178. There, the claim is part of a statement about Tabriz, however, where Della Valle had never been; thus, he did not know by his own experience whether or not Tabriz was surrounded by a wall. It is highly likely that he has taken this idea of wall-free Persian towns from one of the European books he had read at home or while traveling. Moreover, the claim discussed here does not hold true for all or most Persian towns. One example of a walled town was Derbend. Shah Abbas even built new walls there in the 1620s. See, for instance, Paolo Cuneo, "Le Mura di Derbent" *Revista degli Studi Orientali* 59 (1985): 65–6, illustrations 2, 3. Other examples include the royal cities of Qazwin and Isfahan, both of which had rather impressive town walls. See, for instance, Savory, *Iran under the Safavids*, 176.

soldiers who come yearly with the king, or the countless others who meet here to carry on trade or other kinds of business.[69]

The houses – or better, huts – are mostly made from the earth, very rough, and densely covered by thin reeds bound together.[70] These reeds are in their experience suitable for keeping out the rain, which falls in winter not very heavily, but very often. There are many houses the walls of which are also made from reed. That is why they are at the mercy of fires, to which whole parts of the town fall victim.[71] Although I do not believe that things will stay this way in the future, it is no wonder that such a thing happens in young cities. Even when I was there, the grandees were having remarkable houses built, so it is likely that others too will be built more firmly. I have seen more than forty ovens constantly busy making bricks. The king made such an effort to finish the city quickly that the highest satrap of the Mazanderàn region – Mirza Taqì, whom they call vizier (the king himself ordered him to see to my needs) – was able to show me a number of spacious houses, already inhabited; these he had caused to be built himself, from the foundations to the roof, in a space of fifteen days.[72] The palace of the king, which had already been built on the west bank of the river, was daily enlarged. On the east bank, where the river channel is very narrow, trees were planted in straight rows, houses had

---

[69] See Della Valle, *Voyages de Pietro della Vallé*, 4:271, where Della Valle gives the same numbers as learned from an Armenian from Farahabada, except for those of the Georgians and the Armenians. In this letter, he does not mention Armenians among the inhabitants of Farahabada at all and ascribes the number of 40,000 to the Georgians.

[70] In Latin, Della Valle describes the material used for the houses as made from "terra" and "arundum," while in his letters to Schipano he wrote that it consisted of mud and straw, a detail he mentions both in Italian and in Persian: "I muri delle case in Ferhabad gli fanno di una materia usata assai in questa parti, che conforme la chiamano *Cah-ghil, cioè Terra e paglia*, non è altro che terra arenosa, impastatata a modo di calce con un poco di paglia trita mescolata, la quale tuttavia senza pietre, nè altri sassi, così da sè fa buonissima presa." Della Valle, *Viaggi di Pietro della Vallé*, 1:601–2. For the Latin text, see Della Valle, *De recentiori imperio Persarum subiectis regionibus*, 294 (our emphasis). Since the Persian "kah-gil" indeed means "straw-mud," Della Valle's explanation to Schipano is preferable to his choice of words in the geographical text. See F. Steingass, *Comprehensive Persian-English Dictionary* (New Delhi, 1996), 1066, column 2.

[71] See Della Valle, *Voyages de Pietro della Vallé*, 3:233.

[72] Compare to Della Valle, *Voyages de Pietro della Vallé*, 3:233. From 1599, Mazanderan was a crown domain land and thus ruled by a vizier installed by the court. Provinces that were not crown domain lands were ruled by military commanders, the *umara'*. In these provinces, there was a vizier to administer taxes and finance; if appointed by the court, the viziers also supervised the *umara'* to prevent excessive exploitation of the population, and administered justice. See Röhrborn, *Provinzen und Zentralgewalt Persiens*, 94–131.

beautiful gardens and mirrors, and secluded spots were created, suitable for hunting or recreation.[73]

East of Ferhabad, about a mile away, there is another river of the same size called Cinàn or Cinòn. After crossing it and traversing a spacious and fertile plain, one can see the facade of another city, Escrèf; meaning the very noble.[74] This city lies six *ferseng* or Spanish miles east from Ferhabàd, and two miles from the Caspian Sea. It is the newest of all the cities that the same king began to build only a short time ago, on a very pleasant site richly endowed with water, and with woods abounding in all kinds of game. Here the plain meets mountains that are not as high. King Abbas chose this place for himself as a special, secluded, and solitary site of pleasure for diverting his mind. That is why he chose to found here a large city, built in the best manner, with a mixture of native people and immigrants. It has streets marked in order and sequence, markets, temples, bath houses, and other buildings private as well as public for receiving guests. In the year of the Lord 1618, when I was there myself, houses, unfinished and not yet very high, but elegant nonetheless, were being built for the king and the royal ladies, as well as graceful gardens; these things were shown to me by the king's command. Other houses were being erected for the nobles and the king's ministers, albeit only a few, but not at all insignificant.

In the fertile plain between Escref and Ferhabàd are many villages, inhabited partly by Mazanderanians and partly by Georgians, and also many Turcomans.[75] This people are of Scythian origin as the Turks and the Tartars are. In my judgment, they and the Turks continue to use the same language; these are the people who have traversed also very many territories of Asia together with other peoples emigrating from Scythia, devastating the world repeatedly with their raids. As a result, many of them are scattered over the entire empire of the Persians. Many can also be found in the deserts of Arabia and Mesopotamia. Many may be met with too in other territories subjugated by the empire of the Turks, in particular in that part of Asia Minor which they

---

[73] Adorning the interior or exterior of houses, pillars, and other architectural items with mirrors or mirror-tiles was an important element of the Safavid decorative arts.

[74] The manuscript has the correct spelling "Escrèf," while the edition has "Eseref." See Ms Modena γ.S.1.10, f 18a, 13.

[75] See Ms Modena γ.S.1.10, f 18b, 12.

call today commonly Caramania; they wander with their tents from place to place, like the Arabs called Scenitae.[76]

The Turcomans who live, as I have said, in the plains of Mazanderàn have the following custom: after setting up cross-beams, they build their houses very high, and well covered with roofs, but in order to have air in the summer time they are not encircled by covering walls, save for curtains made from the lightest reeds. Like netting, these curtains can easily be raised up or taken away as appropriate, either to open a line of sight for the eye or to allow cooling air to enter. The curtains can also be let down, either at one side only (to keep out, as needed, the sun, or excessive wind), or around the entire house. Those on the interior cannot be seen from the outside through the curtains, but they can see everything that happens outside. For climbing up to these tall houses there are no stairs, only a slightly inclined beam from the ground to the entrance to the sitting room, with indentations scooped out to support the feet. This is done, I believe, either because this is all that is needed, or for greater safety. For these houses are like plains in unprotected areas; if access were easy, they would be exposed at night to savage beasts and evil men.

Yet they also have other houses, more firmly built and made from earth. These houses they mainly use during the winter, for preserving the household furniture as well as animals rather than human beings. Almost all Mazanderanian villagers are accustomed to living in towns and villages in winter time, but move with their flocks in summer, over the peaks, to places where the heat is less and where there is more water and plants. They carry with them tall black tents, according to the custom of the Arabs, woven by the wives from goat-wool, and sufficient for keeping out harsh weather.

Before turning to something else, I want to finish this long account of Mazanderàn with one more point. Mazanderàn, stretching into the interior of the kingdom, and well protected from all sides by the sea and the mountains, which give access to other regions only by passes that are few, narrow, and easily defensible, is considered by King Abbàs to be the safest part of the entire empire. This is why his treasury and some other precious items are held in safe-keeping here. He is convinced, not without reason, that if should happen one day that the inexorable and terrible armies of the Turks, having by some accident defeated all the forces of the Persians, should stream

---

[76] The Skenai were, according to Strabo, a tribe in Mesopotamia. The singular of "Skenai" is "Skenites," from which Della Valle's Latin form "Scenitarum" is derived.

unobstructed through all other regions (which would not be difficult), this one part of Persia, namely Mazanderàn, will be easy to defend.[77]

After Mazanderàn comes the region of Esteràbad, also on the south shore of the Caspian Sea, but towards the east. What else could be the meaning of this name but – because of the abundance of such animals – a "settlement of mules." But I could not determine this with certainty. To the east it is bordered by Chorasàn, and by certain vast districts that lie between the empire of the Persians and the Tartar Uzbags. In the west it is bordered by Mazanderàn; in the north by the Caspian Sea; and in the south by Araq, with the mountains I have so often mentioned running between the two regions. As is the custom in most provinces of Asia, the royal city has received the same name as the region. The soil supports a rich culture of silk, like that of Mazanderàn, I believe. For the rest I have little knowledge, nor have I heard of other cities worth mentioning.

Chorasan could mean "water-mills" in Persian, or "mutes" in Arabic.[78] This is undoubtedly the most fertile region of the entire Persian empire, filled with many excellent and extraordinary cities, foremost among which are Herì, the seat of a governor; Nisciabùr, with its noble turquoise mine; and Mescèd (to give its name in our letters as best as can be done), nowadays known as the place of martyrs, but in ancient times called Senabad. There is the famous, richly built tomb of the eighth successor of Muhammed, because it was here that he was poisoned by the hostile sect of Sonnites. This was Abù l'Hasàn Alì, Erridhà or Rizà (that is, the contented, a common surname), descended from Alì and Fatima, Muhammed's daughter. The Sciàite sect among the Muhammedans of Persia reveres him as a martyr and also calls him *imam*, that is, pontiff, one of twelve they count in succession at the head of their sect. The last imam, hidden away by God, as they believe, still lives, invisible, and is the pontiff of this time until the end of the world. Then he will reappear to establish perfect justice in a world oppressed by injustice. He will convert all peoples into the one community of God, after a certain impious tyrant, called by Muhammedans Deggiàl (that is, the liar) and by us the Antichrist, has been slain by Jesus Christ.[79] This is what

---

[77] See Della Valle, *Voyages de Pietro della Vallé*, 3:222.

[78] Both etymologies are wrong. Della Valle suggests that the region's name Khurâsân is derived either from "khar-âs" (Persian: donkey capstan) or from one of the two plural forms of "akhras" (Arabic: mute, dumb), i.e. "khursân" or "khurs."

[79] The word we translate as "one community of God" is "ovile," i.e. "sheep-fold." Calling the believers "sheep" or "flock" is common in the Catholic Church, while it is less widespread among the various Protestant denominations.

they tell. At Satan's perfidious suggestion, they ascribe to their false pontiff miracles that belong to the Lord, our Redeemer. Between the Sonnites and the Sciàites there is a great and very profound difference in belief regarding this last pontiff, and also the succession of the other, preceding pontiffs; this divides the Persians and the Turks into groups that hate each other irreconcilably, and plague each other with continuous wars. One of these pseudo-pontiffs, as I would say, the eighth in succession according to the Sciàites, was the aforementioned Rizà, to whose tomb in Mescèd many believers flock to venerate it, even from the most remote areas.

To the east and especially the north Chorasàn has as its neighbor, I believe, the Uzbags and some other Tartar tribes, each of which has its own name. Because of the confusion among contemporary authors it is customary to ascribe the name of Tartars to many peoples – to Bactrians and Sogdians as well as to Asian and European Scythians and many others in their vicinity – but it is properly ascribed only to a single tribe of Scythians in the far east of Asia, the Tatars. The others each have their own names, as I have said.

To return to the course of our discussion, Chorasàn adjoins Araq in the west, and in the south Kirmàn and other provinces, if I am not mistaken. I dare not speak of the regions of Sistàn, Zabelistàn, and Sigistàn, since I do not even know for certain if they are adjacent to Chorasàn, or members of Chorasàn, contained partly or completely within it, or whether these regions are now subject to the empire of the Persians.[80] We do have to mention the city of Candahàr and its region, which King Abbàs took by force the year before last from the hands of the Great Mogul, adding it to the Persian empire in a deed of lasting fame. I am sure that it borders on Chorasàn, and lies beyond the city of Herì, but I dare not say with certainty where it is, though I think it likely that it lies to the northeast.[81] From the historical accounts of the Persians I have learned that Candahàr is the capital of the region of Zabelistàn, which, as some of our geographers claim, was called Paropamissum in antiquity.[82]

The region of Kirmàn, retaining until today the name it was given in antiquity, is the fertile Caramania of the ancients. On the east and south I believe it borders the territories of the region of Candahàr, lying between the

---

[80] Sistan and Sigistan designate the same region.
[81] Qandahar lies southeast from Herat.
[82] One of the contemporary geographical works Della Valle used is the *Epitome Geographiae* of Philippus Ferrarius. See note 18.

Persian Empire and the Indus River; one of these may be Sistàn. To the west, it adjoins the region called Persia, to the north Choràsan and part of Araq, if I am not mistaken. In the south, it is next to the region of Macràn, and to that part of the ancient Caramania that ran as far as the end of the Red Sea, and that has had until our time its own prince, in no way subject to Persia. In recent years, while we followed the armies of King Abbàs, renowned for his successes against the Turks who had invaded Agiamia, the brother of the adolescent prince of Macran, a traitor to his homeland, became the first of his people to flee to Persia, to the city of Qazvin. There he met King Abbàs. Led by the desire to become ruler with the help of the Persians, he promised to give his loyalty to the king, and to subdue the entire region of Macran, if given troops.[83] Nonetheless his offer was in vain, at least while I remained at the Persian court. Neither did Persia help him on such an expedition, nor did he make any progress on his own; like an exile and renegade, hating himself, he lived among the Persians as a guest of King Abbàs, almost begging for his living. But after Hormùz had been occupied by the Persians, in May 1622, the region of Macràn and its prince obeyed the king as Persians do, as had never happened previously.[84] I know not if the prince who ruled Macràn had perhaps died, or if the brother who had gone over to the king invaded Macràn, or if the two brothers (presuming both are alive) may have resumed their friendship, with the one who rules now persuaded either by fear of the king (ruling in Hormùz) or by reasons of commercial utility. One common rumor has it that many groups of merchants from an infidel country in India have arrived by ship in Guadel (because of the war one cannot sail as formerly to Hormùz, since Portuguese ships bar the way); having purchased camels for a high price in Guadèl, in the dominions of the prince of Macran, they are said to have traversed the desert of the Ichthyophages, and passed through fertile Caramania, until they came safely to Sphahan, and dispersed from there throughout Persia.

In the region of Kirmàn the ancient pagan worship of the Persian Magi survives until the present day. The people use an ancient language, and differ from others in their appearance, in particular by the color of their dress, which resembles the color of cooked flesh. They cultivate beards and the hair of the head, live their rites, and zealously devote themselves to tending the

---

[83] Compare to Della Valle, *Voyages de Pietro della Vallé*, 4:25.

[84] This and the following four phrases form in the Latin text one single sentence. The subordination of its individual parts under each other is not always clear. Other interpretations than the one given here are possible.

fire, diligently and continuously maintaining it. They are truly the indigenous people among the Persians. Many of them live in the city of Yezd, in the region of Araq, as I believe, between Kirmàn and Sphahàn. To Sphahan not a few of the ancient Persians, called by the Muhammedans Gabri (something like "not circumcised" or "indigenous"), have been brought from Kirmàn and Yezd by King Abbàs.[85] They inhabit one of the four cities that make up the tetrapolis of Sphahan, called Gabrabad, that is, "the settlement of the indigenous." They have built it themselves, as far as the south bank of the Zenderùd (or living river, as it would be in Latin), and as far east as the avenue called Ceharbàgh, meaning "four gardens."[86] This is the avenue that divides Gabrabad from Ciolfa, the city of the Armenians, which also lies on the south bank of the river. North of the river Ceharbagh divides the larger city properly called Sphahan, across the river from Gabrabad, from the recently founded settlement of people from Tebriz, which was at first called Tebrizabàd. Presently, however, the colonists call it after the king's name, Abbasabad, or city of Abbas.

Kirmàn is adjoined by another maritime region, either to the south, or as the Persians say, to the southwest, since it inclines slightly more to the west. This region is called Moghistan, that is, palm-forest,[87] a name it got from its palm trees. There are almost no cities and only a few towns, hardly fortified. Nonetheless there are very many dwellings dispersed among the palm forests, made from wood and palm leaves, not from any other material. This region is either what the ancients called the desert of Caramania, or one of its parts. It is bordered by Macràn in the east, to the west along the coast by the region of Persia, and to the north by Kirmàn, with a chain of mountains dividing Moghistan from Kirmàn. In the south, along the Persian Gulf, we find ports – because of the lack of safety, we might better call them (with Maronian) anchoring places for ships. Among these the best known are Giask, Kuhestèk, Hibrahimi, Duser, and Kombrù, which the Persians have call Abbasì since

---

[85] In modern Persian, *Gabri* can be an adjective or a noun derived from *gabr*. The word used to signify "an ancient Persian, one of the Magi of the sect of Zoroaster, a priest of the worshippers of fire; a pagan, infidel": Steingass, *Comprehensive Persian-English Dictionary*, 1075, column 1; or "Zarathustrier; Zarathustrismus; Gabridialekt; zarathustrisch," according to Heinrich F.J. Junker and Bozorg Alavi, *Wörterbuch Persisch-Deutsch* (Leipzig, 1965), 623, column 1.

[86] The correct name of the river is Zayandah-rud, but in colloquial Persian it is called Zenderud. The name "Caharbagh" also alludes to the theoretical concept of Iranian gardening art and its mystical aspects.

[87] Later, Della Valle chose a different spelling of the word: Moghostan.

they took it from the Portuguese a few years ago, under King Abbas.[88] Straight across from this place, two or three miles away, lies the island of Hormùz; this is, however, the name of the city there, for the island is properly called Girùn.[89] The island is of small circumference and suffers under an unbelievably great heat, which is more unbearable than anywhere else on earth. The whole island is so infertile that one finds no herbs or water, nor anything else at all except salt, the substance of its soil. Nevertheless, it was formerly a very flourishing city, adorned with royal dignity (for much can be accomplished by the accursed hunger for gold), as a famous fortress of the Portuguese and

---

[88] Della Valle overstates the case. Kombru, i.e., Gamerun, was a small fishermen's village. It was turned into a port only during the reign of Abbas. Moreover, Della Valle is overtly partisan ascribing to the Portuguese the right of occupying territories wherever they go while denying the same right to the Safavids or the English. Della Valle's partisanship was religiously based.

[89] This information Della Valle may have taken from al-Jurjani, who called Hormuz the capital of Jarun, put it into the third climate, and ascribed the following geographical coordinates to it: longitude 45° [sic, presumably a scribal error for 85°] 0', latitude 30°30'. Ms Biblioteca Apostolica Vaticano, Città del Vaticano, Vat. P 66, ff 14a and 18a. The same values are given in one set of copies of al-Khazini's geographical table from the twelfth century. David King, *World-Maps for Finding the Direction and Distances to Mecca: Innovation and Tradition in Islamic Science*, vol. 36 of *Islamic Philosophy, Theology and Science: Texts and Studies*, ed. H. Daiber and D. Pingree (Leiden, Boston, and Cologne, 1999), 578; King remarks that the latitude value "probably results from a copyist's error for 32°; 30°." The other set of copies gives for the latitude 30°50'. Ibid., 578. Abu l-Fida' called the island Zarun. He gave the following coordinates for Hormuz, "according to al-Biruni's Qanun: 95° 32°30'; according to a variant [of the Qanun]: 95° 30°33'; according to Ibn Sa'id 94° 28°23'; according to the anonymous Kitab al-atwal: 92° 25°." Abu l-Fida', *Géographie d'Aboulféda*, ed. M. Reinaud, Mac Guckin de Slane (Beirut, 1840), 338–9. The many sources surveyed in King, *World-Maps*, 471, 483, 502, 508, 511, 513, 557, 578, have 84°; 85°; 90°; 92° for the town's longitude and 25°; 25°30'; 26°; 30°30'; 30° 50'; 32°; 32°30'; 35°30'; 36° for the latitude. King called 36° an error for 26° as well as 30°30' an error for 32°30', but did not comment on 35° 30'. Ibid., 471, 502, 509, 578. The differences in longitude result most likely from the usage of different prime meridians. The differences in latitude suggest that different towns were meant. In addition to the island, two towns called Hormuz were known on the Iranian mainland. One of them was at the coast of the Persian Gulf, near to the island of Hormuz. The other one, also called Dih-i Guz, was situated northeast from Jiruft (longitude 83° latitude 30°10' (b) or 31°45' (a) in al-Khazini's table). See W.C. Brice, *A Historical Atlas of Islam*, (Leiden, 1981), 16; King, *World-Maps*, 471. Thus, the second Hormuz on the main land comes close to the values given by al-Khazini and repeated by al-Jurjani, who mistook it, however, for the town on the island. The island's name was known in a truncated form to European mapmakers several decades before Della Valle as "Geru." This name can be found on maps of the Ottoman Empire published by Abraham Ortelius in 1575 and 1580 and by Henricus Hondius in 1613. See Khaled Al Ankary, *La Péninsule Arabique dans les cartes européennes anciennes: fin XV-début XIX siècle* (Paris, 2001), 138–40, 165–7.

the richest trading place in the entire world.[90] Recently, however, as I have said already, the territory has been occupied by the Persians. Its king, who not only paid tribute for long years to the Portuguese, but was subjugated by them, has been brought as prisoner to Persia. The city has been almost completely destroyed, and emptied of inhabitants. Nothing remains but the fortress. Strong currents of war have been set in motion, by the Portuguese to regain Hormùz, and by the Persians to preserve it. May God grant success to our side![91]

In addition to Hormùz, two other islands lie off the coast of Moghostàn. But Larèk is very small and nowadays deserted, though it may once have been otherwise; it is quite uncultivated, with forests, and wild goats. It is in the middle of the Gulf, almost equally distant from Arabia and Persia.[92] The other and larger island, though narrow, is two or three days' journey in length, and is full of villages and rich in fruits and vegetables. Along its entire length the island is close to the coast of Persia. Its common name is Kesem. It has a promontory from which one can look towards Hormuz, where the fortress – built by the Portuguese with so much labor, to secure a supply of water for the city of Hormùz – was conquered by the Persians after a long siege, prior to their destruction of the city.

---

[90] Again, Della Valle overstates the case, expressing his personal dismay over the loss of the island to the Safavids. The remark between parentheses is an indirect quotation of Virgil, 3:57. Why Della Valle added it here remains unclear.

[91] Della Valle sided in this conflict unwaveringly with the Portuguese, mostly because of the shared faith and creed. This, at least, is what he implied in his letters to Schipano.

[92] This is an imprecise claim. Della Valle may have taken it from a European map of Asia or the Arabian Peninsula, since in four maps we have seen (three maps of the Arabian Pensinula, one by Nicolas Sanson printed in 1654, the second by Jan Jansson printed in 1658, the third by Willem Janszoon Blaeu printed in 1662, and a map of Asia (?) by Frederick De Wit published in c. 1670), there is an island situated either between the island of Hormuz and the northern tip of the Arabian Peninsula or southwest from Hormuz. The name of this island is spelled differently: Lorera (Sanson), Lareque (Jansson, Blaeu), or Lenreca (?) (De Wit). This suggests that there was an earlier map on which all these cartographers depended, directly or through intermediaries. Given the spelling of Jansson and Blaeu, this ancestor probably was a Portuguese map. See King, *World-Maps*, 216 and Al Ankary, *La Péninsule Arabique*, 197, 202, 204. Della Valle had seen several European maps of Iran and other parts of the world as he wrote in his letters to Schipano. See Della Valle, *Voyages de Pietro della Vallé*, 6:311. He may also have taken this idea from a sea chart. In his letters to Schipano, he reported about a chart that the captain of the English ship bringing him to Surat had followed from the Straight of Hormuz. In the same letter, he also made clear that he had seen Portuguese sea charts of the Indian Ocean. See ibid. 267, 269.

Another larger island called Bahrein, best known for pearl-diving, formerly obeyed the king of Hormuz, as did the surrounding mainland, but it too is now under Persian rule. It is, however, far from the shores of Moghostàn, and lies in the interior Gulf, close to Arabia. There are other small islands dispersed throughout the Gulf, close to Moghostàn and Persia, either deserted or sparsely inhabited, because of the war, and most of them are also subject to Persia. As for the inhabitants of this region, the poorer men of Moghostàn go naked, barely covering their genitals with a narrow piece of cloth. The rich wear a thin shirt, reaching only to the thighs, or other forms of short clothing, because of the extreme heat. The women wear a tight and very thin chemise reaching to the navel, as is the custom among certain people in India. This chemise is dark blue or mostly black, and covers the arms only half way. Over it and on their heads, they wear another thin garment when they go out. From the navel to their feet they wrap themselves two or three times in a veil which is as long as it is wide, reaching to the ankles, and made either from silk or from a mixture of silk and cotton. Otherwise nude, they wear on their feet sandals made from palm leaves, as the men do. In addition to their gilded bracelets and necklaces, they adorn their nostrils not with small rings, as Arab and Persian women do, but with a gilded disk applied to the right nostril. The disk is either long and narrow, pointing upwards from the nostril, or small and rectangular, having the figure of a rhombus, with two obtuse and two acute angles, one of the pointing upwards. The disks differ according to the gems attached to them. This form of adornment surely comes from somewhere else, far away. The people of Moghostàn are brownish in color, due to the fact that the sun here is too close to the vertex. Nevertheless the women are quite lovely, as is true among almost all Asians.[93] As for food, they eat almost no bread or meat; they eat mostly fish, rice, and grapes that are abundant, and very good. Other fruits are not lacking either, especially quinces, lemon, fennel, and certain other trees mostly unknown in our latitudes.

The air is not very healthy in areas by the sea. Consequently, the region was for me a most unfortunate one. Because it was no longer possible to travel with Portuguese ships to Hormùz due to the war between the Persians and the Portuguese, I waited for English ships to arrive, to travel with them to India. But fortune (as I believe) wished to deny me a happy return to my homeland. My sweet wife Maani Gioredia, a heroic and perfectly virtuous

---

[93] Compare the same discription in Della Valle's letters, which differs only slightly from the one given here. Della Valle, *Voyages de Pietro della Vallé*, 5:375–6.

virgin when I married her, was thereafter a most loyal companion in all joys and pains as well as in the marriage-bed; to her alone could I turn for relief from sorrow and need while traveling.[94] She was in the first bloom of youth, and had always been in good health, but now in the year of Our Lord 1621, in the month of December, she was taken with a very grave fever, within the walls of the city of Mina (one of the most notable of this region, at a latitude of 26 degrees, 35 minutes and 2 seconds from the equator to Arcturus). She first lost her long awaited child, and because of the miscarriage her condition worsened; the whole art of medicine and all useful remedies failed. When it pleased God to call her from this misfortune to an immortal and better life, he left me behind as a widower, bereft of all good things, in mourning and inconsolable so long as I live.

Adjoining the region of Moghostàn is Persia proper, commonly called Faris or Fars, or Faristàn. We might translate it into our language as the "region of the horsemen." Namely, Fars means horseman in Arabic, but in Persian it has no meaning as far as I can tell. It is reasonable to call the Persians horsemen, for in their wars the fighting is always done by cavalry, never by infantry, unless there is need to scale the walls of a town. This is why today both the name and the language of the Persians are common to all peoples of Agiamia. It is by no means a surprise that Persian has certain Arabic names, because the Arab language is very ancient, because the country has a long border with Persia, and because the Arab alphabet, in use for over a thousand years, is spread through the entire Orient more than any other. We might better say that no one should regard it as strange that what the Latins called Persis (just as the ancient Persians did) is now written and pronounced Fars.[95] For the Arabic alphabet, in which the Persian language is now written, does not have a P, and in that region P is commonly equated to F or Ph. In the same manner E, which Arabic does not have as a vowel, is replaced by Aliph.[96] Thus the first syllable of the name for the region changes from Pars to Phars. Because case endings necessary in Greek and Latin are also unknown among the Orientals, the name Persis easily degenerates into Phars or Fars.

---

[94] "… omnis curae casusque levamen," or "(person offering) relief from all sorrow and need": Virgil, 3:709. "when I married her" is an addition to the original.

[95] Compare the same discussion in Della Valle, *Voyages de Pietro della Vallé*, 2:388–9. We follow the manuscript, which has "effertur," while the edition has "effatur."

[96] The manuscript has "E," while the editor replaced it with an incorrect "I." See Della Valle, *De recentiori imperio Persarum subiectis regionibus*, 298.

To the east Persia borders Kirmàn (and perhaps a bit of Moghostàn), to the west Loristàn, to the north Araq, and to the south the remainder of Moghostàn (if there be any) and the Persian Gulf. The region's capital today is Sciraz, not an ancient town, and apparently built by Arab kings. At a distance of ten miles to the north, or rather the northeast, lies the site the Persians call Astehàr.[97] This was once the ancient Persepolis, situated in a large and fertile plain surrounded by mountains on all sides, and watered by small streams and also by a well-known river, which Diodorus Siculus and other ancient authors called the Araxes (though it must be far away from the other river of the same name, among the Armenians), while today's inhabitants call it the Kur. This name Kur does not disagree with the earlier name Cyrus, for the stream flowing from a cave in Persia, where the later King Cyrus was once exposed to the elements. This was why the river was called Cyrus, though its earlier name was Agradatus. The two names Kur and Cyrus are in my view consonant, because both start with K, and we know it was the custom of the ancients to pronounce the Greek Ypsilon of Cyrus as the vowel U. Hence it is certain that Kyros (as Latins say it) and Kuros (as Greeks say it) are the same. When the inflections proper to the Greeks and Latins (but unknown to the Persians and almost all other Orientals) are taken away, the name Kur clearly remains, and this, as I have said, is what the river is now called. One might perhaps also say with reason that the Persian rivers Araxes and Cyrus, mentioned in ancient histories, were one and the same river, namely this one; nothing we know bears witness against this assumption, and no other river in all of this region seems worthy of the name Cyrus. In Media Atropatia there is another river called Kur in the same way, as we know from the reports of our geographers and those of the Persians.[98]

Incidentally, the ruins of Persepolis are still there, as are those of many royal tombs carved out of grottos in the surrounding mountains; the facades are adorned and painted with beautiful and diverse figures that seem to be of

---

[97] In the manuscript, "duodecim" is cancelled and replaced by "decem," while the edition kept "duodecim." In his diary, Della Valle noted that Cehel Minar, the ruins of ancient Persepolis, was ten miles away from Shiraz if one considered the straight distance. Since they had to find a bridge for crossing the river Kur, however, it took them two more miles to reach the ancient site. Ms Biblioteca Apostolica Vaticana, Città del Vaticano, Ottoboniano latino 3382, ff 153b–154a.

[98] See the same discussion in Della Valle's letters to Schipano, where he makes, however, a different and more elaborate kind of argument in favor of his conclusion. Della Valle, *Voyages de Pietro della Vallé*, 5:308–9, 311.

great antiquity. There are also ruins of a very splendid building to be seen on the plain at the foot of the mountain, hidden from the east. These buildings were built with huge pillars, many of which are still standing. Persians call the site "Cehlminàr," that is, "forty lighthouses." They call the pillars lighthouses because the pillars, with their buttresses, resemble the exterior of the towers Muhammedans commonly build next to their temples, to have people called together by an assistant who cries from the top, and also for lighting candles on festival nights.[99]

In light of what Diodorus Siculus says about the sixth year of Alexander's reign, near the end, the admirable character of this building shows that it was once a part of that exalted and splendid palace of Cyrus, burnt by Alexander when he was urged to do so by Thais.[100] But one does not see the mountains at a distance of 400 feet, as Diodorus said, for they are very near, almost connected to the site.[101] Whether the palace that was once here was the site of a temple or a tomb one cannot easily judge, though I would prefer it to have been a temple.[102] The sculptures in particular seem ancient and have an appearance different from anything known in historical reports; in many places they are very numerous. They seem more likely to have adorned a temple than anything else, and appear to march past as if in a profession of sacrifice. There are numerous inscriptions, but one cannot learn anything from them, for their script is today unknown.[103] The form of some of them I have copied elsewhere, in my travel diary. One cannot learn anything from

---

[99] Compare to Della Valle, *Voyages de Pietro della Vallé*, 2:378, 5:312.

[100] See the same statement in Della Valle's letters to Schipano, where he adds it as a conclusion to information taken from Quintus Curtius. Ibid., 5:310.

[101] The same claim can be found in ibid., 5:313, where Della Valle phrases it as a personal observation: "& moi je trouve que les ruïnes touchent immédiatment le pié de la montagne." The palace of Cyrus is, however, not touching the mountains, but other parts of the entire complex are near to them, while still at some distance. Thus, even if Della Valle's protest against Diodorus Siculus's statement would be interpreted as including these buildings too, it would lack force. It would be an interesting exercise to examine all of the Italian traveler's criticisms of ancient authors and see to what extent they are sustained by indisputable observations and information. Such a study may clarify to some extent Della Valle's attitudes towards ancient knowledge.

[102] Compare Della Valle's discussion of the interpretation of this palace in his letters to Schipano, where he also wrote that he would love it to be a temple, but offered some more alternatives of how to view the ruins and their former purpose. Ibid., 5:314–19.

[103] In his letters to Schipano, Della Valle thought that the letters of one of the inscriptions resembled Hebrew letters and that each one of them might represent an entire word. Ibid., 5:319–20.

the histories of the Persians either, since their ancient script and manner of writing were completely lost after the Arabs came. The people of today have no information on ancient matters from the time of Cyrus, though they are rich in tales, uncertain and similar to the prattle of old women.

The town closest to the ruins, half a mile away, is Mehr-chuascon, the meaning of whose name is unclear. After Sciraz, the more noble cities of Persia today are Lar (unless we prefer to reckon it to Caramania), Darabgerd, and Passa. Lar is not far from the border with Moghostàn, and was once the seat of a kingdom, until it was occupied by King Abbas a few years ago. Darabgerd the Persians think was built by Darius, whom they call Darab;[104] today there are few inhabitants. Passa is pronounced locally with a P, but Fassa would be better, according to current orthography (in Arabic script; for, as I have said, the Arabs do not have the letter P, and tend to replace it with F or Ph). Phassa or Passa lies between Sciraz and Lar, somewhat to the east, on a well-maintained road commonly used in winter to bypass the snow-covered mountains.[105] Regardless of its name, one should not have a low opinion of the town; it occupies a graceful site, abundant in fruit of all kinds, and is also memorable because of the ancient Passagardarum; residues of this name still survive. Also worth mentioning is a cypress of great age and size, regarded as holy by local people and religious folk. Five men with arms outstretched can barely manage to encircle its trunk; the longer branches extend out from the trunk about fifteen paces.

For many important aspects of the region of Faristan I have neither the testimony of my own eyes nor information from others. One point that deserves mention is that many towns are now inhabited by Georgian and Circassian Christians, after their settlements had been destroyed by King Abbas. To keep them from returning to their own places far away they have been re-settled here as well as in Mazanderàn. These people, mostly commoners, still follow their inherited religion, albeit in a dull way, due to the ignorance of the priests who guide them. Encouraged by the king, however, the nobles among them, and many of the better sort of people, adopt the errors of the Muhammedans, for want of proper shepherds.

Lor or Loristàn is without doubt the ancient region of the Uxiors, inhabitants of the high mountains between Susiana and Persia. The word Lor

---

[104] Compare to ibid., 5:358.

[105] The same discussion about the town's orthography is found in ibid., 5:351. The manuscript has the correct order as given here, the edition replaced P with F and vice versa. See Della Valle, *De recentiori imperio Persarum subiectis regionibus*, 300.

can have many meanings, the best being lamb and mountain torrent. Both fit this people well, for they inhabit an area well watered by mountain torrents and rivers, and they surely keep many flocks of lamb and sheep. This region adjoins Fars to the east, Chuz in the west, Araq in the north (namely, the province of Hamadàn), and to the south, I think, the Persian Gulf, albeit not directly. There are no excellent cities, but some towns notable more for the number of inhabitants than for their buildings. Still, they like to come out and roam about in tents, together with their flocks in the pasture. The people here are savage, having adhered to the sect of Muhammed only a few years ago, guided mainly by the conversion of their neighbors. That is why they do not yet closely follow its teachings. They bear servitude badly, and hate the empire of King Abbàs. But since no living man dares to introduce changes, they bear their lot unwillingly. They may perhaps shake off the yoke after the king's death,[106] if someone puts the idea into souls already prepared for it.

The last region of the Persian empire is Chuz or Chuzistàn – the ancient Susiana, or one of its parts. (I did not investigate the meaning of the current name.)[107] Its capital today is the city of Sciusetèr; contrary to what some would say,[108] the ancient Susa was not this city but another called Sciuscèn (meaning a multitude of lilies), as is often mentioned in the ancient histories of the Persians. Whether Sciuscen still exists today I do not know, but I assume it was not the same as Sciusetèr.[109]

Chuzistàn is bounded in the north by the Kurds, in the east by Araq and part of Persia, if I am not mistaken, and in the west by the southern limits of Babylonia. In the south it is bordered mainly by Loristan, but also by the Persian Gulf, and by the part of Babylonia that lies east of the Tigris. There is a city in this part of Babylonia, doubtless Haveiza, that is the residence of a free prince of the Arabs; the surrounding land is cultivated by Christian Arabs and by Christian

---

[106] For our translation of "mortuo" as (his), i.e. Shah Abbas's, death, see Otto Güthling, *Langenscheidts Grosswörterbuch Latein: Teil II, Deutsch0Latein*, 16th ed., (Berlin, 1993), 585.

[107] For a discussion of the possible origins of the name see http://en.wikipedia.org/wiki/Origin_of_the_name_Khuzestan.

[108] Della Valle wants to say here that some authors in Christian Europe believed that Shushtar was the place where the ancient capital of Susiana had been located.

[109] This passage indicates more clearly than other parts of Della Valle's text that the author relied more than admitted on Persian (and Arabic) written sources. It also shows that he did not take the trouble to verify all the bits of information he chose to transmit, even if they concerned comparatively important points such as the location of ancient Susa.

Chaldeans from the sect of the Sabaeans.[110] They use either the Chaldean or the Arabic language, but when writing they use a script very different from Arabic or Chaldean. They inhabit many cities of the region of Susiana, especially the area of Kiumalava, adjoining the city of Haveiza.[111] In my view, both cities are properly ascribed to the Chaldean or Babylonian region, where I started and I now terminate my circular description of all of Agiamia.

These are the regions currently subject to the Persian empire. The proper name for them is Agiamia (or Eiran or Eiron, as the Persians say it, if one includes all the lands stretching from the Euphrates to the river Oxus). Their common language is that of the Persians, though there are everywhere people who speak Turkish. This tongue was introduced to Agiamia by the Qizilbascis, when they subjugated it to their rule.

Once the former line of Turkish kings was extinguished, it took many years for Ismail, the first king of the dynasty ruling now, to conquer the empire, using these Turkish soldiers.[112] Ismail was called with the epithet Sophi, the pious, because he adhered to a pious way of life. He was a descendant of the ancient Arabs, from the lineage of that Sciah Sophì, a man in their view not just pious but holy, whom I mentioned in the beginning. As a mark of the new religion, the head-band was folded into a turban with twelve protruding

---

[110] In his letters to Schipano, Della Valle wrote that these Christian Chaldaeans were called St. John's Christians by the Portuguese, who knew all these countries better than anybody else, while some Western European authors called them Sabeans after a certain heretic called Saba. They themselves said they were "Menadi," i.e. Mandaeans. Della Valle also reported that they cooperated closely with the Portuguese against the Safavids and participated as soldiers in manning and defending the Portuguese fortress of Hormuz. See Della Valle, *Voyages de Pietro della Vallé*, 3:343, 6:64–5. On the identification of the obscure Sabaeans with the Christian Mandaeans, see also Kurt Rudolph, *Der Mandäische "Diwan der Flüsse"* (Berlin, 1982), 5–7. As for the rulers of Huweiza, Della Valle is here remarkably brief and obscure, in contrast to his more elaborate description in the letters to Schipano. The province was ruled by a *vali* who was a *sayyid*. That is why the *Tadhkirat al-muluk* declared him to be the most esteemed one among the lords of the marches. For the origins and fortunes of the Musha'sha' dynasty, see W. Caskel, "Ein Mahdi des 15. Jahrhunderts," *Islamica* 4 (1931): 415–22. The area the dynasty governed was called Arabistan after Shah Abbas affiliated it in a stable manner with the Safavid Empire in 1000 h/1590. As a consequence, the traditional name of Chuzistan lost its validity for the southern part of its former territory. See ibid., 416, n. 1.

[111] Della Valle's spelling of "Haveiza" differs from the customary Arabic one, which is "Huwaiza." With regard to the second name's spelling, Della Valle follows the pronunciation of Mandaean inhabitants of the place whom he met in Southern Iran. Della Valle, *Voyages de Pietro della Vallé*, 4:64.

[112] We follow the manuscript, which has "ope," not "opera" as the edition. See Della Valle, *De recentiori imperio Persarum subiectis regionibus*, 301.

points, in honor of the twelve pontiffs of their sect. Ismail allowed soldiers supporting him to dress as he did.[113] The Turkish soldiers were later called by the Turkish word Qizilbasci, that is, red heads.[114] Having built the empire, they retained the right to bear arms and to administer the realm. In our day, however, King Abbas has set above them a new troop of his servants, for keeping down the haughty Qizilbascis, who contended among themselves immoderately. These new soldiers have been brought from other territories, either in Agiamia or elsewhere. They are mostly sons of Christians, trained from childhood as royal slaves, to be incorporated into a troop separate from that of the Qizilbascis. It is said their number has now reached 30,000. Like the Qizilbascis, many of them also participate in the governance of the realm, and have risen to the highest offices and satrapies. Abbas attached to them companies of true Persians, who are called Tat, that is, defenseless subjects. The king uses these Persian troops for campaigns that require irregulars or a supporting militia, but he also employs them for the governance of the realm, for from their ranks come most of those who occupy themselves with justice, taxes, the governance of the people, and other civil services.[115]

Thus apart from the royal family one may say that the forces of the Persian empire are threefold: the Qizilbascis, the Persians, and one other, rather large contingent of servants of foreign origin. Since most of the latter are Georgians, mostly adults from noble families, recently come to Persia, they can never forget their homeland and its fall, despite their conversion to the sect of Muhammed. They cannot forget either the indigenous Georgian princes who survive, many of whom are now in Persia, as I have said. Many of these Georgians rue what they have done. That is why it is not possible to predict the future course of events. With what warlike games and tournaments of the nobles will they celebrate the rites for King Abbas in Persia, where tragic spectacles are never absent from royal funerals? And what can be hoped from his successor? For among the sons of Abbas there remains today only

---

[113] We follow the manuscript, which has "faventibus ipsi," while the edition has "ferventibus ipsis." See Della Valle, *De recentiori imperio Persarum subiectis regionibus*, 301.

[114] Compare Della Valle, *Voyages de Pietro della Vallé*, 2:392.

[115] In his letters to Schipano, Della Valle claimed that Tat was the name of the true descendants of the ancient Persians. He also pretended that Abbas as a rule took from the Tat his viziers, secretaries, and all other officers of the civil administration, adding that the Tat alone served as artillery soldiers and that this new weaponry had been introduced upon the insistence of the Englishman Anthony Shirley. Della Valle, *Voyages de Pietro della Vallé*, 4:92–3, 105. This is, however, at best an exaggeration, as the Tat were only one of the Persian tribes in the Safavid Empire.

a single heir (the others have been killed, or blinded, or being too young). He is an adolescent, called Imam Culi Mirzà, who has never tried his hand in any of the affairs of state.

One might easily judge from the fate of the Mamluks in Egypt. The country of the Mamluks did not touch Egypt, as Georgia touches Agiamia, for it was far away, the entire width of Asia lying between them. Also, because the Mamluks were brought to Egypt as little children sold for money – hence they were called Mamluks, people taken into possession, or slaves – they did not even know their parents. They were not so fortunate as to have nearby princes of their own, or men from the nobility of their race, or any other aid or advantage – unlike the Georgians in Persia (there are three Christian princes of their nation still ruling in Georgia and on the borders of Agiamia). Unfortunately, due to a certain inborn flippancy of spirit, and an excessive simplicity, the Georgians are wanting in concord, and in leadership. But if they ever take over the empire of the Persians – which might easily happen – what is to be expected? Will Agiamia's future rulers be Christians? Or, having slavishly surrendered to the perfidy they have adopted, will they follow the example of the Mamluks, who though Circassian and Christian in origin, in Egypt always remained adherents of the Muhammedan perfidy?[116] I know for sure that those who are once taken with the Muhammedan plague never regain their health. From what I have said already, and from innumerable other examples, I have learned that this perfidious sect possesses some simplistic enticement, so that those who have once completely submitted to it never abandon it again.

But the number of those who have not forsaken the Christian religion is very high, in particular among people of lower station, as I have said. I doubt not that they will persevere, if things proceed well. For experience teaches that people living among infidels – although sometimes oppressed by severe troubles – nevertheless keep the faith and do not forsake it – this I have seen myself. If necessary, they suffer danger to their bodies rather than to apostatize. One example of admirable perseverance and steadfast piety, above all others among the Georgians of today, is that of the glorious heroine I have

---

[116] Compare Della Valle's musings about this subject in his letters to Schipano, where he already introduced the comparison between the Georgians in the Safavid Empire and the Egyptian Mamluks and expressed his hopes that the Georgians would take over power in Persia as the Mamluks did in Egypt. Della Valle, *Voyages de Pietro della Vallé*, 4:71. In contrast to Della Valle's hope, the Georgians defended the Safavid dynasty until it was overthrown by the Afghans in the eighteenth entury.

already mentioned, queen Ketevàn, mother of the prince Teimuràz, who is held hostage in the city of Sciràz.[117]

After their kingdom was lost, the family was led into captivity, the son was beaten and fled; the grandsons, still children, were taken prisoner with their grandmother, and educated in Muhammedan rites, far from her sight, though in the same city. Even today, because of the indulgence of the Persians and her own people, who did not wish to torment her already desperate soul with news of such a cruel and infamous deed, she does not know that these children have been made into eunuchs.[118] When her kinsman, Prince Luarsàb, had been killed in captivity, while she herself was detained, honorably, but distrusted and under careful observation, she suffered her troubles with no less courage than before. Previously, fortune had extinguished the life of her kinsman Constantin, an infidel and a murderer, together with the lives of many Persian soldiers supporting him (Constantin had made war on the queen and her son). Later, however, in the face of inimical fate, she was ready to die in order to save her own endangered people. Subsequently, in order to appease her conqueror, the angry king of the Persians, she turned her face into the danger, of her own free will surrendering herself to him, with her grandsons and daughters; this she did in hopes of securing peace.[119]

Nevertheless, peace was not achieved and she never won her freedom back, but was sent as a prisoner, as I said, into the far away Persia; there – while I was there, in 1622 – she had to abstain from the mysteries of the Christian faith, because ministers of the holy rites were not available. But she always had at her disposal a small chapel, adorned with holy icons,

---

[117] Originally, after Ketevàn in the manuscript, Della Valle had written (but then crossed out): "Ketevàn Dedupali, that is, the queen called Ketevàn as they themselves say." The edition kept this cancelled part. See Della Valle, *De recentiori imperio Persarum subiectis regionibus*, 302. For Della Valle's descriptions of her captivity on the basis of reports by her Georgian retainer and by Mariuccica Tiyatin de Ziba, a young Georgian lady and Della Valle's later second wife, see Della Valle, *Voyages de Pietro della Vallé*, 4:74–5, 108, 109–14.

[118] Compare to Della Valle, *Voyages de Pietro della Vallé*, 4:74.

[119] According to Salia, Ketevan did not deliver herself voluntarily as a hostage; rather, Abbas demanded from Teimuraz that the queen and others of the family become hostages as part and parcel of the negotiations on surrender. Salia, *History of the Georgian Nation*, 291–2. Della Valle knew that Ketevan did not go voluntarily to Abbas since in his letters to Schipano he wrote: "Di far guerra occasione alcuna non vi era, perchè Teimuraz era amico e faceva nel resto ogni ossequio possibile, come si vide, avendo mandato ultimamemente a questo re, per placarlo, quando si faceva la guerra più atroce, infin la madre e due figliuoli, che stanno ora ritenuti in Sciraz ... ." Della Valle, *Viaggi di Pietro della Valle*, 1:663.

burning wax candles, sweet incense, and precious vessels. Piously she visited it regularly with her entire household. She confessed publicly and firmly her faith in Jesus Christ. She observed as best as possible the rites of the religion in her rooms, and did so with such piety of soul that she did not want to allow any of the implements of prayer – for example, the vestments, icons, books, and such things – to come into the hands of the Muhammedans; for of late, many such things had been brought as part of the booty from Hormuz. She did not want to allow by any means that such things should be desecrated by the infidels. On the contrary, in a small holy house of the Lord in her own residence, as I have said, she arranged all things properly and with great reverence, once they had come into her possession, either as gifts from nobles among her own people, many of whom greatly favored her, or because she had ransomed them from others.[120] I can testify to this myself. Two books for religious use, namely a Latin breviary and a small book written in Portuguese for the Holy Sacraments, were saved by her from the hands of the plunderers of Hormuz, and given to me later as a gift in Sciraz (where I stayed for a short time), because they were in our language.[121] I keep them with me like precious gemstones as a memory of this most eminent queen and most excellent lady. That is why no one should fail to be aware that friends are needed, and many of them, to help protect and secure in this situation the Christian faith, particularly that of the Georgians in Persia, which is doubtless close to decay. Since such helpers are lacking today – for there are but a few friars of the Augustinian order and the Discalced Carmelites, living only in Sphahan and Sciraz and doing exquisite work, but surely too few for such an important harvest – why do the Jesuit fathers not hurry hither? This work is their destiny, and they have wandered through almost every region that is accessible; let them come to Georgia, which has so far had no help from us, and to this huge realm of Persia, to bring aid to a small but zealous group of people fighting for our faith. Finally, why do they not penetrate into Asia, into Muhammed's empire, as they have begun work in Constantinople and in the empire of the Moghol and perhaps elsewhere?

You, my revered father Vincislaus, be zealously strengthened in your most holy and pious purpose of working to increase and multiply the Christian

---

[120] See Della Valle, *Voyages de Pietro della Vallé*, 4:75.

[121] Della Valle implies here that he met Ketevan himself, but this was not the case as his letters to Schipano prove. The two books he mentions here he did not receive directly from Ketevan, but through her retainer. Della Valle, *Voyages de Pietro della Vallé*, 4:79, 109–14.

religion, a purpose we share with you; good-bye, and keep us ever in your memory.

Petrus A Valle Peregrinus

Given at Goa, in the capital of the Portuguese in India, in the month of February, in the year of the Lord 1624.

The polar altitude of certain cities in Agiamia which has been differently observed – as will become obvious in the table written down below – by different [people] during my time, namely by Don Garçia a Silva et Figueroa, the ambassador of the Catholic king in Persia, the Scott Georgius Strachan, an educated man, Mullà Zeineddin from Lar, the best astrologer and finally by myself, Pietro della Valle.

	D. Garçia	Georgius Strachan	Mullà Zeineddin	Petrus a Valle
Cehl-minàr	28°56'			
Kasciàn	32°34'			
Kombrù, vel Abbassì portus				26°58'18"25'"*
Lar	27°		27°30'	27°17'1'10'"
Minà				26°35'2"
Qazvìn	35°28'	36°40'**		
Qom		33°4'		
Savà		33°18'		
Sciràz	28°44'			
Sphahàn, sive Ispahàn	31°30'	32°40'		32°23'56"
Sultania	35°57'			

* As it appears in the manuscript. The edited text has 26°52'18"25'". See Della Valle, *De recentiori imperio Persarum subiectis regionibus*, 303.

** As it appears in the manuscript. The edited text has 26°40'. Ibid., 303.

Acknowledgements

We wish to acknowledge courteously that this article could not have been written without the support of the following institutions: Deutsche Forschungsgemeinschaft, Bonn, Germany; Max Planck Institute for the History of Science, Berlin; Germany; British Library, Map Collection (Harley Fellowship), U.K. We also wish to express our warmest thanks for the enormous help given to us by James Tracy, editor of *Journal for Early Modern History*.

V

EARLY MODERN WESTERN EUROPEAN TRAVELLERS IN THE MIDDLE EAST AND THEIR REPORTS ABOUT THE SCIENCES[1]

In 1628/29 François-Auguste de Thou (born 1607, beheaded 1642), the oldest son of the famous French historian Jacques-Auguste de Thou (1553-1617), travelled to and through the Ottoman Empire. In October 1628 he wrote to his uncle, Pierre Dupuy, of his admiration for the Safavid Empire and particularly for Šāh ʿAbbās:

> Three other Capuchins departed for Persia. I do not doubt that they will be welcomed there since it is the most liberal and the best policed country, where justice is provided in the best way. This is due to the prudence of the today (ruling) king who is, as I have been told, another Solomon because one reports about his actions as if they were the same as what antiquity has ever produced at its most excellent. I would have loved nothing better than to be an eye-witness (of them). If it was not for the sure respect for you, Monsieur, (and for you other gentlemen) which made me abstain from this voyage, I assure you that I would have accomplished it. It is not as difficult as one believes, since from Aleppo, you are in less than 25 days in the state of Persia. But one should not think about it anymore.[2]

Although he assured his uncle time and again that his fears about the possible dangers of travelling in the Ottoman Empire were completely unfounded, his sentiments towards the Ottoman dynasty and its state were plainly hostile. January 10, 1629, having arrived in Cairo, he wrote to Nicolas-Claude Fabri de Peiresc (1580-1637), a close family friend who had supported

---

1. I use this expression to indicate travellers from places found today in countries such as France, Germany, England, Italy, or Portugal. Admittedly it is anachronistic since the division of Europe into West and East as its two main components only evolved later. However to call the travellers from Italy, France, and Portugal Southern European and those from Germany and England Northern European or all of them simply European travellers is also unsatisfactory, since the Ottoman Empire included large parts of Southern Europe and I am not dealing with travellers from those regions.
2. "Trois au<tr>es Capuchins sont passes en Perse. Je ne doute point qu'ils n'y soient les bien receus, car cest le païs du monde le plus libre, le mieux policé, & ou la Justice est la mieux faite ce qui est deub<t> a la prudence du Roy d'aujourdhui, que l'on nous dit estre vn au<tr>e Salomon, car l'on conte des actions de lui telles quelles vont du pair auec ce que lantiquité a Jamais produit de plus excellent. Jeusse bien desiré en estre tesmoing oculaire, & n'eust esté certain respect de vous au<tr>es Messieurs, qui eussies trouué a redire a <ce> voiage, Je vous asseure que Je leusse accompli, <qui il> (sic) n'est pas si difficile q<ue> l'on croit, car d'Alep en moins de 25 Journees vous estes dans l'estat de Perse mais il n'y fault plus penser". MS Paris, BnF, Dupuy 703, ff 148b-149.

de Thou's excursion through his vast network of relations with French ambassadors, political envoys, consuls, and merchants in the Ottoman Empire:

> Finally, this country seems to me being one of the most beautiful ones which I ever have seen and this city, for its size and richness has very few in the world similar to it. I think that he who has not seen Egypt cannot claim to have seen the Levant. I leave you pondering what it would be like if it was not in the hands of those miserables who do not think about anything else than ruining the public in order to satisfy their greed, but our sins take away from us this advantage.[3]

De Thou expressed the very same sentiments when he informed Peiresc about the upheaval in Yemen, interpreting the events as a divine reproach against *our cowardliness and neglect* which allowed Muslims rather than Christians to begin the destruction of the Ottoman Empire because they *could not suffer (any longer) the tyranny*.[4] De Thou's letters make it clear that he had acquired opinions in France, which evaluated the two Muslim states and their representatives in fundamentally opposed directions: the Safavids were admirable, valiant knights, the Ottomans were mean, barbarous tyrants.

We are confronted with the same kind of differential portrayal regarding the arts and sciences, when we compare Western European travel accounts of the Ottoman Empire with reports about the Safavid realm. As early as the middle of the 17th century, however, some Western European scholars voiced their dissent to the widespread claim that there were no sciences or arts in the Ottoman realm. In the 18th century, an Italian ecclesiastic, Abbé Toderini, after having visited Istanbul to investigate Ottoman scholarly life, wrote an entire book in order to prove that this claim was flawed. However, Western European public opinion, including its diverse scholarly communities, for two more centuries continued to consider the Ottomans as a dynasty lending no support to the sciences and the people they ruled as likewise disinterested.

This paper wishes to take up again Abbé Toderini's enquiry, albeit in a modified form. Its aim is to show that there was indeed a fundamental difference in the ways in which Western European travellers evaluated the Ottoman and the Safavid arts, sciences, and education and to ask which factors contributed to its creation and stubborn longevity. The paper suggests that the travellers perceived and talked about the arts and sciences in ways which were ultimately linked to two sets of political, religious, cultural, and social features. One was constituted by the multifaceted forms in which the two empires were portrayed and looked at in contemporary Catholic or Protestant countries. The

---

3. "Au reste ce païs ici me semble vn des plus beaux que J'ais Jamais veu, & cette ville po<ur> sa grandeur & richesses a peu de pareilles au reste du monde. & pense q<ue> qui n'a point veu l'Egypte, ne se peut venter dauoir veu le leuant Que s'il estoit hors des mains de ces miserables, qui ne pensent Jamais qu'a ruiner le public po<ur> assouuir leur auarice, Je vous laisse a penser, ce que ce seroit, mais nos peches nous privent de cet aduentage". MS Paris, BnF, Fr. 9537, fol. 299b.
4. *Ibid.*, f 300a.

second was generated by the specific differences which structured journeys by Western Europeans in the two Muslim countries and the modes by which they were integrated into the two societies. In the first section, I shall describe four major forms in which the profound difference in the portrayal of the arts and sciences makes its appearance. In the following two sections, I shall cite sources to illustrate my claim. In the final section I shall present observations and reflections about the political, religious, cultural, and social assumptions and attitudes expressed in these and similar travel accounts which offer clues for understanding the difference.

STATEMENT OF THE PROBLEM

Early modern Western European accounts of journeys in the Middle East differ in several respects from those of their mediaeval predecessors. One of the aspects which makes them different is the inclusion of tales about educational and scholarly matters. Given the context of such reports, it is not surprising that many of them contain at least a few remarks, or even long expositions, about education and science in Ottoman society and its eastern neighbour, the Safavid Empire. What is surprising, however, is that there exists a fundamental difference between the accounts concerning the Ottoman Empire and those, which describe the Safavid Empire.

Descriptions of education and science in the Ottoman Empire tend to be stereotyped with a minimum of specific information about the actual situation in the capital or any of the major cities travellers visited such as Damascus, Aleppo, Alexandria, or Cairo. As a rule, this kind of information referred to medieval Arabic authorities well known in Western Europe. Jewish immigrants from Western Europe were a second source, although it remains doubtful whether remarks pointing to them were based upon direct experience with Jewish scholars. In the later 17th century, geographical, astronomical, or historical Arabic or Persian texts newly edited or translated in Western Europe became a third source for writers on the arts and sciences in the Muslim world, including some travel accounts. A few travellers wrote positively about particular features of education and scholarly life in Ottoman society, while most considered its population as barbarous or at best old-fashioned and backward. When we compare this situation with other themes in Western European travel accounts, we find shifting attitudes. Numerous Western European travellers looked at certain aspects of Ottoman society such as legal practice, the co-existence of divergent religious groups, the social structure and its degree of permeability as pleasantly different, more efficient, or less rigid and less confining. On a general political and religious level, however, most Western European travel accounts display feelings of superiority combined with hostility: the sultans after Süleyman Kanuni were described as foolish and inept drunkards and sexual addicts, the women and eunuchs in the serail were seen as power hungry and immoral, the viziers and governors were often portrayed as greedy, selfish intrigants, the population in the provinces was thought of as "superstitious", but eager to be liberated, preferably by the royal army from the traveller's native country. A comparison between the various travel accounts also reveals, that despite all the differences between the authors the nuclei of the tales told about the arts and sciences correspond to an impressive extent. This nucleus is, in a sense, independent of the attitudes expressed explicitly by the authors of the accounts.

Descriptions of education and science in the Safavid Empire begin in the late 16th century. They were of a more comprehensive nature and presented details which were often unknown beforehand to the European traveller. The corpus of texts studied in Persian *madāris* in mathematics, astronomy, geography, medicine, history, or poetry, was documented with apparently increasing precision. Teaching methods were described, as well as the making of astronomical and mathematical instruments. Western European travellers to Persia more often described encounters with Persian courtiers, scholars, and artisans with whom they discussed religious, metaphysical, astronomical, mathematical, geographical, or medical questions. Some travellers cooperated with local scholars and artisans in astronomical observations and geographical measurements. Safavid physicians used local remedies to successfully cure foreign travellers from life-threatening diseases. There were, of course, also reports to the contrary; for example, how the first royal physician cared for nothing more than plundering the Western European travellers, or how a the Muslim astronomer did not know to design an astrolabe. But, as a rule, the Western European travellers of the 16th and 17th centuries described education and science in Persia in greater detail and often in much friendlier, more sympathetic terms than they did with regard to the Ottoman Empire.

The contrast between Western European reports on the arts and the sciences in the two Muslim countries can be discovered in three further aspects of the travel accounts. The first appears in the lists enumerating the dignitaries and professions of the Ottoman and Safavid courts. In almost all accounts of the Safavids, those lists mentioned the *ḥakīm-bāšī*, the head physician, and the *munajjim-bāšī*, the head astrologer/astronomer, and their respective collaborators. These two functionaries were rarely, if ever, included in the lists describing the dignitaries of the Ottoman courts in the capital and the provinces.

The second aspect concerns the use of contemporary Western European research on Arabic and Persian scientific and other manuscripts by the authors of travel accounts. Some of the travel accounts about Safavid Persia such as the various editions of Thomas Herbert's account (1634; 1637; 1677) drew their information on Persian history, geography, and contemporary politics from a variety of 16th and 17th century Western European publications, presenting some of them as directly based upon Persian material. Others, such as the account by Chardin (first partial account, 1686; first edition of the complete account, 1711), incorporated information about Muslim scientific traditions taken from books published in Paris, Oxford, Leyden, or other Christian European university towns. So far as I am aware, there is only one account of the Ottoman Empire published before 1700 into which this kind of information was integrated. This text is not a travel account in the narrow sense of the word, but a report by Thomas Smith, which I shall discuss below.

The descriptions, sketches, illustrations and paintings of school architecture constitute the third difference between the portrayal of the Ottoman and Safavid Empires in European travel literature. In the case of Safavid Iran mentioning and painting the *madrasa* was the norm, but the *madrasa*, while not completely absent, was relatively rare in accounts of the Ottoman Empire. Even in prominent architectural complexes such as the mosques of the Ottoman sultans in Edirne or Istanbul, the *madāris*, which were an integral part of these structures, were usually ignored in Western European descriptions. This is all the more striking since it is well known that the *madrasa* system played an important role in the organisation of the bureaucratic Ottoman state and in the formation of Ottoman imperial ideology.

The easiest, most seductive interpretation of such findings would be to conclude that there was almost nothing travellers might have possibly discovered to write about. A comparison with Ottoman historical, scientific, and architectural sources, however, proves this to be incorrect. Judging by these sources, there was no deep rift in education and science between the two empires that might be taken as the cause of the difference in Western European perspectives. The major scientific traditions and their authorities in both empires almost coincided. Moreover, by translating Italian, French, or Latin geographical, astronomical, or medical texts into Turkish or Arabic, scientific life in the Ottoman Empire possessed even a closer link to early modern Western European authoritative texts and developments than the Safavid realm.[5]

---

5. See, for instance, what Evliya Çelebi wrote in the middle of the seventeenth century about the Ottoman capital and several provincial towns, among them Bitlis. He claimed that in the Ottoman capital the scholarly professions encompassed about 40,000 people. Besides the scholars of the elementary schools, the diverse types of *madāris*, the mosques, and private households, Çelebi mentioned poets, calligraphers, astronomers, magicians, librarians, physicians, surgeons, and oculists. The corporation of astronomers was said to have counted 70 members, that of the magicians 300. The librarians were said to have been organized in two different corporations: one that was closely related to the *madāris* and the religious and legals scholars comprising 300 members; the other comprising 200 members constituting a sort of flying book trade connected with the crafts of producing paper, book covers, and ink. All these corporations were made up, according to Mantran, of Muslims. The medical corporations, however, included non-Muslim practitioners. Evliya Çelebi enumerated all of them together as 1,000 physicians (in 700 different shops) and 700 surgeons who worked in 400 different shops. See Mantran, 1962, pp. 493-498.

With respect to Bitlis, the site of a Kurdish khan, Evliya Çelebi, describing the ruler's library, not only talked about some 5,000 Arabic, Persian, and Turkish manuscripts on religious, literary, and historical sciences including the ruler's own compositions, but also reported that the library

Thus the fundamental similarity between the tales about the arts and sciences in the Ottoman Empire as told by early Western European travellers can only signify that the reporters followed assumptions, values, expectations, and preconceptions which transcended their relative sympathy or antipathy. Their reports reflected standards of Western European traditions and theories of what was a good travel account which were described in the so-called *apodemic literature*. The character of the descriptions of the arts and sciences in the two Muslim countries implies, however, that these standards did not necessitate a specific investigation at the site visited, or any truly personal experience of what the native population and its experts thought about this or that question of education, science, or art.

We may further conclude that Western European travellers had fewer reasons and inducements to report about Ottoman scientific interests than to report about Safavid scholarly culture. Moreover, as it is well known, there were many prejudices floating through Western European books, pamphlets, or speeches condemning the *Turks* and praising the *Sophi* (that is, the Safavids) which influenced the line the travellers were able to take in their reports about their visits.

EDUCATION AND SCIENCE IN THE OTTOMAN EMPIRE AS DESCRIBED IN EARLY MODERN WESTERN EUROPEAN TRAVEL ACCOUNTS

In 1546, the French Catholic physician, Pierre Belon (1508-1564), went on what might be regarded as one of the earliest scholarly missions sent by the French court to the Ottoman Empire. He was to collect plants, seeds, animals, coins, inscriptions, and manuscripts. Belon's report on his travels, published in 1553, reflected his professional interests in medical and pharmaceutical knowledge and practices available in the Ottoman Empire. He was also interested in customs and habits, and thus included some information on the sciences in general. His accounts of these subjects were positive, though they remain brief and unspecific.

Belon called his general outline of the state of the Ottoman sciences *Des prestres du Turquie, & des sciences des Turcs*. He reported that the Muslim *preachers* do not differ from the lay people in terms of education, code of dressing, marriage, and the earning of their livelihood through civil professions. He declared that *many gain their livelyhood by writing books*.[6] This specificity of Muslim scholars' social embeddedness was, he thought, the reason for the

---

contained 200 European books on geography, including reports on the New World, astronomy, medicine, and human anatomy. Evliya Çelebi somewhat grudgingly admired these European books and the novelties they represented, the art of printing in particular. Çelebi, 1990, p. 293.

6. "Plusieurs gaignent leur vie à escrire des liures", Belon, 1553, p. 346a.

lack of Turkish printing presses in the Ottoman Empire. Belon, in contrast to other travellers, did not conclude that the absence of printing hindered the study of the sciences. He even expressed his surprise that such education was also offered to girls:

> The Turks, according to our emulation, have made such effort that they are today well-versed in the sciences of astronomy, poetry, and philosophy. Not only do the men take pleasure in them, whereas they do not complain about the (money) they spend, but also the male and female children. The schools for boys are, however, separated from that for the girls. The (latter) go to the women and the boys to the men.[7]

Talking about his observations and visits along the routes he travelled, Belon wrote on medical and pharmaceutical shops, authorities, practices, and commodities. The first occasion he had to relate medical and pharmaceutical customs was when speaking of the bazaar of Aleppo. He stated that *those who healed diseases were diligent in preparing remedies corresponding to the singular disease* and that *those who were sick only paid the physicians after they had been healed*. Belon compared this practice with that of ancient Greek and mediaeval Arabic physicians who also had combined the duties of a surgeon and of a druggist with those of a physician proper.[8]

While it has to remain an open question as to what extent Belon's statements truly describe Ottoman medical customs,[9] his list of medical authorities is no doubt based upon the scholastic curriculum in medicine at a Western European university. Not only did Belon mention exclusively ancient Greek and mediaeval Arabic authors whose texts had been translated into Latin, but even mistook the title of an Arabic book for its author.[10]

Belon's description of the medical and pharmaceutical profession given at a later point in his travels depicted what he saw at the market and recounted what he was told by the people he talked to with the help of an interpreter. He claimed that most of the doctors in the Ottoman Empire were Jews, but that there also were a few *Turkish* doctors. Like other Western European travellers of the time, Belon did not differentiate clearly between the different ethnic groups composing the Muslim communities of the Ottoman Empire. In his account, the label *Turk/Turkish* stands for all Muslims. Despite their alleged

---

7. "Les Turcs a nostre emulation ont fait tel effort qu'ils sont maintenant connoiteux des sciences d'Astronomie, Poesie et Philosophie; et non seulement les hommes y prennent plaisir, ains ne plaigent la despence qu'ils font, tant aux enfants masles qu'aussi femelles. Mais les escolles des garsons sont separées des filles, qui vont aux femmes, et les garsons aux hommes". *Ibid.*, p. 346a.
8. *Ibid.*, p. 265a.
9. According to a personal communication by Gianna Pommata, the practice of paying the physician only after the cure had been successfully carried out had come under social pressure. This might have induced Belon to talk about the subject and to link it with practices of acknowledged authorities such as the ancient Greek authors and, within certain Italian and French universities, the mediaeval Arabic authors too.
10. Belon, 1553, pp. 322b-323a.

numerical inferiority, Belon considered the professional standards of these *Turkish* physicians to surpass those of the Jewish doctors. In the same passage, Belon talked once more about remedies and druggists. Again, he plainly favoured the *Turcs* over the *Jews*.[11] Belon's attitude towards the two groups was, no doubt, biased. Although he regarded most of the Jews as immigrants (or the children of immigrants) who had been forced to leave Spain and Portugal, he disapproved of their fortunes in the Ottoman Empire. These sentiments mellowed his perception of the Muslim rulers.[12]

An account which resembles Belon's presentation of medicine, pharmacy, and the sciences in the Ottoman empire while turning its evaluation upside down is that by Leonart Rauwolf, a Lutheran physician from Augsburg, who, in 1573, persuaded his wealthy relatives engaged in trade with the Levant to send him to the Middle East to search for drugs, herbs, spices, and other useful commodities in which to trade. Like Belon, Rauwolf included several descriptive chapters in his discussion of his itinerary. In one of them, dealing with provincial governors, their courts, manners, customs, and officers, he claimed that there are no arts and sciences and no scholars trained in them in the Ottoman Empire.[13] Trying to explain his claim, Rauwolf pointed to the lack of printing and he asserted that the *Turks* and the *Arabians* considered the sciences to be a waste of time.[14] Instead of pursuing serious matters, he claimed, they preferred *frivolous* pastimes and rather marvelled at their own historical narratives, in particular when these narratives denigrated enemies or strangers.[15]

---

11. "Les drogueurs ou materialistes qui vendent ordinairement les drogues par les villes de Turquie, sont pour la pluspart hommes Iuifs: mais les Turcs sont plus scauants en la cognoissance d'icelle, et on plus de matieres medecinales, c'est à dire, des drogues simples en vente en leurs boutiques, que n'auons en Europe: tellement que le meilleur Droguiste de Venise, quelque bien fourny qu'il soit, n'aura pas tant de petites drogueries en sa boutique, qu'un drogueur de Turquie. Nous ne disons pas en quantité de poix, mais en diuersité de nombres des drogues simples.
Quand le medecin a faict sa recepte, il l'enuoye au Droguiste pour auoir des drogues qu'il demande (car il n'y a point de ceux que nous nommons Apoticaires) et là prenant les hards en detail les paye presentement: ...". *Ibid.*, p. 323a.
12. *Ibid.*, pp. 310b.
13. *A Collection of Curious Travels & Voyages 1693*, vol. 1, pp. 81f.
14. *Ibid.*, p. 82.
15. "Concerning the Education of the Youth, they only learn in Schools to Read, and to write the Arabian Alphabete, the Characters whereof are common both to the Turks and Arabians, although their Languages are very differing: Besides these, there are other Schools, wherein the Young Men are Instructed in the Emperour's Laws, and those that go on in their Learning, and take it well, are soon called to high offices, (as Cadi's and Cadileschiers). ... But in Liberal Arts and Sciences, such as we teach in our Countries, they are not instructed, for they have not only none of these Learned Men, but esteem these Sciences a Superfluity, and loss of Time; they rather love old Rhimes, and Ballads that speak of and commend the Mighty Deeds of their Ancient Emperors, and other Champions; or other Fancies that make Foreign Nations, or any of their Enemies ridiculous: ... So that they are rather pleased with the Reading of these frivolous silly Writings, than to learn Arts and Sciences: ... Which you may evidently see, in that they do not esteem, nor will admit of that Noble Art of Printing Books, that might inform them of any thing: Which the Clerks, whereof there is a great number up and down the Cities, like very well, because they daily take a great deal of Money for the Writings of their Prophet Mahomet and others, which maketh them

After having returned to Aleppo from his long journey to *Mesopotamia* and the western frontier of Persia, Rauwolf worked as a physician for some Western European merchants in the town and also for some of the ruling Ottoman families. He obviously felt it necessary to explain to his readers why he had agreed to cure sick Ottomans. The background for such a legitimation of medical practice outside Western Europe was created by the repeated efforts of popes, legal courts, and physicians to deny Jews and Muslims the legal and social acceptance as physicians and healers and to force sick Christians to turn exclusively to Catholic or Protestant doctors. Rauwolf used this explanation as an introduction for a chapter which he entitled *On Turkish Physicians and Apothecaries*. Like Belon, Rauwolf saw that the physicians in the Ottoman Empire came from two different ethnic or religious backgrounds – Turkish and Jewish. Contrary to Belon, however, Rauwolf thought that neither of the two categories was particularly effective. The Muslim physicians were inefficient because they could read only books written in their own language, in contrast to the Jews who, Rauwolf believed, were able to read Greek and Arabic. The Jews were inefficient because only few of them could read Latin, a language in which they possessed scarcely any good books except those gained as booty during the latest Ottoman war against a Christian stronghold (Cyprus). A second feature that decreased the efficiency of Jewish doctors was their negative character traits: covetousness and unreliability during epidemics.[16] The bias in these statements is impossible to ignore. Not only was Arabic the predominant language of medical treatises written by Ottoman Muslims in the late 16th century, but also a number of physicians from the Jewish medical community in the Ottoman Empire had been trained at the best Italian or Spanish universities of the time. Rauwolf did not stop with the textual shortcomings of Ottoman

---

generally very Rich, and wear greater Turbants than the rest, that they may be distinguished from others". *A Collection of Curious Travels & Voyages 1693*, vol. 1, p. 82.

16. "They have a great many Physicians, but they are very unskilful, chiefly the Turks which know none but their own Language, and so cannot read the Authors of Physick that have writ in another Language, as the Jews can. But seeing that the Jews are very much addicted to Covetousness, they endeavour rather to promote their own Interest, than that of their Patients, so that the Turks are but slightly provided with Physicians, and therefore rather die like Flies, than take advise of their Physicians, chiefly of the Jews, which are not content with a small reward; to this add also that the Turks never put any confidence in the Jews, and esteem their Counsel but little; and besides, they believe that God hath already pre-ordained every one his Death, so that he that is born to be drowned cannot be hanged. ... As the Physicians are, so are also the Apothecaries, where you find nothing of any great Compositions, nor purging Electuaries, ... (although they have the best Ingredients thereof, for we have them all sent from them), except they be sent to them from Marseilles or Venice, &c.". *Ibid.*, pp. 214f.

Compare also the following passage: "There are also some Jewish Physicians, which instead of the yellow Turban, wear red high Hats, of Scarlet, they exceed in number the Turkish ones, that go cloathed like the common people. They are commonly more Able and learned, because they can read the Physical Books of Galen and Avicen, &c. in their original Languages Greek and Arabicks which they generally understand. But for the Latin Tongue, very few of them understand that, neither have they any good Books in it, but what they have received in the taking of the Island Cyprus". *Ibid.*, p. 343.

medical knowledge. According to him, both medical communities were also unable to produce appropriate remedies, such as purgatories, and thus had to import them from abroad, in particular from Venice and Marseilles.[17] According to modern research, the views and practices of physicians in mediaeval European countries concerning the usages of purgatories did indeed differ from those in Muslim societies. Rauwolf's final remarks about the unavailability of simple remedies, however, resulted from his inability or unwillingness to acknowledge that grocers in Ottoman cities had duties similar to those of apothecaries in German countries.[18]

The most detailed information on scientific life in the Ottoman Empire provided by a European traveller in the 16th century can be found in two Latin works by Prospero Alpini, one published in 1591 (*De Medicina Ægyptiorvm*), the other published posthumously in 1735 (*Historia Ægypti Naturalis*). In the first five chapters of Book I of the first work, Alpini criticized medical art as exercised in Egypt. He bitterly denounced education, schools, and the licensing of physicians. Acknowledging that medical practitioners of both sexes existed in Cairo and other Egyptian localities, he lamented that nobody pursued medicine methodically, including Hippocratic medicine:

> ... at first I say, that in Cairo and other places of Egypt very many men and women can be found, who exercise medicine publicly in town, but notwithstanding this there is nobody who exercises this art according to any method, not even the Hippocratic one.[19]

He attributed the lack of interest in letters to Eygpt's subjugation by the Turks who did not enjoy the study of the sciences, but indulged in arms, gold, silver, and lewdness. Although there were state schools where various kinds of sciences were taught, there were no exercises in medical studies. Alpini named the Azhar mosque (*Gemehazar*) as the center of studies. It disposed of 300 maydan in gold annually and all expenses for books, food, and other things needed by the teachers and students were supplied publicly. The part of their studies, which alone was considered valuable, concerned the law and institutions of their "pseudo-prophet" Muḥammad. Its students were honored highly by the Turks Other arts and sciences were studied in their entirety by very few people, among them only a minimal number of students of the medical art. Although medicine was usually considered, together with all the other arts and sciences, to be worthy of the greatest respect, it was now considered low and cheap not only because of the people's crudity, but even more so because of those who, across the town, healed by ignorance. And even though the

---

17. *Ibid.*, pp. 214f and 343.
18. *Ibid.*, pp. 215.
19. "... ac primum dico, Cayri alijsq. in locis Ægypti plurimos tum uiros tum mulieres reperiri, qui publice per vrbem medicinam faciunt, non tamen vllos existere, qui hanc artem aliqua ratione atque Hippocratice faciant". Alpini, 1591, p. 1.

Venetian consuls had brought physicians from Europe who also cured Turks, Arabs, and other noble people, the majority was left by the other physicians in a hopeless state (*desperata salus*) and glorified this reduced state (*valetudo reducta*) as health. Alpini concluded that, in Egypt, medicine had sunk to the most ignoble of all the mechanical arts. This deplorable situation, however, Alpini emphasized, was being repaired with diligence by his compatriots.[20] Certain formulations in Alpini's severe criticism, such as his descriptions of the interests of the *Turcs*, his reference to Muḥammad's status of a "pseudo-prophet", or his comparison of the public esteem attributed to different branches of knowledge, imply that his judgment resulted from cultural differences. They suggest that other statements made by him should also be regarded cautiously rather than taken as objective, value-free evaluations. Indeed, in Chapter 2, Alpini modified his criticism by describing contemporary Egyptian physicians as "adhering preferably to (the schools) of the methodicians and empiricists".[21] According to Alpini's summary of their beliefs and practices, it appears that neither were Egyptian physicians without doctrine nor were they truly empiricists. Alpini thought they assumed that each kind of disease was brought on either by heat or cold or they attributed the particular cause of all diseases to extra-natural heat or cold.[22] They applied cold remedies to almost all diseases because they believed that the bodies of all who inhabited Egypt were inclined to the highest and most intemperate heat due to the very hot heaven under which they lived. They considered painstaking observations as ill-famed and vulgar and held that contraries heal contraries.[23] That is why they prescribed cold remedies in particular to fevers, applying them in maximum (dosage) to those, which resulted from putrefaction of the humors.[24] All this, Alpini considered as faulty and against the teachings of medicine.[25] He also disliked the office of the *ḥākim-bāšī* and the monetary components involved in its acquisition as well as in the process of licensing physicians.[26] Despite Alpini's one-sided evaluations of the Egyptian medical community and its social and professional practices, his descriptions are the most explicit, detailed, and profound written on this subject during the 16th and 17th centuries.

In his second work, Alpini gave Chapter I in Book II the title *De scientiis quibus Ægyptii delectantur*. He emphasized that he had chosen this title on purpose because he had already pointed to the Egyptians's inclination towards the sciences in his first work. This statement, however, does not correspond

---

20. *Ibid.*, pp. 1a-2b.
21. "Potius methodicae simulque empiricae ipsos addictos iudicaui". *Ibid.*, p. 3a.
22. "In calorem præter naturam, vel frigidatem". *Ibid.*, p. 3a.
23. *Ibid.*, pp. 3b, 7a-8a.
24. *Ibid.*, p. 3b.
25. "Contra medicine dogmata". *Ibid.*, pp. 3b, 4b-7a.
26. *Ibid.*, pp. 2b-3a.

with what he had claimed in his earlier book. Then he goes on to explain that the Egyptians studied three languages, namely Arabic, Persian, and Turkish, followed by a variety of disciplines such as logic, metaphysics, theology, rhetoric, mathematics, and magic. He named several sources that were available to both the general public and the educated elite during their philological training and called the Azhar mosque the most important school in Cairo.[27] His description of the disciplines that were taught there, and which of the arts and sciences were the most favoured, corresponds rather well with what we know, for instance, of the teaching of Ibn al-Akfānī (d. 1348), in 14th-century Cairo.[28]

Most travel accounts of the 17th century add little information to what was already known, though their tales start to become more lively. This feature allows us to discern their functions more clearly than is the case for the summaries by Belon or Rauwolf. An example of this new narrative style is the account, composed in the form of letters, written by Pietro della Valle to his fatherly friend, Mario Schipano, in Naples.

Pietro della Valle (1586-1652) was a Catholic nobleman from Rome and member of the Accademia degli Umoristi. In 1614, della Valle went on a pilgrimage to the Ottoman Empire. After visiting the holy sites, he decided not to return home, but to go to Persia in order to win over the Safavid shah to the True Faith and to wage war against the *Turks*. In the Ottoman Empire he studied Turkish with a Jewish inhabitant of Istanbul and Arabic with a *Turk* of Cairo. He acquired Arabic and Turkish medical manuscripts, grammars, and dictionaries and collected plants, seeds, drugs, and minerals for Schippano and for himself.[29] In one of his letters, della Valle complained that there were no physicians, nor drugs, nor relief to be found, either in Nablus or in Damascus.[30] This claim is sheer invention, since all these items were available in the market or from the Venetian or French merchants in Damascus. Della Valle himself felt that this statement lacked credibility, since he admitted that his impression

---

27. Alpini, 1735, p. 85.
28. "Dixi aliàs cum de templo Cairi celebri sermonem instituerem, quod vocant Gemelazar, in eo universalem fere omnium disciplinarum Academiam magnis sumptibus ali, in qua Professores, atque studiosi, victum, vestitum, & ad libros etiam, gratias nutriuntur. In hoc inquam celebri Gymnasio omnes disciplinae docentur, quippe logica, naturalis, & supranaturalis philosophia, Rhetorica, Mathematica, Medicina, & Magia tum naturalis, tum supranaturalis: sed omnium maximè astrologiae judiciariae dant operam, atque artibus omnibus divinatoriis, cujusmodi est physionomia etiam eodem modo, quo philosophi ex faciei praesertim lineis, & aliis accidentibus ipsam tractare solent, & Chiromantia ex manuum lineis, quae dividandi occasionem praebet. Omnibus vero praeferunt Geomantiam, quae ars supra punctorum varios, quae ab ipsis formantur figurarum aspectus, suum habet judicium, quam eo certiorem per eas punctorum configurationes fieri exeistimant, si caelesti schemati (vulgus genesim vocat) Astrologia arte supputato illius de quo, sive in cujus gratiam Geomantica figura facta est, fuerit conformata". *Ibid.*, pp. 85-87.
29. See, for instance, della Valle, 1674, Part I, pp. 168, 172 etc.
30. See, for instance, della Valle, 1843, pp. 323-324, 332 etc.

of the deficiency of medical care in Ottoman society possibly resulted from his almost complete lack of effort to meet the local people.[31]

When considering the possible context of this specific tale and, thus, della Valle's motivation in reporting unfounded evaluations as matter-of-fact information, we should note that the story served to legitimize della Valle's belief in predestination, a belief which the traveller himself considered unacceptable in the context of Italian humanism.[32] Della Valle claimed that his servant's sickness and subsequent recovery testified to the correctness of his belief.[33] The details given by della Valle about this recovery reinforce the impression that the entire narrative was meant to defend the author's particular belief. Contrary to della Valle's claim that his servant regained his health with no human help, he reported that after he had called a Maronite priest for the last sacraments, the servant's state improved suddenly for:

> We met, to everybody's great satisfaction, a Jew who, I believe, had formerly been in Christendom. This Jew distilled some water with certain herbs which are, according to the Turks, beneficial for fevers and administered this to him in a well-measured dosage which resulted in the fever beginning to subside as soon as he took it.[34]

Towards the end of the 17th century, the amount of detail in Western European descriptions on the state of art and sciences seems to increase at least in some English texts. This new knowledge was mainly based on studies of Arabic and Persian texts at Western European universities, but not on a closer inspection of local conditions. An example of this type of narrative is the text written by Thomas Smith, after his return from a two-year chaplainship in Istanbul. Smith, who was a fellow of Magdalene College, Oxford and of the Royal Society, used, as one of his main sources for the evaluation of the astronomical and geographical knowledge available in mediaeval Arabic and contemporary Ottoman societies, a text by John Greaves, professor of astronomy at the University of Oxford and himself an experienced traveller to the Ottoman Empire. Whilst Greaves had been much more cautious in his judgments about ancient Greek and mediaeval Arabic, Persian, and Byzantine astronomical or geographical texts, sometimes recommending one, sometimes another, Smith edited this text in such a way that both the ancient Greek and the medieval Arabic sources were rejected for their lack of accuracy and for the unreliability

---

31. *Ibid.*, pp. 311, 322.
32. *Ibid.*, p. 322.
33. *Ibid.*, p. 323.
34. "..., e si trovò un Ebreo, stato, credo, in cristianità, che gli seppe fare un poco di orzata; e con quella, e con certa acqua stillata di erbe, buona, come dicono i Turchi, per la febrem che noi crediamo che fosse acqua di ruta caprara con qualche altra mescolanza, tanto fece, che a poco a poco l'and`liberando dal male:...". *Ibid.*, p. 323.

392

of their data and evidence.[35] Smith's evaluation of Ottoman qualifications in different kinds of arts and sciences is plainly negative.[36]

Increasingly negative attitudes to the arts and the sciences in the Ottoman Empire suggested by the extracts presented here, are less an expression of an evolution than an expression of the genre. The diaries of Antoine Galland, for instance, who worked in the late 17th century as secretary of the French ambassador in Istanbul, tell a markedly different story. Galland made contact with a variety of Ottoman scholars, among them mathematicians, alchemists, astrologers, and librarians. He talked with them about scientific, literary, historical, and religious texts, their personal scientific practices, and new books from Christian Europe. Further examples documenting a greater diversity of interests, attitudes, and expectations towards scholarly life in the Ottoman Empire and its traditional authorities can be found in astronomical texts by Christian authors, Catholic as well as Protestant, such as John Greaves, Ismael Boulliau, Johannes Hevelius, or Edward Bernard; in letters exchanged between scholars in France, Italy, the United Provinces of the Netherlands, or England; and in reports of the missions sent by Mazarin, Colbert, and other French courtiers to the Ottoman Empire. Investigation and discussion of such sources, however, is beyond the scope of this section.

THE ARTS AND THE SCIENCES IN THE SAFAVID EMPIRE, AS DESCRIBED IN EARLY MODERN EUROPEAN TRAVEL ACCOUNTS

The earliest travel accounts relating details on the arts and sciences in the Safavid Empire were written during the last decades of the 16th and the first decades of the 17th century. Between 1593 and 1597, the Portuguese Pedro Teixeira resided in Hormuz.

In his travel report, he wrote:

> The Persians are much addicted to the reading of books, and pride themselves thereon. They are great lovers of poetry, in which they had and have distinguished and erudite works.[37]

In several chapters, Teixeira added some details, which he occasionally misunderstood, about authors and titles of books that were favored in various scholarly disciplines, such as the works of Hippocrates, Democritus, Plato, Socrates, Aristotle, Galen, and other Greek authors in philosophy and medicine; books by Ibn Sīnā on these sciences; the astronomical tables by Naṣīr al-Dīn al-Ṭūsī (d. 1274) called *al-Zīj al-Īlḫānī*, and books on history, historical narratives,

---

35. Greaves, 1693, pp. 88f; Smith, 1693, p. 43.
36. *Ibid.*, pp. 60-63.
37. Teixeira, 1902, p. 251.

and poems such as those on Rostam, Ḫosrow and Šīrīn, or Alexander.[38] Teixeira's major contribution to Western European perceptions of Muslim culture and science consisted in his paraphrasing translations of several Persian historical works, among them the "Rowḍat al-ṣafā" of Mīr-Ḫʷānd.

In 1626, Thomas Herbert (1606-1682), a youth of 20 years, decided to join the entourage of Robert Dodmore Cotton, the English ambassador to Šāh ʿAbbās. The aim of the embassy was to conclude a trading agreement with the shah to deliver raw silk by ship around Africa to England, avoiding the costly and at times difficult roads via the Ottoman Empire to the shores of the Mediterranean Sea. The embassy failed to achieve this aim and its ambassador died in 1628 on Persian soil.

Herbert also fell seriously ill. He recovered, however, thanks to a potent liquor forced upon him by one of his female servants whom Herbert described as having been from Tatary. Herbert sailed home via India where he composed a description of his adventures based upon a diary he had kept while travelling from Bander ʿAbbās via Isfahan to the shah's summer residence, Ashraf, on the coast of the Caspian Sea. This description was privately distributed among the nobles who had made his voyage possible, among them the Earl of Pembroke. The text apparently found the approval of its addressees since in 1634, the first revised version of Herbert's travels was given to the public. During Herbert's life-time, three other revised editions (1638, 1665, 1677) and two translations (1658, 1663) of this travel account were published.

In Herbert's first printed edition no information about the sciences in Persia can be found except for his report about the medical treatment he received during his illness, which he had contracted on the way through the Taurus mountains. Herbert made clear that he was by no means eager to be treated by the Persian physicians, that their skills and remedies did not improve his sad state, and that their thirst for his money depleted his purse:

> I wanted not the helpe and opinion of the Kings best Doctours, who though they hoped of my recouery, gaue me small appearance of it, yet I tooke what they prescribed mee, and gaue them Gold what they desired, so that it became a hard question, whether my spirits or Gold decayed faster. In this weaknesse, I was forced to trauell 300. miles, hanging vpon a Camell, and when I most hoped for recouery, *Morod* their famous *Æsculapius*, seeing no more money, limited my life to fiue days more existence, It was the more terrible, cause hee had seene *Mechà* and neuer after lied, as was told me.[39]

After Persian scientific medicine failed to heal Herbert, folk medicine brought him back to life again with incantations and wine from Shīrāz, although Herbert again did not care for this type of cure nor for the healer and her gender:

---

38. *Ibid.*, pp. 251f, footnote 5.
39. Herbert, 1634, pp. 168-169.

... an old *Tartarian Hecate* my seruant to whom I allowed eight pence daily, inuocated her *Succubi* to succour mee, which not a little hurt me, by forcing me to raile and curse her Orisons, shee whether to hasten the Doctors sentence concerning me, or rather to possesse my linnen (of which I had no small store) aimed to poyson me, and shee knew strong drinke was vtterly forbid me, for feare of inflammation, yet forced by inordinate thirst to call for water, she returnes me old intoxicating *Shiraz* Wine, which insensibly I powred downe, and so immeasurably, it immediately ouercharged my vitall sences, and put mee for foure and twentie houres into a deadly trance, so that it was a thousand to one, but it had kild me: yet by Gods mercy after a virulent vomit and sleepe (which for a moneth before I taste not to any purpose) I recouered (in that time once destinated to be buried by the Natiues, for few friends I had to helpe me) but when they saw me liue, they both admired and reioyced at it, so that by the binding qualitie of that wine and sleepe, I became bound and in small time got strength and action; the olde Whore in this season, opened my Trunckes (while my other seruant sorrowed for me) tooke away my linnen and some moneys. and run whether I neuer pursued her: this sicknesse hapned to mee, in my age of one and twentie, which is one of the Clymacterics.[40]

In the second edition, Herbert repeated the description of his experience with different forms of medical treatment available in Persia adding some information about the remedies given to him by the court physician and the name and ethnic origin of his male servant. The derogatory specification given in both editions to his female servant and healer was *Tartarian hekate* or *hekate from Tartary*. It was, however, not only meant to describe the woman's geographical origin north of Iran. Herbert's reference to the *succubies she implored* suggests this description be read as a word play invoking the idea, born in the Middle Ages, that the Mongols or Tatars came from the netherworld (Tartaros). As a consequence, he not only denigrated the woman as a prostitute, but also as the offspring of Satan. The respective passages in the following quote also illustrate that Herbert not only cut off and added to the narrative of his first edition or profoundly changed the contents of some of its parts, but even rewrote parts that he did not alter in substance:

> I wanted not the help of the Kings best Physitians, they did me little good: I tooke what they prescribed (dry Rice, Pomgranad pills, Barberries, Sloes in broth, and a hundred other things) and gave them what so ere they craved: so that it was hard to judge whether my spirits or gold decayed faster. ... I had then attending mee an Armenian call'd *Magar* and a Hecate of *Tartary*, to whom I daily gave for salary eight pence: many Succuby's shee implored (sore against my will) but finding they had no power to bewitch me; whether to accilerate *Morods* sentence, or whether to possesse my linnen and apparell (of which I had good plenty) I know not, but she resolv'd to poyson me. For, knowing wine was strictly forbidden me, shee presents me in an Agony of thirst, a Violl full of old strong

---

40. *Ibid.*, p. 169.

intoxicating wine, which relisht curiously, and I powred downe without wit or measure: ...[41]

This story also appears in Herbert's last edition, but there the tone is more moderate, less denigrating to the Safavid physician and the woman healer. It is possible that not only age had mollified Herbert's sentiments, but also the taste of the public had changed:

> I wanted not the advice and help of the Archi-ater, the King's doctor; who, albeit he was doubtless a very skilled physician, yet did me little good, so malignant was my distemper; albeit I took what he prescribed (part of which I well remember were pomegranate pills, barberries, sloes in broth, rice and sundry other things) and returned what he expected: so that it was hard to judge whether my spirits or gold decayed faster. ... For I had then attending me an Armenian, called Magar and a Tartarian woman, who (sore against my will) would for my recovery be often invocating her heathenish deities; but finding they had no power, whether to accelerate Morod's sentence or to possess my linen and apparel (of which I had good store) I know not; but no doubt well knowing that wine was by the doctor forbidden me, she nevertheless in an agony of thirst presents me with a phial full of intoxicating wine, which both looked and relished curiously, and I poured down no less insensibly without wit or measure. ...[42]

More direct and more concrete information about Arab or Persian sciences and their authorities can be found in Herbert's second edition onwards, although it also underwent changes in the subsequent editions as other parts of the text. Herbert devoted his attention to two sets of sciences, one set of which he approved, the other one he regarded with suspicion or rejected altogether. The first set encompassed medicine, mathematics, philosophy, geography, and history. The second was comprised of various kinds of occult sciences.

Most of the information about the first set of sciences appears to be slightly embellished, reordered, and misinterpreted extracts of new books about Arabic scientific knowledge printed in Europe in the late 16th and early 17th centuries. An example is the following account in the second edition:

> *Arabia* (denominated from *Arabus* sonne of *Apollo* and Madam *Babilonia*) at this day is more obscured than in ancient times, such time as it was the seminary of famous men: worthily in those dayes called happie, *Pandaya* and *Eudæmonia*. No part bred better Physitians, Mathematicians, and Philosophers. *Galen, Hipocrates, Avicen, Algazales, Albumazar, Abubecr, Alfarabius, Mahomet-ben-Isaac, ben Abdilla, Siet Iooh, ben Cazem, ben Sid'Ally* and others, here borne or educated: the Arabick so inchanted men that it is a common hyperbole amongst them, the Saints in Heaven and Paradize speak it.[43]

---

41. Herbert, 1638, p. 223.
42. Herbert, 1928, pp. 221-222.
43. Herbert, 1638, p. 110.

The text upon which Herbert relied when writing this passage was *De Nonnullis Orientarum urbibus, nec non indigenarum religione ac moribus tractatus breuis* published by two Maronite scholars in 1619 in Paris as an appendix to their Latin translation of the extract of al-Idrīsī's geography, the Arabic text of which had been printed in 1592 in Rome. In Chapter XIII called *De linguis varijs Orientalium, ac praesertim de Arabica, vbi de scriptoribus Arabibus*, Gabriel Sionita and Johannes Hesronita wrote:

> There always was and is an abundance with regard to the Arabic language. The most noble philosophers Averroes, Algazales, Abu-Becr, Alfarabius, who is called the second philosopher by the Muslims, Mohamed Ben-Isaac, who wrote the 'Key of the Orbits' in 663, and Mohamed Benabdilla, (who wrote) of the fundaments and opposites of existence, namely, honored it. The most noble astrologers Giafar Abu Maasciar Belchita, Mohamed Abu Rihan Chorauremzita, (who wrote) the 'Canon on the Comprehension of the Mathematical (Sciences) and the Stars' in 421, Abu-Nasr from Com, (who wrote) about the instructions for astrology in 357, Abu-Giafer Ben Hasan Tusaeus, (who wrote) about the signs of the stars, carefully adorned it. The outstanding mathematicians Abu-Zaid Ben-Hosain, who translated Euclid into Arabic, and Thabet Ben-Corra, who corrected this Euclid from many errors and through comments in 282 Hegyra, also gave lustre to it. The physicians Alfarabius, mentioned above, from whom Avicenna has taken over a lot, Honain Ben Isac from Abad, who wrote much on medical art, Mohamed Ben-Abdillatif with the cognomen Ebn-Elbitar, (who) wrote about the Egyptian plants and their virtues in 646, and Mohamed Ben-Eladib, (who wrote) about the causes of diseases, (did so too). The historians Bidhaui, (who wrote) about califes and sultans, Chalaccan, (who wrote) memoirs about men in 601, Ebrahim Ben-Helal, (who wrote) about the Dailamite empire in 383, Ismael Ben-Aali resp. Abdollah Ben Assad from Iaman (i.e., Yemen), (who) wrote about the events and calamities of empires until 750, (did so too). Ben-Sidi Aali, in his book about the teachings of the Muslims, enumerated one hundred and fifty jurists and (scholars), who wrote about the Coran. (Scholars) of rhetoric and grammarians are almost innumerable. The most praiseworthy (among them) you will find through diligent reading with name, surname, country, and year in Ben-Casem. It is not our intention here to enumerate by turns all Arabic writers, since Thomas Erpenius, a truly very learned man who is able to move freely in all kinds of studies, has promised to bring to light a very extensive catalogue of these (authors).[44]

---

44. "A lingua Arabica semper floruit ac floret; hanc enim philosophi nobilissimi, Averroes, Algazales, Abu-Becr, Alfarabius, qui à Moslemannis secundus cognominatur phylosophus, Mohamed Ben-Isaac, qui firmamentatorum (sic) clauem conscripsit anno 663. & Mohamed Benabdilla de elementorum contrariorum que existentia, ornarunt. Astrologi nobilissimi Giafar Abu-Maasciar Belchita, Mohamed Abu Rihan Chorauremzita de canone in mathesis ac astrorum intelligentiam anno 421. Abu-Nasr Comita de instructionibus in Astrologiam anno 357. Abu-Giafer, & Ben-Hasan Tusaeus (sic) de signis astrorum condecorarunt. Eam etiam illustrarunt Mathematici insignis Abu-Zaid Ben-Honain, qui Euclidem in Arabicam linguam transtulit, & Thabet Ben-Corra, qui eundem Euclidem à multis mendis correxit, atque commentariis anno ab Hegyra 282. illustrauit. Medici Alfarabius surpradictus à quo Auicenna multa desumpsit, Honain Ben-Isac Abadita, qui multa in artem medicam scripsit; Mohamed Ben-Abdillatif, cognomento Ebn-Elbitar de plantis Aegyptiacis earumque virtute scripsit anno 646. & Mohamed Ben-Eladib de causis morborum. Historici Bidhaui de Chalifis ac Sultannis: Chalaccan de hominum memoriis anno

The knowledge gained from Sionita and Hesronita mixed together with other information is offered to the reader, yet again, in the second, general part of Herbert's description of Persia. It appears as a part of Herbert's additions to the first edition, encompassing the portrayal of the entertainments the Persians favoured in peace time, of their manufacturing skills, their love of poetry, and related issues. With regard to the scholarly achievements of the Persians, Herbert focussed upon Persian medicine and aspects of the calendar. He claimed that the physicians were:

> great admirers of Nature, and doat so much thereupon, that they make that ofttimes the first causer which indeed is but instrumentall or secundarie: ...[45]

He evaluated them as moral men whose language and clothing make all who know them esteem and honor them. However, he profoundly disapproved of their inclination towards greed and magic. Nonetheless, he gratified the entire profession with an appreciation in stark contrast to his unwavering refusal to accept their care and cures when he was sick:

> ... and did not avarice (a vice predominating there, and by occasion of sicknesse in me full dearly'exemplified) and Magick studies too far sway them, I could value them above the rest; however as they are, they passe for a generation usefull and exquisite.[46]

Then he informed his reader that the medical profession is ordered by degrees according to skill and seniority, that true doctors and charlatans are known by different names ("Hackeems" versus "Shitan-Tabib", i.e. the "Devills Chirurgion"), and that they are "Masters of much knowledge and ignore not the Mathematiques".[47] Thereafter follows the list of "Arabick" scholarly authorities in which several names specific to Sionita's and Hesronita's account reappear. Herbert also drew upon Leo Africanus's *Descriptio Africae* for this account:[48]

---

601. Ebrahim Ben-Helal de imperio Dailemitico anno 383. Ismael Ben-Aali, & Abdollah Ben-Assad Iamanita (sic) emporum euentus calamitatesque scripsit vsque ad 750. Legislatores, atque ij, qui de Alcorano scripserunt, enumerat centum quinquaginta Ben-Sidi Aali in suo de dogmatibus Moslemannarum libro. Rhetores, Grammaticique innumeri ferè sunt, quos diligenter apud Ben-Casem laudatos inter legendum nomine, cognomine patria & anno reperies. Nec nostrum hûc institutum est omnes Arabicos scriptores recensere, cùm de his catalogum amplissimum Thomas Erpenius vir sanè doctissimus, omnique studiorum genere excultissimus in lucem edendum promittat; ...". Sionita, Hesronita, 1619, pp. 41-42.
45. Herbert, 1638, p. 233.
46. *Ibid.*, p. 233.
47. *Ibid.*, pp. 233-234.
48. Herbert mentioned as poets, among others, Ibnul-Farid ('Umar b. al-Farīd) and Elfargani, an unidentified commentator of Ibn al-Farīd's allegorical poetry. Leo Africanus' book was the only book written in a language accessible to Herbert which mentioned these two authors as poets and also wrote their names in the same way. Herbert, 1928, p. 247; See Jones, 1988, p. 68.

> Many Arabick Writers have flourisht in those parts, most of whose Bookes they read and practise by, namely Galen, Averroys, Hippocrates, Alfarabius, Avycenna, Ben-Isaack, Abu-Ally, Mahumed-Abdilla, Ben-Eladib, Abu becr, Rhazis, Algazallys'and Albumazar. In Geography, Abul-fœda and Alphraganus, from whom they better their discourse, and by such Lectures become admirable.[49]

Several of these authors, such as Muḥammad b. 'Abdallāh, Ibn al-Adīb, or al-Farġānī, are not known to have been relevant for Safavid scholars in general and physicians in particular. Obviously, Herbert had no clear understanding of who these authors had been nor precise information about the scholarly training of Safavid physicians. Nonetheless, he had no scruples about offering this more than imperfect knowledge to his readers as correct descriptions of contemporary Persia. Herbert apparently assumed that what was true, according to Leo Africanus, Gabriel Sionita, and Johannes Hesronita, for Northern Africa and the Ottoman Empire must also apply to the Safavids.

The pressure of Herbert's powerful friends to enlarge his account by more details may have been accompanied by the wish to write something about the sciences in Iran. Satisfying such a demand obviously required that he deliver particular details, such as specific names of scholars; ensuring the correctness of the information appears to have been of less importance. Herbert may have even been convinced that the Oriental autorship of his sources was a guarantee of the truth of his description of the scholarly life in Iran. Such a preference for details derived from reknowned authorities or witnesses not only conforms to the general contemporary interest in particularities, singularities, and curiosities and the frame of the contemporary methods of demonstration and testimony, but also finds its support in the remarkably few changes Herbert introduced in this passage in his last revised edition, adding only one other detail about maps from Abū al-Fidā's *Geography* which appears to be an invention since, according to our knowledge, this work did not contain maps:

> They are masters of much knowledge, and not a little delighted with judicial astrology. Many Arabic writers, learned both in natural philosophy and mathematics, have flourished in those parts, most of whose books they read, namely Hippocrates, Galen, Averroes, Alfarabius, Avicenna, Ben-Isaac, Abbu-Ally, Mahummed-Abdilla, Ben-Eladib, Abu-becr, Rhazis, Algazzallys, and Albumazar. In geography Abul-Foeda, the great Arab cosmographer, whose works they have (one of whose maps I saw at Gombroon, and I thought differed from ours both in lands and seas; it was to be sold, but what money I offered would not be accepted), as also Alphraganus, from whom they better their discourse, and by such helps become admirable. Nor want they knowledge of herbs, drugs, and gums; witness the Maydan in Isfahan, than which no place in the world I think shows greater plenty of herbs and drugs, having also no less choice of fruits, gums, and odours.[50]

---

49. Herbert, 1638, p. 234.
50. *Ibid.*, pp. 244f.

Other features of Herbert's travel account point in the same direction, such as his manifold efforts to give Turkish, Arabic, Persian, and other Oriental equivalents of English, Latin, or, occasionally, Hebrew words and to speak of simple elements of the itinerary in Persian expressions. Herbert many times called, for example, his travel stops *manzeels*. Nonetheless, he had no more than the rudimentary knowledge of Persian a foreigner can acquire while travelling through the country and none whatsoever of Turkish, Arabic, or any of the other contemporary Asian languages he quoted.

Herbert terminated his survey of Persian medicine with a brief enumeration of remedies, in particular the herbs, drugs, and gums he had seen at the central market place of Isfahan, indicating the cures the Persians most favoured and those they used less, i.e., sweating and phlebotomy. He justified this enumeration by his wish to show his readers that the Safavid physicians *have some skill* and that the remedies resemble *European prescriptions*.[51] This approach of putting things into perspective by comparing what he observed or experienced (or read) with English conditions, (whether it concerned the state of the monarchy, the size and natural attributes of towns, or, as in this case, the kind of remedies of the Persian *materia medica*) characterizes many of Herbert's descriptions and evaluations. This approach is Herbert's second most important method for making the unknown familiar to his English audience. The method most often applied by Herbert to achieve this aim, however, was integrating contemporary Persia into the knowledge gleaned from those ancient secular and sacred sources which were well known to the reading public of the time.

Sionita's, Hesronita's, and Leo Africanus's books about Oriental cities and Africa were not the only Western European publications about the Middle East available to Herbert. He also drew on numerous other texts, among them the travel account of the Portuguese physician Pedro Teixeira, which he read in the form of a rather defective summarizing Latin translation by Johannes de Laet (1633) and in the extracts given by Samuel Purchas in his history of the religions since creation (1626), the influential history of Persia by Pietro Bizari (1583), and the Latin extract from an Ottoman genealogy called *Tarich* published by Wilhelm Schickard in 1628.[52] His major source which also influenced his conceptions was Samuel Purchas' *Relations of the World And the Religions Obserued in all Ages and places (sic) Discouered, from the Creation vnto this Present* or, simply, *Pvrchas his Pilgrimage*. Herbert presumably took from it some of the names of those scholars he mentioned, for example that of *Mahummed Abdilla* about whom Purchas wrote:

---

51. *Ibid.*, p. 234.
52. See, for instance, the relevant footnotes in Herbert 1928 as well as the introduction into the new edition of Teixeira's texts by Barajas Sala, pp. XXVf.

> *Ben-Casem* also relates, that *Mohamed Abi Abdillah* professed Philosophie in this Citie (Damascus - S. B.), and to dispute with all commers, and wrote a huge Booke, *De vnitate existendi principiorum*. He dyed there, A.H. 638.[53]

He also changed what had been in Purchas' book a cautious attribution of a statement to some ancient author into a solid general point such as when he stated categorically that "Arabia" has been "denominated from *Arabus* sonne of *Apollo* and Madam *Babilonia*" while Purchas said that "some deriue the name from *Arabus*, the sonne of *Apollo* and *Babylonia*" referring this claim to Solin and Berossus.[54] More important, however, is that Herbert, in his first edition, followed Purchas' conceptual approach to geography by supplementing it with hundreds of details taken from historical books. Purchas had informed his readers:

> My intent is not to teach Geography, but to bestow on the studious of Geographie, a History of the World, so to giue hime flesh vnto his bones, and vse vnto his Theorie or Speculation, whereby both that skill may be confirmed, and a further and more excellent obtained. Geographie without Historie seemeth a Carkasse without life and motion: History without Geographie mooueth, but in moouing wandreth as a Vagrant, without certaine habitation.[55]

Herbert opened his first edition by qualifying his text as one of history which dictated that "truth and simplicity" were the "elements" of its narrative. He emphasized that only additions from "quotations or observations of other men" could bring it to true "splendour and perfection".[56] No wonder, that Herbert filled his work with direct and indirect quotations on geography and history from many authors, mostly those who were part of the early modern Western European intellectual heritage. His description of ancient Persia, while following closely Purchas' work, explicitly mentions almost exclusively ancient Greek and Latin writers and the Bible. Additionally, Herbert claimed that he had also exploited "Persian Histories", a "Persian story", etc.[57] Such claims may refer to Mīr-Ḥvānd's *Rowḍat al-ṣafā*.

Herbert gained most of his knowledge of contemporary Persian geography and of mediaeval and contemporary Persian history from contemporary European historical and geographical books and, perhaps, maps, as well as from medieval and early modern travel accounts. His most important source again seems to have been Purchas' work. With regard to Persian Muslim history, Herbert referred to the *Sefer ha-Yuḥasin*, a work on Jewish chronological history by Abraham Zacuto (about 1450, Salamanca; after 1510, Ottoman Empire).[58]

---

53. Purchas, 1626, p. 242.
54. *Ibid.*, p. 223.
55. *Ibid.*, p. 42.
56. Herbert, 1634, p. 1.
57. Herbert, 1638, pp. 269, 271-275.
58. *Ibid.*, pp. 282-283. *The Jewish Encyclopedia*, 1906, p. 627.

Herbert acquired some knowledge about it third-hand by reading Purchas who, as he himself wrote, had read various books by Joseph Scaliger in which the latter had quoted extracts from Zacuto's book.[59] When summarizing the genealogy of the Safavids, Herbert mentioned *The Annalls of Persia*.[60] Occasionally, Herbert also invoked oral local knowledge, particularly when talking about recent local history.[61]

In the first part of his travel account of Persia, Herbert cited five Muslim representatives of the so-called rational sciences by name. The first, a certain Ibn 'Alī is already mentioned before this first part actually starts; when discussing the different names of the three parts of Arabia (Deserta, Petrosa, and Felix) Herbert reported that *ben Ally* called Arabia Felix *Ajaman* and *Giaman*.[62] In the first part, the same *Ben-Ally* is referred to in a discussion about the presumable age and historical size of Shiraz:

> Antient no doubt she is; her name in history confirming it, *Rocnaduddaule* (Sonne of *Sha-Hussan* Sonne of *Abbaz Viez*, Lord of *Bagdet, Kermoen, Laristan* and *Shyraz* (so 'tis then named)) being here buried *Anno Dom*. 980. of Hegira 360. And questionlesse she has been much greater than at this present. *Vlughbeg* (a learned Geographer and Nephew to *Tamberlang*) gives her in his tyme fifteene myles compasse, *Contarenus* fifteene, and eightie thousand houses. *Barbarus* eightscore yeares ago, gives her twenty; *Teishera* after him, six and thirty myles circuit; *Skikard* upon *Tarich* a like vast circumference: *Iohn* of *Persia* in his time numbred her Inhabitants eightie thousand, *Ben-Ally* thee (sic) houndred thousand: we may not gainsay their reports, because no inquiry can disprove them; let us therefore rest contented in her present description, which I shall present you (God willing) without error.[63]

This *Ben-Ally* might be idential with *Ben-sidi-Ally* mentioned by Sionita, Hesronita, and Herbert in their respective lists of Muslim scholars. In the second part of Herbert's account, at least, it is this form of the name to which he refers twice when describing Persian mores and customs, calling him also "the grand Annalist" and a "right Cabalist".[64] Since both references appear to relate to ḥadīt and Qur'ān, Herbert's characterization of the author does not contradict Sionita's and Hesronita's way of describing him as somebody who wrote on the Qur'an. However, in both cases, Herbert also had access to other sources than the little work of the two Maronites; for example Purchas referred to this author as a source of information on the Ka'ba, Mecca, and the Prophet.[65]

---

59. Purchas, 1626, p. 235.
60. Herbert, 1638, p. 285.
61. *Ibid.*, p. 165.
62. *Ibid.*, p. 110.
63. *Ibid.*, p. 134.
64. *Ibid.*, pp. 235, 240.
65. Purchas, 1626, p. 273.

Uluġ Beg, who of course was Tīmūr's grandson, not his nephew, appears as an authority in geography three more times: once when Herbert discussed the various names of Farahabad near the Caspian Sea, claiming that Uluġ Beg had called the town Strabatt; the second time when he talked about Turkistan giving Uluġ Beg's name in the latinized form "Vlughbeghius"; and the third when he pondered whether Tabriz and Ecbatana were built on the same site.[66] The first and the second of these three references confirm that Herbert gained this knowledge of Uluġ Beg's geographical information neither from oral information in Persia nor from a direct consultation of his *Zīj*, but from European sources, an assumption already suggested by his error concerning Uluġ Beg's parental affiliation to Tīmūr.[67] This indicates that Herbert's inclusion of information on Muslim science in his second edition not only reflects the expectation of the English public, but also illuminates the information on Muslim scholarly traditions that was available in England in the 1630s.

When discussing Turkistan and Transoxania, Herbert mentioned two other Muslim scholars, Naṣīr al-Dīn al-Ṭūsī and Ibn Sīnā:

> Townes of note there, are *Tuz* (in 38 degrees, the birth-place of Nazaraddyn the great Mathematician, & Commentator upon *Euclyde*) ... Townes of account are, *Buchar* and *Seonargant*, (*Maracanda* in *Arrhyan*, *Samrachatan* in *Chalcondiles*, *Paracanda* in *Strabo*, *Sarmagana* in *Ptolemy*,) (*Bokar* and *Samarchand*) the birth places of *Avicen* (call'd *Honain-Ali-ben-sein*) borne *Anno Heg.* 370, a famous scholler, in ninety bookes of Physicks, Chymicks, and Philosophy helping others: ...[68]

In his discussion of the history and geography of Baghdad, mainly based upon his reading, Herbert pretends to rely partly upon a Muslim writer called *Ben-Casen*:

> ... Almansor gave it another name, *Medina-Isalem*, i.e. the City of peace; or as *Ben-Casen* thinks, *Deer-Assala* (sic), i.e. the Church of peace.[69]

While such a name was also mentioned in Sionita's and Hesronita's book, the information concerning Baghdad's epithet cannot be found there. It seems that Herbert took this piece of knowledge from Samuel Purchas who had written:

> Baghdad (which is also called Dar-assalam, that is *The Citie of Peace*) receiued that name of a Monke called *Bachdad*, who as *Ben-Casen* writeth, serued a Church builded in that Medow.

---

66. *Ibid.*, pp. 179, 184, 195.
67. *Ibid.*, pp. 179, 184. The wrong term of Uluġ Beg's relationship to Tīmūr points to an Italian source, since in Italian one and the same word designates a grandson and a nephew (nipote), possibly one of Giovanni Botero's books translated into English in the late 16th and in the 17th centuries.
68. *Ibid.*, p. 184.
69. *Ibid.*, p. 219.

Purchas called *Ben-Casen*'s text from which he had gained the strange information *De viridario Electorum* (The Garden of the Chosen).[70] Nonetheless, the information is insufficient to identify that author and work with certainty.

Herbert's references to the above mentioned Muslim scholars are straightforward and at times admirative. He accepted their knowledge as equivalent in value and meaning to those of the other sources he used, whether ancient, mediaeval, or contemporary. In one case, he even invoked Uluġ Beg and Abū al-Fidā', albeit wrongly so, to persuade his readers of the correctness of his own point of view, namely, that Tauris or Tabriz and ancient Ecbatana were built on the same site. He first claimed that not even a memory survived of ancient Ecbatana:

> ... since it is become a question whether *Tauryz* be old *Ecbatan*; and whether it be in *Media* or no.[71]

Indeed, for instance, Pierre Gilles, some eighty years earlier, had rejected the identification of Tabriz with Ecbatana, although he believed both towns to be in Media:

> From the four castles we proceeded to Tauris, which some believe falsely to be Ecbatana, but Paulus Jovius is wrong, who believes it (being) in Armenia, while it is in Media ...[72]

Herbert knew of other authors (Ptolemy, Niger, Cedrenus, Marco Polo, and Chalcondyles) who differentiated between Tabriz and Ecbatana, and located the first in as different regions as Assyria, Armenia, Persia, Parthia, or Pers-Armenia. The reason for this confusion, Herbert thought, was twofold: first the unacceptable inference from royal titles to geographical locations and second a confusion with regard to Armenia producing the view that a:

> part of *Armenia major* extending South of *Araxis* into *Atropatia*, a part of *Medya*; and from whence the name *Pers-Armenia* is compounded.[73]

Against the separation between Tabriz and Ecbatana and against the assumption that the former was a town outside of Media, Herbert raised three sortes of arguments: geographical, historical, and authoritative:

> If to be under *Baronta*, (*Diodorus, Polybius*, and *Ptolemy* call it *Orontes*,) if to be in 36 degrees 50 minutes, if to have the ruines of *Tobyas* his grave, if to be the buriall place of Kings, if to be the Metropolis time out of mind, if to be the Citie

---

70. Purchas, 1626, p. 242.
71. Herbert, 1638, p. 195.
72. "Inde quartis castris peruenimus Tauricam, quam quidam falso putant Ecbatana, sed falsius Paulus Jouius, qui eam putat in Armenia, cum sit in Media: ...". MS Paris, BnF, Dupuys 16, fol. 3a.
73. Herbert, 1638, p. 195.

from *Ierusalem* N.E. foure hundred forsangs can make it *Ecbatan*; or if the authority of *Ananias, Petrus de la Valle, Leunclavius, Teixera*, and of *Ortelius* will serve, let it be *Ecbatan* and in *Medya*.[74]

However, in order to prove that locating Tabriz outside of Media was incorrect, he furnished a single geographical argument based on authority:

> ... for by *Abulfeda, Vlughbeg*, and others, the latitude of *Tauryz* complies with *Ecbatan*.[75]

This, however, is false, as I have already indicated. First, Abū al-Fidā' and Uluġ Beg differ in what they give as the latitude of Tabriz. Abū al-Fidā', relying here upon al-Bīrūnī, has 39°10'. Uluġ Beg ascribed to Tabriz a latitude of 38°. Second, none of these values agrees with that given by Herbert nor with the latitude of Ecbatana found in Ptolemy's *Geography* (37°45').[76] There are, however, Arabic sources such as the *Zīj* of M. b. M. b. a. Bakr al-Tizzīnī, *muwaqqit* of the Umayyad mosque at Damascus in the late 10th/16th century, which give a latitude value of Tabriz close to that quoted by Herbert – 36°25'.[77] While Herbert may have learned about Abū al-Fidā' and Uluġ Beg from Western European publications of the late 16th and early 17th centuries, his second edition appeared exactly in those years when Edward Pococke and John Greaves had travelled to the Ottoman Empire (visiting Istanbul, Aleppo, Smyrna, and other towns) and had brought back copies of the works by these two scholars as well as al-Tizzīnī's tables and other mathematical, astronomical, geographical, and historical manuscripts. While in 1638, Herbert obviously had believed in the demonstrative efficacy of Abū al-Fidā's and Uluġ Beg's testimonies, forty years later, he had changed his mind and simply omitted this passage.[78] Opinions among English scholars about the value of Arabic and Persian geographical sources had turned from former enthusiastic expectation to disappointed resignation. Herbert's decision to cancel his reference to the two Muslim authorities may reflect this changed intellectual climate. His unstable and at times confused handling of a variety of information, including his description of the route he himself had travelled while in Persia, however, does not allow us to reach such a conclusion with certainty.

Herbert's attitude towards the sciences of medicine and astronomy in Iran is once cautious and then later condemnatory. The first instance occurs when Herbert summarizes the goal of female and male circumcision in Iran based upon Ibn Sayyid 'Alī's authority " or *Ben-sidi-Ally* lyes'.[79] The second relates to

---

74. *Ibid.*, p. 195.
75. *Ibid.*, p. 195.
76. Abū al-Fidā', 1840, p. 400; King, 1999, p. 462; Stevenson, 1932, p. 135.
77. MS Paris, BnF, Arabe 2521, fol. 9b.
78. Herbert, 1928, p. 196.
79. Herbert, 1638, p. 235.

the Persian calendar Herbert's description of which is not only incomplete and partly wrong, but it also motivated him to write some rather strong diatribes against the Persians's attitude toward knowledge in general. His evaluation, as he indicated himself, is partly the outcome of his own fantasies and partly the result of a lack of knowledge:

> They desire rather to tread in an antick path of ignorance, then by any new invention or wholsome study to wrong the judgements of their predicessors: ... And hence it is (as I imagine) that they continue their maimed calculations, out of a blind conceit that antiquity commanded them; for they compute their yeares only by the Moone, not by the course and motion of the Sun; affirming, that the firmament or eight heavens finishes its revolution in two and thirty yeares; which is false; his diurnall motion from East and West compleating it selfe in foure and twentie houres; his other from West to East, but one degree in a hundred years; such is the violence of the first mover. Notwithstanding, it may be they meane the heaven of *Saturne* adjoyning it, (whose revolution comes neere their time) finishing its journey from West to East in 30 yeares. And thus, their Lunarie account is subject to no small errour, reckning (sic) from the Autumnall Æquinox 12 Moones, the number of dayes in a whole yeare 353. Our Solar computation exceeding theirs twelfe dayes at least, every yeare; whereby it comes to passe, that 30 of our yeares make 31 of theirs; whence, the difference arises 'twixt us and them in their Æra or Hegyrath (sic), and doubtlesse by protract, will cause much more confusion.[80]

Herbert reinforced his evaluation of what he perceived as a lack of curiosity and thirst for exotic knowledge when talking about "the Persians in general", while apparently meaning the Safavid military elite:

> Generally, the Persians are facetious, harmlesse in discourse, not very inquisitive of exotique alterations, seldome transgressing this demand, if such and such a Country have good wine, faire women, swift horses, and sharp weapons: choosing rather to fatten themselves by a contented Notion, than by curious inquisition to perplex their other recreations. Few of them know how to read, *Bellona* trayning them up in iron dances; but honour such as have it: the Churchmen, Clerks, and Santos, attracting them. Some skill they have in Musick; the Dorick and Phrygick, a soft and loftie sort of Consort. But above all, Poetry lulls them, that Genius seeming properly to delight it selfe amongst them.[81]

Although it may well be that Herbert met some illiterates among the members of the different courts he came to visit in Iran, his sweeping statement that the military elite was illiterate in general is certainly wrong according to what we know about libraries and courtly education in Safavid times.

While describing his own journey, Herbert occasionally talked about Persian customs based upon beliefs in magic, astrology, divination, or other occult

---

80. *Ibid.*, p. 234.
81. *Ibid.*, p. 235.

sciences. He reported, for instance, that the beliefs of the sultan of *Gombroon* forced him to stay longer than wanted in this unattractive town:

> Fourteene dayes are past since we entred *Gombroon*; the place has no such Magick to perswade us to inhabit here. Our end is travell, why stay we then? sure, wee were stayed three dayes by the Sultans superstition, who upon casting the Dice, if the chance prov'd right, would let us goe; if wrong, *nigro carbone notatus*. The foure and twentieth day the Dice was right, and wee were mounted: ...[82]

In the second part of his account, Herbert briefly took up the issue of "superstition" too. He delivered almost no new information about actual occult practices, nor was he very precise with regard to which of the occult sciences were truly studied in Persian scholarly circles. His attitude towards these sciences and their applications, already made clear by his complaints in the first part of his account, was accentuated by placing their description next to his discussion of pre-Islamic Iranian religion which he called *idolatry* rather than by talking about them in connection with his treatment of the other disciplines:

> They are very superstitious, it may be noted from our adverse fortunes as we travelled; for when we stood at their mercy to provide us Mules, Camells, and Horses, how hasty soever we appeared, they took no notice of it, not cared to set us forward, except, by throwing the dyce such a chance hapned (sic) as they thought fortunate; a ceremony diduced from the Romans who had their *albi & atri dies*. In every mischance also, or in sicknesse they use sorcery, prescribing charmes, crosse characters, letters, anticks, or the like, taken mostly out of their Alcoran. Nicromantic studies are much applauded, as profound, and transcending vulgar capacities, many in those parts make a notable living of it: and few Siets there but can exorcize.[83]

When della Valle finally arrived in the Safavid Empire, he was married to an Assyrian Christian from Baghdad, had learnt some Arabic and spoke fairly fluent Turkish. In Iran, where he stayed for more than six years, he acquired a profound knowledge of Persian. Thus, he was qualified, as almost no traveller before him, to obtain specific, concrete knowledge of the local conditions of the arts and sciences. However, having other obligations, such as the care of his wife and her co-religionists, he did not care to learn about the sciences of the Safavid Empire. Neither did he treat offers from scholars from the court with much esteem, thinking of himself and his European scholarly and literary background as much more sophisticated.[84] His attitude softened with increasing time spent in Isfahan and greater familiarity with Safavid society. He appreciated Persian astronomy, astrology, mathematics, and geography to such

---

82. *Ibid.*, p. 124.
83. *Ibid.*, p. 232.
84. See the summary of della Valle's attitudes, Gurney, 1986, p. 109. See also my own new evaluation of della Valle's printed letters and their tendency to distort della Valle's practice of travelling as well as attitudes: Brentjes, in print [2003].

a degree that he collected manuscripts, planning to translate them into Latin. Together with the Augustinian father Manuel della Madre di Dio, he agreed to visit Mīr Muḥammad ʿAbd al-Vahhābī, a *man of quality*, to see his collection of *curiosities* and to participate in his house with father Manuel in a religious debate. Feeling dissatisfied with his ability to express his thoughts adequately in the course of the discussion, della Valle decided to write down his comments in Persian, to get them approved by the Carmelites, and to engage a skilled Persian scribe to present the text in an acceptable form as a gift to his host.[85] His host appreciated della Valle's gift and annotated it. Della Valle hoped that his apology would induce a response from Shiʿi scholars.[86] Encouraged by Mīr Muḥammad Bāqir Yazdī, known as Mīr Dāmād, Aḥmad b. Zayn al-Dīn al-ʿĀbidīn wrote a reply which was repeatedly copied and distributed free of charge.[87] The mutual discussion of this text even continued while della Valle was already on his way home to Italy through letters written and pamphlets sent by the Carmelites.[88]

As the result of a deep personal crisis, della Valle's attitude softened even more in the last period of his stay in Persia. The crisis was caused by the death of his Assyrian wife from fever in Minab. Della Valle having caught the same fever as his wife, believed he also was going to die, but managed to move on to Lar. There, a friendly and competent Muslim physician born in Shiraz, Ḥakīm Abū al-Fatḥ, nursed della Valle back to life. As della Valle described the treatment, the physician not only took care of the traveller's bodily problems, but also softened his heartache by diverting him with long talks about all sorts of matters, including intellectual subjects, and by encouraging his friends and acquaintances to visit. Della Valle thought that during all his travels he had never seen another town with so many inhabitants so well versed in the sciences as Lar.[89]

Among his visitors della Valle mentioned in particular two lawyers, Rukn al-Dīn and Quṭb al-Dīn, as being skilled philosophers, alchemists, and astronomers. Talking about these Muslim scholars in a language saturated with expressions from the Republic of Letters, he admitted that without their help, trust, and friendship he never would have been able to acquire the best books available and to learn so much truly new and specific information about legal issues and other curiosities which he hoped to put to the service of the public at home:

> Friendship and intimate communication, which I had with these men of letters all the time I lived in Lar, developing with them a more than usual confidence, made it easy for me to know with good grounds many things which, without it, I

---

85. Della Valle, 1658, pp. 251-55.
86. *Ibid.*, p. 254.
87. *Ibid.*, 1658, pp. 500f; see also Gurney, p. 111.
88. *Ibid.*, 1658, pp. 500-505.
89. *Ibid.*, 1658, pp. 359, 361f, 367f.

would have never been able to penetrate. In the first place, with their help and directions, I aquired excellent books, which I keep close to me. Next, also, conversing with them, they told me freely infinitely many particulars of abstruse things, both concerning the law of Mohammed and other curiosities; from which I obtained beautiful information of which I bring with me several note-books, which, if I live, one day may serve something to the benefit of the public.[90]

His new insights included, for instance, information about the teachings of clandestine heretical sects, such as the so-called *ahl al-taḥqīq* which Gurney believes to have been a branch of the *nuqṭā'īs*, a variant of the *ḥurūfīs*.[91] The learned men of Lar also introduced della Valle to scholars and notables of Shiraz who visited the town. This led to conversations with the ruler of Shiraz, Imām Qulī Ḫān, his librarian, Mīr 'Abd al-Ḥasan, and other notables. The increasing use of expressions characteristic of the Republic of Letters to describe the Persians with whom della Valle met and conversed and his growing emotional acceptance of them characterizes the striking difference between della Valle's letters from Isfahan and those from Lar and Shiraz:

> While these people passed by, I was visited several times by different personages of pleasant manners, even though I had not previously met them; who, having heard about me even in the harbour of Combrù, from some friends of mine (among) those men of letters of Lar, such as Moullà Abdì, who went there, and I do not know who else; with much courtesy they wanted to meet me and develop a friendship with me and become friends. Among others, Mirzà Scerèf Gihòn, a man of letters and a curioso, brother of the Seid Scerìf Calantèr of Sciràz, together with another learned (man), called Moullà Hacuerdì, who, coming from the harbour, stopped on their way in Lar for one day only and came to visit me. But, above all, Mir Abdu'l Hasan, the main man of Sciràz, a man of letters and head librarian of the Chan of this City, so famous for its studies among the Persians, because of the reports of my friend Moullà Abdì, had a great desire for my person. The day, he was supposed to arrive in Lar, he sent ahead one of his men in order to invite me to have dinner with him in the house of Cadhì Rokn'eddìn, a common friend of ours, where he was supposed to stay. Likewise, in the name of that Cadhì, the invitation to me was repeated. Thus I went there. The caresses he made to me, the great love that caught me and that he later always manifested to me were extraordinary things. But, to return to al Mir Abdu'l Hasàn, we talked a long time and spent some hours of the night in good conversation. That was not enough, however. It was necessary to promise him that I would come back the next morning for lunch & to spend with him the only day which he was going to spend in Lar. I could not

---

90. "L'amicitia, e comunicatione intrinseca, che io hebbi con questi Letterati tutto'l tempo che in Lar dimorai, arriuando con loro a termini di più che ordinaria confidenza, mi fece strada facile a saper con fondamento molte cose, che, senza essa, non haurei potuto giamai penetrare. In prima, con l'aiuto, & indirizzo loro, mi prouidi di buonissimi libri, che tengo appresso di me: poi anche, discorrendo con loro, mi conferirono liberamente infiniti particolari di cose astruse, tanto della legge di Mahometto, quanto di altre curiosità, che io ne cauai bellissime notitie; delle quali porto con me pieni diuersi scartafacci, che, se io viuo, vn giorno potranno seruire a qualche cosa, a beneficio del publico". Della Valle, 1658, p. 370. I thank Francesca Bordogna for translating these passages into English.
91. Della Valle, 1658, pp. 370-372 and 1674, part III, pp. 169f; Gurney, 1986, pp. 112f.

decline, compelled by his many courtesies and those displayed by the others. Thus, after I went back in the morning, the two of us spent all that day with a few others of similar conversation with the greatest relish, reading books, comparing Authors, examining verses and Poets, & taking other similar pleasures, within secluded chambers; ... .[92]

In 1623, one year after these conversations had taken place, Imām Qulī Ḫān approached the Carmelites to acquire books by Aristotle and Plato in Greek and Latin, Arabic-Latin dictionaries, and the Bible in Arabic.[93]

Della Valle's special friend among all these educated notables, however, was the astronomer Mullā Zayn al-Dīn al-Lārī, whom he described in the most elavating tones:

> Above all, Moullà Zeinèddìn, an excellent mathematician and astronomer, & (excellent) in all the other sciences, (being) not only the most learned person whom I had met in the whole of Persia; but also (a person) who, in our countries would, no doubt, be placed among those of the first rank, grew so fond of me, that every day, at each hour, he was with me, raising my spirits, entertaining (me), talking about matters of learning, with his greatest relish and to my (great) relief. I felt admiration for that great ingenuity, for such a beautiful mind, still young, approximately thirty five years old – not more, who, being so learned, could have kept me, and one hundred others, a long time at school, (teaching us) about everything. In each way he stayed around me and would have died to learn from me

---

92. "Nel passaggio di queste genti, io fui visitato più volte in Lar da diuersi personaggi di garbo, ancorche da me per prima non conosciuti : i quali, hauuta nuoua di me, fin nel porto di Combrù, da alcuni amici miei di quei Letterati di Lar, come il Moullà Abdì, che vi andò, e non sò chi altri; con molta cortesia volsero conoscermi, e far con me amicitia. Trà gli altri, il Mirzà Scerîf gihòn, huomo di lettere e curioso, fratello del Seid Scerîf Calantèr de Sciràz, insieme con vn'altro dotto, chiamato il Moullà Hacuerdì, in vn sol giorno, che venendo amendue dal porto, si trattennero in Lar di passaggio, mi fu a visitare. Ma sopra tutti, il Mir Abdu'l Hasan, huomo principale di Sciràz, letterato, e Bibliotecario maggiore del Chan in questa Città, frà Persiani cosi famosa di studij, per le relationi del Moullà Abdì mio amico, hebbe desiderio grande della mia persona. Il giorno che doueua arriuare in Lar, mandò innanzi vn'huomo suo, ad inuitarmi a cena seco, in casa del Cadhì Rokn'eddìn, nostro comune amico, doue esso haueua da alloggiare; in nome del qual Cadhì, mi fu similmente replicato l'inuito. Vi andai dunque; e futon cose straordinarie le carezze che mi fece, e l'amor grande che mi prese, e che sempre poi mi hà mostrato. ... Ma per tornare al Mir Abdu'l Hasàn, ragionammo quella sera a lungo, e passammo in buona conuersatione alcune hore della notte : non bastò tuttauia; e bisognò promettergli di tornar la mattina seguente a desinare, & a star con lui tutto quel giorno, che solo in Lar doueua trattenersi. Non potei ricusarlo, forzato dalle molte cortesie sue, e degli altri: onde tornatoui la mattina, tutta quella giornata la passammo noi due, con pochi altri di simil conuersatione, con grandissimo gusto, in legger libri, in confrontare Autori, in esaminare versi e Poeti, & in pigliarci altri piaceri di tal sorte, dentro a camere ritirate; ...". Della Valle, 1658, pp. 386f. See also della Valle, 1658, pp. 369f; 396-98; 438f.

93. *A Chronicle of the Carmelites*, 1939, vol. 1, p. 279. Gurney suggests that this request may have been the direct result of the talks between della Valle and the general. Gurney, 1986, p. 113, footnote 53.

some bagatelle, some of those curiosities concerning our countries that I could show him.[94]

Zayn al-Dīn asked della Valle to teach him how to read and write Latin and to explain European astronomical signs and ciphers to him. He also implored the Italian traveller to send him mathematical books once he had returned home, in particular ones written recently. He claimed that despite his inability to comprehend the language they were written in, he nonetheless could put them to good use thanks to the mathematical diagrams and the instruction in Latin della Valle was to give him.[95] Della Valle, however, not only desired to send books from Italy to Zayn al-Dīn, but also wished to take his friend there and convert him to the only true faith. Although he claimed that going to Italy for the sake of knowledge was Zayn al-Dīn's own deepest desire, the Muslim astronomer was unable to travel when della Valle decided to take his leave. The Italian traveller attributed this mishap to Satan's interference:

> But the Devil put himself in the way so that, when I left Lar, one of his brothers, to whom he might have entrusted his house and his pregnant wife with an (almost grown up) daughter whom it was necessary for him to leave (behind), was not here, but absent.[96]

Della Valle was deeply disappointed:

> We visit each other often with letters. I remain, however, greatly tortured about him and in intense pain for not having been able to bring him with me; because, no doubt, in due time, I would have taken him away from Mahometto, and given (him) to God.[97]

---

94. "Sopra tutti, il Moullà Zein'eddìn, Mathematico, & Astronomo eccellente, & in tutte le altre scienze, non solo il più dotto, che in tutta la Persia io habbia conosciuto; ma che ne i paesi nostri ancora anderebbe senza dubbio frà quelli della prima classe; mi si affettionò di maniera, che ogni giorno, a tutte le hore, era meco, e rallegrandomi, e distraendomi, e conferendo cose di studij, con suo grandissimo gusto, e con non poco mio solleuamento. Ammiraua io in quel grande ingegno, in quel così bello spirito, giouane ancora, di circa trentacinque anni e non più, che, con esser tanto dotto, che haurebbe potuto tener me, e cento altri, di tutte le cose, lungo tempo a scuola; in ogni modo me veniua attorno, & andaua morto, per hauer notitia da me di qualche bagatella, ò di qualche curiosità, di quelle che io poteua mostrargli de i paesi nostri". Della Valle, 1658, p. 368. See also della Valle, 1674, part III, p. 168.
95. Della Valle, 1658, pp. 368f and 1674, Part III, p. 168.
96. "Ma il Diauolo si attrauersò, che quando io partij da Lar, non si trouaua iui, ma era assente, vn suo fratello, a chi hauesse potuto raccomandar la sua casa, e la moglie grauida, con vna figliuola grandicella, che gli conueniua lasciare". Della Valle, 1658, p. 369.
The contemporary German translator increased the dramatic of the story writing that the Mullā, not his brother, was absent:
"Es hat aber der Teuffel eine Verhinderung darein gemacht/daß er/als ich von Lar verreiset/eben abwesend gewest/und seinem Bruder sein Hauɔwesen/sein schwangeres Weib/nebenst seiner zimblich erwachsenen Tochter anbefohlen". Della Valle, 1674, Part III, p. 169.
97. "Ci visitiamo spesso con lettere; restando io tuttauia martellatissimo di lui, e con dolore intenso di non hauerlo potuto condur meco; che senz'altro, a lungo andare, l'haurei ritolto a Mahometto, e dato a Dio". Della Valle, 1658, p. 396. See also, della Valle, 1674, part III, p. 169.

He found a certain consolation in exchanging letters with Zayn al-Dīn to check the astronomical measurements he had made while travelling,[98] and Zayn al-Dīn compared the values with Uluġ Beg's astronomical tables. Della Valle also tried, albeit with no success, to meet another of Zayn al-Dīn's brothers, called 'Ināyat.[99] 'Ināyat was a mathematician and astronomer in his own right who had written, among other books, a *taqwīm* for the year 1031/1621 used by della Valle together with other Persian astronomical and astrological textbooks for astronomical observations, calculations of geographical coordinates, or the identification of winds.[100] Finally, in 1623 while in Goa della Valle wrote in Persian a summary of a book on Tychonic cosmology for Zayn al-Dīn. The Latin original had been written in 1613 by the Italian Jesuit Christophoro Borro (1583-1632) who had wished to go as a missionary to China and participated in the Jesuits's visit to Siam writing about it in a travel account. In 1623, Borro was on his way back to Europe.

Borro's book caused a stir in Rome after it had been published in Milan. Della Valle had several reasons for chosing this work in order to inform Zayn al-Dīn about new developments in astronomy in Western Europe. The author of the novelty, Tycho Brahe, was *the most famous of all astronomers/astrologers of our time*. Borro, like della Valle, was an Italian which made their meeting in Goa *full of friendship and conversations*. Furthermore, Borro was an active student of the astronomical sciences *who had checked and found true Tycho Brahe's new cosmological model*. The conviction that the model was true made him write his book to explain the new truth through *the method of theology, mathematics, and philosophy*.[101] Because he was the text's author, Borro could summarize and explain his book to della Valle who could then do his best to render the ideas in Persian.[102]

The text composed by the two Italians consists of a general introduction, four chapters, and two diagrams. In the Introduction, della Valle explained who Borro was, where he had met him, and what the two men had talked about. Moreover, della Valle promised Zayn al-Dīn to send him the books on new European developments in mathematics and astronomy that Borro had mentioned in their talks.[103] The first chapter is called *Faṣl-e avval dar šekl-e donyā* or *Capitolo primo della figura del Mondo* (First chapter of the figure of the world).[104] The second chapter claims to demonstrate that the new model explains all phenomena *Capitolo secondo, nel quale si mostra come con questa figura dal Mondo tutte le apparenze in cielo si saluano* (Second chapter, in

---

98. Della Valle, 1658, pp. 472-474.
99. Della Valle, 1658, p. 459.
100. *Ibid.*, pp. 384f, 399, 472, 511.
101. MS Vat. Pers. 9, ff 3b,9-17 and 4b,1-17 and 5b,1-3. On Borro see also della Valle, 1663, pp. 120, 124f.
102. MS Vat. Pers. 9, f 5b,3-17.
103. *Ibid.*, ff 2a-6b.
104. *Ibid.*, ff 6a,1 and 6b,1.

which is shown, how with this figure of the world all the phenomena in the heaven are saved). In the Persian version, *saluano* is missing: *Faṣl-e devvom ke dar ū namūde mīšavad čun bā īn šekl-e donyā har če ke dar āsmān peydā mīšavad tavānad šod*.[105] The third chapter discusses those phenomena which remained unexplicable in the known cosmological model, but could be better explained now: *Faṣl-e seyyom dar ẓavāhir ke netavānand šod dar towfīq-e šekl-e ma'rūf-e donyā ke dar ānke mā mīgūyim behtar mīšavand* or *Capitolo Terzo della apparenze che non possono saluarsi nella costitution della figura ordinaria del Mondo, che in questa che noi facciamo si saluano meglio* (Third chapter on the phenomena, which cannot be saved in the system of the ordinary figure of the world [but] which can be saved in a better way in this [system] that we make).[106] The last chapter is called *Faṣl-e čahārom ke ḫātime-ye maqālāt-e maḏkūr ast* or *Capitolo Quarto chè è sigillo (cioè Conchiusione) de' sopradetti discorsi* (Fourth chapter, which is the seal (i.e. the conclusion) of the said discourse).[107] The first diagram is placed between the introduction and the first chapter and illustrates the new Tychonic model of the heavens. The sun stands in the center of all the planets except the moon. The latter has an eccentric orb around the earth which is immobile in the center of the universe.[108] The diagram shows additionally the orbs of three comets which appeared according to the Persian version in 1566, 1580, and 1618 and according to the Italian translation in 1577, 1580, and 1615.[109] The second diagram is part of Chapter Two intended to help Zayn al-Dīn to understand a technical expression which della Valle could not render into Persian: *spira*. He decided to give also the Portuguese translation of the word, that is, *parafuso*, because there might be a Portuguese (coming to Lar) who, although unable to understand Latin, could render the word from his own language into Persian (for Zayn al-Dīn):

> zīrā ke dar ānjā balke purtukīzī bāšad ke har čand ke lātīn (sic) nādān (sic) be-zabān-e ḫodaš fahmīde be-fārsī išānrā tarjome bokonad.[110]

During the second half of the 17th and the early decades of the 18th centuries, Western European travel accounts on the Safavid Empire grew ever more rich in details concerning the state of the arts and sciences. The major source for this new and impressively precise knowledge was Raphaël du Mans, a French Capuchin, who arrived in 1644 in Isfahan as a missionary. Although he held the Catholic faith as well as Western European culture and science in general, and their French forms in particular, to be superior, his intimate relations with the Safavid court provided him with concrete insights

---

105. *Ibid.*, ff 10a,1-3 and 10b,1-3.
106. *Ibid.*, ff 17a,2-5 and 17b,2-4.
107. *Ibid.*, ff 22a,1f and 22b,1f.
108. *Ibid.*, ff 77a, b; the model is explained in the following first chapter of della Valle's treatise.
109. *Ibid.*, ff 7a,b; Ecchellensis read 1618: MS Vat. Pers. 10, f 7a.
110. MS Vat. Pers. 9, f 12b,2-4.

Early Modern Western European Travellers in the Middle East... 413

into the textbooks that were read in philosophy, metaphysics, logic, mathematics, physics, or astronomy; the methods that were used for teaching at Safavid *madāris* and mosques; and the economic and social aspects of education and scholarly practice:

> The books here are rather expensive. One calculates per verse. 50 letters make one verse. 1000 of them cost at least 2 abassis and up to 5 abassis, if their scripture is truly perfect. The appreciation usually is for the scripture and not so much for the book's content, if it is not a very rare book. They have here the Almagest[111] of Ptolemy in Arabic, the Spherics of Menelaus and Theodosius, several sorts of theories and mean motions of the planets such as Coage Nescir et Mirza Ouloukbec, Euclid in all his works, some fragments of Archimedes and Apollonius and other ancient authors, also the perspective of Ebne Heissen, books on arithmetic, *elmé hasabe*, algebra, *elgebre*, optics, *menazer*, moving forces, *gerre sakril*. The mathematical sciences are cultivated here more generally, but not on the supreme level as in the West. Here, one finds all the parts of the mathematical sciences, *riassi*. But all these sciences are subordinated under judicial (astrology), *ehkoum*, saying that means without the effects are useless.[112]

This report continues for further three folios in the first of the three manuscripts (1660; 1665; 1684) written by Du Mans about the state of the Safavid Empire. The authors Du Mans claimed to have been studied by Safavid students and scholars correspond rather closely with the manuscripts extant today in Persian libraries and with information found in Safavid historical chronicles.[113] Although Du Mans was not the only source, almost all Western

---

111. In Richard's edition there is a printing error replacing Almageste by Algameste both in Raphael du Mans's text and in Richard's footnote 472. See Richard, 1995, vol 2, p. 124.
112. "Les libvres sont icy fort chers. L'on compte par vers. 50 lettres font un vers. Les 1000 cousteront le moins 2 *abassis*, jusques à 5 *abassis* s'ils sont d'une escripture la plus parfaicte, desorte que l'estime des libvres est d'ordinère à l'escripture et peu à leur contenu, si ce ne sont libvres rares. Ils ont icy l'Almageste de Ptolomée en arabe, les Sphérique de Menelaus et Théodose, plusieurs sortes de théories et moiens mouvements de planettes, comme Coage Nescir et Mirza Ouloukbec, Euclide en toutes ses œu(v)res, quelques fragmens d'Archimède et Apollonius et autres autheurs anciens; aussi la perspective de Ebne Heissen, des libvres d'arithmétique, *elmé hasabe*, d'algèbre, *elgebre*, d'optique, *menaser*, de forces mouvantes, *gerre sakril*, les mathématiques se cultivant icy plus généralement, mais non pas au suprême degré comme en Occident. Icy se treuveront toutes les parties de mathématiques, *riassi*. Mais toutes ces sciences, ils les subordonnent à la judiciaire, *ehkoum*, disants les moiens sans l'effect estre inutiles". Richard, 1995, pp. 124f. While the names of the ancient Greek authors are easily recognizable, the names of two of the three Muslim astronomers are slightly distorted. Coage Nescir stands for Ḫʷāja Naṣīr al-Dīn (al-Ṭūsī) and Ebne Heissen for Ibn al-Hayṭam.
113. In his first report, Du Mans mentioned also the following authors: Aristotle, Plato, Ibn Sīnā. See Richard 1995, vol. 2, p. 127; in his report from 1665, he named Muḥammad Bāqir as the shah's head astrologer. *Ibid.*, p. 270; in the last report from 1684, Du Mans mentioned Ptolemy, Euclid, Menelaus, Theodosius, Abū Maʿšar, Māšāʾallāh, Abū al-Fidāʾ, Ismāʿīl al-Jazarī, al-Fārābī, Abū al-Ṣalt, Ḫʷāje Naṣīr al-Dīn al-Ṭūsī, Uluġ Beg, and ʿAbd al-Raḥmān al-Ṣūfī as the most important authorities of the mathematical and astronomical sciences and Abū ʿAlī b. Sīnā as the fundamental medical authority. The historical chronicle *Rowḍat al-Ṣafāʾ* of Mīr Ḫʷānd, often admired by 16th- and 17th- century European scholars and travellers, is heavily criticized by Du Mans and said to be equally as bad as Pliny's *Historia naturalis. Ibid.*, pp. 304, 352, 358, 360, 362, 370.

European travellers, such as the Protestants Tavernier, Chardin, Kaempfer, or Fryer, and other French Capuchins and Carmelites, such as Gabriel de Chinon, Ange de Saint-Joseph, or François Sanson, profited from his knowledge. Ange de Saint-Joseph, Tavernier, Chardin, and Kaempfer had access to additional Persian sources in fields which had held less attraction for Du Mans such as botany, medicine, and geography. Their reports contain, for instance, data of lost medieval Arabic geographical tables such as the Kitāb al-aṭwāl wa'l-'urūḍ li'l-Furs.[114]

ON SOME FACTORS SHAPING THE DIFFERENT WESTERN EUROPEAN PERCEPTIONS OF THE ARTS AND SCIENCES IN THE TWO MUSLIM SOCIETIES

Travel accounts not only tell stories about the life, customs, structures, and professions in the two Muslim societies and about biblical and ancient history, they also occasionally spell out what motivated their authors and the traditions within which they had evaluated the two Muslim societies in such differing ways. The difference often reflected the two empires' military involvements with Christian countries in Europe. While the Ottomans were engaged in endless wars with one or the other of their European or Asian neighbours and cooperated in some alliances and peace negotiations on behalf of other European monarchies, the Safavids were never directly drawn into any of the European wars, although there were a series of efforts by Western European countries and by the Safavid shahs to build up an alliance against the Ottoman sultans. This difference explains the almost obsessive concentration on matters of war, discipline, weaponry, or fortification in Western European travel accounts about the Ottoman Empire. It does not suffice, however, to explain the differences with regard to the arts and sciences.

A second major difference in Western European perceptions of the Ottoman and Safavid Empires resulted from the former's conquest of Constantinople and the destruction of the Byzantine Empire. The almost mythical reverence of Constantinople as the centre of the (Christian) world and of the oecumene led most Western European travellers to marvel nostalgically over Constantinople's silhouette when arriving from sea, to grieve about its loss, but to show disdain and disappointment with the arrangements of streets, places, and buildings and their architectural qualities as soon as they had entered Istanbul.

The Safavids possessed no such links with Byzantine history or Christian values, which could bring their European visitors to condemn them before getting to know them. Moreover, Persia's connection with ancient Greek history made the region where the Safavids ruled, its history, culture, and reputation

---

114. I thank David A. King, Frankfurt on Main, for this information.

valuable for European travellers. Xerxes, Darius, or Cyrus by virtue of having been of importance for Greece and Persia in ancient times were regarded as cultural heroes. Histories by ancient Greek authors such as Herodotus or Xenophon were used to recognize the people who populated the region in the 16th and 17th centuries as *civilized*. The same authorities, however, were read to report that the *Turks* were descendants of the nomadic, fierce, and brutish *Scythians*. Thus the *Turks* appeared to be *uncivilized*.

The stereotypical categorization of the communities in the Ottoman Empire by Western European travellers and the emphasis put on *our Europe* (an expression mostly used in French accounts) grew so rigid and impressed so heavily on the minds of the readers that, already from the late 16th century onwards, some travellers felt motivated to oppose it strongly, as Henry Blount's explanation of his own travel goals, attitudes, behaviors, and intellectual positions indicates.[115]

Additionally, the differing Western European perceptions of the arts and sciences in the Ottoman and the Safavid Empires seem to express different patterns of travel. Such different patterns led to different degrees of access to information, its sources (local scholars, artisans, libraries, schools, hospitals, etc.), or its means (languages, texts, instruments). They also provided different levels of intimacy with socially or culturally prestigious spaces in the indigenious societies (imperial and provincial courts, private houses of dignitaries, religious meeting places, etc.) where the local values attributed to all kinds of knowledge could be experienced.

In the case of the Safavid Empire, almost all of the travel accounts of the 16th and 17th centuries described the royal court as their ultimate aim and their journey as directed to wherever the court may have been, in Tabriz, Qazvin, Isfahan, or the country-side. The intermediate stops in their travel through Persia were the local courts of provincial governors or semi-independent rulers or the tents of tribal elders, depending upon the precise route of travel followed by the individual traveller. Often it was only in Bandar Abbas, that is, at a point of entry into Persia when coming by ship, and at Isfahan, that is, at a point of arrival on the journey proper, that the Western European travellers met and stayed with other Western Europeans except for those with whom they travelled.

When Western Europeans travelled in the Ottoman Empire, they headed towards a variety of sites, Istanbul being only one of them. Others were the holy places of Palestine or Egypt, the major trading cities on the Arabian shores of the Mediterranean Sea, Cairo, less often Upper Egypt, or the European territories of the empire. Consequently, the travel routes were much more variable, the cultural and natural variations perhaps more drastically felt, and the tensions between the immediate past and the present more palpable. Thus,

---

115. Blount, 1634, p. 513.

there might have been more attractions to the Western European eye which made the traveller ignore or simply forget the prescriptions of the *apodemic* literature.

On the other hand, most of the Western European travellers of the 16th and 17th centuries visited the Ottoman Empire in the company of other Western European travellers, mainly pilgrims, merchants, or diplomats.[116] They travelled from one Western European settlement to another, mostly the houses of consuls or Catholic hospices. They were part of organised tours with tour guides, interpreters, and had travel books to hand. Thus, they often knew what to expect before they arrived. Their aim was not to see the unknown, although in their reports they often claim to have done exactly this. Neither was the aim of the standard Western European visitor to talk to the native population, least of all to its Muslim components. Not only were they incapable of doing so without the help of an interpreter, but many travellers also stressed that the popes had forbidden all faithful Catholics to enter into disputes on religious matters with the *Turks*. Moreover, they claimed that the *Turks* themselves were not eager to talk to their Western European visitors because they hated all that was Christian and regarded themselves as unquestionably superior.

Then, there was the issue of religious differences. Although, both the Ottomans and the Safavids were Muslims and thus spiritually and mentally speaking enemies, *heretics, adherents of superstition*, and followers of *an impostor*, they professed different creeds. The Shi'i creed of the Safavids was recognized as a new imperial religion ordered by an almost, or sometimes even truly, divine ruler. It was portrayed in Western European sources from the early 16th century on as quite close to a form of Catholicism that was permeated by Messianic expectations. Thus, Western European travellers perceived it as unknown, but thought of it as if it was similar to their own beliefs.

The Ottomans, however, followed Sunnī Islam. They were said to adhere more closely to the Prophet Muḥammad and to the Qur'ān, which since the twelfth century had been denounced in Catholic writings as a falsification of the Bible and as a mockery of Jesus Christ's prophecies. Thus, Ottoman religious beliefs were considered familiar to Western European travellers, but different from and inimical to their own beliefs. The truly new developments within the Muslim communities of the Ottoman Empire were perceived as being related to the Dervish orders. Such orders and the strange behaviour of their members attracted the attention of Western European travellers. The *'ulamā'*, that is, the experts of Sunnī knowledge, never appeared as a group or technical name of an intellectual category in these accounts. They were divided into *judges* and *ecclesiastics*. Sometimes, *monks* were mentioned who lived in *cloisters*. These *cloisters* were either attached to the mosques built and donated by the Ottoman

---

116. Western European travellers only exceptionally preferred the company of local travellers. An example for such an exception is Blount.

sultans, their wives, their viziers, or other believers, or they were houses of the Dervish orders. The average Sunnī *ecclesiastic* was believed to have no particular education except in languages, mainly Arabic and Persian. The average *judge*, according to these accounts, had to pass several years of legal training although the practical legal system was often portrayed as unsophisticated but effective. The education of the *monk*, however, remained largely obscure in these travel accounts. Sometimes theology is mentioned, sometimes metaphysics. Very few travellers who had turned into alien residents knew that there existed discussions about the attributes of God.

Finally, Catholic missionaries who were sufficiently widespread in the Ottoman Empire during the 17th century having a presence in Pera, but not in Istanbul proper, had, as far as is known, no part to play in Ottoman court politics. In Safavid Persia, however, most of the Catholic missions were concentrated in Isfahan or in its Armenian suburb New-Julfa. Some of the superiors of these missions entered into a network of relations with the Safavid court from which both sides profited. In some cases, such as that of the Carmelites in the early seventeenth century and the Capuchins in the second half of the seventeenth century, one component of these relations was the exchange of knowledge about religious, medical, astronomical, and, as claimed by missionaries and travellers, but difficult to substantiate, mathematical matters. As a consequence, both sides got to know each other beyond stereotypes. As was noted above, the acquisition of this more intimate knowledge proved influential in all the travel accounts on the Safavids composed during the second half of the seventeenth and the first decades of the eighteenth centuries.

BIBLIOGRAPHY

ABŪ al-FIDĀ', *Géographie d'Aboulféda*, texte arabe publié ... par M. Reinaud et M. Le Baron Mac Guckin de Slane, Paris, Imprimerie Royale, 1840. [Reprint: Beirut, Dar Sader, s.d.]

A Collection of Curious Travels & Voyages, 1693, John Ray (ed.), 2 vols., London.

ALPINI, Prospero,
– *De Medicina Ægyptiorvm*, Venetia, 1591.
– *Historia Ægypti Naturalis*, Leiden, Apud Gerardum Potvliet,1735.

BELON, Pierre, *Les Observations de Plusieurs Singularitez et choses memorables, trouués en Grece, Asie, Iudée, Egypte, Arabie, et autre pays estranges*, Redigées en trois Liures, par Pierre Belon du Mans, Paris, Gilles Corozet, 1553.

BLOUNT, Henry, *A Voyage into the Levant*, in: *Collection of Voyages and Travels. Some now First Printed from the Original Manuscripts, Others Now First Published* in English. In Eight Volumes. With A General Preface, Giving an Account of the Progress of Trade and Navigation, from its First Beginning. Illustrated with Several Hundred Useful Maps and Cuts, Containing Views of the Different Countries, Cities, Towns, Forts, Ports and Shipping: Also the Birds, Beasts, Fish, Serpents, Trees, Fruits and Flowers; with the Habits of the different Nations, all Elegantly Engraved on Copper-Plates, London, 1634. Printed by Assignment from Messierus Churchill, For Thomas Osborne in Gray's Inn, 1752, vol. 8.

BRENTJES, Sonja, *The presence of anciens secular and religious texts in Pietro della Valle's (1586-1652), unpublished and printed writings* (in print) [2003].

ÇELEBI, Evliya, *Evliya Çelebi in Bitlis*, R. Dankoff (ed.), Leiden-New York-København-Köln, 1990.

CHARDIN, Jean, *Voyages du Chevalier Chardin en Perse et autres Lieux de l'Orient*, L. Langlès (ed.), Paris, Le Normant, 1811.

DANNENFELDT, K. H., *Leonhard Rauwolf. Sixteenth-Century Physician, Botanist, and Traveler*, Cambridge, Mass., Harvard University Press, 1968.

De Nonnullis Orientalium urbibus, necnon indigenarum religione ac moribus tractatus brevis, a Gabr. Sionita ... ac Joanne Hesronita ... 1633 Amsterdam, apud J. Janssonium.

Estat de la Perse en 1660. Par Le P. Raphaël Du Mans, Supérieur de la Mission des Capucins d'Ispahan, 1890, Charles Schefer (ed.), Paris, Ernest Leroux.

GREAVES, John, *An Account of the Latitude of Constantinople and Rhodes; written by the Learned Mr. John Greaves, sometime professor of astronomy in the University of Oxford, and directed to the most Reverend James Ussher, Archbishop of Ardmagh*, in: *A Collection of Curious Travels & Voyages*, John Ray (ed.), London, 1693, vol. 2, pp. 84-89.

GURNEY, J. D., *Pietro Della Valle: The Limits of Perception*, BSOAS XLIX, (1986), pp. 103-116.

ḤĀJJĪ ḤALĪFA, *Kašf al-Ẓunūn 'an isāmī al-kutub wa'l-funūn. Lexicon bibliographicum et encyclopaedicum a Mustafa ben Abdallah Katib Jelebi dicto et nomine Haji Khalifa celebrato compositum. Ad codicem Vindobonensium, Parisiensium et Berolinensis fidem primum edidit latine vertit et commentaria indicibusque instruxit Gustavus Fluegel*, Leipzig, Leiden, 1835-1858, 7 vols.

HERBERT, Thomas,
 – *A Relation of Some Yeares Travaile, Begvnne Anno 1626. Into Afrique and the greater Asia, especially the Territories of the Persian Monarchie: and some parts of the Orientall Indies, and Iles adiacent. Of their Religion, Language, Habit, Discent, Ceremonies, and other matters concerning them. Together with the proceedings and death of the three late Ambassadors: Sir D. C. Sir R. S. and the Persian Nogdi-Beg:*

As also the two great Monarchs, the King of Persia, and the great Mogol. [London, Printed by William Stansby, and Jacob Bloome.] Amsterdam, New York, Da Capo Press, Theatrvm Orbis Terrarvm Ltd., [1634] 1971.

– *Some Yeares Travels Into Africa et Asia th Great. Especially Describing the Famous Empires of Persia and Industant (sic). As also Divers other Kingdoms in the Orientall Indies, and I'les Adjacent*, London, 1638, Printed by R. Bl. for Iacob Blome and Richard Bishop.

– *Travels in Persia 1627-1629*, Abridged and Edited by Sir William Foster, C.I.E. with an Introduction and Notes, London, George Routledge & Sons Ltd., 1928.

HESRONITA, Johannes; SIONITA, Gabriel, *De nonnullis orientalium urbibus, necnon indigenarum religione ac moribus tractatus brevis nubiensi geographiae adjectus*, Paris, 1619.

IBN AL-AKFĀNĪ, *A survey of the Muhammedan sciences*, A. Sprenger (ed.), Calcutta. 1849.

JONES, John Robert, *Learning Arabic in Renaissance Europe (1505-1624)*, Phd Thesis, London University, 1988.

KING, David, *World-Maps for Finding the Direction and Distance to Mecca. Innovation and Tradition in Islamic Science*, Leiden-Boston-Köln, Brill, 1999.

MANTRAN, Robert, *Istanbul dans la seconde moitié du XVIIe siècle. Essai d'histoire institutionelle, économique et sociale*, Bibliothèque Archéologique et Historique de l'Institut Français d'Archéologie d'Istanbul, XII, Paris, 1962.

PURCHAS, Samuel, *Pvrchas his Pilgrimage. Or Relations Of The World And The Religions Obserued in all Ages and places Discouered, from the Creation vnto this Present. Contayning A Theologicall And Geographicall Historie of Asia, Africa, and America, with the Ilands adiacent. ...* London, 1626, Printed by William Stansby for Henrie Fetherstone.

RICHARD, Francis, *Raphaël du Mans missionaire en Perse au XVII^{e}s.*, Moyen Orient & Océan Indien XVIe-XIXe s. 9, Paris, Société d'Histoire de l'Orient, L'Harmattan, 1995, 2 vols.

SMITH, Thomas, *Historical Observations relating to Constantinople. By the Reverend and Learned Tho. Smith, D. D. Fellow of Magd. Coll. Oxon, and of the Royal Society*. In: *A Collection of Curious Travels & Voyages*, John Ray(ed.), London, 1693, vol. 2, pp. 35-84.

STEVENSON, Edward Luther, *Geography of Claudius Ptolemy*, New York, New York Library, 1932.

TEIXEIRA, Pedro,
– *Relaciones de Pedro Teixeira del Origen Descendencia y Svccession de los Reyes de Persia, y de Harmuz, Y De Vn Viage Hecho Por El Mismo Avtor dende la India*

Oriental hasta Italia por tierra. Introducción, edición de Eduardo Barajas Sala. Biblioteca de Viajeros Hispánicos 12, Madrid, Miraguana Ediciones & Ediciones Polifemo, s.d.

– *Relaciones de Pedro Teixeira d'el Origen Descendencia y Svccession de los Reyes de Persia, y de Harmuz, y de vn Viage hecho por el mismo Avtor dende la India Oriental hasta Italia por tierra*, En Amberes En can de Hieronymo Verdussen, 1610.

– *The Travels of Pedro Teixeira*, (eds.) W. F. Sinclair, D. Ferguson, London, 1902.

The Jewish Encyclopedia, I. Singer (ed.), New York, London, Funk and Wagnalls Company, 1906.

TOOMER, Gerald, *Eastern Wisedome and Learning. The Study of Arabic in Seventeenth-Century England*, Oxford: Clarendon Press, 1995.

DELLA VALLE, Pietro,

– *Viaggi Di Pietro Della Valle Il Pellegrino Descritti da lui medesimo in Lettere familiari All'erudito suo Amico Mario Schipano. Parte Terza Cioè L'India, Co'l Ritorno Alla Patria*, Roma, 1663.

– *Viaggi di Pietro della Valle il Pellegrino. Descritti da lui medesimo in lettere familiari all'erudito suo amico Mario Schipano. Divisi in tre parti cioè: La Turchia, La Persia e L'India colla vita e ritratto del autore*, Volume Primo, Brighton, G. Giancia, 1843.

MANUSCRIPTS:

MS Città del Vaticano, Biblioteca Apostolica, Vat. Pers. 9.

MS Città del Vaticano, Biblioteca Apostolica, Vat. Pers. 10.

MS Paris, BnF, Arabe 2521.

MS Paris, BnF, Arabe 4348.

MS Paris, BnF, Dupuys 16.

MS Paris, BnF, Dupuy 703.

MS Paris, BnF, fr 9537.

VI

PRIDE AND PREJUDICE: THE INVENTION OF A 'HISTORIOGRAPHY OF SCIENCE' IN THE OTTOMAN AND SAFAVID EMPIRES BY EUROPEAN TRAVELLERS AND WRITERS IN THE SIXTEENTH AND SEVENTEENTH CENTURIES

The historiography of science in respect to the Islamic world has routinely insisted on its Arabic component, often relegating science produced in Persian and Turkish languages to an inferior position in terms of relevance and value. In contrast, historians from Iran, Turkey and Central Asian states have tried to appropriate major Muslim scientists of the past as their ethnic compatriots. Some iranologists from Europe argue that Iran actually contributed a special approach to science and scientific practice by its strong tradition of illuminating scientific manuscripts (astronomy, cosmography, medicine, geography, history) and its attention to technology (ceramics, irrigation) and applied sciences (agriculture, anatomy). For some years historians of science in Turkey have spoken of Ottoman science while historians of science from Algeria, Morocco, and Spain point to the specificity of Arabic science done in the western parts of the Islamic world when compared to Arabic science in the east, i.e. Egypt, Iraq, and Iran. Ideological trends of the twentieth century have shaped these divergent perceptions of the history of science in the Islamic world as much as prejudices and perceptions of a much older origin.

It is with forms of sixteenth- and seventeenth-century presentations of the sciences in two Muslim states of the period that this paper will deal. Its first major claim is that travellers and writers from Catholic and Protestant Europe who visited the Ottoman and Safavid empires and wrote about their travels or the empires' histories and present state of affairs laid the foundations for the current contradictory attitudes towards the history of science in the Islamic world. Its second major claim is that the factors that shaped this newly emerging discourse arose from religious convictions, political enmities, scholarly training, modes of ensuring "politically correct" behaviour, clientele relationships, and social hierarchies in Catholic and Protestant countries in Europe. The most important single factor that contributed to the new discourse was the application of humanist values and styles of writing to the description of contemporary Muslim societies. This application stood in stark contrast to the activities of the travellers with the exception of pilgrims. While the latter could follow well-trodden paths, the former, if they wished to leave such paths, had to "go native", that is they had to adapt to local forms of travelling, dining, and understanding space and culture. When they returned home and prepared their accounts for family and friends or for a larger public, they had to re-navigate their experience, adapt it again to local forms, but this time writing for and reading by a Catholic or Protestant public as well as communicating with Muslim slaves, neighbours, allies, and foes.

VI

The form chosen in this paper to substantiate these two claims is to present three case studies preceded by a general outline of the components of the discourse about the sciences in the two Muslim states in western sources.

The "Turks" have no Science and the "Persians" are the "French of Asia"
Many statements by European writers about the sciences in the Islamic world indicate a contrary perception of the state of the sciences, their sources, offices, professional spaces and architectural settings in the Ottoman versus the Safavid empires. Authors who touch upon such subjects often deny the existence of any science among those they call the "Turks". Those who admit their existence consider them mostly of low or of no value. If particular sciences are mentioned, it is medicine, philosophy, or history, rarely, if ever, astronomy/astrology, mathematics, the occult sciences, botany, zoology, or geography. Both elements point to the prejudicial character of such statements. This character does not mean that all such statements are invariably the same in shape and size. They share some basic properties, but take on a variety of specific appearances.

Most authors of travel accounts agree in ignoring scholarly offices such as the head-astronomer or head-physician at the Ottoman court, although private letters prove that visitors were aware of physicians and astronomers/astrologers working there or at provincial courts. None, however, as far as I can tell, realized that astronomers also worked at mosques. Similar patterns of acknowledgement and ignorance can be found with regard to markets and streets as professional places for the sciences in the Ottoman Empire. They came into view at best for the occult sciences and for scholarly related crafts. Among the latter only those of the druggists and the scribes were mentioned repeatedly. Other scholarly related groups, which according to Evliya Çelebi populated the markets of Istanbul in the middle of the seventeenth century such as the astrolabe- and sea-chart-makers, escaped the attention of the foreign visitors. With respect to teaching, European observers knew of schools for boys where writing, calculating, reading the Qur'an, law, and philosophy were said to be taught and some mentioned equivalent schools for girls. A few admitted to knowing of specific schools for higher learning such as the Azhar mosque in Cairo restricting its scope, however, mostly to religious disciplines and denying occasionally the presence of secular fields of study. They rarely if ever mentioned the madrasa as the most widespread institutional form of higher education in the Ottoman Empire and said nothing about the place of the so-called rational sciences at the Ottoman madrasa. In the abundant descriptions of the Ottoman religious and semi-religious architecture such as mosques, tombs, baths, or inns, we find occasionally a reference to a hospital or to a school attached to such complexes. A few writers acknowledged that dervish orders could house knowledge including some astronomy, astrology or philosophy. Others agreed that the Azhar mosque was a school where a multitude of subjects could be studied.

The attention to the occasional detail does not necessarily express a more correct perception of Ottoman scholarly life. One reason for the overwhelming neglect of hospitals and schools in the descriptions of pre-Ottoman and Ottoman architecture can be found in their architectural similarity with mosques, inns or baths and in the inclusion of such buildings into larger architectural complexes. Alpini who worked between 1581 and 1584 as the physician of the Venetian consul in Cairo and who claimed to have learned Arabic well enough to read medical books in that language did not recognize a hospital in what he transliterated as "Moristan". Despite describing it as the locale where every year the head-physician met with his colleagues to produce the theriaq as part of the yearly royal tribute to be sent to Istanbul, he identified it as a "temple".[1] The lack of difference in architecture was probably not the only and perhaps not even the major reason for Alpini's preference of architectural resemblance over functional difference. Several town views of Cairo made by Venetian and other artists were available since the early sixteenth century and reprinted well into the seventeenth century. In particular those published by the well-reputed Venetian printer and bookseller Matteo Pagano around the middle of the sixteenth century identified the "Moristan" as a hospital. In early modern Venice, painting was regarded as powerful evidence for the truth of a claim, a social setting or a natural event. Hence, Alpini's ineptitude to recognize the "Moristan" as a hospital must be ascribed to his personal context. As I will show later, Alpini composed most of his writings about Egypt, her medicine, plants and customs after his return to Italy in a period of his life when he was searching for an appointment as teacher for remedies and medical plants at his former university in Padua. His books, their structural and rhetorical layout as well as their scholarly contents and presentation were meant to help him achieve his immediate professional goal. His rendition of "Moristan" through "temple" appears to be one of several instances where he seemed to have preferred broad brushes rather than pencils.

    The picture drawn in European sources of the sixteenth and seventeenth centuries about the sciences in the Safavid Empire is profoundly different with respect to its contents, but similar in its quality as a prejudice. The "Persian" variant of the prejudice was more specific than the "Turkish" version. Its specificity was achieved either by consulting books about earlier Arabic and Persian scientific and historical writings newly published in Catholic or Protestant Europe or by relying on oral and written testimony in Safavid Iran. The former reflected both the research interest of early modern academic writers and the expectation of the reading public to find some information about academic issues in any travel account. The latter consisted mostly of information by missionaries plus a few independent observations of the travellers themselves. The different position of the missionaries in the Safavid Empire as compared to the Ottoman Empire increased their access to local forms of knowledge, in particular those available at the court and in its immediate environment. Thus, the information travellers gained in Persia while taken prevalently from a singular

---

[1] P. Alpin, *La Médecine des Egyptiens par Prosper Alpin 1581-1584*. Traduite du latin, présentée et annotée par R. de Fenoyl (Caire: L'Institut Français d'Archéologie Orientale du Caire, 1980), 2 vols., ii, 376.

VI

source had been acquired from a broader spectrum, but filtered through the lenses of the Apostolic missions. As a result, the reports on the sciences given by Catholic and Protestant travellers contain more specific elements which can be confirmed by studying today extant Persian and Arabic treatises and instruments produced in the Safavid period than those given on the Ottoman Empire. The dependence of these reports on either works carried out in Catholic or Protestant countries of Europe or on information collected and filtered by Catholic missionaries in Iran introduced other specific elements into the reports which are partly anachronistic and partly formed by religious, political and scholarly preconceptions.

Most travel accounts and missionary reports on seventeenth-century Iran acknowledge that the Persians were educated and that they possessed sciences, scholars, teaching institutions and professional spaces at the court, in the houses of the nobles and at the markets. The writers insist that the Persians pursued medicine, philosophy, logic, mathematics, astronomy and history, loved excessively poetry and indulged heavily in astrology. The Persians are credited with the application of specific teaching methods of ancient or medieval origin. Many Persians - it is claimed - happily spent money to support scholars, even if only to share the scholar's reputation or fame, and to build madrasas. The writers pretend that the shah's most beloved and honoured court official was the head-astrologer upon whom he lavished not only his trust, but most of his treasury. The court also had a head-physician who supervised a group of lower ranking colleagues. There was a division of labour between the physicians and the druggists. The latter usually worked in separate shops, in the capital, for instance, at the main square built by Shah 'Abbas I where bazaar, mosques, madrasas, and royal palaces met. Some of the travellers even acknowledged that the bazaar also contained shops of instrument-makers some of whom produced splendid items. In other regions of the Safavid Empire, the travellers and missionaries found that the sciences flourished less. According to their narratives, there were no good or simply no instruments available for even the easiest astronomical observations in regions far from the capital. They reported that teachers in madrasas or mosques did not understand Euclid's proofs even in the planimetric books unless the foreign traveller explained them. Whether the Persians possessed maps and were able to draw them is disputed among Catholic and Protestant writers, some claiming they themselves had profited from Persian knowledge in mapmaking while others denied its existence with all force.

Critical remarks, as a rule, concern the comparison of these sciences, their focus, their institutions, their sources or their methods with those in the traveller's homeland. Most writers agreed that the sciences at home were of a higher standard, their pursuit more lively, the outcome more stable, intellectually more attractive, the number of men pursuing them more numerous, all in all, the sciences at home were superior. Within the Republic of Letters various forms of discourse evolved in the sixteenth and seventeenth centuries that insisted upon the scientific superiority of contemporary humanists in Italy, philosophers in

France or members of the Royal Society in England. Regarding Muslim societies, such a discourse was not truly new but had an influential predecessor in the Middle Ages, which claimed that Islam was irrational and the Qur'an incompatible with other scriptures, philosophy and nature. This kind of anti-Islamic rhetoric of medieval Catholicism was learned from five major sources: early Christian polemics against adherents of ancient non-Christian cults and beliefs, early anti-Sunni polemics among Oriental Christianity, early anti-Islamic critique by so-called (Muslim) extremists (ghuluww) and apostates (mulhid), medieval anti-Islamic polemics in Christian circles under Muslim rule on the Iberian Peninsula and (genuine as well as pseudepigraphic) treatises by medieval Jewish converts from the Iberian Peninsula to Catholicism. [2] Several medieval Catholic writers (some of whom even travelled to the Middle East) such as Ricoldo da Monte Croce, Ramon Lull or Roger Bacon concluded from the alleged irrationality of the Qur'an "that there was an acute quarrel between philosophy and religion within Islam itself". [3]

Prospero Alpini's Preposterous Evaluation of Ottoman Egyptian Medicine

The most extensive and detailed evaluation of a particular science and its practice in either of the two Muslim countries can be found in Prospero Alpini's books on Egyptian medicine, plants, natural history and the balm composed between 1582 and 1614. [4] In two of his books, the one on Egyptian medicine (published in 1592) and the one on Egyptian natural history (published posthumously in 1737), Alpini evaluated the character and efficacy of the medical sciences as taught and practised in late sixteenth-century Ottoman Egypt as well as their social standing and procedures of admission to the profession. He claimed that there was almost no teaching of medicine when he practised in Egypt while there was an abundant, almost infinite number of working physicians, men and women. Those practitioners did not follow any theoretical system worth its name, but were mere empiricists. Even so, they had reduced the therapeutic maxims of Hippocratic and Galenic medicine to a mere ghost by

---

[2] N. Daniels, 'Islam and the West', in J. V. Tolan (ed.), *Medieval Christian Perceptions of Islam. A Book of Essays* (New York, London: Garland Publishing, Inc., 1996), 6-7, 57, 63-5.

[3] Ibid., at 65. " (Wilhelm of) Tripoli asserted that the Muslim teachers despise the Qur'an: 'their learned men', added Ricoldo (da Monte Croce) in his Itinerarium, 'entertain no faith in the sayings of the Qur'an, but deride it in secret; in public, however, they honour it on account of fear'. The Caliph, he maintained, had been compelled to prohibit the teaching of philosophy in the schools, so that in Ricoldo's time, when he lived in Baghdad, only the study of the Qur'an had been enforced and encouraged. In consequence, he had found that learned Muslim(s) knew very little of the truth of theology or the subtlety of philosophy. ... Lull also said that the teaching of logic and natural philosophy was publicly forbidden among the Muslim, because it led to heresy and to a denial of the prophethood of Muhammad." Ibid., 66.

[4] P. Alpini, *De Balsamo, Dialogus* (Venice: Franciscus de Franciscis Senensis, 1591). P. Alpini, *De Medicina Aegyptiorum, Libri Quatuor* (Venice: Apud Franciscum de Franciscis Senensis, 1591). P. Alpini, *De Plantis Ægypti liber. Accessit etiam liber de Balsamo, alias editus.* (Venice: Franciscus de Franciscis Senensis, 1592). P. Alpini, *Historiae Ægypti naturalis* ... . (Leiden: Gerardus Potuliet, 1735). French translations: P. Alpin, *Histoire Naturelle de l'Egypte par Prosper Alpin 1581-1584*. Traduite du latin, présentée et annotée par R. de Fenoyl (Cairo: L'Institut Français d'Archéologie Orientale du Caire, 1979). P. Alpin, *Plantes d'Egypte par Prosper Alpin 1581-1584*. Traduite du latin, présentée et annotée par R. de Fenoyl (Cairo: L'Institut Français d'Archéologie Orientale du Caire, 1980). P. Alpin, *La Médecine des Egyptiens*.

VI

believing that all diseases and constitutions in Egypt, due to the climate, were of a hot nature and thus needed to be treated exclusively by cold remedies.

According to Alpini, the medical profession was divided into several specialized fields. It encompassed the well-known ophthalmologists and surgeons as well as other specializations less often found in Europe such as dentists or gynaecologists. Moreover, there were also people curing only specific diseases such as certain kinds of fevers while being ignorant of all other kinds of sickness. The admission as physician lay exclusively in the hands of one person, the so-called hekim-bashi or head-physician, who was attached to the pasha or governor of Egypt. In Italy, Alpini claimed, there was no such concentration of power, but several well-trained physicians examined those aspiring to become a doctor.

The Egyptian system did not only suffer under the lack of theory, teaching and concentration of examining power, it also was corrupt. Money counted more than knowledge both for obtaining the coveted position of the hekim-bashi and for admission as medical practitioner. It was, however, not money that induced men and women to apply for such an admission. An average Egyptian physician could not earn much because the art of medicine was looked upon as a lowly craft. Its reputation and efficacy was so low that it needed Italian physicians to restore it to its former standards and privileges. [5]

All these defects of Egyptian medicine as reported by Alpini did not mean that he implied that there was nothing to learn from it for a European physician. He admits clearly that practices followed in surgery as well as the pharmaceutical value of plants or the production of simple and compound remedies were worth the attention and appreciation of European doctors and students of medicine. Indeed, Alpini's fame as a physician after his return to Italy was built to a remarkable extent upon his application of a variety of Egyptian surgical methods as well as drugs he described in his two books. The same holds true for his fame as a botanist and for his later successful career as a professor for the so-called simple remedies and director of the botanical garden at his home-university of Padua.

The story as described above is more or less the same in Alpini's two books, although the one on Egyptian medicine is much harsher in its formulations than the one on natural history. In the former book, Alpini explained why medicine in late sixteenth-century Ottoman Egypt was in such a desperate shape while everybody in Europe believed that Egypt was the cradle of all medical knowledge and the birthplace of some of the most famous physicians ever born and even Egyptian animals such as the hippopotamus or the ibis knew how to heal themselves and once taught their knowledge to mankind. [6]

His story pretends that all was fine with medicine in Egypt before the Ottomans conquered the country, that is, under the reign of the Mamluks. But

---

[5] P. Alpin, *La Médecine des Egyptiens*, 8-20.
[6] Alpini, *La Médicine*, 6-7.

when the Ottomans drove them out and took over, they mistreated and punished the physicians who wished to take their time for a careful diagnosis and who insisted upon applying remedies which might not please the sick in order to cure not only the symptoms, but also the causes. The "Turks'" rejection of theoretical medicine was caused by their origin from the "Tartars and rude people" which made them a "barbarian race with bestial mores". [7]

After suffering this ordeal for some time, the well-educated physicians decided to strike back by starting to focus upon the treatment of the symptoms and by applying cures which pleased the sick. In this way, they turned into prostitutes, because their complaisance made the sick believe that they were treated properly. After the generation of well-educated physicians had died, there was almost no one left who knew the medical art and only very few continued to care for education. The rulers of the country proved to be enemies of those who wished to teach other than religious and legal knowledge. Thus, the number of students diminished, in particular, in medicine and philosophy. Egypt became destitute of scientific and literary studies as well as of teachers. Later, this method of healing spread from one city to another and all later generations of physicians adopted it since there was not much to learn in order to master it. [8]

Alpini's story is so fantastic that anybody with only a limited knowledge of the history of medicine in Muslim societies or of Mamluk and Ottoman history in general should have been delighted by its ingenuity as well as its lack of foundation. This is, however, not the case. The secondary literature on Alpini or papers using his books as a direct witness for Egypt I have seen, if discussing at all his reports on Egyptian medicine, accept his presentation as a reliable, if "dim view of local custom". [9]

Alpini's story is so fantastic that a substantial effort is necessary to penetrate its various layers, find out its inner conflicts and determine its relationship to the various historical worlds in which he lived. A careful study of Alpini's portrayal of Egyptian medicine reveals first that there are many differences in detail between the presentations in his two books. Furthermore, it reveals that according to his own depictions of Egyptian medical practices, physicians in Ottoman Egypt were by no means mere empiricists, but followed Hippocratic, Galenic and medieval Arabic medical theories. The investigation of other historical documents yields that the entire story is faked at least in three major points - the composition and professional orientation of the medical community in Cairo, the lack of theoretical education of Cairene physicians and the disruptive politics of Ottoman rulers towards the non-religious sciences in Cairo. For my analysis, I used Frank Lestringant's modern edition of the "Cosmographie de Levant", a text by François de Belleforeste, which presented in 1554 André Thevet's travel through parts of the Ottoman Empire (1549-1552)

---

[7] Alpini, *La Médicine*, 23.
[8] Alpini, *La Médicine*, 23-7.
[9] J. Stannard, *Alpini, Prospero*, in C. C. Gillispie (ed.), *Dictionary of Scientific Biography* (New York: Charles Scribner's Sons, 1970), i, 124-5.

on the basis of ancient Greek books. I also used medical writings of older contemporaries of Alpini who worked as physicians in Egypt shortly before he came there, in particular treatises by Da'ud al-Antaki and 'Abd al-Wahid al-Maghribi.

The claim that every physician treats one disease only is clearly borrowed from Herodotus's book on Egypt. It appears in almost identical form in Belleforeste's description of Thevet's travel as well as in Belleforest's source, the 1556-translation of Herodotus's book by Pierre Saliat.[10] Late sixteenth-century Muslim physicians in Ottoman Egypt, on the other hand, were undoubtedly trained in the lines of traditional theoretical medicine. In his work on what the director of the Mansuri hospital in Cairo had to know, 'Abd al-Wahid al-Maghribi presented a brief survey of types of diseases and their appropriate treatments. The author he most often quoted was Hippocrates. Others were Galen, Ibn Sina, Ibn Zuhr, al-Zahrawi, Ibn Nafis and Abu l-'Abbas al-Majusi.[11] Most of these physicians and their works belonged to Alpini's own medical training and were quoted by him repeatedly in his own books.

Members of influential medical families such as the Qusuni family from Cairo continued during Ottoman rule to climb into the highest positions available for a physician qua physician, that of the ra'is al-atibba' or hekim-bashi, as they had done under the late Mamluks. Some of them left Cairo and worked as a physician at the Ottoman court in Istanbul.[12] Except for the deportation of physicians after Selim II had conquered Egypt, a measure not directed against this craft in particular, but against all groups of skill and influence, no militant actions against Egyptian physicians by the Ottoman overlords or their local representatives who mostly were not of Turkish origin are known to have occurred during the sixteenth century.[13]

Moreover, it was standard Ottoman practice to adopt, if possible, local administrative customs and to keep local elites in their offices if they obeyed their new masters. Thus, despite executing the last Mamluk sultan and several of his allies, many office bearers remained in their positions.[14] According to Mantran, there are only very few traces indicating Ottoman efforts to gain control over the religious and intellectual life in post-Mamluk Egypt.[15] If there was a

---

[10] Jean Chesneau, André Thevet, *Voyages en Egypte 1549-1552. Présentation et notes de Frank Lestringant* (Cairo: Cairo: L'Institut Français d'Archéologie Orientale du Caire, 1984), 54-74, 108, 228.

[11] Ms Berlin, Staatsbibliothek, Preussischer Kulturbesitz, Glaser 134, ff 125a-134b.

[12] R. Vesely, 'Neues zur Familie al-Qusuni. Ein Beitrag zur Genealogie einer ägyptischen Ärzte- und Gelehrtenfamilie', *Oriens* 33 (1992), 437-44. D. Behrens-Abouseif, 'The Waqf of a Cairene Notable in Early Ottoman Cairo: Muhibb al-Din Abu al-Tayyib, son of a Physician', in R. Deguilhem (ed.), *Le Waqf dans l'espace islamique outil de pouvoir socio-politique*. (Damas: L'Institut d'Archéologie Français au Damas, 1995), 123-132. R. Vesely, 'Bibliothek eines ägyptischen Arztes aus dem 16. Jhd. A. D./10. Jhd. A. H.', in P. Zemanek (ed.), *Studies in Near Eastern Languages and Literatures*. Memorial Volume of Karel Petrâcek. (Prague: Academy of Sciences of the Czech Republic. Oriental Institute: 1996), 613-30.

[13] D. Behrens-Abouseif, 'The Waqf', 125, 129.

[14] S. Kuri S.J., *Monumenta Proximi-Orientis. I. Palestine-Liban-Syrie-Mésopotamie (1523-1583)* (Roma: Institutum Historicum Societatis Jesu, 1989), 42*-44*.

[15] R. Mantran, *Les Relations entre le Caire et Istanbul durant la Période Ottomane*. Colloque International sur l'Histoire du Caire. (Cairo: Ministry of Culture of the Arab Republic of Egypt, 1969), 301-11.

major rupture in Egyptian medicine for the worse with regard to social standing and reputation, it occurred most likely under the Mamluks, not under the Ottomans. At least this is what Behrens-Abouseif claimed when comparing the Mamluks with their predecessors, the Ayyubids, and their successors, the Ottomans. [16] But even this rupture remains doubtful, partly because of the scarcity of material, partly because of the criteria Behrens-Abouseif applied, and last but not least, because she misinterpreted Alpini's story to refer to the Mamluks rather than to the Ottomans. [17]

The picture of Ottoman behaviour in Egypt after the conquest as I have summarized it on the basis of extant research literature may be as equally flawed as Alpini's story since major changes indeed took place. The ruler of Egypt, for instance, was a foreigner like his Mamluk predecessor, but in a different manner than before. He was not connected with the local elites by any ties. The language of the administration changed from Arabic to Turkish. The previous organisation of the legal system according to the four major Sunna legal schools was replaced by admitting only one legal school, the Hanafi rite, which was preferred in Istanbul. The head-judge would no longer be nominated in Cairo and among local scholars, but chosen in Istanbul and sent from outside into town. All these changes meant a severe rupture in the modus vivendi, which was established between local elites and foreign military rulers in the Mamluk period. The latter obviously were not the only losers due to the new circumstances. The scholars who had sent members of their group to the positions of head-judges and who had acquired the right and the power to participate in decisions over civil matters in town such as appointing professors and heads of schools were now forced to learn a new language, to change their affiliation with a legal school and to migrate for some time to Istanbul if they ever aspired to a high ranking position. We do not know precisely in which ways the mighty religious intellectual elites of the province of Egypt and its capital reacted to these changes and what kind of adaptation took place over time. As late as the second half of the eighteenth century, there seem to have been only few Egyptian scholars who spoke Turkish fluently. The Hanafi head-judge often was sidestepped when conflicts needed to be solved. [18] These changes while severe do not mean, however, that the Ottoman court interfered in any sensible way into the affairs of the Azhar mosque and other religious, educational and medical institutes and the ways in which they were run.

---

[16] D. Behrens-Abouseif, *Fath Allah and Abu Zakariyya: Physicians under the Mamluks* (Cairo: Supplement aux Annales Islamogiques, Cahiers N° 10: 1987), 14-19; D. Behrens-Abouseif, 'The Image of the Physician in Arab Biographies of the post-classical Age', *Der Islam* 66 (1989), 331-41.

[17] Abouseif, 'The Image', 342.

[18] See M. Winter, *Cultural Ties between Istanbul and Ottoman Egypt. (Programme: International Committee of Pre-Ottoman and Ottoman Studies*, 15th CIEPO Symposium, July 8-12, 2002, London, The London School of Economics: Reprographics Department, LSE, 2002), 49. The interpretation of the information given in his lecture and summarized in his abstract is mine. Winter claimed that despite all the mentioned changes, the disturbance of the religious life in Egypt was inconsequential.

Thus, even while there may be a possibility that Alpini captured in his story some local anti-Ottoman sentiments, it continues to differ profoundly from what contemporary Arabic sources have to tell. Despite Alpini's claim that his story was told to him by Egyptian scholars well versed in history, his presentation of late sixteenth-century Egyptian medicine cannot be taken at face value. It can only be understood in the context of Alpini's efforts to secure himself a stable professional career. Alpini's insistence on the necessity of theory and books in his critique at the alleged miserable state of contemporary medicine in Cairo stands in stark contrast to the material emphasis on Egyptian empirical knowledge in his books and in his own medical practice after his return to Italy. The reconfiguration of his own practical behaviour which earned him a high reputation as a practising doctor by a discourse which pushed ancient and medieval theoretical knowledge to the forefront of medicine can only be understood if placed in the frame of debates about practice versus theory in late-sixteenth- century Italy.

Ongaro has already pointed out that Alpini dedicated three of his four books on Egypt to men linked with his former university in Padua and with the Venetian senate. [19] Alpini presented his works as the result of talks with his former teacher Melchior Wielandt held in Padua immediately after his return from Egypt and as responses to requests directed to him by other physicians, among them two whom he praised as the most eminent physicians of his time and who taught at Padua University. The three books appeared in quick succession in 1591 and 1592. Only one year later, in 1593, Alpini was elected to teach Galen and Dioscurides on the simples, a subject not having been taught at Padua since 1568. [20]

This presentation of his books suggests that Alpini conceived of them as a major tool to gain a honourable and reasonably well-paid position, after his bid for the office of city-physician in Bassano had failed in 1591. [21] Thus, it is reasonable to assume that the structure, style and modes of arguing Alpini adopted in these three books were chosen in order to appeal to his potential sponsors, i.e. his former teachers and the curators of Padua University. Presenting himself as a man who had valuable things to teach to coming generations of medical students as well as a Venetian patriot who despised the "Turks" and felt pity for the subjugated Egyptians could at least do no harm. Pride and prejudice acted here as guidelines for deciding upon which kind of rhetoric to choose. They also served for setting hierarchies right. Alpini left no doubt that he himself strongly believed in Italian medicine's superiority. Presenting himself moreover as a man ready to learn medical secrets and

---

[19] P. Alpini, *De Balsamo, Dialogus*. P. Alpini, *De Medicina Aegyptiorum*. P. Alpini, *De Plantis Ægypti liber. Accessit etiam liber de Balsamo, alias editus.* G. Ongaro, 'Contributi alla biografia di Prospero Alpini', *Acta medicae historiae Patavina* 8/9 (1961-63), 76-168, at 93, 99-101. See also A. Minelli (ed.), *The Botanical Garden of Padua, 1545-1995.* Università degli studi di Padova (Venice: Marsilio Editori, 1995).
[20] Ongaro, 'Contributi', 101-02.
[21] Ibid., 98.

practical procedures and cures from foreign men and women fitted well into discussions among early modern physicians about the many useful things that could be learned from women experienced in the herbs or in child birthing, Hindu doctors or savage tribes in the West Indies.

Causes of the Contradictory Prejudices

When asking what may have caused the rift between the two kinds of reports one usually starts by pointing to the direct military confrontation between various Catholic countries in Europe and the Ottoman Empire. In contrast, there were repeated efforts of Catholic princes to build a military alliance with pre-Safavid and Safavid rulers against the Ottomans. I have argued elsewhere that this contrast does not suffice to explain the different perceptions of the state of the sciences in the two Muslim societies by Catholic or Protestant writers from Europe. [22] There were other palpable differences about which the foreign visitors read already at home such as religious difference or different historical relationships and historical evaluations.

The perception of Islam and its adherents was anchored until the early eighteenth century in prejudices born in much earlier times and nourished by medieval translations of the Qur'an and anti-Islamic refutations. Writers of the sixteenth and seventeenth centuries believed in only one truth and one faith. Those who did not share this belief either emigrated, for instance to the Ottoman Empire, or did not expound their belief in travel accounts. Hence, it is not surprising that most writers of travel accounts portrayed Muhammad as an impostor, charlatan, or severely afflicted sick man whose preaching aimed at seducing men by promises of abundant sexual and sensual pleasures. In contrast, the Shi'i creed of the Safavids was seen as something new and potentially less hostile to Christianity. The difference in creed was perceived as the major ideological reason for the repeated conflicts between the two Muslim dynasties. Being the enemy's enemy, the Safavids received a much more favourable treatment in travel accounts than the Ottomans. In particular one Safavid ruler, Shah 'Abbas I (r. 1587-1629), was greatly admired. Several Italian and French travellers used famous heroes of ancient classical mythology and history such as Hercules and Alexander the Great when discussing the shah's merits and stature. [23]

Gender prejudices were a further component of the belief system subscribed to by European writers of the sixteenth and seventeenth centuries that contributed to blackening the reputation of the rulers of both Muslim countries and of their courts. While Ottoman sultans until Selim II (r. 1566-1574) were

---

[22] S. Brentjes, *Early Modern Western European Travellers in the Middle East and their Reports about the Sciences* (Téhran: Institut Français de Recherche en Iran), in press.

[23] Della Valle, for instance, compared Shah 'Abbas with Hercules. P. Della Valle, Delle condizioni di Abbas re di Persia. (Venetia, 1628), 42. François-Auguste de Thou (d. 1642) spoke of the Safavid ruler as the Solomon of his time, because since antiquity nobody had ruled more wisely and more justly. Ms Paris, BNF, Dupuy 703, ff 148b-149.

mostly described as valiant, ferocious warriors, Selim II was mostly seen as an incompetent, cruel drunkard. The marriage of his father Süleyman (r. 1520-1566) to Hürrem was recognized as a breach of previous patterns. The sultana's deadly interference into the succession of the throne in favour of her own sons was interpreted as the beginning of the women's rule. The rise of the Sultan Valide, i. e. the sultan's mother, to political prominence ruling the court from the inner centre of the harem, was denounced as the cause for the withdrawal of many Ottoman sultans of the seventeenth century from public appearance and personal leadership of the army in times of war. The so-called rule of the women and eunuchs was seen as an expression of a fundamental weakness of the Ottoman Empire. [24] Similar developments were "discovered" at the Safavid court after Shah 'Abbas II (r. 1642-1667). But it was mainly in reports about the Ottoman Empire that the notion of decline was used as a category describing the prognosticated and hoped-for outcome of such events since the late sixteenth and throughout the seventeenth centuries. This kind of judgement started in reports of the Venetian bailos in Istanbul sent to the Doge and the Signoria of Venice. [25] From there it spread into reports of French ambassadors and accounts of gentlemen travellers from other Catholic and Protestant countries. Its intellectual basis was the cyclical theory of history subscribed to by many historians and educated travellers of the period. According to this theory the lifespan of every regime consisted of three phases – rise, climax, decline. Some adherents of this theory even believed that the time-span for each phase was meant to be the same for each and every dynasty. They interpreted the long sequence of Ottoman sultans as an indicator for the impending demise of the dynasty. [26]

Additionally, travel accounts show different travel patterns with regard to the two Muslim countries that contributed to different possibilities for accessing local cultures and assessing indigenous population. Travel in the Ottoman Empire could rely on patterns established by pilgrimage and profit from networks and residences of merchants from various Italian and Catalan towns built since the twelfth century in Egypt, Syria, and Anatolia. The founding of embassies in Istanbul since the 1530s and the creation of Capuchin, Carmelite, and Jesuit convents in various Ottoman towns and at some Aegean islands merely added a further component to this set of material, spiritual, intellectual and financial backbones of travel. Experience, recommendation, and support in the form of Franciscan or Dominican priests in Jerusalem, consuls and trading posts for European Christians in Aleppo, Damascus, Alexandria, or Cairo, regular ship

---

[24] L. P. Peirce, *The Imperial Harem. Women and Sovereignty in the Ottoman Empire.* (Oxford: Oxford University Press, 1993).

[25] E. Albèri, *Le Relazioni degli Ambasciatori Veneti al Senato* (Florence: Tipografia all'Insegna di Clio, 1840), Series 3, i; (Florence: Tipografia all'Insegna di Clio, 1844), Series 3, ii; E. Albèri, *Le Relazioni degli Ambasciatori Veneti al Senato durante il Secolo Decimosesto* (Florence: Società Editrice Fiorentina, 1855), Series 3, iii; L. Firpo, *Relazioni di Ambasciatori Veneti al Senato* (Turin: Bottega d'Erasmo, 1984), xiii; M. P. Pedani-Fabris, *Relazioni di Ambasciatori Veneti al Senato* (Padua: Bottega d'Erasmo, 1992), xiv.

[26] J. C. Davis, *Pursuit of Power; Venetian Ambassadors' Reports on Spain, Turkey, and France in the Age of Philip II, 1560-1600* (New York: Harper & Row, 1970).

connections between Livorno, Venice, or Marseille and ports in the Ottoman Empire, and numerous accounts of pilgrimages describing the main sites to be visited created a stable and reliable framework for Catholic and Protestant travellers in the Ottoman Empire. In contrast, the realm of the Safavids did not possess such a well-established and long-trodden network of routes, monuments, hostels, and personal available to visitors. Missionaries flocked to the country only in the early seventeenth century, focused for half a century on the new capital of the empire, Isfahan, before spreading to other towns. While merchants tried already in the course of the sixteenth century to establish trading posts in the Safavid Empire, they too received permission to do so only in the first decades of the seventeenth century. Hence, when official and private travellers other than missionaries and merchants came to the country, they had to rely on local resources and had almost no external support by compatriots and easily accessible sources of orientation. The travel accounts written by English, Italian, French, and Dutch travellers of the seventeenth century, based on the experience of the individual traveller, but more so on the collected knowledge and experience of the missionaries and merchants, filled this gap for their publics as far as sources of orientation and information were concerned. The convents in Isfahan, Shiraz, Baghdad, Basra, and the Caucasus mountains plus the trading posts in Shiraz, Bandar 'Abbas, Basra, and – for some time- at the island of Hormuz contributed the building stones of the slowly emerging network. Compared with opportunities to travel in comfortable familiarity within the Ottoman Empire, the network of Catholic and Protestant points of contact and support always remained weakly anchored and thinly filled. Its major advantage in terms of access to local elite culture was that it was centred around the Safavid court itself, both in the capital and at the Southern shore of the Caspian Sea.

All these factors acted together in producing the different portrayal of the sciences in the two Muslim countries. A close analysis of major travel accounts of the seventeenth century shows, however, that the particular discourse about the sciences under the Ottomans and the Safavids was nourished specifically by one single component. This component shaped the geographical, natural, historical, religious and cultural spaces of the two empires as a historicizing narrative about Scythian barbarians and ancient Persian cultural heroes.

The Historicizing Construction of Western Asia [27]

The construction of the territories ruled by the Ottomans and the Safavids as an entity defined by historical views and beliefs embraced various elements. Political events of major religious relevance such as the fate of the Byzantine Empire were at the forefront of evaluating the Ottoman dynasty. The possibility to mobilize aspects of what ancient writers on history and geography had said

---

[27] Most of what I discuss here applies also to Northern Africa. My decision not to name Northern Africa explicitly is partly a matter of style (trying to avoid too many qualifiers) and an indicator that not all of Northern Africa was part of the Ottoman Empire and so would have no place in this paper.

VI

about the cultural and political places of the Persians dangled as a constant lure before the eyes of the educated writer. Ancient views and values were reanimated for evaluating early modern Safavid rulers and elites. In an analogous manner ideas were derived from ancient books concerning the question from which tribes the Ottomans in particular and the "Turks" in general had sprung. General theories about the origin of philosophy and science including religion and about their subsequent progress and distribution over the world served for turning the pretended lack of science among the "Turks" into an expression of valour. Assumptions about the historical coherence of the world around the Mediterranean Sea and the historical experience with Arabic sciences in Latin translation contributed to set the "Turks" apart from the "Arabs". The "Turks" were cast as the eternal conquerors and oppressors, while the "Arabs" were proclaimed as guardians of ancient Greek knowledge.

Even the dissenters among Protestant authors of travel accounts such as Henry Blount shared some of the ideas forming the images of the "Turks" in Europe in the late sixteenth and throughout the seventeenth centuries. This is particularly true for views about the ethnic origin and its consequence for the status of civilization ascribed to individual tribes and peoples. Blount thought that the alleged "Turks"' ethnic origin from the Asian Scythians conferred military excellence upon the Ottomans as well as a certain ruthlessness that made them much more capable and successful governors of a multinational empire than the Romans ever had been. It was also the reason why the "Turks" had no science, which Blount himself did not hold in high esteem. A mixture of historical and natural factors, however, would guarantee that the "Turks" would eventually appreciate learning:

"To which purpose I have often considered, whether learning is ever like to come in request among the *Turks*, and as far as conjecture may venture, I doubt not thereof, for learning is not admired in the beginning of empires - *emollit mores, nec finit esse feros*, and so weakneth the sword: but when once that hath bred greatnes and sloth, then with other effeminacies come in letters. Thus, in *Rome*, at first, philosophers were banish'd as unactive, but upon the conquests of *Carthage* and *Greece* they crept in; and the *Turkish* empire consists much of those countries, whose air makes speculative wits, and which of old bred the greatest divines, philosophers, and poets of the world: wherefore, though for some ages the *Turkish* race may retain its own proper fierceness, yet in time those subtile climates and mixture of blood with the people thereof, will gentilize and infect it with the antient softness natural to these places. ... Now the natural course of things much follows the sun, who gives life to all; wherefore this *Cyclopaedia* hath been observed to run from east to west. Thus have most civilities and sciences came, as some think, from the Indian gymnosophists into *Egypt*, from thence into *Greece*, so into *Italy*, and then over the *Alps*, into these faint north-west parts of the world, whence if the inquisition hinder not, perhaps they may pass into those new plantations westward, and then return in their old circle among the *Levantines*." [28]

Blount is one of the few authors who spelled out in detail the complex historicizing assumptions and theories that guided Catholic and Protestant perceptions of the "Turks" and their lack of sciences. It is not so much Blount's specific historical theories and assumptions that make me argue that claims derived and revitalized from ancient sacred and secular literature constituted the most important single factor for shaping the perceptions of the state of the sciences in the Ottoman versus the Safavid empires. My point is that the ideas that defined the value attributed to the territories ruled by the two Muslim dynasties as part of the civilized world and to its diverse regions and peoples were historicizing whether they concerned historical subjects, contemporary societies or nature itself. Western Asia, its cultures, social fabric or geographical features, its plants, animals, mountains or skies did not exist as objective facts open to be investigated as to what their meaning and relevance was or could be for the sciences in Europe. To Catholic and Protestant visitors and observers, Western Asia in all its different aspects was an entity where history and present were blended into a unified complex system and where the present was weighed and judged by a past which itself was historically defined.

The direct effect that this historicizing construction of Western Asia had upon the perception of the sciences in those regions is also reflected in the fact that only a few communities were discussed. Many others were excluded from such questioning or reporting. Besides the "Turks" and the "Persians", the issue whether a community had science or not was raised with respect to the Greeks, the "Egyptians", the Arabs, the "Mores" and the Jews. None of the other communities was ever found necessary or worth of discussion by Catholic and Protestant writers in terms of whether they had science or not - not the Maronites who were closest to Catholicism, nor the Nestorians, the Jacobites, the Armenians, the Georgians, the Kurds, the Circassians or the Zoroastrians. They all were good writing material for religious issues, for marriage and burial customs, for the beauty of their women or the variety of their food and clothing. But science was not a subject that came up in their chapters. They either were not present in ancient sources or were despised because of having been purged from the fold of the Church by one or the other ancient concilium.

The Humanist Reconfiguration of Contemporary Western Asia as a Game and a Fake

The historicizing construction of Western Asia, of its cultures and natures went beyond its direct impact upon the presentation of the state of the sciences in those regions. When Blount contemplated cities, valleys or mountains in the European parts of the Ottoman Empire he read Caesar. Pietro della Valle,

---

[28] H. Blount, 'A Voyage into the Levant', in *Collection of Voyages and Travels* (London: Printed by Assignment from Messierus Churchill, For Thomas Osborne in Gray's Inn, 1752), 7 vols., vi, at 539.

VI

in the draft of his dedicatory epistle to the Accademia degli Umoristi, legitimised his travel to the East rather than to the North, the West or the South by Asia's pregnancy with empires, by Egypt's fatherhood of antiquity, and by Greece's motherhood of the letters. He topped this description of Oriental cultural attraction with an indirect quote from ancient historians and poets claiming that there was no stone or shrub without name or fame. [29]

Name and fame were indeed major points of attention when travellers talked about Western Asian nature and culture. Attempts were made to identify rivers, mountains, cities or seas by their historical relevance according to Herodotus, Xenophon, Ptolemy, Strabo, Solin or the Bible. Administrative divisions of the two Muslim countries that dominated published accounts of travellers were foremost those of ancient Greek geography and history. For two hundred years at least, European writers on geography and history were busy describing contemporary Western Asian structures in those terms. [30] Even the measurement of geographical coordinates, the evaluation of specific data and the choice of particular places for studying the tides and the currents was justified by this historicizing perception of the countries south of the Mediterranean Sea. [31]

In contrast, maps and globes indicate that Italian, Dutch and French cartographers tried to incorporate contemporary geographical units, concepts and names into the ancient landscapes not only of Europe, but of Asia and Africa too. The process seems to have started within the editions of Ptolemy's "Geography". Willibald Pirckhaymer's (1470-1530) and Sebastian Münster's (1488-1552) respective Greek and Latin editions contained lists identifying numerous Ptolemaic names of towns or rivers in Asia and Africa with names taken from later written and cartographic sources. In his world-maps as well as in his maps of Asia, Africa, and Anatolia, Giacomo Gastaldi (d. 1566) densely filled the interiors of the two continents, which most maps of the period left rather empty, with towns and villages. These new objects carried ancient Greek and Latin names, corrupt medieval transliterations of Arabic, Persian, Turkish and Mongol names, contemporary local names, partly in distorted Latin, Italian or Catalan forms and partly in very good transliterations, and fantasy names. The high quality of the transliteration of the new local names means that Gastaldi had access to specific and reliable information about Ottoman and Safavid geographical literature and administrative structures. Gastaldi's maps proved highly influential. They were copied by various mapmakers in Venice, Rome, Antwerp and Amsterdam, followed later by their colleagues in London, Paris, Cologne and other towns. Many late sixteenth- and seventeenth-century maps of

---

[29]] Ms Roma, Società Geografica Italiana, 7186, 2 vols., i, 103.
[30] See, for instance, Kh. Al Ankary, *La Péninsule Arabique dans les Cartes Européennes Anciennes. Fin XV- début XIX siècle. Collection Khaled Al Ankary.* Exposition du 15 septembre au 28 octobre 2001 (Paris: Institut du Monde Arabe, 2001).
[31] This was, for instance, the case when in the 1620s and 1630s Nicolas Fabri de Peiresc, Gottfried Wendelin and John Greaves argued for measuring geographical coordinates in Alexandria, Rhodos, Istanbul and Tunis. Another example is Nicolas Fabri de Peiresc's effort to convince Osman d'Arcos, a French convert to Islam in Tunis, to observe the tides at Goletta.

the Safavid Empire and of Anatolia combined ancient classical with contemporary Muslim geography by writing for instance "Fars (or Farsistan) olim Persis" or "Natolia olim Asia Minor". In contrast, ancient sacred and secular geography remained in place for most of the European territories of the Ottoman Empire until well into the eighteenth century and for certain areas such as Palestine or Mesopotamia even longer. [32]

Cartographers such as Gastaldi and geographers and historians such as Filippo Ferrari composed long lists up to long books whose only purpose was to equate ancient and contemporary names of places, rivers, mountains, deserts, seas, and provinces. As the equation of Babylon with Baghdad, Pelusium with Damietta, Ecbatana with Tauris (Tabriz) or Calcedon with Scutari indicate, the writers often failed in their efforts. While they set out to study ancient ruins and monuments in their home countries in order to find some safe ground for their work of identification, when they wrote about Western Asia, they applied indiscriminately unproven historical claims, wrong quotations of geographical coordinates, and falsified eyewitness-accounts as arguments in favour of their specific choices. The French druggist Pierre Gilles (1490-1555), who had toured the Ottoman Empire from 1544 till 1547, and the English leisure traveller Thomas Herbert (1606-1682), who toured Iran in 1627/28, both took contrary stances when it came to the question whether ancient Ecbatana could be identified with Tauris, i.e. Safavid Tabriz. While both correctly believed that Ecbatana was located in ancient Media, only Gilles rejected the wrong identification of Tabriz with Media's old capital:

"From the four castles we proceeded to Tauris, which some believe falsely to be Ecbatana, but Paulus Jovius is wrong, who believes it (being) in Armenia, while it is in Media ..." [33]

Herbert knew of other authors (Ptolemy, Niger, Cedrenus, Marco Polo, and Chalcondyles) who differentiated between Tauris and Ecbatana, and located the first in such different regions as Assyria, Armenia, Persia, Parthia, or Pers-Armenia. The reason for this confusion, Herbert thought, was twofold. The unacceptable inference from royal titles to geographical locations contributed to it as did the many names given by ancient writers to the region of Armenia. [34] Herbert believed that Tabriz sat atop the ruins of ancient Ecbatana. Against their separation and against the assumption that the former was a town outside of Media, Herbert raised three sorts of arguments - geographical, historical, and authoritative:

---

[32] I gained these insights when working on a project financed by a Harley Fellowship in connection with the map collection of the British Library.

[33] "Inde quartis castris peruenimus Tauricam, quam quidam falso putant Ecbatana, sed falsius Paulus Jouius, qui eam putat in Armenia, cum sit in Media: ..." Ms Paris, BNF, Dupuys 16, f 3a.

[34] T. Herbert, *Some Yeares Travels Into Africa et Asia the Great. Especially Describing the Famous Empires of Persia and Industant (sic). As also Divers other Kingdoms in the Orientall Indies, and I'les Adjacent* (London: Printed by R. Bl. for Iacob Blome and Richard Bishop), 195.

"If to be under *Baronta*, (*Diodorus, Polybius,* and *Ptolemy* call it *Orontes*,) if to be in 36 degrees 50 minutes, if to have the ruines of *Tobyas* his grave, if to be the buriall place of Kings, if to be the Metropolis time out of mind, if to be the Citie from *Ierusalem* N.E. foure hundred forsangs can make it *Ecbatan*; or if the authority of *Ananias, Petrus de la Valle, Leunclavius, Teixera,* and of *Ortelius* will serve, let it be *Ecbatan* and in *Medya*." [35]

For proving that Tabriz was not located outside Media, he even used only a single geographical argument based on authority:

"... for by *Abulfeda, Vlughbeg,* and others, the latitude of *Tauryz* complies with *Ecbatan*." [36]

Most of Herbert's arguments in favour of his opinions are false. Ecbatana lies under present-day Hamadan in Khuzistan, while Tabriz is located in Adharbayjan. The Ayyubid prince of Hama, Abu l-Fida' (1273-1331), and the Timurid ruler of Samarcand, Ulugh Beg, (1394-1449) differ in what they give as the latitude of Tabriz. Abu l-Fida', relying here upon the Khwarazmian scholar al-Biruni (973-1048), has 39° 10'. Ulugh Beg ascribed to Tabriz a latitude of 38°, probably derived from the earlier astronomical tables compiled by the Iranian scholar Nasir al-Din al-Tusi (1201-1274). Neither of the two values agrees with that given by Herbert nor with the latitude of Ecbatana found in Ptolemy's "Geography" (37°45). [37] The German scholar Johannes Leunclavius (1533-1593), quoted by Herbert as one of his authorities for identifying Tabriz with Ecbatana, had rejected this equation, both in his own books and when attacking the Italian physician Giovanni Tommaso Minadoi (1545-1618), who had lived from 1576 till 1585 in Aleppo and Istanbul as a physician of the Venetian consuls. Minadoi, when writing about the latest war between the Ottomans and Safavids (1576-1586), had argued in favour of the opinion that both towns were one and the same in terms of geographical location. When criticized by Leunclavius for this wrong view, a fierce fight ensued over who was right. [38]

While the debate about which ancient name applied to which contemporary site or object was led in the sixteenth and early seventeenth centuries with intense seriousness and blithe carelessness, travellers in the later seventeenth century described this game as antiquated and pretended to stick to it merely because of consideration for the uninformed public, which could not travel in person to the sites discussed by the traveller. A substantial conceptual

---

[35] Ibid., 195.
[36] Ibid.
[37] Abu l-Fida, *Géographie d'Aboulféda*. Texte Arabe publié ... par M. Reinaud et M. Le Baron Mac Guckin de Slane. (Paris: L'Imprimerie Royale, 1840; Reprint: Beirut: Dar Sader, s. d.), 400; D. King, *World-Maps for Finding the Direction and Distance to Mecca. Innovation and Tradition in Islamic Science* (Leiden, Boston, Köln: E.J. Brill, 1999), 462; E. L. Stevenson, *Geography of Claudius Ptolemy* (New York: New York Library, 1932), 135.
[38] G. T. Minadoi, *Historia della guerra fra Turchi, et Persiani* (Turin: B. G. Bevilacqua, 1588); Io. Th. Minadoi, *Pro sva de bello persico. Historia Adversus ea quae illi à Ioane Leunclavio obijciuntur. Dispvtatio.* (Venetiis; Apud Nicolaum Moretum, 1595); J. Leunclavius, *Historia Turcorum*. (Frankfurt, 1591).

change occurred, however, only in the eighteenth century when geographers and antiquarians changed the rules of the game and insisted that in order to identify ancient places one had to know contemporary geographical realities. This knowledge was to be supplemented by a serious study of archaeological remains and historical monuments. The mere familiarity with ancient literature did not suffice any longer for answering the long debated question of equality between ancient and contemporary names. [39]

One result of this change was a renewed interest in local knowledge from Western Asia about Western Asia. A second result was the readiness to determine anew the ranking of geographical knowledge as displayed in Greek, Latin, Arabic, Persian or Chinese texts from the past and the present. Moreover, oral, living knowledge held by natives of the mapped lands was integrated into these processes of judging which knowledge was more reliable and who could be trusted. What did not change substantially was the ideology about who possessed scientific knowledge in Muslim countries. The "Turks" continued to be ridiculed by most writers, although a minority wrote against this distortion, as had been the case in the seventeenth century. In contrast to the earlier form of the prejudice, the "Turks" now became portrayed even as the "traitors" of their scientific heritage, developed before them by the "Arabs". [40] The "Persians" simply dropped out of the discourse as a result of the fall of the Safavid dynasty in 1722 and the deep disorder that gripped the country for several decades. The propounded discourse about who had science in the Islamic world camouflaged the use of Arabic, Persian, and Ottoman-Turkish sources and information by geographers and cartographers in Europe.

Principally the same constellation between public discourse and pursued practice can already be found in the early seventeenth century. A few unpublished travel accounts written by French authors show a completely different picture from the one discussed so far. Their authors did not use many ancient terms and names, but talked of the places and territories they saw on their voyages according to their local names, often in distorted transliterations. I assumed first that these travellers had not received the education of young noblemen and sons of rich bourgeois families, i.e. had not read the classical authors and hence did not share the world-view of their co-travellers. Then I thought that they stood at the beginning of a process unfolding in France which applied to the Ottoman Empire the same stick as to the Safavid Empire, that is, replaced the remnants of ancient geography by modern local knowledge. While this appears not to be completely wrong, the unpublished papers of the eminent

---

[39] Clear testimony for this claim comes from Jean-Baptiste Bourguignon d'Anville's book on ancient geography, particularly volume two: *Géographie ancienne abrégée* (Paris: Chez Merlin, Libraire, rue de la Harpe, à l'Image Saint Joseph, 1768), ii.

[40] Thus Voltaire would exclaim, «Quelle difference entre le genie des Arabes et celui des Turcs. Ceux-ci ont laissé périr un ouvrage don't la conservation valait mieux que la conquête d'une grande province». Cited by K. Kreiser, "Haben die Türken Verstand?" – Zur europäischen Orient-Debatte im napoleonischen Zeitalter, in *Ulrich Jasper Seetzen (1767-1811). Leben und Werk*. (Gotha: Forschungs- und Landesbibliothek 1995), 153-73. Reprint: *Türkische Studien in Europa*. Analecta Isisiana, xxxi (Istanbul: Isis, 1998), 121-39.

VI

Italian traveller Pietro della Valle (1586-1652) suggest an altogether different reading of the heavy amount of classical sacred and secular terminology and territorial structuring of Western Asia in published Latin, Italian, French, Dutch, Spanish, Portuguese, and German travel accounts, histories, geographical books, diplomatic reports, political pamphlets and maps.

Della Valle's papers in the Secret Archive and the Apostolic Library of the Vatican contain a number of his original letters to his friend and mentor Mario Schipano, a physician from Naples. Added to these originals are notes that make use of long extracts from books read by della Valle after his return from ten years of travel in the Ottoman and Safavid empires as well as Western India to Italy in 1624. The extracts themselves are preserved in another set of files in the Apostolic Library joined by instructions which book to quote and how to refer to the sources. [41] A comparison of this material with the printed letters proves that almost all authors quoted there had been added to the letters after della Valle's return to Rome. In his original letters to Schipano he had mentioned only a small number of contemporary authors and an even smaller number of ancient authors. Almost no attention is shown to ancient authors in della Valle's travel diary. The amount of classical geographical names in the original letters and the diary is low; local names dominate. The Italian traveller put much effort into learning these local names and sharing them both in transcription and in Arabic letters with his friend.

Mario Schipano, the recipient of the letters, belonged to a circle of scholars in the Accademia dei Lincei who were immensely interested in acquiring and studying Arabic, Persian and Turkish scientific manuscripts. This circle founded and maintained by Prince Federico Cesi (1585-1630) demonstrates that in the early seventeenth century humanist beliefs, active interest in the new sciences, and the focused acquisition of means for studying natural history, medicine, astrology, mathematics, geography and magic in Arabic and Ottoman-Turkish manuscripts not only coexisted, but complemented each other. Della Valle's travel to Western Asia, his immediate efforts to learn first Turkish, then Arabic, and finally Persian, as well as his occasionally unwilling efforts to acquire manuscripts, seeds, minerals, and other items such as mummies deemed worthy for scholarly interest and princely display can only be fully appreciated when placed in the context of the Accademia dei Lincei and the intellectual ambitions of her founder, his advisor Giambattista della Porta (153-1615), and other early members of the circle. [42]

---

[41] Ms Città di Vatican, Archivio Segreto Vaticano, Archivio Della Valle - Del Bufalo 51, letters of della Valle to Schipano (unpaginated); Mss Città di Vatican, Biblioteca Apostolica Vaticana, Ottoboniano latino 3383-85. The volumes 3383 and 3384 contain letters of della Valle to Schipano and other persons. Volume 3385 consists of two parts and contains the results of della Valle's reading after his return to Rome as well as his orders how to quote from his notes.

[42] G. Gabrieli, 'I primi Accademici Lincei e gli studi orientali', *La bibliofila* 28 (1926), 99-115; 100-06, 108, 114. According to the Inventario Codicum, Mss, Bibliothecae Barberini Redactum et Digestum a D. Sancte Pieralisi Bibliothecario, ii, kept in the Biblioteca Apostolica Vaticana, the Accademia dei Lincei owned 20

VI

Most of the Eastern features of della Valle's original letters were banished in the process of preparing them for publication. Their place was filled by quotations from the Bible and the classics to which some contemporary authors were added. [43] The cause for all these changes was the need to receive for every publication in Rome the clearance of the Inquisition. Della Valle worked diligently to prepare a number of texts for print. He approached the Propaganda fide in person for recommending two of his writings for the missionaries. But he managed only twice to get the imprimatur and see his works published. In 1628, his laudatory biography of Shah 'Abbas I appeared. In 1650, the first volume of his letters to Schipano was published. A third work of della Valle, his Turkish grammar, was cleared by a priest of the Inquisition for publication, but never appeared. A few printed pages of his Catholic apology written in Persian in Isfahan and translated into Latin in Rome are extant in della Valle's left papers, but remained unfinished. Apparently, the Propaganda fide was not interested in della Valle's offer. Some other unpublished treatises by della Valle such as his Persian summary of Tycho Brahe's cosmology together with an Italian translation and his Latin geography of Iran were prepared by him for publication too, but never appeared. Although della Valle came from an influential Patrician family in Rome and was befriended by other influential men in the city and in Naples, there were apparently others in the Inquisition and the Propaganda fide who did not wish to see his works published. Some editors of his letters have suggested that della Valle's naive religiosity was at odds with the libertine spirit ruling in Rome and among the cardinals. [44] Whatever the cause for della Valle's misfortunes, since della Valle strongly desired his letters to be published wishing "to live and operate not in a small corner of Rome alone or of Italy, but in the great theatre of the entire universe" he tried his utmost to give the censors no reason to deny their permission for print.

Della Valle's efforts provide us with a unique insight into the gap between individually held beliefs and publicly expressed judgements with regard to the Ottoman and Safavid Empires. In particular, the formulaic view that nothing had changed in Iran and by extension in the whole of Asia since ancient times was only produced by the later integration of ancient authors into the text

---

Arabic, Turkish, and Persian manuscripts, among them 14 texts on arithmetic, astronomy, astrology, geography, and medicine.

[43] F. Gaeta and L. Lockhard, *I Viaggi di Pietro della Valle. Lettere dalla Persia* (Roma: Istituto Poligrafico dello Stato, 1972), i, XIX-XXII. Their claims that the changes in della Valle's letters incorporated due to the Inquisition concerned only "some expressions which seemed to be to lively or improper and cancelled some passages which attacked a certain type of missionary politics or appeared to be equivocal and compromising" are based exclusively on the comparison between the fine copy of the letters preserved in Ms Roma, Società Geografica Italiana, 7186, 5 vols. and the printed version; that is they refer only to the factual interference of the institution in the letters after they were substantially altered by the author in anticipation of its censorship. The latter they described as with della Valle's own words as "formal corrections and the cancellation of banter and things ... (written) in confidence ..." Ibid., at XVIII, XX. As for della Valle's troubles with the Inquisition, the putting of his work on Shah 'Abbas I on the Index and the public critique uttered against it by a Jesuit and professor of theology in Vienna, see ibid., XXI-XXII, footnotes 1 and 2.

[44] Gaeta and Lockhard, 'I Viaggi', i, XIX.

of the letters. This prejudice, which became so influential in the discourses about the Ottoman Empire's incapability for reform in the eighteenth century and about Asia's lack of history in the nineteenth century, was nothing else than a literary fake.

The revision of della Valle's original letters did not only strip the Safavid Empire of its contemporary specificity and mobility, it also eradicated important traces of della Valle's research activities while travelling. Della Valle, the collector of contemporary knowledge in local garb was transformed into della Valle, the owner of true knowledge from ancient books and transformer of an inferior raw nature and culture, which was experienced by the senses and through oral local information, into a superior civilized nature and culture, which was eternalised in ancient and medieval elite texts.

Observations and Reflections

For understanding the various utterances of members of one culture about the sciences in another culture, perceived as profoundly different and even hostile to one's own beliefs and behavioural standards, a historian ideally should engage in a broad spectrum of investigative works and apply a variety of methods for controlling his or her own assumptions as well as the overt and hidden claims and beliefs of the sources. While many historians of present-day Europe and North America seem to accept easily even the worst statement made about a Muslim society, I tend to disbelieve each and every negative statement and to accept all positive statements as unproblematic. Since I know that my attitude is as problematic as the other one I try to control my own preference by intensive questioning and contextualizing of every single detail if possible. I have tried to articulate this approach repeatedly in my paper.

I take an analogous stance against some methodological beliefs of postmodernist doctrine. I do not believe that power and conquest are at the heart of all encounters nor do I believe that communication between different cultures was and is impossible. Travellers, writers, merchants, diplomats or soldiers from Catholic or Protestant Europe did not spent all their energies in constructing a discourse of superiority and uniqueness of their own culture and the non-Western side, even when weaker in some respect, was not prevalently passive, immobile, submissive and silent. Approaching the problem of inter-cultural communications from a comparative angle can open windows for seeing the Easterner ignoring, rejecting, excluding and oppressing the Westerner, but also admitting him or her into their own society and offering support, advice and entertainment. A comparative approach also allows a sharpening of our understanding for the enormous work of adaptation and reformulation carried out while travelling and when writing about the journey.

The encounters between Europeans and inhabitants of the Ottoman and Safavid empires took place between men of different creeds, professions, social status, experience, customs, habits, kinds of knowledge and emotions. Accordingly, the extant historical sources differ in kind, scope, content and rhetoric. Expressions of private beliefs and emotions are only rarely found in early modern Ottoman and Safavid sources, which are overwhelmingly texts of public format on history, biography, religion, the sciences, taxes and legal cases. Expressions of private beliefs and emotions are abundant in early modern Western European sources, which appear to be private utterances but represent a quasi-public and standardized rhetoric written down in semi-public sources such as letters, diaries or reports. Hence, the historian interested in individualized and localized perspectives needs to excavate the occasional slip in Ottoman and Safavid sources and question the formalized public rhetoric with respect to its potential individuality, which often is restricted to the author. With regard to sources from Catholic or Protestant Europe, he or she also needs to excavate the occasional slip into a non-standard deviation from the formalized public forms of private utterances and question the apparently informal public discourse in order to discover its standardized messages.

Religious convictions created the framework for most of the judgements in the travel accounts of Christian writers. They were supplemented by a number of newly emerging concepts such as statehood, civilization and innovation. Other concepts of older origin were joined for the sake of specification and familiarity such as characteristic properties of tribes and peoples, evaluations of rationality and irrationality or judgements of historical, natural and sacred relevance of peoples, animals, countries, regions, cities and monuments. They were expressed in terms of pride, beauty, superiority and ridicule. Whether any of such utterances is a prejudice can be determined by acts of confrontation, i.e. by confronting different sources taken from one culture, by confronting sources taken from different cultures and by confronting different kinds of prejudices. The analysis of such notions often unmasks a historical construction set in scene by the narrating side. The intensity of the construction is culturally and time specific. In the case of early modern European writers, censorship, peer-pressure and a shared educational valorisation of the classics turned the public and semi-public work of historical construction into an elaborate edifice.

Several other elements contributed to shape the statements about foreign sciences in the manner we have encountered them in the various sources presented in this paper. A major element is the incommensurability of cultures, which is partially expressed in the cultural coining of any language. Travellers when trying to explain foreign institutions to readers of their own cultures often did not start with describing their functions and modes of operation, but with choosing a word of their own language which would identify scope and meaning of the foreign thing. Thus, madrasa became a university, then an academy and later a college. A mosque was identified with a temple. The padishah turned out to be a king or a prince. The head-mufti was declared by Catholic writers to be the pope of the Turks. French authors identified the kaziaskar as the first president of the parliament or as the head of the ordinary justice. The fatwa was interpreted as being a statement of Turkish theology. While a few expressions were kept without translation (as for instance dervish, caimacam or deruga) those that were translated acquired wholly new cultural meanings. This transfer of cultural meaning enabled comparison and diminished distance and the feeling of estrangement. It enforced the perspective of universally valid institutions and opened ways for criticism of the foreign as well as of their own political, religious or cultural environment. Through the need for translation cultural meanings, specific to a particular language, slip often silently into the historical constructions of portrayals of foreign cultures, then as today. When trying to understand statements about knowledge and other forms of belief, historians need to address these implicit workings of language and question even seemingly innocuous terms.

A second major element is the tendency for generalization both on the level of historical sources and on the level of research papers by historians. Many travellers when judging the state of the sciences in the Ottoman Empire pretend that what they say applies to all cities and towns, to all of the non-religious or the religious disciplines en bloc or to all members of a religious community. Modern historians have accepted these pretensions uncritically by refraining from questioning which methods and means such a traveller might have possibly applied for collecting necessary and reliable data for this kind of general evaluation. When phrased in this way it becomes clear that in the seventeenth century neither a traveller nor a long-term resident in the Ottoman Empire had the material, social and intellectual means to gain statistically valid information about any theme. What they usually had access to were individual contacts, shared opinions and repeated particular experiences. From there, they drew conclusions and formed generalized judgements. The process of generalizing individual and particular events was guided and regulated by generalizations and preconceptions acquired in the traveller's own culture. Hence, a sound scepticism is necessary when analysing any kind of general statement. This is all the more true for statements about the sciences, since only a few scholarly travellers such as Abbé Toderini in the eighteenth century went explicitly into the Ottoman Empire for studying the local sciences. They went for learning local languages, buying manuscripts, coins, mummies, animals and fruits, collecting plants and seeds, rediscovering ancient monuments, measuring the pyramids, Aya Sofya and the altitude of stars, the sun and the moon and observing eclipses or phases of Venus. Those who were sent for acquiring a comprehensive knowledge of Muslim culture in the Ottoman and Safavid Empires such as François Petis de la Croix in the second half of the seventeenth century achieved indeed a much more intimate knowledge of the various disciplines which formed the educational and literary landscapes in the two countries. But even they tended to focus more on religious, historical, linguistic and philosophical branches than on mathematics, astronomy, astrology, medicine or the occult sciences. The missionaries, on the other side, did not engage into much scientific study in the Ottoman Empire unless they were asked to do so by scholars from Western Europe.

In the Safavid Empire, things were different. Catholic and Protestant scholars rarely came specifically to this country. Mostly they were passing

VI

through as part of the Portuguese, Dutch or English expansion in Asia. Missionaries, in particular the French Capuchins and the Jesuits, collected a fair knowledge about important authors, books and doctrines taught and studied in the Safavid Empire and even engaged in translating some Persian medical texts for the public back in Europe. But they did not address the state of the sciences in the Safavid Empire as a matter that needed a systematic surveying and analysis. Hence, even their general judgements in all probability reflect only the state of affairs in the capital Isfahan in its most basic aspects and the occasional individual encounter in other towns.

A third element is the formative power of the particular interests of the authors and the set of rhetorical, stylistic and related tools available to him. In the paper, the role of this element has been discussed in the case of Alpini's story about the deplorable state of medicine in Ottoman Egypt. The power of the arguments made by the author within his own local context did not depend upon the arguments' reliability and accuracy. The fictitious character of the arguments did not obscure their efficacy, but rather enhanced the latter. Nobody set out to establish the arguments' reliability, not only because it was not meant to be controlled. The arguments' fictitiousness fitted into already operative prejudices and other modes of debates. Their validity apparently was confirmed by earlier practical experiences of confrontation and defeat.

Ideally, a historian is supposed to disentangle all of these different layers of meaning in a statement about the sciences whether it is generally phrased or cast in a particular mode. Since a historian is, however, formed by the incommensurabilities and prejudices of his or her own culture and by his or her own individual interests, preferences and capabilities, it is unavoidable that he or she will end up with only a partially successful excavation and interpretative exploration.

As a result of my research, discussed in this paper, the wide-spread notions of what humanism meant in the second half of the sixteenth and in the first half of the seventeenth centuries and what kind of cultural practices were exercised by humanists of this time need to be reconsidered. Patrons, scholars and educated gentlemen while mostly practising humanism when writing texts for publication cared already much less for ancient authors when they wrote letters that were meant to circulate among their friends and colleagues. When they travelled outside their own world, they often changed not only their clothing, but also some of their perspectives. Numerous scholars of the period, who wished to emulate, restore and complete ancient authors and their writings, approached the latter two points by a detour through the Islamic world. As soon as they travelled physically through the world south and east of the Mediterranean Sea, they had to adapt to the local conditions. Their practice of travel, outside the standardized pilgrimage, was by necessity a journey through and in the contemporary Islamic world, not one through the world of ancient books. They could, for instance, only start in Halab (Aleppo) and end in Baghdad, even when they wrote about this travel as if they had set out from

VI

Hierapolis and arrived in Babylon. While Catholic and Protestant authors wrote often in biting terms about the uneducated and uncivilized "Turks", it was the Ottoman Empire where their envoys and occasionally the scholars and patrons themselves found most of the material they were looking for – manuscripts in several languages and material objects of nature and culture such as seeds, animals, drugs and minerals. The Islamic world was a highly important element in the scholarly projects of the members of the Republic of Letters in numerous European countries. The discourse about the non-scientific "Turks" and civilized "Persians" veiled the impact that the Ottoman and Safavid Empires had upon the new sciences in Catholic and Protestant Europe. Its consequences over the centuries made us blind to the honest turn of major scholars, patrons and gentlemen towards the study of the nature and culture in the Islamic world and the acquisition of the knowledge of its peoples and societies. It is time to recover the contributions provided by the Ottoman and Safavid Empires to the new sciences in Europe during the sixteenth and seventeenth centuries and to restore the honour of those travellers, diplomats, missionaries, scholars, and patrons who pursued seriously and diligently the study of knowledge expressed in Arabic, Persian and Turkish. But it is also time to recognize that our own perceptions of the history of the sciences in the Islamic world have been substantially shaped by the deprivation and the distortion of the sciences of the "Turks" by the writers of these two centuries.

VII

Peiresc's interests in the Middle East and Northern Africa in respect to geography and cartography

January 5, 1635, Nicolas Claude Fabri de Peiresc (1580-1637) wrote a long letter of introducing himself to father Cœlestinus de Sancta Lidvina, a Carmelite missionary in Aleppo and brother of Jacobus Golius, the Leiden professor for Arabic and mathematics.[1] Peiresc used the relation with Jacob Golius he entertained since circa 1629 to persuade the Carmelite of how profitable a "commerce of letters" between the two men could and would be.[2]

Peiresc was in a never ending quest for information about activities of nature, the political climate, commerce, history, languages, religious beliefs and practices in the Ottoman Empire and elsewhere, and for finding the cheapest, but also most reliable ways to acquire manuscripts, antiquities, plants, and animals. Although in 1634-35, he was in more or less regular contact with at least 10-15 men from different countries in Western Europe who, living in various towns of the Ottoman Empire and its North African satellites, contributed to fulfill Peiresc's diverse wishes, he was constantly trying to widen his network within and outside the Empire to complement his group of researching ambassadors, consuls, merchants, ship captains, scribes, physicians, missionaries, or travelers and to reach out as far as Ethiopia, Guinea, India, the top of mountains, or heaven itself. As reimbursement for the exacting demands which Peiresc heaped upon his partners with regard to time, intellectual and physical capabilities, and social relations, he promised as a rule money, not only to pay for the manuscripts, scribes, antiquities, or animals,

---

[1] Tamizey de Larroque has published this letter as the only one among those exchanged between Peiresc and Cœlestinus. He changed, however, for no apparent reason its date into 1633. In general, his edition of the letters to and from Peiresc is highly unreliable because the unavoidable errors of such a huge edition were not only caused by the enormous difficulties presented by the handwriting of at least three of Peiresc's scribes and the material distortion of a number of letters, but much more often by Tamizey de Larroque's own unexplained and often ununderstandable interventions into the wording of the letters. The curator of the Bibliothèque d'Ingiumbertine at Carpentras, Isabelle Battez, - whom I thank for her generous help and her many friendly and generous colleagues for the warm welcome they offered me - has expressed severe criticism at Tamizey de Larroque's edition several times. See, for instance, Passion(s) des Lettres. Peiresc (1580 - 1637) L'universel épistolier. 1998, p. 18:" Cette édition a le merite d'exister et rend bien des services, mais elles n'évite pas de recourir aux originaux, car l'écriture des sécretaires de Peiresc étant souvent peu lisible, Tamizey saute des passages sans le signaler et avec trois lettres en fait une; ou bien élimine ce qu'il juge inintéressant."

[2] In a letter to his friends Dupuy, dated August 23, 1629, he told how he came to hear from J. Golius although his name was distorted into Joly: "Nous pensions que tout commerce fust desja bouclé sur cez bruicts, mais il passa, l'aultre jour, un gentilhomme Breton, qui disoit venir attendre le Chevalier d'Allincourt pour passer en Italie quant et luy, lequel estoit venu de Hollande depuis peu, où il disoit qu'un Professeur en langue Arabique estoit revenu depuis peu du Levant où les Estats l'avoient envoyé avec si gros fonds de credit, qu'il en avoit rapporté 3 ou 400 volumes Arabes entre lesquels il y avoit d'excellentes pieces non encores veües, d'Archimede, Euclyde, Ptolemée, Apollonius Pergasus, et aultres, mesmes de Platon et d'Aristote, et qu'il y avoit des Tables astronomiques d'un Roy du Catay, et des observations continuées en cez pais là durant plusieurs siecles, qui doivent estre de grands thresors. Il le nommoit Mr. Joly, et je pense que ce soit celuy dont Mr Camerarius m'avoit aultres foys escript, par vostre entremise. je seroit bien marry si Mr Gassendi estoit passé si viste en cez pais là qu'il n'eust pas eu le moyen d'en voir quelque chose." Tamizey de Larroque 1890, vol. 2, p. 168.

and the costs of travels necessary to do his bidding, but also for all sorts of fees and arrangements of financing and insuring ships or, as in the case of father Cœlestinus, for personal needs and private wishes. Sometimes, Peiresc went even further. He proposed to make his social relations available, in particular those in Italy and France, and offered himself as a sort of postal deposit and relays station for sending letters, parcels, and other items home, to relatives, friends, or simply to the next point for distributing information or material among the members of the Republic of Letters.

Already in his first letter to the Carmelite, Peiresc drew up a list of his broad interests he wanted the father to take care of: manuscripts, marbles and inscribed stones, ancient temples, plants and animals rarely seen in Western Europe.[3] He also informed Cœlestinus about one of his more specific dreams - to get his hands on a copy of the three hymns of Dionysius, a younger colleague of Aristides, together with the notes since all manuscripts available in Western Europe he had seen or received a description of had been corrupt.[4]

Father Cœlestinus gladly accepted Peiresc's invitation and offers. He directed several of his letters as well as parcels with manuscripts to his brother in Leiden or to his uncle in Antwerp through Aix-en-Provence. Peiresc happily took the occasion to copy them by one of the scribes working for him, to underline what appeared important to him, and to make someone annotate them mostly by repeating the Arabic titles of books given in the letter and adding their translation into French or Latin. Cœlestinus asked Peiresc to send a variety of Latin, French, or Arabic books printed in Western Europe to enlarge the convent's library in Aleppo and to serve some native inhabitants of the town curious either in Catholic faith or in astronomy, astrology, geography, and other sciences. He spent some of the money Peiresc had offered for his private needs and dreams to pay his teacher, copyist, book-seller, informant, and, perhaps, even friend, the dervish Ahmad. He had not, however, foreseen the enormous scope of Peiresc's interests in the Middle East and, in particular, in some of the mountains in Syria and Lebanon as well as in eclipses. In the second letter to Cœlestinus Peiresc spelled out his wishes in an elaborate, but unsystematic form. He wanted the father to spend roughly ten days in the vicinity of Mount Kasios (height: 1770m) North-east of Aleppo between Iskandarun and Antakya. There he should climb up its supposedly 4000 feet to look out for the possible remnants of the ancient cult of Jupiter Casius and, perhaps, for rests of Traian's sacrifice, observe the lunar eclipse of August 1635, investigate the stratification, slope, and other natural properties of the mountain itself, spend (at least) one night on the mountain's top to experience the changing consistency and temperature of the air and to watch for possible indications of winds rising from caves. While marching across the

---

[3] Ms Carpentras, Bibliothèque d'Ingiumbertine, 1874, ff 361a-b.
[4] ibid., f 361b.

mountain, he should put wet paper on places with inscriptions if found for copying most exactly the characters. When all was finished, he should choose another way to climb down than he had used to get to the mountain's top to carry further his investigations of the natural shape of the Kasios. And finally, back to the plain, he was asked to question nearby living peasants whether they had ever seen vapors and fumes to ascend from the mountain in winter times and in case they did so to make them describe what they had seen.[5]

This one letter to father Cœlestinus de Sancta Lidvina summarizes neatly most of Peiresc's geography related interests in the Middle East and North Africa. If compared to other letters and papers of Peiresc it reveals that the study of eclipses, winds, airs, caves, mountains, tides, currents, volcanic eruptions, and earthquakes was not limited to the Middle East and Northern Africa, but it was at the heart of his attention to nature in Western Europe. His efforts to collect such data about the Middle East and Northern Africa were a planned extension of his studies at home. In a sense, they were even more than this. They provided Peiresc with a means to question his interpretations and speculative generalization of what he had observed in France, of what had happened in Southern Italy and Sicily, and of what Galileo had written about in his theory of the tides.

A topic not explicitly present in Peiresc's second letter to Cœlestinus is cartography. It was one of the major motivations to embark upon his efforts to make collaborators observe eclipses in the Middle East and North Africa in 1611-1612 and 1630-1636. Between these two periods, Peiresc encouraged the Maronites Gabriel Sionita (d. 1648) and Johannes Hesronita (d. 1628) to translate into Latin the Arabic fragment of al-Idrisi's "Geography" and pushed the Dutch geographer Petrus Bertius (d. 1628) to produce maps to this text as well as to ancient Greek and Latin authors. Studying ancient and medieval geographical and historical texts and applying recent methods and instruments to engrave historical and modern geographical maps characterized one of Peiresc's various ways to pursue nature and culture in a combined approach. With regard to his efforts to find collaborators in the Middle East and North Africa for observing eclipses, the "nobility" and "celebrity" of a certain place guided his choice of preferable observational sites. When studying mountains, he made "reading nature and culture" complement each other as aspects of one and the same object. His profound interest in the historicity of languages provided occasionally the starting point for an investigation of language(s), text(s), and natural object(s) in the same kind of inquiry.

---

[5] Ms Carpentras, Bibliothèque d'Inguimbertine, 1873, ff 42a-45a.

VII

4

1. Peiresc's network with the Ottoman Empire and its dependencies

Peiresc's network with the Ottoman Empire and its dependencies consisted overwhelmingly of French collaborators. He sought and maintained industriously - direct and indirect - contacts with ambassadors, secretaries of French ambassadors, consuls or vice-consuls, merchants in various Middle Eastern towns, captains whose ships traveled from one Mediterranean port to the other, missionaries mainly from the Capuchin order, but also Franciscans and Jesuits, and at least one French convert to Islam.[6] This part of the network was carried and strengthened by Peiresc's manifold contacts to merchants, ship-owners, and gentry in Marseille and Toulon who organized and maintained the transport of letters and goods between Peiresc and his Middle Eastern and North African partners.[7] Merchants from Italy with strongholds in Marseille, Cairo, Tripoli (Syria), and other Ottoman towns supplemented this web of relations.[8] Through some of his West European partners in the Ottoman Empire and its dependencies, Peiresc had - mostly indirect -

---

[6] 1. ambassadeurs and special envoys:
- François de Savary, comte de Brèves: ambassador in the Ottoman Empire from 1591 to 1605 and owner of the right to farm out the French consulat of Cairo;
- perhaps also Achille de Harlay, Baron de Sancy: ambassador in Constantinople;
- Sanson Napollon (or: Napolon), consul in Jerusalem (around 1625) and special envoy to Algiers, Tripoli, and Tunis (1268-1633);
- Henri de Gournay, comte de Marcheville: ambassador in Istanbul from 1631-1634.
2. secretaries of ambassadors:
- L'Empereur
- Monthoullieu.
3. consuls and vice-consuls:
- Balthasar Viaz (or: Vias) in Algiers;
- Piou in Tunis (?);
- Ant. Espanet (or: Spanet) in Cyprus;
- Angelo de Vento, Gabriel Fernoulx (or: Farnoux), and Esperu (or: Esprit) Laurens in Alexandria or Cairo;
- Viguier, consul for all "Syria";
- Estelle in Sayda;
- L'Empereur in Jerusalem;
- Guillaume Guez in Constantinople;
- F. Bayon in Tripoly/Libya.
4. merchants:
- César Lambert, Jean Magy, Jaques Albert, Jean Allemands etc. in Cairo and Alexandria;
- Balthasar Fabre, Balthasar Claret, Nicolas Gilloux, Mrs. Constans, etc. in Aleppo.
5. ship captains:
- Berenguer (or: Beringuer, Berengier), André Vicard, Louys Lombard, Garnier, Tessier, Baile, Etienne Beaussier, Pascal in North Africa;
- de Ramatuelle Tourtel, Roubault, Charles Blanc, etc. in the Levant;
- Gilles in the Levant and North Africa.
6. missionaries:
- Capucins: Agathange de Vendôme, Cassien de Nante, Michel-Ange de Nante, Gille de Loches, Césarée de Rosgoff (or: Rosgo), etc.;
- Franciscans: Daniel Aymini, Jacques de Vendômes;
- Jesuits: Jerôme Delisle.
7. French converts to Islam:
- Osman d'Arcos, formerly and for Peiresc always Thomas d'Arcos.
[7] de Gastines, L'Empereur, Vias, Jean Guez, Jean-Baptiste Magy - all in Marseille, Honoré Aycard in Toulon, etc.
[8] Santo Seguezzi, Cairo; Louis Gela, Marseille; Mollini, Tripoli.

access to Muslim, Christian, and Jewish inhabitants of these countries: merchants, scholars, local rulers, as well as unnamed scribes, soldiers, and travelers.[9]

In Western Europe, Peiresc turned for information to almost everybody whom he could find. He invited travelers to stop in Aix-en-Provence, stay in his house for some days, and share with him their rare and curious experiences in the Ottoman Empire, Persia, or India.[10] Numerous of his partners in the Middle East and North Africa spent some days at his house in Aix-en-Provence or Boisgency.[11] His interest in such visits became early on common knowledge. February 17, 1626, for instance, Peiresc informed his brother Palamède de Vallavez that he had been sent an old man who had recently returned from Aleppo after having been in Persia:

"Le president Mounyer m'a aujourd'huy envoyé un vieillard venerable nouvellement revenu d'Alep avec des semances de Perse, dont je vous ay creu devoir faire part, en ayant retenu icy un de chasque sorte pour les essayer à Beaugentier, mais je n'y cognois rien. Il dict que les melons sont furieusement grands et excellents, et que les pasteques sont differantes des communes et de trez bon goust, et que la differance se cognoit en ce que la graine de celles icy est amere, et celle des aultres est doulce."[12]

Several of Peiresc's encounters with Oriental Christians, former Muslim slaves in France, Morisco refugees from Spain, and French travelers apparently were one time meetings for the sake of information gathering, discussions on precious stones, medals, or libraries, and acts of hospitality. As early as 1612, Peiresc bought Arabic precious stones and ancient Geek medals from an Armenian trader, called Angelo Michaele Suriano and dressed "à l'Armenienne", who had come from Venice to Aix.[13] Over the years, Peiresc also developed contacts with the Royal galleys at Toulon. There, he could find "Turkish" slaves who might help him in translating texts and

---

[9] 1. merchants:
- Khwaja Abu Bakr "Suala";
- Khwaja "Salaboussati";
- an unnamed Turkish khwaja, owner of a library, all three in Cairo.
2. scholars:
- darwish Ahmad;
- Mohammad al-Taqwi, both in Aleppo.
3. local rulers:
- Fakhr al-Din in Damascus;
- Mohammad, a Ragusian convert to Islam and governor of Suakim;
- a convert from Ferrara well established at the court in Tunis.
[10] Benoît Pellissier or Vincent Blanc from Marseille; le Tenneur (or: Tanneur) and Leger from Aix-en-Provence.
[11] For instance the merchants Gabriel Fernoulx, César Lambert, and Jean Magy or the missionaries Gilles de Loches, Césarée de Rosgoff, Agathange de Morlaix, Charles François d'Angers, Ephrem de Nevers, Léonard de la Tour, Maclou de Pointoise, Pierre de Guingamp, Pierre de Morlaix, and Zacharie de Nogent. See Ms Carpentras, Bibliothèque d'Inguimberinte, 1864, ff ...; Tamizey de Larroque 1898, vol. 7., pp. ...; Apollinaire de Valence 1891, pp. 321, 325, 326, 328, 329, 334, 336; See also Bigourdan 1915, p. 545.
[12] Tamizey de Larroque 1896, vol. 6, p. 396.

deciphering inscriptions. In 1629, while being at Belgentier near Toulon, he talked of such contacts as if they were nothing unexceptional:

"Si nous avions la liberté du commerce de Marseille, j'eusse envoyé querir l'interprete du Roy, pour voir s'en seroit rien deschifré. Mais cela ne se pouvant, si je ne trouve à Toullon quelque Turque qui n'y puisse servir, ..."[14]

One year later, Peiresc wrote to Thomas d'Arcos since two years in slavery in Tunis:

"J'ay veu à Marseille un nommé Sayer que le sieur Napolon ramena à Algers qui avoit afforce libvres curieux, et qui avoit bien leu dans leurs histoires. Je luy monstray des vieilles medailles arabiques, entre lesquelles il y avoit où estoit representé Hercule qu'ils tenoient pour un geant qui eust esté maistre en Affrique."[15]

Peiresc used the occasion to induce d'Arcos to seek out the man if he had come by chance to Tunis and to make him tell Hercules' Arabic name which Peiresc was already told by the former prisoner or slave, but had again forgotten.[16] Apparently, d'Arcos did not find "Sayer" in Tunis, although he had learned from other Muslim informants what they had to tell about a certain giant whose tooth they believed had recently been found, since two years later, Peiresc met another Muslim slave from Tunis whom he asked the same question as he informed d'Arcos:

"Au reste ne trouvez pas si estrange ce que nous ont voulu dire ces Mores concernant le geant dont ils vous parloint, car il ne faut point estre grand Devin ou grand prophète pour rapporter toutes leurs fables à celles d'Hercule qui eut bien autant d'enfans comme celuy dont ils parlent pour le moins et fust empoisonné par sa femme aussy bien que le pretendu Geant; c'est pourquoy j'estois bien ayse d'apprendre en quelle sorte estoit escript dans leurs livres cette fable d'Hercule et son voyage en ce Pais là, pour aller combattre Antée, en allant poser ses colonnes au destroit de Gibartar (sic), et quel nom ils luy donnent, car j'ay veu un celebre esclave Tunequesque [pour Tunisien] qui l'appeloit Carmil ou Carmel en sa langue Moresque."[17]

Students of the Maronite college in Rome or freshly arrived from the Lebanese mountains passed Aix-en-Provence on their way to relatives or friends in Paris paying visits to Peiresc either

---

[13] Ms Pairs, BNF, fr 9530, f 262a.
[14] Tamizey de Larroque 1890, vol. 2, p. 155.
[15] Tamizey de Larroque 1898, vol., 7, p. 87. This was not the only occasion that Sanson Napollon brought North African prisoners from France to one of the three principalities in the frame of the treaties concluded between 1628 and 1632. He died during such a mission May 11, 1633. See, Tamizey de Larroque 1890, vol. 2, p. 529 and footnote 2.
[16] ibid., p. 87.

because they needed money as was the case of Moyse de Giacomo, nephew of Gabriel Sionita, or because they wished to recover manuscripts borrowed by Theophile Minuti who had promised Peiresc would make them printed as implies a letter by Michel Damasceno or simply for the sake of hospitality.[18] Peiresc met a Morisco physician, Hakim Mustafa, on his flight from Andalusia via the Provence to the Ottoman Empire, who was well educated and possessed a rich library.[19] He mentioned this physician in some of his papers and letters as a possible and reliable source for the acquisition of manuscripts from Egypt, information on the Nile, and as an acquaintance of some of his French partners in Cairo such as Jean Magy:

"Il a cogneu le medecin d'Andalusie <+ nommé AQUIN MUSTAPHA mustaffa le P. Gilles de Losches dict qu'il a nom MEMET.>, lequel passa icy et vid Mr. du Vair auant l'expulsion des Morisques. Il va tous les Jours à Jamalasar [Jami'at al-Azhar] qui est la Grand Mosquee et Escolle."[20]

"Il en fault escrire au P. Thomas de Vendosme Capucin, pour marquer exactement le moment du temps de la vrnue (sic, instead of: entrée) de la Goutte, et a cet Aquin Mustafa Espagnol."[21]

Other contacts with former French slaves in North Africa, Maronite scholars in Paris and Rome, or what I think was an Armenian merchant in Marseille, although Peiresc usually called him "my Turk native from Aleppo", were more durable.[22] These men translated for him Arabic or Turkish texts and inscriptions, told him about the tides near Bizerta, or were implored by him to translate Arabic manuscripts belonging to other West European collectors or having been printed in Rome.

Repeatedly Peiresc sought the help of West European orientalists or scholars and clerics with more than a fleeting interest in oriental literature and science.[23] He requested friends who had

---

[17] ibid., p. 105.
[18] Ms Paris, BNF, fr 9543, ff 121a-b (Michel Damasceno).
[19] See for Peiresc's judgment about some of the political consequences of the moriscos' flight from Spain, Tamizey de Larroque 1888, vol. 1, pp. 599-600.
[20] Ms Carpentras, Bibliothèque d'Inguimbertine, 1864, f 256a.
[21] Ms Paris, BNF, Dupuy 661, f 195b.
[22] 1. former French slaves in North Africa:
- Anthoine Armand of Martigues;
- Chevalier de Montmeyan (or: Montmeian).
2. Maronite scholars:
- Gabriel Sionita and Johannes Hesronita in Paris;
- Victor Accurensis Sciala in Rome and Abraham Ecchellensis in Rome and in Paris.
3. a possible Armenian merchant in Marseille:
- Sasson Mattou.
[23] 1. West European orientalists:
- Thomas Erpenius and Jacob Golius in Leiden;
- Gilbert Gaulmin in Paris;
- Samuel Petit in Nîmes, etc.

decided to travel to the Ottoman Empire to take care of his desires and hired special envoys from among his local collaborators for astronomical and geographical observations and members of religious orders for buying manuscripts, ancient Egyptian antiquities, medals, or plants, for copying inscriptions, and for observing and drawing of coastal lines.[24]

It is not very clear why and when Peiresc got interested in the Middle East and North Africa as reservoirs for his own scholarly interests. There is, however, sufficient evidence that it did not only start very early on, but that it was to some extent unavoidable given the immense meaning the trade with the Ottoman Empire had for the towns at the French Mediterranean coast, in particular, for Marseille, Toulon, La Ciotat, or Six Fours. Several of the merchants in Marseille and in Ottoman towns, for instance de Vento, L'Empereur, or Lambert, had built up their own cabinets of curiosity stuffed with pieces from the Middle East, the Red sea, Persia, India, and even China - ancient, medieval, and contemporary - to which Peiresc had access to. In a letter, written November 25, 1606 to Malherbe in Paris, the 26 years old Peiresc almost glowed of excitement over the splendid return of François de Savary from Istanbul:

"Ce soir Mr de Breves, ambassadeur pour le Roy en Constantinoble est arrivé en ceste ville. Mr le premier president du Vair le loge et le festoye magnifiquement. Il raconte des merveilles de ces pays oriantaux dont je vous entretiendrois, si je n'estois bien asseuré que vous en pourrés apprendre aisement tout ce que vous vouldrés, dès qu'il sera à la Cour où il s'en va à grandes journées. Il faict porter de grandz presantz pour le Roy et pour la Royne, et entre aultres un arc avec son quarroys pour Mgr. le Dauphin tout enrichi de diamants qu'on estime beaucoup, un cabinet de six mille escus pour la Royne avec une toillette des plus riches qui se puissent voir, des lions, des leopards, et tout plein d'aultres singularités que vous pourrés voir delà si bon vous semble ..."[25]

- Gilbert Gaulmin in Paris;
- Samuel Petit in Nîmes, etc.
2. scholars and clerics with strong interest in oriental matters:
- Isaac Casaubon;
- Charles de Cassagnes in Marseille;
- Guy Pelletier in Avignon;
- Jean Bourdelot in Paris?;
- Pietro della Valle in Rome, etc.

[24] 1. friends traveling to the Ottoman Empire:
- François-Auguste de Thou, Paris. Other friends either planned or were encouraged by Peiresc to travel also to the Ottoman Empire but their travel either never took place (Gassendi, Bouchard, Holstenius, Gaffarel) or happened after Peiresc's death (Lhuillier).
2. local collaborators:
- Jean Lombard, geometer of Aix.
3. members of religious orders:
- Theophile Minuti, Minime.

[25] Peiresc Lettres A Malherbes (1606-1628). par Raymond Lebègue, CNRS: Paris, p. 10.

Peiresc kept lifelong contacts with de Brèves (d. 1628) and his family. Among his papers preserved at the BnF in Paris, a list of de Brèves' oriental manuscripts can be found although Peiresc wrote in 1628 that he regretted not to have copied this inventory.[26] Peiresc tried repeatedly to win Sionita and Hesronita to edit and translate at least some of these texts. He collected copies of several texts on the Ottoman Empire written by de Brèves as well as his description of North Africa based on the ambassador's experience while traveling home.[27] He took a lively interest in the up and downs of the consulate of Cairo, once even interfering actively into the choice of the next consul.[28]

A few years before de Brèves' passage through Aix-en-Provence, Peiresc had taken already his first steps towards the study of Arabic and other oriental antiquities and acquiring the kind of relations necessary to decipher and interpret them. In 1599 the dragoman, i.e., interpreter, of Marseille, Honoré Juffrin (or: Suffin) reported to Peiresc's father, Raynaud de Fabri, about his modest successes in deciphering Arabic inscriptions on timbales belonging to the church of St. Paul at Narbonne. In this letter, Juffrin also speaks of Raynaud de Fabri having him send an Arabic alphabet which Juffrin intended to send Peiresc to Italy where he was supposed to further his legal training in Padua, but pursued much more actively the study of antiquities and botanical gardens.[29] In 1626, Peiresc again turned to Juffrin for his help in deciphering an Arabic or Turkish plate or buckler ("placque") sent to him by Balthasar de Viaz from Algiers.[30] Two years later, he received from him the translations of "the latest letters from Algiers written to Mr de Guise and Sr Sanson Napolon".[31]

Peiresc brought a set of Arabic medals home from his educational travel to Italy and information on oriental plants acquired from Prospero Alpini, the director of the Paduan botanical garden who had served for two years as physician of the Venetian consul at Cairo. Peiresc sent the medals to Isaac Casaubon (d. 1614) who promised to decipher them. When he died, his heirs sent the collection back to Peiresc with merely one medal having been worked upon. Thus, Peiresc who

---

[26] Ms Paris, BNF, Latin 9340, ff 305a-306b. "Quant aux livres Arabiques de feu Mr de Breves, encores fault il sçavoir au vray ce qu'ils sont devenus, le Maronite [Gabriel Sionita - S. B.] le pourrà bien dire, ou Mr du Val [professeur des langues oriental au Collège Royal - S. B.] mesmes qu'on dict les avoir acheptez qui est voisin de Mr Autin et, je m'asseure, de ses amys. Je me repente de n'avoir eu la curiosité d'avoir coppie de l'inventaire des dicts livres, et si le Maronite l'a il ne seroit que bon de le faire transcrire par nostre coppiste; s'il le veult permettre; sinon je suis bien homme, pour me hazarder, à le demander moy mesmes au dict sieur du Val que j'ay autres foys cogneu assez familièrement pour cela." Tamizey de Larroque 1888, vol. 1, p. 679. See also ibid., p. 695.
[27] Ms Carpentras, Bibliothéque d'Inguimbertine, ...
[28] Aufrère 1990, pp. 90-96.
[29] Ms Carpentras, Bibliothèque d'Imguimbertine, 585, ff 5b, 6b-7a.
[30] Ms Carpentras, Bibliothèque d'Inguimbertine, 1873, f 197a, lettre a Monsieur Gilly.
[31] Tamizey de Larroque 1888, vol. 1, p. 679: "L'interprete du Roy qui se tient à Marseille m'a baillé tantost la version qu'il a faicte, comme il a sceu, des dernieres lettres d'Algers escrittes à Mr de Guise et au sieur Sanson Napolon que je vous [les frères Dupuy - S. B.] envoye."

was now living in Paris as secretary of Guillaume du Vair (d. 1622), the keeper of the royal seals, turned for help to Gabriel Sionita and Johannes Hesronita. About their results he reported in 1617 to Thomas Erpenius, then professor for Arabic at the University of Leiden. He wanted Erpenius to whom he was not yet introduced to search in the Arabic history Peiresc had been told Erpenius was editing and translating for names of "Mesopotamian" kings engraved on some of the medals and for the correct spelling of such names. He also wished to discuss with him certain features of the engravings which either seemed to contradict dress codes ascribed by unnamed West European authors to the prophet Muhammad or appeared to Peiresc's eyes as mixtures of Christian and Muslim customs.[32] Erpenius apparently never answered this letter, at least not immediately, since there is a second copy of it with a postscript, both written almost a year later.[33] This did not prevent, however, Peiresc - according to Gassendi - from encouraging Erpenius to publish Ibn al-Makin's history and from buying its Latin translation in 1625 when it finally had been printed.

Peiresc continued to cooperate with the two Maronites for more than ten years. In 1620-21, he requested and received Hesronita's help when he had gotten from Charles Cassagnes an Arabic-Turkish calendar and dices for prognostication which had been taken from a "Turkish", i.e. e. Northern African, galley conquered by a French vessel near Gibraltar.[34] In 1628, looking back at his relation with the two scholars, he criticized them (too) severely about their apparent lack of continuous and serene service to the "public":

"J'ay cogneu de longue main le sieur Gabriel Sionita et crois qu'il est bien docte en cette langue arabique, mais je ne sçay s'il est porté de si bonne volonté ne son collegue [Johannes Hesronita - S. B.] que sont les Hollandois [Raphelengius, Erpenius, Golius - S. B.], à donner au public les bons livres de cette langue. Ils ont imprimé à Rome avec son compagnon un beau Pere Gaultier auc frais de Mr de Breves, et ont emporté les caracteres à Paris, mais je n'ay rien veu de l'edition de Paris que le traicté du feu roy, et une version latine du geographe de Nubie. Il ne leur manque pas de trez bons livres m[anu]s[crit]s de monsieur de Breves, s'ils vouloient s'excercera les faire imprimer et traduire, mais leur fauldroit de fort sollicitations pour les y embarquer, ... C'estoit pour cela que je tournois mes pensées du costé de Hollande, ou de Rome principalement pour ce livre de droict dont j'escrivoit à Mr Camerarius, attendu qu'en cette matiere je ne pense pas que le sieur Sionita y

---

[32] Ms Carpentras, Bibliothèque d'Inguimbertine, 1809, ff 153a-155a
[33] Ms Carpentras, Bibliothèque d'Inguimbertine, 1873, ff 308a-309a.
[34] Ms Carpentras 114, ff 381a.385b (Translation of the calendar), 390a-b, 394a (Letters by Hesronita), 398a (Letter of Charles Cassange). In 1633, after having loaned his calendar for years to Girolamo Aleandro (1574-1629), Peiresc made the following note summarizing how he came to the book and who was involved in its translation: "Traductions du liuret du Kalendrier Arabe que Les Maronites auoient traduit et que ceulx de Rome auoient long temps Gardé Jusques aprez le decez du Sr. Aleandro. C'estoit Mr. Cassagne qui me l'auoit enuoyé auec les Dais dont ils se seruoient pour jetter leur sort ayant esté prins des Corsaires, qui furent mis à la chaine dans les Galeres du Roy. Le reste du liure est presque tout en Pharsen <sic> ou Persian, que nostre Anthione Arman du Martigues n'entendet pas." ibid., f 386a.

puisse piper, nomplus que son collegue, s'il est revenu du Levant, dont je seray bien aise d'apprendre des nouvelles, si vous en scavez."[35]

Hesronita, however, did not come back from his visit to the Lebanese Mountains but died there. Having been informed about his decease, Peiresc modified his one month-old evaluation of Hesronita's scholarly qualities, leaving the blame alone for Sionita:

" Je plains infimement le pauvre Maronite decedé au Mont Liban, car son ingenuité et zeelle ou passion au bien public ne pouvoient estre assez loués, il estoit beaucoup plus laborieux que les sieur Gabriel, son compagnon, et de beaucoup plus de resolution quand il falloit entreprendre et mettre à execution quelque bon dessein en matiere de libvres, bien qu'il n'eust possible pas tant de science que son compagnon."[36]

The Turkish part of the above mentioned Arabic calendar on astrological fortune telling with dices was rendered into Provençal (?) ("heures deys Jours que soun bouenos per entreprendre qu'auqueis affaires & sy faut gouuarna segun acquesto Tablo") by Anthoine Armand du Martigues:

"Ces Traductions on esteés faictes par Anthoine Armand du Martigues filz de patron Jannot Armand du Martigues dit Troupillon Reeuenu d'Algers en Barbarie, ou il auoit esté miné <sic> esclaue de l'aage de dix ans fut vendu septante cinq piastres a vn nommé Assent bellut bochy quy estoit du Diuan de ceux qui rendoit la Justice lequel l'Enuoyà à lEscolle durant Sept ans, àprez toutesfois l'auoir constrainct à coups de bastons deux mois, aprez sa captiuitté de se faire Turc & de se láissér Circoncire, auquel temps luy fust imposé le nom de Ally & parce quil s'en seruoit d'escriuain de Nauire quand il alloit sur la mer, on l'appelloit Ally ogean c'est Ally escriuain."[37]

Peiresc also maintained contact with two other Maronite scholars, Abraham Ecchellensis and Victor Accurensis. He approved of Ecchellensis' scholarly qualities and recommended him sincerely to his colleagues in Rome.[38]

The first, albeit possibly only indirect, contact with a consul and merchant in the Middle East, Peiresc seems to have entertained September 2, 1613 when Angelo de Vento sent him the description of a consultation the French ambassador to Portuguese India, Marquis de Cavillat, had

---

[35] Tamizey de Larroque 1888, vol. 1, pp. 579-580.
[36] ibid., p. 599.
[37] Ms Carpentras, Bibliothèque d'Inguimbertine, 1774, ff 386b, 388a. The translation runs from ff 388a-395b although it consists partly of a repitition.
[38] Tamizey de Larroque 1890, vol. 2, p.

had with a Muslim diviner in Cairo in 1588. The diviner predicted the immediate outbreak of a revolt against the French king Henri III:

"Finalement il fit entendre audit Marquis par le truchement là present, qu'en France il y auoit de grandes leuees d'armes. Qu'il y auoit au mitan d'vne grande armee vn grand, contre lequel vn autre grand s'estoit rebellé, [qui auoit vne grande balafre a la Joüe droicte], auec de grands appuys et de grandes forces. Mais que le balafré seroit bien tost vaincu et exterminé par le premier grand, de qui il ne pouuoit exprimer le nom, a cause de l'incompatibilité des prononciations Orientales et Françoises. Mais il marquoit qu'il y auoit des R en son nom. Grommelant Ri, Ri, en son langage, pour dire Henry."[39]

The marquis apparently was not truly convinced of the diviner's prediction or preferred a long and at times tedious voyage over the turmoil of the Ligue. In any case, he continued his journey to Istanbul. There, however, he found letters of his sovereign calling him back to France.[40] Peiresc apparently loved this delicious story, since he copied it for himself by his own hand. Then he made one of his scribes copy it and sent it to his very close friends, the brothers Dupuy, Jacques (1591-1656) and Pierre (1582-1652), in Paris.

Peiresc's direct contacts to consuls, merchants, and other partners in the Ottoman Empire and its North African satellites increased during the 1620s and reached their peak between 1628 and 1637. A register made by Peiresc of his letters and parcels sent to friends and acquaintances over a period of ten years (1622-1632) shows 49 entries where the mail was directed to or from the Middle East and North Africa and 35 entries where the mail went to West European orientalists or collectors of orientalia, about two thirds of both categories appearing during the years 1628-1632.[41]

In 1628-29, François-Auguste de Thou (b. 1607- decapitated in 1642), the oldest son of the historian and keeper of the Royal library, Jacques-Auguste de Thou (1553-1617) and his second wife, undertook his only travel to the Ottoman Empire and Theophile Minuti the first of his two voyages. In 1630, the exchange of letters, books, manuscripts, memoirs, and gifts started between Thomas/Osman d'Arcos and Peiresc. The bulk of the mail to and from the Middle East during the years 1628 to 1632 seems to have been connected more or less closely with these three men: 10 letters Peiresc remembered to have written to them and 12 letters appear to be letters of

---

[39] Ms Carpentras, Bibliothèque d'Inguimbertine, 1864, f 295b; see also: Paris, BNF, Dupuy 661, f 187b.
[40] Ms Carpentras, Bibliothèque d'Inguimbertine, 1864, f f 295a-296a; Paris, BNF, Dupuy 661, ff 187a-188a.
[41] Tamizey de Larroque, Ph. 1899: Les petits mémoires de Peiresc. In: Rubens-Bulletin, Jaarboeken ..., Vierde Deel. see in particular, pp. 43-112.

recommendation for the two travelers, letters accompanying those to d'Arcos to their next point of distribution, or letters of thank-saying, letters of credit-transfer, and related issues.[42]

Peiresc referred to the letters of recommendation he had asked for de Thou in France and in the Ottoman Empire in several letters to the brothers Dupuy, for instance, in that dated February 21, 1628:

"Je pensois pouvoir envoyer par cet ordinaire à Mr de Thou les lettres qu'il m'avoit demandées pour les consuls de la nation françoise en Levant et ay desja celles de Mr nostre premier president, de Mr Viguier consul de Syrie à toute les vice consuls de Seitte, Alexandrette et Alep, attendant à ce soir celles du lieutenant de l'admiraulté, mais les meilleures me manquent à mon grand regret, qui sont celles du Sr Sanson Napolon, qui ne s'est pas trouvé à Marseille quand je l'en ay prié, car il a de grandes et puissantes habitudes avec cez Bassa et mesmes avec l'intendant des jardins du Grand Seigneur en Constantinople et envers plusieurs autres, dont j'estime bien plus les cognoisçances que de cez pauvres consuls. Il fauldrà suppleer, Dieu aydant, par le prochain ordinaire. ... Le Sr de Valbelle, lieutenant de l'Admiraulté, vient de m'apporter les lettres de recommandation pour Mr de Thou aux consuls du Levant et en Constantinople, où il a voulu à toute force mettre une lettre de credit de mille escus. J'envoye le tout par cet ordinaire à Lyon soubs l'enveloppe de Mr l'Ambassadeur de France à Venize, selon l'ordre de Mr de Thou et la semaine prochaine l'envoyeray, Dieu aydant, les autres lettres du Sr Napolon."[43]

Peiresc's attention to the Southern parts of the Mediterranean sea as a possible reservoir for observations of nature is attested as early as 1611-1612 when he sent Jean Lombard on a half-year's journey to Malta, Cyprus, Aleppo, and Tripoli in Syria to determine latitudes and - possibly - to test his tables of the satellites of Jupiter.[44] The period of his greatest attention to nature in the Ottoman Empire and its dependencies in North Africa corresponded with the period of his most intense exchange of letters and parcels with the region, the years 1633 to 1637. In 1633, he sent Theophile Minuti on a second research trip to the Ottoman Empire where he wanted him, among other things, to study the coastal line of the gulf of Smyrna. He built up extensive connections with missionaries in Egypt and Syria, in particular French Capucins. When he learned of father Cœlestinus' presence in this area, he rushed to win him for his broad observational program. He pressed Osman d'Arcos to carry out the same variety of inquiries in North Africa. And he almost compelled his partners in this region to engage more men in these activities whether natives or foreigners, scholars or merchants. As a consequence, Giovanni Molino, the interpreter of the Venitian consul in Cairo, Balthasar Claret, a merchant in Aleppo, and Michel-

---

[42] ibid., pp. 69, 80-87, 90, 99, 101-105.
[43] Tamizey-Laroque 1888, vol. 1, pp. 531, 534.
[44] Chapin, p. 17

Ange de Vendôme, a Capucin missionary in the same town, participated in observing the lunar eclipses in 1634 or 1635.[45]

2. Investigations of winds, tides, and vulcanos

Several of Peiresc's scholarly interests were directed - either entirely or partially - towards practical issues such as the types of winds blowing over the Mediterranean sea and at its coasts and the kind of weather they brought with them. While he differentiated at least conceptually between matters to be read in the "book of nature" and affaires to be pursued in the "books of the ancients", he never talked of any kind of difference between research for practical purposes and issues more prone to generalization and speculation. This point can also be formulated in a slightly twisted form. Peiresc did not draw a cut between (mere) "collecting" and (qualified) "observing". This attitude corresponds to Peiresc's lack of social differentiation with regard to collecting information or carrying out observation. He engaged for more than 25 years everybody whom he could find and motivate to participate in his hunt for new knowledge and verification of ancient as well as contemporary hypotheses. Among the people he hired for his investigations in geography related matters were artisans as Simon Corberan, his bookbinder, simple scribes as Gassendi's secretary Antoine Agarrat, mariners from French ships trading with North Africa and the Levant, virtuosi as Jean Lombard, missionaries as Agathange de Vendôme and Cœlestinus de Sancta Lidvina, college and university educated men in the service of the church like Peiresc himself as Thomas/Osman d'Arcos, the former secretary of Cardinal de Joyeuse and later powerful secretary at the court of Tunis, Joseph Gaultier, prior of de la Vallette, Pierre d'Antelmi, canon of Fréjus, and his nephew Nicolas d'Antelmi, Louis Meynier, and Theophile Minuti, Minime, members of the nobility who pursued a military career as Chevalier de Montmeyan, and university alumni recognized as philosophers and astronomers such as Pierre Gassendi and Ismael Boulliau in France or Athanasius Kircher, Gaspar Berti, Andrea Argoli, and Camillus Gloriosi in Italy.

Peiresc's indiscriminating approach in both cases, i.e., the lack of differentiation between practical purposes and general speculation or between collecting and observing and his ignorance of social hierarchies and educational degrees or between qualified and unqualified observers and collectors, was a precondition for his successful organization of research cooperation over large territorial distances and cultural barriers. His letters to the Middle East and North Africa do not support Chapin's claim that Peiresc "favored an expedition devoted to the observation of a single phenomenon by specifically trained personnel".[46] A bundle of material obstacles did not allow a single erudite such an approach how huge his personal wealth might have been. The costs and

---

[45] See, for instance, Ms Carpentras, Biobliothèque d'Inguimbertine, 1832, ff 27a, 33a.
[46] ibid., p. 29.

duration of voyages to the Middle East as well as the time needed for the transport of letters, instruments, instructions, and other items would have rendered the concentration upon one single purpose into an expression of ignorance of the "real world" and of "organizational" stupidity. Peiresc was a stout catholic and greedy collector of all that had won his approval of being rare and curious, but he certainly was no fool.

Between 1633 and 1636, Peiresc collected a number of memoirs and diaries of observations, extracted ancient texts, and wrote down oral information given by Gassendi, French Minimes and Chartreuses as well as his partners in the Middle East Jean Magy, Gilles de Loches, and Césarée de Rosgoff concerning the origins, generations, and movements of winds. This interest is also reflected in Peiresc's letters to Osman d'Arcos and Cœlestinus de Sancta Lidvina. This does not mean necessarily that Peirsc's devotion to this subject arose only then, but reflects only what I was able to read so far. As a consequence, it has to remain an open question whether this interest was motivated by information stemming from the Middle East or by Peiresc's reading of Pliny or by observations of winds and connected meteorological events in the Provence. The material contained in two manuscripts of the library at Carpentras does, however, suggest that Peiresc approached this subject too according to his repeatedly mentioned concept of reading the book of nature together with studying the books of the ancients. The reading of the former, however, had not to be carried out all by himself. As with others of Peiresc's interests in nature, everybody was welcome to be of help. Thus, he not only relied upon Gassendi, French men of the cloth, or French merchants, but also lent his ear to information submitted by Egyptian merchants and soldiers or Christian converts to Islam. The character of the information gathered by Peiresc varies considerably from single notes about particular appearances to diaries containing systematic observations over a longer period of time.

Gassendi, for instance, told Peiresc of a wind which was thought to blow from below the waves of the Mediterranean sea and made drown ships near Martigues.[47] A similar experience was reported by the fathers Dom Polycarpe de la Rivière, prior of the Chartusians of Bompas, and Dom ... (name not given), prior of Villeneuve, with regard to the lake of Geneva.[48] Peiresc added to their statements an extract from the travel account of Sincerus (?), an ancient Latin author, to Gallia emphasizing that this author gave the same description as father de la Rivière. In this case, Peiresc apparently used the ancient author as a confirmation of the modern report.[49] The Chartusians also sent Peiresc a report about an underground lake near Baulme. They insisted that more singularities could be observed at this lake than the Antonine History fol. XLII talked

---

[47] Ms Carpentras, Bibliothèque d'Inguimbertine, 1821, f 131b.
[48] ibid., f 131a.
[49] ibid. f 131a.

about.[50] Peiresc added that one had to observe the effects of the wind or of the vapors which might arise from this underground lake, that one had to do this at night and day-time during diverse seasons, in particular in winter and at the height of summer.[51] He also extracted stories about the prognostic properties of certain lakes and rivers in France from the two ancient books used to evaluate the information sent by the Chartusians.[52]

In 1633, Peiresc received Jean Magy, Gilles de Loches, Césarée de Rosgoff, and apparently also Gabriel Fernoulx in his house in Aix-en-Provence. Magy came in June and the two Capuchins one month later.[53] Fernoulx' visit is suggested by his name being mentioned in the notes Peiresc drew up after his other three visitors had left.[54] Peiresc interviewed them about their experience in Egypt and about what news they had from other parts of the Ottoman Empire. In his later notes, Peiresc found it worthwhile to state that the two Capuchins did not agree in important details with the information given by the merchant on the basis of what a high ranking Ottoman official, the governor of Suakim, had reported during his official visit to Cairo.[55] This treatment of oral or written reports is characteristic of Peiresc's way to digest information and an important step towards distributing it among his most cherished friends and colleagues in the Republic of Letters. In the letters written to them the information acquired a new status, not only by being submitted to the public, but also by Peiresc's way of talking about it. He presented such information usually as reliable knowledge almost never questioning it and only rarely making clear that his informants did not always agree with what the other had reported.

Among all the things Magy may have talked about to Peiresc, the latter focused in his respective notes upon conflagrations in Ethiopia, near Suakim at the Red sea, and earthquakes in Cairo (1632), extraordinary weather appearances and their devastating results in Mecca (1631), particular properties of the hot waters at Tur, a port at the Red sea, the hot waters at Medina, and the Muslims keeping a leg of the prophet there.[56] Magy's informants and commentators of these events were Muhammad Basha, the then governor of Suakim, a convert from Ragusa who had received his training at the serail in Istanbul, the Cairene merchant Abu Bakr "Suala", and the Ottoman soldier "Rajab Chaoux".[57]

---

[50] ibid., f 132a.
[51] ibid., f 132a.
[52] ibid., f 132b.
[53] Aufrère transferred the dating of de Loches' and de Rosgoff's visit upon Jean Magy. Aufrère 1990, p. 290. Compare Ms Carpentras, Bibliothèque d'Inguimbertine, 1864, f 264a. This lack of care for the details is characteristic for Aufrère's book.
[54] Ms Carpentras, Bibliothèque d'Inguimbertine, 1864, f 263a.
[55] ibid., f 264a.
[56] ibid., ff 263a-264a.
[57] ibid., ff 263a-b.

Winds of interest to Peiresc were involved in one of these events - the rainfalls at Mecca. These winds arose from a cave and mattered to Peiresc since he believed in a subterranean origin of winds. The Meccan rainfalls had caused the walls of the Great Mosque to collapse. A few days later, when palisades were errected around the ruins to prevent animals from entering the holy place, a hot, stinky, and unhealthy wind blew from a caverne below the mosque. Numerous people fell sick and several died. Since then, the cave had been sealed. Abu Bakr "Suala" and "Rajab Chaoux", not surprisingly, took this for a portent caused by the vices of the cherif of Mecca who had just rebelled against the Ottoman sovereign.[58]

Peiresc also talked to Osman d'Arcos of subterranean winds. In October 1634, he claimed that observing certain small winds which were born at the aperture of certain caves and run in a more or less limited path through their environments had enabled him to recognize similar effects with regard to winds of a larger extension with a happier success than he (and his collaborators?) had dared to hope.[59] That is why he was obliged to reiterate his earlier implorations that d'Arcos should write for them some small report on the largest winds he had seen in those countries and would have occasion to see in future. This should be done by marking exactly the time of their birth and cessation. If there were caves in the mountains, it should be observed whether there were winds rising from them, at least in the mornings before sunrise, or whether one could see vapors which during wintertimes would make themselves visible as the human breath. In such a case, again the time of ascending, enforcing, and calming had to be taken in.[60] The usage of parts of the human body as a tool for observing or evaluating nature appears repeatedly in Peiresc's letters about winds and other meteorological appearances. It was meant as a means for making things visible and comparable. Peiresc also tried out artificial products such as ink which were meant to function as some sort of analogical tool.

Other winds of interest for Peiresc were tempests occuring at the coasts of the Mediterranean sea. In a letter to Osman d'Arcos, written March 23, 1634, Peiresc asked him to compose a little report about the last tempest which had hit both the French and the North African coasts. It had been of such an extraordinary violence, that many strange incidents had happened about which Peiresc had already collected a series of notes.[61] Peiresc explained in detail what he wanted d'Arcos to pay particular attention to: the time and the places of where the strange events had

---

[58] ibid., f 234b.
[59] Tamizey de Larroque 1898, vol. 7, p. 142. There seems to be something wrong with these phrases in the edition. I did not have the time yet to look for this letter in its original form which is not easy since the codes have been changed since 1898 and there is no concordance.
"et par ce moyen proceder, en observant certains petits ventz, qui naissent à l'orifice de quelques cavernes soubsterraines, et qui ont leur cours plus ou moins limité aux environs. Nous avons recogneu de pareils effetz aux ventz de plus d'estendue avec un plus heureux succez que nous ne l'eussions osé esperer."
[60] Tamizey de Larroque 1898, vol. 7, p. 142.
[61] Tamizey de Larroque 1898, vol. 7, p. 127.

VII

18

happened should be marked as exactly as possible including the moment when the wind had finally died away; the true route of the wind should be described according to the markings of a compass; the point until which it had hit the terra ferma should be noted; people who either lived near those spots or who had traveled with a caravane should be interviewed about their experiences; and finally, if such a tempest or similar events like heavy rainfalls of long duration or long periods of dryness should occur in future, d'Arcos should write down the days where such changes of the usual weather began. Due to the importance of such sea winds for weather conditions, Peiresc also wished to know whether the last tempest had brought with it rainfalls as did the Mistral, since in the Provence the tempest had not acted as "the true Mistral" being more heavily inclined versus West than usually.[62]

This is one of the questions which d'Arcos answered, at least as far as the letters published by Tamizey de Larroque indicate. It remains to be seen whether the unpublished material contains further reports, but given the general spirit found in the published letters, I doubt this. D'Arcos answer was extremely brief, surely insufficient to satisfy Peiresc:

"Vous avez jugé droitement des vents qui nous apportent icy de la pluy, et de la serenité. Les pluvieux sont les septentrionaux et maistraux, et les sereins sont les méridionaux et occidentaux. Les fascheux sont les orientaux et les sirocs."[63]

Thus, Peiresc apparently needled Pierre d'Antelmi in Fréjus to observe maritime as well as subterranean winds, keep a logbook, and summarize his results in relations and letters to Peiresc. Several letters from Antelmi to Peiresc touching these issues, a relation about the wind of the Malignon Mountains, and a daily diary for February 1634, which surprisingly runs over 30 days, are extant.[64]

Instructing his partners what to look for and how to do it characterizes all of Peiresc's cooperative projects whether devoted particularly or exclusively to a study of nature or to an archaeological subject or to a project encompassing a multiplicity of diverse sub-themes and tasks. These instructions should not only guide Peiresc's partners in the Middle East, North Africa, France, or Italy. They also served the purpose of reminding Peiresc what he was pursuing and how it should be done. A frame similar to the instructions was that of the memoir. They sometimes were designed in the same style as the instructions. At other times they were plans of future projects as the memoir written after August 1635 and entitled "Pour les marees, Et les vents, Et les Eclipses". Even in this form the memoirs resembled the instructions in so far as they outlined

---

[62] ibid., f. 127.
[63] Les Correspondants de Peiresc 1972, vol. 2, p. 212.

what had to be done and how it should be done. The first of these two types of guidelines for research, Peiresc drew for his brother's travels to the Spanish Netherlands, The United Provinces, Paris, or for his own travels to England around 1610/11. They were means to organize these travels in terms of people known by letters and to be visited, books or plants to be bought, questions to be discussed with more experienced men of letters, or scholars whose acquaintance Peiresc wanted to make. The instructions and memoirs for research also had a close resemblance to Peiresc's shopping lists drawn up for his brother or for himself. Over the years, Peiresc extended these two tools of organizing travels, adventures, and purchases to cover all of Peiresc's inquiries whether it concerned Philippe Le Bel and his wife Berthe or the tides, winds, and eclipses all over the world as in his memoir from 1635 (?).

In this memoir, Peiresc drew upon this previously collected material and information.[65] It is one of the multiple programmatic plannings pinned down by Peiresc. It envisions to engage observers in England as well as Capucin missionaries in Canada, the New World, and Guinea to carry out systematic observations of winds, tides, and eclipses and to write down their observations in special diaries. Peiresc emphasized the new discoveries obtained due to observations in the Middle East, explained his preference of observing subterranean winds during winter time, and was convinced of not merely collecting information to satisfy his very private curiosity, but to contribute new knowledge of nature.[66]

Peiresc's interests in tides were spurred, if not generated, by Galilei's work on this subject. In 1628, he wrote to the Dupuys:

"J'ay leu tantost couremment cette epistre du Galilei du flux et reflux, et y ay trouvé de bonnes choses à mon gré, et d'aultres où j'ay grande peine de luy accorder; il le fauldrà voir bien à loisir, cependant je l'ay mis ez mains d'un homme qui y ferà les figures necessaires, et aprez eu avoir retenu coppie, je le vous renvoyeray fidelement, avec l'advis de nostre monde de deçà, ..."[67]

The judgment of Peiresc's attitude towards this Galileian text differs in the literature. Tamizey de Larroque thought Peiresc did well not to follow blindly the "very bad" theories of his former teacher and friend of many years.[68] Bernhardt thought that Peiresc did not follow Galilei's theories of the tides since he kept adhering to the idea of antipodes and more generally to Copernicanism. In particular, Bernhardt claimed that Peiresc rejected Galilei's idea that the tides

---

[64] Ms Carpentras, Bibliothèque d'Inguimbertine, 1821, ff 142a-143b, 147a-151b.
[65] Ms Carpentras, Bibliothèque d'Inguimbertine, 1821, ff 279a.
[66] Ms Carpentras, Bibliothèque d'Inguimbertine, 1821, ff 279a-280b.
[67] Tamizey de Larroque 1888, vol. 1, p. 596.
[68] Tamizey de Larroque 1888, vol. 1, p. 596, footnote 2.

resulted from the earth's rotation.[69] The only evidence Bernhardt refers to from among the extant thousands of letters and papers by Peiresc is the extract quoted above.[70] While I still have to dig for more explicit comments on Galilei's work by Peiresc, his remarks from 1628 evidently give no clue as to what he opposed in the text and why.

Several of his letters to the Middle East and North Africa written during the last years of his life, for instance, seven letters to Osman d'Arcos (1634-1636), testify to Peiresc's attention to tides and currents. These letters indicate that Peiresc tried to test and verify information he had received from mariners and other people in France, Italy, and Spain, the former French slave in North Africa, Chevalier de Montmeyan, French ship captains trading with North Africa as Patron Pascal, or the French vice-consul of Algiers, Balthazar de Viaz.[71] Copies of papers summarizing this and other relevant information on tides and currents indicate that close friends of Peiresc as the physician Anthoine Noel, the French ambassador in Istanbul, comte de Marcheville, captains trading with the Ottoman Empire as Gilles, and unnamed mariners were part of Peiresc's network for acquiring these data.[72]

The seven letters to d'Arcos make clear that Peiresc's interest in these matters were not solely spured by Galilei's work. Peiresc preferred to justify his wishes towards d'Arcos by repeated references to concrete new information based upon eyesight, experience, and specific events or locations. In his first letter touching the tides and currents of the Mediterranean sea, Peiresc talked about the Gulf of Martigues and other gulfs of a similar type, of information from France, Italy, and the Kingdom of Valence about the existence of a current in the sea running constantly from East to West while contrary winds could agitate the sea's surface in such a way that the current was no longer visible, and of the current at the coast of North Africa which run perpetually from West to East.[73] The last information reappears in an interview Peiresc had carried out with Patron Pascal as well as with Balthasar de Viaz. Peiresc memorized these talks in an undated document:

"Le Patron Pascal m'a asseure des periodes de ce flux Et Reflux, Et le vice Consul d'Algers p[auure?] Mr. Viaz de ces Coups de mer qui Jettent tant de sable. Et touts deux estoient d'accord qu'il y a plus frequemment vne Corrente de ponant vers le Leuant En la Coste Barbarie, depuis

---

[69] Berhardt 1981, p. 174: "En même temps, il reste critique à l'égard de tel ou tel aspect des idées du grand Pisan: tout en acceptant fermement les antipodes et plus généralement en adhérant au copernicanisme, il n'admet pas la théorie galiléenne des marées et, guère plus que Bacon, il ne semble disposé, bien inspiré en cela, à y voir un effet de la rotation de la Terre."
[70] ibid., p. 174, footnote 34.
[71] Tamizey de Larroque 1898, vol. 7, pp. 128, 141, 171; Ms Carpentras, Bibliothèque d'Inguimbertine, 1821, ff 127a-b.
[72] Ms Paris, BNF, Dupuy 669, ff 75a-78a, 81a-82a, 83a-88a.
[73] Tamizey de Larroque 1898, vol. 7, pp. 127-128.

Algers Jusques à ce Cap de Spac, q[ue] de Leuant En ponant, ou il fault q[ue] ce fo...? des p[ro]<g>nostics? de vents [con]traires quand la mer va de maree contraire, au chemin plus com[m]un du Leuant au ponant."[74]

He wished d'Arcos to figure out where this current made its presence felt, where it started, and whether this point of origin was close to or far away from the straits, i.e., the Straits of Gibraltar (?).[75] He argued that one could draw beautiful consequences from this observation which would concern the discovery of something more than the usual secret of the nature of the tides and their cause as well as the cause and nature of the winds which are almost unknown so far due to the mistakes of people who had wished to abstain from observing general and particular events which one had to do if one wished to know such things.[76]

Half a year later, October 17, 1634, Peiresc informed d'Arcos that he had interviewed at this day Chevalier de Montmeyan who had been for three years enslaved in Barbary.[77] The summary of this interview is preserved Carpentras:

"M.r LE CHEVALLIER DE MONTMEIAN qui à Esté troys ans Esclaue En Barbarie m'a asseuré, q[ue] dans l'Emboucheure de la riuiere qui sert de port aux Galeres de Bezerti, il a veu plusieurs foys le reflux de six En six heures fort reglem[en]t, Et q[ue] les Galeres passent sur le petit destroict, pendant la haulté maree, Et y trouuent neantmoings si peu d'eau qu'elles sont Constraintes de passer quasi toutes riuēs? Et d'aller prendre leur chargement hors de l'Emboucheure de le port (sic) qui peult auoir dix milles d'Estendüe dans la terre ferme En longueur au long de la riuiere, car la largeur n'Estans p[ro]portionnee a Cela. Et me dict de plus auoir apprins des Esclaues desd[ict]z galeres, Et de plusieurs au[tr]es p[er]sones qui faisoient plus Continuelle residance dans le port là, que c'estoit chose Indubitable q[ue] la reciproca[ti]on de ce flux Et reflux dans ce port de six En six heures, Et q[ue] l'Eau y montoit par foys de plus de quattre pieds de hault Et descendoit à p[ro]portion. Et q[ue] le flux se rendoit apparant Jusques au fonds dud[ict] port, à dix milles de son Emboucheure. Il n'auoit rien obserué de semblable à l'Emboucheure de la Goulette, Et de l'Estang de Tunis, Et de Carthage. "[78]

Peiresc evidently hesitated to accept de Montmeyan's information with regard to the coast near Tunis since he asked d'Arcos to tell him whether there was nothing similar in the canal of Goulette to what the Chevalier had reported about the Gulf of Bizerta and whether there was

---

[74] Ms Carpentras, Bibliothèque d'Inguimbertine, 1821, f 127a.
[75] Tamizey de Larroque 1898, vol. 7, p. 128.
[76] Tamizey.Larroque 1898, vol. 7, p. 1128.
[77] Tamizey de Larroque 1898, vol. 7, p. 141.
[78] Ms Carpentras, Bibliothèque d'Inguimbertine, 1821, ff 127a-b.

nothing remarkable to report about the tides and the currents at this part of the coast.[79] He thought that d'Arcos possessed material about these matters from diverse locations. This material Peiresc regarded as capable to prepare the way to great openings through which one could penetrate if not to the true causes, but to the progress and proportions of tides and currents as well as to some rule. This material in d'Arcos possession, Peiresc insisted, seemed to allow a good step forward towards the knowledge of the primary causes by reporting the diversity of the periodes of those vicissitudes at different places of the Mediterranean sea and the Ocean, i.e., the Atlantic.[80] It is not yet clear to me from where Peiresc took this idea that d'Arcos might have stored such information. If this was really the case, than d'Arcos must have been one of the head scribes of the galleys. This is not impossible since d'Arcos spoke repeatedly in his letters to Aycard or de Gastines of "our corsaires" or "our galleys" having left the port. D'Arcos contested, however, to possess such documents.

The remaining five letters not only illustrate that Peiresc's questions to d'Arcos resulted from information received from other sources, but also from experience he had made himself in the Provence. Furthermore, they indicate the interdependence of Peiresc's studies of mountains, winds, tides, and currents. In April 1635, he requested d'Arcos to start a diary on the beginnings of great winds and their spatial orientation. He argued that one could draw conclusions of great utility by comparing them with similar remarks put down by curious people and thus making visible the direct and reciprocal relations which might link "one pole with the other".[81] He added:

"Vous vous moquerez, je m'asseure, de cette badinerie, mais si un jour vous m'en envoyez quelques relations un peu exactes, nous en pourrons tirer des consequences dont vous ne serez pas marry d'avoir esté l'instrument tost ou tard, et si vous avez là des cavernes qui soyent capables de produire du vent, comme nous en avons tout plein en ce pais icy, vous en verriez bien d'autres consequences aussy en son temps et des plus grandes encores s'il y avoit moyen de faire quelque exacte observation de ce qui nous paroit là du flux et reflux de la mer où nous avons decouverts des grands secrets de la nature par la conference de ses periodes en divers lieux de la Mediterranée aussy bien que de l'Oceane. Surtout il faudroit observer aux embouchures des rivieres là où elles se desgagent dans la mer s'il n'y a pas du sable qui gaste la coste et mine la disposition des ports du costé qui est au dessoubz du flux principal de ladicte marée par les plages et bancs de sables qui embouscheure de riviere, et s'il est dans un fond de golfe ou de sein de pleine mer, car tout cella est capable de changer la constitution et disposition des choses et de produire des effectz bien differenz."[82]

---

[79] Tamizey de Larroque 1898, vol. 7, p. 142.
[80] Tamizey de Larroque 1898, vol. 7, p. 142.
[81] Tamizey de Larroque 1898, vol. 7, pp. 146-147.
[82] Tamizey de Larroque 1898, vol. 7, p. 149.

In September and October 1635, he repeated in an abbreviated form the same sorte of questioning, while in May 1636, by now more than impatient about not having received any reply by d'Arcos yet, he once more gave a long and detailed instruction of what he wished him to observe, from whom he had gotten already respective information, whom d'Arcos should approach in Tunis to be of help, and which knowledge from the French coasts, rivers, and mountains should be supplemented and investigated by d'Arcos in Africa.[83]

D'Arcos finally had gotten the one or the other among these seven letters, since he replied twice to the questions raised by Peiresc in a humble, but declining manner. He told him that he himself was too old, too ignorant, too sick to carry out the diverse projects and that others were also incapable of help. While the style and tone of d'Arcos remarks about himself seems to be sufficiently pitiful for not being a mere subterfuge, his setting up of Peiresc's demands suggests that Peiresc indeed had asked too much for somebody with a fulltime job at the court of Tunis whatever his education, health, or degree of curiosity in nature:

"Quant aux flux et reflux des mers de ceste coste, et noter ses plages, seins, bordz, goulphes, encouleures, et les rivieres qui y entrent, leurs arénes et bancs, croissance et decroissance, je desire comme vous le savoir, mais la rechercher moy mesme est impossible, et par information d'autruy je n'en scauray jamais rien de certain, car comme j'ay dit l'ignorance possede tellement ces peuples que la plus part et quasi tous, jusqu'aux plus apparens ne scauroient dire les ans qu'ilz ont, et si quelqu'un semble scauoir quelque chose, ce n'est que ce qui appartiennent aux ceremonies de leur loy, qui ne sont que vanité et superstition. Voilà, monsieur, ce que je puis responde à voz questions, estant marry de ne les pouvoir resoudre, et tres marry de ne vous donner en cela le contentement que je desire, bien que je croy que tout ce qu'il vous a pleu m'escrire a esté plus tost une ostentacion de vostre grand esprit que non l'opinion que je fusse capable de respondre à des choses si sérieuses, rares et exquises."[84]

"... la grande douleur qu je sentois aux piedz, m'estourdissoit tellement la teste que je ne pus alors lire attentivement voz lettres, ni comprendre la docte contenu d'icelles. Je les ay du depuis leües avec plus d'attention et suis resté fort émerveillé d'où vous tirez tant d'excellence de discours et d'érudition: vous asseurant qu'il y a de quoy occuper un cerveau beaucoup plus capable que le mien, bien honteux que je ne saurois satisfaire à voz curiositez, bien que vous me les rendez assez aisées et faciles. Je croy que vous prenez mon plomb pour or, ou que vous voulez eprouver si mon metal souffre la touche de votre pierre. Et aprez auoir bien resué sur voz doctes escritz, j'ay considéré en

---

[83] Tamizey de Larroque 1898, vol. 7, pp. 171-173.
[84] Les Correspondants de Peiresc. 1972, vol. 2, pp. 221-222.

moy mesme qu'il me convenoy vous oster hors d'horreur, et vous dire librement que mon entendement n'arrive pas à de si hautes matières, et que je ne suis pas aigle, sinon un vil reptile qui à peine ne se peut trainer sur la terre. Je me sens neantmoins grandement honoré de la bonne opinion que vous avez de moy, mais je suis bien mortifié quand je m'en estime incapable et que ma suffisance n'arrive à mon souhait, et à vostre desir. Je tascheray de faire le possible pour vous contenter et obeir, ne recusant l'occasion que vous me donnez de faire cognoistre que je scay peu ou rien, estimant que me sera moindre defaut, que non de vous desobeir. Mais parceque voz demandes et recherches, et ma convalescence, requieront du temps à vous respondre, je vous supplie tres humblement me pardonner si je difere (sic) jusqu'à la premiere ocasion (sic) de vous faire veoir mon ignorance m'esforçant de vous complaire si non comme je dois, au moins ce sera comme je pourray."[85]

D'Arcos was by no means an imbecile. This is not only shown by his professional career in France and Tunis, but also by the library he apparently possessed in Tunis and by the numerous treatises on politics, history, creation, Africa, law, etc. he wrote while living in Tunis, sent to Peiresc for approval, and which all seem to be lost nowadays.

As in other cases, Peiresc gave the information he had received from de Montmeyan, Pascal, Viaz, Noel, and other sources publicity by mailing it to several of his Western correspondents. Two occasional remarks by Mersenne from 1634 indicate that he too was involved in Peiresc's search for information:

" J'ay receu des observations des pilotes excellens que la mer n'a nul reflux vers l'equinoctial ni du costé de l'Affrique ni de celuy de l'Amerique ni aux costes du Dannemarc et au delà: et que le plus grand du monde est à St. Michel."[86]

Mersenne repeated this information in very similar termes a few weeks later, replacing the American coast and Danemark by a remark about Norway and about the existence of tides between 26 and 66°.[87]

Copies of his interviews with Montmeyan, Pascal, and Viaz can be found among Dupuys' papers in the BnF. There are also copies of reports to Peiresc extant which are not found among his own papers neither in Paris nor in Carpentras, among them a description of the behavior of the Black sea and the Bosphorus given by the French ambassador in Istanbul, Comte de Marcheville, and

---

[85] Les Correspondants de Peiresc. 1972, vol. 2, pp. 223-224.
[86] Les Correspondants de Peiresc. 1972, vol. 2, p. 510.
[87] Les Correspondants de Peiresc. 1972, vol. 2, p. 521.

captain Gilles, the latter having spent there half a year in 1633.[88] This text is the copy of a survey made by Peiresc on various reports on the tides and currents in divers corners of the Mediterranean sea. It comes as close as possible to a preprint of a treatise on this subject although Peiresc never actually published any of his studies on natural events in such a form. His preferred ways for communicating hypotheses, questions, conjectures, information, or material items were letters, parcels, handwritten surveys, instructions, and memoirs. The surveys on the tides and currents in the Atlantic around Spain, the Mediterranean sea, the Bosphorus, and the Black sea deserve a closer attention which I had no time yet to apply. I give you a copy of the two texts, i. e., Antoine Noel's text on the Atlantic and Peiresc's survey on the Mediterranean and the Black seas, as an appendix to my paper (n° 2).

Immensly fascinated by the outbreak or related activities of several Italian vulcanos, among them the Vesuvius (1631) and the Etna (1634), Peiresc started an extensive study of mostly medieval historical, philosophical, and theological literature, looked for recent travel accounts to Sicily and Southern Italy and descriptions of the actual happenings, and asked his various correspondents to send him their newest knowledge on vulcanos and earthquakes. Papers and letters in four of the manuscripts at Carpentras testify to Peiresc's curiosity in this matter and to his handling it by the combined approach of "reading the book of nature", in this case through the eyes of travelers, together with the books of the "ancients", in this case mostly manuscripts written and books published during the last 300 years.

Several folios in Ms Carpentras, Bibliothèque d'Inguimbertine, 1821 portray Peiresc's study of medieval books and search for contemporary reports on Italian vulcanos. He tried to construct an orderly series of all available information on earlier outbreaks of the Etna and the Vesuvius. Within this series, he noted the appearance of new mountains in the Mediterranean sea, the occurences of earthquakes, the details of the vulcanic eruptions, and known witnesses.[89] He wrote to Italy to acquire information about what books had been published since the 16th century about the behavior of the Vesuvius among them "distinta relatione de l'Incendio del seuo Vezuuio 1631 con la relatione del Incendio di Pottuoli de l'anno 1534. Scritta da Michel Angelo Mazino di Casuello" or "dicorzo (sic) Astronomico delle Ecclissi di Angelo Perroti (sic) con la risolutione di trenta questiti e con discorzo filosophico sopra incendio del Vesuuio de Padre Zacharia di Napoli Abbate di San Seuerino".[90] He asked a second correspondent to inform him about Latin books on the subject who did not only compile a list of books but sent Peiresc extracts carefully annotated with his own comments.[91] In 1636, he acquired a copy of a handwritten report on the eruption of

---

[88] Ms Paris, BNF, Dupuy 669, ff 83a-88a.
[89] Ms Carpentras, Bibliothèque d'Inguimbertine, 1821, ff 195a, 196a.
[90] Ms Carpentras, Bibliothèque d'Inguimbertine, 1821, f 243a.
[91] Ms Carpentras, Bibliothèque d'Inguimbertine, 1821, 248a.

26

Etna by Antoine Leal, Chevalier of Malta, directed to the rector of the Jesuit college in Aix-en-Provence.[92]

One of Peiresc's closest friends and supporters in his exchange of letters and parcels with the Ottoman Empire and its North African dependencies, Honoré Aycard, actively participated in Peiresc's study of the vulcanic activities.[93] In three letters from February 1632, Aycard made clear that he had repeatedly exchanged opinions with Peiresc on this matter and wrote Peiresc about his efforts to collect the newest news possible. He informed Peiresc about his meeting with a Palermian "Jurat" (?) who had passed by Toulon on his way to Spain and about a handwritten report on Sicily as well as a relation on the conflagration of a mountain "Somme" (?) printed in Naples.[94] The traveler from Palermo told Aycard that the fire of Mount Gibel Stromboli (sic) and the Vulcan all together were only a corn-flower compared with Vesuvius' fire and that January 3, when he had left Naples the fire had truly diminished although the mountain continued to spit fuming ashes and boiling waters.[95]

When Jean Magy visited Peiresc in Aix-en-Provence in late June 1633, he told him about the reaction of Muhammad Basha, governor of Suakim, to the news about Vesuvius marvelling at the coincidence of this conflagration with a similar, but subterranean and more durable one in Ethiopian soil near the borders of his province.[96] He also promised Peiresc to send "very punctual relations on the precise days and of all these incidents fine and accordingly attested in a good demonstrative form".[97] One month later Peiresc interviewed the Capucins Gilles de Loches and Césarée de Rosgoff about the Ethiopian event. In his notes of this meeting, Peiresc wrote that the two fathers had confirmed its taking place, but thought that it had begun before Vesuvius had started to throw out fire and that it had happened further away from the Ottoman border than Muhammad Basha had claimed.[98] They had added that the conflagration had occurred near Mount Sem where some hundred Jews lived whose villages had been ruined due to their favors rendered to the "Schismatic" Coptes against their sovereign, the prince of the Abyssins, who was a "good Catholic".[99]

Peiresc apparently regarded the information about the subterranean eruption in Ethiopia, its temporal coincidence with the Vesuvian conflagration, the people living in the Ethiopian

---

[92] Ms Carpentras, Bibliothèque d'Inguimbertine, 1810, ff 102a-103a.
[93] Aycard had also relations of his own to the Middle East and North Africa, in particular, to Constantinople, Smyrna, and Tunis.
[94] Ms Carpentras, Bibliothèque d'Inguimbertine, 1821, ff 265a-267a.
[95] Ms Carpentras, Bibliothèque d'Inguimbertine, 1821, f 266a.
[96] Ms Carpentras, Bibliothèque d'Inguimbertine, 1864, f 263a.
[97] Tamizey de Larroque 1890, vol. 2, p. 556.
[98] Ms Carpentras, Bibliothèque d'Inguimbertine, 1864, f 264a.

mountains, and their fate as hot news. He immediately shared the reports with some of his correspondents, among them the brothers Dupuy and Philippe Fortin de la Hoguette, a low ranking French officer and member of the scholarly circle of the brothers Dupuy.[100] In his first respective letter to the brothers Dupuy (July 4, 1633, i.e., only four days after Magy's visit), Peiresc accepted not only all information given by Magy as reliable, but even turned Muhammad Basha into Magy's "particular friend" and a greatly honest and curious man, despite his huge body.[101] In a letter to the brothers Dupuy written after the Capuchins' visit and dated in Tamizey de Larroque's edition July 23 in obvious contradiction to Peiresc's own note dating of this visit July 25 and 26, Peiresc submitted all the details he had memorized from this visit modifying somewhat the interpretation of why the Fallashas had been hit by the fire.[102]

With regard to the different opinions of his visitors about the timing of the event, he apparently was insecure whom to follow. He characterized the Capuchins' information as given "without precise certainty" and added that "the Marseillaises" insisted on their contrary opinion only admitting if there had been indeed a time gap it had been truly small.[103] This suggests that Peiresc has had a second interview with Magy which could not have taken place after the Capuchins had visited Peiresc since in his letter dated July 4, Peiresc had said that Magy would leave for Cairo July 12.[104] In his second letter, he described Magy as already on his way to Cairo having left the evening of (Mary) Magdelene, i. e., July 22.[105] In a third letter to the Dupuys (September 19), it becomes clear that Peiresc had entertained in that summer a fourth visitor from Cairo, the former consul Gabriel Fernoulx. He seemed to have been in Aix during the first half of September, but he

---

[99] Ms Carpentras, Bibliothèque d'Ingiumbertine, 1864, f 264a.
[100] Ms Carpentras, Bibliothèque d'Inguimbertine, 1809, f 182a; Tamizey de Larroque 1890, vol. 2, pp. 555-556, 569-570.
[101] Tamizey de larroque 1890, vol. 2, p. 555: "Et cez jours cy depuis la closture de nostre parlement ont esté employez en une conversation bien agreable avec un marchand de Marseille qui a esté vingt ans au Cayre, de qui j'ay bien appris de plus belles curiositez que de toutes les relations que j'en avois veües soit imprimées ou m[anu]s[crite]s: entr'aultres il m'a asseuré tenir de la bouche de memet-Bacha, de Suachem, son amy particulier, Ragusoys de nation, trez vaillant homme et trez robuste, et quasi en demy geant, mais grandement curieux et honneste, que pendant l'incendie du Mont Vesuve prez de Naples, il s'embrasa une aultre gueulle de feux soubsterrains sur les borned de l'empire du prebstre Jean et du pais de Suachem sur la mer Rouge, d'où l'on voyoit des flammes et la fumée, dont les pais circonvoisins furent touts desolez à plus de troys lieües è l'entour, et le feu y duroit encores avec violence environ le mpys de mars de l'am 1632 que ce Bassa se retira au Cayre. Or le mesme hyver, y eult untremblement de terre jusques au Cayre mesme, et peu temps devant, aprez une furieuse tempeste à la Mecque dans les ruines de la grande mosquée qui en fut abbattüe, la terre s'entr'ouvrit et en sortit quelque peu de temps un vent si puant et si infect, si chauld et si mallin que plusieurs eu furent malades, et aulcuns en perdirent la vie, et si cela eust duré, le lieu eu eust esté inhabitable, mais cela se recombla bien tost et cessa d'incommoder le peuple qui imputoit le tout au chastiment des faultes de leurs chefs."
[102] Peiresc wrote that the Jews had been punished because they were partisans of the new Ethiopian king who was an ennemy of the Catholic christians. Tamizey de Larroque 1890, vol. 2, p. 570.
[103] Tamizey de Larroque 1890, vol. 2, p. 570.
[104] Tamizey de Larroque 1890, vol. 2, p. 556.
[105] Tamizey de Larroque 1890, vol. 2, p. 570: "Ce qu'il dict de plus pour le temps est qu'il tient, bien que sans certitude precise, que cet embrasement là aye prevenu celuy du Vesuve de quelques moys, mais les Marseillois opiniastrent le contraire [et] disent que s'il y a de la differance elle est fort petite, ...".

might have seen Peiresc also earlier, if not in Aix, then possibly in Marseille. It was, perhaps, Fernoulx whom Peiresc interviewed after the Capuchins' visit with regard to his knowledge about the timing of the Ethiopian conflagration.[106] Early September, in any case, in a letter to de la Hoguette, Peiresc had made up his mind and favored Magy's report, i.e., the story of the Ottoman eyewitness Muhammad Basha, over that of the two Capuchins:

"... Au reste vous auez fort bien Jugé que ce mont de Sem nest pas loing de la mer rouge Car noz marseillois nous disent auoir apprins de la bouche de memes (sic) Bassa du Suachem dont la demeure estoit au bord de la mer rouge que de ce mesme lieu Ilz en voyoient la fumee et les flammes. ne doubtant pas que le voysinage de la mer ne Contribue quelques dispositions a celz embrasementz et a leur dureé ..."[107]

In this letter to de la Hoguette, Peiresc described not only Muhammad Basha's story about the Ethiopian conflagration, but also presented the other pieces on Medina and Mecca as undisputable data. On this base, Peiresc set out to offer bold generalizations about the subterranean connection between the Arabian Peninsula and Ethiopia via the Red sea in analogy to the same type of deduction derived from his collected material about the Etna, the Vesuvius, the Stromboli, and the Pozzuolo:

"de l'autre costé mesme de la mer rouge, qui est à l'orient du mont Sinai, Il y à des bainds Chaudz en la ville de Medina Nebie, et al Tor, et dict on que prez de la Mecque Il y eu (sic) cez anneés dernieres du vent pestifer, venu dessoubz terre qui tua vn nombre Infinis de personnes et de Chameaux dont estoit composeé la Carauane, Ce qui pourroit Induire aussy Je ne sçay quelle Correspondance de là au mont de Sem, par dessoubz lad[icte] mer rouge, si tant est que la matiere ou s'entretiennent cez feu sousterrains soit assez profoinde (sic) dans la terre pour prendre quelque correspondance d'vn lieu à l'autre par dessoubz la mer rouge, Comm'il semble quil y en ayt du Mont Æthna au Vesuue et aux autres lieux d'autour de pozzuolo aussy bien qu'auec le Vulcan et le Strombole ..."[108]

Peiresc argued that although time could bring the conflagrations to cease on the earth's surface, they continued to be active underground causing the vulcanos to erupt time and again. Earthquakes might contribute to hinder or even close the underground communication between such locations, but he believed the disposition to reopen either at the old apertures or at new ones would continue to exist. He wondered whether the fire would not be capable to push up naturally

---

[106] Tamizey de Larroque 1890, vol. 2, p. 602.
[107] Ms Carpentras, Bibliothèque d'Inguimbertine, 1809, f 182a.
[108] Ms Carpentras, Bibliothèque d'Ingiumbertine, 1809, ff 182a-b.

new mountains or islands where it would open up spirals for the underground fire enclosed under the sea. To lend some credibility to this assumption, Peiresc referred to mountains and elevations under the surface of the sea between Sicily and Syria which could be capable - when hit by the full force of the sea agitated by the sirocco - to imprint some movement and compression upon the deepest bowels [entraillez] of these burning chimneys [fournaises] so that they excited noise and made the fumes and flames to move upwards towards their gulf. According to the mariners, the most reliable signs for a coming sirocco were exactly these fumes and flames. Quasi as a sideremark, Peiresc seems to propose the derivation of one of the fables of Greek mythology - that of Aeolus' power over the winds - from such natural portents.[109] The pondering of mariners' narratives about the sirocco induced Peiresc to extend his generalizations, now not only assuming a subterranean linkage between the Italian vulcanos and in analogy to it between the Arabian Peninsula and Ethiopia, but a more widespread connection between the Etna, the dead vulcanos of "Greece" and "Palestine", and the region of the Red sea. Assuming that the fires by producing greasy and bituminous matter form a crust or a kind of [bource] ? or a furnace capable to bear the marine waters and to hinder them to enter the enflamed caves, it would be much easier to understand and conceive of that the Mediterranean sea being agitated at the Syrian coast and driven towards Sicily exercised such a great charge upon the enflamed caves enclosed by the sea that there would be enough compression to push the fume and the flames out and to produce the extraordinary noise which proceeded the sirocco sometimes.[110] Finding obliging matter due to its greasiness and compressing the underground void, the sea - as if through a sponge - made come out the fume, flames, and noise through the gulf of Mount Etna and those of the Vulcan, the Stromboli, and others whose fume covered incessantly the sea and was brought by the next sirocco even until the Provençal coast. There, its stench and blackness could be smelt up to Froins and the Islands of Ieres, but not further because the coast turned to the North. Peiresc, for once again back to single details, justified this claim by his personal experience of contracting a disease near Froins which lasted for eleven months. The disaster motivated him to spend some time investigating its causes although it did not render him overly curious.[111] This was reserved to his

---

[109] "... et c'estoit fondeé l'ancienne fable du regne d'Æole sur les ventz, s'il pouuoit eu predire certainement quelques vns par telz signes de ces montanges bruslantes, la cessation desquelz pouuoit produire la succession des ventz Contraire selon la Commune vicissitude des choses de ce monde ..." Ms Carpentras, Bibliothèque d'Ingiumbertine, 1809, f 183a.

[110] "Que s'il pouuoit estre loysible de supposer vne Communication soubsterrain aussy bien du Mont Ætna en ceux de la grece et de la palestine qui ont burslés ou produit des eauc chaudes, et auec ces autres d'autour de la mer rouge, supposant aussy que telz feux en fondant cez matieres grasses et bytumineuses se forment vne Crouste ou vne espece de bource ou de foruneau capable de soustenir l'eau marine et de l'empescher d'entrer dans cez Cauernes enflameés, ... Il seroit bien plus facile de Comprendre et de Concepuoir que la mer mediterraneé se trouuant agiteé du costé de la Syrie et porteé vers la Sicile fit vne si grande charge sur cez antres ou Cauernes enflameés couuertes de la mer quelle y fist asséz de Compression pour en exprimer la fumeé et les flammes et las bruict extraordinaire qui procede le vent Syroc de Certain temps ..." Ms Carpentras, Bibliothèque d'Inguimbertine, 1809, f. 183a.

[111] Ms Carpentras, Bibliothèque d'Inguimbertine, 1809, ff 183a-b.

later years since this letter and Peiresc's ruminating about the winds, subterranean caves, vulcanos, fossiles, and earthquakes goes on for another two folios of very narrow handwriting[112].

Peiresc's general ideas on vulcanic activities and subterranean connections between various parts of the ancient world were not born in a minute of overly strong excitement, but based upon serious occupation with all the material he had collected. A first, much shorter version of Peiresc's ideas on how to interpret the eruptions of Vesuvius and the Ethiopian mountain, is contained in the first letter to the brothers Dupuy reporting of Magy's visit.[113] A second version which appears almost to be a draft of his letter to de la Hoguette is found in Ms Carpentras, Bibliothèque d'Ingiumbertine, 1821. It documents Peiresc's efforts to arrange his source material, compose his arguments, and present his deductions.[114] They resemble closely another piece of one folio in the same manuscript containing Peiresc's comments on some of the astronomical observations he had carried out in Aix-en-Provence either together with Gassendi or Joseph Gaultier, prior of de la Valette, and the discussions these men have had in order to evaluate and interpret the observational results.[115] Thus, even if the notes on the vulcanic activities indeed served as a draft for Peiresc's letter to de la Hoguette they reflect his style of working in a much broader sense. They were not simply a means to organize his correspondence in a pleasing and persuasive way. Neither did Peiresc merely collect information or material items, read and extracted ancient books, or took a carriage in order to make a promenade in the Provençal mountains to observe their alignments with the cardinal directions or their stratifications. He spent evidently hours of solitude in one of his several studies, analyzing his material, reflecting upon it, and writing down his results in a form which resembles those of his instructions and memoirs.

3. Peiresc's interest in Arabic geographies and mapmaking

Peiresc's exchange of letters with Lucas Holstenius, librarian in Rome in the service of Cardinal Barberini, treats time and again Holstenius' project, started before 1622, but never finished, to edit all the so-called minor Greek and Latin geographers. Peiresc supported it by searching for ancient Greek manuscripts extant in Western European libraries as well as in those of the Ottoman

---

[112] Ms Carpentras, Bibliothèque d'Inguimbertine, 1809, ff 182a-184b.
[113] Tamizey de Larroque 1890, vol. 2, p. 555-556: "Il y a des bains et aultres eaux-chauldes non seulement à Medina Nebits et au Tor, entre le Mont Sinai et la Mecque, mais en d'aultres endroits, qui sont indices manifestes des exhalaisons que les feux soubsterrains poulsent à la surface de la terre, de sorte qu'il n'y auroit pas grande merveille quand il s'y ouvriroit des gueulles de feu semblables à celles du MontÆthna et du Vesuve; mais cela ayt paru en mesme temps, c'eust esté grande merveille, s'il s'y trouvoit du rapport des temps á peu prez, car il fauldroit conclurre <sic> que la source de ce feu vinsse de bien profond et de bien prez du centre de la terre."
[114] Ms Carpentras, Bibliothéque d'Inguimbertine, 1821, ff 198a-b.
[115] Ms Carpentras, Bibliothèque d'Inguimbertine, 1821, f 219a.

Empire, in particular in Cyprus.[116] Among other things, he looked for a copy of Dionysios of Byzantium's description of the Bosphorus which Pierre Gilles had found fragments of in Istanbul during his visit of the Ottoman Empire in the middle of the 16th century.[117] He also encouraged Holstenius to rectify ancient maps of oriental countries by comparing them, for instance, with the travel accounts published in England by Hakluyt and Purchas. He diligently tried to procure for himself a copy of Purchas' latest edition of the entire collection, asked Henri de Valois who was of Scottish origin to translate for him at the least its tables of contents, and offered Holstenius to lend him these volumes to facilitate his studies and hasten the publication of the ancient geographers.[118]

In three of the many letters discussing Holstenius' work on the geographers and Peiresc's efforts to support him, he informed Holstenius that he had already pushed the Dutch geographer Petrus Bertius (d. 1629) along similar lines.[119] In the first of the three letters, Peiresc told Holstenius that while he had suggested Bertius to work on the ancient geographers his protegé had already begun to draw a map on al-Idrisi's 12th-century Arabic geography.[120] Two years later, when Holstenius reported to him the first progress in his own work on the ancients, Peiresc not only congratulated him warmly, but came back to Bertius' maps both of the ancient Greek and Latin and of the medieval Arabic geographers, thus again suggesting a link between the two projects. This time, Peiresc claimed explicitly also to have caused the drawing of the map to the

---

[116] Tamizey-Larroque 1894, vol. 5, p. 547: "Il fault advoüer qu'il [Holstenius - S. B.] a un genie nompareil à cette entreprinse des geographes, et que seulement le catalogue qu'il en a dressé merite d'estre fort estimé. Mon regret est de n'avoir de quoy l'ayder en son entreprinse de rien qui vaille, quelque diligence dont je puisse user pour escrire à gents de nostre cognoisçance touchant les livres qu'il vouldroit trouver, si ce n'est qu'un bonheur inesperé nous fist avoir du Levant quelque aultre rencontre de livres qui fussent de cette nature dont j'attends la résolution dans Pasques prochaines Dieu aydant."

[117] "Quant au Dionysius Byzantius, je ne m'estonne poinct que vous en faciez si grand cas comme vous faictes, estant tel qu'on le peult juger par les parcelles dont s'est servi P. Gillius. Ce seroit grand dommage s'il estoit perdu. Je feray de bon coeur tout ce qui me sera possible, pour tascher de le vous faire avoir s'il est en main de persone tant soit peu traictable. J'en a y desjà escript en beaucoup de divers endroicts, ..." Tamizey de Larroque 1894, vol. 5, p. 261.

[118] "Au reste, si pour accelerer vos geographes vous avez de besoing des volumes des Navigations du Purchas, je vous envoyeray le mien trez volontiers; n'en faictes pas de difficulté de l'accepter. ... ... j'y joinct ... les cartes postumes de la geographie ancienne du pauvre deffunct Mr Bertius, lesquelles il avoit entreprinses à ma persuasion, mais vous les ferez bien mieux, si vous voulez, et y joindrez, si vous me voulez croire, celles de la geographie de Strabon et aultres autheurs selon leurs sentiments. J'y ay joinct aussy les peregrinations et voyages de Purchas, afin qu'il ne tienne poinct à cela que vous ne puissiez travailler plus commodement sur la geographie de cet Orient et altres contrées mieux descrittes dans les receueils dudict Purchas que dans les aultres autheurs de nos temps." Tamizey de Larroque 1894, vol. 5, pp. 288, 364. See also ibid., p. 350.

[119] See the previous footnote.

[120] Tamizey de Larroque 1894, vol. 5, pp. 260-261: "J'avois autres foys voulu disposer le bon homme Bertius d'entreprendre quelques carthes de l'antiquité, differentes selon la diversité des sentiments de ceux qui ont descript le monde ou quelque porcion d'iceluy. Entr'autre une ou plusieurs selon la doctrine et les suppositions de Pline, et ainsin des autres anciens autheurs, soit pour Strabon, Solin, Mela, Pausanias, Stephanus, Arrianus (principalement pour sa mer rouge et son expedition d'Alexandre), soit pour cez autres petits geographes grecs qui estoient dans la bibliotheque du roys, en conservant tousjours tant que faire se pourroit la vraye figures des terres, et rivieres, et y accomodant seulement les noms anciens. Il avoit desjà commancé par la carthe de ce geographe Arabe nubien, qui luy estoit fort bien reussie, ..." (1627)

"Geographia Nubiensis" and even to possess Bertius' autograph which he offered Holstenius to further his own research:

"Au reste vous m'aviez faict plaisir de me dire que vous ayez desjà dressé voz tables sur voz petits geographes et que le pauvre feu Mr Cluverius eusse dessein d'entreprendre celles de Strabon, mais il falloit que la posterité vous en eusse l'obligation à vous quelque jour à la suitte de voz dicts geographs et des aultres principaux autheurs, car pour celles du bon homme Bertius, il y a quelque chose à desirer, qui ne vous seroit pas eschappée à vous. C'estoit pour l'amour de moy qu'il avoit dressé la carte sur la geographie arabe du Nubiensis et j'en ay son autographe au net qu'il me voulut donner, et que je voulois faire imprimer à Paris, sans qu'il ayma mieux attendre une aultre edition de Nubiensis."[121]

Holstenius answered that he once had seen in Bertius collection or cabinet a map of the "Geographia Nubiensis" which was arranged according to the climates and which would be in the interest of the public to draw into light:

"Sed ut ad Bertium redeam, memini mihi visam olim in ipsius Museo tabulam Geographiæ Nubiensis secundum climata accomodatam, quam in lucem protrahi publice interesse existimo."[122]

While I don't know yet whether Holstenius ever visited Paris, it is clear that he had studied in Leiden. Thus his remark might refer to this time. If this is the case - which I think is a reasonable assumption since it wouldn't make sense for Holstenius to talk to Peiresc about a map of this geography in Bertius' possession in Paris who would presumably have known of it from his stay there - then it must have been an Arabic map since Bertius only can have started with his own map in Paris if Peiresc's claim about his encouraging Bertius to draw it is reliable. It is, however, unclear how Bertius might have had acquired this Arabic manuscript. Moreover, in a letter written by Peiresc to the brothers Dupuy in 1628, the former reported about visitors he had recently entertained. These visitors had only returned from Persia where they had seen an Arabic geography with maps which differed from al-Idrisi's work implying therewith that the latter's geography was well known among the people in Aix enabling them to judge the contents of other Arabic geographical manuscripts and their maps:

"Nous avons eu icy Mr le Tenneur (filz du greffier du conseil, mon bon voisin et ancien amy) ensemble M. Leger, qui reviennent de Perse, où ils ont sesjourné longuement, et veu

---
[121] ibid., pp. 377-378.
[122] ibid,, p. 378, footnote 2.

familiairement le Prince de ce pais là. ... Ils ont veu une Geographie arabique avec des chartes differante de celle du Nubiensis."[123]

Marina Tolmaschewa has found circa ten years ago a copy of the printed version of Bertius' map in the Newberry Library in Chicago. She has suggested in her paper that Bertius prepared his map on the base of Arabic maps of al-Idrisi's "Geography" but could not identify any possible source among the today extant Arabic manuscripts of this text. Peiresc's letters solve at least one puzzle Marina faced - the question what might have induced Bertius to produce his map of the "Geographia Nubiensis". She thought it was a rather outlandish project since 17th-century West European cartography was much superior in comparison with the medieval Arabic author and could have had no use of such a map.[124] The results of my research, in contrast, suggest that West European cartography of the 17th century depended profoundly on books. Arabic and Persian geographies were acknowledged as important literary sources by mapmakers and scholars alike. This process apparently started in the middle of the 16th century when Jacopo Gastaldi (d. 1566) designed his maps of Anatolia and Asia in Venice on the basis of Venetian diplomatic letters, portolan charts, and Turkish, Persian, and possibly Arabic written and oral sources.

A third scholar whom Peiresc cajoled to join maps to his edition of the Greek polyhistor Solinus was Claude de Saumaise in Leiden. He drew his attention - as he had with Holstenius - to the maps Bertius already had produced.[125]

Peiresc wrote about his part in Bertius' work on the ancient and medieval geographers to the brothers Dupuy too:

" J'ay veu avec grand plaisir les livres dont vous m'avez daigné retenir l'assortiment, entre lesquels j'ay esté bien aise de trouver le Typus orbis terrarum du bonhomme Bertius in fol° que je luy avois autres foys voulu mettre en teste, et luy proposois de le representer en differantes cartes, selon la differance des suppositions des divers aultheurs principaulx, comme Pline, Strabon, et autres dont nous n'avons pas des carthes."[126]

He told the Dupuys that it had been he who had - using the power of his patron and friend Guillaume du Vair - made Sionita and Hesronita translate into Latin the Arabic extract of al-Idrisi's

---

[123] Tamizey de Larroque 1888, vol. 1, p. 621.
[124] Tolmaschewa 19
[125] Tamizey de Larroque, 1888, vol. 1, p. 56: "Je vouldrois qu'il [Saulmaise - S. B.] y fit mettre quelques carthes accommodées à la geographie du dict Solin, à quoy le bonhomme de Bertius le serviroit bien je m'asseure s'il vouloit; à qui j'avois une foys mis enteste d'entreprendre des cartes de geographie accommodées à chascun des anciens geogrpahes grecs et latins, et possible seroit ce une trez bonne piece et d'un grand soulagement pour l'intelligence plus facile des dits autheurs." (1625)

"geography" which Giovanni Baptista Raimondi (1536?-1614) had printed in 1592 in the Medici Press, Rome:

"... (mais il leur [Sionita et Hesronita - S. B.] fauldroit de fortes sollicitations pour les y embarquer,) comme je fis lorsqu'il fut question de l'edition du dict Geographie de Nubie où je fis intervenir l'authorité de feu monseigneur le G[arde] d[es] S[ceaux] du Vair, encores y eust-il bien de la peine."[127]

The Arabic manuscript had come in the 1580s together with another hundred or so Arabic and Syriac codices from Antakya to Rome. They were brought by the Jacobite patriarche Ni'amatallah (d. 1587) who had agreed to negotiate the acceptance of the Catholic creed by his church. The patriarche had stipulated that the entire collection was to be transferred after his death to Raimondi.[128] Multiple copies of the contents of this collection as well as of Raimondi's publishing plans regarding Arabic, Syriac, Ethiopian, and other oriental manuscripts are extant among the papers of Peiresc and the brothers Dupuy.[129] Acquiring copies of most of the big and several of the smaller French, Italian, and also some Dutch, English, or former Byzantine libraries was a central means of the Provençal erudite to keep himself informed about which oriental, Greek, and Latin manuscripts were available in Western Europe and which he had to persuade people in the Middle East to search for.

An anonymous evaluation of the Latin translation of the "Geographia Nubiensis" is extant among Peiresc's papers in Carpentras. The above-described context suggests that its author was Bertius. Among other things, Bertius stressed the differences of opinion regarding the choice of the prime meridian and the arrangement of the climates which characterized al-Idrisi's work and the position adopted by modern geographers. If Peiresc's retrospective descriptions of his interests in designing maps to accompany the edition of ancient and medieval geographers can be trusted, the bringing to light of such and other differences was one of his major aims. It remains, however, an open question whether the elucidation of such differences served a historical purpose or was part of a comparison between the "book of nature" and the "books of the ancients" as was, for instance, his delving into Aristides and the gulf of Smyrna.

The Latin translation and publication of the "Geographia Nubiensis" was an immediate and long-lasting success. Father Cœlestinus repeatedly asked Peiresc to send the book for his convent's library in Aleppo. French geographers of the 17th and 18th centuries, among them the royal

---

[126] Tamizey de Larroque 1890, vol. 2, p. 64, see also ibid., 1888, vol. 1, p. 56.
[127] ibid. 1888, vol. 1, p. 579.
[128] Ms Florence, 13. II. III, ff.
[129] Mss Carpentras, Bibliothèqie d'Inguimbertine, ; Paris, BNF, Latin 9340.

geographers Nicolas Sanson, Guillaume Delisle, and Jean Bourguignon d'Anville, used it to draw historical and contemporary maps of the Middle East or to discuss the reliability of ancient Greek geographical literature with regard to Egypt and the correctness of identifications between historical and modern cities in China proposed by some Jesuits measuring and mapping the Middle Empire. Even Peiresc himself took much pride in it. He recommended it to Thomas d'Arcos time and again, and insisted he include it in his own "Relation of Africa":

"Je pense que vous aurez veu là un livre de Geographie Arabe, dont le text Arabique fut imprimé à Rome in-4° en mesme temps que le Nouveau Testament, qu'il vous pleut m'envoyer dernièrement; et la version latine en a esté imprimée à Paris, quand j'y estois, soubz le nom de *Nubiensis*, lequel descript tout le plein de particularitet de son pais de Nubie, en traictant la Geographie Universelle. Si vous ne l'avez veu, je vous en fairay avoir un, Dieu aydant, et contribueray tout ce qui me sera possible, pour accelerer la perfection de vostre relation Affricaine, lequel je cheriray plus particulièrement que voz autres œuvres, puisque vous me dictes de l'avoir mise en françois pour l'amour de moy, dont je me tiens fort redevable à vostre honnesteté; et certainement le subject en est fort de mon goust, et je pense qu'il rencontrera le goust plus commun, attendu que vous pouvez enseigner des choses de cez Pais barbares, si peu frequentez <sic>, lesquelles nous ne sçaurions apprendre d'ailleurs."[130]

As a postscript to this letter from March 1633, Peiresc informed d'Arcos that he had read some parts of his book, but found no references to the "Geographia Nubiensis" whose author had reported things about Africa which were almost unknown to other classical books. Peiresc promised d'Arcos to send him a copy.[131] D'Arcos answered him in June 1633, that he had been told about the "Geographia Nubiensis" some time ago, that he knew that its Latin translation had been published in Paris, and that he would like to see what the "Nubian" had written.[132] In March 1634, Peiresc informed d'Arcos that the "Geographia Nubiensis" was on its way from Paris to Aix.[133] D'Arcos confirmed its arrival via Honoré Aycard in August 1634.[134]

The entire year of 1634, Peiresc continued to be fascinated with d'Arcos description of Africa. He marveled at the great number of books d'Arcos had available "in those countries there", many of them so rare "in these countries here" that one does not know how to find them, in particular Marmol's description of Africa and other "ancient" Spanish writers.[135] Peiresc continued to instruct d'Arcos how to improve his book. He proposed him to include measurements of the

---
[130] Tamizey de Larroque 1898, vol. 7, pp. 109-110.
[131] ibid., p. 115.
[132] Les Correspondants de Peiresc 1972, vol. 2, p. 208.
[133] Tamizey de Larroque 1898, vol. 7, p. 125.
[134] Les Correspondants de Peiresc 1972, vol. 2, p. 215.

geographical latitudes of Tunis and Carthago, of Tunis since it was the place where d'Arcos dwelled, Carthago since it had been so noble and famous.[136] Peiresc recommended d'Arcos to ask the "grenadins", i.e., the Moriscos fled from Spain, whether they disposed of instruments suitable for measuring the altitude of the sun rather exactly and insisted that d'Arcos carried out such observations several times, principally around the two solstices. His reasoning was that since d'Arcos had wanted to describe such places he was obliged to ensure himself of their true position.[137] He continued this letter by proposing d'Arcos if he once had started with the business of measuring the sun's altitude, he also could engage himself in observing the next lunar eclipse (March 14, 1634) since this would be a beautiful means to determine Tunis' longitude. After giving him some instructions on how to do this, Peiresc emphasized that such a deed would greatly enhance the value of d'Arcos' "Relation":

"... par consequent de la situation de la ville de Thunis, ce qui seroit pour donner un grand credit à vostre Relation d'Affrique."[138]

Peiresc argued that a good book on strange countries was one where his author had added his very own experience of geography and natural curiosities and replaced hearsay by verified eyesight. [139] He strengthened his effort to persuade d'Arcos not only to go on working on his beloved text, but also to carry out the diverse observations and inquiries Peiresc had asked him to undertake by explaining what had turned Leo Africanus' "Africæ Descriptio" into such an instant and long-lasting bestseller - namely adding his own doings and observations and quoting from manuscripts unavailable in Western Europe.[140]

According to one of the 17th- or 18th-centuries' catalogues of Peiresc's left papers in Carpentras Peiresc possessed copies of (extracts of) two works composed by the Ayyubid prince Abu l-Fida' (d. 1321) - his geography "Taqwim al-buldan" and his history of Muslim rulers. While the latter is lost, the former reappears under the header "Extraits de la Géographie d'Abu l-Feda" in the description of Ms 1774 by the 19th-century librarian of the "d'Inguimbertine".[141] It owes its

---

[135] Tamizey de Larroque 1898, vol. 7, p. 116.
[136] ibid., pp. 126, 153, 164.
[137] ibid., p. 119: "Et si vous aviez là de cez grenadins ou autres qui eussent des instrumenz propres à mesurer la haulteur du soleil bien exactement, à quelque journée bien seraine sur le midy, je desirerois bien que vous en eussiez faict l'observation diverses foys, principalement au plus grand ou au plus petit jour de l'année, pour voir la vraye Latitude ou Elevation Polaire du lieu où vous estes, laquelle manque à vostre Relation Affricaine, sinon par le dire d'aultruy; estimant que puisque vous en avez voulu faire la description, vous estes obligé d'en veriffier vous-mesmes le point de la situation."
[138] ibid., p. 120.
[139] ibid., pp. 120-121, 163.
[140] ibid., p. 121: "Ce qui a rendu plus recommandable la relation de Leon a esté ce qu'il y a entrelassé de son propre faict et de ses propres observations, aussy bien que de celles d'aultruy, si ce n'est quand c'estoit aprez des livres manuscrits que nous n'avions point en l'Europe."
[141] Ms Carpentras, Bibliothèque d'Inguimbertine, 1774, ff 182a-195b.

naming to Peiresc who himself had written "EX GEOGRAPHIA ISMAELIS ABULFEDA" on the first page of a French translation of a Latin geography which Peiresc declared to have been printed on a wooden table in Venice.[142]

Abu l-Fida' was known in Western Europe as an important Arabic geographer since the middle of the 16th century when Guillaume Postel had brought the first manuscript of his work back from his voyage through the Ottoman Empire. Jacopo Gastaldi may have used a few names from it from 1550 onwards for his maps of Asia and North Africa. Ramusio published some years later a brief extract of Abu l-Fida's tables of geographical coordinates. Abraham Ortelius - based upon Gastaldi and Masius - gave the Ayyubid prince not only a place in the map of Asia, but also an entry in his list of eminent geographers. Since Peiresc also had bought and distributed several copies of the " Africæ Descriptio" composed by the Muslim jurist, traveler, diplomatic envoy, captive of Christian pirates, Catholic convert, and papal protegé Leo Africanus, his interest in Abu l-Fida's geography comes as no surprise. The author of the text he had acquired was, however, not the Ayyubid prince, but a person named Ahmad of Tunis. Peiresc evidently had not read his copy since it made clear already on the second folio of Peiresc's copy that Abu l-Fida' was merely the authority and example which should lend credit to another author's work:

"Le verteux Emir Ismael pour faire Sçauoir Les acroustement de La terre Il traicte en Ses Liures quil a escripte de La Longueur et de La Lergeure <sic> du monde et des Climats des pays des villes et generalement a escript de toute <sic> ce qui en despend nous aussy selon le liure dudict autheur auons dechiffré et faict La description des Lieux et fait La Ressemblance du monde et des Pays qui sont en Italie auec La nouuelle terre vrayment ..."[143]

Almost at the end of the text, after the description of Malabar, there is a fascinating story of the life and fate of its author. He was a born Muslim who studied all his life law and the "book of the stars" in Fez - where a renowned mosque, the Qayrawiyin, operated also a school. Then he was made a slave in the countries of the "francs", i.e., Catholic Europeans, and sold to a generous master who did not interfere into his religious beliefs, but promised him freedom when he would have finished his translation of the cosmography into Turkish which Ahmad had composed in the language of the "francs" on the base of the books of Plato, Socrat, Abu l-Fida' (?; aboulfetah), and the great doctor Locma (?).[144] After emphasizing once more the importance of the discovery of

---
[142] ibid., f 182a.
[143] ibid., 1774, f 182b.
[144] ibid., ff 193b-194b: "Au Nom de dieu misericordieux et pieux
O doctes ez Scauants sur qui La benediction de dieu soit SCACHEZ quil est ainsy ce pauure et foible de puissance lequel a besoing de La misericorde de dieu son Riche Seigneur assauoir moy qui suys Le pelerin ahmet de la ville de thunis de mon Jeune age Jusques a present du coste de Loccident estudiant a Lescolle qui est en la ville de fez Jay esté grande quantite de de <sic> temps en qualité descolier et presque toute may vye à

VII

38

the new world by the Spanish and the Portuguese, Ahmad of Tunis repeated that he wrote this text in Turkish due to the command of his master and because of the great expansion of this language in the world. Finally he expressed his eagerness to be told of the faults in his description of the world and closed with the words: "mais dieu scait la verité".[145]

While this translation seems to have been unknown in modern literature, the map claimed to have been drawn by Ahmad of Tunis and printed in 1588 in Venice, as a woodcut has been known since decades. It raised a profound dispute as to whether the map was genuine. It has been proposed that Gastaldi may have drawn the map and two Venetian translators of Ottoman and Safavid diplomatic letters composed the text. The existence of the French translation of the map's text among Peiresc's papers indicates that contrary to current knowledge the map and its story circulated outside of Venice.

Among Peiresc's left papers in Carpentras there are two more sets of maps and related letters. One concerns the position of ancient Carthago, the other the form of the Gulf of Smyrna. The second case was turned into a question for research by Peiresc himself, while in the first case, his interest was piqued by claims that the ancients' description of the geographical position of Cartage was badly lacking making all maps of the Mediterranean sea highly imprecise and that modern authors thought that Carthago's or Tunis' true geographical position was on the same meridian as that of Rome. That is why he insisted on d'Arcos observing lunar eclipses in and around Tunis.[146]

Lestude pour apprendre Les Loys et comme Jay eu eu <sic> atteint la doctrine comme Je desiroit au Liure des astres Jay esté fait esclaue au pays du francs et ay este achepte d'vn genereux chef dudict pays Lequel estoit vertueux homme aymant La Science et durant mon esclauitude ny manque pas vn foys ma priere selon La reigle des mussulmans et comme Le debuoir est en ay faict Lexpedition et La doctrine que Jay apprise en ces quartiers La m'est plus agreables <sic> que Silz m'auoyent donné toute sorte de dignitez et faict toute sorte de courthoisye et en ces pays La Jay faict La figure et description du monde comme Je paroit selon Le traicté de Liures des auteurs filosophes assauoir platon socrat aboulfetah et le tresgrand docteur Locma (?)/ et dans Ladicte description est donné a congnoistre generallement et particulierement toutes Les despandances des cieux et de la terre / et ceste composition est extremement profitable a tous Les mussulmans qui La voudront Regarder et principalement aux grands Elle a esté traduitte par moy de Langue franque en turquesque et Lay tiré de Leur propre escripture et pour ceste occasion en Recompense m'ont Jurez de me donner Lettre de Liberté Mais en verité de dieu Jusques a ce que Jay eueu <sic> perfectionné ce tout de la facon de vous voyez Les maulx et cruautez que que <sic> Jay endurez sur <sic> sont en sy grand nombre qui ne ce peult dire Mais dieu soit Loué cest pourquoy le don d'Intelligence et proué par ceste oeuure car Je suis la cause du bien de tous Le mussulmans cest pourquoy Je desire contentement et destre exant du pays des francs Retournant en Joys et en santé au pays des mussulmantz."

[145] ibid., f 195b.
[146] Tamizey de Larroque 1898, vol. 7, p. 133: "Car si vous l'observez on s'en pourroit servir pour veriffier ce que tiennent aulcunz modernes que Carthage ou Thunis sont soubz le mesme meridien de Rome; ... ."
ibid., p. 179: "Vous ne sçauriez croire de quelle importance seront voz observations en cela, à cause des vieilles presupositions qui avoint esté faictes de la distances de Carthage d'avec Arbelles où fust donnée ceste celebre bataille du temps d'une Ecclypse notable qui fust veüe en mesme instant à Carthage soubz une heure differemment supputée. Car c'est possible de cela principalement que viennent les distances mal mesurées de toutes nos cartes geographiques depuis Carthage jusques au fonds de la mer Mediterranée, qui se sont tousjours

In Ms Carpentras, Bibliothèque d'Inguimbertine 1831, several maps of the Gulf of Carthago or its parts can be found. The larger less perfectly drawn map seems to be at the origin of if not all, than most of the other maps given not only the more sketchy character of the drawing, but also the more extensive list of explanations and the amount of Provençal (?) words or orthography in this list. The large maps are clearly based upon contemporary knowledge of the region, referring as they do to Muslim historical buildings, Spanish fortresses, and Turkish battles. It is equally obvious that at least their inscriptions have been devised by a West European because of Carthage's presence. The second, more expertly drawn version is accompanied by rearranged markings and inscriptions which seem to focus more clearly than the older map upon ancient sites. Peiresc extracted some details from these maps using them to reconstruct the Roman locations of power as described in an ancient Latin text. A copy of a text by Peiresc to an anonymous (?) describing the difficulties of such a comparison between a modern map and ancient descriptions of Carthage's environment is extant in Ms Paris, BnF, Dupuy 663.[147]

In Ms Carpentras, Bibliothèque d'Inguimbertine 1809, the map of the Gulf of Smyrna can be found.[148] This map was meant to check an argument Peiresc wished to make about the interpretation of specific Greek, Latin, and French expressions by representing nature as exactly and faithfully as possible. In an incomplete copy of a letter written in 1633 to Henri de Valois, Peiresc informed him how he had come to this map and that he had given order to someone to prepare a more exact map of this gulf:

"Au rest Je vous enuoye vn peu de griffonement du Golphe & de la multiplicité des portz de Smyrne tel que l'ont peu desseigner des matelotz qui en sont reuenuz de plus fraische datte sur le credit de leur memoire et de l'Imagination quilz y en auoient retenüe. J'ay donné charge à dautres qui S'y en Vont en bref, d'en faire portraire vn autre sur les lieux plus exactement ..."[149]

The person whom he had given not only the order to produce a new map of the Gulf of Smyrna, but also rather precise instructions how to proceed, was the Minime Theophile Minuti. Peiresc described these particular instructions to Minuti in his letter to Valois telling him that he wanted his envoy to climb up diverse mountains or valleys more elevated than the gulf itself. The aim of this tour should be to recognize better not only the position and figure of places, but the proportion of their distances and the symmetry the gulf possibly showed. Peiresc hoped that this

---

continuées de siecle en siecle, avec la mesme erreur de plus de deux ou trois cents lieües de trop, ce qui est quasi incroyable si l'on ne le voyoit et si l'on ne le touchoit au doit, comme on fait à present."
[147] Ms Paris, BNF, Dupuy 663, ff 154a-155b.
[148] Ms Carpentras, Bibliothèque d'Inguimbertine, 1809, f 170a.
[149] ibid., f 169a.

new drawing would be more similar than the one he was sending to Valois to a vase of such a form as the ancient author Aristides had chosen to compare the gulf with:

"... et de monter pour cet effect sur diuerses montagnes ou Collines plus esleueés d'alentour pour mieux recongnoistre non seulement la Conformation & figure des lieux, mais à peu prez la proportion des distances, et <u>Symmetrie</u> quil y peult auoir, possible beaucoup <u>plus semblable que le Griffonement y Joint, à vn vase tel qu'Aristide auoit choisy pour le Comparer.</u>"[150]

In a letter to the brothers Dupuy from November 7, 1633, Peiresc confirmed that this "better drawing of the Gulf of Smyrna" had been made, but was not in his hands yet.[151]

Peiresc believed to have figured out that Aristides' form either had been that of a vase or of a cup or of a certain plate used for serving fruits, since he held it difficult to understand that a gulf with a number of ports could have had any relation or conformity to a vase with several spouts. To justify his assumption, Peiresc discussed and interpreted Greek, Latin, and French words referring to nature (sources of fountains or rivers) and to culture (cups and special plates or basins) in comparison with his observations of the spring areas of rivers in the Provence.

In his opinion, the Greek "krounois" and the Latin "salientes" - the mother sources of fountains or rivulets - corresponded only too well to what the clock-makers and other artisans called "goderons" with regard to the circumference of a plate or a little basin if one supposed that both, the Greek and the Latin word took on the specific meaning of sources of rivulets and rivers the majority of which went back to diverse veins and roots. The combination of these veins and roots could produce a river or a creek which was encompassed at its "head", i.e., its spring, by more or less smaller rivulets. The particular sources of these rivulets break the earth neighboring the mouth of the river and undermine the roundness of its borders making the river's source look like a set of small ports or semi-round water-basins resembling the form of the basin which is called "goderonné". This could be observed truly easily in the spring area of the river Argens near St. Maximin and several others which Peiresc had seen as long as such rivers did not spring off rocks of irregular figure which prevented the waters from gnawing the terrain according to their nature.

Two more times, Peiresc bolstered his argument by interpreting language. The Greek word "fiale" (bowl) Aristides used to describe an aspect of a gulf could only be taken to mean a cup or "escuella" the circumference of which was not purely circular but more like a vase or of such a figure which being filled with liquor appeared to be surrounded by many small ports or semi-round

---

[150] ibid., f 169a.
[151] Tamizey de Larroque 1890, vol. 2, p. 642.

(things) coming close to the figure of those which surrounded that gulf. The object which "we called in French commonly 'un godet' (a small bowl)" is what the ancients called "poculum" (goblet, pitcher). Peiresc admitted not to know whether the French word "goderons" which he earlier had argued to represent fairly well the meaning of the Greek "krounois" and the Latin "salientes" was derived as a sort of diminutif from "godet" since several small 'godetz' or 'goderons' brought together formed a greater 'godet goderonné', i.e., a bowl surrounded by 'goderons' or smaller 'godets'.

Goblets or pitchers of this form came from "Constantinople" which were very good to drink of because they did not have a turned over border as the plates or basins. That is why these Turkish goblets made from boiled leather beautifully painted and enriched by gilding represented much better the "poly-nozzled or 'goderonnées' phioles" than the plates or basins. Peiresc advised de Valois to have a look at some of them in the cabinets of curiosity of Paris where he believed they could be found without difficulty. There he could see for himself the likeness between the Turkish goblets when filled with water and a large port surrounded by many small ports.[152]

The subject must have aroused de Valois' curiosity since he answered Peiresc a brief fortnight later kissing him humbly the hands for the pencil drawing of the Gulf of Smyrna but rejecting all of Peiresc's ideas and arguments whether they concerned the conformity of the gulf's natural figure with the poly-nozzled vases referred to by Aristides or Peiresc's philological interpretations. With regard to the first point, de Valois remarked:

"Pour ce qui est du Crayon du Golphe de Smyrne quil vous à pleu m'enuoyer Je vous en baise humblement les mains mais Je n'y ay pas encores apperceu la Conformité & la ressamblance que luy donne Aristides auec ces vases polukrounois. Et pour vous parler franchement J'estimeroit sauf vostre correction que le mot de polukrounoiV s'entendroit mieux de plusieurs petitz tuyaulx qui estoient allentour de cez vases ornéz & enioliuéz, Ce que les anciens appelloient amblemata."[153]

He accepted Peiresc's interpretation of krounos as the mother source of fountains or creeks and gave as an example the name of a fountain devoted to Athena. He added that the Greek word also could mean a spout as "in Pollux and the Greek-Latin Glossary".[154] If the word, however, was used together with that of "fiale" (bowl) it could by no means in the world be interpreted as a "source" even if there was a "polukrouna pege" (a poly-nozzled spring). De Valois insisted that "polukrounois" with regard to bowls could only refer to spouts.[155] To take the blow out of his

---

[152] Ms Carpentras, Bibliothèque d'Inguimbertine, 1809, ff 169a-b.
[153] Ms Carpentras, Bibliothèque d'Inguimbertine, 1810, f 174a.
[154] ibid., f 174a.
[155] ibid., f 174a: "Il fault donc par necessité quil s'entende de tuyaux".

adversity, de Valois added that he believed nonetheless in Peiresc's information begging him not to take badly his deviating opinion and ensuring him that he always bowed his head to Peiresc's judgments.[156] These reassuring remarks also responded to Peiresc's own words of playing down his interest in the subject, his conjectures, and his arguments.[157]

Peiresc not only limited himself in this particular study to look at goblets from Istanbul and to think about languages, he also used his connections with North Africa to ask for more vases he could investigate. In a letter written March 22, 1633 to Osman d'Arcos, Peiresc informed his correspondent that he now had adopted a taste for all kinds of ancient vases or "escuellons" given that they were made from metal. He already possessed a good number mainly made from copper or silver. He wanted d'Arcos to buy him all he could acquire, even broken, as long as they could be restored to recognize their form and figure.[158] Although Peiresc did not explain to d'Arcos the reason for his sudden interest in such matters and although this letter was written seven months before the two others referring to the Gulf of Smyrna, his insistence upon form and figure seem to relate the three letters to each other.

---

[156] ibid., f 174a.
[157] Ms Carpentras, Bibliothèque d'Inguimbertine, 1809, f 169b.
[158] Tamizey de Larroque 1898, vol. 7, pp. 112-113: "Je suis maintenant entré en goust des Vases antiques ou Escuellons de toute sorte, pourveu qu'ils soint de metail, en ayant rassemblé un grand nombre de cuyvre, aulcuns mesmes d'argent, qui ne laissent pas d'estre bien asseurement antiques; s'il s'en desterroit par hazard de par de là, vous m'obligeriez grandement d'en faire achepter et retenir pour mon compte tout ce que vous en pourriez retenir commodement, encores qu'ils soint rompuz et fracassez, pourveu des pièces on puisse commodement reprendre la forme et figure des Vases; je ne les payerois pas pour cela moins volontiers, et vous fairay fort soigneusement rembourser des fraiz que vous y employerez."

Appendix

1. Ms 1874, Carpentras, Bibliothèque d'Inguimbertine

ff 361a-361b Peiresc an Celestine

f 361a Monr mon Reuerend P. la grande vertu et profonde Erudition de Monsr Golius vre <digne> frere luy a acquis et consequemment a tous les siens, et particulierement a ceux qui luy appartienent (so) de si prez, come uous faictes beaucoup plus d'Auys; et de seruiteurs, qui (so) uous ne pensés l'un et laultre, et le renom de vre pieté, et merite particulier ne luy en acquiert pas moings aussy bien qu'a uous. Cest pourquoy uous ne trouuerés pas estange sil uous plaict que sans que J'aye l'honeur (so) destre cogneu de uous Je me dispence comme Je faicts de uous offrir montres humble seruice par cette lre non quil ne uous fusse desia bien acquis; mais peut uous en metre (so) en notice, et uous Inuiter d'en disposer auec toute liberté et authorité. En quoy uous m'obligerés infiniment et receures de ma part toute sorte d'obeissance et de sincere correspondance qui pourra dependre de moy & de mon foible credit. Ce sera toutes et quant foys? il uous plairra (so) et ne sera jamais asses tost a mon gré; cepandant uous receurés auec la presente vne (so) petit pacquet lequel ma esté reccomandé de la part de Monsr Golius que Je n'ay pas deu laisser passer D'oultre moi? sans l'accompagner de ce mien petit compliment uous suppliant de l'agreer et de ne me point espargnes, si Jugés que J'aye aulcun moyen de uous donner des preuues de mon seruice pour les interets de Monsr vre frere ou pour les vres particuliers s'il se peult rien faire pour uous soit a Rome ou Jay quelques habitudes que Je uous offre de bon coeur soit en ce Royaulme ou bien sur les lieux mesmes ou uous estés ou je ne doubte pas que uous n'ayés des habitudes beaucoup meilleurs que moy, et plus de credit mais ce peu que J'ay (so) en puis auoir uous est tous desuoué au moindre clin doeil qu'il uous plaises m'en donner, et possible ne uous y sera til pas Inutil si uous en uoulés faire l'essay comme Je uous en supplie que si la commodité de me trouuer icy porté quasi au lieu d'entrepos le plus propre pour entretenir vre commerce auec Monsr vre frere uous peult seruer de rien, assurés uous que Je reputeray ce singuliere faueur d'en estre l'instrument et l'entretenir /361b/ ce? que uous my? trouuerés tousiours prest a contribuer toute sorte de Candeut et de bonne uolonté Ayant depuis peu enuoyé de mes liures MSS a Monsr Golius, et luy prins le soing de m'en faire transcrire des siens quand il a pressenty?, quils pouuoint estre de ma curiosité sans mesme Je l'en eusse requis tant il est honestes (so) et enclin a me uouloir du bien plus que Je n'en scauroys auoir merité, Aussy n'en seray Je Jamais ingrat si Je puis trouuer d'asses dignes moyens de m'enreuancher, et luy feray tusiours tres bonne part de touts mes liures plus rares quand il vouldra comme Je mose promettre de sa Deboneteté (so) qu'il ne me refuseroit pas la communication de quelques vns des siens au besoing ce qui faict que Je les ayme quasi tout aultant entre ses mains que

VII

44

je scauroys faire dans les miennes? propres. et quil peult fre (= faire) estre des miens comme des siens p. (?Pre, pro?) prés. Ce quil estoit bien experience (so) et uos fre P~~remier~~ auoir, a telle fin que Je uous trouuéz bien et me fre addresse d'aulcune chose pour la seruice et ...? vre frere seulm.t ou liures vous puissiéz estre tout? asseurer que J'auray tous les soings et mes possibles de les luy fre ... ... ? fidelem.t et le plus diligem.t que fre ce pourra. Et que vous en soyéz hors de regret?. Quoy que Je crois bien que vous pouues? prendre? d'autres meill. addresses à droictues? du Leuant en Hollande ou que se vous vouléz en prendre à Mars. Il ne vous y manque pas des iseulz (so) de la nation bien plus rapat. ? que mes de vous y seruire mais en tous cas Il ~~Il ne vous manque pas des gentz~~ me peult bien ...? peruins de vous fre ... ? de ma bonne volonté pour ...? qui peult escheoir en telle conieuct...?, que les autres addresses ne seroient pas à tous de Commodité que de Coustume. Que si vous rencontriéz ... despences que vous ne Jugeussiéz pas tant du goust et de la porteé de Mr vre frere que vous pouuéz faire bien recongnoistre, ceque vous poussiéz ...? que J'eusse aulcun moyen de les fre valloire, Je seray tres ayse de vous en auoir l obligation et quil vous plaist m'en laisser la p.ference sur les autres qui ne seront pas voz seruiteurs plus a/offreéz? que moy. Et feray punctuellem.t payer les sommes qui vous en pourréz ordonner sur moy auec tous les droicts distraist? et proffictz maritimes comme se lois? tous.rs pratiqm.t lors que d'autres de mes amys m'ont daigné rendu de pareilz offres. Qui ont tous.rs trouué de pardelà, asséz de credit? sur moy mais pour ce peine? commun? là, principalem.t en? ...? des liures dont le ...? est le ...? de tous. Que si vre Curiosité vous à porté à faire des obseruations des autres singularitéz que se peuuent rencontrer en cez pais là, comme sont les anciennes fabriques, les marbres et autres pierres escriptes, en Grecs en latin (so) ou autres langues orientales, mais soitent (so) de bonne antiquité. Et mesmes pour les animaulx estranges et les plantes non communes. Vous nous obligeriéz grandem.t si vous n'auiéz pas de ...? que nous en dicssions? quelque participation que nous messagerons? ains la discursion et d'estre dun requise et taschierons de les fre valloir selon leur? ... ... ?

Monsieur de Peiresc a Aix en prouence ce 5. Januier 1635.

Si vous rencontriéz la par hazard soit chéz les moynes Grecs ou les Dreuilz (so), quelque bon liure vn peu ancien d la musique non seulem.t en grec, mais en Arabe ou autre langue orientale, pricipalem.t de ceux? ou ils? pourroient ...? Construeéz quelques notes de l'ancienne musique. J'y employerois volontiers mon argent et vous aurois a? l'obligation de la Charitable assistance que vous m'y auriéz daigneé despoueoir?. Mr Gs vre frere m'a faict offrir ce quil en à tant d'Auicenne que d'un autre en Arabe, et J'en ay recouuré vn troisi. en Cayre en Arabe, aussy que Je luy ay enuoyé por le Conferer sur les siens, mais Il n y à pas decouuert? à tous cela asséz dequoy satisfre à nre appetit. Et J'entendz quil s'en trouue là quelques bons volumes en mains de quelque pbre. Grec bien jaloux de les monstrer qu'a des amys bien confidentz. Je voudrois sur tous vn Exemplre bien fidelem.t transcript et portraict sur quelque bien ancien Ms des trois hmynes de Dionysius qui soit dernier l'Aristides auec les notes parce quelles sont fort corrompues en tous les exemplre que nous en auons peu voir de par decà. vous feréz oeuure bien meritoire ...? le public si vous auiéz donné moyen de restaurer ce beau sens? de l'antiquité. y ayant des braues hommes qui trauaillent maint.nt en diuers lieux de l'Europe sir la restauration de la plus ...? musique des anciens Grecs et Romains.

2. Ms Dupuy 669, Paris, BnF

ff 75a-78a: A. Noel's relation of the tides and currents near Gibraltar
ff 83a-88a: Peiresc's survey of information about the tides, currents, and winds in the Mediterranean and Black seas

untranscribed, nice handwriting

3. Ms Carpentras, Bibliothèque d'Inguimbertine, 1821,

ff 279a-280b: Pour les marees, Et les vents, Et les Eclipses

Parceque l'on tient que les plus haultes Et plus apparantes MAREES du monde soient aux Costes de la Basse Bretagne, s'il y auoit moyen d'En faire obseruer bien excatement les periodes En cez lieux là, par des persones vn peu Curieuses de marquer non seulement les heures bien precises du flux Et de reflux ord.re Journalier, tant pour le montant Et pour le decours, que pour le plain, Et le plus bas, mais aussy la differance de Haulteur Et Bassesse du[dict] <flux Et> reflux, durant toute vne Lunaison pour le moings, Et sur tout durant les deux plus haultes Et plus basses marees de l'annee, voire s'il Estoit possible durant vne ou deux annees Entieres.

Joignant cez obseruations auec d'autres qui se font ailleurs, En mesme temps, Il s'En tireroit de meruelleux secours pour penetrer, sinon aux vrayes Causes, de ce flux Et reflux, au tout le moings, à la Cognoissance d'vne bonne partie de l'ordre que la nature y peult tenir.

Dont on a desia faict de bien rares descouuertes par diuerses obseruations dans la mer Mediterranee qui n'Est pas du tout exempte de ce flux Et reflux comme lon le Croid (sic) plus Communement.

Mais il fauldroit En mesme temps faire marquer la qualité des vents <soit secs ou humides> qui regnet sur la face de la mer ou de la terre, Et les periods de leurs commancements Et de leur fin, principalement de Ceulx qui sont bien Grands Et Impetueux, Et de Longue duree. pour En

VII

46

Examiner les periodes, Et les causes plus naturelles. qui ne se soient pas si incogneües si l'on y preuoit garde de plus prez que l'on ne faict.

A celle? fin de pouuoir juger de ce que peult Contribüer l'vn à l'autre par la vicissitude ord[inai]re des choses, En diuerses contrees Et saisons, Et par la Concurrence de diuers Euenments de plus ou moings grande Efficace ou par le manquement des choses mesmes, auxquelles bien souuent l'on <Impute Et> attribüe des Effects, qui n'En procedent nullement, quoy que l'on En aye voulu Croire Jusques a present.

Et ne fauldroit pas mesmes negliger, de faire obseruer si les troys Cauernes de la Coste du Sud de Belle isle ne sont point Cappables de produire quelque vent pour petit qu'il puisse Estre, selon la diuersité des saisons.

Ce qui se recognoistrà principalement En Hiuer pendant la plus grand froid, si l'on en void sortir de la vappeur espassie en forme de fumee, comme la respiration des hommes se rend visible en ce temps là, bien que imperceptible à noz ieulx tout le reste de l'annee.

Et se pourà Encores plus sensiblement recognoistre En faisant ~~fermer~~ boucher les ouuertures desd[ictes] cauernes, Et y laissant seulement quelque petit soubspirail par ou l'on puisse faire sortir l'air Enfermé, Et le voir Couuertir En Vent sensible En sortant.

Mais il En fault faire l'Espreuue à diuerses foys, Et a diuerses heures Et saisons, pour recognoistre lesquelles sont plus sortables, et plus conformes, à la disposition naturelle, de paroistre plus ou moings fortement Et plustost à vne heur de la nuict ou du Jour qu'à vne autre. S'En Estant trouué En des Cauernes de Prouence, qui ont des heures Certaines de leur naissance vne fois Chasque nuict, et de leur dureé vniforme journellement durant des moys Entiers.

Si ce n'Est quand d'autres plus grands vents regnent au dehors, qui en font <cesser ou> changer les Effects, si sensiblement Et apparement, qu'il s'En fit de tres belles consequances Et notices, de la Chose du monde quasi la plus Incogneüe, pour estre inuisible comm'il est.

Car de mesmes que plusieurs fontaines font vn ruisseau Et plusieurs ruisseaux vne Riuiere, Et qu'vne pluye faict couller plusieurs Gouttieres de diuers toicts En mesme temps, par la Cheutte d'vne mesme quantité de matiere d'Eau, Cappable de former tout d'vn Coup de Grands torrents,

Ainsin plusieurs Cauernes produisent diuers petits ruisseaux de vents En certaines vallees, qui se Joignant et acquierent assez de force pour aller des lieües Entieres, Et quelque foys assez loing dans la mer, d'ou se forment les petits vents de terre, que les mariniers trouuent En certain temps, quasi à Couuersture de Chascune Vallee qui abouttit au bord dela mer.

Mais sur tout il fault faire obseruer se (sic) le flux des Marees, Et particulierment des plus grandes, ne vient pas plus tost d'vn Costé d'autre <que d'vn autre>. Et particulierement s'il ne vient pas du Septentrion plus Communement qu'il ne paroit d'y retourner, prinipalement Entre l'Angleterre et la france sur la poincte plus aduancee, vers l'isle d'OVISSANT. ou aulcuns disent que la mer à vne pente <ou Courant> perpetuelle trez apparante versle midy, sans retourner en arriere que fort imperceptiblement. Ce qui auroit bien de besoing d'estre verifié sur les lieux en diuers temps et en diuerses saisons.

Cez bons Peres capucins et autres persones bien intentionnes vers le public qui sont employees (sic) en cez missions estrangeres, tant de Canada, et de Terre neufue que de la Coste de la Guinee, pourroient tenir des petits Journaulx, des marees et des vents, qui seroient d'vne merueilleuse vtilite dans la Comparaison des vnes aux autres et de la differance des lieux en mesme temps, et des retardement ou anticipations des effects que l'on ... [illisible - S. B.] peut attendre.

mais il fauldroit les faire accoustumer à bien marquer les heures seurement, par quelque obseuation de la haulteur du soleil au Jour, ou de la haulteur de quelque Estoille fixe la nuict de peur que les horologes communes ne <les> trompent.

Et qu'ils prinsent des habitudes à pouuoir obseruer la haulteur du Pole des lieux ou ils se trouueront resider, par l'obseruaion de la haulteur du soleil à l'heure du midy et peu au parauant et aprez, et de quelques Estoilles fixes.

Que s'il y auoit moyen de les disposer à obseruer quelques ecclipses, ou renontres du corps de la Lune auec quelque estoille fixe, com'il arriue assez souuent. Il s'en tireroit d'autres bien grands aduantages, pour regler la vray situation desdz. lieux, et et (so) les Consequances qui se peuuent tirer des obseruations qui s'y seroit faictes ou qui s'y feront à l'aduenir.

L'on a commancé d'en faire obseruer vne au Leuant du moys d'Aoust dernier, tant au Cayre, qu'en Alep, Et de les faire Comparer, à ce qui s'en est remarqué en mesme temps à Rome et Naples, et ailleurs, d'ou il s'est trouué de quouy conuaincre? de faulx toutes les Cartes, d'vne longue distance de Marseille en Leuant, de plus d'vn tiers du Chemin qu'il y à effectiuement.

VII

4. Ms 1821 Carpentras, Bibliothèque Inguimbertine

ff 127a-b Peiresc
Anmerkung Peiresc: 1634. Juin, Juillet
FLVX ET REFLVX COVRANTE D'AFRIQUE

LE COVRANT DE LA MER NOIRE penetre l'Hellespont Et l'Archipelago Et trauerse toute la mediterranee Jusques aux Sirtes de Lybie. audroict de la Candie, au Golfe du Cap St. André, Et de celuy de Spac Et de la ville du Souchon, que les Grenadins ont entreprins dhabiter.

Il y a là des bas fonds Et bancs de sable que la mer faict mouuoir tantost d'vn Costé tantost de l'autre, auec telle violence, que parfoys vn Coup de mer Jetterà soisante quintaulx de sables dans vn nauire, ce qui Est bien dangereux.

Dans le port ou petit Golfe le flux Et reflux de la mer y Est fort reglé de six En six heures, Et y a de plus haultes marees, Et de plus basses, qui laissent à sec des nauires En des lieux ou d'ord.re ils peuuent Estre En basse maree.

De Thunis à l'Entree de ce Golfo de Spac n'y a que 150. Milles,

Le Patron Pascal m'a asseure des periodes de ce flux Et Reflux, Et le vice Consul d'Algers p<ar?> Mr. Viaz de ces Coups de mer qui Jettent tant de sable. Et touts deux estoient d'accord qu'il y a plus frequemment vne Corrente de ponant vers le Leuant En la Coste Barbarie, depuis Algers Jusques à ce Cap de Spac, que de Leuant En ponant, ou il fault que ce fo...? des pro<g>nostics? de vents contraires quand la mer va de maree contraire, au chemin plus commun du Leuant au ponant.

M.r LE CHEVALLIER DE MONTMEIAN qui à Esté troys ans Esclaue En Barbarie m'a asseuré, que dans l'Embouchure de la riuiere qui sert de port aux Galeres de Bezerti, il a veu plusieurs foys le reflux de six En six heures fort reglement, Et que les Galeres passent sur le petit destroict, pendant la haulté maree, Et y trouuent neantmoings si peu d'eau qu'elles sont Constraintes de passer quasi toutes riuès? Et d'aller prendre leur chargement hors de l'Embouchure de le port (so) /127b/ qui peult auoir dix milles d'Estendüe dans la terre ferme En longueur au long de la riuiere, car la largeur n'Estans proportionnee a Cela. Et me dict de plus auoir apprins des Esclaues desdz. galeres, Et de plusieurs autres persones qui faisoient plus Continuelle residance dans le port là, que c'estoit chose Indubitable que la reciprocation de ce flux Et reflux dans ce port de six En six heures, Et que l'Eau y montoit par foys de plus de quattre pieds de hault Et descendoit à proportion. Et que le flux se rendoit apparant Jusques au fonds dud. port, à dix milles de son

Emboucheure. Il n'auoit rien obseruer de semblable à l'Emboucheure de la Goulette, Et de l'Estang de Tunis, Et de Carthage.

5. Ms 1821, Carpentras, Bibliothèque d'Inguimbertine

maps of of the Gulf of Carthago/Tunis

I did not add the three larger maps to the appendix since it is too time-consuming to glue all their separate pages 20 times or so together. You can have a look at them at the wall besides my room. I will bring them also to the seminar.

6. Ms 1809, Carpentras, Bibliothèque d'Inguimbertine

ff 182a-184b (Peiresc an de la Hoguette)
ohne Anfang

182a ... Au reste vous auez fort bien Jugé que ce mont de Sem nest pas loing de la mer rouge Car noz marseillois nous disent auoir apprins de la bouche de memes (so) Bassa du Suachem dont la demeure estoit au bord de la mer rouge/que de ce mesme lieu Ilz en voyoient la fumee et les flammes. ne doubtant pas que le voysinage de la mer ne Contribue quelques dispositions a celz/telz? enbrasementz et a leur dureé puisque nous voyons, que l'eau de la fontainne ardente, estant conduitte sur la terre disposeé au feu, y faict conceuoir les flammes et leur (l'eau?) sur de base, comme si les flammes penetroient a trauers de l'eau, pour former vne pyramide de feu ou de flamme sur ceste eau, sans que l'eau courrint? de challeur apparauent?. non plus que les eaux ne seruent pas à esteindre le feu Grecs vis a Cause de la Camphora?, et autres matieres grasses et bitumineuses, que se voyent communement à l'entour de cez grandes fournaises ongueulles de feu sousterrain, et qui font opiniastre(r)? sil se peut dire, le feu, a brusler, quand Il s'y est vne foys attacheé leur legereté? les faisant surnager, quand cez matieres sont iecteéssur vn grand fondz d'eau, et leur graisse empeschant que l'eau ne peu (so) estre, ou s'incorpore(r) dans la substance d'icelles, auquel cas elle sembleroit pouuoir plus commodement estendre les flammes y attacheés. Or y Joignant ceste seicheresse que vous auéz obserueé aux riuages de la mer, la disposition y est tousiours tant plus grande à conceuoir le feu Mais ce que J'y trouue le plus estrange, est de voir que le feu puisse venir de si profond, comme Il fault quil vienne, puis quil a faict esleuer des Isles au milieu de la mer, et faict ouurir des gueulles de feu au minton? dicelles, comme grarrure? d'aulcunes de celles de la mer de Naples aussy bien que de celle de la Grece Car Il faudroit presupposer quil eusse prins la naissance dans les entrailles du Mont Ætna, ou du mont vesuue, qui n'en sont guieres

VII

50

moins esloignéz, l'ung que l'autre, Et sembleroient Induire Je ne scay quelle necessité de Correspondance de l'on à lautre, par dessoubz le lict de la mer, puis que dans polluy? se nomment les plus? brulantes du Wulcan/ et de Stromboly. Et du faict de? la plus part des sources d'eaux chaudes tant en ceste ville qu'ailleurs ordiniers? lieux de ma congnoiss. Ilz semblent quilz ayent leur naissance directement de bas en hautz restant? derriers? le centre de la terre, et tirant a la surface d'icelle, au lieu que les autres sources froides; ont? leurs deriuations de hault en bas, ou laterales Et Je pense que ce soit pour cela, que noz eaux chaudes ... villes ont perdu? leur primitif degré de challeur par la meslange de quelques autres froides sans que depuis le temps de Strabon/182b/ qui en à remarqué l'alteration; on ayt Jamais peu empescher ceste melange parue quelle se faict trop proffond en terre, pour y pouuoir aller mattre Curieux et empeschent qui y seroit necessaire. Estant bien certain que leur Challeur prouient du feu qui est par dessoubz ainsy quil s'est veriffié? aux termes de Pozzuolo à Cherdroict? desquelz s'ouurit vne gueule? de feu soubzterrain au temps du pape Paul III. dont les baueruces? f...? vne montagne bien haulte dans 24 heures laq.lle J'ay veue? Jusques au Sommet ou Il est Demeuré vne forme de grand Theatre? ou de Chauderon? dont la gueule sest resonneé? par le Croublent/Croulent? des terres de cà et de la que les pluyes y ont trouueés. Le pic de Temerse? dans l'une des Canaries que l'on tient des plus haultes montagnes du monde semble auoir esté formé dans le milieu de l'ocean par de semblables embrasemenz, dont la gueule est encores ouuerte sans brusler toutesfois et appelleé la Caldara del diauolo, à cause que si lon y Jette des pierres, elles font vn bruict qui resonne et retentie? comme si elles tomboient sur des Chauderons? à cause des metaulx qui y ont esté fonduz et brusléz en sorte? que possible ne sont ilz plus cappables de se refondre/refoudre? or comme dans ces puis Septentrionaux et au milieu des vndes Il y a des montaignes bruslantes aultant et plus normalle? ...? que les nostres. et d'autres dans le feu est cessé, comme on dict du trou de St. patric en hibernie, et comme auoit esté long temps nostre vesuue, Il y en à encor ce dict vn, dans l'amerique Et y en à ou/du? dauantage dans la Grec quil ny en à pntilmt.? comment l'Innondu? de Sodom et Gomora, nà laissé que des marques fumestes? de ce quil y à rauagé autresfois. de lautre costé mesme de la mer rouge, qui est à l'orient prez du mont de Sinai, Il y à des bains Chaudz en la ville de Medina Nebie?, et al Tor, et dict on que prez de la Meque Il y eu cez années dernieres du vent pestifer, venu dessoubz terre qui tua vn nombre Infinis de personnes et de Chameaux dont estoit composeé la Carauane, Ce qui pourroit Induire aussy Je ne sçay quelle Correspondance de là au mont de Sem, par dessoubz lad. mer rouge, si tant est que la matiere ou s'entretiennent cez feux sousterrains soit assez profoinde dans la terre pour prendre quelque correspondance d'vn lieu à l'autre par dessoubz la mer rouge, Comm'il semble quil y en ayt du Mont Æthna au Vesuue et aux autres lieux d'autour de pozzuolo aussy bien qu'auec le Vulcan et le Strombole (so?) Car encores que la summission? de temps? fasse d'aullcunesfois? cesser les embrasemenz appartenant? à l'exterieur, et combler les gueulles et ouuertures ie n'estime? pas pourtant quele (so) se cesse par dedans puis qu'on le void rallumer de temps en temps. estant bien certain qu'encor que le monte (so) uour? de Pottulo, n'ayt pas bruslé depuis que sa gueulle se fust refermeé/refumeé? le feu n'en peut pas estee? acheué d'esteindre au fondz puis que la fumeur/fumee? soit encores à la Solfatroza?, et á la fumarola qui en sont si proches. et pense bien que le passage ou la communication de l'un de cez lieux à autre se peult embarasser et cloire? pour quelque temps par les tremblementz de terre et croullementz (so) des rochers et des terres aussy bien que les gueulles mais Je doubte que/183a/que la disposition n'y puisse demeurer de se r'ouurir plus en des lieux qu'en d'autre. Et ne sçay s'il ne se pourroit faire naturellemnt (quelque difficulté que nous ayons à le concepuoir) que comme au bord de la mer, et bien auant dans les ondes erassez/ecassez? loing dudict bord. le feu a esté capable de pousser des montaignes et des Isles nouuelles, ou Il l'ouuroit des souspivaulx/ souspiraulx? du feu sousterrain embrasé par dessoubz la mer. Il se soit poussé de semblables montaignes ou enleueures pardedans le fondz de la mer d'entre la Sicile et de la Syrie que ne soient (so) pas arriueés asséz hault pour paroistre sur le niueau des ondes marines, et pour? s'entr'ouurir comme les autres lesq.lles estant heurteés par le gros de la mer agiteés du Siroc soient Cappables d'Imprimer quelque mouuemt. et Compression dans les plus profondes entraillez de cez fournaises bruslantes en sorte qu'elles en irritent le bruict & en augmentans? la fiumeé (so) et les flammes à leur gueulle tantes et quantesfois que le vent Syroc se met sus et les foussent paroistre si long temps à laduance comme l'on dict, Car les mariniers n'en ont point de signes plus Certains que ceux là ne disent ilz, et c'estoit fondeé l'ancienne fables du regne d'Æole sur les ventz, s'il pouuoit eu predire certainement quelques vns par telz signes de ces? montaignes bruslantes, la cessation desquelz pouuoit produire la succession des ventz Contraire selon la Commune vicissitude des chose de ce monde Que s'il pouuoit estre loysible de supposer vne Communication soubsterrain aussy bien du Mont Ætna en ceux de la grece et de la palestine qui ont bruslés ou produit des eaux chaudes, et auec ces autres d'autour de la mer rouge, supposant aussy que telz feux en fondant cez matieres grasse et bytumineuses se forment vne Crouste ou vne espece de bource? ou de fourneau capable de soustenir l'eau marine et de l'empescher d'entrer dans cez Cauernes enflammeés, comme la Charge et froideur de l'eau pourroit empescher ce feu de p...? telle crouste si ce n'est par quelque accident extraord.re Il seroit bien plus facile de Comprendre et de Concepuoir que la mer mediterraneé se trouuant agiteé du costé de la Syrie et porteé vers la Sicile fit vne si grande charge sur cez antres ou Cauernes enflammeés couuertes de la mer quelle y fist asséz de Compression pour en exprimer la fumeé et les flammes et la bruict extraord.re qui procede le vent Syroc de Certain temps plus ou moins long selon que le vent est plus pu moins fort et Impetueux Car ce heure? de la mer trouuant des matieres obeissantes en quelque façon pour la melasse? ou graisse d'icelles, et comprimer le viude sousterrain en faict sortir comme par vne syringe la fumeé et les flammes et le bruict; par les gueulles du mont Ætna, et de ceux du vulcan et de stromboli et autres, dont la fumeé couure Incontinant? la mer et est porteé par le Syroc Subsequent Jusques à nostre Coste de prouence vers froins et les Isles dyeres Jusques ou, elle conserue sa puanteur et noirceur, mais elle ne se sent pas plus auant, à cause que la Coste se tourne et deslire au Septentrion de là deshors? dont J'ay esté vne foys en ma vie tesmoing oculaire estant

VII

a Roqiebiant? prez de froins, et en contractay vne maladie de vnze mois, laquelle me rendit? Curieux d'en examiner les causes./183b/ <sans>? estre trop curieusement. Car Considerant que dans la Holande sur le Chariot a voille Et allant aussy viste que le vent puis quil n'y est aps Sensible a l'atouchement, ains Seulement par l'ouye du bruict & par la veüe du Sable quil charrie en l'air on faict 14 leües (so) par heure a peu préz come (so) vn bon vent en pouppe, il falloit bien du temps au? vent Syroc S'il Commence a se iettér (so) de la terre dans la mer, audroict de la Syrie pour arriuer en Sicile, com'il Se voy d'ailleurs Et y peust ? bien arriuer aussy tard Comme om void En telles occasions Et Estre preuenu par le feu qui a ses mouuement beaucoup plus vistes & plus Soudains que? le Simple vent, Et qui à vn chemin possible plus Court par dessoubz la Conuexité de la mer. Et quand mesmes on feroit difficulté d'admettre Cette Crouste bithumineuse y obeyssante ou susceptible de Compression Je ne sçay s'il ne se pourroit poinct supposé quelque Chose d'approchant à cela pour les rochers les plus durs, Sy on peust aduoüer que les Cauernes soient bien grandes Et bien vastes. Car en ce Cas Elles sont succeptibles (so) de quelque compression Et obeissance à vne Grosse Charge Extraord.re Comme elle est (l'est?) quand le vent l'agite. Cequi se veriffie ai mouuement sensible que Jay veu a Paris du Clocher de St. Jacque de la Bocherie quand les Grosses cloches sonnent, bien que ce soit vne Tour qarree? assez grosse & assez massiue dont le mouuement est imperceptible (so) En bas vers les fondements, mais en hault il est Sy Sensible qu'un (so) a peine de se tenir de bout sur la tarasse (so) qui est au Sommet de la Tour. Jy fut mené pour voir cette merueille par feu Monsieur le Feure precepteur du Roy à present heuresement reinant, Et y ay mene l'Eminnentissime Cardinal Bagny, Et plusieurs autres personnes d'importance qui ne trouuoient pas cela moins extraord.re que de voir ceste pierre prope à Esmeraldre? comme des? Quiaes/Queues? laquelle vient des Indes, Et laquelles peult se loyer ? Et Pbeyr iusques à certaine proportion & portion d'un cercle, selon sa longueur? plus ou moins grande. Le mouuement aux choses les plus solides ne vous estantz imperceptible (so) que pour trop proche du centre comme en ceste Tour l'Esloignement du Centre le rend sy preceptible (so) Comme il estant Sommet. vous aurez bien de quoy vous mocquer de moy, que ie vous ote entretenir de telles reueries? de filbureux mais scay bien pourtant que vous ne laisserez pas de me pardonnér?, tout cela comme sy ie vous desois? la pensée qui me vint a l'aduis de l'Embrasemt du Vesuue, ceque la mer s'estoit abaisseé Jusques dans le port de Naples en que les Galleres Et les barques cy touchoient le fonds en quelques endroictz. à scauoir que les grand Coups de? bruicts comme du Tonnere, qui carsoient de sy grands tremblements de terre pouueroient auoir faict leffect de la Saucsisse? Et auoir faict entroüir en quelque endroict des racines du veslune? Et en y loulty? assez grande Cantilte? deau pour abbaissér le Niueau de la mer Jusques aupoinct quil le fust, mais que le fardeau? de la Montaigne, layant faict retombé Sur le mesme lieu/184a/ dont Elle auoit este Elleuer ou arracheé, s'estoit en fin rebousche, par la qualitté grasse de ces matiers bythumineuses, que le vilence (so) du feu y pouuoit opposér puis quil y en auoit sy grande quantittés quil en vomissoit par le plus hault de la Gueulle de la Montaigne Et quil en poussoit de sy

VII

53

grosses riuieres & ruisseaux bruslantes Et Courant par fois de bien largezCampagnes Comme vn lac de feu Et qui Scayt Sy les eaux pareillement bruslantes ou bouillantes que la montaigne vomit par diuerses ouuertures laterales, qui fermerent des Torrents lesquelz firent des grands rauagés Et Creuements des terres, Et noyerent des grandes Campagnes revindrent par de ces eaux Englouttics de Ceste maniere Comme des Riuieres des fourneés/tourneés a ce qu'on presuppose. Car bien que les tremblements de terre, Et les fois que le Niueau de la mer s'abbaissà de la Sirte. Et puis ne tarda guieres de receuoir à Sa premiere hauteur à Cause que la Surfasse (so) de la mer voisine auoit de quoy fournir & Suppléer bien tost tout ce qui en pouuoit auoir esté Engloutty. Voire ie ne Scay Sy les Coquellages Et plantes & fruicts maritimes qui se trouuent à certains Niueaux quasy de Toutes les Montaignes de Prouence Et qui nous contraignent d'aduouer que le Niueau de la Mer Est autrefois montent (so) iusques là, bien quil soit a vne hauteur fort Considerable par dessus le Niueau de la mer d'a present. Ne pourroit poinct faire Comprendre que les Embrasement Soubzterrains fument auoir engloutty & tiré ailleurs, toutte leau qui y manque a present d'vn niueau à l'autre qui est de plus de cent toises de heuteur ou de differance. Mais enfin ieu? diray trop pardonnez moy Je vous supplie Tres humblement, Monsieur, Et faisei ? la fauour (so) de me renuoyer ceste lettre Originellement quand vous y auez vne fois ietté la Veüe, afin quil n'en demeure rien Car Jaurois grande honte quelle feust veüe par dautres que vous, que pouuez excusér & pardonnér mes fautes Et impertinences, parce que vous me tenez pour vostre seruiteur Comme ie suis de bon Coeur. Nous auons en icy de nouueau liure Imprimé En Angleterre de Veritate, Et renetaon.? d'vn homme qui n'est pas du Commun Et crois bien que vous lauez veu, ou que vous ne tarderez pas ayant les bonnes Correspondances que vous auez en ce pays là. dont il est sorty despuis peu Encor vne belle piece de St. Clement pape disciple de St. Pol aux Corinthiens, Extraicte d'vn Exemplaire Escrit enuiron le temps du Conscile (so) de Nice, dont est faicté (so) mention En plusieurs des St. peres Grecs mais elle estoit perdue despuis fort long temps Surquoy Monsieur ie finiray demeurant Monsieur Vostre très humble & tres obeissant Seruiteur ...? ce 6 Septembre 1633

Le honneur de la presente vous parlera d'vn tres bonnes lhomme que nous auons icy qui meriteroit bien de lEmploy? Si l'occasion. S'en/184b/presente pour la forte des Canons du Roy Car il excelle en ce mestier Et Jentends que vous y auez maintenant du pouuoir aultant pour le moings comme il faut pour cela Et pour beaucoup plus puis que la Charge de Grand Me. Est passeé En Sy bonnes mains.

7. Ms 1821, Carpentras, Bibliothèque d'Inguimbertine

ff 198a-b: Peiresc's notes on vulcanic activities and their interpretations
f 219a: Peiresc's notes on some astronomical observations and their interpretation

VII

8. Ms 1774, Carpentras, Bibliothèque d'Inguimbertine

ff 182a-183b, 193b-194b, 195b: Extracts of Ahmad of Tunis' "Geography"

only partly transcribed in my paper; not a too nice handwriting

9. Ms 1831, Carpentras, Bibliothèque d'Inguimbertine

maps of Carthago and the respective coast

10. Ms 1809, Carpentras, Bibliothèque Inguimbertine

ff 169a-171a (Peiresc an de Valois)
Note by: <FIA>LE POLUKROUNOIS

without beginning

Au reste Je vous enuoye vn peu de griffonnemt. du Golphe & de la multiplicité des portz de Smyrne tel que l'ont peu desseigner des matelotz qui en sont reuenuz de plus fraische datte sur le credit de leur memoire et de l'Imagination quilz y en auoient retenüe. J'ay donné charge à dautres qui S'y en Vont en bref, d'en faire portraire vn autre sur les lieux plsu exactemt. et de monter pour cet effect sur diuerses montagnes ou Collines plus esleueés d'alentour pour mieux recongnoistre non seulmt. la Conformation & figure des lieux, mais à peu prez la proportion des distances, et Symmetrie quil y peult auoir, possible baucoup plus semblable que le Griffonemt. y Joint, à vn vase tel qu'Aristide auoit choisy pour le Comparer. Que J'auois creu pouuoir estre d'un vase, Tasse, ou bassin goderonné comme l'n faict communemt. les platz à seruir de fruictz Car Il est malaisé de comprendre, qu'un Port ou vn Goulphe de plusieurs portz aye peu auoir aulcune relation ou conformité à vn vase qui fust accompagne de plusieurs tuyaux Et les mots par lesquelz les Grecz nommoient krounouV (so), Ce que les Latins Salientes, les meres sources des fontaines & ruisseaux, Quadrent ? fort bien à ce que les Orpheures & autres artisantz appellent Goderons, a la Circonference d'un plat ou d'un petit bassin, supposé que l'un & l'autre mot Grec & Latin Soient prins en la propre Signification des sources des ruisseaux. & des riuieres, la plus part desquelles puiennent de diuerses veynes & surgeons. l'assemblage desquelz est Capable de former vne riuiere & ruisseau enuironné en Sa teste de plus ou moins grand nombre de moindres ruisseaux dont les particulieres sources /169b/breschent la terre qui borde la teste de la riuiere qui plus qui moi<ns>? et rompantz la rondeur de ce bord par leur enfoncemt. dans le terrain, forment la representation de diuers petitz portz ou demy rondz pleins d'eau <&>? la mesme figure des bassins qoderonnéz (so). Ce qui se void fort naifuement represente en la <u>Source de nostre Riuiere d'Argens</u> prez de St.? Maximin & en plusieurs autres que J'ay veües, quand elles ne viennent pas de rochers de forme irreguliere, qui ne laissent pas agir les eaux, selon leur nature de ronger le terrain d'ou elles sortent. Et le mot <u>de Fialh</u>, dont se sert Aristide, monstre bien, puis quil est <u>comparé à l'aspect d'un Golphe</u> de mer quil ne peut estre prins en cet endroict là que pour vne Tasse ou escuella (so) dont la Circonference soit consideréé non puremt. Circulaire mais comme <u>faicte en rose</u> (SO, STATT VASE?) ou en telle figure, qu'estant pleine de liqueur elle semble enuironneé de diuerz petitz portz, ou demy rondz approchant de la figure de ceux qui enuironnoient ce Goulphe; Et d'aultant que nous appellons communement en langue françoise <u>vn godet</u>, Ce que les anciens appelloient <u>poculum</u>, Je ne sçay si le mot de <u>Goderon</u> ne seroit point venu de quelque allusion ou diminutif de Godet, Comme si plus.rs petitz Godetz, ou Goderons assembléz, formoient vn plus grand godet goderonné, ou bien enuironné de goderons ou de petitz godetz. Il en vient de Constantinople de trezbeaux de ceste forme là, qui ne sont que le cuir bouilly, mais si bien peintz & enrichiz de doreures, quilz sont excellentz & fort commodes pour la boisson, par ce qu'ilz n'ont pas de bord r'abbatre comme les plats & les bassins, & les fruictiers, & representent mieux ces <u>phioles Polycronnes ou goderonneés</u>. Ne doubtanz pas qu'il ne s'en trouue plus.rs dans les Cabinetz des Curieux à Paris, ou vous prendréz plaisir de voir la grande conformité qu'ilz ont auec vng grand port enuironné de plusieurs petitz portz quand elles sont remplies d'eau: Entre les Curiositéz de la maison de <u>Montmorrency</u> qui ont esté vendües depuis peu, J'entendz quil y en auoit <u>vne d'Agathe</u> qui s'est vendüe à plus.rs orpheures 5. ou 600 ... (livres?) laquelle estoit de ceste forme là. Mais Je ne sçay Si vous ne trouueréz point mauuaise /170a unfoliiert - Zeichnung des Golfs von Smyrna: ASMIEROV - so); 170b gibt es nicht; 171a/ la longuer & confusion de ce chetif discours, que ie m'aurois pas faict si libremt. ne si confidemmt. à vn autre que vous, qui me tesmoignéz tant de cordialle affection, que Je me prometz l'excuse & le pardon de tous les manquemtz. que ie sçaurois faire, & que Je vous supplie de m'octroyer s'il vous plaist. Et de mettre à part parmy vos dignes estudes ce que vous obserueréz de plus extraord.re concernant la figure des vases, et de leurs ornementz & enrichissemtz, principalemt. dans les Autheurs Grecs, Surquoy possible auray ie le moyen quelque Jour de vous desduire quelque autre resuerie aussy pardonnable que celle cy, mais commandez moy Je vous supplie en toute authorité &cs. a Aix ce 6 Nouemb. 1633.

VII

11. Ms 1810, Carpentras, Bibliothèque Inguimbertine

f 174a (de Valois an Peiresc)
Anmerkungen von Peiresc: 1633 22. Nouembre VALOYS
POLUKROUNOIS

Coppie de lre escripte a Monsr de peiresc par le Sr. de Valoys de Paris le 22. Nou. 1633

(without beginning and end)

Pour ce qui est du Crayon du Golphe de Smyrne quil vous à pleu m'enuoyer Je vous en baise humblemt. les mains mais Je n'y ay pas encores apperceu la Conformité & la ressemblance que luy donne Aristides auec ces vases polukrounois. Et pour vous parler franchemt. J'estimerois sauf vostre correction que le mot de polukrounoiV s'entendroit mieux de plusieurs petitz tuyaulx qui estoient allentour de cez vases ornéz & enioliuéz, Ce que les anciens appelloient amblemata. Ce la mot de krounos se peult prendre vrayemt. en deux façons, tant pour les meres sources des fontaines comme vous le prenéz, d'ou est appelleé vne fontaine à Athenis enneakrounos (sic) par ce que c'estoit vne fontaine amassee de q. petites sources, ou bien Il se prend pour vn Tuyau comme dans Pollux & dans le Glossaire grec latin mais ce mot estant Joint auec vne tasse polukrounos fiale (sic), Il ne se peult entendre en façon du monde d'une Source, bien si il y auoit polukrounos pege (sic). Il fault donc par necessité quil s'entende de tuyaux. J'en croiray neantmoins vostre aduis, Et vous prie bien fort de ne trouuer pas mauuais que ie vous descouure ainsy libremt. mon petit Jugemt, lequel Je soubmetz tres volontiers a vostre Censure. Et doresnauant s'il se presente quelque chose de cette matiere Je vous le communiqueray auec la mesme liberté pour en apprendre vostre Jugement auquel Je deffere Infiniemt.

VIII

Astronomy a Temptation? On Early Modern Encounters across the Mediterranean Sea

The question of the conference whether astronomy turned during the early modern period into a discipline providing other areas of intellectual enterprise with guidance can be looked at, from my point of view, from six different angles, if not more. The aspect which comes to mind most quickly is model building and the epistemological as well as ontological status of models. The immediate follow-up concerns methods of producing new results, new claims, and new evidence. A third aspect can be seen in the tools needed for making the methods work as well as the impact of these tools on the methods and the models. A fourth point relates to the patterns used for making innovations acceptable and winning opponents over. As a fifth aspect we may discuss the question whether there was a new diversification of the field of practitioners of astronomy and whether this diversification was followed suit in other disciplines. Finally, the usage of parts of observational practice, reasoning, modeling, questioning, lobbying, and instrumentation from astronomy in other disciplines or even other spheres of culture – if it takes place – can be taken as a measure for reputation and attraction and hence may provide people with guidance for extra-scholarly activities such as having fun, spending leisure time in an exciting manner or promoting religious goals. It is this last aspect that motivated the choice of the title of my paper. The field of new instruments and new designs of longer known types induced Jesuits in the Ottoman Empire to use them as a means to tempt Orthodox Greek and Jewish youngsters into closer contact with Catholics, their beliefs, and rituals. Sighting tubes of various sizes and types tempted French scholarly travelers, Venetian merchants, and English ambassadorial ladies to break rules of good behavior and spy in the backyards of those secluded Oriental houses hoping to get a glimpse on the members of the harem or any other deliciously scandalous scene.[1]

---

[1] An example is Balthasar de Monconys who watched in 1648 in Pera at least twice an Ottoman backyard with a telescope and once the sultan

In the same time, they wrote with utter disdain that the Ottoman sultans, in particular the allegedly mad Ibrahim who is described as having cared for nothing else than his pleasures and war, used the very same instruments for the very same purposes.[2] It is quite remarkable that the new astronomical, mathematical, and botanical instruments arrived within a very short time in the Middle East and were some decades later already objects of trade in the Kashmir mountains.[3] One traveler, the Italian nobleman Pietro della Valle, who wrote an amazing eulogy of Shah 'Abbas I after his return to Rome, even claimed that European embassies not only brought telescopes and other astronomical instruments as gifts to the Safavid court between 1617 and 1622, but also a piece which he called "microscope".[4] In della Valle's eyes, there was obviously a mutual relationship between the new exciting instruments and the valiant Safavid shah, the new Hercules, as della Valle praised him – the one ennobled the other.[5]

Hence, it is no exaggeration to claim that within the sphere of cross-cultural encounters in astronomy between people from various

---

himself in his private rooms (June 16: l'apresdisné ie vis le G. S. [Grand Seigneur, S. Brentjes] souper dans son lit, mangeant baucoup & des deux mains auidement, gesticulant ou parlant par signes, puissant de bout dans vn pot d'argent). Iovrnal des Voyages de Monsievr de Monconys 1665, pp. 389-390, 393.

[2] Mss Paris, BnF, fr 13039, f 26b; Paris, BnF, Dupuy 18, ff 37a, 41a, 70b.

[3] Oral information by A. Klein-Franke.

[4] I thank B. Hoppe for her information that this name was applied to single lenses before the actual invention of the instrument.

[5] "Ma in somma Abbàs, [...], si mosse à guisa d'vn nuouo Hercole, domator de' Tiranni, [...]" Della Valle 1628, p. 25. "Quando poi d'Europa, ò d'altre parrti gli è portato, ò à vendere, ò in presente, come spesso auuiene, qualche cosa curiosa d'artificio strano, & à lui ignoto, come sono stati già horiuoli galanti, i cannocchiali da veder di lontano, ruote d'archibugi, della quale non fà stima, perche per la guerra poco seruono, stromenti artificiosi, come farebbe hora questo altro occhiale, che chiamano Microscopio, perche rappresenta grosse le cose minutissime, ouero l'archibugio à vento, nuouamente inuentato, & altre machine ingegnose di tal sorte, non si curro egli d'hauerle, nè di conseruarle, ma le guasta subito, e le disfà tutte di sua mano, perche vuol vederle dentro minutamente come stanno, & intenderne, e saperne con essattezza tutto l'artificio." Della Valle 1628, p. 44.

Catholic and Protestant European states and inhabitants of the Ottoman Empire, the Safavid Empire, and the realm of the Sa'dite dynasty around Marrakesh the usage of astronomical instruments was the most important aspect. This is true when one looks at such cross-cultural astronomical activities from a quantitative angle, that is how often instruments were carried along on such travels, were acquired while abroad, and were used for various activities. This is also true when one looks at astronomical activities from the aspect of problem solving. Here too, instruments and observations were at the forefront of what travelers from non-Muslim Europe took with them on their voyage, used in their own astronomical activities in Muslim territories, and tried to make European residents – missionaries and merchants – as well as Christian, Jewish, and Muslim locals engage in.

1. The quantitative aspect

Since the second half of the 16th century, an increasing number of travelers to the East undertook their journeys with instruments in their luggage. Most often it was an astrolabe, which the travelers used at leisure time in order to observe solar or stellar altitudes and then calculate terrestrial latitudes. Pietro della Valle, for instance, received in summer 1621 an astrolabe as a gift by Paolo Maria Cittadini from Bologna, the Papal general vicar of the Armenian Catholic community near Nakhichevan and envoy of Shah 'Abbas to the pope, who had brought the instrument from India.[6] The instrument probably was a Portuguese or Spanish astrolabe from Goa, since della Valle never became truly proficient in reading Hindi, although he may have been capable of writing it.[7] He used the astrolabe from that time onwards to determine the latitudes of all Iranian and Indian towns he visited or came through claiming that this activity contributed to correct the many

---

[6] Della Valle 1843, vol. 2, pp. 134-5, 219.

[7] Hindi or Sanskrit words are noted in Devanagari letters in della Valle's diary, but it is impossible to tell whether it was the traveler who wrote them or one of the Indians he met in various Iranian towns and later in India or to estimate on the basis of their existence della Valle's proficiency in reading the script.

faulty Western maps of Asia.[8] For the calculations he used a method from a manuscript shown to him in Isfahan by the same Dominican Paolo Cittadini and a hand-made copy of Giovanni Antonio Magini's ephemerids.[9] Della Valle did not explain what language the manuscript was written in nor did he describe the method he borrowed from it. When he encountered some difficulties because of lacking information about Eastern places in Magini's tables, he talked to a local astronomer and friend in Lar, Mulla Zayn al-Din. Later on his travel he used two Persian ephemerids, one of them by Mulla Zayn al-Din's brother 'Inayat. He considered them insufficiently accurate. In order to solve his difficulties, he wrote Zayn al-Din a letter and asked for information from Ulugh Beg's tables and explanations how to use the data.[10]

Della Valle was not the only European traveler in the Safavid Empire who determined latitudes and measured altitudes. George Strachan was a younger son of Scottish nobility who had studied at the university of Paris. He came to the East to earn the much lacking funds by posing as a would-be physician of one of the heads of the tribes of the Arabian desert and acting later in some unspecified function for the English East India Company.[11] While in Iran, he determined the

---

[8] Della Valle 1843, vol. 2, p. 219.
[9] Della Valle 1843, vol. 2, pp. 101, 177, 303, 336. Ms Città del Vaticano, Ottoboniano latino 3383.
[10] Della Valle 1843, vol. 2, pp. 419-420, 452-453.
[11] Della Valle 1843, vol. 2, pp. 437-438 (Il signor Giorgio Strachano adunque è nativo di Scozia, e Merniese di patria: nato gentiluomo, di famiglia nobile, ma cadetto nella sua casa, e, per conseguenza, con poco di vivere nel sue paese. Da piccolo perciò fu allevato in Francia, dove studio in Parigi molto bene: ed essendo dotato di acutissimo ingegno, fece profitto grande non solo nelle lettere latine, greche ed ebraiche, ma nelle scienze ancora, possedendo fondatamente la filosofia, la teologia, le leggi, le matematiche ed ogni sorta di curiosa erudizione. Fatto uomo, ebbe gusto di veder mondo, e di sapere a questo fine varie lingue. Pratico Italia e Roma, e forse alter parti di cristianità. Passato in Levante, dimorò qualche tempo in Constantinopoli, dove dal mio signor di Sansy, ambasciador che ivi era allora di Francia, poco prima di me, fu accolto ed accarezzato con la solita sua gran cortesia più mesi. Da Constantinopoli andò on Soria, vide il monte Libano, e, capitato in Aleppo, per desiderio d'imparar bene la lingua araba, avendo saputo vhe l'emir Feiad, principe del Deserto ivi vicino, cercava ivi un medico, benchè non avesse egli mai studiato in medicina, si fines di

Encounters in astronomy

latitudes of Qazwin and Isfahan.[12] Another contemporary of della Valle was the old and ailing ambassador of the Spanish crown to Shah 'Abbas, Don Garcia de Silva y Figueroa. The ambassador is credited by della Valle in his Latin geography of Iran with having determined the latitudes of nine Iranian localities during his visit in 1617 to 1619.[13] The travel account, published under the ambassador's name, but written by one of his secretaries, ascribes some of the observations explicitly to the ambassador, while others are reported in an impersonal style.[14] Contrary to the claims of della Valle, the French translation of the ambassadorial account contains only geographical latitudes of seven places the ambassador traveled through. One of these places, i.e. Hormuz, is not mentioned by della Valle. Another place, i.e. Lar, is given a latitudinal value different from the one quoted by della Valle and clearly mistaken.[15] One of the coordinates mentioned by della Valle as the results of de Silva y Figueroa's measurements, i.e. the latitude of Soltaniye, was not

---

esser tale; e provveduto di alcuni libri a questo effetto, andò per medico a sevirlo. Stette da due anni con l'emir nel deserto: nel qual tempo e la lingua araba apprese ottimamente, e di tutte le cose più abstruse de' maometani acquistò pienissima notizia."

[12] Ms Città del Vaticano, Ottoboniano latino 3384. Della Valle 1977, p. 302.

[13] Garcia de Silva y Figueroa 1667, pp. 136, 144, 227; Della Valle 1977, p. 302.

[14] Garcia de Silva y Figueroa 1667, p. 136: "La ville de Schiras est située à 28. degrez & 44. minutes de la ligne, le Pole Arctique s'éleuant d'autant sur son horizon, selon l'obseruation que l'Ambassadeur en a faite plusieur fois, pendant le seiour qu'il y fut depuis le 24. Octobre 1617. iusqu'au 8. Auril de l'année suiuante, [...]" Garcia de Silva y Figueroa 1667, p. 219 describing the position of Qom, where the embassy arrived June 8, 1618, merely states: "Sa situation est à trente trois degrez, quatre minutes, de deçà la ligne."

[15] Garcia de Silva y Figueroa 1667, p. 365: "En prenant icy la hauteur du Soleil exactement, nous trouuasmes que la situation de cette Ville est à plus de dix-sept (sic) degrez & vn tiers, & à vingt minutes moins qu'Ormus." According to della Valle, the ambassadorial value was 27°. Della Valle 1977, p. 302. While the value of the French translation could be an error either of the translator or the printer, the phrase about the difference between Lar and Hormuz does not make sense at all, since Lar is north of Hormuz, not south as implied by the phrase. The latitude given in the French version of the account is 26° 4'. Garcia de Silva y Figueroa 1667, p. 43.

determined by the ambassador himself, since he never traveled there.[16] The travel account does not specify whether the ambassador used an astrolabe he himself had brought to Iran or whether he used the small and simple quadrant, which one of his servants had received as a gift from a friend in Goa. Hence, the ambassador's astronomical observations may well have been the result of fortune rather than intent. But even so, the fact that the secretary deemed it worthwhile to attach such astronomical activities to the ambassador's noble Castilian name testifies to the esteem attributed to the handling of astronomical instruments, tables, and formulas in the early 17th century.

Scholars traveling in various functions – as scholars pursuing their own scholarly interests and pleasures like the French astronomer Ismaël Boulliau, secretaries of embassies or in search for a salaried job, like Adam Olearius who had studied in Leipzig and Engelbert Kaempfer who had received his training in Leiden – pursued astronomical observations as one among several scholarly activities while in the Ottoman Empire or in Safavid Iran.[17] Merchants such as Jean-Baptiste Tavernier and Jean Chardin equally devoted time, money, and patience to labor with astrolabes for obtaining the latitudes of the towns on their itinerary – at least they claimed in their travel accounts that they did so.[18] Della Valle's, De Silva y Figueroa's, Olearius', Tavernier's and Chardin's travel accounts as well as Kaempfer's diary illustrate that in the course of the 17th century, using astrolabes brought from home together with tables and astrolabes accessed abroad became an acceptable practice both in the fields of lay astronomy and travel account writing. The start for including descriptions of such observations into accounts of travels to the Middle East can be found in texts of late-16th-century travelers.

Between 1581 and 1583, the young, Jean Palerne, former maître d'hôtel of François, Duke of Anjou and Alençon, the brother of King

---

[16] Garcia de Silva y Figueroa left Qazvin, after having met Shah Abbas there, July 27, 1618 and traveled through Sava, Qom and Natanz back to Isfahan. Garcia de Silva y Figueroa 1667, pp. 241-260.

[17] Ms Paris, BnF, Dupuy 18, f 175a; Olearius 1647, pp. 255, 258, 333, 357-358 et alia; Haberland 1990, p. 141.

[18] Voyages du Chevalier Chardin 1811, vol. 2, pp. 165, 328, 377, 385, 392, 407, 413 et al.

Henri III, undertook out of curiosity an extensive travel through some of the provinces of the Ottoman Empire. He went first to Egypt and from there to Palestine, Syria, Cyprus, some of the Aegean Islands, and Istanbul. He returned home across the Balkans and Italy. Palerne did not travel alone, but in company with other curious young men. One member of this group came from England and carried an astrolabe with him for measuring the latitudes of major cities while traveling. Palerne claims that the Englishman was also capable to determine the longitude of the cities with this instrument. For Alexandria, the English traveler "found that it had circa sixty degree & thirty minutes (of longitude) & thirty one degree of latitude, in elevation of the Arctic pole."[19] Palerne was very impressed. He decided to add to each description of a city the values determined by his English companion. In order to increase the profit of his audience when encountering these numbers, he added a brief course on the celestial and terrestrial spheres and how to determine terrestrial latitudes and longitudes as his English friend had taught him.[20]

As the case of the ambassador's servant shows European visitors to the Middle East also used other instruments than astrolabes. They either brought the instruments along for previously planned projects as in the case of John Greaves or acquired them in the Ottoman Empire itself as in the case of Balthasar de Monconys. John Greaves was professor for geometry at Gresham College in London and later Savilian professor for astronomy at the University of Oxford. He wanted to re-determine the latitudes of Istanbul, Rhodes, and Alexandria since he judged both ancient Greek and medieval Arabic data of these three places sadly lacking.[21] In order to do the necessary measurements with sufficient accuracy, Greaves designed and ordered a new large quadrant as well as a big sextant. Both instruments are kept today at the History of Science Museum in Oxford. Balthasar de Monconys, a French traveler and well-connected amateur-scholar of the first half of the 17th century, was less lucky. His visit to Cairo, Aleppo, Istanbul, and a number of Anatolian towns was part of a more substantial travel

---

[19] D'Alexandrie à Istanbul 1991, p. 79.
[20] D'Alexandrie à Istanbul 1991, pp. 79-80.
[21] Ms Oxford, Bodleian Library, Add. A 380, ff 153-156. For a general survey of Greaves' Oriental interests see Toomer 1996, pp. 138-141.

program covering most countries of Catholic and Protestant Europe. Before starting to sail across the Mediterranean Sea, de Monconys had ordered an unspecified number of telescopes at home for shipment to Cairo. The ship got lost in a storm and the French traveler had to reorder the instruments. This was not only a financial loss, but also a loss of time, one would think. But according to de Monconys' travel log, he had no problems to replace the lost instruments by buying in Cairo at least one telescope and other mathematical or astronomical instruments.[22] In other cases, instruments were specifically produced in France, the United Provinces, or Germany in order to be used as tools for observations carried out by astronomical laymen, to serve as diplomatic gifts as already mentioned, and to be used by crews of merchant and war ships sailing to Ottoman islands and harbors. The last activity took on systematic forms in the late 17th and throughout the 18th century, at least when we look at France, its Royal Academy and the office of hydrography of the French navy.[23] A map drawn at the Dépôt des Plans de la Marine in 1737 registered 78 astronomical measurements made by French mariners and scholars in the Mediterranean Sea between 1696 and 1735. One third of these measurements were carried out in localities of the Ottoman Empire and its African dependencies.[24] But it is highly likely that English and Dutch sailors in the Mediterranean Sea also engaged in such enterprises.

---

[22] De Monconys 1665, p. 260 (June 5, 1647: [...] l'apresdiné ie fus chercher des instruments chez vn Affendi pour prendre la hauteur des piramides croyant d'y aller; [...]), p. 262 (June 7, 1647: [...] puis l'achetay des longues vuës: [...]), p. 275 (July 23, 1647: [...] ie me levay au cry du premier More, & ie fus essayer mes lunettes à la Lune, où distinctement ie fis voir à Monsieur Daniel l'ombre qui faisoit vn petit corps de la groseur d'vn pois dans les parties claires de la lune, outré plusieurs autres belles choses; ie vis aussi Saturne en cette figure.).

[23] Mss Paris, BNF, fr n.a. 1030, ff 191a-191b, 228a-228b; fr 5580; fr 5581, ff 6-7, 10-13, 31-34. 43-49; fr n.a. 6503, ff 583a-586b, 588a-600b, 608a-608b; Rés. Ge DD 226(5), 226 (12), 226 (32), 226 (39), 226 (40), 226 (47), 226 (48); Ge A 1212; Ms Paris, Bibliothèque de l'Institut 2721; Ms Archives du minstère de la Marines 2JJ52, n° 35; Atlas de Toutes les Parties Connues du Globes Terrestre [ca. 1780], pp. 6-9.

[24] Ms Paris, Bibliothèque de l'Institut 2721, n° 129.

Beside measurements of solar altitudes and calculation of geographical latitudes, the observation of heavenly events such as eclipses or the appearance of comets was another astronomical activity of travelers whether they owned instruments or not. Numerous lunar eclipses made Western travelers comment on what they pretended was the superstitious nature of the "Orientals". Visitors of Aleppo in the Ottoman Empire and of Isfahan in the Safavid Empire described popular customs of protection against such events. Copper pots, pans, and tools for beating on the pots and pans were carried up on the roof and the men created as much noise as possible in order to drive the dragon away who had swallowed the moon or was in the process of doing it.[25] Several travelers watched comets, often informed about their appearance by servants who had seen them earlier than their educated masters, and described color, form, and path of the object.[26] In at least one case, astronomical observations served primarily for alchemical experiments.[27]

2. Problem solving

The three major practical astronomical problems pursued by scholars or special envoys from Catholic or Protestant Europe in the Ottoman Empire and to a lesser degree in other Muslim countries were the corroboration of Galileo's observation of the moons of Jupiter, the determination of terrestrial latitudes and longitudes, and measurements of the length of 1° latitude. The first activity is exclusively connected with the Provençal scholar and mediator of the commerce of letters, books, information, and objects of knowledge, Nicolas Fabri de Peiresc. In 1611, he financed for one of his servants a trip to Ottoman Tripoli and Aleppo with the explicit task to observe with a telescope the moons of Jupiter and their phases.[28]

Peiresc also engaged in the determination of latitudes and longitudes. He organized the well-known multicultural and cross-religious project

---

[25] Della Valle 1843, vol. 1, pp. 338, 500.
[26] Della Valle 1843, vol. 2, pp. 838; Garcia de Silva y Figueroa 1667, pp. 272-273; Ms Paris, Bibliothèque de l'Institut, Godefroy 68, f 5a.
[27] The traveler in question was Balthasar de Monconys.
[28] Ms Carpentras, Bibliothèque Ingiumbertine 1803, ff 250a-276a.

of observational astronomy. I will treat here only the instruments involved in the project as far as it concerns the Middle East. The French Capuchin missionaries Agathange de Vendôme and Cassien de Nantes, cajoled by Peiresc into observing the upcoming lunar eclipses in 1635 and 1636, complained about the lack of even astrolabes in Cairo.[29] Their letters made Peiresc design and produce small quadrants, buy a few small telescopes, draft a list of steps to follow and a list of errors to avoid when observing a lunar eclipse, and send all this to Cairo, Aleppo, and Tunis. When one of the ships carrying the parcel destined for Cairo seemed to have lost course, he sent a replacement.[30] Agathange also searched for a native astrologer, but the one he found had lost his entire collection of astronomical instruments some years earlier and now used only bookish knowledge. The local astrologer whose religious affiliation is not spelled out by the Capuchin recommended Agathange to build a big quadrant for measuring the altitude of the polar star.[31] For Alexandria, the missionary negotiated with the captain of an English ship who just visited Cairo to do the same after his return to the port.[32] Peiresc too invested a substantial amount of money, planning, and networking in this project. He wrote to several astronomers in Paris, Tübingen, Rome, and Naples as well as to the Cardinals Antonio and Francesco Barberini.[33] He asked Schickard in Tübingen and Gassendi in Digne for instructions enabling the untrained missionaries in the Ottoman Empire and his informant in Tunis to observe reliably the eclipses. Peiresc's servant Corberan built a quadrant for one of the Capuchins whom Peiresc invited on their journey to the Middle East to his house in Aix-en-Provence in order to show them how to measure altitudes and observe the heavens.[34] The quadrants and perhaps even the small telescopes that were shipped to Cairo, Aleppo, and Tunis were probably also produced by Peiresc's servants.

---

[29] Correspondance de Peiresc 1891, p. 170.
[30] Correspondance de Peiresc 1891, pp. 52, 137-141, 168, 188-189, 234-235, 240-243, 246-247 et alia. Lettres de Peiresc 1898, vol. VII, pp. 149-155 et alia.
[31] Correspondance de Peiresc 1891, pp. 211-212.
[32] Correspondance de Peiresc 1891, p. 212.
[33] Correspodance de Peiresc 1891, p. 233.
[34] Correspondance de Peiresc 1891, pp. 234-235.

Having no idea about the precise shape of the landscape around Cairo and Aleppo, Peiresc proposed to Agathange to climb upon one of the pyramids and to Jacob Golius' brother in Aleppo, the Carmelite Celestinus de Sancta Lidvina, to get to the top of a 2000m-mountain near Antioch. While Celestinus indeed set out for the mountain al-Khanzir and enjoyed climbing to its top, Agathange categorically refused to set a foot on the wall of a pyramid, not only because it was cumbersome to do so and needed money for bribing some local guards, but because mountains hindered the clear sight Peiresc wanted the missionary to have.[35] Finally, Agathange, Cassien, and Celestinus found collaborators in the Carmelite missionary Michelange de Nantes the Armenian interpreter J. Molino of the Venetian consul in Cairo, Monsieur Claret, a French merchant in Aleppo, and a few local servants who observed the lunar eclipses in Cairo and in the environment of Aleppo.[36] Pereisc's contact in Tunis, the French convert to Islam Osman, previously Thomas d'Arcos, sent Peiresc a very brief statement about the beginning of the lunar eclipse in Tunis comparing its time with the information given by Andreas Argoli in his tables printed in 1623.[37] He promised to observe the solar eclipse that was expected for February 20, 1636, four days after his letter was written, if possible and according to Peiresc's instructions.[38] Osman's observations were never mentioned again, neither by himself nor by Peiresc, Gassendi who compiled the report about all the observational results received in Aix, or current historians. Osman himself sent half a year after his letter promising to observe the solar eclipse an apology to Peiresc giving his increasing gout, his detoriating eyesight (Osman was in his mid-sixties), and his lack of erudition as the major factors for his faling ability to serve Peiresc in his intellectual queries.[39]

Many other scholars and travelers engaged in determining latitudes as already pointed out. Traveling to the Ottoman Empire for

---

[35] Correspondance de Pereisc 1891, p. 154.
[36] Correspondance de Peiresc 1891, pp. 170, 217-219.
[37] Les Correspondants de Peiresc 1972, vol. XV, pp. 36-37; Ms Paris, BnF, Dupuy 688, ff 19a-20a; Paris, BnF, fr 9539. ff 194a-195a.
[38] Les Correspondants de Peiresc 1972, vol. XV, p. 37.
[39] Les Correspondants de Peiresc 1972, vol. XV, p. 40.

determining longitudes became an almost standard routine in the late 17th and during the 18th century. In this context, new instruments were carried across the Mediterranean Sea, among them the new types of clocks. Various French travelers from religious orders, the naval forces, and privately endowed sailed in the last years of the 17th and in the course of the 18th centuries to the Aegean Islands, the Arab coastal towns, and Istanbul and traveled over land with the express purpose of observing eclipses of the moon and of the moons of Jupiter. They submitted later their results to the Royal Academy where they became available to the royal geographers Guillaume de l'Isle, Jean Baptiste Bourgignon d'Anville, and others. Several of these travelers boasted of a royal order for their observations after they had solicited support through the academy's head-astronomer, for instance Jean-Dominique Cassini, and other members.[40] Charles Marie de la Condamine's travel through the Ottoman Empire and the results he achieved there convinced the Royal Academy to finance the well-known expedition to Peru for a variety of objectives, among them measuring the length of one degree of latitude.[41] The Royal Society was also involved in this kind of activity. Its members sent lists of questions with sailors, merchants, and other travelers to the Middle East, as was their behavior with regard to other territories in Asia.[42] In 1760, after leaving Italy where he held a professorship for mathematics at the Collegium Romanum in Rome and traveling to Paris and London, Roger Boscovic was asked by the Royal Society to sail to California in order to observe the transit of Venus. He declined and the Society proposed him to go to Constantinople for the same purpose. The travel was badly planned and Boscovich arrived too late in the Ottoman capital where he stayed, due to illness, for another seven months.[43]

---

[40] Ms Marseille, Bibliothèque municipale 943, pp. 252-314; Jauffatet (sic) 1828, p. 204.
[41] Laissus 1981, pp. 269-273.
[42] See, for instance, Hall 1994, pp. 147-157.
[43] Boscovich 1922, p. viii.

3. Astronomical theories and models

When looking at the more theoretical aspects of the question outlined in the introduction to this paper, the material available to come to a conclusion is more limited. Traveling from Italy to the Arab provinces of the Ottoman Empire for scholarly purposes starts at latest in the early 16th century. The first scholars undertaking such voyages were physicians and druggists such as Andrea Alpago, Pierre Belon, and Pierre Gilles from Italy and France. They journeyed across the Mediterranean Sea in the service of the Venetian bailo in Damascus or in the entourage of Valois diplomatic envoys. The frame for enabling these scholars to go to the Ottoman Empire thus was trade and political alliance-building against Catholic neighbors. Astronomy neither was a pioneer here nor a discipline that provided the traveler with specific points for research. A third French traveler who went like Belon and Gilles in the 1540s and then again in the 1550s with a French ambassador to Istanbul and passed through some of the Arabic territories of the Empire was Guillaume Postel. He was the first scholarly traveler known to me who was interested more in the traditional disciplines of the quadrivium than in medicine, botany, and drugs. Postel bought astronomical manuscripts in Arabic alongside with texts on geography, mathematics, and religious topics. As Saliba has shown Postel also worked with some of these manuscripts, annotated them and tried to access their contents. Two of the manuscripts Postel worked with was on model-building within the hay'a tradition of Arabic and Persian astronomy.[44] Despite the fact that most travelers sent by the pope, royal or ducal courts, universities, or other, more loosely knitted institutional as well as individual patrons to the Ottoman Empire, Morocco, Iran, or even India for buying Oriental manuscripts, brought home Arabic and Persian texts on the models constructed by Ibn al-Shatir, Nasir al-Din al-Tusi, and Qutb al-Din al-Shirazi such as the merchant brothers Vecchietti who were closely linked to several popes in the late 16th century, to the court of Florence, and to prince Federigo Cesi, the founder of the Accademia dei Lincei, Jacob Golius from the University of Leiden, or John Greaves from the University of Oxford, none of them seem

---

[44] Saliba undated, Section 4.

to have had a more than passing interest in this kind of manuscripts. At least, no current research has been carried out whether the manuscripts they bought contain annotations from their or other hands and if so what happened to the acquired knowledge. And even if Greaves or Golius should have spent time with the theoretical texts they bought, they never published their findings. Hence, theoretical astronomy of Arabic and Persian provenance was not what interested these scholars in their quest for Oriental manuscripts.

There is, on the other hand, evidence available that Ottoman scholars and even the broader Ottoman educated elite were informed about the newly developed astronomical models of Copernicus and Tycho Brahe. The earliest known translation of a Latin astronomical text describing these models into Arabic and then into Ottoman Turkish was done in the 1660s by a person called Köse Ibrahim Efendi Tezkereci Zigetvari. Not much is known about his life. His name implies that he came from the Hungarian parts of the Empire and that he worked as a special scribe in the Ottoman army. In the early 1660s he presented the head-astrologer of the Ottoman court, Müneccimek Efendi, with an Arabic version of a rather mediocre Latin text by a French author called Noel Durret and devoted to Cardinal Richelieu in 1637. The story of this translation and its later fate as told by Köse Ibrahim and a later editor called Çesmi Efendi is full of contradictions and surprises. This suggests that some interesting conflicts surrounded the introduction of at least this particular text into the Ottoman scholarly and political milieu. In this introduction, the translator tells a strange history of astronomy, which includes the ancients, medieval Muslim, Christian, and Jewish authors and sources and reaches until early modern authors such as Brahe and Kepler.[45] He also tells a strange story about his shifting patrons from the court astronomer to the head-judge of the Ottoman army and the Grand vizier during the so-called Uyvar-campaign after he just had convinced the court astronomer that the foreign tables were reliable and produced the same calendar as the tables of Ulugh Beg and the court astronomer had gratified him with a huge amount of money as large as the treasure of Egypt.[46] Not only the fact that Köse

---

[45] Ihsanoglu 1992, pp. 71-72.
[46] Ihsanoglu 1992, p. 72.

Ibrahim publicly insults a high ranking and well-establish official of the Ottoman court after he had made him pay for something he had not ordered is a surprising element. The answer of the court astronomer when told that the two tables yielded the same calendar is another puzzling piece. He said that he was glad that the translator had soothed his doubts and that he was now convinced that their tables, that is tables by Muslim authors used by Ottoman astronomers, were trustworthy. There can be no doubt that this is what the Turkish text says. I have checked it several times with two colleagues at Istanbul University.[47] One fascinating point is that the court astronomer seems to be made saying that Ottoman astronomers in the mid-17th century did not trust any longer their own tables and took their apparent agreement with any tables from Western Europe as sufficient proof for their reliability. The only way in which I can understand such a statement is that the Ottoman court astronomer was well aware of the flourishing state of astronomy in Catholic and Protestant states of Europe. Müneccimek's answer implies moreover, as I have already indicated, that Ulugh Beg's tables were not considered any longer as reliable. Such a statement is per se not very surprising, not only because these tables were compiled in the 15th century, but because there is a long standing tradition of criticizing and re-fashioning astronomical tables in Islamic societies. What I find surprising is the solution chosen by the court astronomer – he agrees to accept an unknown foreign author and his work, which at the beginning of the story he had denounced as "another European vanity" rather than pointing to observation or calculations carried out by Ottoman astronomers trained at the imperial schools and affixed as muwaqqits to numerous mosques and schools in the capital and other major towns of the empire. Moreover, he did not bother to point to the Copernican model described in the book and its conflict with the geocentric model he himself followed. Theoretical themes apparently were not at the forefront of what the court astronomer worried about and was interested in.[48]

---

[47] I thank Feza Günergun and Mustafa Kacar for their support.
[48] Ihsanoglu came to a different evaluation of this passage based on a different translation of Müneccimek's answer. Ihsanoglu 1992, 75-76.

English and French sources of the 1640s and 50s support the hypothesis that people in mid-17th century Istanbul were well informed about the works of Copernicus and Brahe and their implications for cosmology. John Greaves and Ismaël Boulliau both report about their talks with either astronomers or dervishes in Istanbul and Pera. Greaves who lived several years in the Ottoman Empire in the late 1630s claimed to have read with much pleasure with Ottoman astronomers Tycho Brahe's book "Progymnasta" which they knew already.[49] Boulliau who paid in 1645 a visit to Istanbul wrote to the brothers Pierre and Jacques Dupuy in Paris and later to Prince Leopold of Tuscany that Adam Efendi, the head of a Dervish convent in Pera, admitted to know Copernican and other non-geocentric models of the universe when asked by the French astronomer.[50] Adam Efendi dismissed the models since they contradicted the doctrines of the three prophets Musa, Isa, and Muhammad, while Greaves' guests showed more interest in comparing the instruments and observational skills of Tycho Brahe with those of Ulugh Beg.[51] Theory and modeling then does not appear to have attracted much attention nor does it seem to have caused much uproar. This seems to be confirmed by the relative ease with which late 17th-century and 18th-century Ottoman authors presented or dismissed the various new cosmological models introduced to them in geographical and astronomical books mostly from the United Provinces and France. While taking some time to ponder the religious ramifications, they seem to have followed more or less the lead of these books.[52]

As for the Safavid Empire, there is one case of efforts to make the new model of Tycho Brahe accessible to an Iranian astronomer. Moreover, Capuchin and Carmelite missionaries claimed time and again that they used their special skills in mathematics and astrology to gain access to Safavid noble families and the ear of Safavid politicians and bureaucrats. While the Persian paraphrase of Tycho Brahe's cosmological model is extant in two copies in the Vatican Library and hence can

---

[49] Hyde 1712, vol. III, p. 86.
[50] Ms Paris, BnF, fr 13039, f 24a.
[51] Ms Paris, BnF, fr 13039, f 245; Hyde 1712, vol. III, pp. 86-87.
[52] Ihsanoglu 1992, pp. 76-96.

be studied, there is no evidence to back the missionaries's claims about their skills and the use they put them to. Having discussed the Persian presentation of Tycho Brahe's model written by Pietro della Valle 1624 in Goa after a lengthy talk with the Jesuit Christofero Borro in a different paper, I wish to focus briefly on the problem of the claim that the missionaries in Iran used the mathematical sciences for religious goals. Not alone that no result of such efforts has survived in contrast to medicine, theology, and language studies, given the open-minded attitude of most of the Safavid shahs of the 17th century towards religious debates, the missionaries simply did not need to enter their true business through the backdoor of mathematics and astrology. There were plenty opportunities for direct, straightforward religious debate in the Safavid capital as well as in other towns of the empire. Dictionaries composed in the period, mostly Italian-Turkish-Persian, Italian-French-Persian, or Latin-Persian, contain only a very insubstantial amount of mathematical, astrological, and astronomical words.[53] Parts of the little mathematical vocabulary found in these dictionaries result from a literal translation such as seh konj = three corners for triangle.[54] The missionaries and their local helpers obviously did not know Persian mathematical terminology as used in scientific writings. Pietro della Valle's Persian description of Tychonic cosmology suffers under the same lack of familiarity with Persian scientific terminology.[55] Hence, the discourse of "mathematics and astrology to promote Catholicism" rather addresses the audience at home than reflects missionary activities in Safavid Iran.

---

[53] Mss Città del Vaticano, Biblioteca Apostolica, Borgiano persiano 8, 14, 15; Paris, BnF Arabe 4353; Paris, Mission Etrangère 1069; Roma, Biblioteca Nazionale Centrale, Or. 63, Gesuitici 964 (Or.3093).
[54] Ms Città del Vaticano, Biblioteca Apostolica, Borgiano persiano 14, f 31b (second pagination in the second half of the manuscript).
[55] Brentjes 2002, in print.

4. Oriental astronomy in Catholic and Protestant Europe

Astronomical treatises from the Middle East gained new attention of professional astronomers in Catholic and Protestant Europe in the late 16th and 17th centuries after they seem to have been recommended to courts and universities in Italy by Byzantine visitors already in the late 15th century. In the framework of recovering ancient Greek knowledge, scholars, among them astronomers, in England, France, the United Provinces, Spanish Flanders, and the Holy Roman Empire learned Arabic, some also studied Persian and Ottoman Turkish, in order to be able to work with the newly acquired texts. Greaves in Oxford worked with Ibn al-Shatir's, Nasir al-Din al-Tusi's, and Ulugh Beg's astronomical tables and translated the star catalogue and the table of geographical coordinates, among other things. Golius in Leiden also studied Tusi and Ulugh Beg and used their texts as well as others in his notes to his translation of al-Farghani's introduction into astronomy. Claude Hardy in Paris labored long hours in order to translate parts of Tusi's tables. Johannes Hevelius corresponded with the Royal Society about editing and translating the tables. Medieval tradition and early modern search for a more comprehensive and more reliable mapping of the heavens met in these efforts. This meeting of the two encounters between East and West in astronomy is neatly demonstrated by a series of frontispieces in the works of Cellarius, Landsberge, and Hevelius.[56] It also found expression in the mapping and naming of the moon by Riccioli.[57]

---

[56] See p. 38. – I thank Volker Remmert, Mainz, Germany for bringing to my attention the images in the works of Landsberge and Cellarius.

[57] I thank Kerry Magruder, Norman, OK, USA for directing me to Riccioli's map of the moon and the discussion about which names to choose.

Encounters in astronomy

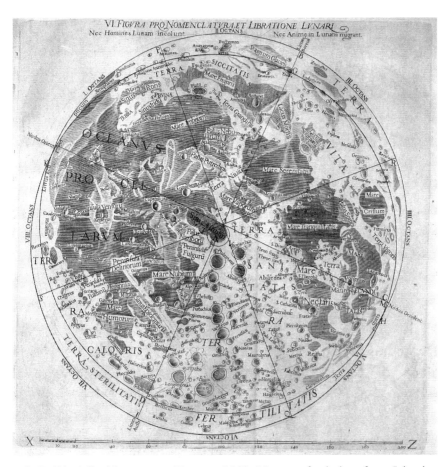

J. B. Riccioli, Almagestum Novum, 1661: Names of scholars from Islamic societies perceived as scholars from the Middle Ages (Albategni = al-Battani, Alfraganus = al-Farghani, Arzachel = al-Zarqallu et al.) and as early modern scholars (Abilfedea = Abu l-Fida').

Image courtesy History of Science Collections, University of Oklahoma Libraries, Norman, OK, USA.

J. Hevelius, Selenographia, 1647: Ibn al-Haytham and Galilei as the foundational fathers of the new science of the moon.

Image courtesy History of Science Collections, University of Oklahoma Libraries, Norman, OK, USA.

5. On the reliability of the sources

Any representation of the self is loaded with bits and pieces declaring how the author and his culture saw themselves and wanted the readers to agree with. There is a huge number of papers and books analyzing this phenomenon from various angles and offering opposing theoretical approaches for explaining it. Since my paper is not aiming at another theoretical excursion into the multi-layered structure of self-representational writings, a category to which travel accounts belong, all I wish to do here is indicate with a few examples that even reports on simple astronomical activities during a travel are by no means simple, straightforward, one-dimensional products of writing and hence cannot be taken at face-value.

A closer inspection of most of the reports about astronomical observations found in 16th- and 17th-centuries travel accounts on the Middle East yields sufficient evidence to assume that not all coordinates given by the traveler were indeed the product of his own observations of the skies, but often fruits of his diligent reading. Tavernier and Chardin, for instance, sought and gained access to local astronomical knowledge. Chardin quotes from at least one, if not more unspecified Persian tables and from Persian astrolabes.[58] Tavernier included in his travel account a table of geographical coordinates of

---

[58] Voyages du Chevalier Chardin 1811, vol. 2, pp. 88, 300, 318, 336, 383. Langlès identified Hamdollah b. Abi Bakr Mustoufi Qazvini's (ca. 1280-after ca. 1340) "Nozhat al-qolub" as one of the Persian sources Chardin used in his travel account. Chardin referred to it as "La géographie persane". Voyages du Chevalier Chardin 1811, vol. 2, p. 336, footnote 4. On other pages of his account, Chardin talks of several Persian geographical and historical sources as his basis. He claimed, for instance, to have taken all the longitudes of Persian locations from "the newest Persian tables". Voyages du Chevalier Chardin 1811, vol. 2, p. 383. Langlès, however, believed that at least some of Chardin's claims represent direct or indirect quotations from al-Qazvini without giving the latter's name. Voyages du Chevalier Chardin 1811, vol. 2, pp. 392-393, footnote 3. Langlès himself was not always well informed, because he did not know that al-Qazvini had also written a book on history "Tarikh-i Guzideh" to which Chardin referred explicitly. Voyages du Chevalier Chardin 1811, vol. 2, p. 395 and footnote 1.

admittedly Iranian provenance.[59] The attitudes towards cultural borrowing however differed between professional and lay astronomers. Astronomy as a pastime was less rigid towards foreign knowledge than astronomy as a field of scholarly expertise. As a result of a lower urge for reliability, lay astronomers accepted occasionally more accurate values than professional astronomers.
Palerne, for example, enlisted latitudinal and longitudinal values for Cairo, Tor, Rama, Jerusalem, Damascus, Famagosta, Rhodes, Dandili, and Istanbul.[60] Several of the longitudinal values such as 62°15' for Cairo (Ptolemy: Babylon) or 69° for Damascus go back to Ptolemy's "Geography", while others come from other tables or maps such as 70° for Jerusalem. The comparison with Ptolemy's data implies that some of the latitudinal values were rather taken from a table than read from an instrument.[61] This result implies that while astronomical measurements may well have been regarded as an enjoyable and worthy pastime of a traveler, including such values into a travel account was as least as much, if not more a part of the act of writing the report as it was part of the travel. Interpreting astronomical observations in accounts about travels to the Middle East as an amalgam of literary fiction and traveling reality is supported by the fact that Palerne, della Valle, and other travelers like them did not bring an astronomical instrument with them from their hometown, but encountered it in the possession of a co-traveler or received it as a gift after they had arrived in the country they wished to visit. The emergence of such an amalgam indicates the increasing desire to portray a higher educational or scholarly level both of the traveler and of the act of traveling, a desire which corresponds closely to what Stagl has described as the contents and purpose of the apodemic literature, i.e. theoretical texts on how one should travel, which persons, places, and objects a traveler should visit, and how he

---

[59] Tavernier 1681, pp. 148-158.
[60] D'Alexandria à Istanbul 1991, pp. 97, 154, 172, 176, 211, 221, 227, 237, 248.
[61] Palerne's latitudinal values for Alexandria, Cairo, and Damascus agree with those given by Ptolemy for the same three cities, if we identify Cairo with Babylon.

should record his experience.[62] Visiting scholars, libraries, bookshops, exhibits, and public lectures was one set of activities recommended in the apodemic literature. Such visits were not seen as passive undertakings, but demanded an active involvement on the side of the visitor who was supposed to follow the rule of polite behavior, participate in debates, express his thoughts, share information about similar places and objects he had visited elsewhere, and report about whom he met and what he saw either by telling his friends at home or new acquaintances on later stages of his travel of his experience or by writing an account on his travel. Demonstrating scholarly knowledge and skills was an important part of this kind of theoretically informed culture of traveling. The increasing presence of astronomical instruments, measurements, and observations in travel accounts on the Middle East since the late 16th century testifies to the successful extension of this mode of travel to a cultural region outside of the realm for which it was devised. It also emphasizes the relevance of astronomy, even if only on a rather elementary level, within this extended cultural praxis of traveling.

The most remarkable latitudinal value in Palerne's travel account is that of Istanbul given as 41°.[63] The standard values in printed versions of Ptolemy's "Geography", in texts attached to maps in the new atlases of the last third of the 16th century, and in Medieval Latin, Arabic, and Persian tables of geographical coordinates range from 43° to 45°. In works of Ottoman scholars as early as the 14th century and very widespread in manuscripts of the 16th and 17th centuries, the almost correct values 41°, 41°15', 41°20', and 41°30' appear.[64] The earliest reference in Western sources to one of these values as obtained by observations made by Ottoman astronomers is known from a letter of Godfried Wendelin to Nicolas Fabri de Peiresc. Wendelin informed Peiresc that he had received a letter by the Dutch consul to Istanbul, Cornelius Haga, who apparently was quite impressed by the accuracy of the Ottoman result. Wendelin, however, was less willing

---

[62] Stagl 2002.
[63] D'Alexandrie à Istanbul 1991, p. 248.
[64] Two randomely chosen examples of manuscripts where such values appear are Mss Paris, BnF, Arabe 2240, p. 285; Berlin, Preussischer Kulturbesitz, Staatsbibliothek, Wetzstein II 1149, ff. 61a, 91b.

to trust the professional skills of scholars from a different culture. He proposed Peiresc to organize an expedition to Istanbul and other places in the Ottoman Empire in order to determine in personam what the true latitude of this and other cities may be. If such a travel for establishing direct control over astronomical knowledge could not be done, Wendelin argued, it was better to trust the results of a culture whose scholarly proficiency in general and astronomical expertise in particular had long been established and proven. Rather than believing in the Ottoman result of 41°15', Wendelin opted for maintaining the 43° of Hipparch and Ptolemy as the true latitude of Constantinople.[65] Palerne who had parted company with his English travel fellow in Damascus may either have found access to another instrument for determining the latitude of Istanbul or he asked for its value while visiting the town. Whatever the case, the latitude he reported in his account goes back to a more recent observation than the longitude he chose and it is only known from Ottoman tables and marginal notes. Palerne's longitudinal value of 56° however comes ultimately from Ptolemy's work.

There is a profound difference between the attitudes of the two men towards the values of Istanbul's geographical coordinates. Wendelin, himself a skilled and well-known astronomer, who had studied and taught at least one Arabic astronomical text in Latin translation – Abd al-Rahman al-Sufi's book of the stars, wished to maintain cultural control about the values and their accuracy. Rather than writing to the Dutch consul for proof that the new Ottoman result was indeed reliable, he preferred adhering to a less exact value because of the established reputation of ancient astronomy and geography if he could not induce a trusted member of the Republic of Letters to finance a skilled astronomer from his own culture to verify the reliability of the achievement of a foreign culture. Wendelin evaluated, shaped, and directed astronomy by specific cultural norms. Palerne, on the other hand, while being an educated man, was not even an amateur of astronomy, if his self-portrayal is trustworthy. We do not really know what made him include the geographical coordinates, the brief chapter on cosmography, and the story of about his encounter with the Englishman pursuing observations with an

---

[65] Mss Paris, BnF, n.a. lat. 1637, f 62a; Dupuy 663, f 27b.

astrolabe as a pleasant pastime. The values he included in his report document however his syncretistic approach. He probably used tables and maps from where he took the Ptolemaic values and the wrong, but widespread claim that the small Egyptian town of Esna was situated on the Tropic of Cancer and hence was ancient Syene. His values for the latitude of Istanbul and for the Dardanelles suggest that he relied – directly or indirectly – on Ottoman knowledge. The identification of Tor at the eastern border of the Red Sea with a place called Elim rather than the Ptolemaic Elana as editors of the "Geography" early in the 17th century did points to Palerne's reading of pilgrimage accounts or maps of the "Holy Land". This mix of plausible sources for Palerne's pretended direct observations carries the explicit cultural message that astronomy is capable of increasing the status of the traveler and his account. The origin and reliability of the values do not matter for achieving this goal. The syncretism even enforces the claim that the values come from direct observations, since no reader checking them would have found them in a single and easily accessible table.

The exploitation of astronomical observations for determining geographical latitudes as a literary device establishing reputation was not limited to young adventurers and amateurs of travel. The secretary of Garcia de Silva y Figueroa used them for demonstrating the social and cultural superiority of his master. The ambassador's servant like Palerne never had worked with an astronomical instrument before he got one in Goa as a good-buy gift. His gift-giving gave him some basic explanations as to how to use the quadrant for observing solar altitudes. When the servant tried to apply the instrument to such a purpose he is described in the ambassadorial travel account as incapable and in need of help. It remains unclear who supplied this help, since the ambassador did not dare to expose himself to the sun.[66] The secretary's elaboration that only one of the three men

---

[66] Garcia de Silva y Figueroa 1667, pp.8-9: "Deux iours auparauant (i.e. April 4, 1617), l'on auoit veu entre les mains d'vn des domestiques de l'Ambassadeur, vn méchant quadran de bois de prés d'vn quart d'aulne de diameter, qu'vn de ses amis luy auoit donné à Goa, & luy auoit enseigné quelques regles pour prendre l'éleuation du Soleil: mais comme il ne les auoit bien comprises & qu'il n'auoit point de table pour les maisons du

explicitly credited in the account with astronomical measurements and calculations – the ambassador, his servant, and the Persian captain of the ship they traveled with – indicates that evaluating the reliability and accuracy of astronomical observations was seen as a prerogative of the ambassador. He was not only learned enough to take over what the servant pathetically failed to do, but could also control the results of the experienced Persian captain achieved with an instrument unknown to the Spanish embassy and unfamiliar to the pilots of the Spanish crown with the help of the lowly and unreliable quadrant and prove him wrong. Astronomy appears here not only as an accidental pastime, but as a domain of knowing and doing of the nobles and the West, as a field where guidance was closely connected with social status and cultural origin. In such a frame, it did not truly matter that all of the places were indeed measured by the noble symbolic author of the account as it did not matter that he had not written the account himself to be claimed as its author.

Soleil, ny de sa déclinaison de la ligne Equinoxiale, comme les Pilotes en vsent ordinairement en Europe, il n'y reüssit point du tout. Car deux ou trois jours auant que de dire à personne, qu'il auoit cet instrument, il voulut prendre l'éleuation du Soleil, mais trouuant, ainsi qu'il confessa depuis, tantost cinquante & tantost soixante degrez d'éleuation, & dauantage, il resolute, enfin, de dire, qu'il auoit ce quadran en sa possession, & en fit voir vn de la façon que nous venons de dire. Et parce qu'il estoit prés de midy, l'Ambassadeur voulut qu'il prist l'éleuation en sa presence; mais il fut trouué si ignorantm qu'il ne sçauoit pas seulement comment il falloit poser le quadran, ny s'il deuoit prendre l'éleuation à midy ou à quelque autre heure du iour, parce qu'auparauant il s'en estoit seruy à toutes les heures. Et d'ailleurs, l'Ambassadeur ne s'osant exposer au Soleil, l'on trauailla beaucoup à prendre ce iour-là l'éleuation, auec le peu de certitude que l'on pouuoit se promettre de ce meschant instrument, Neantmoins, le Soleil n'estant pas fort esloigné de la ligne, l'Ambassadeur jugea, en gros, & sans tables, que le Pilote qui sousenoit, que nous estions à dix-huict gedrez & demy, plus ou moins, s'estoit trompé, & que nous ne pouuions auoir cette hauteur, & qu'ainsi nous deuions ester à l'Est & West de Curia Muria, ou de Matraca, en la coste d'Arabie."

6. Return to temptation

As far as I know there is no modern history of the Catholic missions in the Ottoman and Safavid Empires. These missions for sure play no role in current history of science, not even the Jesuits are taken care of. The reason for this neglect stems probably from several sources. One such source is that the Middle East in general is neglected in early modern studies of history of science. Another point is that the missions in the Middle East were neglected for a long time in historical research. A third aspect is that all the major school projects planned in the 16th and 17th centuries in the Ottoman Empire never came to work except for grammar schools for children where the basics of catholic religion were taught. The foundation of three colleges in Rome for the Maronites, the Greeks, and the Neophytes who all received their education at the Collegium Romanum at the end of the 16th century made appear a direct investment in higher learning in the Ottoman Empire superfluous, expensive, and too far from direct control. A fourth moment, according to Capuchin sources, was the many struggles between the various orders about who had the right to preach and save souls in the Ottoman Empire in general and in the so-called Holy Land in particular. These fights absorbed much energy, time, and even money when they became too rabble-rousing so that the Ottoman administration was asked to crush them or felt it necessary to interfere. A fifth, perhaps not final, but amusing point was that the Middle East apparently presented too many temptations to the missionaries, at least in the eyes of their superiors in France and Rome.

February 11, 1755, the superior of the Capuchin province of Lille sent a set of rules to all the missionaries in the Ottoman Empire, which touched in 19 points upon standards of etiquette, the strict obeisance to the father superior in all important as well as unimportant things, and a variety of details such as book loan, fasting, letters of recommendation for locals, creation of women convents, borrowing of money, behavior inside and outside the convent, and also in points 8 and 10 on two scholarly subjects. Number 8 accepts grudgingly the practice of medicine as a necessary evil, as "moyen nécessaire pour s'entretenir en l'amitié des grands", which by no means should be exercised by all missionaries since such a practice only causes strife and envy. Number

10 admonishes the missionaries to study as much as possible and not to spend their time "with childish and useless things like feeding the birds or other animals, playing instruments etc."[67] Being a Capuchin in the Ottoman Empire apparently was no easy life and the missionaries tended to stray. How much they gave into the temptation to circumvent their rigid lifestyle is reflected in a second ordinance issued in December 18, 1755 to all the missionaries in Syria. In this ordinance the superior of the province Lille forbade with all rigor all missionaries and lay brothers to sleep over night outside of the convent, to cover when sleeping with valuable cloth, to dress shirts and slippers, in particular when leaving the convent, to shed the holy habit, and to go to public bathes because they might be confronted with "libertés sensuelles, propres aux idolatres et aux infidels, pardonnables peut être à des séculiers; mais indignes des Capucins qui doivent ètres des modèles de pureté et de mortification".[68]

7. Conclusions

No straightforward, unequivocal picture emerges from the narratives, the practices, and the objects as to whether astronomy provided indeed travelers to the Ottoman and Safavid Empires with guiding principles for what they should look for, buy, ask for, talk about, and observe. The numerous astronomical manuscripts brought home by merchants, envoys, diplomats, scholars, and gentlemen-travelers from Italy, France, England, Germany, the United Provinces of the Netherlands, and the Habsburg Empire as well as the manifold other activities undertaken by such travelers, their meetings with local scholars, their selling of astronomical and other instruments, their usage of such instruments for religious purposes, and the social and cultural esteem allotted to such instruments and their application indicate indisputably the appreciation of astronomy by a large circle of educated and professional men and a few women traveling in the Middle East. The travelers' stories show furthermore that they expected the local experts to share their preferences and the practices followed by their own countrymen. If their expectations matched

---

[67] Ms Paris, Bibliothèque des Capucins, 1189, pp. 99-102.
[68] Ms Paris, Bibliothèque des Capucins, 1189, pp. 95-96.

their experience, the scholarly proficiency of local experts was acknowledged and occasionally even praised. If the travelers encountered unknown instruments and practices, efforts to learn how they functioned or what their principles were prove to be the exception. The values most often formulated were those of superiority and exclusivity. The travelers' and their countrymen's knowledge, instruments, and skills were presented as yielding more exact results and hence being more reliable in precarious situations and as more complex and hence necessitating more specialized knowledge than that found among the locals whether aboard a ship or at a court. Astronomy served to establish cultural and social hierarchies and as a yardstick to ascribe to men and peoples places on the constructed scales of superiority. Seen from this perspective, astronomy appears to have functioned rather as a guide for orientation in cultural and social spaces than as a guide for acquiring pure knowledge. It may have been precisely this capacity that tempted most writers of travel reports to introduce some elements of astronomy into their accounts.

Bibliography

Atlas de Toutes les Parties Connues du Globe Terrestre, dressé Pour l'Histoire Philosophique & Politique des Etablissemens & du Commerce des Européens dans les deux Indes [ca. 1780] [Rigobert Bonne, Genève].
Boscovic, R. 1922: Theoria Philosophiae Naturalis – A theory of natural philosophy. Latin-Engl. ed. from the text of the 1st Venetian ed. in 1763. With a short life of Boscovich. Open Court Publ. Co.: Chicago, London.
Brentjes, S. 2002: Pietro della Valle's Persian summary of Tycho Brahe's cosmology for the astronomer Zayn al-Din Lari. First National Conferenc on Iranology, Tehran, June 19-21, 2002; in print.
Correspondance de Peiresc avec plusiuers Missionaires et Religieux de L'Ordre des Capucins 1631-1637 Recueillie et Publiée par le P. Apollinaire de Valence. Alphonse Picard: Paris, 1891.
Les Correspondants de Peiresc 1972: Lettres Inédites publiées et annotées par Philippe Tamizey de Larroque. Slatkine Reprints: Geneva, vols, I-XXI.
Della Valle, P. 1628: Delle conditioni di Abbàs Re di Persia All'Illustriss. & Reuerendiss. Sig. Francesco Cardinal Barberino Nipote di N. S. Papa Vrbano VIII. Pietro della Valle il Pellegrino. In Venetia, M.DC. XXVIII. Reprint Edition 1976 by the Imperial Organization for Social Services: Tehran.

Della Valle 1977: De recentiori imperio Persarum subiectis regionibus. Gamalero, E. (ed.) in Studi Iranici 17, pp. 287-303.
Haberland, D. 1990: Von Lemgo nach Japan. Das ungewöhnliche Leben des Engelbert Kaempfer 1651 bis 1716. Westfalen Verlag: Bielefeld.
Hall, M. B. 1994: Arabick Learning in the Correpsondance of the Royal Society 1660-1677. In Russel, G. (ed.), The 'Arabick' Interest of the Natural Philosophers in Seventeenth-Century England. E. J. Brill: Leiden, New York, Köln, pp. 147-157.
Hevelius, J. 1647: Selenographia. Hünefeldt: Dantzig.
Hyde, Th. 1712: Geographiae Veteris Scriptores Graeci Minores. Accedunt Geographica Arabica etc. (Oxford: E Theatro Sheldonia, 1712), vol. III, text n° 10:Tabulae Geographicae Nassir Eddini & Ulug Beigi. (Lectori).
Jauffatet, I. (sic; the correct name seems to be: L. Jauffret) 1828: Notice sur la vie et sur les ouvrages du P. Louis Feuillée Religieux de l'ordre des Minimes. Imprimerie D'Archard: Marseille.
Laissus, Y. 1981: La Condamine, Charles Marie de. In DSB, (ed.) Ch. Gillispie, Charles Scribner & Sons: New York, Supplement I, pp. 269-273.
Lettres de Peiresc Publiées par Philippe Tamizey de Larroque. Imprimerie Nationale: Paris, 1898, vol. VII,
Monconys, B. de 1665: Iovrnal des Voyages de Monsievr de Monconys, [...] Publié par le Sieur de Liergves son Fils. Horrace Boissat & George Remevs: Lyon.
Olearius, A. 1647: Offt begehrte Beschreibung Der Newen Orientalischen Reise. Jacob zur Glocken: Schleswig.
Riccioli, J. B. 1661: Almagestum Novum. Heir of Victor Benatius: Bonn.
Saliba, G. undated: Whose Science is Arabic Science in Renaissance Europe? www.columbia.edu/%7Egas1/project/visions/case1/sci.1.html.
Stagl, J. 2002: Eine Geschichte der Neugier: die Kunst des Reisens 1550-1800. Böhlau: Wien.
Tavernier, J. B. 1681: Beschreibung der Sechs Reisen Welche Johan Baptista Tavernier, Ritter und Freyherr von Aubonne. In Türckey/Persien und Indine/innerhalb vierzig Jahren/durch alle Wege/die man nach diesen Ländern nehmen kann/verrichtet. Johann Hermann Widerhold: Genf.
Toomer, G. 1996: Eastern Wisedome and Learning. The Study of Arabic in Seventeenth-Century England. Clarendon Press: Oxford.
Voyages du Chevalier Chardin, en Perse, et autres lieux de l'orient. Nouvelle edition par L. Langlès. Le Normant: Paris, 1881, 11 vols.

Manuscripts

Ms Berlin, Preussischer Kulturbesitz, Staatsbibliothek, Wetzstein II.
Ms Carpentras, Bibliothèque d'Inguimbertine 1840.
Ms Città del Vaticano, Biblioteca Apostolica, Borgiano persiano 8.
Ms Città del Vaticano, Biblioteca Apostolica, Borgiano persiano 14.
Ms Città del Vaticano, Biblioteca Apostolica, Borgiano persiano15.
Ms Marseille, Bibliothèque municipale 943.
Ms Oxford, Bodleian Library, Add. A 380.
Ms Paris, Archives nationales, Archives du minstère de la Marines 2JJ52.
Ms Paris, Bibliothèque des Capucins,1189.
Ms Paris, Bibliothèque de l'Institut 2721.
Ms Paris, Bibliothèque de l'Institut, Godefroy 68.
Ms Paris, BnF, Arabe 2240.
Ms Paris, BnF, Arabe 4353.
Ms Paris, BnF, Dupuy 18.
Ms Paris, BnF, Dupuy 663.
Ms Paris, BnF, Dupuy 688.
Ms Paris, BnF, fr. 5581.
Ms Paris, BnF, fr. 9539.
Ms Paris, BnF, fr. a.n. 1030.
Ms Paris, BnF, fr. a.n. 6503.
Ms Paris, BnF, n.a. lat. 1637.
Ms Paris, BnF, Rés. Ge DD 226 (5, 12, 32, 39, 40, 47, 48).
Ms Paris, BnF, Ge A 1212.
Ms Paris, Mission Etrangère 1069.
Ms Rome, Biblioteca Nazionale Centrale, Gesuitici 964 (Or. 3093).
Ms Rome, Biblioteca Nazionale Centrale, Or. 63.

INDEX

Abad, see Ibadi, al-: V 396
Abadan: IV 5–6
Abbas, Shah, see Abbàs, ʿAbbas I, ʿAbbās: IV 3, 13, 19
   King: IV 29, 33, 36, 42, 48, 51
Abbas/Abbàs: IV 19, 24, 26, 37
   King: IV 24, 26, 31, 39–41, 49
ʿAbbas I, Shah, see Abbas/Abbàs; ʿAbbās: xxii; I 452, 456; III 6, 19; VI 232, 239–40, 249; VIII 16–17, 19
   king of the Persians: IV 19
ʿAbbas II, Shah: xxii
ʿAbbās, Šāh, see Abbas, Abbàs, ʿAbbas I: V 379, 393
Abbasabad: IV 41
Abbasì, portus, see Bandar/Bander ʿAbbas; Combrù; Gambrun; *Gombroon*; Kombrù: IV 41
   portus: IV 55
ʿAbdallah b. Asad, see Ben Assad, Abdollah
Abd al-Rahman al-Sufi: VIII 38
   book of the (fixed) stars: VIII 38
ʿAbd al-Wahid al-Maghribi, see Maghribi, al-, ʿAbd al-Wahid: VI 236
Abdì, Moullà, see ʿAbdi, Mulla: V 408
ʿAbdi, Mulla, see Abdì, Moullà: V 408
Abdilla, Mahummed, see *Abu Abdillah*; *ben Abdilla, Mohamed*; Benabdilla, Mohamed; Ibn ʿAbdallāh, Muḥammad; Mahummed-Abdilla: V 399
Abhar, see Abher
Abher, see Abhar: IV 21
Abilfedea, see aboulfetah, Abu l-Feda/Abulfeda/Abul-fœda, Ismael; Abu l-Fidaʾ/Abū l-Fidāʾ; Abufedda, Ismaël: VIII 33
aboulfetah, see Abilfedea; Abu l-Feda/Abulfeda/Abul-fœda, Ismael; Abu l-Fidaʾ/Abū l-Fidāʾ; Abufedda, Ismaël: VII 37
Abu l-ʿAbbas al-Majusi, see Majusi, Abu l-ʿAbbas, al-: VI 236
Abu Abdillah, Mohamed, see *Abdilla, Mahummed*; *ben Abdilla*; Benabdilla, Mohamed; Ibn ʿAbdallāh, Muḥammad; Mahummed-Abdilla: V 400

De vnitate existendi principiorum: V 400
Abbu-Ally: V 398
Abu Bakr al-Razi, see Abubecr/Abu-becr; Abu-Becr; Razi, al-, Abu Bakr; Rhazis: I 442
Abu Bakr "Suala": VII 16–17
Abubecr/Abu-becr, see Abu Bakr al-Razi; Abu-Becr; Razi, al-, Abu Bakr; Rhazis: V 395, 398
Abu-Becr, see Abu Bakr al-Razi; Abubecr/Abu-becr; Razi, al-, Abu Bakr: V 396
Abufedda, Ismaël, see Abilfedea; aboulfetah; Abu l-Feda/Abulfeda/Abul-fœda, Ismael; Abu l-Fidaʾ/Abū l-Fidāʾ; Abufedda: II 146
   Sultan de Hamah: II 146
   Takouim al Buldan: II 146
Abu l-Feda/Abulfeda/Abul-fœda, Ismael, see Abilfedea; aboulfetah; Abu l-Fidaʾ/Abū l-Fidāʾ; Abufedda, Ismaël: II 141; V 398; VI 246
   "Extraits de la Géographie d'Abu l-Feda": VII 36
   "EX GEOGRAPHIA ISMAELIS ABULFEDA": VII 37
Abu l-Fidaʾ/Abū l-Fidāʾ, see Abilfedea; aboulfetah; Abu l-Feda/Abulfeda/Abul-fœda, Ismael; Abufedda, Ismaël: I 452, 454; II 123–4, 141, 146; V 398, 403–4; VI 246; VII 36–7
   Geography: V 398
   Taqwim al-buldan: II 123, 146; VII 36
Abu-Giafer Ben Hasan Tusaeus, see Coage Nescir; Naseruddin; Nasir al-Din al-Tusi/Naṣīr al-Dīn al-Ṭūsī; Ṭūsī, al-, Abu Jaʿfar b. Ḥasan, Naṣīr al-Dīn/Tusi, al-, Abu Jaʿfar b. Hasan, Nasir al-Din; Nazaraddyn: V 396
Abù l'Hasàn Alì, Erridhà or Rizà, see Abu l-Hasan ʿAli al-Riza: IV 38
Abu l-Hasan ʿAli al-Riza, see Abù l'Hasàn Alì, Erridhà or Rizà
Abu l-Hasan Saʿid b. ʿAli al-Jurjani, see Jurjani, al-, Abu l-Hasan Saʿid b. ʿAli: III 11, 13
Ketab-e masalek al-mamalek: III 11, 13

2 INDEX

Abu Ishaq Ibrahim ibn Muhammad al-Farisi al-Istakhri, see Istakhri, al-: IV 5
Abu l-Qasim Ibn Hawqal, see Ibn Hawqal: IV 5
Abu Maasciar Belchita, see Abu Ma'shar al-Balkhi; Albumazar; Balkhi, al-, Abu Ma'shar: V 396
Abu Ma'shar al-Balkhi, see Abu Maasciar Belchita; Albumazar; Balkhi, al-, Abu Ma'shar
Abu-Nasr, from Com: V 396
  instructions for astrology: V 396
Abu Rihan al-Biruni, see Abu Rihan, Mohamed, Choraurezmita; Biruni/Bīrūnī, al-, Abu Rayhan: II 142
Abu Rihan, Mohamed, Choraurezemita, see Abu Rihan al-Biruni; Biruni/Bīrūnī, al-, Abu Rayhan: V 396
  'Canon of the Comprehension of the Mathematical (science) and the Stars': V 396
Abu l-Su'ud, see Ebussud Efendi: I 448
Abu-Zaid Ben-Hosain, see Ishaq b. Hunayn: V 396
Abu Zayd Ahmad b. Sahl al-Balkhi, see Balkhi, al-, Abu Zayd Ahmad b. Sahl: IV 4–5
Accademia degli Umoristi: IV 2
Accurensis, Victor: VII 11
Achmad, Pierre: II 145–6
Adana, see Adena: II 132
Adem/Adam Efendi: II 136; VIII 30
Adena, see Adana: II 132
Adharbayjan, see Adherbaigian; Adilbegian; Azerbayjan: VI 246
Adherbaigian, see Adharbayjan; Adilbegian; Azerbayjan: IV 21–2, 30
Adilbegian, see Adharbayjan; Adherbaigian; Azerbayjan: III 2
Adrianople, see Adrinople; Edirne: II 146
Adrinople, see Adrianople; Edirne: II 145
Aegean Islands: VIII 21, 26
Æole, see Aeolus: VII 51
Aeolus, see Æole: VII 29
Affrique/Afrique, see Africa: VII 6, 24, 48
Africa, see Affrique/Afrique: I 449; IV 7–8, 16; V 393, 399; VI 244; VII 24, 35
  North: VII 3, 7–8, 14, 17, 20, 37, 42
  Northern: I 449; II 123; IV 16; V 398; VII 3
Agarrat, Antoine: VII 14
Agathange de Vendôme, see Vendôme, Agathange, de: VII 14; VIII 24–5
Agem, see Agiam; Agiamia; Azimia: III 8; IV 21
Agiam, see Agem; Agiamia; Azimia: III 8; IV 21
Agiamia, see Agem; Agiam; Araq of Agiamia; Azimia: III 8; IV 21–2, 24, 30–32, 40, 45, 50–52, 55
Agra: xx, xxv
Agradatus: IV 46
Ahmad, dervish, see Aḥmad b. al-Ḥājj Ḥusām al-'Akalshānī: VII 2
Aḥmad b. al-Ḥājj Ḥusām al-'Akalshānī, see Ahmad, dervish: xxviii
Aḥmad b. Zeyn al-Dīn al-'Ābidīn: V 407
Ahmad of Tunis, see Ahmet, Hajji: VII 37–8, 54
  „Geography": VII 54
Ahmet, Hajji, see Ahmad of Tunis: IV 8
  Map: IV 8
Aix-en-Provence: VII 2, 5–6, 9, 16, 26–8, 30, 32, 35, 43, 55; VIII 24–5
Ajaman, see Giaman; Iaman; Yemen: V 401
Albania: IV 26, 28
Albategnius, see Battani, al-: VIII 33
Albumazar, see Abu Maasciar Belchita; Abu Ma'shar al-Balkhi; Balkhi, al-, Abu Ma'shar: V 395, 398
Alep, see Aleppo; Halab; Halep: VII 5, 13, 47
Aleppo, see Alep; Halab; Halep: xx–xxiii, xxvii–xxviii; II 125, 127, 132; IV 11; V 379, 381, 385, 387, 404; VI 240, 246, 253; VII 1–2, 5, 7, 13, 34; VIII 21, 23–5
Alexander, the Great: IV 47; V 393; VI 239
Alexandrette, see Iskandarun/Iskenderun: VII 13
Alexandria/Alexandrie: xxvii; II 127, 133, 142–3; V 381; VI 240; VIII 21, 24
Alfarabius, see Farabi, al-: V 395–6, 398
Alfraganus, see Alphraganus, Farghani/Farġānī, al-; Golius, Jacob, Elemens d'astronomie d'Alfergánie: VIII 33
Algazales, see Algazallys/Algazzallys; Ghazali, al-: V 395–6
Algazallys/Algazzallys, see Algazales; Ghazali, al-: V 398
Algeria: VI 229
Alger/Algiers, see Algers; Algiers
Algers, see Alger/Algier; Algiers: VII 6, 11, 20–21, 48
Algiers, see Alger/Algier; Algers: VII 9, 20
Alì, see 'Ali: IV 38
'Ali, see Alì
'Ali Oğlan, i.e. 'Ali, the footboy, see Ally ogean, i.e. Ally, the scribe
Alingià, see Alinja: IV 23
Alinja, see Alingià
Allaci, Leo: III 17
Ally ogean, i.e. Ally, the scribe, see 'Ali Oğlan, i.e. 'Ali, the footboy: VII 11

INDEX

Almansor, see al-Mansur: V 402
Alpago, Andrea: I 439, 446; VIII 27
Alphraganus, see Farghani/Farġānī, al-;
    Golius, Jacob, Elemens d'astronomie
    d'Alferganie: V 398
Alpini, Prospero: I 439, 445–6, 450; V 388–9;
    VI 233–4, 237–8; VI 253; VII 9
  De Medicina Ægyptiorvm: V 388
  Historia Ægypti Naturalis: V 388
  Natural History of Egypt: I 445
Alps: VI 242
America/Amerique/amerique: VII 24, 50
  North: VI 250
Amsterdam: VI 244
Ananias: V 404; VI 246
Anatolia, see Natolia: IV 8; VI 240, 244–5;
    VII 33
Andalus, al-, see Andalusia/Andalusie: I 448
Andalusia/Andalusie, see Andalus, al-: VII 7
Ange de Saint-Joseph: V 413
Angelo, Jacopo d': IV 7
Angleterre, see England: VII 47, 53
Annals of Persia: V 401
Antaki, al-, Da'ud: VI 236
Antakya, see Antioch: VII 2, 34
Antalya: II 138
Antée: VII 6
Antelmi, Nicolas d': VII 14
Antelmi, Pierre, d', canon of Fréjus:
    VII 14, 18
Antioch, see Antakya: VIII 25
Antwerp: VI 244; VII 2
Anville, Jean Baptiste Bourguignon de,
    see Bourguignon, Jean-Baptiste
    d'Anville: II 132, 140–46; VII 35;
    VIII 26
Apamea, see Hama: III 14
Apennines: IV 31
Apollo: V 395
Apollonios/Apollonius: II 140; V 413
  Conics: 140
Aquin Mustafa Espagnol, see Aquin
    Mustapha/mustaffa, also Memet;
    Hakim Mustafa: VII 7
Aquin Mustapha/mustaffa, also Memet, see
    Hakim Mustafa; Aquin Mustafa
    Espagnol: VII 7
Aquinas, Tomas, of: I 464
Arabia/Arabie: I 451; II 141, 143, 146; IV 21,
    36, 43–4; V 395, 400
  Deserta: V 401
  Felix: V 401
  Petrosa: V 401
Arabian desert: III 23; VIII 18
Arabian Peninsula, see Peninsula, Arabian:
    VII 27

Arabus: V 395, 400
  sonne of *Apollo* and Madam *Babilonia*:
    V 395, 400
Arach, see Araq, Iraq: III 1, 15
Araq/Aràq, see Arach, Iraq: III 8; IV 21–3,
    30–32, 34, 39–42, 49
  of Agiamia: III 8; IV 21–2
  of Arabia: III 8; IV 21
Araxes, see *Araxis*: IV 24, 46
Araxis, see Araxes: V 403
Archimedes: II 140; V 413
  Liber Assumptorum: II 140
Archipelago: VII 48
Arcos, Thomas, d', see Osman: VII 6, 12–15,
    17–18, 20–24, 35–6, 38, 42; VIII 25
  relation Affricaine, see Relation
    d'Affrique; "Relation of Africa":
    VII 35
  relation d'Affrique, see relation
    Affricaine; "Relation of Africa":
    VII 36
  "Relation of Africa", see relation
    Affricaine: VII 35
Ardebil: IV 22
Argens, river near St. Maximin: VII 40, 55
Argoli, Andrea: VII 14; VIII 25
Aristides/Aristide, Aelius: VII 2, 34, 40–41,
    45, 54–6
Aristotle: I 454, 458, 461; V 392, 409
  Aristu: I 458
  Politics: I 454, 461
Armain, Pierre: II 142
Armand, Anthoine, Martigues, du, see
    Martigues, du, Armand, Anthoine:
    VII 11
Armand, Jannot, Martigues, du, called
    Troupillon, see Martigues du, Armand,
    Jannot, called Troupillon: VII 11
Armenia: IV 22–5, 28; V 403; VI 245
Arnaout-Beligrad, see Belgrade: II 145
  Belgrade des Albanois: II 145
Arrian, see Arryan
Arryan, see Arrian: V 402
Arvieux, Laurent de: II 123, 141
Arzachel, see Arzaqallu, al-: VIII 33
Ascichaer, see *eski cheher*; Eskishehr: II 132
Ashraf, see Escrèf: V 393
Asia/Asie: I 455; II 121, 133, 140; III 1;
    IV 4, 7–8, 16, 39, 52, 54; VI 230,
    244, 249–50, 253; VII 33, 37;
    VIII 18, 26
  East: IV 7
  Minor: I 451; IV 36; VI 245
  South: IV 7
  Western: I 454; II 123; IV 16; VI 241,
    243, 245, 247–8

Assemani, Joseph S.: II 141
Assent bellut bochy: VII 11
Assyria: IV 24; V 403; VI 245
Astarbad, see Esterabàd
Astehàr, see Istakhr: IV 46
Athena: VII 41
Atlantic: VII 22, 25
Atlas: IV 4
    Catalan: IV 4
Atropatene: IV 28
Atropatia: IV 46
Augsburg: I 439; V 386
Auicenne, see Avicen; *Avicenna*; Ibn Sina: VII 44
Austria: II 123
Avicen, see Auicenne; *Avicenna*; Ibn Sina: V 395, 402
    call'd *Honain-Ali-ben-sein*: V 402
Avicenna, see Auicenne; Avicen; Ibn Sina: I 446, 464; V 396, 398
Averroes, see Ibn Rushd: I 464; V 396, 398
Aycard, Honoré: VII 22, 26, 35
Azerbayjan, see Adherbaigian; Adilbegian: I 452; III 2
Azimia, see Agem; Agiam; Agiamia; Araq of Agiamia: III 1

Babylon: xviii; I 443; III 8, 14; IV 8, 11, 19–21; VI 245; VIII 36
Babylonia: III 23; IV 49
Bachdad, see Baghdad: V 402
    Monke: V 402
Bacon, Roger: VI 233
Bactrians: IV 39
Bagadat, see Baghdad: I 464; IV 11
Baghdad, see *Bagadat*: xviii; III 14, 19; IV 6, 8, 11, 19, 21; V 402, 406; VI 241, 245, 253
Baghdadi, al-, Ibn 'Abd al-Latif, Muhammad, see Ben Abdillatif, Mohamed; Ibn 'Abd al-Latif al-Baghdadi, Muhammad
Bagny/Bagni, Jean-François, Cardinal: VII 52
Bah Kuja, see Baku, Vahcuh: IV 28
Bahr, see Bohar
    Bahr al-Qulzum, see Bohar Corsun; Mare Coruzum; Sea of Corusum
    Bahr-bela-ma: II 143
    mare-sine aqua: II 143
Bahrein: IV 44
Baldi, Bernardino: II 123
Balkans, the: VIII 21
Balkhi, al-, Abu Ma'shar, see Abu Maasciar Belchita; Abu Ma'shar al-Balkhi; Albumazar

Balkhi, Abu Zayd Ahmad b. Sahl, al-, see Abu Zayd Ahmad b. Sahl al-Balkhi
Bandar/Bander 'Abbas, see Abbasì, portus; Combrù; Gambrun; *Gombroon*; Kombrù: xx; V 393, 415; VI 241
Barbarie/Barbary: VII 11, 21, 48
    la Coste Barbarie: VII 20, 48
Barbaro, Josaphat, see Barbarus: I 452
Barbarus, see Barbaro, Josaphat: V 401
Barberini, Antonio, Cardinal: VIII 24
Barberini, Francesco, Cardinal: VII 30; VIII 24
Barhebraeus: II 141
Baronta, see Orontes: V 403; VI 246
Basra: xx, xxi; I 454; VI 241
Bassano: VI 238
Bathman: II 143
    Wadi: II 143
Batn: II 143
Battani, al-, see Albategnius: VIII 33
Baulme: VII 15
Baydawi, al-, see Bidhaui
    about caliphs and sultans: V 396
Beaugentier: VII 5
Behrens-Abouseif, Doris: VI 237
Belgentier: VII 6
Belgrade/Belgrade, see Arnaout-Beligrad: I 463; II 145–6
Belleforest, François, de: VI 235–6
    "Cosmographie de Levant", see Thevet, André: VI 235
Bellet, Isaac: II 145
Belon/Bélon, Pierre, see Belonio: I 439, 440–42, 450; II 132; III 4–5, 20; IV 11–12; V 384–7, 390; VIII 27
    L'histoire naturelle des Estranges Poissons Marins, Avec la vraie Peinctvre & description du Daulphin, & de plusieurs autres de son espece (1551): I 441
Belonio, see Belon/Bélon, Pierre: III 12
ben Abdilla, see *Abdilla, Mahummed*; Benabdilla; Ibn 'Abdallāh, Muhammad; Mahummed-Abdilla: V 395
Ben-Aali, Ismael, from Iaman, i.e. Yemen, see *ben Ally*/*Ben-Ally*; Isma'il b. 'Ali: V 396
    about the events and calamities of empires: V 396
ben Ally/*Ben-Ally*, see Ben-Aali; Isma'il b. 'Ali: V 401
Benabdilla, Mohamed, see *Abdilla, Mahummed*; *ben Abdilla*; Ibn 'Abdallāh, Muhammad; Mahummed-Abdilla: V 396, 398

INDEX

Ben-Abdillatif, Mohamed, see Ibn 'Abd al-Latif al-Baghdadi, Muhammad; Baghdadi, al-, Ibn 'Abd al-Latif, Muhammad: V 396
Ben Assad, Abdollah, see 'Abdallah b. Asad: V 396
   about the events and calamities of empires: V 396
ben Cazem, see *Ben-Casem*; *Ben-Casen*; Ibn al-Qasim: V 395–6
Ben-Casem, see *ben Cazem*; *Ben-Casen*; Ibn al-Qasim: V 399
Ben-Casen, see *ben Cazem*; *Ben-Casen*; Ibn al-Qasim: V 402–3
   De viridario Electorum (The Garden of the Chosen): V 403
Ben-Eladib, Mohamed, see Ibn al-Adib, Muhammad: V 396, 398
   on the causes of deseases: V 396
Ben-Helal, Ebrahim, see Ibrahim b. Hilal: V 396
   about the Dailamite empire: V 396
Ben-Isaac, Mohamed, see Ibn Ishaq, Muhammad; *Mahomet-ben-Isaac*: V 396, 398
   'Key of the Orbits': V 396
ben Sid'Ally, see Ben-Sidi Aali; *Ben-sidi-Ally*; Ibn Sayyid 'Ali: V 395, 404
Ben-Sidi Aali, see *ben Sid'Ally*; *Ben-sidi-Ally*; Ibn Sayyid 'Ali: V 396
Ben-sidi-Ally, see *ben Sid'Ally*; Ben-Sidi Aali; Ibn Sayyid 'Ali: V 401
   Book about the teachings of the Muslims: V 396
Ben al-Wardi, see Ibn al-Wardi: II 141, 143
   La Perle des Merveilles: II 141, 143
Berlin: xvi, xviii; IV 56
   Max Planck Institute for the History of Science: IV 56
Bermond, Christophe de: II 130
Bernard, Edward: II 142; V 392
Bernhardt, J.: VII 19
Bernier, François: II 125
Berossus: V 400
Berthe, Queen: VII 19
Berti, Gaspar: VII 14
Bertioli, Antonio: I 445
Bertius, Pierre/Petrus: II 123; VII 3, 31–4
Bezerti, see Bizerta: VII 21, 48
Bianco, Andreas: IV 6
Bidhaui, see Baydawi, al-: V 396
Biruni/Bīrūnī, al-, Abu Rayhan, see Abu Rihan al-Biruni; Abu Rihan, Mohamed, Choraurezemita: II 143; V 404; VI 246

Bitlis: III 20
Bizari, Pietro: V 399
Bizerta, see Bezerti, Gulf of: VII 7, 21
Blaeuw, Willem Janszoon: I 454
Blaudon, see *bouladin*: II 132
Blount, Henry: I 450, 460–64; V 415; VI 242–3
Bohar, see Bahr
   Bohar Corsun, see Caspian Sea; Chualenska More; Hircanian/Hyrcanian Sea; Mar di Bachau; Mare Coruzum; Mare de Bachu; sea of Bachu; Corusum; Cunzar; Giorgian; Terbestan: III 2
Boisgency: VII 5
Bokar, see Buchar; Bukhara: V 402
Bologna: VIII 17
Bompas: VII 15
Bonn: IV 56
   Deutsche Forschungsgemeinschaft: IV 56
Borelli, Alfonso: II 140
Borro, Cristoforo/Cristofero/Christophoro: xxvi; I 451; V 411; VIII 31
Boscovic, Roger: VIII 26
Bosphorus, see Gulf: VII 24–5, 31
Bots, H.: I 464
Boucher, G. de la Richarderie: I 449
   Bibliothèque des Voyages: I 449
Bouladin, see Blaudon: II 132
Boulliau, Ismaël: I 450; II 123–5, 132–9; V 392; VII 14; VIII 20, 30
Bourguignon, Jean-Baptiste, Anville, d': II 123, 132, 140–46; VII 35; VIII 26
Bouseh: II 141
Bousir: II 141
   Bousir Kouridas: II 141
Brahe, Tycho: V 411; VIII 28, 30–31
   "Progymnasta": VIII 30
Bretagne
   Basse: VII 45
Brevedent, Charles Xavier de: II 144
Brèves/Breves, de, Savary, François, see Savary, François, Brèves/Breves, de: VII 8–10
Britain, see Great Britain: II 123
Buache, Philippe: II 142
Buchar, see Bokar; Bukhara: V 402
Bukhara, see Bokar; Buchar
Burke, Peter: xvii
Busenas, de, Monsieur: II 129

Caddusians: IV 23
Caesar: VI 243
Cairo, see Cayre: xx, xxii–xxiii, xxv, xxvii; I 439, 445–6, 461–2; II 125, 127, 129–31, 133, 144; V 379, 381, 388,

Cairo (cont.)
    390, 415; VI 230–31, 235–8, 240;
    VII 4, 7, 9, 13, 16, 27; VIII 21–2,
    24–5, 36
  Azhar, al-, mosque, see Gemehazar;
    Jamalasar; Jami'at al-Azhar: I 446;
    V 388, 390; VI 230, 237
  Gemehazar, see Azhar, al-; Jamalasar;
    Jami'at al-Azhar: V 388
  Jamalasar, see Azhar, al-; Jami'at al-
    Azhar; Gemehazar: VII 7
  Jami'at al-Azhar, see Azhar, al-;
    Jamalasar; Gemehazar: VII 7
  Mansuri hospital: VI 236
  "Moristan": VI 231
Calcedon, see Scutari: VI 245
California: VIII 26
Camerarius, Joachim: VII 10
Cambridge: xvi
Canada: VII 19, 47
Canaries: VII 50
Candahàr, see Kandahar: IV 39
Candie: VII 48
Cap de Spac, see Golfe de Spac; Golfo de
  Spac: VII 21, 48
Caramania, see Kirman: IV 39–40, 48
Carmel, see Carmil: VII 6
Carmil, see Carmel: VII 6
Carpentras: VII 15, 21, 24–5, 34, 36, 38–9
  Bibliothèque d'Inguimbertine: VII 25, 30,
    36, 39, 43, 45, 48–9, 53–4, 56
Carthago/Carthage: xviii, xix; VI 242; VII 21,
  36, 38–9, 49, 54
Casaubon, Isaac: VII 9
Cassagnes, Charles: VII 10
Cassien de Nantes, see Nantes, Cassien, de:
  VIII 24–5
Cassini, Jean-Dominique: VIII 26
Castorîa, see iol-Kioster: II 145
Cavillat, de, Marquis: VII 11
Cayre, see Cairo: VII 44, 47
Cedrenus, Georgius: V 403; VI 246
Cehlminàr/Cehl-minàr, see Chehel Minar:
  IV 47, 55
Celestine, see Celestinus/Cœlestinus de
  Sancta Lidvina: VII 43
Cellarius, Christopherus: VIII 32
Césarèe de Rosgoff, see Rosgoff, Césarée, de:
  VII 15–16
Cesi, Federico, Prince: IV 47; VI 248; VIII 27
  Accademia dei Lincei, see Florence:
    VI 248; VIII 27
  "forty lighthouses": IV 47
Çesmi Efendi: VIII 28
Çelebi, Evliya: VI 230
Chagatai, Khan, see Giagatà

Chalaccan: V 396
  memoirs about men: V 396
Chalcondiles, see Chalcondyles;
  Chalkondyles, Laonikos: V 402
Chalcondyles, see Chalcondiles;
  Chalkondylos, Laonikos: V 403;
  VI 245
Chaldea: I 440
Chaldeans: IV 50
Chalkondyles, Laonikos, see Chalcondiles;
  Chalcondyles
Champigny, Pierre, de: II 127
Chardin, Jean: I 452–4, 456, 459; II 124;
  V 383, 413; VIII 20
Charles I, King: I 452, 460
Charles V: II 125
Chatay: II 140
Chehel Minar, see Cehlminàr/Cehl-minàr:
  III 12
Chesi, see Chisi, Kish: IV 5
China: I 448; II 126, 143; III 7; IV 19; V 411;
  VII 8, 35
Chingiz Khan, see Zinghiz Khan: III 6
Chirman, see Caramania; Kirman: III 1
Chisi, see Chesi, Kish: IV 5–6
Chorasàn/Chorasan, see Corasan; Corasani;
  Khurasan: IV 21, 32, 38–40
  "water-mills": IV 38
  "mutes": IV 38
Chosistân, see Chuz; Chuzistàn; Cusistan;
  Khuzistan: II 146
Chuz, see Chosistân; Chuzistàn; Cusistan;
  Khuzistan: IV 49
Chuzistàn, see Chosistân; Chuz; Cusistan;
  Khuzistan: IV 49
Chrysocca, Georgius, see Chrysococces,
  Georgius: II 140
Chrysococces, Georgios, see Chrysocca,
  Georgius: II 139–40
  "Persian Syntaxis": II 139
Chrysolaras, Manuel: IV 5, 7
Cinàn, see Cinòn: IV 36
Cinòn, see Cinàn: IV 36
Ciolfa: IV 41
Ciotat, La: VII 8
Circan, see Sirjan (?): III 2
Città del Vaticano: III 11, 13, 15–16, 18
  Archivio Segreto/Secret Archive: III 15;
    VI 248
  Biblioteca Apostolica Vaticana: III 11, 13,
    15–16, 18; VI 248
  Vatican Library: VIII 30
Cittadini, Paolo Maria, Papal general vicar:
  VIII 17–18
Claret, Balthasar: VII 13; VIII 25
Clusius, Carolus: I 442, 448

INDEX

Cluverius, Philippus: I 452; VII 32
Coage Nescir, see Abu-Giafer Ben Hasan Tusaeus; Naseruddin; Naṣīr al-Dīn al-Ṭūsī/Nasir al-Din al-Tusi; Nazaraddyn; Ṭūsī, al-, Abu Ja'far b. Ḥasan, Naṣīr al-Dīn/Tusi, al-, Abu Ja'far b. Hasan, Nasir al-Din: V 413
Cochichin: xx
Colbert, Jean-Baptiste: xx; V 392
Cologno: VI 244
Colzum, see Qulzum: II 142
Combrù, see Abbasì, portus; Bandar/Bander 'Abbas; Gambrun; Gombroon; Kombrù: V 408
Condamine, Charles Marie, de la: VIII 26
Constantin, King: IV 53
Constantinoble, see Constantinople; Istanbul: VII 8
Constantinople, see Constantinoble; Istanbul: xviii; I 441, 449; II 124, 133–6, 139, 142; IV 54; V 414; VII 13, 41, 55; VIII 26, 38
    Aya Sofya, see Istanbul: II 135–7; VI 252
    Hippodrome, see Istanbul, Akmeidan: II 137
Contarenus, see Contarini, Ambroglio: V 401
Contarini, Ambroglio, see Contarenus: I 452
Conti, Niccolo: IV 7
Copernicus, Nicolaus: II 139; VIII 28, 30
Corasan, see Corazani; Khurasan: III 1
Corazani, see Corasan; Khurasan: III 1
Corberan, Simon: VII 14; VIII 24
Cotton, Robert Dodmore, Sir: V 393
Celestinus/Cœlestinus de Sancta Lidvina, see Celestine: VII 1–3, 13–15, 34; VIII 25
Crescentis, Crescentio, Cardinal: IV 11
Crete: II 134
Cunningham, Andrew: I 447
Curtius, Quintus: III 12–13
Cusistan, see Chosistân; Khuzistan: III 1
Cyprus: V 387; VII 13, 31; VIII 21
Cyrus, see Kur; Kuros; Kyros: III 22; IV 46–8; V 415
    King: IV 46
    River: IV 46

Damas, see Damascus: II 143
Damasceno, Michel: VII 7
Damascus, see Damas: xxvii; I 439; V 381, 390, 404; VI 240; VIII 27, 36, 38
Damietta, see Pelusium: II 144; VI 245
Damvile, Mr., see Bourgignon, Jean-Baptiste, Anville, d': II 145
Dandili: VIII 36

Danemark, see Dannemarc: VII 24
Dannemarc, see Danemark: VII 24
Danube: II 146
Dar-assalam, see *Deer-Assala* (sic); *Medina-Isalem*; Madinat al-salam: V 402
    The Citie of Peace
Darab, see Darius: IV 48
Darabgerd: IV 48
Dardanelles: VIII 39
Darius, see Darab: III 22; IV 48; V 415
Deer-Assala (sic), see *Dar-assalam*; *Medina-Isalem*; Madinat al-salam: V 402
    Church of peace: V 402
Deggiàl, see Dajjal: IV 38
    Antichrist: IV 38
Delisle, Guillaume see Isle, Guillaume, de l': II 123, 143; VII 35
Demir-Capi, see Porte de fer, la, (on the Danube): II 146
Democritus: V 392
Derbend/Derbènd: III 10; IV 28–9
    Bab elabvàb, see Bab al-abwab: IV 28
    Caspian Doors, Porta<e> caspia<e>: IV 28
    Caucasian Doors, see Porta<e> caucasia<e>: IV 28
    Demir-capi, see Porta ferrea: IV 28
    Der Ahanin, see Porta ferrea: IV 28
    Iron Doors, see Porta<e> ferrea<e>: IV 28
Descartes, René: I 457
Dieppe: xvi
Digne: VIII 24
Diodorus, see Siculus, Diodorus: V 403; VI 246
Dionysius: VII 2, 45
Dionysius of Byzantium: VII 31
Dioscorides, see Dioskurides: III 20
Dioskurides, see Dioscorides: I 442; VI 238
Djargument: III 2
Duchateland, Jesuit: II 145
Dupuy, Jacques: II 125, 132–3, 135–6, 138; VII 12–13, 19, 24, 27, 30, 32–4, 40; VIII 30
Dupuy, Pierre: II 125, 132; V 379; VII 12–13, 19, 24, 27, 30, 32–4, 40; VIII 30
Durret, Noel: VIII 28
Duser: IV 41
Duval, Pierre: II 123

East India Company: VIII 18
Ebn-Elbitar, see Ibn al-Baytar: V 396
    Egyptian plants and their virtues: V 396
Ebne Heissen, see Ibn al-Haytham: V 413
Ebussuud Efendi, see Abu l-Su'ud: I 448
    Grand Mufti: I 448

Ecbatan, see Ecbatana; Ekbatana; Tabriz;
    Tauris: V 403–4; VI 246
Ecbatana, see Ecbatan; Ekbatana; Tabriz;
    Tauris: IV 9; V 402–3; VI 244–6
Ecchellensis, Abraham: II 123, 140; VII 11
Edirne, see Adrianoupolis; Adrinople: V 383
Edrisi, see Idrisi, al-: II 141, 144
Egypt/Egypte, see Masr: I 440, 445–6, 451;
    II 126, 133, 141, 144, 147; IV 52;
    V 380, 388–9, 415; VI 229, 234–8,
    240, 242, 244; VII 13; VIII 21
  Ottoman: VI 233–6, 253
  post-Mamluk: VI 236
  Southern: II 144
  Upper: V 415
Eiran, see Eiron; Iran: IV 50
Eiron, see Eiran; Iran: IV 50
Ekbatana, see Ecbatan; Ecbatana; Tabriz;
    Tauris: xviii
Elana: VIII 39
Elichmann, Johann: II 134
Elim: VIII 39
Elizabeth, Queen: III 1–2
Elsear, Père, see Elzéar de Samsaye; Père
    Elzear, Capuchin: II 127, 129
Elzear, Père, Capuchin, see Elsear, Père;
    Elzéar de Samsaye: II 130
Elzéar, Samsaye, de, see Elsear, Père; Père
    Elzear, Capuchin : II 131
Empereur, Jean l', see Lempereur: II 136
Emessa, see Emissa; Homs: III 14
Emissa, see Emessa; Hhams; Homs: III 14
Empereur, L', Lempereur, Jean: II 136; VII 8
Empire/s: V 396
  Byzantine: V 414; VI 241
  Habsburg: VIII 42
  Iranian: III 22
  Muslim: II 125
  Ottoman: I 435–44, 447–50, 454–5,
    461–2, 464; II 121–5, 127, 129, 132,
    134, 136, 139, 143, 145, 147; III 3–7,
    11, 13, 15, 17, 20, 22–3; IV 9–12,
    14, 16; V 379–88, 390–93, 398,
    400, 404, 414–17; VI 230–32, 235,
    239–41, 243, 245, 247–50, 252, 254;
    VII 1, 4–5, 7, 12–13, 20, 26, 30–31,
    37; VIII 15, 17, 20–27, 41–2
  Persian: III 8; IV 19, 21–2, 29, 39–40,
    49–50
  Roman: I 461
  Safavid: I, 435–8, 454–5, 464; III 1,
    4–7, 11, 15, 23; IV 9–12, 14; V 379,
    381–3, 392, 406, 413–15; VI 230–32,
    241, 243, 245, 247–50, 252–4;
    VIII 17–18, 23, 30, 41–2

Turkish: III 8; IV 21; VI 242
Turks, of the: III 8; IV 21
England, see Angleterre: I 448, 452, 460, 463;
    III 1; V 393, 402; VII 19, 31;
    VIII 21, 32, 42
  Royal Society, see London: VI 233
Enguichar, see *yeni cheher*; Yenishehr: II 132
Erevan, see Irovan
Erpenius, Thomas: III 20; V 396; VII 10
Escrèf, see Ashraf: IV 36
  the very noble: IV 36
eski cheher, see *Aschichaer*; Eskishehr: II 132
Eskishehr, see *Aschichaer*; *eski cheher*
Esna: VIII 39
Esterabàd, see Astarabad: IV 30, 38
Esther: IV 21
Ethiopia: II 144; VII 1, 26, 28–9
Etna, see Mont Æthna; Mont Ætna; Mount
    Etna: VII 25–7, 29
Euclid, see Euclyde: I 453; V 413; VI 232
Euclyde, see Euclid: V 402
Eudæmonia: V 395
Eulaios: IV 5
Euphrates: IV 50
Europe: I, 436–7, 445, 449, 452, 455; II 135,
    138; IV 1, 3–4, 7–8, 10, 16, 19, 23;
    V 389, 395, 411, 414–15; VI 229,
    232, 234, 239, 242–4, 247, 250,
    253–4; VIII 29
  Catholic: III 2, 11; IV 1, 3–4, 8, 10;
    VI 229, 231, 250–51, 254; VIII 22–3,
    29, 32
  Central: I 437
  Christian: V 392
  Northern: IV 7
  Protestant: III 2, 11; IV 1, 3, 10; VI 229,
    231, 250–51, 254; VIII 22–3, 29, 32
  Western: I 436–7, 445, 449, 451, 453,
    455–7, 459, 465; II 121–4, 126, 147;
    V 381, 387, 411, 414; VI 252; VII 1,
    3, 34; VIII 29
Eygur, see Uighur: II 144

Fabri, Nicolas Claude, Peiresc, de, see
    Peiresc, de, Fabri, Nicolas Claude:
    xix, xxi; I 445, 448; II 124–5, 133,
    136; V 379–80; VII 1
Fabri, Raynaud: VII 9
Famagosta: VIII 36
Farabi, al-, see Alfarabius
Farahabad, see Ferhabàd: III 15–17, 19
Farghani/Farġānī, al-, see Alphraganus;
    Golius, Jacob, Elemens d'astronomie
    d'Alfergānie: II 141–2; V 398; VIII 32
  Introduction into Astronomy: II 142

INDEX

Faris, see Fars; Faristàn/Faristan; Farsistan; Pars; Persia; Persis; Phars: IV 45
Faristàn/Faristan, see Faris; Fars; Farsistan; Pars; Persia; Persis; Phars: IV 45, 48
Fars, see Faris; Faristàn; Farsistan; Pars; Persia; Persis; Phars: III 2; IV 22, 45, 49; VI 245
Farsistan, see Faris; Faristàn/Faristan; Fars; Farsistan; Pars; Persia; Persis; Phars: IV 22; VI 245
Fassa, see Passa; Passagardum; Phassa: IV 48
Fatima: IV 38
    Muhammed's daughter: IV 38
Fayyum, see Fioum
Ferhabàd, see Farahabad: IV 33–4
    laetitia colonia: IV 33
Fernoulx, Gabriel: VII 16, 27
Ferrari, Filippo: III 4–5, 15–16, 18, 20–21, 23; IV 11, 14; VI 245
    Epitome Geografica: III 12, 20; IV 11, 14
Feure, le, Monsieur, precepteur du Roy: VII 52
Fez: VII 37
Findlen, Paula: I 448
Fioum, see Fayyum: II 141
Firuz-cuh: IV 31
    Victorious Mountain: IV 31
Florence: II 131–2, 139–40; IV 5–6; VIII 27
Fortin, Philippe, Hoguette, de la, see Hoguette, Fortin, Philippe, de la: VII 27–8
France/france: I 448, 457–60; II 122, 130, 133–4, 143, 148; V 380, 392; VII 3, 5, 12–13, 16, 18, 20, 24, 47; VIII 22, 27, 30, 32, 42
    Dépôt des Plans de la Marine: VIII 22
François I: II 125
François, Duke of Anjou and Alençon, brother of King Henri III: VIII 20–21
Fréjus: VII 14, 18
Froins: VII 29
Fryer, John: V 414
Fück, Johann: xii

Gabrabad: IV 41
Gabriel, Chinon, de: V 414
Gaffarel, Jacques: II 125
Gagnier, Jean: II 123, 141
Galen: V 392, 395, 398; VI 236, 238
Galilei, Galileo, see Gallo, Galilaeo: II 139; VII 3, 19–20; VIII 23, 34
Galland, Antoine: II 124, 132, 142; V 392
Gallia: VII 15
Gallo, Galilaeo, see Galileo, Galilei: II 130

Gambrun, see Abbasì, portus; Bandar/Bander 'Abbas; Combrù; *Gombroon*; Kombrù: I 452
Ganca, see Ghiengé
Gassendi, Pierre: II 124–5, 132, 136; III 18; VII 10, 14–15, 30; VIII 24
Gastaldi, Giacomo see Gastaldi, Jacopo: I 454; II 123; III 1, 2; IV 8–9; VI 244–5
    Persia Nova Tabula: III 1
Gastaldi, Jacopo, see Gastaldi, Giacomo: II 123; VII 33, 37
Gastines, de: VII 22
Gaulmyn, Gilbert: II 124–5, 132
Gaultier, Joseph, Vallette, de la: II, 125; VII 10, 30
Genoa: IV 3, 5
Georgia: I 456; IV 2, 34, 52, 54
Germany: II 148; VIII 22, 42
Gessner, Conrad: I 448
Ghazali, al-, see Algazales
Ghiengé, see Ganca: IV 25
Ghilàn, see Gilan: IV 23, 30, 32, 34
Giagatà, see Chagatai, Khan: III 6
Giagataiini: III 6
Giagataio: III 6
Giask, see Jask: IV 41
Gibartar, see Gibraltar: VII 6
Gibraltar, see Gibartar: VII 10, 21, 45
    Straits of: VII 21
Gilan, see Ghilàn: III 1
Gilles: VII 20, 25
Gilles de Loches/Losches, Père, see Loches/Losches, Gilles, de: VII 7, 15–16
Gilles, Pierre: III 4–5; V 403; VI 245; VII 31; VIII 27
Giròn, see Jirun: IV 42
Giustino, see Justinus/Iustinus; Iustinianus, Marcus: III 13
Gloriosi, Camillus: VII 14
Goa: xx, xxvi; III 8, 20; IV 2, 13, 55; V 411; VIII 17, 20, 31, 39
Goldgar, A.: I 464
Golf von Smyrna: VII 55
Golfe de Spac, see Cap de Spac; Golfo de Spac: VII 48
Golfe du Cap St. André: VII 48
Golfo de Spac, see Cap de Spac; Golfe de Spac: VII 48
Golius, Jacob: xxvii, xxviii; II 141–2; VII 1, 10, 43–4; VIII 27–8, 32
    Elemens d'Astronomie d'Alferganie: II 141
Golphe ... de Smyrne, see Golf von Smyrna; Gulf, Smyrna, of: VII 39, 41, 54, 56

Gombaud, Monsieur: II 130
Gombroon: see Abbasì, portus; Bandar/ Bander 'Abbas; Combrù; Gambrun; Kombrù: V 406
Goulette, la: VII 21
Gournay, Henri, de Marcheville, de, Comte, see Marcheville, de, Comte, Gournay, Henri, de: VII 20
Goutte, la: VII 7
Great Britain, see Britain: II 148
Greaves, John: xxvii; II 123, 138; V 391–2, 404; VIII 21, 27–8, 30, 32
Grece, see Greece: II 140
Greece, see Grece: I 463; II 135; V 415; VI 242, 244; VII 29
Grillet: I 127
Grosrichard, A.: I 456
Guadel/Guadèl: IV 40
Guinea/Guinee: VII 1, 19, 47
Guise, de, Henri II, Duke: VII 9
Gulf: IV 4–6, 43–4
    Arabian: III 2
    Bizerta, of: VII 21
    Bohar Corsun: III 2
    Carthago, of: VII 39, 49
    Martigues, of: VII 20
    Persian, see gulph of Persia: IV 4–6, 41, 46, 49
    Smyrna, of, see Golphe ... de Smyrne: VII 34, 38–42
gulph of Persia: III 1
Gurney, J.D., V 408

Hacuerdì, Moullà, see Haqvirdi, Mulla: V 408
Haga, Cornelius: VIII 37
Hajji Khalifa: I 446; II 141–2
    Jihan numa: II 141
    Kashf al-zunun 'an isama al-kutub wa'l-funun: I 446
Ḥakīm Abū l-Fatḥ: V 407
Hakim Mustafa, see Aquin Mustapha: VII 7
Hakluyt, Richard: VII 31
Halab, see Alep; Aleppo; Halep: VI 253
Halep, see Alep; Aleppo; Halab: II 143
Hama, see Apamea: III 14; VI 246
Hamadan, see Hamadàn: III 8; IV 21; VI 246
Hamadàn, see Hamadan: IV 49
Hamdallah al-Mustawfi al-Qazwini: I 454; II 124
    Nuzhat al-Qulub: I 454; II 124
Haqvirdi, Mulla, see Hacuerdì Moullà
Hardy, Claude: II 125; VIII 32
Harlay de Sancy, Achille de: xxiv
Harvey, J.: I 447–8
Haveiza: IV 49–50

Haye, Jean, de la, Seigneur de Vantelet, see Vantelet, Jean de la Haye, Seigneur de: II 136
Heidelberg: II 123
    Palatine Library: II 123
Hellespont: VII 48
Henri III, King: VII 12; VIII 21
Henri de Valois, see Valois, Henri, de: VII 31, 39
Hentsch, Th.: I 456
Her, el: III 19
Herat, see Herì
Herbelot, Barthélemy d': II 142
    Bibliothèque Orientale: II 142
Herbert, Thomas: I 452, 457; II 124; V 382, 393–406; VI 245–6
Hercules/Hercule: VI 239; VII 6; VIII 16
Herì, see Herat: IV 38–9
Hermes Trismegistos: II 126
Herodotus/Herodotos: I 454; III 4, 18; V 415; VI 236, 244
Hesronita, Johannes: II 123, 141; V 396–9, 401–2; VII 3, 9–11, 33–4
    De Nonnullis Orientarum urbibus, nec non indigenarum religion ac moribus tractatis breuis: V 396
Hevelius, Johannes: V 392; VIII 32, 34
    Selenographia: VIII 34
Hhams, see Emessa; Emissa; Homs: III 14 hibernie: VII 50
Hibrahimi, see Ibrahimi: IV 41
Hipparch: VIII 38
Hippokrates: V 392, 395, 398; VI 236
Hoguette, Fortin, Philippe, de la, see Fortin, Philippe, Hoguette, de la: VII 27–8, 30, 49
Holande, see Holland: VII 52
Holland, see Holande
Holstenius, Lucas: VII 30–33
Holy Land/«Holy Land»: I 443, 454; II 135; VIII 39, 41
Homs, see Emessa; Emissa; Hhams: III 14
Honain ben Isac, from Abad (sic), see Hunayn b. Ishaq al-Ibadi; Ibadi, al-, Hunayn b. Ishaq, Abu Zayd: V 396
Hondius, Jodocus: III 2
Hormuz/Hormùz, see Ormus: IV 40, 42–4, 54; V 392; VI 241; VIII 19
Ḥosrow: V 393
Hubert, Etienne: I 447
Hunayn b. Ishaq, see Honain ben Isac, from Abad
Hungary: I 463
Hürrem: VI 240
Hüseyin Efendi: II 138

INDEX

Hyde, Thomas: II 124, 142
Hyrcania, see Ircania: III 5, 15

Iaman, see Yemen: V 396
Ibadi, Hunayn b. Ishaq, Abu Zayd, al-, from al-Hira, see Honain ben Isac, from Abad (sic); Hunayn b. Ishaq al-Ibadi
Iberia: IV 25–6
Ibn ʿAbdallāh, Muḥammad, see *Abdilla, Mahummed*; *ben Abdilla*; Benabdilla; Mahummed-Abdilla: V 398
Ibn ʿAbd al-Latif al-Baghdadi, Muhammad, see Baghdadi, al-, Ibn ʿAbd al-Latif, Muhammad; Ben Abdillatif, Mohamed
Ibn al-Adīb, see Ben-Eladib, Mohamed: V 398
Ibn al-Akfani: I 446; V 390
  Irshad al-qasid ila asna al-maqasid: I 446
Ibn Ali, see Ibn Sayyid ʿAli; *ben SidʾAlly*: I 452
Ibn al-Baytar, see Ebn-Elbitar
Ibn al-Haytham, see Ebne Heissen: VIII 34
Ibn Hawqal, Abu l-Qasim, al-: IV 5
Ibn al-Makin: VII 10
Ibn al-Makki: I 439
Ibn al-Nafis: I 439; VI 236
Ibn al-Qasim, see *ben Cazem*
Ibn Rushd: I 442
Ibn Sarabiyun: I 442, 446
Ibn Sayyid ʿAli, see Ben-Sidi Aali; *ben SidʾAlly*; *Ben-sidi-Ally*: V 404
Ibn al-Shatir: VIII 27, 32
Ibn Sina, see Avicen; Auicenne; *Avicenna*: I 439, 442, 446, 451; V 392, 402; VI 236
  Canon: I 447
Ibn al-Wardi, see Ben al-Wardi: II 124, 141–2
  Kharidat alʿajaʾib: II 124
  La Perle des Merveilles: II 142
Ibn Zuhr: VI 236
Ibrahim, Sultan: II 134; VIII 16
Ibrahim b. Hilal, see Ben-Helal, Ebrahim
Ibrahimi, see Hibrahimi
Ichthyophages: IV 40
Idikou: II 144
Idrisi, al-, see Edrisi: I 454; II 123, 141, 143, 146; V 396; VII 3, 31–3
  le géographe de Nubie: VII 10
  "Geographia Nubiensis": VII 32–5
  Geographie Arabe, called *Nubiensis*: VII 35
  Geographie de Nubie: VII 34
  Geography: II 123, 146; V 396; VII 3, 31, 34
Ierusalem, see Jerusalem, Quds, al-: V 403; VI 246

Ieselbas, see Yesilbaş: III 2
Imām Qolī Ḫān, V 408–9
Imam Quli Mirzà: IV 52
ʾInayat: III 11; V 411; VIII 18
  Taqvim/taqwīm: III 11; V 411
India: I 440, 451–2; II 126, 132, 141, 147; III 4, 13, 15, 18, 20, 22; IV 6, 19, 44, 55; V 393; VII 1, 5, 8; VIII 17, 27
  Western: III 5; VI 248
  Indies: I 440
  East: I 440
  West: I 440; VI 239
Indus: IV 40
Ioeuttem, see *yrchilirmak*: II 132
Iohn of Persia, see *Siet Iooh* (?); Juan, Persia, of: V 401
Iol-Kioster, see Castorîa: II 145
Iran: I 453; III 2–3, 7, 15, 20–22; IV 1–3, 6, 9, 11, 14–15, 17–18; V 398, 404–6; VI 232; VIII 18, 20, 27, 31
  "the kingdom of the Sophi": IV 3
  Safavid: I 456; III 2–3, 7, 20, 22; IV 1, 3, 14, 17; VI 229, 231, 245, 249; VIII 20, 31
Iraq, see Arach, Araq: II 143; IV 5; VI 229
  Arabic: IV 5–6
Ircania, see Hyrcania: III 1
Irovan, see Erevan: IV 23, 25
  Three-Churches IV 23–4
Isa, see Jesus: VIII 30
Isaac: II 131
Isac, Rabi: II 128
Isfahan, see Isphahan; Sphahan; Sphahanum: xx–xxiii, xxv–xxvi; I 454; III 6, 13, 17, 20; IV 1; V 393, 398–9, 406, 408, 415, 417; VI 241, 249, 253; VIII 18–19, 23
  Maydan: V 398
Ishaq b. Hunayn, see Abu-Zaid Ben-Hosain
Iskanderun/Iskandarun, see Alexandrette: xxvi; VII 2
Islands of Ieres: VII 29
isle, Belle: VII 46
Isle, Guillaume de lʾ: II 123, 143; VIII 26
Ismail, Shah: IV 50
  Sophì: IV 50
Ismail Efendi Emin: II 138
Ismaʿil b. ʿAli, see Ben-Aali, Ismael; *ben Ally*
isnik, see Iznik; *Zenie, Ville de*: II 132
Isphahan, see Isfahan; Sphahan; Sphahanum: IV 21
Istakhr, see Astehàr
Istakhri, Abu Ishaq Ibrahim ibn Muhammad al-Farisi, al-: IV 5

Istanbul: xviii, xx–xxvii; I 447, 450–51, 462;
  II 125, 132, 136–7; III 5, 14, 20;
  IV 11; V 380, 383, 390–92, 404, 417;
  VI 230–31, 236–7, 240, 246; VII 8,
  12, 20, 24, 31, 42; VIII 21, 26–7,
  30, 36–9
Akmeidan, see Constantinople,
  Hippodrome: II 137
Aya Sofya, see Constantinople, Aya
  Sofya: VI 252
Istanbul University: VIII 29
Italy: I 460; II 123, 133, 148; III 3, 7; IV 8,
  15, 31; V 392; VI 232, 234, 238, 242,
  249; VII 4, 18, 20; VIII 21, 26–7, 42
Iustinianus, Marcus, see Justinus/Iustinus;
  Giustino
Izalgik: II 146
Iznik, see *isnik*; *Zenie, Ville de*: II 132

Jacout, see Yaqut al-Hamawi al-Rumi: II 141
Jask, see Giask
Jenkinson, Anthony: III 1
Jerusalem, see Ierusalem, Quds, al-: xxiv;
  I 443; II 131, 133, 136; IV 16;
  VI 240; VIII 36
Jesus Christ, see Isa: IV 20, 38, 54; V 415
Jirun, see Girùn
Jode, Gerard, de: I 454
Jovius, Paulus: V 403; VI 245
Joyeuse, François, de, Cardinal: VII 14
Juan, Persia, of, see *Iohn of Persia*;
  Siet Iooh (?): I 452
  secretary of Shah Abbas I: I 452
Juffrin, Honoré, see Suffin, Honoré: VII 9
Jupiter: VII 13; VIII 23, 26
Jupiter Casius: VII 2
Jurjani, al-, Abu l-Hasan Saʿid b. ʿAli, see
  Abu l-Hasan Saʿid b. ʿAli al-Jurjani:
  III 11, 13
  Ketab-e masalek al-mamalek: III 13
Justinus/Iustinus, see Iustinianus, Marcus,
  Giustino: III 11, 18

Kaʿba: V 401
Kabul: III 1
Kacheti: IV 26–7
Kaempfer, Engelbert: I 452; V 414; VIII 20
Kasciàn, see Kashan: IV 21, 31, 55
Kashan, see Kasciàn
Kashgar: II 141
Kashmir: VIII 16
Kasios, see Mount Kasios: VII 3
Kepler, Johannes: VIII 28
Kesem, see Qeshm: IV 43
Ketevan/Ketevàn, Dedupali = Queen: IV 20,
  26, 53

Khuzistan, see Chosistân; Cusistan: II 146;
  III 1; IV 5–6; VI 246
Khurasan, see Chorasàn; Corasan; Corazani:
  III 1
Kia-ho-tchin: II 144
  la ville du confluent: II 144
King, David A.: I 452
Kiosek-Feraoun: II 142
  Le Balcon ou le Portique de Pharaon:
  II 142
Kircher, Athanasius: VII 14
Kirman, see Chirman; Kirmàn: III 1
Kirmàn, see Chirman; Kirman: IV 39–41, 46
Kirnë: IV 6
Kirwitzer, Vincislaus Pantaleone: III 7; IV 2,
  17–18, 54
Kish, see Chesi, Chisis: IV 5–6
*Kitab al-atwal waʾl-ʿurud li-lʾfurs/Kitāb
  al-aṭwāl waʾl-ʿurūḍ li-lʾFurs*: I 452;
  V 414
Kiumavala: IV 50
Koehler, Bernhard: II 123
Kombrù, see Abbasì, portus; Bandar/Bander
  ʿAbbas; Combrù; Gambrun;
  Gombroon: IV 41, 55
Köse Ibrahim Efendi Tezkereci Zigetvari,
  see Zigetvari, Köse Ibrahim Efendi
  Tezkereci: VIII 28–9
Krafft, Johann Ulrich: I 444
Ktesiphon: IV 11
Kuhestak, see Kuhestèk
Kuhestèk, see Kuhestak: IV 41
Kur, see Cyrus; Kuros; Kyros: III 12, 15;
  IV 46
Kurdistan: IV 21
Kuros, see Cyrus; Kur; Kyros: IV 46
Kyros, see Cyrus; Kur; Kuros: IV 46

Laertios, Diogenes: I 442
Laet, de, Johannes: V 399
Lambert: VII 8
Landsberge, Johan Philip, see Lansbergius,
  Philippus: VIII 32
Lansbergius, Philippus, see Landsberge,
  Johan Philip: VIII 32
Lar: xxvi; I 453; III 1, 12; IV 48, 55; V 407–8,
  410; VIII 18–19
Larek, see Larèk
Larèk, see Larek: IV 43
Larroque, Tamizey, de, see Tamizey de
  Larroque: VII 18–19, 27
Latium: IV 19
Laurestan, see Lor; Lorestàn; Luristan;
  Lurestan: II 146; III 1
Leal, Antoine, Chevallier of Malta: VII 26
Lebanon: VII 2

Leger, M.: VII 32
Legzì, see Lexghì: IV 29
Leiden: xvi, xxvii; IV 1; V 383; VII 1, 10, 32–3; VIII 20, 32
　University of Leiden: VIII 27
Leipzig: VIII 20
Lempereur, Jean, see Empereur, L': II 136; VII 8
Leo Africanus: V 397–9; VII 36–7
　Descriptio Africae: V 397; VII 36–7
Leopold, Prince of Tuscany: II 133–5, 139–40; VIII 30
Leuant, see Levant: VII 20–21, 44, 47–8
Leunclavius, Johannes: V 403; VI 246
Levant, see Leuant: I 460; II 126, 134; V 380; VII 11, 13–14
Levantines: VI 243
Lexghi/Lexghì, see Legzì: IV 27, 29
Lhuïllier/Lullier, François: I 125; II 138
Lille: VIII 41–2
Livorno: II 139; VI 241
Loches/Losches, Gilles, de, Père: VII 7, 15–16, 26
Locma, see Luqman: VII 37
Lombard, Jean: VII 13–14
London: xvi; IV 1, 56; VI 244; VIII 26
　British Library: IV 56
　　Map Collection: IV 56
　Gresham College: VIII 21
　Royal Society: V 391; VIII 26
Lop: II 144
Lor, see Laurestan; Loristàn; Lurestan; Luristan: IV 48
Loristàn, see Laurestan; Lor; Lurestan; Luristan: IV 46
Lorraine: IV 8
Louis XIV: I 439
Luarsàb, Prince: IV 25, 53
Lukian: II 135
Lull, Ramon: VI 233
Luqman, see Locma
Lurestan, see Lauristân; Loristàn; Luristan: III 1
Luristan, see Lauristân; Loristàn; Lurestan
Lyon: II 124, 126, 127, 145
　Academie des Beaux-Arts: II 145
　Academy of the Arts: II 145

Maani Gioredia: IV 44
Macràn/Macran, see Makran: IV 40–41
Mada'in, al-: III 13; IV 11
Madinat al-salam, see *Dar-assalam*; *Deer-Assala* (sic); *Medina-Isalem*
Magar: V 394–5
Maghribi, al-, 'Abd al-Wahid, see 'Abd al-Wahid al-Maghribi: VI 236

Magis, Monsieur: II 130
Magini, Giovanni Antonio: VIII 18
Magrepli, Soliman, afendi: II 127
Magy, Jean: VII 7, 15–16, 26–7
Mahamet Cherebi, see Mohammad Chelebi: II 128
Mahomet-ben-Isaac, see Ben-Isaac, Mohamed; Muhammad b. Ishaq: V 395
Mahometto, see Mohammad; Muhammed; Muḥammad: V 410
Mahummed-Abdilla, see *ben Abdilla*; Benabdilla; Mohamed, Ibn 'Abdallāh; Muḥammad: V 398
Majorca: IV 4
Majusi, al-, Abu l-'Abbas, al-, see Abu l-'Abbas al-Majusi: VI 236
Malabar: VII 37
Malherbe, François, de: VII 8
Malta: VII 13
Manastir, see Monasterio, Niška Banja in Serbia (?): II 145
Manlich emporium: I 444
Mans, Raphael/Raphaël, du, see Raphael/Raphaël du Mans: V 413
Mantran, Robert: VI 236
Manuel della Madre de Dio: V 407
Manus Salofiensis, Jacobus: I 446
Maqrizi, al-: II 141–2
Mar di Bachau, see Bohar Corsun; Caspian Sea; Chualenska More; Hircanian/Hyrcanian Sea; Mare Coruzum; Mare de Bachu; sea of Bachu; Corusum; Cunzar; Giorgian; Terbestan: III 1, 2
Maracanda, see *Paracanda*; *Samarchand*; Samarkand; *Sarmagana*; *Samrachtan*: V 402
Maragha, see "Marga": xxviii; I 452; IV 5–6
Marc Anton: III 20
Marcheville, de, Comte, Gournay, Henri, de, see Gournay, Henri, de, Marcheville, de, Comte: VII 20, 24
Marc-Pol, see Polo, Marco: II 144
Mardians: IV 23
Mardochai: IV 21
Mare de Bachu, see Bohar Corsun; Caspian Sea; Chualenska More; Hircanian/Hyrcanian Sea; Mar di Bachau; Mare Coruzum; Sea of Bachu; Corusum; Cunzar; Giorgian; Terbestan: III 1
Mare Coruzum, see Bohar Corsun; Caspian Sea; Chualenska More; Hircanian/Hyrcanian Sea; Mar di Bachau; Mare de Bachu; Sea of Bachu; Corusum; Cunzar; Giorgian; Terbestan: III 2

"Marga," see Maragha: IV 5
Marmol/Mármol, Luis, Carvajal, de: VII 35
 Descripción general de Africa: VII 35
Maronian: IV 41
Marrakesh: VIII 17
Marseille: xxv; V 388; VI 241; VII 4, 6–8,
 13, 47
 Chamber of Commerce: xxv
Marsigli, Luigi, de: I 450
Martigues: VII 15
 Gulf of: VII 20
Martigues, du, Armand, Anthoine, see
 Armand, Anthoine, Martigues, du:
 VII 11
Martigues, du, Armand, Jannot, see Armand,
 Jannot, Martigues, du, called
 Troupillon: VII 11
Maruan el Hamar, see Marwan b. ʻUmar,
 Caliph: II 141
 dernier des Khalifes de la race d'Ommiah
 (Umayyads): II 141
Marwan b. ʻUmar, Caliph, see Maruan el Hamar
Mashhad, see Mescèd
Masius, Andreas: VII 37
Masr, see Egypt/Egypte: II 141
 Royaume: I 141
Mattioli, Pietro Andrea: III 20; IV 8
Mauro, Fra: IV 7
Mazandaran, see Mazanderàn/Mazernderàn;
 Mesandaran: III 1, 4, 15; IV 21
Mazanderàn/Mazenderàn, see Mazandaran;
 Mesandaran: III 5; IV 30, 32, 34–5,
 37, 48
Mazarin, Cardinal: xx; II 138; V 392
Mazerat, Monsieur: II 128
Mazino, Michel Angelo, Casuello, di: VII 25
Mecca, *Mechà*, Mecque: I 445, 457; V 401;
 VII 16–17, 28
 Kaʻba: V 401
Mechà, see Mecca: V 393
Media, see Medya: IV 5, 22–3; V 403;
 VI 245–6
Medici, see Rome, Medici Press: II 123, 139
Medina, see Madinat al-salam; Medina-
 Isalem; *Deer-Assala* (sic); *Dar-
 assalam*; Medina Nebie: VII 16, 28
Medina-Isalem, see *Deer-Assala* (sic); *Dar-
 assalam*; Madinat al-salam; Medina;
 Medina Nebie: V 402
 City of peace: V 402
Medina Nebie, see *Deer-Assala* (sic); *Dar-
 assalam*; Madinat al-salam; Medina;
 Medina; see Medina-Isalem:
 VII 28, 50
Mediterranean, see Sea, Mediterranean: I 447
Mecque, see Mecca: VII 28

Medya, see Media: V 403–4; VI 246
Mehr-chuascon: IV 48
Membré, Michele: IV 8
Menander: II 137
Menelaus: V 413
 Spherics: V 413
mer de Naples: VII 49
Mer Est: VII 53
Mer Noire, see Sea, Black: VII 48
mer rouge, see Sea, Red: VII 28, 49
Mercator, Gerhard Jr.: I 454; III 2
Mercier, Raymond: II 140
Mercure de France: II 145
Mersenne, Marin: II 125, 133; VII 24
Mesandaran, see Mazandaran; Mazanderàn/
 Mazenderàn: III 1
Mescèd, see Mashhad: IV 38–9
Mesopotamia: IV 36; VI 245
Meynier, Louis: VII 14
Michaelis, Johann David: II 123
Michel-Ange de Vendôme, see Vendôme,
 Michel-Ange, de: VII 14
Michelange de Nantes, see Nantes,
 Michelange, de: VIII 25
Middle East: I, 437–9, 441–3, 445–7, 450,
 456, 459; II 121–2, 125, 128, 130,
 134; III 23; IV 4, 14; V 386, 399;
 VI 233; VII 2–3, 8, 11–12, 14–15,
 17, 19–20, 34; VIII 16, 20–21, 26,
 32, 35–7, 41
Milan: V 411
Mina/Minà, see Minab: IV 45, 55
Minab, see Mina/Minà: V 407
Minadoi, Giovanni Tommaso: VI 246
Minuti, Theophile: VII 7, 12–14, 39
Mir Abdu'l Hasan, see Mīr ʻAbd al-Ḥasan:
 V 408
Mīr ʻAbd al-Ḥasan, see Mir Abdu'l Hasan:
 V 408
Mīr Dāmād, see Mīr Muḥammad Bāqir Yazdī:
 V 407
Mīr-Ḫʷānd: V 393, 400
 Rowḍat al-ṣafāʼ: V 393, 400
Mīr Muḥammad ʻAbd al-Vaḥḥābī: V 407
Mīr Muḥammad Bāqir Yazdī, see Mīr Dāmād:
 V 407
Mirza Ouloukbec, see Ulug-beg; Uluġ Beg;
 Ulugh Beg; *Vlughbeg*;
 "Vlughbeghius"
Mirza Scerèf Gihòn, see Mirza Sharaf Jahan:
 V 408
Mirza Scerif, Calantèr of Sciràz, see Mirza
 Sharif, Qalantar of Shiraz: V 408
Mirza Sharaf Jahan, see Mirza Scerèf Gihòn
Mirza Sharif, Qalantar of Shiraz, see Mirza
 Scerìf, Calantèr of Sciràz

Mirza Taqì: IV 35
Missions Étrangères, see Paris: xxi, xxvi; IV 1
Moghistan/Moghostan/Moghostàn: IV 41, 43–6, 48
  palm-forest: IV 41
Mohammad, see Mahometto; Muhammed; Muḥammad: I 462
Mohammad Chelebi: II 128
Molino, Giovanni/J.: VII 13; VIII 25
Monasterio, see Manastir: II 145
Monconys, Balthasar de: II 124, 126–32; VIII 21–2
Montagne: II 143
  Alaki: II 143
Mont
  Æthna, see Etna; Mont Ætna; Mount Etna: VII 28
  Ætna, see Etna; Mont Æthna; Mount Etna: VII 49, 51
  Liban, see Mountains, Lebanese: VII 11
  Sem, de: VII 28, 49–50
  Sinai: VII 28, 50
Montmeyan/Montmeian, de, Chevalier/Chevallier: VII 14, 20–21, 24, 48
Montmorrency, de: VII 55
More, Chualenska, see Bohar Corsun; Caspian Sea; Hircanian/Hyrcanian Sea; Mar di Bachau; Mare Coruzum; Mare de Bachu; Sea of Bachu; Corusum; Cunzar; Giorgian; Terbestan: III 2
"Mores": II 137; VI 243
Morin, Jean B.: II 125
Morocco: VI 229; VIII 27
Morod, see Murad: V 393–5
  physician of Shah 'Abbas: V 393
Moses, see Musa
Mounyer, president: VII 5
Mount
  Aethna, see Etna; Mont Æthna; Mount Etna: VII 27
  Etna, see Mont Ætna; Mont Æthna: VII 29
  Gibel Stromboli, see Strombole; Stromboli; Stromboly: VII 26, 28–9
  Kasios, see Kasios: VII 2
  Sem: VII 26
  "Somme": VII 26
  Vesuvius: VII 28
mountain
  Khanzir, al-: VIII 25
Mountains
  Caucasian, see Caucasus: IV 28; VI 241
  Lebanese, see Mont Liban: VII 11
  Malignon: VII 17

Taurus: III 8; IV 21, 30, 32
Moyse de Giacomo: VII 7
  nephew of Gabriel Sionita: VII 7
Muḥammad, see Mahometto; Mohammad; Muhammed: V 388–9; VIII 30
Muhammad Basha, governor of Suakim: VII 16, 26–8
Muhammed, see Mahometto; Mohammad; Muḥammad: IV 34, 38, 49; VII 10
Muhammad b. Ishaq, see Ben-Isaac, Mohamed; Mahomet-ben-Isaac
Müneccimek Efendi: VIII 28–9
Münster, Sebastian: IV 8–9; VI 244
Murad, see Morod
Murad III: II 124
Murtada b. al-Khalil: II 141
Musa, see Moses: VIII 30
Muscovites: I 455

Nablus: V 390
Nachcivan/Nachcivàn, see Nakhichevan: IV 6, 23
Nahr-Eddahab: II 143
  fleuve d'or: II 143
Nakhichevan, see Nachcivan/Nachcivàn: VIII 17
Nantes, Cassien, de, see Cassien de Nantes: VIII 24–5
Nantes, Michelange, de, see Michelange de Nantes: VIII 25
Naples: xvi, xxiv; I 447; III 6, 20; IV 2, 11; V 390; VI 248–9; VII 26, 47, 52; VIII 24
  Accademia dei Lincei: VI 248; VIII 27
Napoli, Zacharia, die, Padre, Abbate di San Seuerino: VII 25
Napolon/Napollon, Sanson: VII 6, 9, 13
Narbonne: VII 9
  St. Paul: VII 9
Naseruddin, see Abu-Giafer Ben Hasan Tusaeus; Coage Nescir; Naṣīr al-Dīn al-Ṭūsī/Nasir-al-Din al-Tusi; Ṭūsī, al-, Abu Ja'far b. Ḥasan, Naṣīr al-Dīn/Tusi, al-, Abu Ja'far b. Hasan, Nasir al-Din; Nazaraddyn: II 141
  Tables Astronomiques: II 141
Naṣīr al-Dīn al-Ṭūsī/Nasir-al-Din al-Tusi, see Abu-Giafer Ben Hasan Tusaeus; Coage Nescir; Naseruddin; Ṭūsī, al-, Abu Ja'far b. Ḥasan, Naṣīr al-Dīn/Tusi, al-, Abu Ja'far b. Hasan, Nasir al-Din; Nazzaraddyn: V 402; VI 246; VIII 27, 32
Natolia, see Anatolia: VI 245

Nazaraddyn, see Abu-Giafer Ben Hasan Tusaeus; Coage Nescir; Naseruddin; Naṣīr al-Dīn al-Ṭūsī/Nasir al-Din al-Tusi; Ṭūsī, al-, Abū Ja 'far b. Ḥasan, Naṣīr al-Dīn /Tusi, al-, Abu Ja'far b. Hasan, Nasir al-Din: V 402
Negrone, Francesco, Fra, Father, Franciscan: III 11, 13, 21
Nellen, H.J.M.: II 121, 122, 134, 147
Nemek-zàr: IV 32
 "the place of salt": IV 32
 "the salt-works": IV 32
Netherlands, The, see United Provinces of the Netherlands, the: II 148
 Spanish: VII 19
New-Ciolfa, see New Julfa: IV 24
New-Julfa, see New-Ciolfa: xxii; IV 1; V 417
Ni'amatallah, Ignatius, patriarch of Antioch: VII 34
Nice: VII 53
Nicholay, Nicholas, de: I 450
Nicople: II 146
Niger, Sextius: V 403; VI 245
Nile: II 129, 143; VII 7
Nisciabùr, see Nishapur: IV 38
Nishapur, see Nisciabùr
Niška Banja in Serbia (?), see Manastir, Monasterio
Noah: IV 23
 ark: IV 23
Noel, Anthoine: VII 20, 24–5, 45
Noir, Jean-Jacques, Le, Roule, du: II 144
Norman: VIII 33–4
Norway: VII 24
Nubie: VII 35

Ocean: IV 4, 6
 Atlantic: IV 4
 India: IV 6–7
Old-Ciolfa: IV 24
Ok (Oklahoma): VIII 33–4
Olearius, Adam: I 453; II 124; IV 16; VIII 20
Ongaro, G: VI 238
Orient: III 3
Orléans: I 458; II 140
Orontes, see Baronta: V 403; VI 246
Ormus, see Hormuz/Hormùz: IV 40, 42–4, 54; V 392; VI 241
Ortelius, Abraham: I 454; II 12; III 2; IV 9; V 404; VI 246
Osman, see Arcos, Thomas, d': VII 12–15, 17–18, 20, 42; VIII 25
Ovid: III 15
Oxford: xvi, xxvii; V 383, 391; VIII 32
 History of Science Museum: VIII 21
 Magdalene College: V 391

Oxford Botanical Garden: I 448
University of Oxford: V 391; VIII 21, 27
Oxus: IV 50

Padua: I 445; VI 231, 234, 238; VII 9
 Padua University: VI 238
Pagano, Matteo: VI 231
Palermo: VII 26
Palerne, Jean: VIII 20–21, 36–8
Palestine: II 131; V 415; VI 245; VII 29; VIII 21
Panagioti, Nikousios: II 137
Pandaya: V 395
Paolo, Giovan: I 445
paradize: V 395
Paris: xvi, xxi, xxiii, xxvi; II 133, 138, 140–41, 145; IV 1; V 383, 396; VI 244; VII 6–8, 10, 12, 19, 24, 32, 35, 41, 52, 55; VIII 18, 24, 26, 32
 Bibliothèque nationale de France/BnF: II 124, 132, 141, 146; VII 24, 39, 45
 Clocher de St. Jacques de la Bocherie: VII 52
 Institut de France: II 143
 Library: II 143
 Jeunes des Langues: II 143
 Missions Étrangères: xxi, xxvi; IV 1
 Observatoire: II 145
 Royal Academy of Inscriptions and Letters: II 140, 143
 Royal Academy of the Sciences: II 140, 143; VIII 22, 26
 Royal Library: II 139, 143–4; VII 12
Paropamissum: IV 39
Pars, see Faris; Fars; Farsistan; Phars; Persia; Persis: IV 45
Parthia, see Partia: III 15; VI 245
Partia, see Parthia: III 1
Pascal, Patron: VII 20, 24, 48
Passa, see Fassa; Passagardum; Phassa: IV 48
Passagardum, see Fassa; Passa; Phassa: IV 48
Paul III, pope: VII 50
Peiresc, de, Fabri, Nicolas Claude, see Fabri, Nicolas Claude, Peiresc, de: V 379–80; VII 1–45, 48, 53–4, 56; VIII 23–5, 37–8
Pelusium, see Damietta: VI 245
Pembroke, Earl of: V 393
Peninsula, Arabian, see Arabian Peninsula: VII 28–9
Pera: II 136; V 417
Perroti, Angelo: VII 25
Pers-Armenia: V 403; VI 245
Perse, see Faris; Faristàn/Faristan; Fars; Farsistan; Pars; Persia; Persis; Phars: VII 32

INDEX 17

Persepolis: III 15; IV 46
  Naqsh-e Rostam: III 15
Persia, see Faris; Faristàn/Faristan; Fars;
  Farsistan; Pars; Perse; Persis; Phars:
  I 448, 451–5, 457–9; II 132, 143;
  III 1, 8, 13, 21; IV 3, 6, 21–2, 24–5,
  38, 40–41, 43–6, 48–9, 51–5; V 379,
  382, 387, 393–4, 397–9, 401, 407,
  409, 414–15; VI 231, 245; VII 5,
  8, 32
  Ancient: V 400
  Safavid: V 383, 417
Persis, see Faris; Faristàn/Faristan; Fars;
  Farsistan; Pars; Perse; Persia; Phars:
  III 2; IV 45; VI 245
Peru: VIII 26
Pétis de la Croix, François: xxvi; VI 252
  Father: xxvi
Phars, see Faris; Fars; Faristan/Faristàn;
  Farsistan; Pars; Persia; Persis: IV 45
Phassa, see Fassa; Passa; Passagardum:
  IV 48
Philippe, Le Bel, King: VII 19
Philippines: III 8; IV 2
pic de Temerse (?): VII 50
Pietro, Sieur: II 131
Pirckhaymer, WIllibald: VI 244
Pisa/Pise: II 131; IV 6
Piscatoris, Monsieur: II 130
Pitton, Joseph de Tournefort: I 439
Plato: II 123; III 15; V 392, 409; VII 37
Plessy: II 127
Pliny/Pline: I 442, 444; III 10; VII 15, 33
Plutarch: I 442
Pococke, Edward: xxvii; V 404
Poland: IV 6
Pollux: VII 41, 56
Polo, Marco, see Marc-Pol: II 144; IV 4–6;
  V 403; VI 245
Polybios: V 403; VI 245
Poncet, Jacques Charles: II 144
Porta, Giambattista, della: VI 248
Porta\<e\> caspia\<e\>, see Caspian Doors:
  III 10; IV 28
Porta\<e\> caucasia\<e\>, see Caucasian Doors:
  III 10; IV 28
Porta\<e\> ferrea\<e\>, see Demir-capi; Der
  Ahanin; Iron Doors: III 10; IV 28
Porte de fer, la, see Demir-Capi: II 146
Portel, Monsieur: II 131
Portugal: II 135; IV 3; V 386
Postel, Guillaume: II 123; VII 37; VIII 27
Pozzuolo/pozzuolo, see Mount: VII 28, 50
Propaganda fide, see Rome: xxi; III 17; IV 1,
  23; VI 249
Prouence, see Provence: VII 46, 53

Provence, see Prouence: VII 7, 15, 17, 22, 40
Ptolemy/Ptolémée: xi; I 454; II 141; III 1;
  IV 3, 5–9; V 402–4, 413; VI 244–6;
  VIII 36, 38
  Almagest: V 413
  Geography: xi; III 1; IV 3, 5–9; V 404;
  VI 244, 246; VIII 36–7, 39
Purchas, Samuel: V 399–402; VII 31
  Relations of the World And the Religions
  Obserued in all Ages and places (sic)
  Discouered,
  from the Creation vnto this Present =
  Pvrchas his Pilgrimage: V 399
Pythagoras: II 126

Qayrawiyin: VII 37
Qazvin, see Qazvinum, Qazwin: III 15–17,
  19; IV 21, 40, 55; V 415
Qazvini, Yahya b. ʿAbd al-Latif al-, see
  Yahya b. ʿAbd al-Latif al-Qazvini:
  III 12
  Lubb al-tavarikh: III 12
Qazvinum, see Qazvin; Qazwin: IV 31
Qazwin, see Qazvin; Qazvinum: VIII 19
Qeshm, see Kesem
Qizilbascis: IV 50–51
  red heads: IV 51
Qizil-uzen: IV 22
  blackberry-red: IV 22
  golden-colored: IV 22
Qom: IV 21, 55
Quds, al-: xxiv
Qulzum, see Colzum
Qushji, Ali: II 124
Qusuni, al-, family: VI 236
Quṭb al-Dīn ʿAbd al-Ḥayy b. al-ʿIzz Ḥusaynī:
  xxvi; V 407

Rabia: III 2
Rabi-Isac, see Isac, Rabi and Isaac: II 127
Ragusa: VII 16
Raimondi, Giovanni Baptista: III 20; VII 34
  Medici Press, director, see Rome: VII 34
«Rajab Chaoux»: VII 16–17
Rama: VIII 36
Ramusio, Giovanni: IV 8; VII 37
Raphael/Raphaël du Mans, see Mans,
  Raphael/Raphaël, du: I 455–60;
  V 412
  L'Estat de la Perse en 1660: I 455
Raphelengius, Franciscus, see Ravelingen,
  Frans, van: III 20; VII 10
Rau, Christian: xxvii
Rauwolf, Leonhard: I 439, 442–4; V 386–8, 390
Ravelingen, Frans, van, see Raphelengius,
  Franciscus: VII 10

Razi, al-, Abu Bakr, see Abu Bakr al-Razi; Abubecr/Abu-becr; Abu-Becr; Rhazis
Reiske, Johann Jacob: II 123
Reland, Adrien: II 124
Renan, Ernest: x
Renaudot, Théophraste: II 125
Republic of Letters: xix, xxi, xxviii; I 435, 438, 454, 457, 464–5; II 121–2, 124, 129, 135, 147; III 19, 22; V 407–8; VI 232, 254; VII 16; VIII 38
Rhazis, see Abu Bakr al-Razi; Abubecr/Abubecr; Abu-Becr; Razi, al-, Abu Bakr: V 398
Rhodes: VIII 21, 36
Riccioli, J.B.: VIII 32–3
   Almagestum Novum: VIII 33
Riccoldi da Monte Croce: I 464
Riccoldo da Monte di Croce, see Riccoldi da Monte Croce: I 464; IV 9; VI 233
Richard, Francis: xv
Richelieu, Cardinal: xx; VIII 28
Rincke, Friedrich Theodor: II 123
Rivière, Polycarpe, de la, Dom: VII 15
Rocnaduddaule (sic), see Rukn al-Dawla, Hasan b. Buya: V 401
   Sonne of *Shah-Hussan* Sonne of *Abbaz Viez*, Lord of *Bagdet*, *Kermoen*, *Laristan* and *Shyraz*: V 401
Rokn'eddin, Cadhi, see Rukn al-Dīn: V 409
Roger I, King: II 144
Roi de Sicile: II 144
Rome: xvi, xx, xxi, xxii, xxiii; III 7–8, 13–15, 19, 21–2; IV 1–2, 11, 13, 19–20, 23; V 390, 396; VI 242, 244, 248–9; VII 6–7, 11, 34, 38, 43, 47; VIII 16, 24, 26, 41
   Accademia degli Umoristi: V 390; VI 244
   Collegium Romanum: VIII 26, 41
   Inquisition: III 18–19; VI 249
   Medici Press, see Medicis, Raimondi, Giovanni Baptista: VII 34
   Propaganda fide: xxi; III 17, 19; IV 1, 23; VI 249
Roque, de la, M. (Monsieur): II 123
Rosgoff, Césarée, de: VII 15–16, 26
Rostam: V 393
Roumelie, see Rumelia: II 145
Rukn al-Dawla, Hasan b. Buya, see *Rocnaduddaule* (sic)
Rukn al-Dīn: V 407
Rumelia, see Roumeli
Russell, Gül: xii
Russia: IV 7
Rustam Beg: I 452

Sabaeans: IV 50
Saida, see Seitte
St Clement, pope: VII 53
Saint George, see Lusavereius, the illuminator: IV 23
St Maximin: VII 40, 55
St Michel: VII 24
St Patrick: VII 50
St Pol: VII 53
Salah (?) al-Din Efendi: II 138
Salah al-Din al-Ayyubi: II 141
Salamanca: V 400
Saliat, Pierre: VI 236
Saliba, George: VIII 27
Samarcand: VI 246
Sanson, François: V 414
Sanson, Nicolas, de: I 454; II 123
Sarì, see Sarù: IV 34
   saffron-colored: IV 34
Sarù, see Sarì: IV 34
Satan: II 139; IV 39; V 394, 410
Saumaise, Claude, de: VII 33
Savà: IV 55
Savary, François, de Brèves/Breves, see Brèves/Breves, de, Savary, François: VII 8
Sayda: xxi; II 125, 133
Sayer: VII 6
Scaliger, Joseph: V 401
Scenitae: IV 37
Scervàn, see Servan; Shirvan: IV 30, 34
Schantariah: II 141
Schickard, Wilhelm, see *Skikard*: I 452; III 18; V 399; VIII 24
   Tarich: V 399
Schip(p)ano, Mario: I 447; III 3–4, 7, 18, 20, 22; IV 11–15; V 390; VI 248–9
Schüller, Volkmar: xviii
Schulte, Abraham: II 123
Sciah Sofi, see Sciah Sophì: IV 22
   "chosen and upright king": IV 22
   "pious king": IV 22
Sciah Sophì, see Sciah Sofi: IV 50
Sciraz/Sciràz, see Shiraz: IV 20, 27, 48, 53–5
Sciuscèn, see Shushan: IV 49
Sciusetèr, see Shushtar: IV 49
Sclavonia: IV 8
Scopia, see Scople; Skopje: II 145
Scople, see Scopia; Skopje: II 145
Scutari, see Calcedon: VI 245
Scythia: III 6; IV 36
Scythians: III 6; IV 39; V 415
   Asian: IV 39; VI 242
   European: IV 39

INDEX 19

Sea: II 123, 132, 140–41, 143; III 1–2, 10; IV 4, 21
    Black, see Mer Noire: II 132; III 1; IV 4, 29; VII 24–5, 45
    Bachu, of, see Bohar Corsun; Caspian Sea; Chualenska More; Hircanian/Hyrcanian Sea; Mar di Bachau; Mare Coruzum; Mare de Bachu; sea of Corusum; Cunzar; Giorgian; Terbestan: III 2
    Bohar Corsun, see Caspian Sea; Chualenska More; Hircanian/Hyrcanian Sea; Mar di Bachau; Mare Coruzum; Mare de Bachu; sea of Bachu; Corusum; Cunzar; Giorgian; Terbestan: III 2
    Caspian, see Bohar Corsun; Chualenska More; Hircanian/Hyrcanian Sea; Mar di Bachau; Mare Coruzum; Mare de Bachu; sea of Bachu; Corusum; Cunzar; Giorgian; Terbestan: II 123, 140–41; III 1–2, 10; IV 4, 21–3, 28–30, 33–4, 36, 38; V 393, 402; VI 241
    Corusum, see Bohar Corsun; Caspian Sea; Chualenska More; Hircanian/Hyrcanian Sea; Mar di Bachau; Mare Coruzum; Mare de Bachu; Sea of Bachu; Cunzar; Giorgian; Terbestan: III 2
    Cunzar, see Bohar Corsun; Caspian Sea; Chualenska More; Hircanian/Hyrcanian Sea; Mar di Bachau; Mare Coruzum; Mare de Bachu; Sea of Bachu; Corusum; Giorgian; Terbestan: III 2
    Giorgian, see Bohar Corsun; Caspian Sea; Chualenska More; Hircanian/Hyrcanian Sea; Mar di Bachau; Mare Coruzum; Mare de Bachu; Sea of Bachu; Corusum; Cunzar; Terbestan: III 2
    Hircanian/Hyrcanian, see Bohar Corsun; Caspian Sea; Chualenska More; Mar di Bachau; Mare Coruzum; Mare de Bachu; sea of Bachu; Corusum; Cunzar; Giorgian; Terbestan: III 2; IV 21
    Mediterranean/Méditerranée: I 447; II 143; III 1; V 393, 415; VI 242, 244, 253; VII 15, 17, 20, 22, 25, 29, 45; VIII 15, 22, 26–7
    Red, see mer rouge: IV 40; VII 8, 16, 26, 29; VIII 39
    Terbestan, see Bohar Corsun, Caspian Sea; Chualenska More; Hircanian/Hyrcanian Sea; Mar di Bachau; Mare Coruzum; Mare de Bachu; sea of Bachu; Corusum; Cunzar; Giorgian: III 2
Seitte, see Saida: VII 13
Selim II: I 448; II 236, 239
Senegerie, de la, Monsieur: II 129
Sepid-rud: IV 22
    white river: IV 22
Serapion, see Ibn Sarabiyun: I 446
Serva, see Scervàn; Servan; Shirvan: III 1
Servan, see Scervàn; Serva; Shirvan: III 1
Sharaf al-Din al-Samarqandi: I 452
Shiniz: IV 5
Shiraz/Shīrāz, see Sciraz: I 452; V 393–4, 401, 407–8; VI 241
Shirazi, Qutb al-Din, al-: VIII 27
Shirvan, see Scervàn
Shushan, see Sciuscèn
Shushtar, see Sciusetèr
Siam: xx, xxv; V 411
Siah-cuh: IV 31
    Black Mountain: IV 31
Sicard, Claude: II 144
Sicile/Sicily: II 144; VII 26, 29, 51–2
Siculus, Diodorus, see Diodorus: III 4–6, 10–13, 18; IV 46–7; V 403
Siet Iooh, see *Iohn of Persia* (?): V 395
Sigistan/Sigistàn, see Sijistan; Sistàn: III 1; IV 39
Sijistan, see Sigistan/Sigistàn; Sistàn: III 1
Silistra: II 146
Silva et Figueroa, Garçia a, Silva y Figueroa, Garçia/Garcia da, Don: IV 55
Silva y Figueroa, Garçia/Garcia da/de, see Silva et Figueroa, Garçia a, Don: III 12; VIII 19–20, 39
Simon: IV 25
Sincerus: VII 15
Sionita, Gabriel: xxvii; II 141; V 396–9, 401–2; VII 3, 7, 9–11, 33
    De Nonnullis Orientarum urbibus, nec non indigenarum religion ac moribus tractatis breuis: V 396
Šīrīn: V 393
Sirte: VII 53
Sirtes de Lybie: VII 48
Sistàn, see Sigistan/Sigistàn; Sijistan: IV 39–40
Six Fours: VII 8
Skikard, see Schickard, Wilhelm: V 401
    Tarich: V 401
Skopje, see Scopia, Scople
Smith, Thomas: V 383, 391–2

Smyrna, see Gulf, Smyrna, of: II 133, 136–9; V 404; VII 13
Socrat: VII 37
Sogdiana: III 6
Sogdians: IV 39
Solfatara, see Solfatroza (?)
Solfatroza (?), see Solfatara: VII 51
Solin, see Solinus: V 400; VI 244
Solinus, see Solin: VII 33
Solomon: III 19; V 379
Soltaniye, see Sultania; Sultaniye: VIII 19
Sophì/Sophi, see Sophie: IV 50; V 384
Sophie, see Sophì/Sophi: III 1
Souchon: VII 48
Spain: I 460; II 135; III 21; IV 8; V 386; VI 229; VII 5, 20, 25, 36
Sphahan/Sphahàn, see Isfahan; Isphahan; Sphahanum: IV 24, 40–41, 54–5
Sphahanum, see Isfahan; Isphahan; Sphahan/Sphahàn: IV 21, 24, 30, 32
Stagl, Justus: VIII 36
Stephanos, see Stib: II 145
Stib, see Stephanos: II 145
Strabatt, see Astarabad: V 402
Strabo/n: I 454; III 4–5, 10–11, 13, 18; V 402; VI 244; VII 32–3, 50
Strachan, Georgius: IV 55; VIII 18
Strombole, see Mount Gibel Stromboli; Stromboli; Stromboly: VII 28, 50
Stromboli, see Mount Gibel Stromboli; Strombole; Stromboly: VII 28–9
Stromboly, see Mount Gibel Stromboli; Strombole; Stromboli: VII 50
Suachem, see Suakim: VII 28, 49
Suakim, see Suachem: VII 16, 26
Suffin, Honoré, see Juffrin, Honoré: VII 9
Suleiman, Sultan, see Süleyman: I 448; II 125
Sultania, see Soltaniye, Sultaniye: IV 21, 55
Sultaniye, see Sultania; Soltaniye: IV 6
Surat: xx; III 20–21
Suriano, Angelo Michaele: VII 5
Susa: IV 49
Susiana: III 8; IV 5, 21, 48–50
Süleyman, see Sulaeiman; Sultan: II 125; V 381; VI 240
  Kanuni: V 381
Syene: II 142; VIII 39
Syria/Syrie: II 143; VI 240; VII 2, 4, 13, 29, 51–2; VIII 21, 42

Tabaristan, see Taperistan: III 1
Tabriz, see Ecbatana; Ekbatana; Tares; Tarsi; Tauris; *Tauryz*; Tebriz: III 2; IV 6; V 402–4, 415; VI 244–6
  Safavid: VI 245
Tagargar: II 141

Taheràn, see Tehran: IV 31
Tajan, see Tegginé-rud: IV 33
Tamberlang, see Timur/Tīmūr: V 401
Tamizey de Larroque, Philippe, see Larroque, Tamizey, de, Philippe: VII 17, 19, 27
Tantabec, see Tencabash, Tenkabach: II 144
Taperistan, see Tabaristan: III 1
Tares, see Tabriz; Tarsi; Tauris; *Tauryz*; Tebriz: III 2
Tarsi, see Tabriz; Tares; Tauris; *Tauryz*; Tebriz: III 2
Tartaros: V 394
Tartars, see Tatars: IV 28–9, 36, 38–9; VI 235
Tartary, see Tatary: V 394
Tasso, Torquato: III 11–12
Tat: IV 51
Tatars, see Tartars: V 394
Tatary, see Tartary: III 6; V 393
Tauris, see Ecbatana; Ekbatana; Tabriz; Tares; Tarsi; *Tauryz*; Tebriz: IV 9; V 403; VI 244–5
Tauryz, see Tabriz; Tares; Tarsi; Tauris; Tebriz: V 403–4; VI 246
Tavernier, Jean-Baptiste de: I 452, 456; II 124, 132; IV 15; V 414; VIII 20, 35
Tbilissi, see Teflis, Tiflis: IV 25
Tebriz, see Tabriz; Tares; Tarsi; Tauris; *Tauryz*: IV 22, 41
Tebrizabàd: IV 41
Teflis, see Tbilissi; Tiflis: IV 25
Tegginé-rud, see Tajan: IV 33
  rapid river: IV 33
Tehran, Taheràn: IV 31
Teifashi, al-: II 142
Teimuraz/Teimuràz, Prince: IV 20, 26–7, 5
Teishera, see Teixera; Teixeira, Pedro: V 401
Teixeira, Pedro, see Teishera; Teixera: I 454; II 124; III 11; V 392–3, 399
Teixera, see Teishera; Teixeira: V 404; VI 246
Tencabash, see Tantabec; Tenkabach: II 141
Tenkabach, see Tantabec; Tencabash: II 144
Tenneur, le, Mr.: VII 32
Terre neufue, see World, New: VII 47
Thabet Ben-Corra, see Thabit b. Qurra: V 396
Thabit b. Qurra, see Thabet Ben-Corra
Thais: IV 47
Theodosius: V 413
  Spherics: V 413
Theophrast: I 442, 444
Thévenot, Melchisédec de: II 123, 125, 132, 141
Thevet, André: VI 235–6
  «Cosmographie de Levant», see Belleforest, François, de: VI 235
Thomas de Vendôme, see Vendôme, Thomas, de, Père: VII 7

INDEX 21

Thou, François-Auguste, de: II 125, 133, 136; V 379–80; VII 12–13
Thou, Jacques-Auguste, de: II 133; V 379; VII 12
Thunis, see Tunis: VII 36, 48
Tibi, Bassam: x
Tiflis, see Tbilissi, Teflis
Tigris, see Tygris: IV 49
Timur/Tīmūr, see *Tamberlang*: V 402
Tizzīnī, al-, M.b.M.b.a. Bakr: V 404
  Zīj: V 404
Tobbat: II 141
Tobyas: V 403; VI 246
Toderini, Giambattista, Father, Abbé: I 450; V 380; VI 252
Tole, Monsieur: II 129
Tolmaschewa, Marina: VII 33
Tor, al, see Tur: VII 28, 50; VIII 36, 39
Torc, see Turks: II 141
Tott, François, de, Baron: I 450
Toulon: II 145; VII 4–6, 8, 26
Tours: II 126
Tournon, François, de, Cardinal: I 439
Tracy, James: IV 56
  Journal for Early Modern History: IV 56
Traian: VII 2
Transoxania: V 402
Tripoli: I 442–4; VII 4, 13; VIII 23
Troye: I 458
Tübingen: xvi; VIII 24
Tunis, see Thunis: xviii, xix; VII 6, 14, 21, 23–4, 36–8, 49; VIII 24–5
Tur, see Tor: VII 16
Turcomans: IV 36–7
Turcs, see Torc; Turks: II 145; V 384, 388–9
Turfan: II 144
Turkey, see Turky: I 441; II 143; VI 229
Turkistan, see Turquestan: V 402
Turks/"Turks"/Turks, see Torc, Turcs: I 441, 455, 461, 463; II 134, 137, 141; IV 19–20, 22–4, 26, 36–7, 40; V 384–6, 390–91, 415–16; VI 230, 235, 238, 242–3, 247, 251, 254
Turky, see Turkey: I 461
Turquestan, see Turkistan: II 141
Turquie, see Turkey; Turky: V 384
Tus, see *Tuz*
Tuscany: II 133; VIII 30
Ṭūsī, al-, Abu Jaʿfar b. Ḥasan, Naṣīr al-Dīn/ Tusi, al-, Abu Jaʿfar b. Hasan, Nasir al-Din, see Abu-Giafer Ben Hasan Tusaeus; Coage Nescir; Naseruddin; Naṣīr al-Dīn al-Ṭūsī/Nasir al-Din al-Tusi; Nazaraddin: xxviii; I 450; II 124, 139, 141; III 11; V 392, 402; VI 246; VIII 27, 32

Tuz, see Tus: V 402
Tygris, see Tigris: III 1

Uighur, kingdom, see Eygur: II 141
Ulug-beg, see Mirza Ouloukbec; Uluġ Beg; Ulugh Beg; *Vlughbeg*; "Vlughbeghius": II 141
  Tables Astronomiques: II 141
Uluġ Beg, see Mirza Ouloukbeg; Ulug-beg; Ulugh Beg; *Vlughbeg*; "Vlughbeghius": V 402–4, 411
  Tīmūr's grandson: V 402
Ulugh Beg, see Mirza Ouloukbec; Ulug-beg; Uluġ Beg; *Vlughbeg*; "Vlughbegius": I 451–2; II 124, 141; VI 246; VIII 18, 28–30, 32
  New Tables: I 451
United Provinces of the Netherlands, see Netherlands, The: V 392; VII 19; VIII 22, 30, 42
Urmia, lake: IV 4
USA: II 148; VIII 33–4
Uxiors: IV 48
Uyvar: VIII 28
Uzbags, see Uzbegs: IV 38–9
Uzbegs, see Uzbags
Uzun Hassan: I 452

Vah Kuh, see Baku, Bah Kuja: IV 30
Vair, Guillaume, du, keeper of the royal seals: VII 7–8, 10, 33
Valbelle, Antoine, de: VII 13
Valence, Kingdom of: VII 20
Vallavez/Valavez, Palamède, de: VII 5
Valle, Petrus, a, Peregrinus, see Valle, Pietro, della: IV 55
Valle, Petrus, de la: V 404; VI 246
Valle, Pietro, della, see Valle, Petrus, a, Peregrinus, Valle, Petrus, de la: xvii, xviii, xxiii, xxiv, xxv; I 447, 451, 452, 453; III 3–23; IV 2–3, 6, 11–15, 17–18, 55; V 390–91, 406–12; VI 243, 248–50; VIII 16–20, 31, 36
  Latin geography of Iran: III 3, 22; VI 249; VIII 19
Valois/Valoys, Henri, de: VII 31, 39–42, 54, 56
Van: IV 24
Van, lake: IV 4
Vantelet, Jean de la Haye, Seigneur de, see Haye, Jean, de la, Seigneur de Vantelet: II 136
Vatican City, see Città del Vaticano: xxvi
Vattier, Pierre: II 142
Vecchietti, Gerolamo: I 451; VIII 27
Vecchietti, Gioambatista: I 451; VIII 27

Vendôme, Agathange, de, see Agathange de
    Vendôme: VII 14; VIII 24
Vendôme, Michel-Ange, de, Michel-Ange de
    Vendôme: VII 13–14
Vendosme/Vendôme, Thomas, de, Père, see
    Thomas de Vendôme: VII 7
Venice/Venise, see Venize: xvi, xxiii; I 460;
    II 131, 134; III 1; IV 6, 8; V 388;
    VI 231, 240–41, 244; VII 5, 33, 37–8
    Signoria: VI 240
Venize, see Venice/Venise: VII 13
Vento, de, Angelo: VII 8, 11
Venus: VIII 26
Vergil, see Virgil: III 4, 10, 15–16, 18
Vesuue, see Mount Vesuvius; Vezuuio:
    VII 28, 50, 52
Vesuvius, see Mount Vesuvius; Vesuue;
    Vezuuio: VII 25–6, 28
Vezuuio, see Mount Vesuvius; Vesuue;
    Vesuvius: VII 25
Viaz, Balthasar, de: VII 9, 20, 24, 48
Vidini: II 146
Vienna: IV 1
Viguier, Sr.: VII 13
Villeneuve: VII 15
Virgil, see Vergil: IV 18
Viviani, Vincenzo: II 140
Vlughbeg, see Mirza Ouloukbec; Ulug-beg;
    Uluġ Beg; Ulugh Beg;
    "Vlughbegius": V 401, 404; VI 246
    Nephew to *Tamberlang*, see Timur/
        Tīmūr: V 401
"Vlughbegius", see Mirza Ouloukbec;
    Ulug-beg; Uluġ Beg; Ulugh Beg;
    Vlughbeg: V 402

Waquet, F.: I 464
Wendelin, Gottfried: II 124; VIII 37–8
Wielandt, Melchior: VI 238
Witkam, Justus: xv, xxvii, xxviii

World
    Islamic: VI 229
    New, see Terre neufue: II 121; VII 19

Xavier, Jerónimo: xxv
Xenophon: III 4–5, 18; V 415; VI 244
Xerxes: V 415

Yahya b. ʿAbd al-Latif al-Qazvini, see Qazvini,
    Yahya b. ʿAbd al-Latif, al-: III 12
    Lubb al-tavarihk: III 12
Yaqut al-Hamawi al-Rumi, see Jacout
Yazd, see Yezd
Yemen, see Ajaman; Giaman; Yaman: II 143;
    V 380
Yesilbaş, see Ieselbas
Yezd, see Yazd: IV 41

Zabelistàn, see Zabulistan: IV 39
Zabulistan, see Zabelistàn
Zacuto, Abraham: V 400–401
    Sefer ha-Yuḥasin: V 400
Zahrawi, al-: VI 236
Zayn al-Dīn/Zayn al-Din/Zeyn al-Dīn, Lārī,
    al-, Mullā/Mulla, see Zeineddin/
    Zeineddìn, Moullà/Mullà: xxvi;
    I 453; III 12; V 409–12; VIII 18
Zebekier: II 127
Zeineddin, Mullà, see Zayn al-Dīn/Zeyn al-
    Dīn/Zayn al-Din, Mullā/Mulla:
    IV 55; V 409
Zende-rud/Zenderùd: IV 24
    living river: IV 41
Zengian: IV 21
Zenie, Ville de, see isnik; Iznik: II 132
Zigetvari, Köse Ibrahim Efendi Tezkereci,
    see Köse Ibrahim Efendi Tezkereci
Zigetvari: VIII 28–9
Zinghiz Khan, see Chingiz Khan: II 144
Zoroastre: II 126